# THE YALE EDITIONS OF
# *The Private Papers of James Boswell*

## RESEARCH EDITION

*Journals*

*Life of Johnson*

# James Boswell

## THE JOURNAL OF HIS GERMAN AND SWISS TRAVELS, 1764

EDITED BY

MARLIES K. DANZIGER

EDINBURGH UNIVERSITY PRESS
Edinburgh

YALE UNIVERSITY PRESS
New Haven and London

© Yale University, 2008

Edinburgh University Press, 2008
22 George Square, Edinburgh

Yale University Press
New Haven and London

Set in Goudy by the
Yale Boswell Editions, New Haven,
and printed in Great Britain by
Antony Rowe Ltd, Chippenham, Wilts

A CIP record for this book is available
from the British Library

Edinburgh University Press
ISBN–13 978 0 7486 1806 4

Yale University Press
ISBN–13 978–0–300–12360–9

Library of Congress Control Number: 2008924506

This paper meets the requirements of ANSI/NISO Z39. 48–1992 (Permanence of Paper).

Published by Yale University Press with the assistance of the Annie Burr Lewis Fund.

*Boswell's Journals, Volume 1*

*General Editor: Gordon Turnbull*
*Associate Editor: James J. Caudle*

JAMES BOSWELL:
THE JOURNAL OF HIS
GERMAN AND SWISS TRAVELS,
1764

The preparation of *James Boswell:*

*The Journal of His*

*German and Swiss Travels, 1764*

was generously supported by

the National Endowment for the Humanities,

the James J. Colt Foundation,

and

the Henry Luce Foundation

# Editorial Committee

# Advisory Committee

# General Editorial Note

THE research edition of the Private Papers of James Boswell consists of three co-ordinated series: Boswell's journals in all their varieties, his correspondence, and the *Life of Johnson*. The undertaking is a co-operative one involving many scholars, and publication is proceeding in the order in which the volumes are completed for the press. The present volume is the first to appear in the research series of journals.

The correspondence is appearing in three kinds of volumes: *single-correspondent* volumes; *subject* volumes of letters related to a topic or theme; and *miscellaneous-correspondence* volumes of the remaining letters in chronological sequence. *Boswell's* Life of Johnson: *An Edition of the Original Manuscript* is presented in an arrangement which shows the method and progress of the composition.

The parallel 'reading' or trade edition, based for the most part on Boswell's journal, began publication in 1950, and was completed in 1989. While the annotation of that edition primarily turned inwards towards the text, the annotation of the research edition turns outwards from the text as well so as to relate the documents to the various areas of scholarship which they can illuminate: history (literary, linguistic, legal, medical, political, social, local), biography, bibliography, and genealogy, among others. The comprehensiveness and coherence of the papers that Boswell chose to preserve make them highly useful for such treatment.

# Contents

# Acknowledgements

THIS edition, twenty years (with interruptions) in the making, has benefitted from the work of many people, ranging from experts in German and Swiss culture to the Boswellians, past and present, associated with the Yale Boswell Editions, as well as friends and interested persons in other places. Editorial work on the documents began, in fact, long ago. In the mid-1930s, Helen Randall established a draft and notes for the Swiss portion of the journal. Shortly after World War II, Robert Warnock, outstanding among the early editors, amassed information for the notes on the German journals and also prepared an extensive Biographical Register, which, though it was eventually abandoned, provided a useful starting point for this edition's work in biographical identification. In addition, Warnock left the Boswell project a generous bequest, which has been used to fund the Warnock Fellowships for senior scholars (including me) as well as Warnock Internships for graduate students who have undertaken, among other tasks, many of the time-consuming searches of historical and biographical sources.

Since then, information has come from German librarians and archivists as well as from my personal visits to the places recorded in Boswell's journal. To cite only a few, Bellevue, the splendid mansion of the de Spaens destroyed by bombs in 1945, was vividly described by Ursula Geisselbrecht-Capecki, a local historian who came to meet me in Kleve to illustrate the past of the now-deserted property. The documents concerning Dessau in the Landesarchiv Oranienbaum were made available to me by Marlies Ross, while identifications of other little-known Dessau figures were provided by letter by Erhard Hirsch, also of Dessau. Helmut Roob of the Forschungbibliothek Gotha took me to the vicinity of Gotha by automobile at a time when petrol was expensive in the former DDR (East Germany). Above all, Hans-Joachim Reuter of Kassel and now of Munich made many of Boswell's experiences comprehensible to me through a five-day automobile trip, following Boswell's route from Nijmegen to Brunswick-Wolfenbüttel. In a continuing friendship, he has been indefatigable in finding material in other parts of Germany. In Scotland, Susan L. Burnett invited me to her family home, Kemnay House in Aberdeenshire, to browse productively among the papers of her ancestor Alexander Burnett, Boswell's friend in Berlin.

In Switzerland, Andreas Fankhauser, Staatsarchivar in Solothurn, and Maryse Schmidt-Sourdez, librarian of the BPU Neuchâtel, went out of their way to be helpful. François Matthey, Director of the Musée J.-J. Rousseau at Môtiers, came especially to that mountain village to open Rousseau's quarters for me. Carlos and Brigitte Palacios enabled me to retrace Boswell's trip from Yverdon to Môtiers and to identify the mountain, actually a pasturage at elevated height, that Boswell called *Lapidosa*. In Geneva, Charles Wirz, until recently Director of the Institut et Musée Voltaire, freely shared his vast knowledge of both Rousseau and Voltaire. My notes to the text point to many other details that became clear from my personal visits.

Among those with other specialized knowledge, Philippe-Henri Morbach, an archivist as well as a member of the Grande Loge de France, provided very helpful information about Freemasonry. Gordon Williams, Thomas A. Thacher Professor

Emeritus of Latin and Classics, Yale University, has kindly provided eloquent translations from the Latin.

At Yale, invaluable research has been accomplished by the Warnock interns, notably by Jenny Davidson, Gabrielle Gopinath, Eric Lindstrom, Elisa P. Milkes, Hannibal Hamlin, Hiba Hafiz, Rebecca C. Johnson, Michele Martinez, Carrie Roider, John Staines and Juliette Wells. Equally important over the years has been the assistance of the knowledgeable staff of the Boswell Editions' office: Rachel McClellan, the late Irene Adams, and more recently the ever-helpful Nadine Honigberg. The staff of Yale's Beinecke Rare Book and Manuscript Library has been unfailingly patient. Nancy E. Johnson is mainly responsible for compiling the index. And the talented cartographer Stacey Maples of the Yale University Map Collection has rendered Boswell's routes clear and vivid in the accompanying maps, even drawing in their topographical setting.

My personal thanks go to my former colleague and friend Gerald M. Pinciss of Hunter College and the Graduate School of the City University of New York, for repeatedly reading drafts and offering sensible, insightful advice drawn from his deep knowledge of Shakespeare and the Renaissance. Grateful thanks furthermore go to members of my immediate family: to the late Ruth and Kurt Mitchells (my sister and brother-in-law), who encouraged me to spend several summer months at their home on the shores of Lake Geneva, and to my son Charles, who kindly took time from his legal practice and his own book to drive me between Westchester and New Haven, as my work required.

Further special thanks go to my fellow Boswellian editors past and present, in particular Thomas Crawford of Aberdeen for his support while at work on the first volume of the Boswell-Temple correspondence, and more recently James J. Caudle for his knowledge of early Boswellian material. In addition, my gratitude is due to Mark Spicer for his expertise in technical matters, especially in styling, copy-editing, and setting the type in its finished form. He patiently served as a sounding board for my questions on British usage, and he provided useful reminders of the editorial practices in previous volumes of the Boswell editions. Above all, my grateful acknowledgement goes to Gordon Turnbull, General Editor of the Yale Boswell Editions, whose remarkable knowledge of Boswell was acquired during his many years of involvement with the Boswell project, and who has proved to be a talented, tactful editor throughout. While I take full responsibility for any errors that may have inadvertently crept in, I trust that our combined efforts have minimized them and have, in fact, enriched this volume.

Following in Boswell's footsteps has truly been, for me, the scholarly journey of a lifetime.

MKD
Scarsdale, New York
June 1, 2007

# Editorial Procedures

## The Texts

### Sequence

THE entries are presented in chronological order, beginning with the brief notes (memoranda) which Boswell wrote late at night or early in the morning, then proceeding to the fuller version of the journal written later, often covering several days. The dating of the memoranda differs by a day from the date of the journal entries, as indicated in the heading for each memorandum. Boswell's ten-line verses, recorded on separate sheets starting in October, are added under each appropriate date. Material such as separately recorded anecdotes (known as 'Boswelliana') is added in the notes where appropriate.

### Transcription

In conformity with the plan of the Research Edition, the manuscript documents in this edition have been printed to correspond to the originals as closely as is feasible in the medium of print. Changes have been kept within the limits of the conventions stated here. No change that could affect sense has been made silently.

### Spelling

For English words, the spelling of the original has been retained. Words or phrases written in French where apostrophes are omitted, but easily understood by a phonetic reading, are allowed to stand without comment (e.g., 'cest lhomme' for 'c'est l'homme', 'lecosse' for 'l'Écosse'). In a few instances, small square brackets are supplied to facilitate the reading (e.g., 'n[ ]ose' where Boswell wrote 'nose'). French accents—erratic and inconsistent—have been retained as Boswell wrote them.

Names of persons are given as Boswell wrote them, often phonetically (e.g., 'Boik' for 'Poigk', 'Pergo' for 'Perregaux'), and clarified in the notes.

### Punctuation

Punctuation follows Boswell's where possible. In keeping, however, with the other research volumes in this series, missing periods are supplied at the end of a sentence, and omitted capitals are supplied after periods. Where both periods and capitals are omitted, they are supplied in small square brackets. Where the end of a line stands in place of punctuation (a frequent occurrence in the memoranda), a dash in square brackets is added. Colons are substituted without comment for the periods Boswell habitually used to introduce quotations.

### Quotations

Primary quotations are indicated by single quotation marks, secondary by double. Omitted quotation marks are supplied where one is introduced and the other is missing at the beginning or end of a passage.

## Abbreviations

The following abbreviations, contractions, and symbols are expanded: abt (about), agst (against), wd (would), wt (with), ye (the), yr (your), yt (that). However, & (and) and &c (etc.) are retained as Boswell wrote them.

## Brackets

Parentheses replace square brackets in the text, brackets being reserved for editorial use.

## Devices of emphasis

Underlinings for purposes of emphasis are printed in italics.

## Interlineations and marginalia

All such insertions are indicated in the notes.

## Deletions in the manuscript

Some deletions are Boswell's, whether undertaken at the time of writing or a few years later. More are due to censorship by later owners of the manuscript, chiefly by Lady Talbot of Malahide, who inherited the papers and scored out numerous passages before selling the manuscripts in the mid-twentieth century. She did so for reasons of propriety, e.g., to eliminate seemingly risqué descriptions, or from family pride, so as to exclude allusions to madness in Boswell's ancestors (see *Pride and Negligence*, pp. 89, 96–97, 101, 110). Most of these deletions, ranging from a few words to paragraphs, have been reconstructed by later Yale editors and are so described in the notes.

# The Annotation

## Footnotes

These are intended to elucidate the text and extend the historical, social, or cultural frame of reference. Such explanatory notes follow the journal. They are provided for the memoranda when no clarification is offered in the journal entries.

## Place names

German and French place names in the notes follow twenty-first century practices (e.g., 'Kassel' for 'Cassel', 'Bern' for 'Berne'). Where two versions of a name, or two different names, are in use (e.g., 'Hannover' in German, 'Hanover' in British usage; 'Solothurn' in German, 'Soleure' in French), both are mentioned.

## Tense

Boswell's time of writing is regarded as the present, and events are discussed from his point of view. Accordingly, while the main tense in the notes dealing with Boswell's experiences is the present, events in the past are presented in the pluperfect (e.g., 'he had been educated ...'), but historical facts are presented in the simple past, and future events use the 'would' form (e.g., 'he would become ...').

## Sources

When an abbreviated source is given, the full citation appears either in the preceding note or in the following list of Cue Titles and Abbreviations.

# A Note on Distances and Currency

THE distances travelled by Boswell are difficult to gauge. The very concept of a mile differed from one German principality to another, and beyond that from one European country to another (see *Encyclopaedia Britannica*, 1773, s.v. 'Miles', iii. 245–46; *Lexikon zur Geschichte der Kartographie*, ed. Ingrid Kretschmer, Johannes Dörflinger, and Franz Wawrik, 1986, ii. 478–79). In addition, detailed information about Boswell's route (for instance, whether he was proceeding along the northern or southern side of a mountain or river) is usually lacking and makes it impossible to be certain about some of the distances he covered. Under the circumstances, the distances mentioned here, except for a few given by Boswell himself, are taken wherever possible from Thomas Nugent and John George Keyssler, travellers of Boswell's own time who described many of the routes taken by Boswell. Even this choice, however, leaves uncertainties. Nugent's measuring is vague, as when he states that one German mile is 'better than four English miles' (Nugent, i. 'Of Miles'). At best, twenty-first century readers will have an indication of what distances Nugent, Keyssler, and Boswell *thought* they were covering.

Since kilometres have long been used on the Continent, both miles and kilometres are provided in this edition. Kilometres are calculated at 1.609 km per mile, the standard measurements adopted long after Boswell and included here to give twenty-first century readers a rough impression of the distances he covered.

The worth of the currency recorded in Boswell's Expense Account is also uncertain. This money was in coins, since paper money was not yet in use. But the value was determined not by a standardized amount identified on the coins but by the metal content and weight of the individual pieces. While the value of big coins, made of gold (e.g., ducats) or silver (e.g., Taler, écus), was relatively stable, smaller coins, minted by different principalities, could be adulterated at their source or 'clipped' while in use — that is, diminished in size, weight, and value by having little bits of their metal, usually silver, sliced off. Boswell resorted to the book-keepers' so-called 'accounting' currency, unchanging hypothetical Taler or écus, assigned to coins whose value had been highly variable during the Seven Years' War, and was still not certain. For further details, see the introduction to the Expense Account (Appendix 3).

# Cue Titles and Abbreviations

THIS list omits the more familiar abbreviations of standard works of reference and periodicals, such as DSH, OCD, OED, and N & Q.

*Note:* All manuscripts referred to in the footnotes without mention of a repository are in the Yale collection. Catalogue numbers are supplied in some instances in order to facilitate identification.

ACV: Archives cantonale vaudoise.

ABBAW: Archive of the Berlin-Brandenburgische Akademie der Wissenschaften.

ADB: *Allgemeine Deutsche Biographie*, 56 vols., 1875–1912.

Adelung-Jöchers: Johann Christoph Adelung, *Fortsetzung und Ergänzungen zu Christian Gottlieb Jöchers allgemeinem Gelehrten-Lexico*, 7 vols., 1784–97.

*Adres-Calender: Adres-Calender der Königlich Preussischen Haupt- und Residenzstädte Berlin und Potsdam*, various years.

AE: Andrew Erskine.

AEB: Archives de l'état de Berne.

AEN: Archives de l'état de Neuchâtel.

*Album Studiosorum: Album Studiosorum Academiae Lugduno Batavae*, 1875.

*Ann. Reg.: The Annual Register*, 1758–1862.

*Ayr and Wigton:* James Paterson, *History of the Counties of Ayr and Wigton*, 3 vols. in 5 parts, 1863–66.

Baedeker, *Die Schweiz:* Karl Baedeker, *Die Schweiz*, 1930.

Bailey: James Boswell, *The Hypochondriack*, ed. Margery Bailey, 2 vols., 1928.

Bengesco: Georges Bengesco, *Voltaire: Bibliographie de ses Œuvres*, 1882–85.

BCU/D: Bibliothèque cantonale et universitaire/Dorigny, Lausanne.

BU: *Biographie universelle, ancienne et moderne*, with supplement, 85 vols., 1811–62.

*Book of Company:* James Boswell's *Book of Company at Auchinleck 1782–1795*, ed. The Viscountess Eccles and Gordon Turnbull, 1995.

Borgeaud: Charles Borgeaud, *Histoire de l'université de Genève*, 4 vols., 1900–34.

*Boswelliana: Boswelliana. The Commonplace Book of James Boswell*, ed. Rev. Charles Rogers, 1874. The greater part of the manuscripts Boswell himself labelled 'Boswelliana' was published in Rogers's book and is now in the Hyde Collection at Harvard University. The Yale collection also contains some 'Boswelliana' papers (M 24–69).

Both, *Friedrich II:* Wolf von Both and Hans Vogel, *Landgraf Friedrich II von Hessen-Kassel: ein Fürst der Zopfzeit*, Veröffentlichungen der Historischen Kommission für Hessen, 1973.

Both, *Wilhelm VIII:* Wolf von Both, *Landgraf Wilhelm VIII. von Hessen-Kassel*, 1764.

BP: *The Private Papers of James Boswell from Malahide Castle in the Collection of Lt.-Colonel Ralph Heyward Isham*, ed. Geoffrey Scott and F. A. Pottle, 18 vols., 1928–34; index, 1937.

BPUN: Bibliothèque Publique et Universitaire de Neuchâtel.

*Braunschweig—Das Bild der Stadt: Braunschweig—Das Bild der Stadt in 900 Jahren*, 2 vols., 1985: Richard Moderhack, *Braunschweigs Stadtgeschichte* (vol. i); Franz-Josef Christiani, Matthias Puhle, Heinrich W. Schüpp, and Gerd Spies, eds, *Brauschweigs Stadtbild* (vol. ii).

*Braunschweig und Umgebung: Braunschweig und Umgebung: Historisch-topographisches Handbuch* [1877]. Anon.

Brockhaus: Brockhaus, *Die Enzyklopädie*, 20 vols., 1996.

*Burke's Peerage: Burke's Peerage & Baronetage*, 106th ed., 2 vols., 1999.

Burnett of Kemnay Archives: The Burnett of Kemnay Archives, Kemnay House, Kemnay, Aberdeenshire.

Casanova: Jacques Casanova de Seingalt, *History of My Life*, trans. Willard R. Trask, 12 vols. in 6, 1966–71.

*Cat. Ferney: Voltaire's Catalogue of His Library at Ferney*, ed. George R. Havens and Norman L. Torrey, *SVEC* 9 (1959). Includes 'List of the books in Voltaire's library'.

'Cat. of Books': 'A Catalogue of Books belonging to James Boswell, Esq.', 1770–80, National Library of Scotland MS. 3285.

*Catalogue*: Marion S. Pottle, Claude Colleer Abbott, and Frederick A. Pottle, *Catalogue of the Private Papers of James Boswell at Yale University*, 3 vols., 1993.

CC *Rousseau: Correspondance complète de J.-J. Rousseau*, ed. R. A. Leigh, 52 vols., 1965–1998.

Cheyne: George Cheyne, *The English Malady*, 1733.

Choisy: Albert Choisy, *Généalogies Genevoises: Familles admises à la Bourgeoisie avant la Réformation*, 1947.

*Comp. Peer.: Complete Peerage of England, Scotland, Ireland, Great Britain, and the United Kingdom*, ed. G. E. C[okayne], rev. Vicary Gibbs, H. A. Doubleday, and others, 13 vols., 1910–59.

*Corr. 1: The Correspondence of James Boswell and John Johnston of Grange*, ed. Ralph S. Walker, 1966 (Yale Research Edition, Correspondence: Volume 1).

*Corr. 2: The Correspondence and Other Papers of James Boswell Relating to the Making of the* Life of Johnson, ed. Marshall Waingrow, 2nd edition corrected and enlarged, 2001 (Yale Research Edition, Correspondence: Volume 2).

*Corr. 3: The Correspondence of James Boswell with Certain Members of the Club*, ed. Charles N. Fifer, 1976 (Yale Research Edition, Correspondence: Volume 3).

*Corr. 4: The Correspondence of James Boswell with David Garrick, Edmund Burke, and Edmond Malone*, ed. Peter S. Baker, Thomas W. Copeland, George M. Kahrl, Rachel McClellan, and James M. Osborn, 1987 (Yale Research Edition, Correspondence: Volume 4).

*Corr. 5: The General Correspondence of James Boswell, 1766–1769*, Vol. 1: 1766–1767, ed. Richard C. Cole, with Peter S. Baker and Rachel McClellan, and with the assistance of James J. Caudle, 1993 (Yale Research Edition, Correspondence: Volume 5).

*Corr. 6: The Correspondence of James Boswell and William Johnson Temple, 1756–1795*, Vol. 1: 1756–1777, ed. Thomas Crawford, 1997 (Yale Research Edition, Correspondence: Volume 6).

*Corr. 7: The General Correspondence of James Boswell, 1766–1769*, Vol. 2: 1768–1769, ed. Richard C. Cole, with Peter S. Baker and Rachel McClellan, and with the assistance of James J. Caudle, 1997 (Yale Research Edition, Correspondence: Volume 7).

*Corr. 8: The Correspondence of James Boswell with James Bruce and Andrew Gibb, Overseers of the Auchinleck Estate*, ed. Nellie Pottle Hankins and John Strawhorn, 1998 (Yale Research Edition, Correspondence: Volume 8).

*Corr. 9: The General Correspondence of James Boswell, 1757–1763*, ed. David Hankins and James J. Caudle, 2006 (Yale Research Edition, Correspondence: Volume 9).

*Corres. Voltaire: Les Œuvres Complètes de Voltaire: Correspondence and related documents*, definitive edition by Theodore Besterman, 51 vols., 1968–77.

*Corres. Walpole: The Yale Edition of Horace Walpole's Correspondence*, ed. W. S. Lewis and others, 48 vols., 1937–83.

Courtney: C. P. Courtney, *Isabelle de Charrière (Belle de Zuylen)*, 1993.

Cranston, *Jean-Jacques: The Early Life*: Maurice William Cranston, *Jean-Jacques: The Early Life and Work of Jean-Jacques Rousseau, 1712–1754*, 1983.

Cranston, *The Noble Savage*: Maurice William Cranston, *The Noble Savage: Jean-Jacques Rousseau, 1754–1762*, 1991.

Cranston, *The Solitary Self*: Maurice William Cranston, *The Solitary Self: Jean-Jacques Rousseau in Exile and Adversity*, 1997.

CSD: *The Concise Scots Dictionary*, ed. Mairi Robinson and others, 1985.

Cuthell: Edith E. Cuthell, *The Scottish Friend of Frederick the Great*, 2 vols., 1915.

DDE: *Deutsche Biographische Enzyklopädie*, 1995–.

DBF: *Dictionnaire de biographie française*, 1933–.

Deneke: Bernward Deneke, *Hochzeit*, 1971.

DHBS: *Dictionnaire historique et biographique de la Suisse*, 7 vols., 1921–33, supplement 1934.

*Dizionario Biografico degli Italiani*: multiple vols., 1960–.

*Dict. of Art: The Dictionary of Art*, ed. Jane Turner, 34 vols., 1996.

*Dict. de Rousseau: Dictionnaire de Jean-Jacques Rousseau*, ed. Raymond Trousson and Frédéric S. Eigeldinger, 1996.

DSB: *Dictionary of Scientific Biography*, 18 vols. in 10, 1970–90.

*Dict. SJ*: Samuel Johnson, *A Dictionary of the English Language*, 2 vols., 6th ed. 1785.

Douglas, *Baronage*: Sir Robert Douglas, *The Baronage of Scotland*, 1798.

*Earlier Years*: Frederick A. Pottle, *James Boswell: The Earlier Years, 1740–1769*, 1966, repr. 1985.

Eigeldinger: Frédéric S. Eigeldinger, *Des Pierres dans mon jardin: Les années Neuchâteloises de J. J. Rousseau*, 1992.

Elcho: 'Le Journal de Lord Elcho' (later Lord Wemyss), BPUN MS. MSA 795.

*Extremes: Boswell in Extremes, 1776–1778*, ed. Charles McC. Weis and F. A. Pottle, 1970.

*Fac. Adv.: The Faculty of Advocates in Scotland, 1532–1943*, ed. Sir Francis J. Grant, 1944.

*Fasti Scot.: Fasti Ecclesiae Scoticanae*, ed. Hew Scott, 1915.

Felsenstein: Frank Felsenstein, *Anti-Semitic Stereotypes*, 1995.

*Ferney-Voltaire: Ferney-Voltaire, Pages d'Histoire*, 1st ed. 1984, 2nd ed. 1990.

FLB Gotha: Forschungs Landesbibliothek, Gotha.

'Fourierbuch': 'Fourierbuch', FLB Gotha Chart A 1660.

Galiffe: J.-A. Galiffe et al., *Notices généalogiques sur les familles genevoises*, 7 vols., 1829–95; repr. ed. Slatkine, 1976.

GD: George Dempster.

GLA Karlsruhe: General Landes Archiv, Karlsruhe.

*Grand Tour I: Boswell on the Grand Tour: Germany and Switzerland, 1764*, ed. F. A. Pottle, 1953.

*Grand Tour II: Boswell on the Grand Tour: Italy, Corsica and France, 1765–1766*, ed. Frank Brady and F. A. Pottle, 1955.

*Great Biographer: Boswell: The Great Biographer, 1789–1795*, ed. Marlies K. Danziger and Frank Brady, 1989.

Grellet: Pierre Grellet, *Les Aventures de Casanova en Suisse*, 1919.

GStA PK: Geheimes Staatsarchiv Preussischer Kulturbesitz.

Hamberger-Meusel: Georg Christoph Hamberger, *Das Gelehrte Teutschland; oder, Lexikon der jetztlebenden teutschen Schriftsteller*, cont. by Johann Georg Meusel, 22 vols., 1783–87.

*Handbuch: Handbuch der Historischen Stätten Deutschlands*, 12 vols., 1976–96.

Hartwig: Theodor Hartwig, *Der Übertritt des Erbprinzen Friedrich von Hessen-Cassel zum Katholicismus*, 1870.

*Hebrides: Boswell's Journal of a Tour to the Hebrides with Samuel Johnson LL.D., 1773*, ed. from the original MS. by F. A. Pottle and C. H. Bennett, new ed. 1961.

Hess: Ulrich Hess, *Geheimer Rat und Kabinett in den Ernestinischen Staaten Thuringens*, 1962.

Hirsch: Erhard Hirsch, 'Progressive Leistungen und reaktionäre Tendenzen des Dessau-Wörlitzer Kulturkreises', Ph.D. diss., Martin-Luther-Universität Halle-Wittenberg, 1969.

Hof Etat: Hof Etat vom Jahr 1764, Brunswick, Nds.StAWf, 1 Alt 25 228-228/1.

Hochfürstl. Sachsen-Gothaischer Hof-Calender: Hochfürstl. Sachsen-Gothaisch- und Altenburgischer Hof- und Adress-Calender, 1764.

Holborn: Hajo Holborn, *A History of Modern Germany, 1648–1840*, 1966.

*Holland: Boswell in Holland 1763–1764*, ed. F. A. Pottle, Heinemann ed. 1952, McGraw-Hill ed. 1952.

Horn: D. B. Horn, *British Diplomatic Representatives, 1689–1789*, 1932.

HUA: Het Utrechts Archief.

IGI: International Genealogical Index, compiled by the Church of Jesus Christ of Latter Day Saints. Summary lists of births, baptisms, marriages (but not deaths). See: www.familysearch.org

Impey and MacGregor: Oliver Impey and Arthur MacGregor, eds., *The Origins of Museums*, 1985.

Isenburg: Wilhelm Karl Prinz von Isenburg, *Europäische Stammtafeln*, 5 vols., 1953, repr. 1975–78.

Jamieson: John Jamieson, *An Etymological Dictionary of the Scottish Language*, 1880, repr. 1966.

JJ: John Johnston of Grange.

Keyssler: John George Keyssler, *Travels Through Germany, Bohemia, Hungary, Switzerland, Italy, and Lorrain …*, 2nd ed., 1757.

Klebe: Albert Klebe, *Gotha und die umliegende Gegend*, 1796.

Kneschke: Ernst Heinrich Kneschke, *Neues allgemeines deutsches Adelslexicon*, 9 vols. 1859–70.

Kohn: George C. Kohn, *Dictionary of Wars*, 1986.

*Later Years*: Frank Brady, *James Boswell: The Later Years, 1769–1795*, 1984.

Lauts: Jan Lauts, *Karoline Luise von Baden*, 1980.

*Laird*: *Boswell: Laird of Auchinleck, 1778–1782*, ed. Joseph W. Reed and F. A. Pottle, 1977.

Lehndorff, *Dreissig Jahre*: Ernst Ahasverus Heinrich von Lehndorff, *Dreissig Jahre am Hofe Friedrichs des Grossen aus den Tagebüchern des Reichsgrafen Ernst Ahasverus Heinrich von Lehndorff*, ed. Karl Eduard Schmidt-Lötzen, 1907; *Nachträge*, 2 vols. 1910, 1913.

*Letters JB*: *Letters of James Boswell*, ed. Chauncey Brewster Tinker, 2 vols., 1924.

Leuschner: Hans Leuschner, *Friedrich der Grosse: Zeit—Person—Wirkung*, 1988.

Lewis and Short: Charlton T. Lewis and Charles Short, *A Latin Dictionary*, 1879, repr. 1969.

*Life*: *Boswell's Life of Johnson, Together with Boswell's Journal of a Tour to the Hebrides and Johnson's Diary of a Journey into North Wales*, ed. G. B. Hill, rev. L. F. Powell, 6 vols., 1934–50; vols. v and vi, 2nd ed. 1964.

Lincoln: Eleanor Terry Lincoln, 'James Boswell, Reader and Critic', Ph.D diss., Yale University, 1938.

*Lit. Car.*: Frederick A. Pottle, *The Literary Career of James Boswell, Esq.*, 1929.

Littré: Émile Littré, *Dictionnaire de la langue française*, ed. intégrale, 1962.

Livet: Georges Livet and Francis Rapp, *Histoire de Strasbourg*, 4 vols., 1987.

*Lond. Journ.*: *Boswell's London Journal, 1762–1763*, ed. F. A. Pottle, 1950.

Loertscher: Gottlieb Loertscher, *Altstadt Solothurn, Schweizerischer Kunstführer*, rev. ed. 1987.

Löffler: Fritz Löffler, *Der Zwinger zu Dresden*, 1981.

LSAO: Landeshauptarchiv Sachsen-Anhalt, Aussenstelle Oranienbaum, Dessau.

Lustig: *Boswell: Citizen of the World, Man of Letters*, ed. Irma S. Lustig, 1995.

Lüthy: Herbert Lüthy, *La Banque protestante en France*, 1961.

Macdonald: Donald J. MacDonald, *Clan Donald*, 1978.

MacDonogh: Giles MacDonogh, *Frederick the Great: A Life in Deed and Letters*, 1999.

*Marggräflich Baden-Badischer Calender*: *Marggräflich Baden-Badischer Staats-und Addresse-Calender*, 1766.

*Markgräflich Baden-Durlachischer Calender*: *Markgräflich Baden-Durlachischer Staats-und Adresse-Calender*, 1767.

May: Georges May, *Rousseau*, 1994.

McCusker: John J. McCusker, *Money and Exchange in Europe and America, 1600–1775*, 1978.

McLynn: Frank McLynn, *Charles Edward Stuart: A Tragedy in Many Acts*, 1988.

*Militairisches Pantheon*: *Militairisches Pantheon oder biographisches Lexikon aller Helden und Militairpersonen welche sich in preussischen Diensten berühmt gemacht haben*, 1797.

Moderhack, *Braunschweigische Landesgeschichte*: Richard Moderhack, *Braunschweigische Landesgeschichte im Überblick*, ed. Richard Moderhack, *Quellen und*

*Forschungen zur Braunschweigischen Geschichte* 23 (1976).

Mörz, *Haupt- und Residenzstadt*: Stefan Mörz, *Haupt- und Residenzstadt: Carl Theodor, sein Hof und Mannheim*, 1998.

MN: Musée Neuchatelois.

Montet: Albert de Montet, *Dictionnaire Biographique des Genevois et des Vaudois*, 2 vols., 1877–1878.

Namier and Brooke: Sir Lewis Namier and John Brooke, *The House of Commons 1754–1790*, 3 vols., 1964.

NBG: *Nouvelle biographie générale depuis les temps les plus reculés jusqu'à nos jours*, ed. J. C. F. Hofer, 46 vols., 1853–66.

NDB: *Neue Deutsche Biographie*, multiple volumes, 1953–.

*New Grove 2: The New Grove Dictionary of Music and Musicians*, 2nd ed., ed. Stanley Sadie and John Tyrell, 2001 .

Nicolai: Friedrich Nicolai, *Beschreibung der Königlichen Residenzstädte Berlin und Potsdam*, 3 vols., 3rd ed. rev. 1786.

Nds.StAWf: Niedersächsisches Staatsarchiv Wolfenbüttel.

Nl. Formey: Nachlass Formey in SBB-PK.

Nugent: Thomas Nugent, *The Grand Tour*, 4 vols., 2nd ed. corr. 1756.

OCCL: *The Oxford Companion to Classical Literature*, ed. Sir Paul Harvey, 1946.

OC *Charrière*: Isabelle de Charrière/Belle de Zuylen, *Œuvres complètes*, ed. Jean-Daniel Candaux et al., 10 vols., 1979–84.

OC *Voltaire*: *Les Œuvres Complètes de Voltaire*, Voltaire Foundation, Oxford, multiple volumes, 1968–.

*Œuvres de Fréderic le Grand*: *Œuvres de Fréderic le Grand*, ed. J. D. E. Preuss, 31 vols., 1846–57.

OC *Rousseau*: *Œuvres Complètes de J.-J. Rousseau*, ed. B. Gagnebin et al. Ed. Pléiade, 5 vols., 1959–95.

OGS: *Ordnance Gazetteer of Scotland*, ed. Francis H. Groome, 2nd ed. 1901.

*Ominous Years*: Boswell: *The Ominous Years, 1774–1776*, ed. Charles Ryskamp and F. A. Pottle, 1963.

Osten: Jenny von der Osten, *Luise Dorothee, Herzogin von Sachsen-Gotha*, 1893.

Oxford DNB: *The Oxford Dictionary of National Biography*, ed. Brian Harrison, founding ed. Colin Matthew, 2004.

*Panorama: Panorama der Fridericianischen Zeit*, 1985.

Philippi, *Landgraf Karl*: Hans Philippi, *Landgraf Karl von Hessen-Kassel*, Veröffentlichungen der Historischen Kommission für Hessen, Marburg, 1976.

Philippi, *Das Haus Hessen*: Hans Philippi, *Das Haus Hessen*, 1983.

*Pol. Corr.*: *Politische Correspondenz Friedrich's des Grossen*, 46 vols., 1879–, 1939.

Pomeau, *La Religion de Voltaire*: René Pomeau, *La Religion de Voltaire*, 1969.

Pomeau, *Voltaire*: René Pomeau, *Voltaire en son temps*, 5 vols., 1995.

*Poststrassen: Poststrassen, Postkutschen, Postreisescheine*, ed. Christian Springer, 1982.

*Pride and Negligence*: F. A. Pottle, *Pride and Negligence: The History of the Boswell Papers*, 1982.

Rachel and Wallich: Hugo Rachel and Paul Wallich, *Berliner Grosskaufleute*, 2nd ed., 1967.

Reg. Let.: JB's register of letters sent and received (Yale MS. 251–55).

*Repertorium*: *Repertorium der diplomatischen Vertreter*, vol. 1: ed. Ludwig Bittner and Lothar Gross, 1936; vol. ii: Friedrich Hausmann, 1950; vol. iii: Otto Friedrich Winter, 1965.

Rentsch: Dietrich Rentsch, *Barockstadt Rastatt*, 1985.

*RHV: Revue Historique Vaudoise.*

Ribbentrop: Philip Christian Ribbentrop, *Beschreibung der Stadt Braunschweig*, 2 vols., 1789 and 1791.

Robert: *Le Grand Robert de la langue française*, 2nd ed. 1985.

Rowlands: John Rowlands, *Holbein: The Paintings*, 1985.

SächsHStA Dresden: *Sächsisches Hauptstaatsarchiv Dresden*.

Savory: Sir Reginald Savory, *His Britannic Majesty's Army in Germany During the Seven Years War*, 1966.

SBB–PK: Staatsbibliothek zu Berlin–Preussischer Kulturbesitz.

Schaab: Meinrad Schaab, *Geschichte der Kurpfalz*, 2 vols., 1988.

Schmincke: Friedrich Christoph Schmincke, *Versuch einer genauen Beschreibung der Residenz- und Hauptstadt Cassel*, 1767.

Schnegg: Alfred Schnegg, archivist, AEN, letters to Robert Warnock, 1955.

*Search of a Wife: Boswell in Search of a Wife, 1766–1769*, ed. Frank Brady and F. A. Pottle, 1956.

Seydewitz: Max Seydewitz, *Dresden, Musen und Menschen*, 1971.

Sedgwick: Romney Sedgwick, *The House of Commons 1715–1754*, 2 vols., 1970.

Sgard: Jean Sgard, *Dictionnaire des journeaux*, 2 vols., 1991.

Siebigk: Ferdinand Siebigk, *Das Herzogthum Anhalt*, 1867.

Sigrist: Hans Sigrist, *Solothurnische Geschichte*, vol. 3, 1981.

SJ: Samuel Johnson.

StASo: Staatsarchiv des Kantons Solothurn.

Stavan: Henry Anthony Stavan, 'Voltaire et la duchesse de Gotha', SVEC 185 [1980]: 27–56.

Stewart: Maj.-Gen. David Stewart, *Sketches of the Character, Manners, and Present State of the Highlanders of Scotland*, 3rd. ed., 2 vols., 1825.

SVEC: *Studies on Voltaire and the Eighteenth Century.*

Thiébault: Dieudonné Thiébault, *Mes souvenirs de vingt ans à Berlin*, 5 vols., 1804.

Thiele: Andreas Thiele, *Erzählende genealogische Stammtafeln zur europäischen Geschichte*, 4 vols., 2nd ed. c. 1991–96.

Thieme-Becker: Ulrich Thieme and Felix Becker, *Allgemeines Lexikon der Bildenden Künstler*, 37 vols., 1907–50.

ThStA Gotha: Thüringisches Staatsarchiv, Gotha.

H. Tronchin: Henry Tronchin, *Théodore Tronchin: un médecin du XVIIIe siècle*, 1906.

Vallière: P. de Vallière, *Honneur et fidelité: histoire des Suisses au service étranger*, 1913.

Vehse: Eduard Vehse, *Geschichte der deutschen Höfe*, 48 vols., 1851–60.

Volkland: Walther Volkland, 'Die Bau– und Kunstdenkmäler der Stadt Gotha', *Gotha: Das Buch einer deutschen Stadt*, ed. Kurt Schmidt, 1938.

Voss: Jürgen Voss, *Universität, Geschichtswissenschaft und Diplomatie im Zeitalter der Aufklärung: Johann Daniel Schöpflin*, 1979.

Wagner: Henry Wagner, 'Descendants of Sir James Kinloch, Bart.', *The Genealogist*, n.s. 14 (1897–98): 200–03, 261–63.

Weich: Karl Weich, *Mannheim—das neue Jerusalem: Die Jesuiten in Mannheim*, 1997.

Weinart: Benjamin Gottfried Weinart, *Topographische Geschichte der Stadt Dresden*, 1777.

Wettiner: Albert, Duke of Saxony, *Die Wettiner in Lebensbildern*, 1995.

WJT: William Johnson Temple.

Wurzbach: Constant von Wurzbach, *Biographisches Lexikon des Kaiserthums Oesterreich*, 60 vols. in 36, 1856–91.

Yale *Life* MS. Ed.: *James Boswell's* LIFE OF JOHNSON: *An Edition of the Original Manuscript in Four Volumes*, Vol. 1: 1709–1765, ed. Marshall Waingrow, 1994; Vol. 2: 1766–1776, ed. Bruce Redford, with Elizabeth Goldring, 1998.

Zedlitz-Neukirch: L. von Zedlitz-Neukirch, *Neues preussisches Adels-Lexicon*, 6 vols., 1836–43.

# Introduction

> I am preparing *my* Travels ... and believe they may be ready for
> publication next winter. They will not have much of inanimate
> subject matter, though I flatter myself there will be some good
> touches too on several topics of that nature. But for
> conversations, with Voltaire, *Rousseau*, ... Abbé Jerusalem of
> Brunswick, ... and a wonderful number of other persons, with
> letters, anecdotes, etc., etc., etc., they will be, I *say it*, delightful.

WHEN Boswell wrote these lines to his friend and executor Sir William Forbes on
11 May 1793, he had already published his major biographical works, *The Journal
of a Tour to the Hebrides* (1785) and *The Life of Samuel Johnson* (1791), his second
edition of which would appear two months later. Looking for a new project,
Boswell sensed that the journal kept at the time of his travels on the Continent,
undertaken nearly thirty years earlier, offered rich material for revision and
publication as well. He had, in fact, discussed this ambition with Johnson some
fifteen years earlier than his letter to Forbes, but Johnson, who expressed himself
no admirer of most contemporary travel writing, was discouraging.[1] Yet the
portion of his Continental diary relating to his adventurous trip to Corsica and his
meetings there with General Pasquale Paoli, the leader of the patriot insurgents,
had indeed been revised for publication and put to strikingly successful use,
forming the basis of his first acclaimed book-length work, *An Account of Corsica*,
in 1768. Moreover, the journal he kept at the time of his Scottish tour with
Johnson in 1773, revised with the help of his friend and editor Edmond Malone,
had been greeted with similar success on publication with the expanded title of
*The Journal of a Tour to the Hebrides, with Samuel Johnson, L.L.D.* But in 1793,
Boswell was in poor health, financially distressed, a professional failure in his
transfer from the Scottish to the English bar, and struggling as the widowed father
of five children. He would not have the opportunity to revise or expand his journal
in the two years he had left to live. Even so, in its fresh and originally written state,
this journal, in the words of Frank Brady (the twentieth-century biographer of
Boswell's later years), provides 'some of our finest glimpses' of several of Boswell's
eminent European contemporaries. '[G]iven fullness and continuity,' Brady
rightly observed, 'his "Travels" would have been a worthy companion piece to the
*Hebrides*'.[2]

Boswell had actually recognized the value of his Continental travel journal
while still in the process of writing it. 'What a rich treasure for my after days will
be this my journal,' he noted near the beginning of his trip in Brunswick, and he
promised himself a treat in reading it at a later time.[3] The present volume,

---

[1] *Life* iii. 300–01, 17 Apr. 1778.
[2] *Later Years*, p. 476.
[3] Journ. 11 Aug.

covering the period of Boswell's German and Swiss travels from the time he left Holland to the beginning his journey in Italy, Corsica and France, confirms Boswell's sense that it was a treasure on many counts. As this introduction and the journal itself will show, it offers, beyond the compelling record of his experiences and the characteristically perceptive Boswellian observations of characters among the high and the low, an unparalleled view of conditions of travel in eighteenth-century German and Swiss territory as well as of many other aspects of the period's culture. Written in the aftermath of the Seven-Years' War, the diary illuminates the customs as well as the religious and intellectual climate of western Europe at a time when the realms of landgraves, margraves and dukes were not yet absorbed into our modern nation-states. In addition, the journal sheds new light on Boswell's own complex personal and journalistic motivations.

This volume is the first to appear in the Yale research edition of Boswell's journals, the scholarly series envisaged since the establishment of the Yale Boswell Editions as a more thoroughly researched and annotated parallel to the popular 'trade' or 'reading' edition published in thirteen volumes from 1950 to 1989. *Boswell on the Grand Tour: Germany and Switzerland, 1764*, edited by Frederick A. Pottle, appeared in 1953 as the third volume in the 'trade' series, following *Boswell's London Journal 1762–1763* (1950) and *Boswell in Holland* (1952). For the research edition, the text has been newly transcribed from the manuscripts, with deletions made by their later owners restored. The many passages in Boswell's idiosyncratic French, which had been given in English in the 'trade' volume, are presented as close to the original as possible. Furthermore, the journal is placed here in the context of its attendant writings, including Boswell's preliminary essay on travelling in Germany, the short and often revealing notes ('memoranda') he wrote for each day of travel, the doggerel verses 'Ten Lines a Day' he dashed off daily starting Oct. 1, the autobiographical 'Ébauche de ma vie' written for Rousseau (together with its drafts, outlines, and related letters), and his detailed expense accounts. The volume's annotation not only corrects several errors of fact found in the 'trade' volume and other earlier editions of Boswell's writings, it also offers new historical or biographical details concerning German and Swiss personalities, topics and political issues with which modern readers will not be familiar. All aspects of the volume's materials have been researched afresh—a task helped by the increasingly accessible archives in the former Democratic Republic of Germany ('East Germany'). Moreover, improved library facilities, the completion of major editions such as R. A. Leigh's monumental *Correspondance complète de J.-J. Rousseau* in 52 volumes (1965–98), and extensive work in local history have helped to explicate materials by means not available to the earlier Yale editors.

## I. Boswell on the Continent

Boswell's German and Swiss journal, a segment of the personal diary he kept for much of his adult life, is also a detailed record of his travel experiences. Compared with other travel books written in his time, it is unusually full and informative. Thomas Nugent's *Grand Tour* (4 vols. 2nd ed. corr. 1756), which the notes to the present volume often invoke for corroborating information, offers brief, straightforward descriptions of a few noteworthy places, but concentrates mainly on routes and itineraries. Boswell combines the factual, his observations of what he saw, with the psychological, his personal reactions, experiences, interests, and varying moods. At his liveliest and best, he presents himself, in moments of self-dramatization, as 'young Boswell on his travels', or even occasionally as a self-deprecating figure, for instance when he is wrapped up *'like an Egyptian mummy'* perched precariously on his primitive cart-like vehicle.[4] Not only does this young traveller become a memorable figure, but the journal also offers a fascinating cast of other characters, the many men and women in all stations of life whom he encountered and inscribed into his own record.

The present volume, as mentioned earlier, covers only part of Boswell's experiences on the Continent. He had already spent ten months in the Netherlands where, following his father's footsteps, he had rather reluctantly pursued his law studies. His subsequent travels, which would continue for more than a year after he crossed the Alps into Italy, suggest not so much professional preparation as the traditional eighteenth-century Grand Tour—a phrase used as part of the title of the 'trade' edition of the Continental journals. But Boswell's own title, 'Journal of my Travels', is more appropriate. For he took an unusual path, avoiding most of France, spending time at the German courts, visiting Swiss cities and mountain villages, journeying up and down Italy, and eventually making a daring detour to the seldom-visited island of Corsica. More importantly, he was not the typical participant in the Grand Tour, a wealthy aristocrat who had time and money at his disposal, would mingle on equal footing with upper-class society, and could look forward to a secure future on his return. Although Boswell came from an established landed Scottish lowland family, was heir to an attractive estate in Ayrshire, and was proud of ancestors related to the earlier royal families of Scotland, his immediate family and his own prospects were professional, in Scots law. On his journey, while he cultivated persons of distinction and high birth, he extended his acquaintances to the middle and lower classes, indeed across the entire social range. In addition, his wish to meet two of the great literary men of his time, Rousseau and Voltaire, was remarkably ambitious, the result of an adolescent aspiration he had shared in Edinburgh with his college friend, William Johnson Temple. The actual fulfillment of this dream represents a high point for this portion of his travels. Altogether, young Boswell had broader interests and wider experiences than probably any other young Briton on any version of the Grand Tour in his day.

Before actually embarking on this phase of his journey, Boswell had tried consciously to prepare himself. In Holland starting in April 1763, he had practised French conversation, improved his wardrobe, and mingled with good society to which he had been introduced by his Dutch relations. Along with his law studies, he enjoyed more pleasant social experiences. Towards the end of his stay in Holland, he had carried on mild flirtations with Catherina Elisabeth (Hasselaer) Geelvinck, an attractive young widow, and with the young author Belle de Zuylen (later Mme de Charrière), the intelligent, headstrong daughter of one of the first

---

[4] Journ. 8 Oct.

families of Utrecht. But he had also suffered from periods of intense loneliness and depression. In the throes of various kinds of insecurity, he complained of the 'narrow' education he had received at the hands of his boyhood tutors in Edinburgh, and he was keenly aware of a need to become what he termed 'retenue'—restrained, decorous, manly, no more a youthful rattle. Now, at the age of twenty-four, imbued with a sense of adventure and curiosity as well as a sincere desire to broaden his experience through travel and meetings with interesting people, Boswell was coming to a new chapter of his life in regions largely unknown to other young British men of his day.

## II. Boswell's Itinerary

The beginning of his German travels was determined by an old family friend who had agreed to let Boswell accompany him from Utrecht. George Keith, 10th Earl Marischal, a respected diplomat in the service of Frederick II of Prussia and a former Jacobite who had grown disillusioned with that cause, was returning to Potsdam after a short stay in his native Aberdeenshire. He was accompanied by his ward, Emetulla de Froment, an indolent young Turkish woman, who is one of the many remarkable figures introduced in these journals.

During the first few days (18–25 June), the party journeyed east through Westphalia, stopping overnight at small towns with differing histories that reflected the turbulent political and religious dissensions of the seventeenth century. Most of the towns—Kleve, Wesel, Vellinghausen, Herford, Minden— had been absorbed into Prussia by treaty and were primarily Protestant (Lutheran), although Catholic worship was tolerated. Other towns, like Haltern and Rietberg, had reverted to Catholicism, reflecting the changing religion of new rulers. Hanover, though administered independently, was 'British' through the 'personal union' of its rulers, the Hanoverian King Georges, who had come to the English throne as descendants of James I (James VI of Scotland) after the death without an heir of Queen Anne, and had continued to regard themselves kings of England but also Electors of Hanover (so called because they were among those entitled to elect the ruler of the Holy Roman Empire).

In Brunswick, scene of the travellers' first somewhat longer stay (26–28 June), they reached the sociable court of the ducal family of Brunswick-Lüneburg. From there, Boswell could have proceeded directly south to Kassel, Frankfurt, and Mannheim, all of which he was planning to visit, but he chose to continue east, accompanying Lord Marischal as far as Potsdam and then escorting Mme de Froment to Berlin. In this, the largest and most interesting city he would visit, Boswell stayed for more than two months (from 5 July to 23 Sept.). During that time he returned to Potsdam to visit Lord Marischal, and for two weeks in August he also returned to Brunswick, from which he went on a day's excursion to the former ducal residence at Wolfenbüttel and summer palace at Salzdahlum.

Boswell began a new stage of travelling—to smaller and much less well-known German courts—on 24 September. After a day in Coswig, in the tiny duchy of Zerbst, he spent a week in the duchy of Anhalt-Dessau, residence of the militaristic pro-Prussian Dessauers. For one full day he also made a trip to Wittenberg, the 'cradle of the Reformation', even though that meant going further east than was called for by his main itinerary. By 1 October, abandoning an earlier scheme to reach Geneva by late November and Rome by Christmas, Boswell decided to spend more time in German and Swiss territory. His itinerary, written out at this time and revised a few days later, reveals his ambitious plan to see ten more German courts (see App. 1). Fulfilling this plan, he proceeded southward, spending a day in the Prussian town of Halle to see its salt manufactory, then four days in the university town of Leipzig (3–7 Oct.). From there he travelled to Dresden, his farthest point east, where he spent five days at the Polish-Saxon court (9–12 Oct.).

To visit the next court of his choice, Saxe-Gotha, Boswell had to reverse direction, travelling westward. To his chagrin, he had to retrace his route to Leipzig, and not finding a seat in a large passenger coach, proceeded slowly, with frustrating delays (14 to 15 Oct.) in a private coach or 'Extra'—a term for 'Extra-Post' that belied its name by actually offering no special advantage.[5] In the event, he gave up the visit to Weimar planned on his itinerary but spent four days (16–20 Oct.) at the well-organized court of Saxe-Gotha. Then, trying to fit in as many courts as possible, he headed north to Kassel, stopping at the residence of the dowager duchess of Saxe-Weissenfels in Langensalza just long enough to be invited to dine (21 Oct.). He came to Kassel hoping to meet the young landgrave, Friedrich II of Hesse-Kassel, but hearing only perfunctory greetings, left disappointed after four days (23–27 Oct.). Returning to his main route south, Boswell travelled to Frankfurt, from which he made a one-day detour east to Hanau, the residence of Friedrich II's estranged wife, Princess Mary. But because he had come from the court in Kassel, he was not received at hers. On his return to Frankfurt on the following day, Boswell took a boat south along the river Main from Mainz to Worms, and from there a coach to Mannheim, the residence of the Elector Palatine. Finding this court not hospitable to strangers, Boswell left after a few days (2–8 Nov.).

Continuing southward to Karlsruhe, Boswell experienced an unexpected change of fortune when he was warmly received by Margrave Karl Friedrich of Baden-Durlach. Boswell extended his stay from the planned three days to seven for what became the high point of his visits to the German courts (9–16 Nov.). Then, proceeding still further south, he came to one more small court, this one in Rastatt, the residence of the Catholic Margrave of Baden-Baden. On the stretch between Mannheim and Rastatt, presumably feeling the pressure of time, Boswell omitted other tempting places listed on his itinerary: Darmstadt, ducal residence of Hessen-Darmstadt; Heidelberg, precursor of Mannheim as residence of the electors palatine; and Stuttgart, residence of Karl (II) Eugen, Duke of Württemberg, at whose splendid court Boswell had planned to spend four or five days. Even with these omissions, he managed to see twelve courts in the span of five months, nine of them while journeying from Dresden to Rastatt during his last six and a half weeks (9 Oct. to 19 Nov.).

Now close to but not yet in Swiss territory, Boswell had to pass through Strasbourg, formerly German but annexed to France at the end of the seventeenth

---

[5] See Journ. 13 Oct., 'Ten Lines', 14 Oct., and Mem. dated 15 Oct.

century. He stayed for two and a half days (20–22 Nov.), just long enough to meet a few key members of the local French society. Pressing southwards, he then took in several Swiss towns: Basel (24–26 Nov.), Solothurn, known to him by its French name, Soleure (27–28 Nov.), and Bern (29–30 Nov.). From there he veered west to Neuchâtel, the Prussian dependency where Lord Marischal had served as Frederick II's governor. Realizing that Rousseau had found refuge nearby in the mountain village of Môtiers (a place not mentioned in his planned October itineraries), Boswell energetically sought out 'the wild philosopher' (Journ. 3 Dec.). For the next three weeks, Boswell travelled back and forth in the region: from Neuchâtel to Môtiers (3–5 Dec.), from Môtiers to Neuchâtel (6–9 Dec.) and to nearby Colombier to see Lord Marischal's pensioned retainers (10–11 Dec.), on to Yverdon, less than nineteen miles (30 km) south-west on Lake Neuchâtel, to meet some fellow Scots (12–13 Dec.), and back to Môtiers for his much hoped-for intimate conversations with Rousseau (14–15 Dec.). He returned to Yverdon for a few more days (16–19 Dec.) on his way to Lausanne, where he stayed for a full day of sociability (21 Dec.). On the following day he reached Geneva, which interested him (given his rigorous Scots religious upbringing) as the city of Calvin, and also as a point of departure for Voltaire's château at Ferney in French territory close by. Boswell went to Ferney on the afternoon of 24 December and stayed there from 27 to 29 December, having gained permission from Voltaire to spend two nights at the château. Before, during, and after these visits to Ferney, he mingled with Genevan society. On 2 January 1765 he left Geneva for the Alpine route to Turin, his German and Swiss travels now complete.

## III. Conditions of Travel

The journal, recording all these movements, provides a vivid account of the physical experience of travelling in German and Swiss territory in the mid-eighteenth century. The types of available vehicles, the state of the roads, the discomforts and even dangers of moving from place to place come to life through Boswell's personal experiences, as do the social implications of choices made by him and his fellow travellers.

Private carriages for several passengers could be hired by the well-to-do, as Boswell did for Lord Marischal and his group. Large stage coaches were run by the princes of Thurn und Taxis, who had a monopoly protected by the Holy Roman emperors. These Boswell must have taken for longer stretches along major roads. Less well known are the regional coaches he used in Prussia and in Hessen once he travelled on his own. His description of the cheap public conveyance called the *journalière*, which operated between Berlin and Potsdam, emphasizes its primitive construction. No more than an open cart made of wooden planks placed over wheels, it left its passengers at the mercy of the elements, even of tree branches at eye level.[6] Worse than this open *Postwagen* were the vehicles enclosed with leather covers that let in little air and blocked the view to the outside. After Boswell banged his head against the iron rods on the roof of one of these

---

[6] See Journ. 4 Aug.

'monstrous machines', which were part of the local 'Hesse Post', he preferred the open conveyances.[7] But gentlemen did not use such vehicles, open or closed. Boswell carefully changed to the more respectable Extra-Post, reserved for one or two passengers, to enter Brunswick 'as a gentleman' on his return visit in August. Yet the Extra-Post, more costly than the local coaches, brought new problems with it, since the wheels had to be greased at frequent intervals—an activity reported as 'Smear-Gelt' (German: *Schmiergeld*) in Boswell's expense account. And the Extra-Post could be slower when fresh horses were not available, as Boswell was chagrined to find on his unexpectedly prolonged trip from Dresden to Gotha.

The journal, furthermore, vividly shows the deplorable state of the roads, which were usually rough and bumpy. Wrapping himself up in his greatcoat against the cold, Boswell feared he would be helpless if the coach overturned.[8] When such an accident actually happened, on the way to Kassel, he and the other passengers were left in a ditch, in the dark, and in the rain.[9] Nor was there much choice of routes even between major places. Boswell, having travelled from Leipzig to Dresden, had to return to Leipzig before he could take the main route south to Gotha, Mannheim, and Karlsruhe. A few days later, in Langensalza, the roads 'overflowed with liquid mud'.[10] Perhaps that was why Boswell accepted an invitation in Langensalza to ride in a coach for even a short distance. Possibly for the same reason, he engaged a sedan chair in Kassel.

Safety in the town and city streets was also a concern. In Brunswick, no one was allowed on the street at night without a light, as Boswell discovered when he came close to being arrested (undismayed, he considered the experience 'an Adventure').[11] In Leipzig, the famous bridge with its elaborate one-way system for pedestrians and vehicles inspired him to write down the regulations for the flow of traffic. And lodgings for travellers varied considerably in quality. They could be pleasantly luxurious, as they were for Boswell in Berlin, but inns *en route* were often as uncomfortable as the vehicles. On the way to Frankfurt, where he had his worst experience, he lodged in a room with fourteen other adults and three children, though being acknowledged as 'Herr Baron', he was given the one available bed .[12] On several occasions, seeking better air, Boswell chose to sleep on a bare floor or on straw—even in a stable in spite of the possible danger of being trampled by the horses.[13] Fortunately, he had the courage and resilience required of travellers, especially in the autumn and winter months.

Travel in Swiss territory, rarer in this period and therefore a topic seldom considered in modern studies of eighteenth-century travel, offered even more limited choices of transport. To judge by Boswell's expense account, he took the Thurn und Taxis stage coaches on the main routes to Basel and Bern, and later from Lausanne to Geneva. For shorter distances—from Geneva to Ferney, for instance—he hired a private chaise or coach, which in the event proved

---

[7] See Journ. 27 Oct.
[8] See Journ. 8 Oct.
[9] See Journ. 22 Oct.
[10] See Journ. 21 Oct.
[11] See Journ. 18 Aug.
[12] See Mem. dated 30 Oct.
[13] See Journ. 24 Aug., 3 Oct.

inconvenient since he had to cut short his first meeting with Voltaire because the gates of Geneva closed early in winter. To reach Môtiers and other places in Neuchâtel, Boswell had to hire a horse, for whose upkeep he was responsible. At the very end of his time in Swiss territory, he had to entrust himself to the extremely primitive 'Alps machine'—logs tied together and carried by porters—in which he finally crossed the mountains into Savoy and Italy.[14]

## IV. The Courts and Courtiers

Viewed in a broader historical context, Boswell's German and Swiss travel journal focuses on a period of peace just fifteen months after the end of the Seven Years' War, when England, Prussia, and a few supporting German principalities had been pitted against France, Russia, and other German states, and contrary to expectation, had prevailed on the Continent. Frederick II himself had spent the war years on the battlefields. Other princes, including the Duke of Brunswick and the Landgrave of Hesse-Kassel, had been in exile while their territory was occupied by enemy forces. But by 1764 these rulers or their successors had resumed their power. They were back in their palaces, surrounded by their picture galleries, *objets d'art*, and other displays of wealth. In short, as observed by Boswell, life at the courts had become normal again. Yet residual signs of the Seven Years' War, as well as of earlier conflicts, lingered. Soldiers brutally punished as deserters aroused Boswell's sympathy, as did veterans in Prussia recalling their wartime hardships. The ruins of Dresden, caused by Prussian troops, called forth his indignation. In any case, with historical hindsight, readers of the twenty-first century will sense the precariousness of the period of peace enjoyed by Boswell and the rulers he visited, unaware as they were of the religious, social and political pressures and tensions that continued to fester under the surface. These would come to the fore twenty-five years later, when the French Revolution would bring yet more difficult times and even more drastic changes to western Europe.

More specifically, Boswell's journal extends our knowledge of the social reality of the German courts. It illuminates, for example, the vital importance of their unquestioned hierarchy. Their vertical organization began with a ruling prince and his successor, the *Erbprinz* (hereditary prince), and extended through the ranks of marshals, chief and subordinate chamberlains, masters of the horse, wine stewards, captains and officers of the life guards, ladies in waiting, down to lowly servants (even an official duck-catcher in Baden-Durlach), all named in the respective court calendars. Characteristically, Boswell's journal, recording his often friendly rapport with several of these officials, gives human faces to the hierarchies. Details of the courtiers' provenance and personal histories, offered in the annotation of this edition, deepen our understanding of these courts into whose life Boswell's record offers such revealing glimpses. In Brunswick, the presence of a Teutonic Knight (Ekhard von Stammer), of a young chamberlain from the provinces (Christian Ludwig Gottlob von Plessen, of Mecklenburg), along with a foreign-born diplomat (Feronce von Rotenkreuz) suggest the varied

---

[14] See Journ. 6 Jan. 1765.

backgrounds of the courtiers, while the presence of the wealthy Russian Shuvaloffs at one extreme and of the impoverished Italian nobleman Cavalcabò, in search of a position, at the other suggests the differing financial resources as well as the cosmopolitanism of this court. Boswell notes a similar social order in much smaller courts such as Saxe-Gotha, which covered a mere fifty square miles after being subdivided among seven siblings in an earlier generation. There he quickly established friendly relations with the leading chamberlain, the master of horse, the wine steward, and above all the marshal, all mentioned by name and most of them happily ready to have social conversations with Boswell.[15] Even the still smaller domain of the dowager duchess of Saxe-Weissensfels in Langensalza had a lady-in-waiting and 'grand maître' (major-domo) as well as a court chaplain, the latter glad to escort Boswell on a walk through the town.

All these courts functioned according to strictly enforced protocol. The letters of introduction with which Boswell had provided himself opened doors. Farewell calls strengthened recently established social bonds and laid the groundwork for further correspondence with a number of the people he met. Meals featured ceremonial beginnings and endings, as during Boswell's stay in Gotha. Yet along with the striking social rigidity of certain customs, Boswell benefitted from the quite remarkable hospitality extended to strangers at several of the courts. Those of Brunswick, Saxe-Gotha, Baden-Durlach (in Karlsruhe) and Baden-Baden (in Rastatt) provided him with an astonishing number of free meals, usually at the well-set table of the prince or of a high-placed courtier. Details from the so-called *Fourier-Buch* in Gotha, named for the official in charge of social arrangements, show the seating of guests, menus, and number of footmen in attendance, corroborating Boswell's journal entries. The journal itself also reveals that Boswell took such hospitality for granted. When no invitations were offered, for instance in Kassel and Mannheim, he felt slighted and aggrieved.

The aristocratic style of life which dominated the courts extended to their dress code. Elegant clothing was expected, and Boswell, having improved his wardrobe before leaving Utrecht, was pleased to have a 'suit of flowered Velvet of five colours' to wear in Gotha.[16] To attend a ball at that court, he was able to borrow a domino costume—*de rigueur* for the occasion. Special dress was also required for official mourning. This could last many months, as Boswell discovered when, unprepared for such a contingency, he could not be introduced at the court of Dresden because it was in mourning for the preceding Elector, Friedrich Christian of Saxony (who had died 27 Dec. 1763), and would continue to be in mourning for two more months to complete the customary year-long period. Only by ingeniously adding a few pseudo-military touches to his coat did Boswell eventually persuade the British envoy to arrange an introduction to Prince Xaver of Saxony, who had, in fact, recently published a detailed dress code while he served as 'administrator' in the minority of the young prince.

---

[15] See Journ. 17 Oct.
[16] Journ. 19 Oct.

Still more obviously contributing to the aristocratic tone of the courts was the widespread use of titles. Many persons, Boswell soon noticed, were styled *baron*, and he was convinced, not without foundation, that by the standards of the German courts he himself was also entitled to call himself such.[17] On several occasions, notably in Kassel and Langensalza, he was received at court only after identifying himself as a nobleman. Even the least socially conscious court he visited, that of Baden-Durlach in Karlsruhe, had its special distinction, the Order of Fidelity, which the ruling margrave awarded only to persons of aristocratic family. So eager was Boswell to win this honour that he unashamedly resorted to flattery and hypocrisy—'the skills of a courtier'—to curry the margrave's favour, and might well have succeeded, had the unexpected news of the death of his mother not prevented him from returning to Karlsruhe.

A monarchist even before he arrived in German territory, Boswell took a special interest in the princes. He managed to meet and describe several of them, starting with Karl I, Duke of Brunswick, a traditional absolute ruler who lived opulently, apparently oblivious to the financial problems he was causing for his realm. Boswell relished being at the Duke's table and meeting the ducal family, which included the newly arrived Princess Augusta, sister of George III, an English princess who had just been married to the hereditary prince of Brunswick. In contrast to these welcoming princes, the Electors in Mannheim were obnoxiously haughty, determined to prove their 'grandeur' by hardly deigning to address an unknown visitor. Two Irish members of their court, the uncle and nephew Harold, had difficulty even in arranging a speedy introduction for Boswell. Fortunately, the margrave of Baden-Durlach unexpectedly proved friendly and accessible to the unknown young Scot.

The most imposing ruler described in Boswell's journal, the one who caught his attention early in his German stay, was undoubtedly Frederick II of Prussia. Already known as 'the Great', he was the hero of the first Silesian and subsequent Seven Years' War as well as 'defender of the Protestant cause'. Boswell shows him unforgettably in the guise of brilliant soldier-king, striding majestically among his officers at parade.[18] Another side of the monarch is suggested in the display of his books, published under the pseudonym of *philosophe de Sanssouci* (a name inspired by the summer palace Frederick II had commissioned in happier days). At the time of Boswell's visit, the King was living in Potsdam, bent on rebuilding Prussia after its near-defeat in the Seven Years' War, but not deigning to receive a visiting stranger. In spite of Boswell's repeated efforts to be introduced, even those close to the King could not or would not arrange a meeting (though the reason for Boswell's failure to meet the King, unknown to him, and long unknown to scholars of his writings, has become clear from the family archives of Boswell's friend Alexander Burnet[19]). But Boswell's estimate of Frederick dropped precipitously after seeing the ruins of Dresden,[20] and his estimation fell further when he heard soldiers' tales concerning the King's wartime conduct.

---

[17] See Journ. 1 Oct. and n. 5.
[18] See Journ. 13 July.
[19] See Journ. 7 Sept. n. 3.
[20] See Journ. 9 Oct. and n. 8.

## V. The Bürger and Expatriate Scots

Beyond his accounts of the rulers and their courts, Boswell provides a rare view of the style of life of the *Bürger* (the citizens or bourgeois) in Berlin and nearby Charlottenburg—the bankers, jurists, and government officials who lived in their own circles though they owed their positions to the King. One of these, the manufacturer Johann Andreas Wegely, whose family had profited from the Seven Years' War, entertained guests in his summer house ('campagne') in Charlottenburg, near Berlin, and even had a decorative grotto in his garden. Others had experienced more difficult times, notably the entrepreneur Johann Ernst Gotzkowsky, who had made and lost his fortune as owner of a chinaware factory during and after the war. Recently declared bankrupt, he was now managing the factory for the King, though he was allowed to live on the premises. Carl David Kircheisen, president of police as well as mayor of Berlin, seems to have had limited resources, for he was pleased to take Boswell in as a paying lodger, but Kircheisen was nonetheless able to play host at a wedding in his town house, allowing Boswell to witness a modest though extended four-day celebration.[21] Kircheisen is of interest, furthermore, because he was a freemason, a member of the first lodge in Prussia formed in 1740. Possibly his warm feelings for Boswell were strengthened by his recognizing the young man as a brother mason. Boswell had joined the Canongate Kilwinning Lodge No. 2 in Edinburgh and had already served as junior warden.[22] That this bond was not mentioned in Boswell's journal probably reflects their obedience to the masonic code of silence. A similar silence was observed by Prince Ferdinand of Brunswick and Margrave Karl Friedrich of Baden-Durlach, both of whom were especially kind to Boswell (princes as well as Bürger could belong to masonic lodges). Other unidentified masons may well be commemorated in Boswell's journal.

Another group in the orbit of the Prussian court consisted of assorted Scots. Some were diplomats, such as the British envoy Andrew Mitchell and his secretary Alexander Burnet, who resided in Berlin and befriended Boswell there. Others were Scottish expatriates such as the privateer John Wake, who had taken on Prussian citizenship to strengthen his claim for compensation for his wartime losses in the service of Prussia. Still another group, the Kinlochs, had settled in the Swiss mountains, where Boswell would meet them a few months after leaving German territory. Sir James Kinloch had left his native Scotland in 1730 to avoid prosecution for bigamy, and had subsequently fathered an extended family in the vicinity of Yverdon, in Utrecht, and elsewhere on the Continent.[23]

But the most impressive Scot described in Boswell's journal was undoubtedly Lord Marischal, the warm friend of Frederick II and by this time another voluntary expatriate. Lord Marischal's stories, recorded succinctly in Boswell's memoranda, amount almost to an anecdotal survey of key developments of recent Scottish history. In one of the more dramatic moments of the journal, Lord Marischal is recorded as overcoming his noticeable early coolness towards Boswell by handing

---

[21] See Journ. 17–20 July.
[22] See Journ. 17 Nov. and n. 6.
[23] For his remarkable story, see Journ. 13 Dec. n. 2.

him a copy of John Barbour's *Brus*, which he inscribed with the memorable Latin phrase 'Scotus Scoto' ('From one Scot to another'). This gesture affirmed Boswell's national self-consciousness. His journal in London of 1762–63 had recorded his aspirations to acquire an English sensibility, in part by shaking off his Scottish upbringing and even some of his Scottish acquaintances, about whom his feelings fluctuated considerably and could best be described as inconsistent. Several of his comments in the Continental journals show his complicated national feelings, at times pro-Jacobite, but in general staunchly Hanoverian. Lord Marischal's gesture led to a notable turning point in Boswell, a moment after which he seems to have felt less ashamed of his fellow Scots. At his last public appearance in Prussia, he is to be found at a military parade in Potsdam ostentatiously sporting a Scottish 'bonnet'.

The importance of national identity recurs as a theme in this journal in other respects, too. The well-known admiration for the French language and culture at the German courts is confirmed in many ways, including Boswell's use of the language as his chief means of communicating with most of the people he met in German terrirory. Even the theatrical performances he saw at several of the courts—for instance in Prussia and Gotha—belonged to the French repertoire. But German language and literature were coming more and more to be appreciated. Boswell saw German examples of serious or polite literature, for example, in the translations from David Hume's *History of England*, which the margraval librarian Friedrich Valentin Molter included in his anthology for the court in Karlsruhe. More importantly, Boswell had several meetings with Johann Christoph Gottsched, the leading academic in Leipzig, who had devoted his career to improving the quality of German literature and the taste of the theatre-going public.

On another front, residual national tensions between the British and the French brought Boswell into great personal difficulty in a significant episode in Berlin. There he aroused the anger of a French captain in Prussian service by thoughtlessly making an anti-French remark (a prime example of his lack of 'retenue'). He quickly found himself in peril when the captain indignantly called him *faquin*, a loaded and calculated insult referring to a scoundrel of the lowest social class. The contretemps escalated into an affair of honour: for the captain, because the French nation had been insulted, and for Boswell because the honour of his family and of the Scots had been impugned. As a consequence, Boswell felt obliged to agree to a duel he did not want. Only the eventual proffering of apologies from both sides extricated the two equally unwilling opponents from a highly dangerous situation.

## VI. Religious Issues

Closely related to the issue of national identity was the question of religious identity, illuminated by the ways in which Boswell's journal draws attention to its fluidity and complexity in eighteenth-century western Europe. Different religions were practised within a very few miles of each other. In Westphalia, as noted earlier, Boswell saw strongholds of Protestantism such as Kleve and Herford, and of Catholicism in Rietberg, which had reverted to this religion in the early seventeenth century with the ruling Kaunitz family. In Prussian territory and in Brunswick, Protestantism, particularly Lutheranism, was the prevailing religion, though Duke Anton Ulrich had temporarily brought the realm back into the Catholic church. Further to the south, Catholicism was the dominant religion. These changes were of great interest to Boswell, who had, distressed by his own Scots Calvinist religious education, come to favour a 'decent system of mild Christianity' and had recently, after various other youthful experiments that included receiving the Roman Catholic communion, committed himself to the Church of England.[24] At the same time he remained attracted to the pomp and ceremony—the processions, the masses, the music—which he observed in the Catholic churches he visited whenever he had the opportunity.

The various religious points of view are personalized in the journal through Boswell's conscious efforts to talk with knowledgeable clergymen. Several of these men were what later centuries would call 'enlightened Protestants', well-read in the works of contemporary philosophers while giving preeminence to the Bible, especially the Gospels, as sources of truth. These clergymen, mostly from German and Scandinavian states, belonged to what is often termed the 'Northern Enlightenment'. Basically conservative, though aware of contemporary secular and advanced intellectual currents, they remained within their church and did not raise the disturbing questions posed by the more radical Enlightenment of the French, represented notably by Voltaire.

The German clergyman presented most fully and favourably in the journal is Johann Friedrich Wilhelm Jerusalem, the court chaplain and leading educator of Brunswick. He had been an abbot (*Abt* in German, hence called *abbé* by Boswell) of a Lutheran seminary. Known for fostering religious tolerance in Brunswick and disapproving of all sectarianism, he concentrated on the basic truths of Christianity as encoded in the Gospels. He had the ability to express difficult concepts simply, and to use personal experiences as a pedagogical device. In a memorable passage of the journal, Boswell sets down Jerusalem's own words to describe how he had sought solace when he thought he was dying, had not found Plato and the classics reassuring, but had then been soothed by reading the New Testament. The abbot's easily comprehensible lessons, gently taught, were understandably congenial to Boswell, the more so as they differed markedly from the Calvinist teachings of the Edinburgh kirk ministers and his intensely pious mother, who had left Boswell with painful memories. But in another subject of anxious interest to Boswell, the relative claims of divine foreknowledge and free will, Boswell did not accept Jerusalem's traditional view that the two concepts could be easily reconciled.

In Kassel, where the religious situation was more complex than in Brunswick, several generations of staunch Calvinist landgraves had been followed recently by a new landgrave, Friedrich II, who had secretly converted to Catholicism in younger days but had been forced to retain Calvinism as the state religion. Boswell had no opportunity for a personal talk with the landgrave but was befriended by a local clergyman, Jean-Jacques de la Porte, who authenticated the strange story of

---

[24] See Journ. 22 June.

Friedrich's conversion by pointing out a grotto in which Friedrich had secretly practised his Catholic worship. La Porte was a Huguenot, and one of three pastors for the sizeable French congregation which had settled in Kassel after the Revocation of the Edict of Nantes (1685) had led to the expulsion of non-Catholics from France. He was on good terms with the landgrave in spite of their different religions, and remarkably tolerant of the landgrave's flaws. But La Porte was firm in maintaining his own beliefs. Among various anecdotes, he described how the Landgrave had boasted that one of his prayers had been fulfilled, and how he, la Porte, ever the Protestant, had not hesitated to rebuke his ruler for believing that the saints or the virgin Mary would dispense such special favours. Boswell thoroughly approved of this clergyman, whom he found rational and independent.

Mannheim offered Boswell an opportunity to explore yet another religious point of view, for in the Palatinate, Catholicism had gained a strong hold through the Jesuits who had settled there. Boswell lost no time in seeking out a Jesuit attached to the local college. 'Le père Monier', as Boswell called him, has been tentatively identified in a study of the Jesuits in Germany as the Père Monet or François le Moine, formerly Prefect at the Jesuit college in Reims, who had recently been expelled from France with others of his order.[25] Like Jerusalem and La Porte, he was willing to be drawn into a discussion of thorny religious issues, and Boswell soon raised the troubling question of the eternity of punishment. This had been, according to his 'Ébauche de ma vie', one of the first great principles inculcated in him—it was, in fact, accepted by both Catholics and Calvinists—but he found it difficult to accept the idea of an unpardoning deity. The journal records a battle of wills between Boswell, who was hoping for a forgiving attitude, and the Jesuit, who remained intransigent. Amusingly, Boswell, having recorded both points of view, gives himself the last word by expressing the hope that they would meet in heaven. The Jesuit, on the other hand, insisted that a belief in eternal punishment was an essential part of his religion. Their verbal sparring thus ended in a stand-off. These and other spirited exchanges on his travels were excellent preparation for his meetings with Rousseau and Voltaire, whom Boswell had no qualms about asking outright questions concerning their religious beliefs while maintaining his own.

Religious affiliation in the Swiss territory Boswell visited was equally varied. In Basel, Protestant since the Reformation, Boswell recorded the defacement of Catholic images he was shown by a worldly guide, Emanuel Wolleb. On the other hand, in Solothurn, seat of the French ambassador to the Swiss cantons, Boswell was made aware of the prevailing Catholicism by the several churches and monasteries in close proximity (though the Swiss regiments stationed there presumably practised the religion of their homes). Bern, Neuchâtel, and Geneva were Protestant and offered him no surprises. But Geneva, historically 'the city of Calvin', unexpectedly proved to be far from austere in the actual practice of its citizens. Boswell, invited to a social gathering in the heart of the old town, was startled to find card-playing and general merriment on Sundays, and was shocked particularly by the presence of a clergyman among the guests. Evidently he could not erase his own childhood Calvinist training from his memory.

---

[25] See Journ. 7 Nov.

## VII. Intellectual Pursuits and the Cult of Sentiment

In a more secular cultural context, Boswell's journal reflects two opposing and seemingly incompatible trends of the mid-eighteenth century: the intellectually driven Enlightenment and, in a phrase that speaks for itself, the so-called cult of sentiment. One or the other of these trends shaped the personality or interests of many persons whom Boswell met, and in some respects they came together in Boswell himself.

About Boswell's intellectual interests, there can be little doubt. Even before arriving on the Continent, he had been a member of the Select Society of Edinburgh, an exclusive discussion group which brought together ambitious young Scots for meetings on intellectual subjects, and which counted David Hume and the historian William Robertson among its members. Moreover, while in Holland, Boswell had started to compile a Scots dictionary with the aim of collecting and preserving expressions that might otherwise be forgotten—an Enlightenment project emulating in a small way Johnson's *Dictionary of the English Language* and possibly also in a more limited form the *Encyclopédie* just being launched in Paris by Diderot and d'Alembert. Indeed, Boswell's projected dictionary offered a plausible entrée, or common ground, for meeting established scholars or intellectuals.

Yet during the first part of his German travels, Boswell, busy with new acquaintances, was in no hurry to seek out intellectual companions. When he finally spent a day at the *Académie royale des sciences et belles lettres* in Berlin, he was not impressed by that seemingly august body founded by Leibniz and still tightly controlled by Frederick II. The journal confirms the King's well-known preference for French or at least non-German members, but this preference did not necessarily ensure distinction. The Perpetual Secretary, Jean-Henri-Samuel Formey, though a prolific writer and influential leader in his Huguenot community of Berlin, struck Boswell as self-centred and a bore. A more impressive academician known to Boswell from their days in Utrecht, the mathematician-astronomer Jean Salvemini de Castillon, who had just been appointed to the mathematics section of the Academy, gave Boswell an opportunity to discuss weighty philosophical concepts such as free will and divine prescience, but he found Castillon's reasoning hard to summarize.[26] The actual meeting of the Academy, which Boswell attended thanks to Castillon, was particularly disappointing, since the paper delivered by Joseph Dufresne de Francheville on the making of ambergris was of little interest, and indeed erroneous in its conclusion about how ambergris is produced.[27]

Intellectual life at the University of Leipzig proved more congenial to Boswell. Gottsched—referred to by Boswell as 'one of the most distinguished literati' in Leipzig[28]—quickly became interested in Boswell's planned Scots dictionary, which he recognized as a scholarly interest they had in common. At Gottsched's suggestion, Boswell sought out Karl Andreas Bel, the university librarian, who was

---

[26] See Journ. 29 Aug.
[27] See Journ. 13 Sept. n. 7.
[28] Journ. 4 Oct.

also editor of the *acta eruditorum Lipsiae*, the oldest German periodical, written in Latin, that reviewed recently published works of literature and scholarship. Bel showed Boswell the newest issue of the *acta*, reading it aloud just before sending it to the printer. In addition, Bel introduced Boswell to other members of the university: Johann Bartholomäus Rogler, compiler of a dictionary incorporating words from Johnson's work, and Christian Fürchtegott Gellert, professor of philosophy and a poet who was much admired in Leipzig for his *Fables* and religious poems. Encouraged by the warm reception he received, Boswell, with increased self-confidence, went on to meet other intellectuals. These included the political philosopher Emmerich de Vattel, who had written about the rights of nations in wartime in his *Droit des gens* while living through the bombardments of Dresden; Bartholomew Tanner, the first professor of English at the university of Strasbourg, who gave Boswell a copy of his inaugural address; and Jean-Daniel Schöpflin, professor of history and rhetoric at the University of Strasbourg, member of many learned societies and author of a seven-volume survey (in Latin) of the history of Baden-Baden and Baden-Durlach. Though Boswell's journal does not provide details about his meeting with Schöpflin, its success is suggested by the letter this eminent scholar wrote to Margrave Karl Friedrich of Baden-Durlach referring to Boswell as 'un jeune homme qui ira loin'.[29]

Not only his meetings with stimulating intellectuals but also his visits to their libraries and related collections of medals, coins, and busts (the precursors of modern museums) reveal the broadening of Boswell's intellectual horizons. The private libraries of Jerusalem, Gottsched, the margravine of Baden-Durlach, and Schöpflin all caught Boswell's attention. So did the imposing ducal library in Wolfenbüttel, which Boswell described in detail after a day's visit. These libraries aroused Boswell's own ambition for improving the library at Auchinleck, in the hope of making it not just a large but—his favourite term of praise—a 'noble' one.

Not to be overlooked in the range of Boswell's intellectual interests are his responses to works of art, which he recorded in many entries of his journal. Though he lacked a sophisticated vocabulary to express his enthusiasm, he responded best when he had a personal connection to a work. He was struck by the Flemish portrait of a beautiful young woman in Kassel because it reminded him of Belle de Zuylen. And in Basel he showed keen interest in the works of Hans Holbein the Younger, at least in part because of a complicated association of ideas linking Lord Auchinleck with his favourite author Erasmus as well as Holbein, who had illustrated Erasmus's *Encomium Moriae* with drawings.[30] Boswell was so enthralled by the Passion cycle of paintings in Basel, which he attributed to Holbein (though it may have been created rather by a contemporary of Holbein's), that he took notes on each of its eight panels and later had his law clerk copy the notes in a neater hand.

While the journal shows Boswell actively engaged in these various intellectual pursuits, it also reveals his involvement with the emotional side of the period, the cult of sentiment. With its emphasis on feelings, especially distressing or mournful ones, this mood, well known in Britain through the fictional writings of Henry

---

[29] See Journ. 21 Nov. n. 13.
[30] See Journ. 26 Nov. n. 7.

Mackenzie, Samuel Richardson, and Laurence Sterne, figures prominently in Boswell's journal. Two of its key terms, 'spleen' and 'hypochondria' (sometimes abbreviated as 'hypoc') appear often, used interchangeably and broadly without invoking the bodily organs that had originally inspired their names. These terms refer to a malaise that had been called 'melancholy' in Shakespeare's time and would later be called 'depression'.[31] Indeed, as shown in his fragmentary jottings of 1764 (App. 1), Boswell, in response to the emotional life he was experiencing in this portion of his travels, was already drafting early versions of the series of seventy essays he would write in later life under the revealing pseudonym 'The Hypochondriack'.

The journal shows that this mood was anything but unique to Boswell, or restricted to the British Isles. Indeed, spleen or hypochondria was a complaint to which an astonishing number of his contemporaries could admit. His fellow sufferers included Lord Marischal (Mem. dated 21 June), Mme de Froment (Mem. dated 27 June), Castillon (Journ. 3 Sept), Kircheisen (Journ. 17 Sept.), and General Weiligh (Mem. dated 23 Sept.), to name only a few in Prussia; as well as Jerusalem, Plessen, and Cavalcabò in Brunswick (Journ. 21 Aug.). Jerusalem, in particular, spoke eloquently of having suffered from black moods which brought him close to despair (Journ. 11 Aug.). He also told the pathetic story of a young tutor who was painfully incapacitated by his failed suicide attempt, illustrating the dangers of uncontrolled depression. Boswell realized that spleen was not just 'the English malady', as some of his contemporaries believed, but a more universal human condition, one extreme manifestation of the cult of sentiment's exaggerated awareness of the operations of one's own inner life.

Boswell's daily entries, especially in his memoranda, give a much fuller account of the complaint than other, more public sources. The journal provides a survey of some of Boswell's attempts to trace it to empirical causes (bad weather, lack of sleep, a raging headache and fear of oncoming fever) as well as of the means of combatting it (mainly by exercise). Boswell concluded that often his spleen or hypochondria was not just an inexplicable feeling but a physical complaint. With this insight he was echoing the ideas of Dr. George Cheyne, the author of the *English Malady* (1733), who regarded spleen and hypochondria as 'nervous diseases' caused by disturbances of the circulation or perspiration and other secretions.[32] Although Boswell also refers to his 'nerves' or 'nervous disorder' or to a 'nervous fluid' that was 'disordered',[33] he was more interested in locating his distresses in the circulation of the blood. Sluggish circulation, he believed, was a cause of depression while, conversely, brisk circulation was a sign of vigour and youth.[34] Knowing that physical activity could ward off or overcome his depression, Boswell took the time, especially in Berlin, for horseback riding and lessons in fencing. His particularly exciting days in Dessau, which included two spectacular stag hunts, notably left him free of depression.

---

[31] For a fuller discussion of these terms, see Mem. dated 20 June n. 4 and 21 June n. 2, Journ. 26 June n. 9.

[32] See Cheyne, ch. vii.

[33] Journ. 6 Aug., 3 Nov.

[34] See Journ. 18 June.

Yet at least as often, psychological or existential causes for depression, especially what Boswell terms 'speculation'—the tendency to brood introspectively or to analyze too much—occupied Boswell's thoughts on his condition. Such thoughts could intrude suddenly in an otherwise comfortable setting, for instance during a pleasant dinner in Brunswick: 'All was noble & fine. Yet did my abominable Speculation analyse All into insipidity at last'.[35] Boswell's sense of the value of human life suffered when he speculated about the insignificance of the many Prussian soldiers expendable in battle, worth no more than 'a barrel of herring', or of himself, who was 'nothing in the multitude of Beings'.[36] Repeatedly, he brooded about agitating subjects, 'metaphysics, fate, free will, the origin of evil, and all those beautiful themes', phrases drawn from his conversation with Andrew Mitchell. That discussion ended with Mitchell and Boswell agreeing that to be 'busy and cheerful' was preferable to 'dark speculations'.[37] In the background of these troughs of low spirits were Boswell's memories of Scotland and his dreary Calvinist childhood, seldom mentioned in the journal, but emerging in full force in the 'Ébauche de ma vie' he wrote to introduce himself to Rousseau.

## VIII. Women

Boswell's interest in women remains a key component of his general reputation. Any attractive woman, especially a young one who showed an interest in him, gained his attention. But this journal introduces a wide spectrum of women differing in age, social standing and authority. Indeed, the journal shows that Boswell's relations with them were more varied and his attitudes correspondingly more complex than one might expect from his generally libertine reputation. His interest in women here only occasionally includes amorous possibilities. His sexual activity during this portion of his Continental travels was, in fact, far less frequent than amorous fantasies, whose objects range from (improbably enough) the princesses in Brunswick to bourgeoise young women in Berlin, for one of whom, the sprightly young Caroline Kircheisen, Boswell wrote his charming 'Verses written on a Post-Wagon' after leaving her father's house (see App. 1). The figure of Belle de Zuylen also recurs in his memory, usually with conflicting feelings, as he was both attracted and disturbed by her.

But strong-minded women were not necessarily threatening to Boswell, as seen by his admiring description of the talented, highly intellectual Karoline Luise, Margravine of Baden-Durlach. She had established a gallery of small-scale paintings and works in crayons, some of them her own work, and was setting up a collection of scientific specimens on the model of the *Encyclopédie*, for which she enlisted Boswell's help. A commanding figure in her society, she inspired Boswell to wish for such a wife for himself.[38]

---

[35] Journ. 27 June.
[36] Journ. 13 July, 9 Aug.
[37] Journ. 2 Aug.
[38] See Journ. 14 Nov.

Other mature women appear in the journal as appealing figures. Henriette Kircheisen, wife of the Berlin mayor and mother of the lively Caroline, had loyally cared for her husband during his most difficult wartime years, as she told Boswell, and baked 'fine cakes' for Boswell himself during his last days in Berlin.[39] Mme de Poigk (Boswell's 'Boick'), governess to the Brunswickian princesses, became Boswell's confidante and an amused observer of his quandary about which princess to court on a given evening. On the other hand, hearing of the many 'gallantries' of Mme von Brandt, lady in waiting to the Queen of Prussia, made him wish to stay in Berlin long enough to benefit from her experience in that particular regard.[40]

Yet another mature woman, with whom Boswell actually formed a friendly relationship towards the end of his Swiss stay, was Rousseau's housekeeper and former mistress Thérèse Levasseur. Not only was she devoted to Rousseau, protecting him from intrusive visitors, but fortunately she also took a liking to Boswell and paved the way for his interviews with the great man. The garnet necklace Boswell sent her on his last day in Geneva, presumably to thank her for her kindness, seemed to mark the end of their acquaintance at this time—though it would grow into a brief sexual affair when he escorted her from Paris to England in 1766.

Still lower on the social scale were two figures who illustrate the vulnerable position at this time of unattached working women. A beautiful laundress in Brunswick inspired Boswell with such tender feelings that he asked her to come with him to Scotland, an offer she had the good sense not to accept. He made a similar offer to a servant at the inn in Colombier, Caton Otz, the daughter of the local butcher (she, too, declined to go with him). Neither of these women could be considered marrigeable for one of Boswell's standing as the son of a Scottish judge and hereditary landowner, but neither was a sexual partner.

On one occasion in this part of his travels, however, Boswell engaged in quick sex with a young woman who came to his room selling chocolate. She was the wife of a Prussian soldier, and pregnant, so seemed quite safe. This episode, an example of the rakish behaviour thought typical of Boswell, was so unusual for him by this time that it caused him great feelings of guilt, and made him vow to refrain from such activity until he could discuss the matter of sex and morality with Rousseau.

All in all, Boswell's varied experiences with women in German and Swiss territory can be seen as part of the process of deepening his knowledge of the world. They were also stages that led him, a few years later, to seek a suitable permanent partner in marriage at home.

### IX. Rousseau and Voltaire

'Voltair, Rousseau, immortal names!'. These names had inspired Boswell and his college friend William Johnson Temple as early as 1759 to daydream about spending a summer in Geneva, where they hoped to meet both men and to 'enjoy the benifit of their conversation'.[41] This plan, never carried out by Temple for

---

[39] Journ. 17 Sept.
[40] Journ. 18 Sept.
[41] From WJT, ?Spring 1759, *Corr.* 6, pp. 16–17, 18 n. 5.

financial reasons, would set an ambitious goal for the end of Boswell's German and Swiss travels.

By the time he reached Swiss territory, Boswell had in some measure overcome his initial insecurities, his sense that he had suffered from a 'narrow' education, and was insufficiently 'retenue'. In a significant change, he had come to think in more positive terms: 'I must be Boswell and render himself as fine a fellow as possible'; 'I must be Mr. Boswell of Auchinleck and no other. Let me make him as perfect as possible'.[42] The compliments he began to record at this time, particularly Jerusalem's expression of fulsome esteem and Vattel's assurance that he was 'bien instruit', attest to the young man's deepening sense of personal 'merit'. This term, which was becoming a favourite of Boswell's, refers not simply to intrinsic worth, but to proving himself by passing various tests or trials. He had experienced such success on earlier occasions, as when he managed to be received by the professors in Leipzig without formal introduction—an achievement he considered a 'fair tryal of my real Merit'.[43] Now he was ready for the most important tests of his merit, the meetings with Rousseau and Voltaire. And he was clear about his motivation: 'My romantic Genius which will never be extinguished, made me eager to put my own merit to the severest tryal'.[44] Yet to achieve the hoped-for meetings was no easy matter, since neither Rousseau nor Voltaire was in good health, and neither was especially interested in talking with eager young strangers. That Boswell succeeded in having extensive discussions with the two leading *philosophes* of his time was indeed an extraordinary feat.

Boswell's records, especially of his conversations with Rousseau, offer not only a remarkably full and many-sided view of this famous man but also a uniquely personalized window on the range of ideas expressed within the radical Enlightenment. Boswell's impassioned letter asking for an interview emphasizes the 'merite singulierre'—a phrase memorable in spite of its flawed adjectival-noun agreement—that makes him worthy of being seen and judged by Rousseau, and also suggests the impact of the writings of the *philosophe* on an impressionable young man. This letter, read together with the earlier drafts Boswell was replacing, itself mirrors the sentimental effusions of Rousseau's St. Preux in *La Nouvelle Héloïse*. Boswell's elevated mood, which continued with his walk in a snowy Alpine landscape, reveals the kind of passion for nature popularized by Rousseau, and little on display elsewhere in Boswell's writing. In other words, Boswell approached Rousseau already in a Rousseauistic state of mind.

In the account of his actual meetings with Rousseau, recorded in detailed memoranda as well as written up fully in the journal, Rousseau's 'sentiment' can be seen yielding on occasion to pointed and clear-headed ripostes. When Boswell mentions his short-lived conversion to Catholicism, including his thought of possibly entering a monastery, Rousseau's response is brusque: 'Quelle folie'.[45] Boswell's direct question about whether Rousseau was a Christian—in a memorable moment in which they exchange piercing looks—yields another

---

[42] Journ. 20 July, 9 Aug..
[43] To JJ, 6 Oct, *Corr. 1*, p. 136.
[44] Journ. 3 Dec.
[45] See Mem. dated 6 Dec., Journ. 5 Dec.

forceful answer—'Je me pique de l'étre'—followed by Rousseau's declaration that he believes in the Gospel and the Trinity, though he cannot be sure of more.[46] This limited affirmation of traditional beliefs is of high value to students of Rousseau in view of his difficulties with the ecclesiastical and civil authorities of Paris, Bern, and Geneva, who had questioned his religious orthodoxy, had refused him residency, and had ordered the burning of his books. As for the important issue of how to expiate for one's wrongdoing, a nagging question for Boswell, Rousseau again gives firm advice: 'Faites du bien. Vous acquiterez tout le mal'.[47]

When asked by the dazzled Boswell whether he would become his mentor, Rousseau quickly refuses, asserting that he can care only for himself. Rousseau's characteristically rational, judgmental approach, suggested in these exchanges, continues even after his reading of the 'Ébauche de ma vie', which Boswell had left during his absence from Môtiers. Hearing of Boswell's changes of religion, Rousseau bluntly declares that the young man has become bogged down (*fariné*) in religious uncertainties and should stay away from clerics.[48] Told about Boswell's guilt-ridden affair with a young married woman in Scotland, Rousseau strongly advises Boswell to tell her that his conscience forbids their continuing their relationship. On polygamy, in which Boswell half-seriously claims an interest on the model of the Biblical patriarchs, Rousseau insists on obedience to the laws of one's own society. In short, Rousseau emerges as stern judge of behaviour, independent in his thinking, strong-minded in his opinions, much more given to practical rationality than to sentiment.

Yet as the discussions continue, the initial unfamiliarity gives way to a warmer, less preceptorial relationship between the philosopher and his young visitor. Boswell even feels free to tease Rousseau about his *figmagairies* (whims), and he relishes the intimate domestic scene to which he has been invited in the kitchen of Rousseau's simple rented house. Boswell records every course of the frugal but hearty meal prepared by Thérèse Levasseur, then focuses on a charming moment of Rousseau singing to his dog while the dog dances around his platter. The scene continues the mood of sentiment with a prolonged tender farewell—Rousseau offering an embrace and kisses which make Boswell think of him as 'St. Preux attendri', a merging of Rousseau with his sentimental hero. At this point Boswell senses an invisible thread or bond of affection linking him with Rousseau. Finally, as if unwilling to end the farewell, Boswell introduces a quotation from *Emile* that suggests he and Rousseau speak the same emotional language. The scene as a whole is infused with the tone and style of the cult of sentiment.

The meetings with Voltaire were more difficult to achieve than those with Rousseau, since the available time was limited not only by the early closing, already mentioned, of the Geneva gates, but also by Voltaire's habit of emerging from his room only towards the evening. Boswell overcame these obstacles by appealing to Mme Denis, Voltaire's niece and hostess, in an amusing letter asking for an overnight stay, and was quickly granted permission in a letter written

---

[46] Journ. 5 Dec.
[47] Ibid.
[48] See Mem. dated 15 Dec.

ostensibly by her but actually by Voltaire himself. Once at Ferney, Boswell recorded his impression of an aristocratic atmosphere at the estate and among its occupants. The two-storey house, though not yet expanded by wings at the time of Boswell's visit, was already known as the *château*. Voltaire, served by footmen and a secretary-librarian, behaved like a *grand seigneur*. In the subsequent meetings, he was surrounded by sophisticated cosmopolitan friends and admirers very different from the simpler company in Môtiers.

The conversations recorded by Boswell at Ferney offer an unusual view of Voltaire by showing his command of English and his interest in English literature. Having mastered this language in the 1740s during his stay in England, Voltaire uses it with wit, imagination and even a sprinkling of no longer fashionable English curse words. Boswell's notes reveal Voltaire's extensive knowledge of English literature, as well as his awareness of the latest literary trends, such as the interest in the newly 'discovered' Ossian. Characteristically critical when confronting writings that might compete with his own reputation, Voltaire shows little appreciation for Shakespeare, whom he credits with writing two good lines but not six.[49]

Compared with his literary opinions, Voltaire's statements on religious subjects seem sparse, at least partly because significant pages of Boswell's record were lost after being written on separate sheets of paper. Yet Voltaire—or Boswell summarizing Voltaire—shows a remarkable gift for focusing quickly on key issues: the soul (not knowable), public worship (acceptable on limited occasions), one universal deity only, and the brotherhood of man.[50] He does not accept a belief in the Trinity, the concepts of sin, eternal punishment, and an organized church. Voltaire's beliefs were those of a deist or theist, as he called himself, and as such accorded with the ideas of the radical Enlightenment. Such thoughts were far from being acceptable to conservative Christians, such as Samuel Johnson and Boswell. Indeed, the latter accused Voltaire to his face of being 'a bad man', and of being an 'infidel'.[51] Nonetheless, Boswell was elated with his experience. He had succeeded in being admitted to serious discussions first with Rousseau and then with Voltaire. By each one, furthermore, Boswell had been promised a correspondence in the future. Above all, he had proved himself. He had held his own in the presence of two of the most famous men in Europe. The triumph for Boswell had been the endorsement of his 'mérite singulierre'.

## X. The Journal

Journal-writing was already a habit for Boswell when he embarked on his Continental travels. He had recorded his experiences and thoughts in his 'Journal of my Jaunt, Harvest 1762' and had continued at greater length in his London journal of 1762–63 and in his journal in Holland (regrettably lost when sent back to Scotland). He evidently had an irrepressible urge to write, and felt impelled to

---

[49] See Journ. 27 Dec.
[50] See Mem. dated 30 Dec.
[51] Journ. 28 Dec.

record his own experiences. The very activity of writing brought him pleasure, as well as solace.

On his travels, Boswell recorded his activities late at night or on the following morning. Usually he contented himself with short 'memoranda' written in brief phrases that served as reminders of actual happenings or of expectations for the next day. The memoranda included snatches of conversations, even of anecdotes heard from others. A little later, he wrote up the journal, several days' worth at a time, with more attention to coherent exposition. When he came to Rousseau, Boswell set down their conversations at much greater length in his memoranda, and often retained their wording in the fully written journal.

Boswell was methodical in keeping his journal more or less up to date. He made a point of writing it up just before leaving a place, most tellingly at the end of his stay in Rastatt: 'Enter not Suisse — till Germ[.] journalised'.[52] Yet he had mixed feelings about his daily record keeping, taking it seriously while also observing himself with a touch of self-irony, as when he likened himself to a pedantic German professor producing his annual folio.[53] And he amused himself by engaging in brief dialogues with himself, as in the following example in which his thoughts about journal-keeping can be seen to fluctuate:

> At night Indolence made me think: Why give myself so much labour to write this Journal, in which I realy do not insert much that can be called usefull — Beg your pardon. Does it not contain a faithfull Register of my variations of mind? Does it not contain many ingenious observations & pleasing strokes which can afterwards be enlarged? Well, but I may die. True but I may live, & what a rich treasure for my after days will be this my Journal.[54]

Boswell considered this 'treasure' as 'a reservoir of ideas' for later interpretation rather than a factual 'history'.[55] Yet the journal is, for the most part, remarkably accurate in the verifiable details of its reporting. Later editors, for example, who doubted the existence of a 'Mme. de Buick' or 'Boik' at the Brunswick court, were proved wrong when archival documents revealed a 'Frederique von Poigk' active there for many years.[56] The curious flakes Boswell observed floating down on his way to Dresden did not come from trees, as one might assume, but consisted, as Boswell correctly explained, of gossamer produced by spiders in late autumn.[57] Inevitably, Boswell made occasional mistakes. An acoustical problem misled him into calling the great bell of a church in Erfurt 'die grosse Susanne' instead of 'Osanna', for 'Hosanna': 'in praise of God'.[58] But such slips are few, and on the whole negligible.

---

[52] Written in the margin of the Mem. dated 20 Nov.
[53] See Journ. 10 July.
[54] Journ. 11 Aug.
[55] See Journ. 18 Oct.
[56] See Journ. 12 Aug and n. 6; Mem. dated 13 Aug.; and *Grand Tour* I, p. 59 n. 2.
[57] See Journ. 7 Oct. and n. 3.
[58] See Journ. 16 Oct. and n. 4.

The writing in the journal varies, like Boswell himself, in mood and skill. Often pedestrian in recording a day's activities, it is enlivened by Boswell's bursts of enthusiasm, as when he describes being thrilled by the beauty of the young laundress in Brunswick,[59] or by the 'glorious chace' of a stag in Dessau.[60] The style rises in intensity at a few key moments, notably in recording his view of Frederick II striding among his officers on parade (an attempt at the lofty writing of the sublime)[61] and in describing his walk in the snowy Jura mountains as he prepares himself for his first meeting with Rousseau (an attempt to capture a Rousseauesque moment in nature).[62] Boswell displays at times an attractive sense of humour, along with gifts for playful detachment and self-dramatization, as when he refers to himself repeatedly as 'Young Boswell of Auchinleck ... upon his travels'.[63] And he comments amusingly on his own writing, for instance on noticing a redundancy in the phrase 'printed editions': 'Poh! what language is this! A printed Edition. One might as well say a written Manuscript. But I journalise in haste: so let errors be pardoned'.[64]

About a third of the Journal is written in French, attesting to Boswell's increasing fluency in that language and earnest desire to improve himself in it. But though his comprehension seems to have improved, his writing often sounds like a direct transliteration of the English, and his recording of names can be puzzling until one recognizes that it is phonetic, as in 'du Foin' for de Faugnes and 'Pergo' for Perregaux. His memoranda, written even more hastily than the journal, are disorganized, rapid and disjointed outpourings of ideas and feelings. They are instructive and revealing in their own way, often disclosing, for example, more of Boswell's 'spleen' than the fully written journal. Most of his admonitions to himself to be more controlled ('retenue') in his utterances appear only in the memoranda, as do the frequent reminders to himself to write up the journal. Some of the memoranda, tantalizingly elliptical, give only brief phrases that refer to anecdotes Boswell wished to remember, and thus supplement the fully written journal and afford an even more comprehensive record of the time. Several of these concern Frederick II of Prussia, others concern Lord Marischal, still others focus on interesting personalities such as the notorious Lord Baltimore travelling with his harem, or the strangely named 'Tibi' whose 'curious story', too long for the journal and then lost in being recorded on separate pages, is now known to concern General Oglethorpe and his loyalty to Marshal James Keith mortally wounded on the battlefield.[65]

To publish the writings associated with his German and Swiss travels was not just an idea that occurred to Boswell later in his life. It was a scheme he considered while he was still in the midst of the experience. In October he mentioned a vague plan to revise his journal in a few years' time, to 'abridge it in a more elegant

---

[59] See Journ. 13 Aug.
[60] Journ. 28 Sept.
[61] See Journ. 13 July.
[62] See Journ. 3 Dec.
[63] Journ. 7 July.
[64] Journ. 26 Nov.
[65] See Journ. 28 Aug. and n. 1.

style'.[66] And he expected to publish reports of his meetings with Voltaire, first as a 'sketch' in a London newspaper and then in a full report after Voltaire's death. The 'eight quarto pages' he had already written immediately following his last meeting with Voltaire would presumably have been the basis for such a report.[67] But these pages, too, were lost. Except for the *Account of Corsica* (1768), he did not live, as noted at the beginning of this Introduction, to revise his Continental travel journals as he intended.

Years later, Boswell did however receive a touching reminder that his experiences abroad had not been forgotten. James Boswell the younger ('Jamie'), then a youth of sixteen, tried to console his despondent father with the thought that being known to Voltaire, Rousseau, and other famous persons of his day was surely preferable to being 'a rich, though dull, plodding lawyer'.[68] Other, more private documents, most notably the 'Ébauche de ma vie', which Boswell retrieved from Rousseau but had no thought of making public, have come to be valued for their biographical, social, and historical information. The present volume allows modern scholars, in a way that Boswell's real but unfulfilled ambitions could not, access to what it is no exaggeration to call, in his own ebullient term, 'a treasure'.

MKD

---

[66] Journ. 25 Oct.
[67] See To WJT, 28 Dec., *Corr.* 6, p. 125.
[68] See From James Boswell Jr., 18 Oct. 1794, quoted in *Great Biographer*, p. 305.

JAMES BOSWELL:
THE JOURNAL OF HIS
GERMAN AND SWISS TRAVELS
1764

## Monday 18 June

[MEM. dated Tuesday 19 June[1]] Yesterday after being up all night set out in high spirits. All things gay blood quick just as in youth amaz'd at Utrecht so chang'd[2] — Sleepy but genteel — My Lord silentish — Nimeguen Graham on ramparts. At night Turk in your room — was truly devout & swore new virtuous conduct & to be allways master of self & at last fine fellow, to die in respected peace. This day no Zelide wait.[3] Mark accts. paid[4] — Be active.

[J.] ... At seven we set out in a coach and four. My blood circulated just as briskly as in my days of youth.[5] I was drowsy, & now & then nodded. My Lord Marischal was pretty silent.[6] So was Madame de Froment.[7] I laid my account with[8] little conversation. We came at night to Nimeguen.[9] I met Captain Mungo Graham of Gordon's Regiment,[10] who accompanied me round the Ramparts. We saw a very ancient Castle, in which it is said that Julius Caesar lived. We also mounted a tower from whence we had a most extensive and noble Prospect.[11] At night I was in a charming frame, quite blissfull.

[1] Unless otherwise noted, JB's memoranda, written after the experiences of the day, give a date one day later than the journal entry.

[2] From the depression which had engulfed JB on his first coming to Utrecht in Aug. 1763 and more recently in Mar. of this year (To WJT, 16 Aug., 23 Mar. 1764, *Corr.* 6, pp. 61–62, 87; To JJ, 23 Sept., 20 Jan., 9 Apr. 1764, *Corr.* 1, pp. 111–15, 117, 123). JB had suffered depression periodically since boyhood.

[3] JB was either waiting for word from Belle de Zuylen (1740–1805) or deciding not yet to write to her. She was the clever, high-spirited young woman who had captured his imagination in Utrecht and with whom he was now beginning a secret correspondence. Born Isabella Agneta Elisabeth van Tuyll van Serooskerken and a member of one of the oldest families of Holland, she chafed at what she regarded as the stiff conventionality of Dutch society and, styling herself Zélide, expressed herself in a free, libertine vein that at once attracted and troubled JB (Courtney, pp. 5–7, 96–110; Geoffrey Scott, *The Portrait of Zélide*, 1925, pp. 4–12; *Earlier Years*, pp. 137–39). She had revealed contradictory feelings about JB in a letter begun 14 June though not completed until three days later. In his brief reply written in French this very day, just before leaving Utrecht, he had denied being in love with her but had called himself her faithful friend (OC *Charrière*, i.

189–92, 192–93; English translations in Holland, Heinemann pp. 289–94, McGraw-Hill pp. 297–302).

[4] JB had kept an expense account (Yale MS. A 30) in Holland and may have written his last entry, dated 17 June, on this day. He would not record further expenses until 8 July ('Depensés á Berlin', A 32; see App. 3).

[5] Although perhaps used as a vague metaphor here, the notion that the brisk circulation of the blood was a sign of good health and well-being is expressed several times in this journal (e.g., Journ. 3 July and n. 13; Mems. 1, 14, 22 Aug.; Journ. 29 Aug., 11 Sept). It was presumably inspired by the discovery of the English physician William Harvey (1578–1657) that blood circulates from the arteries through the heart to the veins (described in his Lumleian lectures of 1618, pub. in 1628 as *Exercitatio de motu cordis et sanguinis* [*Essay on the Motion of the Heart and Blood*], DSB, vi. 151–58). Even though the implications of this discovery were still not widely accepted and did not affect medical treatments, the importance of good circulation was recognized by, among others, Dr. George Cheyne (1671–1743) in his seminal treatise on depression, *The English Malady* (1733, p. 192).

[6] George Keith (?1693–1778), 10th Earl Marischal of Scotland, was returning to Potsdam at the urgent invitation of Frederick II, who had taken a great liking to him and whom he had served in various

3

diplomatic capacities since 1747. Scion of one of the principal noble families of Scotland, he had joined the Jacobite uprising of 1715 and had been attainted the following year, forfeiting his rights not only to his family's property but also to his title of nobility. He had nonetheless continued to use his title, styling himself 'Earl Marischal' or 'Maréchal d'Écosse' while living on the Continent (see Cuthell, i. 34–36, 64; AEN, *Actes de Chancellerie*, vol. 29; MS. BPUN, 1595). For almost thirty years he had worked for the Stuarts in Spain and France, even leading the unsuccessful 'Glenshiel' expedition to recapture Scotland in 1719, but had become increasingly disenchanted with the Jacobite cause and had refused to take part in the uprising of 1745 (see Journ. 23 July; 6 Dec. and n. 5). Accepting employment from Frederick II in 1747, he had served as his ambassador to France from 1751 to 1754, as governor of the Prussian territory of Neuchâtel from 1754 until his unofficial retirement in 1763, and as Frederick's special envoy to Spain in 1759 (Cuthell, i. 244–300, ii. 3–4, 70–73, 101, 162). In return for diplomatic services to the British Court in 1759 (see Journ. 23 June n. 3), he had been pardoned by George II on 14 Feb. of that year and had been granted permission, by a special act of Parliament passed in Feb. 1762, to inherit and repurchase the family estate of Keith Hall in Aberdeenshire. He had returned to Scotland in 1763 with the intention of settling there and had repurchased several other family estates that were just coming on the market, but finding the Scottish winter too harsh and local rural society too limited, he was now leaving his native country for good (Cuthell, ii. 70–73, 177, 182–85, 193). For JB's eager anticipation of travelling with Lord Marischal and his admiring first impression of him, see To WJT, ?11 June, *Corr.* 6, p. 100 and 'Abrégé d'un Voyage en Allemagne' (App. 1).

[7] Emetulla (Emet Ulla, Marie Emeté) de Froment (d. 1820) was the Turkish ward of Lord Marischal, whose brother, James Francis Edward Keith (1696–1758), fieldmarshal in Russian service at the time, had rescued her in 1737 when his troops captured Ochakov during the Russo-Turkish War of 1736–

39 (Cuthell, i. 186, 191; *Earlier Years*, pp. 141–42; Kohn, p. 400). The date of her birth appears as 1717 on her death certificate (AEN, Neuchâtel-Décès 1804–1827, p. 345) but was more likely 1725 since she had been a child when found by Keith (J.-H. Bonhôte, 'Note sur Emétulla', *MN* 2 [1865]: 28). She was said to have been the daughter of a captain of the élite Turkish troops known as janissaries (see J.-H. Bonhôte, 'Un Gouverneur de Neuchâtel, Milord Marischal', *MN* 2 [1864]: 47). In Apr. 1763 she had married Denis-Daniel de Froment (for whom see Journ. 5 July and n. 3; AEN, *Actes de Chancellerie*, xxvii. 61–62). She had stayed with Lord Marischal in Scotland from Apr. of this year and was now returning to Prussia with him.

[8] 'Expected', a Scotticism later accepted as standard English (OED, s.v. 'account', 15).

[9] A town in the eastern part of the Netherlands close to the border of the German territory of Westphalia, known in the twentieth and twenty-first centuries as Nijmegen (in the middle ages it was Nimwegen). JB and his companions, coming from Utrecht, had covered about 42 miles (c. 67.6 km) in a single day (Nugent, ii. 398).

[10] Mungo Graham (d. 1778) was captain-commander of a grenadier company in the Scots Brigade, which had served in the Netherlands from 1572 and would continue to do so until 1782 (James Ferguson, *Papers Illustrating the History of the Scots Brigade*, 1899–1901, ii. 281, 423, 430 and n. 2; see also i. 3–8; ii. 496–97). Graham's regiment, commanded by Col. James Gordon (d. 1776), was stationed at Nijmegen from 1763 to 1766 (Ferguson, ii. 122 n. 2, 393).

[11] The remains of an ancient fortress, the Valck-Hof, which had been built by Charlemagne on foundations dating from the time of Julius Caesar ('Nimeguen', *A Gazetteer of the Netherlands*, 1794). The Belvédère tower, on the other side of a nearby ravine, offered 'one of the finest prospects of the neighbouring country that can be imagined' (Nugent, i. 197). It overlooked an idyllic pastoral landscape and the river Waal, a side arm of the Rhine.

## Tuesday 19 June

[SPECIAL MEM., undated, written 18 or 19 June]
Nimeguen Memorandum

In sweet fine spirits you saw all well. You adored God [—] you resolved to have uniform command of Passions — to keep up the character which Zelide has — to suffer in silence & never to own — never to be too strict — to judge by reason allways — but get command of self. Habit is much. Now form — above all rétenue.[1] Be fine with Zelide love her.

[J.] François has given me an excellent character.[2] We dined at Cleves.[3] I went and payd my respects to Mr. & [M]adame Spaen at Bellevue, from whence there is indeed a fine Prospect.[4] It was pleasant to see the German Baron's Castle — a hall adorned with guns — an english Clock that plays ten tunes, and cost £1000.[5] At night we came to Wesel[6] where we had a jolly, talking Landlord. I find Madame de Froment very lively, altho' she has an indolence or, as the french say, a *nonchalance*[7] that is terrible. She does not dress. Scarcely even will she speak. I talked with her in rather too gallant a strain.

[1] Lit. 'Restrained, reserved' (Robert, s.v. 'retenue'), an uncommon term (not in *Dict. SJ* or the OED for the eighteenth century), associated by JB with self-restraint in speech, 'the power of suppressing what it is improper to utter' (*Hypochondriack* no. XXIII [Aug. 1779], in Bailey, ii. 284). JB adopted it from the French, spelling it with various accents (most often 'retenué' in London; in Holland usually without an accent, except for 'retenúe' on 5 Oct. 1763 and 19 Feb. 1764, and 'reténu' on 20 May 1764). JB had used the expression close to 40 times in the London memoranda, and about 30 times in the Dutch memoranda. But he had omitted it in the fully written journal, suggesting that the term was a private one, usually self-admonitory: 'Be retenué'. Recently he had also noted approvingly 'you was sensible, prudent, *retenu*' and had promised himself 'a new course of *retenue*' to cultivate a 'mild and grave dignity' in conversation. The pose was in keeping with the self-control, prudence, and high-minded morality with which he wished to impress Belle de Zuylen (25, 28 Feb., *Holland*, Heinemann pp. 164–65, McGraw-Hill pp. 168, 170; see Courtney, pp. 98, 102–04).

[2] François Mazerac (d. 1790) had served as JB's valet in Utrecht for nine months (To WJT, 23 Sept. 1763, *Corr.* 6, pp. 69–70). At JB's whimsical request, he had written a character reference for his master on the model of the reference a servant might expect. This eight-point summary, submitted sealed and only now read by JB, mentioned certain flaws—being careless about money and possessions, studying too intently, arriving later than his invited guests, retiring to bed too late—but emphasized his good heart and punctual religious obser-

vances, and ended with a burst of affection (*Holland*, Heinemann pp. 283–84, McGraw-Hill pp. 290–91, and App. IV).

[3] A town in German territory a little more than 12 miles (19.3 km) from Nijmegen (Nugent, ii. 398). Formerly an independent duchy, Kleve had become part of Prussia as a result of the Treaty of Xanten in 1614 (R. von Thadden, *Prussia: The History of a Lost State*, 1981, p. 189).

[4] Alexander Sweder, Baron de Spaen (1703–68), and Elisabeth Agnes Jacoba, *née* van Nassau La Lecq (1724–98), had befriended JB in The Hague. JB had written to Mme de Spaen from Utrecht to practise his French (28 Mar. 1764), and she had replied with an invitation to their country seat, Bellevue (10 Apr. 1764). Their correspondence would continue until 1773. The Baron, now an adjutant-general in the army of the Netherlands (he would be appointed major-general in 1766), was a German nobleman by birth. He had served in the Prussian army until he took part, in 1730, in the ill-fated attempt of the future Frederick II to escape from his tyrannical father, Friedrich Wilhelm I (1688–1740), King of Prussia. De Spaen had destroyed incriminating papers when the plot was discovered but had been imprisoned and exiled (A. J. van der Aa, *Biographisch Woordenboek der Nederlanden*, 1852, repr. 1969, p. 237). He had been more fortunate, however, than his friend and fellow conspirator, Lt. Hans Hermann von Katte (1704–30), who had also been arrested and then summarily executed (see MacDonogh, pp. 49–50, 61–73). JB had alluded to these events in his memorandum of 30 Dec. 1763 (*Holland*, Heinemann p. 108 and n. 3, McGraw-Hill p. 111 and n. 3).

Bellevue, the most imposing mansion in its neighbourhood, took its name from the 'prospect' which opened from a terrace or 'Belvedere' especially built on a promontory a short distance from the house. From there the picturesque medieval Schwanenburg ('Swan's Castle') and the Stiftskirche Maria Himmelfahrt ('Collegiate Church of the Ascension of the Virgin') could be seen rising above an arm of the Rhine. De Spaen, whose forebears had come from the region, had purchased the estate in 1752 (Ursula Geisselbrecht-Capecki, *Die Bellevue*, 1994, illus. 1 and 2, and pp. 13–14, 60 n. 31).

[5] This clock was a prize possession of de Spaen from before his marriage in 1749 ('Inventaris Familiearchief No. 162: Inventar der von Alexander Sweder van Spaen in die Ehe mit E. A. J. von Nassau-LaLecq gebrachten Güter von 1750'). It was the work of the London clockmaker Charles Clay (fl. from 1716, d. 1740), who is credited with inventing mechanical musical clocks (Geisselbrecht-Capecki, pp. 16, 62 n. 52; Cedric Jagger, *Royal Clocks*, 1983, pp. 76–82). Such clocks, often elaborate and expensive, were housed in long, upright cases, produced their tunes by bells with one or two hammers, and could play automatically every few hours (Anthony Bird, *English House Clocks: 1600–1850*, c. 1973, pp. 187–88).

[6] A town in Prussian territory, at the confluence of the Rhine and Lippe, 16 miles (25.8 km) southeast of Kleve (Nugent, ii. 410).

[7] 'Apathy', 'indolence', 'lethargy'. The term was already in use in this sense in the eighteenth century (Robert, s.v. 'nonchalance').

## Wednesday 20 June

[MEM. dated Wednesday 20 June, covering 19 and 20 June] [Y]esterday you was well & easy & grave but talkd too gallant with [M]ad. From. You learnt that grave composed passions are happiest. But still you thought of sad exitus[1] [—] at night, Haltern bad inn.[2] This day go on [—] your'e[3] losing change of ideas [—] your'e seeing world [—] mind strengthens [—] you'll have no spleen[4] for a long time — youll be well & devout.

[J.] We pursued our journey peacably; but, were still silent in the coach. At night we had a sad Inn.[5]

[1] 'Departure' (OED, s.v. 'exitus'). Possibly a thought about dying, which had been on JB's mind when he expressed the hope 'to die in respected peace' (Mem. dated 19 June); alternatively, regret about having left Utrecht just as he and Belle de Zuylen had formed a bond.

[2] MS. 'At night ... inn', an interlineation.

[3] JB's consistent way of writing 'you're'.

[4] 'Excessive dejection or depression of spirits; gloominess and irritability; moroseness; melancholia' (OED, s.v. 'spleen', 8.c). SJ had defined it, in one of several senses used since the Renaissance, as 'Melancholy; hypochondriacal vapours' and had linked it with the bodily spleen, supposedly 'the seat of anger, melancholy, and mirth' (*Dict. SJ*, 'Spleen', 1 and 5). JB uses the term frequently in this period as he monitors his emotional state (see Mems. dated 25, 26, and 28 June).

[5] At Haltern (see Journ. 21 June and n. 7).

## Thursday 21 June

[MEM. dated Thursday 21 June][1] [Y]esterday a procession [—] went into church — swore one god — no gloom — die in Serenity — chace Hypochondria — well on Journey — My Lord silent & sowrish — talk'd of Hypocs even in Spain.[2] Lady seven years there[3] — was o<n> guard, resolved firm at night. Fellinghausen — Inn bad ... table, &c. This day go ...[4] on [—] journal &c. —

[M]ajor of brigade[5]

[MEM. dated Friday 22 June] Yesterday you was quite well all fine all noble at night at ———⁶ where [M]arischal Broglio slept. Table — Straw. — Quite Campaign which you dreaded at Auchinleck. This day go on brace nerves — Be manly — Things pass, but may last long. Clear short Journ & begin new life —

[J.] We were now in a Roman Catholic town.⁷ It was *Fete Dieu* so that there was to be a Procession.⁸ I went into the Church, adored my God, and resolved to be a worthy man.⁹ All seemed noble and well. At night we came to an Inn in the territory of Cologne where Marechal Broglio has slept.¹⁰ A dreary Inn it was. I was laid upon a table covered with straw with a Blanket and a sheet; and above me I had a sheet and a feather-bed. Thus was I just in the situation of a bold Officer. Thus did I endure the very hardships of a German Campaign which I used to tremble at the thoughts of, when at Auchinleck.¹¹

---

¹ From here to 24 June JB was hazy about dates. This memorandum refers to the procession at Haltern as 'yesterday', 20 June, but it actually took place this very day (see Journ. and n. 8).

² 'Hypocs', short for hypochondriacs, those suffering from hypochondria. 'A morbid state of mind, characterized by general depression, melancholy, or low spirits, for which there is no real cause' (OED, s.v. 'hypochondria', 2). This complaint, evidently familiar also to Lord Marischal, is closely related to the 'spleen' mentioned in the memorandum of 20 June. SJ had defined 'hypochondriack' as melancholy and also as 'disordered in the imagination'. He had found the source of this state in the 'hypochondres', the region of the abdomen flanking the ribs, close to the liver on one side and the spleen on the other. That SJ neither equated 'spleen' and 'hypochondria' nor clarified the differences between them suggests that these were closely related but loosely defined concepts in his time. JB seems to have used the terms interchangeably and no longer linked them to the physical organs that gave them their name.

³ Mme de Froment had accompanied Lord Marischal during some of the years he had spent in Spain (see Journ. 23 June n. 3).

⁴ MS. A single word (not deciphered) after 'bad', another such word after 'go', both blotted out by ink or a stain. Apparently Vellinghausen (for which see n. 10 below) had an inn as bad as the one at Haltern.

⁵ MS. Phrase written in a different quill, perhaps referring to an unidentified anecdote about a major in the Scots Brigade.

⁶ MS. Long dash, for Vellinghausen. In this memorandum JB repeats the last part of

the preceding one and, in effect, writes two memoranda for 22 June.

⁷ The town, Haltern, was one of several pockets of Catholicism in a region that had been predominantly Protestant since the Reformation. It belonged to the bishopric of Münster and had remained strongly Catholic in spite of the brief appearance of radical Anabaptists in the 1530s and of Calvinists who had openly or surreptitiously practised their religion from about 1570 until the edicts of 1624 and of 1629 forbade all forms of Protestant worship (Manfred Wolf, 'Geschichte der katholischen Kirchengemeinden', *Haltern: Beiträge zur Stadtgeschichte*, 1988, pp. 195–203).

⁸ *Fête-Dieu*, the Feast of Corpus Christi, falls on the Thursday after Trinity Sunday (thus JB gives the correct date). In Catholic countries this feast, which celebrates the mystery of the Eucharist, is marked by joyful outdoor processions honouring the Host just consecrated at a Mass (NCE, iv. 345–47). At Haltern the Corpus Christi procession was one of several such religious processions organized each year. The townspeople's fervour had been fuelled by reports of recent miracles that included sightings of lights and unexpected healings of the sick (Wolf, pp. 204–05).

⁹ The small church of St. Sixtus, in the centre of the town, could provide only 475 seats for its much larger congregation. It had been repeatedly rebuilt since its founding in medieval times but was again in need of repairs, which would not be undertaken for another eighty years (Wolf, pp. 181, 195–204, 210).

¹⁰ The inn was in Vellinghausen (see Mem. dated 21 June), a village in the terri-

tory of Mark, which was a dependency of Prussia (it did not belong to Cologne, a large bishopric nearby but on the other side of the Rhine). Victor-François, Duke de Broglie (1718–1804), Commander-in-Chief in Germany, Marshal of France, and Prince of the Holy Roman Empire since 1759, had stayed there the night of 15 to 16 June 1761. During the battle fought just before and after this night, Broglie had engaged British, Hanoverian, and Brunswickian forces under the command of Prince Ferdinand of Brunswick-Lüneburg (1721–92) and the Marquis of Granby (1721–70). Broglie's efforts had been hampered by receiving only half-hearted support from Soubise (1715–87), another Marshal of France, and the battle had ended with heavy losses and the withdrawal of the French. Nonetheless, Broglie would come to be considered 'the most capable French commander of the Seven Years' War' (Savory, pp. 26 n. 1, 320–26; see also Richard Waddington, *La Guerre de Sept Ans*, 1899–1914, v. 105–07).

[11] In his earlier journals JB had not mentioned experiencing this dread while at Auchinleck. However, in his 'Journal of My Jaunt Harvest 1762' (Yale MS. J 2), written in the vicinity of, though not actually at Auchinleck, he had recorded hearing 'such terrible descriptions of the great expence fatigue & danger of a German Campaign, that my blood run cold in my veins or rather stood still' (Journ. 7 Nov. 1762). And while in London, he had been told by his cousin

Capt. James Webster (1740–81) of the 'allmost incredible' fatigues of a German campaign (Journ. 20 Dec. 1762). Earlier, he had been more enthusiastic about military life. As he recalled in his autobiographical sketch written for Rousseau, he had thought of joining a highland regiment in America at the beginning of the Seven Years' War until his father objected ('Ébauche de ma vie', Outline 1, Yale MS. L 1109, App. 2, III.D; *Earlier Years*, pp. 31–32). He had hoped for a commission in the Foot Guards in London in 1762, though attracted primarily by the glamour of their uniform and way of life (To AE, 8–9 May 1762, published in *Letters between the Honourable Andrew Erskine and James Boswell, Esq.*, 1763, Letter XXVIII; *Corr. 9*, pp. 247–49; Journ. 6, 11, 13, 27 Dec. 1762, 9–10 Jan. 1763). Furthermore, he had found inspiration in the actions of another eager young military man, the son of his hoped-for patroness, the Countess of Northumberland, in his 'Verses on Lord Warkworth's Going a Volunteer to Germany, 1760' (included in *A Collection of Original Poems by the Rev. Mr. Blacklock and other Scotch Gentlemen*, published by Alexander Donaldson in 1760):

> May I his virtue ever present find
> To rouse each spark of courage in my mind:
> That if high fate shall call me forth to wield
> The steely weapon in the tented field,
> I may th'applause of my dear country gain,
> Glorious reward of danger, toil, and pain.

## Friday 22 June

[MEM. dated Saturday 23 June][1] [Y]esterday you heard Storys of Highlander in year 15 weep because Macdonald retired from his foe.[2] Faith very uncertain. My Lord never had Absurditys yet in mind you kept plain Christianity. At night you came to ——— belonging to Count ——— glorious Spirits walk'd out [—] Crucifix — olive [—] kneeled devout [—] mounted on Table slept sound — was just as well as mild as gay as ever.

[J.] My Lord told me so many curious storys, that I began to think Faith very uncertain. Yet I resolved to maintain a decent system of mild Christianity.[3] He told me that he had never been opprest with religious Prejudices. At night we came to          [4] a Popish Town. I walked without the Gates in delightfull humour. I was struck at the sight of an Image of the Pope, with a Crucifix in one hand, and an Olive-branch in the other.[5] I was filled with pleasing reverence. I kneeled, and with warm devotion adored my God and was gratefull to the Saviour of the World. A Poor man came to me; I gave him Alms. I was very happy. I slept upon a great table in the common hall of the Inn.

[1] MS. 'SATUR' written over 'Friday 22'

[2] JB made a separate record of this anecdote of the weeping highlander. During the Jacobite uprising of 1715 this man had appeared, without shoes, yet had rejected Lord Marischal's offer of footwear, declaring: 'Sir, ... I want no shoes; I am crying to see a Macdonald retire from his enemy' (*Boswelliana*, p. 236). The Macdonald in question was probably Donald Macdonald (d. 1718), 11th Baron and 4th Bt. of Sleat, who had brought his clan members from the Isle of Skye to fight under the Earl of Mar (1675–1732) but whom illness had forced to return home before the indecisive battle of Sheriffmuir on 13 Nov. 1715 (see Alexander Mackenzie, *History of the Macdonalds*, 1881, pp. 224–29; Donald J. Macdonald of Castleton, *Clan Donald*, 1978, p. 424). Lord Marischal had gained first-hand knowledge of these events while serving the Earl of Mar as major-general of the horse (Mackenzie, p. 227; Cuthell, i. 41).

[3] JB had recently adopted a moderate Christianity, as expressed in his 'Inviolable Plan' (16 Oct. 1763, Yale MS. M 88; see *Holland*, App. I, Heinemann p. 376, McGraw-Hill p. 388). After a sustained adolescent religious crisis, during which he had experimented briefly with methodism and Roman Catholicism, he had now committed himself to the Church of England, taking the sacrament on 26 Dec. 1763 (*Holland*, Heinemann p. 104, McGraw-Hill p. 107).

[4] MS. Blank. The town was Rietberg, described as 'belonging to Count ———' in the memorandum dated 23 June. It was in the domain of the Austrian statesman Count Wenzel Anton von Kaunitz (1711–94; see Wurzbach, ix. 69–70; Franz Szabo, *Kaunitz and Enlightened Absolutism*, 1994, p. 17). This small independent territory had become Lutheran during the Reformation but had reverted to Catholicism when its ruler, Count Johann III (1601–25), converted to the old religion in 1601 (Erika Heitmeyer, 'Die katholische Pfarrei St. Johannes Baptista in Rietberg', *700 Jahre Stadt Rietberg*, 1989, pp. 351–53). It had remained Catholic when the arranged marriage of the present Count's father, Maximilian Ulrich (1679–1746), and Maria Ernestine Franziska (1686–1758), Countess of Rietberg, brought it into the possession of the Kaunitz family in 1700 (Grete Klingenstein, *Der Aufstieg des Hauses Kaunitz*, Schriftenreihe der historischen Kommission bei der Bayerischen Akademie der Wissenschaften, 1975, xii. 80–82, 324).

[5] The statue had been made in 1723 by a local sculptor, Johann Baptist Drütigen of Paderborn, and stood at the end of the road coming from the palace. It did not, as JB thought, commemorate a Pope but St. John Nepomuk (1350–93), patron saint of Bohemia, as shown in the inscription (still there in the twenty-first century) which identifies the saint and the donors, the Count and Countess von Kaunitz. St. John Nepomuk, a legendary figure not to be equated with the historical John of Pomuk, had supposedly been martyred in 1393 by being thrown off a bridge in Prague because he refused to divulge the secret of his queen's confession. He had been canonized in 1721 (Manfred Beine and Käthe Herbort, 'Rietberg', *post* 1989, p. 37). Soon after his death statues of him were placed on bridges and altars, churches were named after him, and songs and plays celebrated him. This vogue would earn him the epithets 'bridge saint' as well as 'patron saint of the baroque' (Käthe Herbort, 'Der Brückenheilige Johannes v. Nepomuk und seine Standbilder', *Heimatjahrbuch Kreis Gütersloh*, 1992, pp. 67–68).

## Saturday 23 June

[MEM. dated Sunday 24 June].[1] [Y]esterday after hard sleep on table in great room — You was well — My Lord praised Spain — never betray trust — Irish & Spaniards do ill throw dice — Spaniard also — Mcdonald in Spain — Campbell never take law while I've broad sword — Mcdonald run from siege Gibralt. Others come by sea[2] [—] bold fine fellow [—] come to Herford — charming — Ideas quite altered one God. This day Journ — up — bravo.

[J.] My Lord was eloquent in the praises of Spain, where he past twenty years. He talked of the beautifull Country the charming Climate, the excellent People who were never known to betray their trust.[3] My desire to go to Spain was increast.[4] His Lordship also talked of the Scots Highlanders with respect and affection, as the most brave and most generous People upon earth, and abused the harsh absurdity of our Government, for taking their cloaths from them and extirpating their language by which means they will be at last reduced to a level with the other Inhabitants of Scotland; and so we shall lose the best Militia upon earth. The proper method was surely not to destroy the Highlanders, but to render them attached to the Government, which would be no difficult matter, as the Chiefs are no longer disaffected.[5] We came at night to Herford.[6] I found myself a new man. My ideas were altered. I had no gloomy fears. I talked with Madame de Froment, who had been educated Mahometan & who still beleived that the Great Prophet was sent from God.[7] This opened my mind. I resolved to be prudent, nor to own my many waverings. I was quite happy. I determined to get free of the clouds which hung upon me. I determined to be manly and content.

[1] MS. Written below a deleted 'Saturday 23 June'

[2] Snatches of unexplained anecdotes about the siege of Gibraltar of 26 Apr. to 12 June 1727, in which Lord Marischal and other Scottish Jacobites had participated on the Spanish side. The Spaniards had been trying to recapture the rock held by the British and ceded to them in 1713 by the Treaty of Utrecht (Philip Dennis, *Gibraltar and Its People*, 1990, pp. 25–30; Cuthell, i. 141–43). The hardships of the campaign— torrid heat and sickness as well as fierce bombardment by the British garrison—had caused the defection of many of the 2000 men led by the Conde de las Torres (d. 1749; William Smith, 'The Late Siege of Gibraltar', 1728, BL Add. MS. 36680). The siege had been brought to an inconclusive end by the unexpected arrival of a ship with orders to both sides to cease fighting while the preliminaries of a peace were negotiated (Cuthell, i. 142–43).

Neither the Campbell nor the Macdonald can be identified with certainty. The hostility between their clans, hinted at here, dated at least from the sixteenth century and reflected the continuing power struggles among various clans (see T. C. Smout, *A History of the Scottish People*, 1969, pp. 48, 103–06, 111–13, 224, 341–42). The two-edged broadsword with its distinctive basket-hilt was the traditional weapon of the highlanders ('Highland Broadsword', *The Encyclopedia of the Sword*, 1995, p. 291).

[3] Lord Marischal had been in the military service of Spain from 1719 to 1746 (Cuthell, i. 85, 225) and had lived there for long periods in 1728–31, 1734, 1736, 1737,

and 1740–41 (Cuthell, i. 145–52, 176–79, 189–91). He had grown especially fond of Valencia (Cuthell, i. 133). As recently as 1759 he had been in Madrid as Prussian ambassador. While engaged in negotiations to end the war, he had been able to warn the British government that the Spaniards, neutral to this point and inclined towards the British, were being wooed by the French. His warning, which had prepared the British for the Bourbon Family Compact between France and Spain subsequently signed in Aug. 1761, had paved the way to his being granted a pardon (see Journ. 18 June n. 6; Cuthell, ii. 81–85, 87).

[4] JB's interest had been aroused by SJ's remark that much of Spain had not yet been 'perambulated' and that JB might usefully provide a report on that country (Journ. 25 June 1763). JB expressed his enthusiasm for Spain more fully in his 'Abregé d'un Voyage en Allemagne' (M 93), very likely written on this day (*Catalogue*, i. 72; see App. 1). But his hopes to travel there would never be fulfilled.

[5] In reprisal for the highlanders' part in the Jacobite rebellion of 1745, the Disarming Act of 1746 had forbidden the wearing of tartans, kilts, and other accoutrements of highland dress (19 Geo. II, c. 39). The use of Gaelic had not actually been outlawed but had been discouraged by the act of 1752 'for the better civilizing and improving the Highlands of Scotland', which had established new schools 'for instructing young persons in reading and writing the *English* language' (25 Geo. II, c. 41). The chiefs of highland clans who had survived the battle of Culloden (16 Apr. 1746), or

had replaced those killed, had apparently come to accept the Hanoverian rule. In the Seven Years' War, the highlanders, serving in their own regiments on the British side, had shown extraordinary bravery (Stewart, ii. 98).

⁶ Described as 'charming' in the memorandum dated 24 June, Herford was a picturesque, prosperous town about 34 miles (c. 54.7 km) from Rietberg (Jens Jürgen Schulz, 'Häuser und Ihre Geschichte', *1200 Jahre Herford*, ed. Theodor Helmert-Corvey and Thomas Schuler, 1989, pp. 68–69). It had been a stronghold of Protestantism since the Reformation in spite of attempts by occu-

pying troops to recatholicize it in the 1620s and 1630s. Tension between Lutheran and Reformed (Calvinist) Protestants had disturbed Herford until the Reformed church became dominant in the late 1720s (Christine and Lutz Brade, 'Religion Prägt das Leben', *1200 Jahre Herford*, pp. 293–97).

⁷ Mme de Froment had only recently been converted to Calvinism, the official religion of Neuchâtel. She had been baptized there on 24 Jan. 1763 and given the name Marie Emeté (J.-H. Bonhôte, 'Un Gouverneur de Neuchâtel', *MN* 1 ⌜1864⌝: 47; Cuthell, ii. 157–58).

## Sunday 24 June

[MEM. dated Monday 25 June] Yesterday You was noble. You past thro Minden & heard a little Mass & was devout but had not one single Sunday idea. My Lord said, Campbell's saying 'I beleive' is not enough — Tis his trade as was his petitioning against letters on Sunday &c.¹ — resolv'd to keep counsel — adore God — be good & never own waverings[.] [A]t night Hannoverian house great *salle*, Cows horses — Dog chain'd — Cocks & hens. This day go on bravo!

[J.] We dined at Minden.² But I had not time to view the field of Battel.³ I went into a Roman-Catholic Church, & heard Mass, and was devout, & had not one Scots Sunday idea. My Religion now is chiefly devotion. Pomp of worship aids me in this. I see a probability for the truth of Christianity. I shall be an amiable Man.⁴ My 'life shall be in the right'.⁵ We came at night to an Inn in the territory of Hannover. Thus was I laid. In the middle of a great German Salle upon straw spread on the floor was a sheet laid, here 'great Boswell lay'.⁶ I had another sheet and a coverlet. On one side of me were eight or ten Horses, on the other, four or five Cows. A little way from me sat on high a Cock & many Hens, and before I went to sleep the Cock made my ears ring with his shrill voice, so that I admired the wisdom of the Sybarites who slew all those noisy Birds.⁷ What frightened me not a little, was an immense Mastiff chained pretty near the head of my Bed. He growled most horribly, and rattled his chain. I called for a piece of bread & made a freindship with him. Before me were two great folding doors wide open, so that I could see the beauties of the evening Sky. In this way however did I sleep with much contentment, and much health.

¹ George Campbell, D.D. (1719–96), Professor of Divinity and Principal of Marischal College, Aberdeen, had tried to make a case for Christian belief in his *Dissertation on Miracles*, 1762, in answer to David Hume's sceptical essay 'Of Miracles', first pub. 1748 in *Philosophical Essays Concerning Human Understanding* (later entitled *An Enquiry Concerning Human Understanding*, 1756). Countering Hume's argument for a presumption against miracles, Campbell had insisted on a presumption in their favour and had claimed that 'some original grounds of belief' precede experience (Pt. I, secs. i–ii, iv–v). Lord Marischal, a sceptic and friend of Hume's, clearly disapproved of Campbell's

argument, as well as of the public protest against the use of mails on Sundays in which Campbell had joined (Lord Marischal to Hume, 28 Oct. 1763, quoted in Cuthell, ii. 180).

[2] Minden, about 18 miles (c. 29 km) from Herford, had been a bishop's see until the Reformation but was now a Protestant town belonging to Prussia (Nugent, ii. 113–14).

[3] In this major battle of the Seven Years' War, fought on 1 Aug. 1759 about 1.5 miles (c. 2.4 km) northwest of Minden, Prince Ferdinand of Brunswick-Lüneburg had defeated a superior force of French led by Broglie and by Louis-Georges-Érasme, Marquis de Contades (1704–95), another marshal of France (see Savory, Sketch VI [3] and pp. 161, 178–79). Neither of the town's two gates was convenient for a visit to the battlefield: the Mühlentor, through which JB and his companions had no doubt entered, faced south, and the Weserthor, through which they would have to leave, faced east.

[4] The church was either the cathedral or one of the other two large churches that had remained Catholic even though Minden was by this time predominantly Protestant. JB had become interested in Roman Catholicism in 1759, and had even undergone a month-long conversion in London in 1760 (for this important episode, see his confession to Rousseau, Journ. 5 Dec. and n. 4, and F. A. Pottle's appendix, 'Boswell's Conversion to Roman Catholicism', *Earlier Years*, pp. 569–70). Although JB had meanwhile found a safer religious haven in the Church of England (see Journ. 22 June n. 3), he would feel drawn to the forms of

Catholic worship for the rest of his life. At the same time, he had developed an abhorrence for the austere Scottish Calvinism which his mother and the local clergy had tried to inculcate in him as a child, and he would retain bitter memories all his life of the strict, joyless observance of Sundays in Scotland (see 'Ébauche de ma vie', Yale MS. L 1107, App. 2, III.A; French theme, 29 Jan., Yale MS. M 87).

[5] Quoted from Pope, *Essay on Man*, iii. 305–06:

> For Modes of Faith, let graceless zealots fight;
> He can't be wrong whose life is in the right....

JB was responding to the differing 'modes of faith' he had observed in the span of a few days.

[6] An allusion to Pope's description of 'the worst inn's worst room' where 'Great Villiers lies' (*Moral Essays*, iii. 299–305). The location of JB's inn cannot be precisely determined, but it could not have been near Hameln (correcting *Grand Tour I*, Heinemann p. 10 n. 3, McGraw-Hill p. 11 n. 8), which was not on the direct route from Minden to Hanover.

[7] The luxury-loving Sybarites were so determined to avoid disturbing noises that they had prohibited even roosters within Sybaris, their Greek city in southern Italy which had flourished from 720 to 510 B.C. (Athenaeus, *Deipnosophistae*, xii. 518, Loeb ed., trans. C. B. Gulick, 1933 (vol. 5); see also J. S. Callaway, *Sybaris*, 1950, pp. 1–2, 14).

## Monday 25 June

[MEM. dated Tuesday 26 June] Yesterday you was still fine & had ideas quite changed — gold spoons steal quite natural. My Lord made Johnson say jokes on Hannover. Came to Hannover. My Lord many storys told him. You had been idle dog resolved now do well. This day determine thus. Spleen is going. After despair, you've much Joy. Your'e reserved & not absurd. Continue & your'e sure of bliss [—] adore God — At night clear up Journ short & now be happy — but Baron exchequer.[1]

[J.] My Lord joked on the tea-spoons, which seemed of Gold. Ay ay the money of old England in the Hannoverian Dominions. He assumed the character of Dictionary Johnson, in order to joke in this manner.[2] He talked of somebody having stolen gold spoons. Very natural said I. Hear the Scotsman, said he. We came to Hannover where we dined.[3] My Lord went & waited on the Countess of Yarmouth.[4] My old Mrs. Webster ideas of

King George's Palace at Herenhausen &c were all realised.[5] We had a very amusing day of it. I made my Lord laugh by saying that all the Girls we met, were like the Princesses of our present Royal family.[6]

[1] For the Baron of Exchequer, John Maule (1706–81), see Journ. 10 July and n. 4. The Court of Exchequer, which he headed, had supreme jurisdiction over revenue cases. The position was well paid and respected but not overly strenuous (see Journ. 24 Feb. 1763; To JJ, 11 May 1765, *Corr. 1*, p. 165 and n. 6).

[2] Hanover had been joined with England earlier in the century by the quirk of fate that had brought to the British throne the offspring of Sophie (1630–1714), granddaughter of James I (1566–1625) of England, who was also James VI of Scotland. Sophie was the wife of the Elector Ernst August (1629–98) of Hanover, and her son, George Louis (1660–1727), had come to England as George I to succeed Queen Anne (1665–1714), whose children had all predeceased her. Hanover had however remained largely independent. It had its own government and ministers who reported directly to the King, and was linked to England primarily through the 'personal union' of the ruler. Both George I and George II (1683–1760) had considered themselves as much Electors of Hanover as Kings of England and had spent summers in their German residence. Unlike these rulers, George III (1738–1820), the grandson of George II, was proud to have been born and educated a Briton (see his speech to Parliament, 18 Nov. 1760, *Ann. Reg.* 1760, p. 248). He had disliked Hanover in his youth and would not visit it when he became king, although he would still regard it as his inheritance (Philip Konigs, *The Hanoverian Kings and their Homeland*, 1993, pp. 34, 51–52, 63–71, 124–30).

Lord Marischal's joke refers to the first two Georges, who, as many Englishmen had feared, had spent considerable amounts of money in their Hanoverian homeland. SJ had displayed what JB called a 'warm anti-Hanoverian zeal' in the lifetime of George II, ridiculing him frequently (*Life* i. 141; see Robert DeMaria Jr., *The Life of Samuel Johnson*, 1993, p. 215).

[3] Hanover was a substantial, handsome town, although it had dwindled in importance since the seventeenth century, when it had flourished as ducal residence of the Calenberg branch of the Guelfs and as centre for trade in Lower Saxony (Carl-Hans Hauptmeyer, 'Die Residenzstadt', *Geschichte der Stadt Hannover*, 1992, i. 144–57).

[4] Amalie Sophie Marianne von Wallmoden (1704–65), Countess of Yarmouth, had been the acknowledged mistress of George II for more than twenty years. She had recently returned to her native Hanover (*Ann. Reg.* 11 Apr. 1763, p. 68). Hers was a prominent local family, and she owned a house granted her by George II in 1740 (Arnold Nöldeke, *Die Kunstdenkmäler der Provinz Hannover*, 1932, reissued 1979, i. 319).

[5] Herrenhausen had been the favourite summer residence of both George I and George II. It was about 2 miles (c. 3.2 km) northwest of the town of Hanover and linked to it by a broad avenue lined by more than 1300 linden trees (Nugent, ii. 240; Hauptmeyer, i. 137). The palace had been built around a large half-timbered building that had been dismantled at its original site at Koldingen in 1665 and reassembled 10 miles (16.1 km) further north. The building had been extended in various directions, its simple core hidden under a more elaborate exterior, and its rooms made increasingly sumptuous over the years (Udo von Alvensleben and Hans Reuther, *Herrenhausen: Die Sommerresidenz der Welfen*, 1966, pp. 5–7, 25–28). Possibly JB had heard this odd history in Edinburgh from his maternal aunt Mary (Erskine) Webster (1715–66). She was married to Alexander Webster, D.D. (1707–84), minister of the Tolbooth Church in Edinburgh since 1737, chaplain to Frederick Louis, Prince of Wales (1707–51) from 1748, and a convinced Hanoverian (*Fasti Scot.* i. 119–20; *Book of Company*, p. 13). JB seems not to have visited the famous 'Great Garden' of Herrenhausen.

[6] The sisters of George III—Augusta (1737–1813), for whom see Journ. 27 June and n. 14, Elizabeth Caroline (1740–59), Louisa Anne (1749–68), and Caroline Matilda (1751–75)—were considered rather plain. For their Hanoverian features, see copies of their portraits by J.-E. Liotard in the file of 'The Family of George III', Heinz Archive, National Portrait Gallery, London.

## Tuesday 26 June

[MEM. dated Wednesday 27 June] [Y]esterday my Lord told storys of old Soldier who when Dr. Oliphant said He first cure & then beat — said you can neither do one nor t'other.[1] Also some little neat ones. You was noble — arrived at Brunsvic — well stroled fine —[2] Father's letter to restrain[3] — resolved to manage — Lord Galloway old fool opera Girl — your sister in wrong — Saint in heaven — what! pimp for you sound whores[4] — At night indolent.[5] Turc talked of Hypochond. This day swear conduct pay visits — Be alive. Bring up Journ — Pray.

[J.] We arrived at Brunswic before dinner. My Lord drest dined & went to Court.[6] I stroled about; found it a large & handsom Town, with a number of old Buildings.[7] At night Madame de Froment & I supt tête â tête. She talked of the Hypochondria which she had severely felt. She understood it perfectly. She told me of a Gentleman whom his freinds wanted much to settle in Business; but, he said he would not stir two steps to get two thousand Pounds. She said that the Imagination & all the faculties of the mind were confounded, & could judge of nothing; so that all things appeared one undistinguished black Mass. Exercise & dissipation[8] with moderate employment she said were the only Remedies. I was amused with all this;[9] but kept myself snug.

[1] An unidentified anecdote, perhaps about Dr. Charles Oliphant (1666–1719), fellow of the College of Physicians in Edinburgh (P. J. and R. V. Wallis, *Eighteenth-Century Medics*, 2nd ed. 1988, p. 442). He had been embroiled in professional squabbles about his pamphlet on treating fevers, and his 'contumacy' had led to his temporary expulsion from the College of Physicians (see W. A. Greenhill, *Life of George Cheyne*, M.D., 1846, p. 17 and note d). His wartime experiences are not recorded.

[2] MS. Short word '–f–', perhaps 'aft', blotted out by JB.

[3] Lord Auchinleck had written two encouraging letters to JB with advice on how to overcome the depression that JB had finally admitted to having experienced in Holland (letters of 20 and 23 Mar., not recovered, mentioned by Lord Auchinleck in his letters of 2 and 15 Apr.). Lord Auchinleck had linked it to his own father's 'melancholick turn' (2 Apr.). He had urged JB to refrain from idleness and 'gloomy thoughts', and instead to occupy his mind by intellectual pursuits (15 Apr.).

[4] The point of this apparently scandalous anecdote, either provided by Alexander Stewart, 6th Earl of Galloway (1694–1773), or concerning him and an opera girl, is obscure. JB, who had stayed at Galloway

House from 25 to 27 Sept. 1762, had described the earl as 'a man of great quickness and uncommon spirits ... a Man of Pleasure' ('Journal of My Jaunt Harvest 1762', 25 Sept. 1762). By his first marriage he was Lord Marischal's brother-in-law, and he was also an old friend of Lord Auchinleck's. Married twice, he had fourteen children in all, and would eventually die in Aix-en-Provence (*Comp. Peer.* iv. 164–66).

[5] MS. Following 'indolent', one word ending in 'd' inked out and subsequently erased.

[6] They had travelled 28 miles (45.1 km) from Hanover to Brunswick (see Nugent, ii. 215).

[7] Brunswick had been a prosperous member of the Hanseatic League, the powerful mercantile association that linked independent cities in Northern Germany and the Baltic from the mid-thirteenth to the seventeenth centuries. It had remained quasi-independent from the Guelf dukes, to whom it had been granted by the Holy Roman Emperor in 1235, until it was captured in 1671 by Duke Rudolf August (1627–1704) of the Guelf house of Brunswick-Lüneburg (*Braunschweig—Das Bild der Stadt*, i. 15, 19–20, 22, 28, 34–35, 56–57, 120). In JB's time it was still surrounded by walls, within which it had a number of remarkable old buildings

ranging from the Gothic Old City Hall, first documented in 1302, to medieval half-timbered houses, to the 'Gewandhaus' of the tailors' guild with its Renaissance ornaments (P. J. Meier and K. Steinacher, *Kunstdenkmäler des Herzogthums Braunschweig*, [1926], ii. 5, 44–47, 72–93). In the early eighteenth century it had been enriched by handsome private houses, some with baroque façades, many others with ground floors of stone, upper storeys half-timbered, designed for the wealthy by Hermann Korb (1656–1735) and situated on broad streets paved with stones (Meier and Steinacker, ii. 72–73; *Braunschweig—Das Bild der Stadt*, i. 59, 64–66; illustr. in ii. 80–81, 95–100, 103–04, 108–11, 140–41).

[8] Diversion (OED, s.v. 'dissipation', 5).

[9] Mme de Froment's description of this incapacitating black mood presumably amused JB because it so well matched his own experience (for an account of which see Allan Ingram, *Boswell's Creative Gloom*, 1982, pp. 18–24). For her subsequent further interpretation of the causes and cures of 'hypochondria', see Journ. 3 July and n. 13).

## Wednesday 27 June

[MEM. dated Thursday 28 June] Yesterday you waited on Feronce found him gay formed polite — was too neuf [—] said la *Religion d'Hollande* &c.[1] This was absurd. At 2 presented to Duke & to Dutchess — Ladies of the Court &c. honour[2] dind — Prince Ferdinand electrified — quite great man silent, hard true old German Court. English — Richards amiable Mckenzie — Lord Hope poh — no characters — All ceremonies[3] — Stanmer good man — then Hered Prince kist her hand, talked much to him charming Prince — then visited Madam Baswitz — Madam Bloem bel esprit knew Miss Carter & english Books[4] — Feronce vain — no matter — talked with him on immortality — curious. At night court — cards — supper [—] affraid of spleen — This day march — go on[.]

[J.] The fiend laid hold of me. I was heavy & gloomy, & aukward & lazy. At breakfast we had Mr. Mckenzie of Seaforth, a lively pretty young man, with the most perfect elegance of manners, having been abroad a great many years.[5] I was bashfull before him. Such is the effect of a narrow education.[6] At eleven I waited on M. de Feronce Conseiller prive &c du Duc de Brunswic. I had a letter for him from young Count Bentinck at the Hague. I found him a man of polite science, lively & easy.[7] He sent to all the Grands Mareschals & Grands Maîtres,[8] & all the great folks, who appointed me to be at Court by two. Feronce went with me. He presented me to M. de Stanmer, a Knight of the Teutonic Order, for whom I had also a letter from Count Bentinck.[9] I was next presented to all the Grands &c & to the Dames d'honneur.[10] Next the Duke came out, to whom I was presented, & next to the Dutchess.[11] At three we sat down to dinner. I was quite struck to find myself at table in the Palace of Brunswic, with that illustrious family. I sat opposite to Prince Ferdinand whose Presence inspires animated Respect. He absolutely electrifyd me. Every time that I looked at him, I felt a noble shock.[12] We had a splendid dinner & plenty of Burgundy & other wines. After dinner we went into another room & had coffee,[13] after which M. de Stanmer went with me to the Court of the Hereditary Prince. I kist the hand of the Princess, & I was politely received by the Prince.[14] I next went with the gay[15] Feronce & payed some visits to Ladies whom he presented me to, and at seven I returned to the reigning Court, where I played at Whist.[16] We had here of english Lord Hope & his

Tutor, Mr. Rouet, & his Brother of the Guards.[17] Mr. Richards an amiable Dorsetshire man, and Mr. William Hall of Scotland.[18] We supt with the Court. All was noble & fine. Yet did my abominable Speculation[19] analyse All into insipidity at last.

[1] 'Neuf': 'inexperienced' (*Larousse Dictionnaire français-anglais*, new ed. 1981). 'La Religion d'Hollande': JB's code words for Calvinism, which had been the state religion of Holland since 1622 (*The Oxford Dictionary of the Christian Church*, 2nd ed. 1974, p. 224). JB's meaning here is, however, uncertain.

[2] The ladies of honour ('dames d'honneur') ment. in the journal; see n. 10.

[3] For Lord Hope, a young Englishman traveling with his tutor, see n. 17. JB seems to be recording an anecdote about a derogatory remark of Hope's concerning people who value ceremony but lack character. Hope had revealed his own disregard for 'ceremony'—i.e., good manners—at a meeting with the Prussian princesses in Berlin which had caused the Chamberlain of the Queen of Prussia, Count von Lehndorff (1727–1811), to write disapprovingly about Hope's sitting 'with crossed legs propped up on a table as if he were in a tavern' (20 Nov. 1761, *Dreissig Jahre: Nachträge*, i. 286, 326).

[4] Madame Baswitz was presumably the wife of Baron Henning Adam von Bassewitz (see Journ. 8 Aug. and n. 5). JB quotes her description of a Madame Bloem, who was probably the 'Madame de Blum' whom Elizabeth Carter (1717–1806) had found particularly 'amiable and agreeable' at Spa a year earlier (To Mrs. Vesey, 26 July 1763, in *A Series of Letters Between Mrs. Elizabeth Carter and Miss Catherine Talbot*, ed. Montagu Pennington, 1808, ii. 94). Carter had published poetry—*Poems upon Several Occasions* in 1738 and *Poems on Several Occasions* in 1762—as well as Sir Isaac Newton's *Philosophy explain'd for the use of the ladies* in 1739, trans. from Francesco Algarotti's *Newtonianismo per le dame*, and an important translation of Epictetus in 1758. She had also contributed Nos. 44 and 100 to SJ's *Rambler*. Her various writings earned her the sobriquet 'the learned Miss Carter' (*A Dictionary of British and American Women Writers 1660–1800*, ed. Janet Todd, 1987, pp. 75–76).

[5] Kenneth Mackenzie of Seaforth (1744–81) was traveling with his Huguenot tutor (see Journ. 11 Aug.). He belonged to the Protestant branch of a Jacobite family that had formerly been Catholic. His father, who had been attainted for joining the uprising of 1715, had been pardoned the following year

and had been allowed to repurchase his forfeited estates in 1741 after converting to Protestantism. Later, in 1766, Mackenzie would be created Baron Ardelve and Viscount Fortrose, and in 1771 Earl of Seaforth. He would serve as M.P. for Caithness from 1768 to 1774 and raise a regiment of foot, the 78th Seaforth Highlanders, in 1778, but would be forced to sell his estates to cover his debts in 1779. He would die at sea while taking his regiment to India (*Scots. Peer.* vii. 512–13; Namier and Brooke, iii. 88–89).

[6] JB's education was 'narrow' only in the social sense, in not providing the gentlemanly training that youngsters of the English upper classes received in their public schools (*Earlier Years*, pp. 23–24). In other respects, his was the sound education appropriate to his station. He had started in 1746 at a school for small boys in Edinburgh run by James Mundell (d. 1762), and from 1748 had been taught by private tutors: John Dun (c. 1723–92), a divinity student with a taste for literature, and then the more rigid, dogmatic Joseph Fergusson (c. 1719/20–92). Both however lacked polish and were treated like servants in Lord Auchinleck's household ('Ébauche de ma vie', Yale MS. L 1107, App. 2, III.A, nn. 11, 21; Yale MS. L 1111 [discarded portion], App. 2 III.E; *Earlier Years*, pp. 18, 20). From the age of thirteen JB had taken a general education course at Edinburgh University, and starting in Oct. 1758 had begun a few months' study of law. He had spent close to a year at Glasgow University, where he had heard lectures by Adam Smith and others, then ran away from the university to London in Mar. 1760 (F. A. Pottle, 'Boswell's University Education', *Johnson, Boswell, and Their Circle*, 1965, pp. 230–53; *Earlier Years*, pp. 23–25, 38, 42). JB would later send his sons Alexander ('Sandy', 1775–1822) and James ('Jamie', 1778–1822) respectively to Eton and Westminster School (*Great Biographer*, p. 8; Journ. 6 June 1790; To Malone, 8 July 1789, *Corr. 4*, p. 364).

[7] Jean-Baptiste Feronce von Rotenkreutz (1723–99), an accomplished diplomat, had distinguished himself by winning financial support for Brunswick through a subsidy agreement with England in 1759 and by arranging the marriage of the Hereditary

Prince to an English princess in 1762 (see n. 11). He had come to Brunswick as secretary of legation (*Legationssecretär*) in 1748 and had been privy counsellor of legation (*Geheimer Legationsrat*) since 1761, when he was also ennobled (Nds.StAWf 3 Alt 552, pp. 3, 7, 26). Appointed finance minister in 1773, he would negotiate further British subsidies in return for the use of Brunswickian troops in Europe and America in 1776 (Otto von Heinemann, *Geschichte von Braunschweig und Hannover*, 1892, iii. 295–97, 376).

Feronce, who had been born in Leipzig of Franco-Swiss parents, had presumably become a man of 'polite science' from his studies at the universities of Jena, Halle, and Göttingen as well as from his travels in Holland, France, and various German places before coming to Brunswick (ADB). He had been described even more favourably by Count Christian Bentinck de Varel (1734–68), in his letter to JB of 5 June (Yale MS. C 143), as 'very sensible, quick, & sprightly, knows a great deal, writes very good prose, & pretty poetry; a little wicked, but good Company'. Bentinck, whose wife was a cousin of Belle de Zuylen, was providing JB with several introductions and served as an intermediary in the correspondence between him and Belle (see From Belle de Zuylen, 19 June 1764; To Belle de Zuylen, 9 July 1764, OC *Charrière*, i. 193–96, 196–204).

[8] The ducal household included two marshals, one chief chamberlain, and eighteen chamberlains (*Hof Etat*, pp. 1–2).

[9] Ekhard (Eckhard) August von Stammer (1705–74), lord of Ballenstedt und Asmusstedt, was chief master of horse (*Hof Etat*, p. 14). He was described by Bentinck as 'honest, good, worthy' as well as 'plain & good naturedly civil' (From Bentinck, 5 June). Descended from an old Anhalt family, he had started at the Brunswick court as a page in 1717, had risen through various ranks as cavalry officer and chamberlain, and had held his present position since 1756 (Nds.StAWf Pagenbuch VI Hs 2 Nr. 4, p. 14; VI Hs 10 Nr. 15 Bd. 1, pp. 26, 58, 87). As a Teutonic Knight, he belonged to the prestigious order of warrior monks (parallel to the Templars and Knights of St. John), whose mission had begun during the crusades and who had ruled over Northern Europe, notably Prussia, from 1230 to 1550 (*Deutsche Orden*, 1980, pp. 48–63). Von Stammer would become head of the order's local house and of the entire Saxon branch in 1773 (Johannes Voigt, *Geschichte des Deutschen Ritter-Ordens*, 1857–59, i. 1–4, 128–54; ii.

687; Voigt, *Geschichte Preussens*, 1827, ii. 28–36, 77–81, 125–32). The date of von Stammer's birth and the spelling of his first name are taken from his monument in the order's church at Lucklum (P. J. Meier, *Die Bau- und Kunstdenkmäler des Herzogthums Braunschweig*, 1890–1910, ii. 84).

[10] Ladies in waiting. There were six, all chosen from respected families (*Hof Etat*, p. 20).

[11] Karl I, Duke of Brunswick-Lüneburg (1713–80), belonged to the Guelf line of Brunswick-Bevern through his father, Ferdinand Albrecht II (1680–1735), who had succeeded for a few months his cousin Ludwig Rudolf (1671–1735), the last of the main line of Brunswick-Wölfenbüttel (Isenburg, i. Tafeln 72–73; see also Journ. 1 Aug. n. 6). Duke Karl, a pleasure-loving ruler and patron of the arts, had presided over an opulent court for almost thirty years. He was especially fond of French drama and Italian opera, both of which he encouraged and supported financially in his theatres. During the recent war he had first sided with Prussia and then, while the French occupied Brunswick from Aug. 1757 to Feb. 1758, had chosen neutrality and exile in Blankenburg, which his family had inherited from earlier branches of the Guelfs (*Braunschweig—Das Bild der Stadt*, i. 70; ADB; *Herzog August: Sammler, Fürst, Gelehrter*, 1979, pp. 125–26). The Duchess, Philippine Charlotte (1716–1801), was the daughter of Friedrich Wilhelm I of Prussia and was devoted to her brother, the recently victorious Frederick II of Prussia. She was interested in religion and philosophy as well as the arts. Unlike her husband, she admired German literature (Selma Stern, *Karl Wilhelm Ferdinand, Herzog zu Braunschweig und Lüneburg*, Veröffentlichungen der historischen Kommission für Hannover, Oldenburg, Braunschweig, 1921, vi. 3–4, 48).

[12] JB gave WJT (for whom see Journ. 3 July, n. 10) a similarly glowing account of this meeting with Prince Ferdinand, Duke of Brunswick-Lüneburg (the younger brother of the reigning duke), describing him as 'the General that made Broglio and his foppish legions fly, and sent shame and terror to the gates of Paris' (23 July, *Corr.* 6, p. 105). Ferdinand had been in the service of Frederick II since 1740 and had been named commander-in-chief of the Anglo-Hanoverian troops in 1758 after the Duke of Cumberland (1721–65), the notorious 'butcher of Culloden', was dismissed for prematurely capitulating to the French at Kloster-Seven (Heinemann, iii. 277–83; Savory, pp. 47 ff.,

67 ff., 112 ff.). So successful had Ferdinand been at Minden (see Journ. 25 June n. 3) that the bells of Edinburgh had pealed for him (*Scots Mag.* 1759, xxi. 370), and he had won further renown for his victory at Vellinghausen (see Journ. 21 June n. 10).

[13] Coffee, brewed or boiled roasted beans served with sugar, was usually imported from Turkey. It had long been appreciated by Muslims as a non-alcoholic drink, and had been popular as a stimulant since the seventeenth century in more northerly countries, especially after heavy eating or drinking (John Chamberlayne, *The Natural History of Coffee, Thee, Chocolate,* 1682, p. 6).

[14] On 16 Jan. of this year Karl Wilhelm Ferdinand (1735–1806) had married Princess Augusta (1737–1813), the daughter of the Prince of Wales (1707–51) and Augusta, Duchess of Saxe-Gotha (1719–72), and sister of George III. The young couple had recently returned to Brunswick by way of Holland, where JB had caught a glimpse of them on 10 Feb. (French theme, Yale MS. M 87, quoted in *Holland,* Heinemann pp. 140–41, McGraw-Hill pp. 144–45). In 1773 the Prince would take control of the affairs of Brunswick with the help of Feronce, curbing his father's extravagances, and economizing further when he succeeded his father as Duke of Brunswick-Lüneburg in 1780 (Stern, vi. 65–70; Gerd Biegel, *6. Februar 1794,* Veröffentlichungen des Braunschweigischen Landesmuseums, 1994, lxxiv. 35–36). He would serve as Prussian field marshal against Holland in 1787, would fight against the French revolutionists in 1793, and would die in advanced age of wounds received in the battle of Jena-Auerstedt against Napoleon (Heinemann, iii. 272, 282–83, 294–309, 333–37).

[15] MS. 'gay' scored out by a modern hand.

[16] JB's favourite card game, usually played by four participants (two sets of partners) with a full deck of 52 cards. Each player showed one card at a time to win a 'trick'

over the other players, and the partners, combining their tricks, had to gain a total of seven or more to win. The challenge was to calculate what cards were held by one's partner on the one hand and by the opponents on the other (Edmond Hoyle, *A Short Treatise on the Game of Whist,* first pub. 1742, 1746, pp. 2–52). The game, believed to have originated in England, was a precursor of bridge.

[17] Charles Hope (1740–66), *styled* Lord Hope, son of John, 2nd Earl of Hopetoun, had been traveling on the Continent since 1760 (Lehndorff, *Dreissig Jahre: Nachträge,* i. 285–86). He would die at an early age on his return from a voyage to the West Indies (*Scots Peer.* iv. 497). His tutor, William Rouet, had taught at Glasgow University as Professor of Oriental Languages from 1751 to 1752 and Professor of Ecclesiastical History from 1752 to 1761. He had resigned from his position in Dec. 1761 after the university rejected the Earl's offer to pay for a substitute (W. Innes Addison, *Matriculation Albums of the University of Glasgow,* 1913, p. 5; J. D. Mackie, *The University of Glasgow,* 1954, pp. 188, 192–94).

Lord Hope's brother, James Hope (1741–1816), later 3rd Earl of Hopetoun, had entered the 3rd Regt. of Foot in 1758, had fought at Minden in 1759, and had just left military service. A Representative Peer for Scotland in 1784–90 and 1794–96, he would also raise and command the Hopetoun Fencibles, and would be created Baron Hopetoun of Hopetoun in 1793 (*Scots. Peer.* iv. 500).

[18] Neither one has been further identified.

[19] 'Abstract or hypothetical reasoning on subjects of an abstruse or conjectural nature' (OED, s.v. 'speculation', II. 6). JB had recently tormented himself with questions about virtue and vice, personal annihilation, Christian beliefs, and other religious or philosophical issues (see To WJT, 22 May and ?11 June, *Corr.* 6, pp. 98–101).

## Thursday 28 June

[MEM. dated Friday 29 June] Yesterday you waited on Abbé Jerusalem quite learned & mild — was twice adying read Plato's Phaedon poor — happy to be Christian. Then waited on Prince Ferdinand — noble above humanity — Highlanders pleas'd with heath — but not long enough — then Princesses — then dind Hered Prince. Princess affable talked of Eglint — March &c with ease — afternoon Feronce — night court fine with Dame d'honneur yet gloomy — well with Rouet [—] after supper much convers with Duke [—] cordial leave of all —

This day set out — Be gay — mem firm Laird of Auchinleck habits of retenue — Prudence &c — Manage Father with affection.

[J.] I waited on Lord Hope & the other english, found them at breakfast, talking like Virtuosos.[1] Left them soon. Waited next on the Abbé Jerusalem for whom I had a letter from Count Bentinck. I found him a learned agreable Man with a pleasing simplicity of manners.[2] He told me he had a conversation of two hours with The King of Prussia, whom he found as great a Man as fame had reported him to be. He talked on a variety of subjects with a remarkable force and fluency. The Abbé said that he lost all fear for the King; so that at last he wished to bring him on the Subject of Religion on which he doubted not to give his Majesty some arguments that would not be without weight.[3] The Abbé said he defended no Sect; but the genuine Christian Religion itself. He said he had been twice just adying, and took up Plato's Phaedon, which was the support of the Ancients in the gloomy hour. I was struck, said he to find it so weak. I applied to the Religion of Jesus, and had full contentment of mind. Thus said he, I have had a tryal of my Religion.[4] I was pleased with this Anecdote of the worthy and amiable Abbé. But I was not at ease myself. My Faith was confused. Objections rose thick against Revelation.[5] Yet I hoped at last to attain stability. I said to the Abbé that in travelling we meet with painfull circumstances. We make a good acquaintance and we must be obliged to quit. Je trouve said I, que Je pourrois etre tres heureux avec la Conversation de Monsieur l'Abbé, et demain Je dois le quitter, et peutetre Je n'aurrois jamais le bonheur de le revoir. I dined with the Hereditary Prince. The Princess was excessively affable. She talked to me with the greatest ease of the Catch Club, Lord Eglintoune Lord March, and other English topics.[6] After dinner she spoke english to My Lord Marischal, Mckenzie, Richards and me. She was just a free english Lass. I can get no bread & butter here of a morning, said She. The Butter is bad and they have only brown bread. A Cumberland Squire's daughter could not have been more easy.[7] I then payed a visit to Feronce, saw his Library which was not great, but very well-chosen & elegant. I was gloomy, & talked to Feronce of that distemper. He said it was merely corporeal; for he had heard of a Girl of twelve who hanged herself, & she could not have much thought.[8] I then went to the reigning Court. The Palace is ancient, and the rooms filled me with respect. The great Court looks noble alltho' the front is only wood cut in imitation of stone, except a small part of it newly built.[9] I ought to be tied to the Halberts, and lashed unmercifully for neglecting to relate that this day at two I was presented to Prince Ferdinand. He received me in his Bedchamber.[10] It was splendid. The Canopy was sumptous. He had a number of pretty pictures, and an elegant collection of Books. He talked a good time to me. It was luxury. I stood with a mind full of the ideas of the last glorious war. I was talking to a distinguished Heroe. He had a force & yet an affability of address. He seemed a man of strong judgment and clear ideas. He told me that the Scots Highlanders were happy when they met with heath; but complained that it was short, and nothing like their heath.[11] All my Speculation could not annihilate the satisfaction of this Interview. At night Rouet and I talked a good deal. He was a sensible forward fellow. After supper the Duke of Brunswic honoured me with a pretty long conversation, and I am sure that his Highness was pleased. Here now do I find myself in the very sphere of magnificence. I live with Princes, and a Court is my home. I took leave of the Duke, and a cordial adieu of all the Courtiers. I found myself allready liked by them with affection. They asked me to return to Brunswic in August when I would see the Fair.[12] I said I probably should have that pleasure. I went home in vast spirits. I could scarcely sleep.

[1] Connoisseurs of works of art or, more likely, dilletantes (OED, s.v. 'virtuoso', 2).

[2] Johann Friedrich Wilhelm Jerusalem (1709–89), court chaplain and educator, was the most respected clergyman in Brunswick, known for his piety, learning, and tolerance. JB calls him abbé, a style used not only for a French priest but also for an abbot (Larousse, s.v. 'abbé'). Jerusalem had headed the Lutheran seminary of Riddagshausen since 1753 and, for the four previous years, the monastery of Marienthal near Helmstedt (Nds.StAWf VI Hs 10 Nr. 6 and Nr. 10; Wolfgang Erich Müller, *Johann Friedrich Wilhelm Jerusalem*, 1984, pp. 1–8). In Brunswick he was addressed as *Abt* (i.e., 'abbot'—see Journ. 22 Aug.). Bentinck described Jerusalem as 'a worthy man who has all the good natuir [*sic*] the affability & the modesty of a Child, with the most deep & sublime Study, & the most refined taste' (From Bentinck, 5 June).

[3] Frederick II was known for his religious scepticism and scorn for traditional Christianity. But Jerusalem's hopes of engaging Frederick's interest in religion were not wholly unrealistic. The King had written poems expressing his belief in a providential God, had accepted deistical ideas, and had strongly supported Protestant values. Some later scholars would conclude that in spite of his reputation, he had not been 'irreligious' (J. D. Preuss, *Friedrich der Grosse*, 1833, iii. 152–202; Nicholas Saul, 'Friedrich II und die religiösen Strömungen seiner Zeit', in *Panorama*, pp. 62–67).

[4] Plato's *Phaedo* presents the dying Socrates' tentative thoughts about the immortality of the soul. The upright Cato of Utica (95–46 B.C.) was said to have sought strength in this work before committing suicide (OCCL, s.v. 'Cato, Marcus Porcius'). In seeking consolation in the classics, Jerusalem reflected Enlightenment thinking, while in finding such consolation rather in

the Bible, he revealed his even stronger faith as a Protestant. Eventually, Jerusalem would come to be characterized as an 'enlightened Lutheran', who drew on several of the intellectual currents important in his day: English latitudinarianism, deism, and the Leibniz-Wolffian thought that had recently been formulated in German universities (see Wolfgang Erich Müller, 'Von der Eigenständigkeit der Neologie Jerusalems', *Neue Zeitschrift für Systematische Theologie und Religionsphilosophie* 26 [1984]: 289–309).

[5] In earlier moments of religious perplexity JB had been encouraged to think about revelation by SJ and had continued to do so in Holland (Journ. 22 Oct. 1763, 18 Mar. 1764; *Holland*, Heinemann p. 49 and n. 2, McGraw-Hill p. 50 and n. 7). JB had also been exchanging views on revelation with Belle de Zuylen, who had expressed certain doubts in her letter of 18–19 June (OC *Charrière*, i. 193–94; *Holland*, Heinemann p. 298, McGraw-Hill pp. 306–07). The topic was of special interest to Jerusalem. In his major published work he would argue that revelation was God's gift to humanity in general and not to individuals, though with the consolation that individuals could understand the purpose of their suffering in the universe (*Betrachtungen über die vornehmsten Wahrheiten der Religion*, 'Reflections on the Foremost Truths of Religion', 1768, i. 85–95, 101–03; Müller, *Jerusalem*, pp. 98–99). In later volumes Jerusalem would develop the theory that revelation was granted in three stages: by God the Creator in Genesis, through Moses, and through Christ (vol. 2, 1772; vol. 3, 1774; see Müller, *Jerusalem*, pp. 66–76). JB, as his journal entry makes clear, did not fully accept Jerusalem's views.

[6] Alexander Montgomerie, 10th Earl of Eglinton (1723–69), and William Douglas, 3rd Earl of March (1724–1810), had become Lords of the Bedchamber on George III's accession to the throne in 1760. Eglinton was

also a close friend of the Princess's brother, Edward Augustus, Duke of York (1739–67). Both Eglinton and March were members of the Catch Club, founded in 1761 by John Montagu, 4th Earl of Sandwich (1718–97), to encourage the composition of catches (humorous rounds), canons, and glees (*New Grove 2*, 'Sandwich, 4th Earl of [John Montagu]'; see also French theme, ?26 Oct. 1763, Yale MS. M 87). Eglinton, an Ayrshire neighbour with a London residence, had befriended JB during his first stay in London in 1760 and had introduced him to the circles of 'the great, the gay, and the ingenious' ('Memoirs of James Boswell, Esq.', *Eur. Mag.* May 1791, see *Lit. Car.* p. xxxi). In showing him the pleasures of the capital, Eglinton had weaned JB from his Catholicism and had paved the way for his return home (*Earlier Years*, pp. 47–48; 'Ébauche de ma vie', App. 2, III.A, n. 36). It was during his second visit that JB had learned to sing catches from Eglinton and had been pleased to hear him say 'there were not five people in the whole Catch Club who had a better ear than I had' (Journ. 23 Mar. 1763). For JB's enthusiastic singing, see Morris R. and Melita Ann Brownell, 'Boswell's Ballads: A Life in Song', *Boswell in Scotland and Beyond*, ed. Thomas Crawford, Association for Scottish Literary Studies, Occasional Papers 12 [1997], pp. 119–22.

[7] Augusta had no particular link with Cumberland, a county in the Lake District, but she apparently reminded JB of a simple, hearty country girl. Her natural amiability had already impressed her mother-in-law (Duchess of Brunswick to Frederick II, 23 Feb. 1764, *Aus Den Briefen der Herzogin Philippine Charlotte von Braunschweig*, ed. Hans Droysen, Quellen und Forschungen zur Braunschweiger Geschichte, 1916, viii. 184) and would soon be noted by Count Lehndorff in Berlin (21 July 1764, *Dreissig Jahre: Nachträge*, i. 406).

[8] Not identified.

[9] The palace, called the *Graue Hof* (Grey Court) after the Cistercian monastery that had once stood in its place, was built between 1716 and 1721 by Hermann Korb but incorporated a much earlier building erected by thirteenth-century Templars. Its central court was dominated by a splendid staircase emerging from a massive central *corps de logis* (P. J. Meier and K. Steinacher, p. 42). It would eventually burn down during an uprising in 1830 (*Braunschweig und Umgebung* [1877], pp. 54–55).

[10] Prince Ferdinand was living in the palace while a residence was renovated for him on the Burgplatz at the centre of the town (see Peter Königfeld and Reinhard Roseneck, *Burg Dankwarderode*, 1995, pp. 37–38).

[11] By 'heath' the highlanders had evidently meant the shrubs and heather they had known in their native Scotland (OED, s.v. 'heath', 2.b and 'heather', 1.a). They would have seen such heath, which requires sandy, arid soil, in several parts of Westphalia.

Prince Ferdinand had met various groups of highlanders under his command during the recent war. About 300 men, recruited by Major Robert Keith (1730–95), a cousin of Lord Marischal, had arrived in Germany in Aug. 1759 and had fought so valiantly a few days later that the Prince had asked for more such troops. A full regiment, the 87th Highlanders, also known as 'Keith's Highlanders', had arrived in Nov. 1759 and had been followed by the 88th Highlanders in June 1760. After the battles of 1759, 1760, and 1761 Prince Ferdinand had singled out these Scottish forces for special praise (Savory, pp. 477–78; Stewart, ii. 91–96; see also James Ferguson, *Papers of The Scots Brigade*, ii. 412 and n.).

[12] Brunswick's trade fairs, held in Feb. and Aug. of each year, were high points of social as well as mercantile activity (*Braunschweig—Das Bild der Stadt*, i. 60). For JB's return visit, see Journ. 7–22 Aug.

## Friday 29 June

[MEM. dated Saturday 30 June] Yesterday after restless night you set out early — dull day. Happiness equal to desires — at night — very dreary & changefull.

[J.] After a restless night, I rose fallen not a little. At six we set out. We had a so so day of it.

## Saturday 30 June

[MEM. dated Sunday 1 July] Yesterday set out early was much better — never own'd uneasiness but appeared composed — lost all foreign ideas — thought yourself just in Scotland — Time & space annihilated. Lord M — chatty afternoon. King of Prussia. Sottise des hommes — coups de hazard never vain — praises Daun & Czarine.[1] Marquis d'Argens Hyp'd — waistcoat 4 years grown to skin — goodnatur'd. My Lord's sound mind — This day be bold — *think* you have fine days before you yet.

[J.] I was exceedingly melancholy; but I had fortitude enough to conceal it. My thoughts were horrid; yet my manners were cheerfull. I lost all foreign ideas. I thought myself just in Scotland. How strange is the mind of Man. How are our ideas lodged? How are they formed? How little do they depend upon realitys! In the afternoon My Lord was very chatty. He told me that the Marquis d'Argens was a good-natured amiable man, and much liked by the King of Prussia. He is now old. He has married an Actress, whom he keeps in great subjection. He has made her learn greek, & I don't know how many things, merely to make her of use to him in his studies.[2] He is a miserable Being, for, he is Hypochondriack & terrified for death. He had worn a flannel underwaistcoat four years & durst not take it off, for fear of catching cold. The King drove out one fear by another, & told him that if he persisted to wear that waistcoat, his perspiration would be entirely stop'd, & he must inevitably die. The Marquis agreed to quit his waistcoat. But it had so fixed itself upon him, that pieces of his skin came away with it.[3] My Lord as usual laughed at Religious gloom. I told him he had the felicity of a sound mind, which every body has not. Good heaven! how fortunate is one man above another! We slept at Magdebourg.[4]

---

[1] Fieldmarshal Leopold Joseph von Daun (1705–66) was the leading Austrian general fighting against Prussia in the Seven Years' War. He had won important victories at Kolin on 18 June 1757 and at Hochkirch on 14 Oct. 1758 (Franz-Lorenz von Thadden, *Feldmarschall Daun*, 1967, pp. 263–78, 362–69). The Czarina Elisabeth (1709–62) had strongly supported her Austrian ally. So pleased had she been with Daun that she had sent him a jewelled sword after the battle of Hochkirch (von Thadden, pp. 367, 413). Lord Marischal's anecdote concerns Frederick II's generous tribute to two of his fiercest opponents in the recent war, all the more remarkable because James Keith, his favourite general, had been killed at Hochkirch.

[2] Jean-Baptiste de Boyer, Marquis d'Argens (1704–71), sceptic, wit, and prolific miscellaneous writer of essays, memoirs, novels, and secret histories, was the director of theatre and long-time friend of Frederick II. In 1749 he had married Babet Cochois (fl. 1735–62), an actress in the French Theatre of Berlin (*Archives biographiques françaises*). They were said to have married without Frederick's knowledge or consent, but other reports suggest that they actually had his approval from the start and had been given the opportunity to live in one of his palaces during the Seven Years' War (Thiébault, v. 355–56; J. J. Olivier, *Les Comédiens français dans les cours d'Allemagne au XVIIIe siécle*, 1902, ii. 39, 99 n. 39, and 100; Lehndorff, *Dreissig Jahre*, p. 303). After her marriage the marquise had retired from the stage and had helped her husband with his writings. Talented in painting and music, she was interested in philosophy as well, and she had mastered French, German, and Italian. She also knew some Latin and had learned a little Greek to please the marquis, but refused to study Hebrew, whose letters she found 'trop barbares' (Thiébault, v. 352; Olivier, pp. 36–39).

[3] The Marquis d'Argens was known to suffer from imaginary illnesses, a weakness that inspired many practical jokes. For similar anecdotes, see Thiébault, v. 345–46,

357–58.
[4] MS. 'Magdebourg' written over 'Brunsw.' Magdeburg was about 50 miles (c. 80.5 km) from Brunswick.

## Sunday 1 July

[MEM. dated Monday 2 July] Yesterday you was pretty well.

[J.] I was in moderate spirits & pretty well.

## Monday 2 July

[MEM. dated Tuesday 3 July] [Y]esterday you arrived at Potzdam just as at *Laird's* house.

[J.] We talked of the Spaniards. My Don Quixote Humour got up. I said I should be infinitely happy to be a Colonel in the Spanish Service. My Lord amused us with a fine fancifull story of my making a conquest of Portugal, and marrying an Infanta, and afterwards called me constantly the great *Colonello*.[1] At night we arrived at Potzdam, which is a very pretty Town. The King has built houses like those of the People of quality in London, & has let them to Taylors and Shoemakers and other Tradesmen.[2]

[1] To conquer Portugal would have meant recapturing the country which Spain had been forced to evacuate by the Treaty of Paris of Feb. 1763, after an occupation of eleven months (*Ann. Reg.* 1762, p. 6; W. N. Hargreaves-Mawdsley, *Eighteenth-Century Spain 1700–1788*, 1979, pp. 102–08). Hostilities between the two countries actually dated back at least to Spain's occupation of Portugal from 1580 to 1640 (Douglas L. Wheeler, *Historical Dictionary of Portugal*, 1993, p. xvii). JB's self-consciously Quixotic fantasy of a Spanish military career was probably inspired by the experiences of Lord Marischal, who had been officially accepted into Spanish service in 1721 and had been commissioned as a *Capitán General* in Va-

lencia in 1734 (GStAPK, VI. HA Familienarchive und Nachlässe, Nl George Keith, II Nr. 1, Bl. 5, 11).
[2] By order of the King, good housing had been provided to encourage new settlers to work in local trades. Depending on their origin, they lived in the Dutch, French, or Italian district in houses constructed with uniform façades that reflected their nationality (Jakob Friedrich von Bielfeld, 19 Nov. 1754, Letter 85, *Lettres familières*, 1763, ii. 326; *Potsdam*, ed. Martin Uhlemann and Otto Rückert, 1986, pp. 31, 49). So fast had the houses sprung up, that they had become known as 'les champignons de Frédéric' (Thiébault, i. 284; Nicolai, iii. 1250).

## Tuesday 3 July

[MEM. dated Wednesday 4 July] [Y]esterday you was fine. My Lord took you to Parade presented you to Prince of Prussia & Comte D'ainhault. You saw old Earl with aparts. as in abbey. Din'd — saw Palace — King's Books remember'd Temple. Evening Mad:[1] From[.] wrong to approach [—] was virtuous. This day [S]ans [S]ouci.

[J.] My Lord Marischal carried me to the Palace where he has an appartment assigned him by the King.[2] He seemed just like one who comes

23

to a good freind's house in the country, when the freind is of somewhat higher rank than the guest. Just as I come to Eglintoune. It was fine to see the old Scots Nobleman lodged in the Palace of Prussia, just as if he had been in the Abbey of Holyroodhouse.[3] At ten he carried me to the Parade, which was full of Prussian officers, all bold-looking, all gay, all well-drest.[4] He presented me to the Prince of Prussia[5] calling me 'd'une tres bonne maison et fort galant homme' he also presented me to Count Danhalt the lover of Zelide; he has never seen her, but has heard so much of her charms, that he has sent formal proposals to her.[6] I then waited on Mr. Catt Reader to the King to whom I had a letter from M. de Zuyl. He was sick & could not go out with me; but he was civil. I found him dry & even insipid.[7] Madame de Froment & I dined téte á teté, after which we went & were shown the Palace which is magnificent. The King's Concert-Room is very elegant.[8] We looked thro' a glass door & saw his Bedchamber, & a neat little library. All his books were bound in red turkie & handsomly gilt.[9] They made me think of my dear Temple. They would have pleased him much.[10] In the Antichamber were a good many Books, but our Conductor would not allow us to lift any of them, for, he said, the King knew the exact place of every one of them. I saw Œuvres de Voltaire, & a fine quarto Edition of the Œuvres du Philosophe de Sans-Souci.[11] Great & pleasing were my thoughts. At night Madame de told me how hypochondriack she had been. 'Toutes mes pensées etoient tristes. Les Beautés de la nature m'insultoient. J'etois au desespoir. Pourtant sans aucun changement exterieur J'ai devenu tout d'un coup parfaitement heureux. J'avois une gayeté d'imagination. Je me trouvois seule dans ma chambre au soir. Je voulois avoir de compagnie pour leur communiquer mon Bonheur. J'ouvrit ma fenêtre. J'étois enchanté avec tout ce que Je voyoit. La Lune les Astres La Campagne Le Lac tout me paroissoit riant.[12] Je me dit "Mon Dieu! est il possible? D'ou vient toute cette felicité?" En verité Monsieur, notre Bonheur depend du façon que notre sang circule.'[13]

This description struck me very much. Some weeks ago at Utrecht when I felt an amazing flow of sudden felicity, I thought it quite singular;[14] but I find that I have just had the very same distemper with my Turkish Lady. This is curious to find the same Spleen over the whole globe.[15] I was in the humour of gallantry tonight. I was pleased with the romantic idea of making love to a Turk. However I talked morality at last & thought myself a Johnson.[16] She seemed too indolent in Body & too vivacious in mind to be a very rigid Lady. Besides her ideas were quite different from mine. Her Religion was of a kind very different from mine. Bless me. What are mortals?

---

[1] 'Mad' scored out (see Editorial Practices), possibly by a modern owner of the MS who wished to eliminate a reference to madness and who did not realize that JB's 'Mad:' referred to Madame de Froment.

[2] The Potsdam Palace, a huge building consisting of a substantial *corps de logis* and two wings, was situated on the outskirts of the town, with its main entrance facing the gardens and the river Havel beyond. Formerly the chief residence of the militaristic, spartan Friedrich Wilhelm I (see Journ. 19 June n. 4), the palace had been expanded and lavishly redecorated for Frederick II by Georg Wenceslas von Knobelsdorff (1709–53), his favourite architect (see Bielfeld,

Letter 85, 19 Nov. 1754, ii. 326–28; Edwin Redslob, *Barock und Rokoko in den Schlössern von Berlin und Potsdam*, 1954, pp. 38–39).

[3] For Eglinton, see Journ. 28 June, n. 6; *Corr. 9*, pp. 18–19 n. 1; Eglinton's seat was in Kilwinning parish, Ayrshire, on the left bank of Lugton Water. The abbey and palace of Holyrood House included apartments for several noblemen. JB associated the place with Mary, Queen of Scots, who had lived there from 1561 to 1567, and Prince Charles Edward Stuart, who had stayed there briefly in 1745 (Charles Mackie, *The History of the Abbey*, 1819, pp. 76–90; see also To JJ, 17 Aug. and 13 Sept. 1762, 22 Feb. 1763, *Corr. 1*, pp. 13, 15, 49 and nn. 6, 50). For JB's enthusiasm for Mary and Holyrood House, see Jayne Elizabeth Lewis, *Mary Queen of Scots*, 1998, p. 110.

[4] The parade ground occupied a large area between the palace's ornamental gardens and the Havel (Nicolai, iii. map). The officers were assembled for one of several reviews that Frederick II conducted there each year for his best troops, as his father had done before him. Frederick also instituted new manœuvres at his parades and expected representatives of his other regiments to carry them back to their respective troops (Bielfeld, 19 Nov. 1754, Letter 85, ii. 329).

[5] Since Frederick II was childless, his nephew Friedrich Wilhelm (1744–97) had become Prince of Prussia—that is, Hereditary Prince—on the death of his father, Prince August Wilhelm (1722–58). The young man was in Potsdam with his regiment, the Prinz von Preussen (No. 18), which was stationed there (Detlef Kotsch, *Potsdam: Die preussische Garnisonstadt*, 1992, p. 73). Long groomed for a military career by Frederick II, he had been made an officer at the age of ten and had taken part in the battle for Schweidnitz in 1762. But he was now no longer enthusiastic about military life (W. M. Bissing, *Friedrich Wilhelm II, König von Preussen*, 1967, pp. 12–19). According to Baron J. H. von Ried, Austrian envoy to Berlin, 'The heir apparent, whom no one credits with great intellect, is big, well built, plays the foreigner, and has nothing Prussian about him apart from his uniform' (To the Emperor Francis I, Sept. 1763, quoted in G. B. Volz, *Friedrich der Grosse im Spiegel seiner Zeit*, 1926, ii. 210). Friedrich Wilhelm II would prove to be less bellicose but also less effectual than his uncle when he finally succeeded to the throne in 1786. He would try to preserve the interests of Prussia by negotiation, especially with Austria and Russia, and would be called on to arbitrate disputes involving Poland and Denmark. During the French Revolution he would join Austria in a vain attempt to support the French monarchy, but his military intervention in 1792 would soon be beaten back, and the Treaty of Basel in 1795 would force him to give up Prussian territory west of the Rhine (ADB; Holborn, 357–73). For his later life, see Wilhelm Bringmann, *Preussen unter Friedrich Wilhelm II (1786–1797)*, 2001.

[6] Friedrich, Count of Anhalt (1732–94), had been the Prince of Prussia's adjutant-general since 1757 after serving as aide-de-camp to Frederick II (ADB). An illegitimate son of Wilhelm Gustav, Hereditary Prince of Anhalt Dessau (1699–1737), he owed his title not to Prussia but to the Holy Roman Emperor (see Journ. 25 Sept. n. 13). He belonged to a famous military family, had distinguished himself in many recent battles, and was highly respected in both Dessau and Prussia (*Militärisches Pantheon*, pp. 62–63). He had heard about Belle de Zuylen from Henri-Alexandre de Catt (1725–95), who had served as tutor to her family before becoming Frederick II's Reader in 1758 (P. Godet, *Madame de Charrière et ses amis*, 1906, i. 68 and n.; Courtney, pp. 87–89).

[7] The letter JB was bringing to Catt had come from Belle's father, Diederik Jacob van Tuyll, Heer van Zuylen (1707–76), who a few weeks later would report to JB that Belle had dissuaded the Count from undertaking his long-postponed visit, thereby ending his courtship (11 Dec., Yale MS. C 3175, quoted in translation in *Holland*, Heinemann pp. 314–16, McGraw-Hill pp. 323–25).

Catt had gained his position in Prussia by making a favourable impression on Frederick II while the latter was travelling incognito in Holland in 1755 (MacDonogh, p. 241). Less impressed by Catt, Andrew Mitchell (1708–71), British envoy to Prussia, called him 'Chatty' and declared him 'the silliest, vainest, emptyest, fellow I ever was acquainted with' (To Alexander Burnett, 15 Feb. 1765, Bundle 82, Burnett of Kemnay Archives; for Burnett, see Journ. 15 July, n. 4).

[8] The concert room held a special piano and the King's tortoise-shell music stand. Lavishly decorated, it had walls, chairs and settees covered in green and gold, a ceiling of gilded stucco, and a rock-crystal chandelier (Nicolai, iii. 1140–41).

[9] The bedroom was elegantly furnished in silver and blue (Nicolai, iii. 1141–43). Some of the King's books, bound in morocco leather ('red turkie'), were kept in an alcove beyond the bedroom.

[10] WJT was one of JB's closest friends. They had met in Robert Hunter's Greek class at Edinburgh University in 1755 and would remain lifelong friends and correspondents. WJT's literary interests, which he shared with JB, evidently included an appreciation for handsome bindings. WJT had studied law at Trinity Hall, Cambridge, from 1758 to 1761, had taken chambers in the Inner Temple in 1763, but had returned to Cambridge in June of that year with thoughts of entering the ministry. After earning his LL.B. from Trinity Hall, Cambridge, in June 1765, he would be ordained in Sept. 1766 and become rector at Mamhead, Devon, in Sept. 1766, later moving to a similar position at St. Gluvias, Penryn, Cornwall, in 1777 ('Brief Chronologies of the Lives of James Boswell and William Johnson Temple', *Corr.* 6, pp. xviii–xx; Journ. 3 Apr., 7 July 1763).

[11] Frederick II kept almost identical collections in his residences in Potsdam, Sanssouci, Berlin, Charlottenburg, and Breslau so that he could read a book without interruption when he moved from one of these places to another (Thiébault, i. 147–48). He owned seven different editions of Voltaire's works published by 1764, hence the set seen by JB cannot be specifically identified (Bogdan Krieger, *Friedrich der Grosse und seine Bibliotheken*, 1914, pp. 167–68). The edition of Frederick's works, named after his summer residence of Sanssouci, was either the 1750 or the 1752 quarto, both in three volumes (Joachim Gustav Leithaeuser, *Verzeichnis sämtlicher Ausgaben der Werke Friedrich des Grossen*, 1877, p. 35).

[12] Presumably at the château of Colombier, on Lake Neuchâtel, where Mme de Froment had resided with Lord Marischal while he served as Governor of Neuchâtel.

Her appreciation for natural beauty reflects the ideas recently popularized by Rousseau, especially in his *Julie, ou La Nouvelle Héloïse* (1761). She had known Rousseau while he was under the protection of Lord Marischal (see Journ. 3 Dec. n. 29). For JB's visit to Colombier, see Journ. 11 Dec.

[13] A physical explanation not mentioned by Mme de Froment the first time she revealed her 'hypochondria' (see 26 June and n. 9).

[14] In mid-Apr. JB had suddenly and inexplicably experienced 'a glow of delight … a real ecstacy' after a period of prolonged depression (To WJT, 17 Apr., *Corr.* 6, p. 92). JB had associated his sense of well-being with briskly circulating blood on his first day of travel (Journ. 18 June).

[15] JB here contradicts the widely held opinion, popularized by Dr. Cheyne in his *English Malady*, that spleen and hypochondria were typically English complaints (pp. i–ii; see also Roy Porter, *Mind-Forg'd Manacles*, 1987, pp. 83–89). JB would meet many more sufferers in the course of his travels and would again make the point, in his first *Hypochondriack* essay of 1 Nov. 1777, that such depression was not confined to the British (Bailey, i. 107).

[16] SJ, who had befriended JB in London soon after their inauspicious first meeting on 16 May 1763, had profoundly influenced JB's thinking and remained a moral guide even at this distance: 'Since my being honoured with the friendship of Mr. Johnson, I have more seriously considered the duties of morality and religion and the dignity of human nature. I have considered that promiscuous concubinage is certainly wrong' (Journ. 16 July 1763).

## Wednesday 4 July

[MEM. dated Thursday 5 July.] [Y]esterday you saw Gallery at Sans Souci noble rich — All choice pieces — But was hyp'd & had no pleasure — dind quiet then journ. then walked in garden then home too famil with ———. Have a care [—] at night merely from talking grew well. This day be alive — be manly fear not censure — If pleasure be a deception, so is pain. Enter Berlin content. Pursue Plan[1] — Forget dreary ideas & sensual Turkish ones — Be Johnson. But take fresh German &c.[2]

[J.] At nine the Inspecteur of the gallery at Sans Souci waited on me & I carried him in a coach to the Retreat of the Great Frederic. The King has here apartments for himself & four freinds. The Building is light and elegant.³ But the Gallery is truly superb. It is very long very lofty & very richly finished. The Collection of Pictures is not as yet very numerous, but they are all fine pieces, and I was told by Lord Marischal that there is not a better collection in one place.⁴ I was unlucky enough to be gloomy, & could not relish this rich scene as Boswell himself relishes Beauty. I speculated on the *ennui* of terrestrial existence. I waited on Lord Marischal, who, as one of the King's particular freinds is lodged here. I then saw the foundation of an immense Palace which the King is building near this.⁵ I returned to Potzdam, din'd quiet, journalised and walked & chatted till Bedtime.

¹ JB's 'Inviolable Plan', formulated in Holland on 16 Oct. 1763. It consisted of idealistic resolutions to avoid the gloom caused by idleness and to devote himself to piety, morality, study, temperance, good conversation, and exercise (*Holland*, App. I; *Earlier Years*, pp. 127–28).

² Perhaps a girl; see 'But think to have fine Saxon girls' (Mem. 21 July).

³ Frederick II's country retreat was 'about a mile' from the centre of Potsdam (Nugent, ii. 196). A miniature palace of only twelve rooms, it had been planned by Frederick II with Knobelsdorff, had been built from 1745 to 1747, and was the quintessence of German rococo. It stood at the top of six glassed-in terraces that protected carefully nurtured vines. The most important feature of its interior was the oval marble hall, modelled on the Roman Pantheon, in which Frederick had held his famous dinners with philosophers, musicians, and other congenial friends before the Seven Years' War and especially during Voltaire's stay from 1750 to 1753 (Willy Kurth, *Sanssouci*, 1964, pp. 16–40; Nicolai, iii. 1212–17; Edwin Redslob, *Barock und Rokoko in den Schlössern von Berlin und Potsdam*, 1954, pp. 42–48). Four rooms were indeed available for guests, but which friends, apart from Lord Marischal, habitually occupied them at this time has not been determined.

⁴ JB's guide, Matthias Oesterreich (1716–

78), had been Director of the picture gallery since 1757 (see *Corr.* 6, p. 113 n. 21). The gallery, next to the palace, was a classical Palladian building designed by Johann Gottfried Büring (b. 1723) and built from 1755 to 1763. It housed a newly assembled collection of old masters, taking no works from other Prussian palaces (Frederick II to Wilhelmina, Margravine of Bayreuth, 30 Nov. 1755, *Œuvres de Frédéric le Grand*, xxvii. 277). The first catalogue, Oesterreich's *Beschreibung der königlichen Bildergalerie und des Kabinets in Sans souci* (1764), lists 70 paintings (not counting those in the King's cabinet), including two da Vincis, two Raphaels, six Titians, twenty-five Rubens, two Rembrandts, and seven Van Dycks. Some of these, however, would later be attributed to lesser masters (Kurth, p. 96 n. 56).

⁵ Frederick II's largest and most ambitious palace, the Neue Palais, planned as early as 1755 and built from 1763 to 1768. Designed by Büring and Heinrich Ludwig Manger (1728–90), it would consist of some 200 rooms when completed. Frederick used it to provide work for his artists and craftsmen and also to give the impression of continued financial strength in spite of his wartime losses (Georg Holmsten, *Friedrich II in Selbstzeugnissen*, 1969, pp. 155–56; *Potsdam*, ed. Martin Uhlemann and Otto Rückert, 1986, p. 47).

## Thursday 5 July

[MEM. dated Friday 6 July.] [Y]esterday at nine you left Potzdam in sweet spirits, & conducted in coach mad. de Froment. She seemed tender as much as her nonchalance would allow [—] wanted you to be *ami* [—] you said Je ne connois assez.¹ You arrived at Berlin, all gay. Froment a good lively frenchman. Honest Macpherson an excellent Highlander — din'd then call'd on Mr. Mitchell — & on Banker none at home [—] saw Palace superb — walk'd with From &c. by water side. 'Twas delightfull. The fiend fled. Today go on.

[J.] I hired Post-Horses for my Lord's Coach, & set out free and happy to conduct Madame de Froment to Berlin. We had a pleasant jaunt, & arrived about two at *Rufin's* in the *Post Straas*.[2] Here we found M. de Froment, a lively frenchman pretty much mellowed,[3] and Lieutenant Lauchlan Macpherson late of Frazer's Highlanders. He is son to Breckachie.[4] He is a fine, honest, spirited fellow. We dined & then I drest & Macpherson accompanied me to Mr. Mitchel's the British Envoy, & to my Bankers; but, we found none of them at home.[5] I was struck with the Beauty of Berlin. The Houses are handsom and the streets wide long and straight. The Palace is grand.[6] The Palaces of some of the Royal family are very genteel.[7] The Opera-House is an elegant Building, with this Inscription. Fridericus Rex Apollini et Musis.[8] At night we sauntered in a sweet walk under a grove of Chesnut-trees by the side of a beautifull Canal, where I saw a variety of Strangers.[9] The foul fiend fled.

[1] MS. 'Wanted ... assez' scored out by a modern hand.

[2] Berlin was about 16 miles (c. 25.8 km) northeast of Potsdam (Nugent, ii. 420). JB's inn, operated by a Frenchman named Rufin, was called *Die Drei Lilien* (*Adres-Calender*, 1763, p. 238). It was situated on one of the main streets of 'Berlin', the oldest section and the one that gave the city its name. This part of town was like an island, enclosed by the river Spree to the south and west, and by remnants of fortifications to the north and east (Nicolai, i. 1, 9–10).

[3] Denis-Daniel de Froment (d. 1810), Emetulla's husband, was a Huguenot Frenchman born in Uzès, Languedoc (AEN, Neuchâtel-Décès 1804–1827, p. 28). He had left the Regiment of Monfort, in the service of Sardinia, in Mar. 1763 with the rank of lieutenant ('luogotenente') of infantry (R. Segreteria di Guerra, Lettere all'Ufficio generale del Soldo, vol. 13; Regi Viglietti Assenti nell'Armata, Arma di fanteria, 1763, vol. 37). His marriage would soon end in divorce (registered in Berlin on 16 Jan. 1765), and he would continue to live in Prussia, compensated by an annual pension of £800 paid him by Lord Marischal (From Lord Marischal, 24 Oct. 1767, *Corr. 5*, pp. 244–45 and n. 5).

[4] Lauchlan Macpherson (d. 1767) was the second son of Duncan Macpherson, Laird of Breakachy, Inverness-shire. He was now on half pay, his regiment having been disbanded in 1763. Trained as a surgeon, he had served in the 78th Regt. of Foot, called Fraser's Highlanders, as ensign from 1759 and as lieutenant from 1760. He would return to London in Oct. of this year, fearing the loss of his half pay (From Alexander Burnett, 20 Oct.; From Lord Marischal, 18 Nov.), and would join the Independent Company of Foot in Senegal, where he would soon succumb to 'the curst air of Africa' (From Lord Marischal, 14 Apr. 1767, *Corr. 5*, pp. 144–45).

[5] Andrew Mitchell (1708–71) had been Minister Plenipotentiary since 1756 (*Repertorium*, ii. 161). He was a friend of JB's father (From Lord Auchinleck, 2 Apr.). The firm of JB's bankers, Splitgerber and Daum, founded in 1712, was regarded as 'la première, la plus riche, et la plus solide maison de commerce de toute l'Allemagne' (Thiébault, ii. 32). Its premises were located in the Gertraudenstrasse in 'Altköln', the district adjacent to the original 'Berlin' but separated from it by the ubiquitous Spree and, together with it, the oldest part of the city (Nicolai, i. 66). The firm would flourish in the same location into the twentieth century (Friedrich Lenz and Otto Unholtz, *Die Geschichte des Bankhauses Gebrüder Schickler*, 1912).

[6] The royal palace, in a central position in Altköln, was a monumental baroque building constructed around two large courtyards and embellished by splendid façades, the whole influenced by both Roman architecture and Versailles (Nicolai, i. 97–115; Redslob, pp. 12–16). It dated from the fifteenth century and had been remodeled from 1699 to 1708 by the prominent architect Andreas Schlüter (1660–1714), then up to 1713 by his successor Johann Friedrich Eosander von Göthe (1670–1729). In the nineteenth century it would become a symbol of the Prussian-German state. Reduced to ruins in World War II, it deliberately would not be rebuilt, and then

totally obliterated by the Communist East German government in 1950 (Renate Petras, *Das Schloss in Berlin*, 1992, pp. 116–32).

[7] Nearby were the palaces of Frederick's younger brother Prince Heinrich (1726–1802); of his sister Sofie (1719–65), married to Friedrich Wilhelm, Margrave of Brandenburg-Schwedt (1700–71); and of his sister Amalia, Abbess of Quedlingburg (1723–87). See Nicolai, i. 169–74; Isenburg, i. Tafel 63.

[8] The opera house, in the shape of a Greek temple, bore Frederick's dedication to Apollo and the muses on its entablature.

Designed by Knobelsdorff, it had been commissioned in 1740 and inaugurated in 1742 when not quite finished. It could seat about 2400 persons comfortably, 4500–5000 when necessary (August Brass, *Chronik von Berlin*, 1843, pp. 353–55; Nicolai, i. 169–70).

[9] The chestnut trees were presumably part of the Kastanienallee in the Lustgarten, near the palace, cathedral, armory, and River Spree (Nicolai, ii. 941). The canal was one of several which, together with the Spree and its tributaries, made Berlin a city of waterways.

## Friday 6 July

[MEM. dated Saturday 7 July.] Yesterday you called on Bankers found Schickler a fine jolly fellow & young Splitzerber who went with you to look at lodgings & then in coach carried you to his Cousins[1] an immense dinner — bold Germans 3 hours at table — then hour on water — then supper — home in coach sung english songs was fine — at night quite happy, & relishd present happiness. This day go on — Love God — fear not — youll grow strong — Study french.[2] Improve more & more.

[J.] I went to my Bankers, and found Mr. Schickler a fine jolly generous fellow and young Splitzerber a good bluff dog; he has been three years in London.[3] He went with me to look for lodgings, but I found none to my mind. He then carried me in his coach to the Campagne of Heer Schickler that is to say a house & Garden. We dined in a handsom Summer-house which projects upon the River, and commands a view of Berlin and it's beautifull vicinity.[4] We were fifteen or Sixteen at table. I was enlivened by seeing the hearty Germans. After being three hours together at table, we played at nine-pins.[5] I then took a tour in Schickler's Boat. At nine we had a cold collation & good wine. Splitzerber carried me home in his elegant coach & sung many english Songs in The Jovial Crew, Artaxerxes etc.[6] I was firm & gay and sound as ever. Am I indeed the dull dog of Utrecht.

[1] Actually, his brother-in-law (see n. 3).

[2] JB already knew enough French to read light fiction while in London (Journ. 16 Jan. 1763). Starting in early Oct. 1763 he had practised the language more seriously in Utrecht at weekly meetings with other young people, and he had written 'French themes' almost daily—232 in all—between Sept. 1763 and May 1764 (Yale MS. M 87; *Catalogue*, i. 70; *Earlier Years*, pp. 126, 128–29).

[3] Johann Jacob Schickler (1711–75) had just taken over the management of Splitgerber and Daum together with Friedrich Heinrich Berendes (1729–71) following the

death of their father-in-law, the original David Splitgerber (1683–1764); see Hugo Rachel and Paul Wallich, *Berliner Grosskaufleute*, 2nd ed., 1967, ii. 209–22 and Tafel IV. The present David Splitgerber (1741–1823), who had also inherited part of the firm from his father, was primarily a sportsman. He had been in London during the early 1760s (see n. 6 below). In 1765 would be named master of the hounds to Prince Ferdinand of Prussia (1730–1813). Subsequently, in 1789, he would be ennobled by Friedrich Wilhelm II, successor to Frederick the Great, and he would retain his share of the bank until bought out by the next generation of Schicklers in 1795 (Rachel and Wallich, ii. 222 and Tafel IV).

⁴ Schickler's country house ('campagne') was about 4 miles (c. 6.44 km) from the centre of town on the Spree, across from Treptow (Journ. 29 Aug.).

⁵ 'A game in which nine skittles are set up to be knocked down by a ball or bowl' (OED), similar to the more modern game of bowling.

⁶ *The Jovial Crew; or The Merry Beggars* had had 31 performances at Covent Garden in 1760, when this ballad opera was at the height of its popularity. Based on a play by Richard Brome (d. 1652) first produced in 1661, it was reworked as a comic opera in 1731, presumably inspired by Gay's *The Beggar's Opera*, and revived again in the 1760s (*Lond. Stage*, pt. 3:1, p. 115; pt. 4:2, p. 774). JB had seen one of only seven performances at Covent Garden three years later (see Journ. 13 Jan. 1763). JB had also seen *Artaxerxes*, with music composed by Thomas Arne and a libretto based on Metastasio's *Artaserse* (1730), on 21 Apr. 1763, in its second year at Covent Garden (*Lond. Stage*, pt. 4:2, p. 915; *New Grove 2*).

## Saturday 7 July

[MEM. dated Sunday 8 July.] Yesterday you dined with M. & [M]ad. Froment. [Y]ou drank Punch with Captain Wake. At night you was all joy. You was young Boswell of Auchinleck on his travels at Berlin & had [M]cpherson an honest lively highland Officer of Frazer's Regiment in the room with you. All well.

[J.] If ever Man underwent an Alteration it is the man who writeth this journal. I drank punch at the lodgings of Captain Wake a Scots Privateer.¹ At night, I was Young Boswell of Auchinleck upon his travels, and had with me Macpherson a brave Highlander. He was quite the man for me. He had good health, good sense & good-humour. He awaked well. He never speculated. He was gay. I was the same, and gloom fled from my mind.

¹ John Wake (dates unknown) of Prestonpans was a shipowner commissioned by Frederick II to harass Swedish and Austrian shipping. As a privateer, he operated his vessel for his own gain but with official approval. Although he had successfully captured several enemy ships and had been in Berlin since 1762, he had not yet obtained the prize money due him (see Journ. 7 Sept. and n. 3; Hans Szymanski, *Brandenburg-Preussen zur See*, 1939, pp. 105–06). For the differences between privateers and pirates, see Janice E. Thomson, *Mercenaries, Pirates, and Sovereigns*, 1994, p. 22.

## Sunday 8 July

[MEM. dated Monday 9 July.] Yesterday you waited on M. Mitchell found him easy & freindly. Mad Zuyl trop d'esprit pour les Hollandois. Beau compliment au ministre. Turned it off — lesson never to blunder out. Din'd table d'hote¹ — drank too much slept after dinner — was all relaxed went to coffeehouse played Billiards walked — parc — home well & content.

[J.] I waited on Mr. Mitchell and found him a knowing amiable easy man. He was very polite.² He talked of Mademoiselle de Zuylen 'Elle a beaucoup d'Esprit'. Oui said I trop d'Esprit pour les Hollandois. And who was in the room but Mr. Verelst the Dutch Envoy. Mr. Mitchell turned it off with a smiling reply. 'Monsieur, c'est un beau Compliment que vous faites au Ministre d'Hollande'.³ Blockhead that I was. Let never Man blunder out reflections against any country, when he does not very well know his company. I din'd too heartily this day, and Macpherson and I must needs have our sleep after dinner. I dozed like a very Bum-Baillif; but when I awoke relaxed were my nerves, and like unto a lump of clay on a Barrel of Edinburgh Twopenny was my mighty head.[4] It was indeed fitter for knocking other People down, than for holding itself up. However out went the Highlander & I, took a dish of coffee and a game at Billiards,[5] and then away we went & took a hearty Walk in the Park which is a noble thing just by this beautifull City. It has a variety of walks both for Coaches & Horsemen as well as for those who love the milder movement of their own limbs.[6] We grew as fresh and as strong and as content as men of the last century. Macpherson is a true Philosopher, tho he knows not what Philosophy means.

[1] 'A common table … [for] a public meal served … at stated hours and at a fixed price' (OED, s.v. 'table d'hôte').

[2] Mitchell was greatly admired in Berlin society for his forthrightness and ready wit (Lehndorff, 15 June 1756, 27 Jan. 1757, *Dreissig Jahre: Nachträge*, i. 69, 82; Thiébault, iii. 272–82).

[3] Dirk Hubert Verelst (1717–74), Dutch Envoy Extraordinary and Minister Plenipotentiary to Frederick II, had been in Berlin since 1758 (A. J. van der Aa, *Biographisch Woordenboek der Nederlanden*, 1852, repr. 1969, vii. 43).

[4] 'Bum-bailiff: A bailiff of the meanest kind; one that is employed in arrests' (*Dict. SJ*, quoted in OED); 'relaxed': enfeebled, from 'to make loose or slack; to enfeeble or enervate' (OED, s.v. 'relax', 1.b); 'Edinburgh Twopenny', weak ale or beer sold at twopence a Scots pint, which was equal to about 3 imperial pints, or 1.7 litres (CSD). JB would mention it fondly in a letter to a fellow Scot in Berlin: 'When the Scots Twopenny froths we say it laughs' (To Alex-

ander Burnett, 27 Dec., Burnett of Kemnay Archives).

[5] 'Billiards et Caffé, 6 Gr' (Exp. Acct. 9 July, App. 3). 'Gr.' stood for 'Groschen', a small monetary unit made of silver. If this was a so-called 'good' Groschen, it represented $1/24$th of a Taler, a larger silver coin of relatively stable value (Albert R. Frey, *Dictionary of Numismatic Names*, 1947, pp. 103, 240). But at this moment the value of some of the coins was uncertain because their silver content had been diminished during the war, and these were in the process of being replaced in Prussia (Friedrich von Schrötter, *Das Preussische Münzwesen im 18. Jahrhundert*, 1902–11, iii. 206).

[6] The park was the Tiergarten, a large expanse alongside the Spree that had been remodelled by Frederick II according to plans by Knobelsdorff. It provided broad avenues for carriages and narrower paths for pedestrians as well as streams, ponds, mazes, and a pheasant preserve. Dogs and shooting were prohibited (Nicolai, ii. 943–47).

## Monday 9 July

[MEM. dated Tuesday 10 July] [N]othing[1]

[MEM. dated Wednesday 11 July][2] [Y]esterday you waited on Prof. Castillon was cordially received. At night drank tea at President's de la Ville: an honest rough fellow — his Lady genteel all fine — had lodging at 15 crowns a month. At night enterd it — quite gay — just like Digges[3] — happy as ever.

[J.][4] Who will say that I am not a man of Business? I who write my Journal with the regularity of the German Professor who wrote his folio every year. I waited this day on Professor Castillioni whom I had known at Utrecht.

He received me well, & I saw him with other eyes than when I groaned in gloom.[5] I drank tea at the house of The President de Police M. Kirkeiser a hearty cordial Saxon.[6] I found his Lady well-bred, & his son lively.[7] My worthy M. Schickler recommended me to the President who agreed to let me have an apartment in his house, at the rate of fifteen crowns a month.[8]

[1] MS. 'nothing' squeezed in.

[2] Confused about the dates, JB interpolated 'Wednesday, 11 July' in mistake for 10 July. This memorandum covers the events of Monday 9 July.

[3] For Digges, see Journ. 10 July, n. 3.

[4] On this day JB also composed what F. A. Pottle considered his most important letter to Belle de Zuylen (Grand Tour I, Heinemann p. 21 n. 2, McGraw-Hill p. 22 n. 1). Writing in English except for a few phrases in French, JB described why she would not be a suitable wife for him, offered advice in the persona of 'mentor' on how to live more calmly, then asked whether she could submit her will to his and whether she might have eloped with him if he had insisted (Holland, Heinemann pp. 299–308, McGraw-Hill pp. 307–17, OC Charrière, i. 196–204, original in BPUN; see also Courtney, pp. 102–04). To these contradictory messages, she replied with an apparently soothing letter to him in Brunswick (see Journ. 25 Aug.), and a long letter of 27 Jan. 1765, in which she 'reviewed' their relationship and offered no more than friendship (OC Charrière, i. 367–68; English translation in Holland, Heinemann pp. 320–22, McGraw-Hill pp. 329–32).

[5] JB had come to know the mathematician Jean Salvemini de Castillon (1708–91) the preceding autumn (Journ. 1 Oct. 1763, Holland, Heinemann pp. 37–38, McGraw-Hill pp. 38–39) and had privately mocked him for his bad teeth (French theme, c. 20 Oct. 1763, Yale MS. M 87, quoted in Holland, Heinemann pp. 48–49, McGraw-Hill pp. 49–50). Castillon had changed his original name, Giovanni Francesco Mauro Melchior Salvemini, to that of his birthplace in Tuscany. He had earned a doctorate in jurisprudence in Pisa in 1729 but, suspected of being a freethinker, had soon left for Swiss territories (NDB, iii. 174–75). He had directed a school in Vevey from 1737, had taught in Lausanne from 1745 as well as in Bern from 1749. Two years later he had moved to Utrecht, where he taught mathematics and astronomy at the university until he was appointed to the mathematics section of the Prussian Academy in 1764. A productive scholar, he had edited Newton's minor mathematical and philosophical works (1744), the Leibniz-Bernoulli correspondence (1745), and Euler's Introductio in Analysin infinitorum (1748). He had written an answer to Rousseau's Discours sur l'origine de l'inégalité (in 1756, two years after its publication); had translated Pope's Essay on Man into Italian (1760) and Locke's Elements of Natural Philosophy into French (1761); and had published a commentary on Newton's Arithmetica (also 1761), which had probably brought him the invitation to Berlin. One year after meeting JB he would also publish a translation of George Campbell's Dissertation on Miracles. Castillon would be appointed royal astronomer in 1765 and eventually head of the Academy's mathematics section in 1787 (DSB, iii. 119–20).

[6] Carl David Kircheisen (1704–70), a native of Dresden, Saxony, had been Polizei-Director (chief of police) since 1741, Geheimer Kriegsrat (privy counsellor for war) since 1744, and Stadt Präsident (president of the city council) from 1746 (Stadtrath Klein, Erinnerungen an Karl David Kircheisen, 1821, pp. 5, 9, 12; titles from the Adres-Calender, 1764, p. 175). He had begun his long service in Prussia under Friedrich Wilhelm I in 1732 and had been named mayor of Berlin in 1733. In spite of these and other honours, he struck JB as simply 'a rough-voiced hard-headed warmhearted Saxon' (To WJT, 23 July, Corr. 6, p. 106).

Tea was evidently a favourite drink of the Kircheisens and their bourgeois friends (Journ. 16, 18, 25, 29, 30 July). Both green tea, brewed from young unfermented leaves, and black tea, brewed from older fermented leaves, were imported from China and had been introduced in Germany by way of Holland in the mid-seventeenth century. Tea was credited with preventing a wide range of illnesses as well as encouraging sobriety (J. Ovington, An Essay upon the Nature and Qualities of Tea, 1699, pp. 31–35; William H. Ukers, All About Tea, 1935, i. 28–35). JB had expressed his fondness for green tea in London (Journ. 13 Feb. 1763) and would drink it often in Berlin until he developed misgivings about it and about coffee (for which, see Journ. 29 Sept., 28 Oct.).

[7] Henriette (Lauer) Kircheisen was the

daughter of a Prussian captain of artillery (Klein, p. 39). JB described her to WJT as 'well-bred agreable & gay'. Their younger son, Friedrich Leopold (1749–1825), whom JB considered 'a lively spirited young fellow', was studying at the Joachimsthal Gymnasium. He already showed an interest in the law and would become a prominent jurist (Corr. 6, p. 106 and 114 n. 42; ADB; Zedlitz-Neukirch, iii. 110). The Kircheisens lived in the Altköln district in their own house close to the St.-Petri-Kirche (Adres-Calendar, 1764, p. 175).

[8] A crown appears to have had the same value as a Taler, and a Taler the same as the Dutch Daalder. While in Prussia JB, still noting his expenses in D. (for Daalder) and Gr. (for Groschen), recorded 30 D. for two months' lodging (Exp. Acct. 19 Sept., App. 3).

## Tuesday 10 July

[J.][1] At night I entered to my Apartment. I had a handsom parlour gayly painted & looking to St. Peter's Church a noble Building.[2] I had a genteel large Alcove with a pretty silk bed. I was quite happy, quite Digges,[3] quite as if I had never felt the heavy hand of the Dæmon of gloom. I find that my happiness depends upon small elegancies. I am a kind of Baron Maule. I will take care to have all the elegancies of life.[4]

[1] Because of his problem with the dates, JB leaves no further memorandum for this day.

[2] The St.-Petri-Kirche, an eclectic baroque building (Nicolai, i. 122–24), was erected after a fire destroyed an earlier church in 1730. Founded in the late twelfth or early thirteenth century, it served one of the oldest congregations in Berlin (Klaus Koziol, Kleine Chronik der St.-Petri Kirche, 1965).

[3] JB greatly admired his friend West Digges (?1725 or 1726–86), an English actor who had made his name in Edinburgh, for his dashing portrayal of Gay's Macheath and for his 'deportment of a man of fashion' (Journ. 1 Dec. 1762). JB had assumed Digges's name in taking lodgings for his rendez-vous with the actress 'Louisa' (Journ. 12 Jan. 1763). See also Corr. 9, p. 3 n. 1.

[4] JB liked to fantasize about living in the manner of John Maule (1706–81), Baron of Exchequer, and of enjoying respect yet an easy life—'otium cum dignitate' ('leisure with dignity', Cicero, Pro Sestio, xlv. 98; see Journ. 24 Feb. 1763; To WJT, 23 July, Corr. 6, p. 108 and n. 57). JB had already mentioned Maule's position, though not his name, in Mem. dated 26 June.

## Wednesday 11 July

[MEM. dated Thursday 12 July][1] [Y]esterday Froment took house. You dind with him — then you & Mcpherson went & playd at Billiards & walk'd[.] Mitchel advised Potzdam lazy & hesitating. Mcpherson prevailed. Find him better than Philos.

[J.] M. de Froment took lodgings very near me. I agreed with him to dine at his lodgings when not otherwise engaged. He had dinner from a tavern, & we payed half an Ecu a head.[2] This Regulation[3] is exceedingly convenient for me. I am allways sure of dining agreably.

[1] MS. 'Thursday' inserted above deleted 'Wednesday', making the day and date correct.

[2] An écu appears to have been worth 18 Groschen, the sum JB regularly recorded for 'Diner' on 14, 17, 19, 24, 25, and 26 July. Robert Warnock calculated that since JB equated six écus with a British pound (Journ. 1 Oct), half an écu would have been 1s 8d.

[3] 'Standing rule' (OED, s.v. 'regulation', 2).

## Thursday[1] 12 July

[MEM. dated Friday 13 July] Yesterday you payed visit to [M]ad. la Presidente. Madle. tres belle — quite pleas'd [—] at 12 Journalierre — Polish Col. — sulky a little — had a dusty journey to Potzdam [—] found Scott — honest Aberdeenshire Man — supt with him. Mac & I straw bed.

[J.] I was advised by Mr. Mitchel to accompany Macpherson to Potsdam, in order to see some of the entertainments given to the court of Brunswic.[2] I was indolent, but resolved. In the morning, I waited on Madame la Presidente, and was presented to Mademoiselle. She was seventeen, comely, fresh, good-humoured & gay, and had an ease of Behaviour that pleased me greatly.[3] I was quite in pleasing frame. I must observe of myself, that from my early years I have never seen an agreable Lady, but my warm Imagination has fancied as how I might marry her, and has suggested a crowd of Ideas. This is very true; but very very absurd. At twelve Macpherson and I got into the *Journalière* a sad machine but cheap, for, you pay but twelve Gros for four German miles.[4] We had with us a Polish Colonel a sulky dog;[5] but Macpherson's *Braid*[6]-sword kept him quiet. We had a dusty Journey to Potsdam. We waited on Captain Scott of the Regiment du Prince de Prusse. We found him a worthy, plain hearty Caledonian. He is an Aberdeenshire Man son to Scott of Achtiedonnel a branch of the family of Gallowshills. He has been fifteen years in the service, and has distinguished himself as a very brave officer.[7] He gave us a good supper, english Beer & good wine, & Macpherson and I were laid upon the floor, on two hard beds and clean straw, like two immense Highlanders. Hearty were we and as content as human existence could allow.

[1] MS. Written over a deleted 'Wednesday'.
[2] The Duke of Brunswick and his family were in Potsdam from 9 to 24 July to celebrate the engagement of Princess Elisabeth to the Prince of Prussia (Karl H. S. Rödenbeck, *Tagebuch oder Geschichtskalender aus Friedrichs des Grossen Regentenleben*, 1841, ii. 241–42). For JB's view of the betrothal feast, see Journ. 21 July.
[3] This was Mme Kircheisen's daughter Caroline (b. 1747). JB described her in similar terms to WJT: 'She is seventeen, she is handsom she is good humoured and clever' (23 July, *Corr.* 6, p. 106).
[4] The journalière was part of a regional system for transporting persons and letters ordered by Frederick II in the 1750s to compete with the imperial postal system run by the princes of Thurn und Taxis (Gottfried North, 'Die Post', *Panorama*, pp. 636–38). The name promised daily service but during JB's stay in Berlin the journal-

ière actually covered the 16 miles (25.8 km) between Berlin and Potsdam twice a day, leaving at 1 P.M. and also at 7 A.M. (*Adres-Calender*, 1764, p. 244).
[5] Not identified.
[6] 'Broad': the broad sword carried by highland troops (see Mem. dated 24 June, and n. 2). It was part of the full dress uniform of Fraser's Highlanders, the regiment to which Macpherson belonged (J. R. Harper, *The Fraser Highlanders*, 1979, pp. 27–28; Stewart, ii. 88).
[7] James Scot (born c. 1729) was a descendant of the mid-seventeenth-century George Scot who is considered the 'progenitor of the Scots of Auchty-Donald in Aberdeenshire'. George Scot's older brother James had been granted the barony of Galashiells by charter of 1642, and a fifth descendant, John (1732–85), represented the Galashiells branch in JB's time (Douglas, *Baronage*, pp. 220–21). James Scot's father, William, had owned the

manor of Auchtydonald (Alexander Hep-
burn, 'Description of the Countrey of Buchan
Aberdeenshire', 1721, quoted in Walter Macfarlane, *Geographical Collections*, 1906, i. 45).
JB's Scot, whose first name is known from
his letter to Alexander Burnett of 2 Apr.
1772, Bundle 74, would later command the

garrison of the fortress Spandau, near Ber-
lin, and would eventually advance to the
rank of major-general (Scot to Alexander
Burnett, May 1798; from Alexander
Burnett to Scot, Jan. 1799, Bundle 86,
Burnett of Kemnay Archives).

## Friday 13 July

[MEM. dated Saturday 14 July] [Y]esterday rose sound as a highlander — break —
saw[1] My Lord — Parade [—] saw the *King* blue noble — sun shone quite show.
Officers bowed — King like loadstone — or storm — dind guard — supt too — Stories
of Prussian wars & Mac America — saw strong sense. Defended morality —

[J.] I rose fresh as a Roe on the Braes of Lochaber.[2] I find that if I had got a
Commission in a Highland Corps, I should have been as stout a Donald as
the best of them.[3] I waited on my good Lord Marischal, whom I found as
contented and as chearfull as ever. I then went to the Parade. I saw the
King. It was a glorious Sight. He was drest in a Suit of plain blue, with a Star,
& a plain hat with a white feather. He had in his hand a cane. The Sun
shone bright. He stood before his Palace, with an air of iron confidence that
could not be opposed. As a Loadstone moves Needles, or a Storm bows the
lofty oaks, did Frederic the great make the Prussian Officers Submissive
bend, as he Walked majestic in the midst of them.[4] I was in noble spirits, &
had a full relish of this grand scene, which I shall never forget. I felt a crowd
of ideas. I beheld the King who has astonished Europe by his warlike deeds.
I beheld (pleasant conceit!) the great defender of the Protestant Cause,
who was prayed for in all the Scots Kirks.[5] I beheld the 'Philosophe de Sans
Souci'. I have realy a little mind, with all my Pride. For I thought one might
well endure all the fatigues of war, in order to have an opportunity of
appearing grand as this Monarch. My Lord Marischal told me I could see no
shows here, & advised me to post back to Berlin, & get introduced at
Court.[6] Scott was this day upon guard. Macpherson and I dined with him,
then played at Billiards & walked: then sup'd with him. Never were fellows
more jolly. Scott gave us Storys of Prussian Wars, and Macpherson of
American ones.[7] I saw that Prussian officers live just as well as others; and
for the common Soldiers, they placed themselves on a seat before the guard-
room, & sung most merrily. My ideas of the value of men are altered, since
I came to this countrey. I see such numbers of fine fellows bred to be
slaughtered, that human Beings seem like Herrings in a plentifull season.
One thinks nothing of a few Barrels of Herring; nor can I think much of a
few Regiments of men.[8] What am I then a single Man? strange thought! let
it go. I slept sound one night more as a Highlander.

[1] MS. Inadvertent full stop after 'saw'
[2] *Braes*, Scots for 'hillsides', referring to
the rough mountainous environs of Lochaber, Inverness-shire, in the western high-

lands. Lochaber was the home territory of
some of the 'Donalds', notably the Macdonalds of Keppoch, who were known as
'Clanranald of Lochaber' (Donald J. Mac-

Donald, *Clan Donald*, 1978, p. 361). It was also the native place of JB's companion, Macpherson of Breakachie.

[3] For JB's wish to join a highland regiment, see Journ. 21 June, n. 11. One such regiment, Montgomery's Highlanders (77th Regt. of Foot), had been organized by JB's friend and neighbour Lord Eglinton in 1757 and had served abroad from 1758 to 1763 (*The Service of British Regiments in Canada and North America*, compiled by Charles H. Stewart, pp. 322, 435–36).

[4] JB's elevated style, aspiring to the Longinian sublime, emphasizes this high point of his hero worship. The King was wearing the outfit he habitually wore after 1750, the plain blue uniform of his life guards adorned only with the star of the Order of the Black Eagle (for which see Journ. 21 July n. 8) and a hat with one white ostrich feather (Vehse, iv. 86). For JB's earlier view of a parade in Potsdam, see Journ. 3 July and n. 4.

[5] At the height of his popularity in England, after his victories over the French at Rossbach on 5 Nov. and Leuthen on 5 Dec. 1757, Frederick had been hailed as 'the great support of the Protestant religion on the Continent of Europe' (*Whitehall Evening Post*, Nr. 1851, 24–26 Jan. 1758), and as 'our able and active ally, the defender of the Protestant cause in Germany' by Philip Yorke, Lord Royston (1720–90), in the House of Commons on 1 Dec. 1757 (quoted in Manfred Schlenke, *England und das Friderizianische Preussen*, 1963, pp. 234–49). Frederick's birthday, on 24 Jan., had been

celebrated throughout England and Scotland in 1758 and 1759 (Schlenke, pp. 244–48 and n. 380). His popularity had however waned later in 1759 and especially in 1760 when critics had questioned his service to Protestantism in attacking not only Austria, a Catholic country, but also the neighbouring Protestant state of Silesia (Schlenke, pp. 249–59).

[6] Ceremonial functions such as greeting strangers at court were fulfilled by Elisabeth Christine, Queen of Prussia (1715–97), who lived in Berlin separated from Frederick II (see Journ. 15 July and n. 6).

[7] Scot's regiment (the Regt. des Königs No. 18—Prinz Friedrich Wilhelm von Preussen) had seen action in nearly all the major battles of the Seven Years' War: at Prag, Schweidnitz, and Leuthen in 1757; at Zorndorf and Hochkirch in 1758; and at Liegnitz and Torgau in 1760 (Alexander von Lyncker, *Die Altpreussische Armee, 1714–1806*, 1937, pp. 46–48). Macpherson's regiment, Fraser's Highlanders, had taken part in the attack on Quebec in 1759; the Battle of the Heights of Abraham, by then in British hands, in 1760; and the mission to retake St. John's, Newfoundland, in 1762 (J. S. Keltie, *History of the Scottish Highlands*, n.d. [188–?], iv. 476–81).

[8] This view of men seen *en masse* is offset by JB's sympathy for an individual soldier, whose punishment as a deserter he would witness a few weeks later (see Journ. 4 Sept. and n. 1).

## Saturday 14 July

[MEM. dated Sunday 15 July.] [Y]esterday up fine — leave of Mac — good journey — after dinner Mitchel Yorke I am *an Ambassador* told story too vivacious — This day Church. Be grave & think & at nine for heal<th>.[1]

[J.] I left Macpherson at Potzdam where he waits the Instructions of Lord Marischal, who took a liking to him in Scotland, & made him come to Berlin, to see the world a little, at his Lordship's expence. This is very genteel in My Lord, who is a kind of lowland Chieftain of the Macphersons.[2] I rumbled in the *Journalière* to Berlin having for company amongst others Madll. Dionisicus,[3] daughter to the Cook of Prince Ferdinand of Prussia.[4] I talked words of German to this lass. I dined at Froment's, & after dinner went to Mr. Mitchel's. We talked of Sir Joseph Yorke, whom he called Sir Joé. I told him that he seemed so anxious lest People should not know that he was Embassador, that he held his head very high, & spoke very little. And as in the infancy of painting People generally wrote 'This is a Cow' 'This is a Horse' So from Sir Joé's mouth cometh a label with these words 'I am an Embassador'.[5] What a difference between this buckram knight[6] & the amiable Mr. Mitchel. The family of my good *Heer Présidént*[7] were happy to see me.

[1] MS. 'healt', corner torn off. JB's meaning is unclear.

[2] Lord Marischal's estates were in Aberdeenshire, but his family was thought to be descended from the Clanchattan, which had settled in Lochaber in the western highlands in the thirteenth century (Alexander D. Murdoch, ed., *The Loyal Dissuasive by Sir Aeneas Macpherson*, 1902, p. xcvi; Alan G. Macpherson, *The Posterity of the Three Brethren*, 1966, p. 11). The Macphersons were highland descendants of the same clan. Lord Marischal himself had attested to the longstanding family relationship in a letter to 'Cluny Macpherson'—Ewan Og Macpherson (1706–64), head of the Cluny branch and a Jacobite on the run—by expressing 'real concern in what ever regards you and your clan, as being of the same origine [sic], if old tradition does not fail, and having ever a warm heart towards you and them' (draft in GStAPK, VI.HA Familienarchive und Nachlässe, Nl George Keith, II Nr. 2 Bl. 98). For a summary of the connection between the Lords Marischal and the Macphersons, see Alan G. Macpherson, 'On the Death of Marshall Keith and the Clan Consciousness of James Macpherson', *From Gaelic to Romantic: Ossianic Translations*, ed. Fiona Stafford and Howard Gaskill, 1998, pp. 54–56).

[3] MS. 'Dionicus' with 'si' inserted above 'ic'. The name is given as 'Dionisius' in *Grand Tour I*, Heinemann p. 24, McGraw-Hill p. 25.

[4] Three cooks were employed by Prince Ferdinand (1730–1813), youngest brother of Frederick II (Nicolai, i. 268). No further details about this young woman or her father have been found. JB spent '3 D' ('Daalder'; that is, Taler) on this jaunt (Exp. Acct).

[5] Sir Joseph Yorke (1724–92) had become British ambassador in the Hague in 1761 after serving as minister there from 1751. While respected and esteemed in some quarters, he was also known for his 'pride and hauteur' (Richard Rigby to the Duke of Bedford, 27 July 1764, quoted in *Oxford DNB* [DNB archive] and Namier and Brooke, ii. 679). JB had waited on him in the Hague at the insistence of Lord Auchinleck, who considered an acquaintance with the British ambassador socially useful (From Lord Auchinleck, c. 10 Dec. 1763, Yale MS. C 224). At one of several ambassadorial balls JB had then attended, he had been struck by Yorke's 'dry insolence' (4 June, *Holland*, Heinemann p. 262, McGraw-Hill p. 269). JB would repeat the cutting description of Yorke in *Boswelliana*, p. 237.

[6] Buckram was 'coarse linen or cloth stiffened with gum or paste', here used figuratively to mean 'stuck up' (OED, s.v. 'buckram', 2 and 4.b). The phrase 'buckram knight' suggests Falstaff, another boastful knight, the more so as he is associated with imaginary 'rogues in buckram' from whom he claims to have escaped (*1 Hen. IV*, 2. iv. 217).

[7] 'Heer': Dutch for 'Herr' (in English: 'Mr.'). Possibly JB was also reminding himself of the German pronunciation by doubling the vowel in Herr and placing a mark on the accented last syllable of President.

## Sunday 15 July

[MEM. dated Monday 16 July.] [Y]esterday you dined with Mr. Mitchel where all was well & easy but your mauvais honte made you silent [—] then played at Billiards with Secretary Burnet — At six went with Envoy in coach to Mont Bijou the seat of the Princess of Prussia & there was presented to the Queen the Princess &c &c all very easy & well. A pretty garden. Was not affraid but was aukward — home — undrest — met black girl[1] — had no cond[2] walk'd came home.

[J.] I dined at Mr. Mitchel's. He has an elegant house and a good table.[3] He is polite and easy. His Servants are good people, civil and attached to their Master. After dinner, I played at Billiards with Mr. Burnet Secretary to Mr.

Mitchel a very good sollid clever young fellow.[4] At six The Envoy carried me to Mont Bijou the Campagne of the Princess of Prussia.[5] Here I was presented to the Queen with whom the King has never lived. She has been handsom, and is very amiable, altho' she stammers most sadly.[6] I was presented to I don't know how many Princes & Princesses. I was aukward, but not affraid.

[1] MS. 'Undrest ... girl' scored out, possibly by JB, one or two words illegible. 'Undrest' here means changed from court dress; 'black', dark complexioned.

[2] 'Cond': condom, a protective sheath made of thin material such as animal bladders or animal skins. It was used by the male partner during sexual intercourse, usually to prevent venereal disease more than to avoid conception (Angus McLaren, *A History of Contraception from Antiquity to the Present Day*, 1990, pp. 157–58).

[3] Mitchell lived in rented quarters in the so-called Boden house situated on the Gens d'Armes Market (*Adres-Calender* 1764, p. 199).

[4] Alexander Burnet or Burnett (1735–1802) of Kemnay, Aberdeenshire, had studied at the University of Leiden and had served as Andrew Mitchell's secretary from 1756, accompanying him and Frederick II on several campaigns of the Seven Years' War (*Boswelliana*, pp. 227–28; Andrew Bisset, *Memoirs and Papers of Sir Andrew Mitchell*, 1850, i. 27n; Susan Burnett, *Without Fanfare*, 1994, pp. 109–13). He would eventually become Mitchell's heir (Sir Andrew Mitchell's last will and testament, 10 Dec. 1770, Bundle 82, Burnett of Kemnay Archives).

Mitchell would be named K. B. in Dec. 1765 (Namier and Brooke, iii. 143).

[5] Monbijou, situated just outside the city in the Spandauer Vorstadt, had been the summer residence of Frederick II's mother, Queen Sophia Dorothea (1687–1757). Originally a compact little mansion, it had been extended by east and west wings designed by Knobelsdorff. Its garden, in the Dutch style, went down to the Spree (Folkwin Wendland, *Berlins Gärten und Parke*, 1979, pp. 245–47). The public was admitted (Nicolai, i. 42–43; ii. 930). Monbijou was now used primarily by the widowed Luise Amalie, Princess of Prussia (1722–80), sister of the Queen and mother of the present Prince of Prussia.

[6] The Queen, Elisabeth Christine, was at Monbijou while her own residence at Schönhausen was being renovated (Lehndorff, May 1764, *Dreissig Jahre: Nachträge*, i. 398). Eldest daughter of Ferdinand Albrecht II (1680–1735), Duke of Brunswick-Bevern, and Antoinette Amalie (1696–1762), Princess of Brunswick-Wolfenbüttel, she had left her large, genial family in Brunswick to enter an arranged marriage with Frederick II of Prussia insisted upon by his father. The relationship had been unhappy almost from the start, and since 1745 Frederick had refused to have her near him. 'Madam has become more corpulent' was said to have been his only comment to her after returning from his seven-year absence in the war (Lehndorff, 30 Mar. 1763, *Dreissig Jahre*, p. 457; Eufemia von Adlersfeld-Ballestrem, *Elisabeth Christine, Königin von Preussen* [1908], pp. 108–46).

JB did not know that the Queen was particularly agitated on this day because, as reported by her chamberlain Count Lehndorff, Frederick had not yet invited her to the engagement of her niece to the Prince of Prussia. When she was finally summoned only two days before the event, she was delighted (July 1764, *Dreissig Jahre: Nachträge*, i. 402–04).

## Monday 16 July

[MEM. dated Tuesday 17 July] Yesterday you went at seven & saw *manége*[1] — You was pleased. You din'd with Verelst whom you found easy & cordial. Antipathy fled.[2] You had also Comte gay & lively [—] you had Abbey ideas of Lord Somerville. Tea [M]ad[.] La Presidente — then in Carosse in Wood with Monsieur — supt — lively, then walk'd fine — quite in taste, quite new man. This day translate a little Erskine.[3] Mem your'e Laird of Auchinleck & Temple's freind. Write Temple — Your'e the same man. Your'e doing well — you'll be quite rid of gloom[.]

[J.] I dined with M. Verelst the Dutch Minister and dined heartily. His Excellency was phlegmatic, but not unjolly. We formed a trio at table with the assistance of a German Count who had great vivacity & usage du monde.[4] I had old Abbey, Lord Somerville ideas.[5] I drank tea at home (for so I call my Landlord's) then went with Heer Présidént in his chaise, & took a drive in the Park. Came home supt with the family, & after supper went with the Ladies and the young Kirkheisen & walked *sous les marauniers.*[6] Is not this living? It is. I am quite a new man.

[1] The royal riding academy, which was close to the royal stable and palace (Nicolai, i. 118; ii. 719–20).

[2] Possibly JB's previous 'antipathy' had been caused by his embarrassing blunder at their first meeting (see Journ. 8 July). He may have been put off also by Verelst's habit of using cosmetics or at least blackening his eyebrows (Lehndorff, *Dreissig Jahre*, p. 457; *Nachträge*, i. 334).

[3] JB had begun to translate John Erskine's *Principles of the Law of Scotland* (1754) into Latin while in Holland. He had planned to gather annotations from his law professor, Christian Heinrich Trotz (1706–73), and hoped, as Trotz had suggested, to have the completed work published (French theme, c. 16 May, Yale MS. M 87, quoted in *Holland*, Heinemann p. 239, McGraw-Hill p. 245). The project, like many others of JB's, was not completed. For Trotz, see *Biografisch Archief van de Benelux.*

[4] That only men were present at this small dinner party may have been owing to the fact that Verelst's wife had left him because of his infatuation with a Frau von

Kraut. Neither his wife nor Frau von Kraut had been well liked, and he had become more popular in Berlin society after freeing himself from both (Lehndorff, Jan., 15 May 1759, Mar. 1762, *Dreissig Jahre: Nachträge*, i. 192, 209, 334). The German count has not been identified.

[5] Presumably the count's cultivated manners reminded JB of James Somerville (1697/8–1765), 12th Lord Somerville (for whom see *Corr.* 9, p. 12 n. 2). He was the first of the older men who became father figures and mentors for JB. Somerville had taken an interest in JB's writings, which they had discussed in his private apartments in Holyrood House next to the Abbey Church. Somerville was also a patron of actors, protecting them from restrictive laws and the general opposition to stage performances in Edinburgh. His noble family, commission in the dragoons, and success in court and literary circles in London all made him a powerful model (*Earlier Years*, pp. 36–37). See also *Comp. Peer.* xii, pt. 2, pp. 104–05.

[6] The Kastanienallee (see Journ. 5 July and n. 9).

## Tuesday 17 July

[MEM. dated Wednesday 18 July.] Yesterday at five you went in coach to Heer Beemer's where you had fine Ball & collation in Garden & saw the vivacity of German Ladies & Comtes &c was quite charmed; danced & learnt to be an easy man without affected timid consequence. Home too late.

[J.] Our family carried me at five to Heer Beemer's a Conseiller de guerre where was a fine Ball.[1] I must explain this matter a little. Madll. Schartow an amiable young Lady lost her parents in her infancy. My worthy President Kirkheisen took her to his house, where she has lived as if she had been their own child. Heer Steelow who has a little office that enables him to live genteely, made love to her, and was accepted. Heer Beemer is her Uncle & gave this Ball to the *Promis & Promise* and their freinds.[2] Here I saw the vivacity of German Ladies and Counts & Captains & Heeren.[3] We had at ten o clock a collation in the Garden; three or four tables with cold meat & Pastry & sweetmeats & fruits & Wine of different sorts. Beemer was a big, gallant Allemand, his Wife hearty even to excess. She was a most singular figure. She had no cap, & her hair dangled about her head. While she ran from table to table, with bottles in her hand, & health most florid in her face, she seemed quite a female Bachanalian.[4] I was just celebrating the *Orgies*. Her daughter was little & lively & kind.[5] '*Je vous supplie Monsieur, goutez ceci*' was her byword. I eat much, & drank much, & found Animal life of very great consequence. I danced a great deal, & was an easy man, without affectation and timid consequence. We went home late.

[1] Friedrich Ehrenreich Behmer (1721–76) lived in his own house in the Friedrichsstadt, a prosperous district that had grown at the eastern border of Neukölln where the Kircheisens lived (Nicolai, i. 180). He was a respected jurist, at this time *Geheimer Justiz-und Tribunals-Rat* (privy counsellor in tribunal), director of the court of public works, and member of the college of examiners (*Adres-Calender*, 1764, pp. 203, 69, 98). He had written several belletristic and legal works in French and Latin, including a defence of Frederick's title to Silesia, 'Vindiciae suprematus in Silesiam Borussici' (MS. deposited in the royal Prussian library; Adelung-Jöchers, i. 1602–03).

[2] Johanne Elisabeth Schartow was the daughter of a Prussian counsellor of war and of the crown lands in Stettin. The bridegroom, George Friedrich Stielow, was an attorney and bureaucrat specializing in medical matters, listed as 'Königl. Preuss. Ober Medicinal Fiscal und Advocatus-Ordinarius' (Register of Marriages, St.-Petri-Kirche, 1764, p. 28).

[3] 'Herren'; that is, 'gentlemen'

[4] Charlotte (Menzel) Behmer would behave even more unconventionally in later years, when Behmer served as vice-president of one of Catherine the Great's tribunals in St. Petersburg. To his wife's cousin Jean-Henri-Samuel Formey (for whom see Journ. 1 Aug. and n. 4), he would complain about her 'frivolité et l'etourderie' (in a letter dated only 'le 25'), while she, in turn, accused him of bad temper and arrogance (To Formey, 21 Apr. 1774, Nachlass Formey, SBB-PK). By then Behmer had written his major work on civil law, *Novum jus controversum*, 2 vols., 1771 (Carlos Denina, *La Prusse littéraire*, 3 vols. 1790, i. 249–50; J.-H. Formey, *Souvenirs d'un citoyen*, 2 vols. 1789, i. 102).

[5] Caroline (To Formey, 13 Oct. 1786) and Albertine (To Formey, 30 Jan. 1788), both unmarried at the time of their letters (Box 44 file 97, Nachlass Formey, SBB-PK).

## Wednesday 18 July

[MEM. dated Thursday 19 July.] [Y]esterday young Kirkheysen showed his prints & pebbles &c & violin & miss her drawings & china all fine. You din'd house: good party — tea & coffee — at 7. Parson Lutheran marriage — then cards then splendid supper — quite German — was romantic — was infidel — was averse to Scots advocates & Edinr[1] but was silent — sugar & devices, then to Bride's — mounted coach saw them abed. Le President kist you — jamais Cœur mieux placé. La Providence a fait notre connoissance — all fine &c. This day restrain a little[.]

[J.] Young Kirkheisen showed me his prints & pebbles,[2] & Mademoiselle her drawings & Books & China. I love young People who have tastes of this kind. They never tire. I dined with Heer Présidént. The young Couple were there. At five the company came & we had tea & coffee; & at seven a Lutheran Parson performed the ceremony of marriage according to the German service-book.[3] It was very decent. We then had cards, and at ten a most elegant supper.[4] It was quite German, quite hearty, & quite easy; for, altho' this Nation loves form, custom has rendered it easy to them. We had sugar figures of all sorts. A Gentleman broke those figures in a Lady's hand, and in the ruins was found a device one of which is curiously baked in each figure. They are generally amourous or witty. I sat by my dear Mademoiselle Caroline whom I find more & more agreable. She said she imagined the British Nation to be rude like Russians or Turks. How excellent was this. What would I have given that Mr. Samuel Johnson had heard a German talk thus! Heer President embraced me with cordiality & cried 'Mon cher Anglois jamais un homme avoit le cœur mieux placé. C'est la Providence qui a vous envoyé en ma maison.' Prodigious! Is this the gloomy Wretch who not long ago laid it down as an impossibility that he could ever have a happy hour. After this can I dare to oppose sickly Theory to bold Practice? I hope not. I hope to be free of sickly Theory. After Supper we conducted the young couple to the house of Heer Steelow.[5] I mounted on the back of the Calash quite english.[6] At Heer Steelow's we had a collation and good wine. We laughed much and many a joke went round. The Ladies were free & vivacious. We put the Bridegroom & Bride to bed in night gowns.[7] They got up again, & wished us good night. How pleasant a scene was this! & how innocent! Some years ago, it would have quite filled my Imagination with fine sentiments. But now I am too old, I have seen too much. My taste is too much corrupted. However here was one day of sure satisfaction.

[1] That is, Lord Auchinleck's career plans for JB.

[2] Agates or other gems 'found as pebbles in streams, esp. in Scotland' (OED, s.v. 'pebble', 2.c).

[3] The clergyman belonged to the St.-Petri-Kirche, where the marriage was recorded. Possibly he was the church's *pastor primarius*, Johann Peter Süssmilch (*Adres-Calender*, 1764, p. 119). Unlike a Catholic wedding, which was always performed inside a church, this one took place in the Kircheisens' house as was permitted for distinguished members of a Protestant congregation (Paul Graff, *Geschichte der Auflösung der alten gottesdienstlichen Formen in der evangelischen Kirche Deutschlands*, 1937, i. 335–37). The German (i.e., Lutheran) Service Book provided a succinct 'agenda' for the ceremony based on Luther's widely used *Traubüchlein* of 1529 known also as the *Order of Marriage for Common Pastors* (*Luther's Works*, 1965, liii. 110–15; see Ludwig Ernst Borowski, *Preussische Kirchen-Agenda, die liturgischen Formulare der lutherischen Gemeinden*, 1789, pp. 37–51). The very sparseness of the proceedings reflected Luther's emphasis on marriage as a civil and contractual matter rather than on its spiritual significance (D. G. Rietschel, *Lehrbuch der Liturgik*, 1909, ii. 251–59; Kenneth Stevenson, *Nuptial Blessing: A Study of Christian Marriage Rites*, 1983, pp. 125–34).

[4] This 'supper' seems to have taken the place of the elaborate feast that was the usual high point of a traditional wedding (Deneke, pp. 109–16).

[5] Stielow lived in the Horch house on the Fischmarkt, which was in Altkölln close to the Kircheisen's house (*Adres-Calender*, 1764, p. 180; Nicolai, i. 125–26).

[6] The vehicle, also known as 'caleche' or 'calèche', was a light carriage with low wheels and a folding hood (OED, s.v. 'calash', 1; Ralph Straus, *Carriages and Coaches* [1912], pp. 140, 155). The procession of friends taking the bridal couple to their home was a time-honoured tradition at German weddings (Deneke, pp. 103–06).

[7] The 'bedding' of the young couple was also an old tradition. It was often accompanied by loud music and raucous jokes, but could include blessings on the couple and their progeny (Deneke, pp. 129–32). This one appears to have been quite modest, decent, and restrained.

## Thursday 19 July

[MEM. dated Friday 20 July.] [Y]esterday at 11 you waited on Bride & Bride-groom all gay again. At dinner was too lively: 'Mon homme est hors de lui.' Check this. Madame said vous avez beaucoup besoin de la compagnie. Got Reid's Book — quite pleased. Common sense reignd. Was all elevated, was in delightfull Mood — Young Dog[1] too forward — walk'd with him — This day Journ — morning & at 10 Mitchell & be sober. Letter to Verelst, recollect — resolve Advocate genteel & London once a year [—] you love libr<ary> & all — [D]ine not Fro<m to>day.

[J.] At eleven I waited on young Couple. Our jokes were still gayer. We had a fine breakfast. The Weather was charming, which gave me delicious spirits. I was too *high* at Froment's. He said 'Mon homme est hors de lui'. Madame said Vous etes naturellement trop serieux. Vous avez beaucoup besoin de la Compagnie gâye. This is exceedingly true. I found among My Lord Marischal's Books 'An Inquiry into the human Mind on the Princi-ples of Common Sense' by Professor Reid of Aberdeen. I found it a treasure. He discovered strong reasoning & lively humour. He insisted much on the original Principles of the Mind, which we cannot doubt of, and which cannot be proved; because they are realy Axioms: He drove to pieces the sceptical Cobweb.[2] I found myself much refreshed and very happy. At night I walked with the Young Kirkheisen sous les marauniers. He was too forward. I checked him.

[1] Presumably young Leopold Kircheisen
[2] In his *Inquiry*, published in this year, Thomas Reid, D.D. (1710–96) rejected the scepticism and far-reaching empiricism ex-pressed by David Hume in his *Treatise of Human Nature* (1739; CBEL: 1740). Adopt-ing a modified empiricism, Reid argued that the observation of our mental processes as well as common sense make us aware of certain innate principles of the mind that are impervious to rational questioning, and that reading Hume had placed him 'only in an enchanted castle, imposed upon by spe-ctres and apparitions' (*Inquiry*, ed. Timothy Duggan, 1970, I. vi). Reid's image may have inspired JB's rejection of 'the sceptical cob-web', which also alludes to Hume's rational scepticism. In May of this year Reid had suc-ceeded Adam Smith as Professor of Moral Philosophy at Glasgow University (Keith Lehrer, *Thomas Reid*, 1989, pp. 4, 8). He would become the chief exponent of the Scottish School of Common Sense Philo-sophy.

## Friday 20 July

[MEM. dated Saturday 21 July] [Y]esterday you din'd at Splitzerbers' &c. The morning you was dull & had been with Mitchel who gave fine ideas — At night Ball in garden — was quite illumed — but too singular — no matter. Be self. Be original. Be happy. You was so certainly. Add to this learning & taste, & devotion & *retenue*. Marry not — but think to have fine Saxon girls &c & be with Temple. Continue Journ — Go. Keep firm abroad another year — or marry Zelide. Go home with design to *try*[1] & if bad Spain or [F]rance &c &c. &c —

[J.] I past the morning with Mr. Mitchel who talked of parliamentary Affairs while he sat in the house. He revived in my mind true english

Ambition.[2] I dined at Heer Schickler's. At six in the evening I went in our family coach to Heer Splitzerber's Garden, where the young Couple gave a fine Ball, and most excellent Supper.[3] I danced a great deal & was in true gay vigourous spirits. I must mention a particular circumstance or two in a german Marriage. There is a Poem of Hymenaeal guise composed, & every guest receives one.[4] The Bride stands in the center of a ring of Gentlemen and they dance arround her. She is blindfolded, & holds in her hand an emblematical crown of Virginity, which she puts on the head of what Gentleman she pleases, and he is considered as marked out to be the first married of the Company. He again takes the Bride's place, & in the same manner crowns a Lady.[5] I was rather too singular. Why not? I am in reality an original character. Let me moderate & cultivate my Originality.[6] God would not have formed such a diversity of men if he had intended that they should all come up to a certain standard. That is indeed impossible while black brown and fair, serious lively and mild continue distinct qualitys, Let me then be Boswell and render him as fine a fellow as possible. At one we went home. I made Mademoiselle[7] play me a sweet air on the Harpsichord to compose me for gentle Slumbers. Happy Man that I am.

---

[1] Conflicting possibilities: to stay abroad in spite of his father's resistance and possibly to marry Delle de Zuylen, or to practise law in Scotland, as his father wished.

[2] Mitchell had been M.P. for Aberdeenshire from 1747 to 1754, and for Elgin Burghs from 1755. He would retain this seat in the House, *in absentia*, for the rest of his life (Namier and Brooke, iii. 143). As a Scot who had been active in English politics and was now a respected English diplomat, Mitchell evidently inspired JB to thoughts of similar success.

[3] The garden, a long, narrow property in Neukölln close to the Spree and the town's fortifications, was large enough to accommodate two summer houses, one in Chinese style (Nicolai, i. 135–36; ii. 934). Purchased thirty years earlier by the original Splitgerber, it was separate from the family's imposing house in the Gertraudenstrasse in Altkölln, which was near the Kircheisens' house (Nicolai, i. 125).

[4] The poem was entitled 'Der Demoiselle Schartow bey ihrer Verbindung mit dem … Herrn Stielow, zugeeignet von einem bekannten Freund und Diener' ('Dedicated to Miss Schartow on her union with Herr Stielow, by a friend and servant'). According to German custom, it had been printed in advance and was anonymous. JB's copy is preserved (P 158).

[5] A crown of jewels or flowers as symbol of virginity, often associated with the Virgin Mary, had been a traditional part of the bride's wedding outfit since the middle ages but was no longer taken seriously in the eighteenth century (Deneke, pp. 88–93). Here it had become part of a game that prefigures the British and American custom of throwing the wedding bouquet to signify who will marry next.

[6] The wish to 'Be self' (Mem. for this day) and to cultivate his originality marks an important change in JB's development from his wish to model himself on others ('Be Johnson', 'Be Maule').

[7] Caroline Kircheisen.

## Saturday 21 July

[MEM. dated Sunday 22 July] [Y]esterday morning Madll had a present of cherries for you. You visited new pair. You din'd Froment who talked of Scots familiarity — kick on backside. You was too echauffé — you must not lose reins. At 3 — you set out in coach — was hypish but said nothing. Saw Garden at Charlot. Then Wegel's — jolly people — Then Comedy full of gay ideas too libertine[1] — restraind. Supt in grotto — too free. This day church — at 10 Hubner — Be mild —

[J.] Scarcely had I got up when Mademoiselle sent me a rural present of luscious cherries.[2] At dinner, Froment talked of Scotland and the grievous dullness of our women qui sont la à bailler toujours. Nor did he neglect to mention the sad familiarity amongst our men. Un homme la vous donne votre nom de Batême. Ah Jacques! et peutêtre un coup de Pied sur les fesses. He said I must lay my account to be very miserable in Scotland for fourteen or fifteen years. This sounded very hard. But I hope it shall not be so. At three I had a coach, & carried three Germans to Charlottenbourg, one of which was Heer Hubner a Clerk in Chancery, a genteel eventempered fine fellow, much at ease.[3] We went to Heer Wegli's a rich merchant who has a *Campagne* here.[4] We went & saw the garden at Charlottenbourg, which is spacious and elegant,[5] and afterwards to a Comedie françoise played for the entertainment of The Court of Brunswic.[6] No Strangers were invited to the feasts: So, I was only a simple Spectator.[7] I had a full view of The King. I was very well amused. I spoke some time with My Lord Marischal, who at seventy five was much pleased with shows and gayety, & Ribbands & Stars, as any young Courtier in Christendom.[8] With all this He is the old Scotch Earl and has strong sense & much knowledge. It is hard that I can see him so little. We returned to Wegli's & supt, & went home gay.

[1] MS. 'too libertine' scored out, possibly by JB.

[2] JB was so fond of the cherries, now in season, that he himself had bought some on 11, 14, and 20 July (Exp. Acct., App. 3).

[3] Very likely Carl Friedrich Hübner, *Geheimer Kanzellist* (privy chancery clerk), a bachelor who lived in the house of a widow in the Scharrenstrasse (*Adres-Calender*, 1764, p. 107). The street was next to the Petrikirche (Nicolai, i. 119–21) and hence close to JB's lodgings (*Adres-Calender*, 1764, pp. 107–08).

[4] Johann Andreas Wegely (1712–71), who had acquired this house in 1752, owed his wealth to the family woolen business, which had supplied the Prussian army with textiles during the Seven Years' War (Wilhelm Gundlach, *Geschichte der Stadt Charlottenburg*, 1905, i. 150; ii. 356; Gisela Zick, *Berliner Porzellan der Manufaktur von Wilhelm Caspar Wegely*, 1978, p. 35, correcting *Grand Tour I*, Heinemann p. 29 n. 1, McGraw-Hill p. 30 n. 3, which takes him for his brother, Wilhelm Caspar Wegely [1714–64], owner of the first porcelain factory in Berlin from 1751 to 1757, and also assumes that financial losses caused this factory to be 'converted' to a woolen manufactory; actually, the woolen business flourished before and after the porcelain venture; see Zick, pp. 9–10, 35 and n. 200, where Pottle's misidentification is noted).

[5] The garden of Charlottenburg Palace had been inspired by the grounds of Herrenhausen in Hanover (see Journ. 25 June, n. 5), where the Electoress Sophie Charlotte (1668–1705) had grown up. Her husband, Friedrich III (1657–1713, Elector of Brandenburg, who had taken the title of Friedrich I, first King of Prussia, in 1701, had built her a summer palace that he had called 'Charlottenburg' after her death. Built from 1695 to 1701, it had been a restrained baroque building, designed by Johann Arnold Nering (1659–95) and then by J. F. Eosander von Göthe. A new wing designed by Knobelsdorff had established symmetry, making it an example of 'Friderician rococo'. It was now one of the residences of Frederick II (Martin Sperlich, *Schloss Charlottenburg*, 1974, p. 20; Nicolai, iii. 1006–16; Redslob, p. 21, Mathilde Koop, *Kurfürstin Sophie von Hannover*, 1964, p. 221).

[6] The play was *L'Embarras des richesses* (1725), a revival of a three-act harlequinade by Léonor-Jean d'Allainval (1700–53) that had been previously performed at the Prussian court in 1743 (*Berlinische Nachrichten*, No. 88, 24 July 1764; Jean-Jacques Olivier, *Les Comédiens français dans les cours d'Allemagne*, 1902, repr. 1971, ii. 101 and n.; DBF, i. 86).

[7] JB made a separate record of his experience as onlooker, using the third person to describe himself: 'All the ladies and gentle-

men pressed eagerly to get places at the windows of the palace, in order to see the royal families at supper. Boswell found this a little ridiculous, so came up to his acquaintances and said, "allons, allons, je vous en prie voyons la seconde table; je vous assure il vaut mieux la peine; ces gens mangent plus que les autres?"' (*Boswelliana*, p. 237). The ground floor had a number of French windows which allowed spectators to look in (Sperlich, p. 16).

[8] JB believed that Lord Marischal was seventy-five years old ('Abregé d'un Voyage en Allemagne' [June 1764], App. 1; To WJT, 23 July). Lord Marischal himself never divulged his age, and neither church nor baptismal records are available for this information. He would have been seventy-

one if born in 1693, as specified in *Scots Peer*. viii. 485, or seventy-nine, as proposed as the most likely of three possibilities by his friend d'Alembert in his obituary, *Eloge de Milord Maréchal*, 1779, p. 65 n. 2.

Lord Marischal was especially proud of his *Schwarze Adlerorden* (Order of the Black Eagle), a radiating eight-pointed star worn on the breast. He had been granted this insignia on his appointment as envoy to France in 1751 and had worn it also for his official portrait as governor of Neuchâtel (*Das Buch vom Schwarzen Adler-Orden*, ed. Louis Schneider, 1870, p. 92; illustr. in *Grand Tour I*, facing p. 6). The decoration was Frederick II's highest honour (Brockhaus, i. 146, s.v. 'Adlerorden').

## Sunday 22 July

[MEM. dated Monday 23 July.] [Y]esterday you entered a moment St. Peter's church & was not gloomy. Youll cure your *kirk* prejudices at last. You took coach & drove to Charlottenburgh to Wegil's[1] — saw the garden to great Advantage — Mem — take *ideas* of some of the Beauties for Auchinleck. You Sat by Madll. Scheenmark you was too open you must learn *usage du monde de badiner sans que le cœur s'y mêle.* You then played at round &c & betted crown [—] have care you have gaming spirit — in Garden Hered Prince nam'd you — & Duke spoke — saw King —

[J.] I entered a moment St. Peter's Church, was devout & not gloomy. I hope to get free of my dreary Associations of sadness to public worship in any form. I fear however, that the Presbyterian *Kirk* cannot be overcome. I went to Charlottenbourg, & dined with our family at M. Weglis.[2] His Garden is splendid. We dined in a Grotto richly adorned with Shells & Seaweed and all manner of fine things.[3] After dinner I played at a Game which I know not the name of. We were seated upon elbow chairs fixed on a round plain of boards which was whirled about very fast. Every[4] one had a pole in his hand, with which our business was to catch some iron rings which were loosely fixed in a Beam above the plain on two sides.[5] I was Blockhead enough to bett against a Lady an ecu (3 shillings) each ring. I lost 18 ecus. I have realy the spirit of gaming. Happy is it for me that I am tied up.[6] We next went to the Royal Garden & amongst other Spectators heard or saw a Concert. I also saw the King a long time in the Garden. General Weiligh Cousin to Mr. Spaen whom I was recommended to, stood by me.[7] I was quite enthusiastic & talked of the King with prodigious warmth. The gallant Weiligh held me by the Arm, & said 'tranquilisez vous Monsieur'. An excellent Anecdote. As I stood among the crowd, the Duke of Brunswic walked past. He made me a most gracious bow, & made me come out to him; took me by the hand, and talked to me some time. I told him I intended to have the honour of paying my respects at Brunswic, at the *Foir*.[8] He said I should be very wellcome. How worthy and how amiable a Prince is this! He made me very happy. The Hereditary Prince also named me. I returned to Wegli's, & eat a bit of supper. There was here a Mademoiselle Scheenemark[9] very handsom and very clever, but too theatrical. She pleased me not a little. I went home calm.

[1] A second visit in two days to Charlottenburg, only 5 miles (8.1 km) from the centre of Berlin. For the costs of JB's carriage to Charlottenburg, see Exp. Acct. 21 July and 22 July, App. 3.

[2] See Journ. 21 July and n. 4.

[3] Presumably the grotto was in the garden. Such playful rococo architecture had originated in the Boboli Gardens in Florence and had been developed in France at Fontainebleu, the Tuileries, and Versailles before being adopted at Herrenhausen in Hanover as well as at Monbijou in Berlin and at Sanssouci in Potsdam (Udo von Alvensleben and Hans Reuther, *Herrenhausen*, 1966, pp. 156–57). The taste for grottos had now been acquired also by a wealthy German merchant—and would soon inspire JB to order a 'Grand Grotto' to be built into a cliff at Auchinleck (From Bruce, 26 Nov. 1768, *Corr. 8*, p. 18 and n. 5).

[4] MS. 'Eevery'

[5] This game, called *Ringelstechen* or *Ringelspiel*, was played on a primitive merry-go-round. Originally used as training for battle and in chivalric tournaments, it had become popular in various domesticated forms in the eighteenth century (Walter Endrei and László Zolnay, *Fun and Games in Old Europe*, 1986, pp. 145, 150).

[6] 'tie up': 'to bind, restrain, or confine strictly' (OED, s.v. 'tie' *v*., 13.c). JB was restrained by a promise he had made to Tho-

mas Sheridan (1719–88) not to lose more than three guineas at a sitting. Sheridan, father of the playwright Richard Brinsley Sheridan and another of JB's early mentors, had previously rescued him from gambling debts (Journ. 7 Jan. 1763; from Thomas Sheridan, 1 Oct. 1763, Yale MS. C 2485; Mem. dated 11 May).

[7] Friedrich Wilhelm von Wylich und Lottum (1716–74) was a distant cousin of de Spaen's through Florentine Anne (de Spaen) (b. 1681), who had married Dietrich von Wylich (1677–1709) of a collateral line (Königl. Herolds-Amt, GStAPK, I. HA Rep. 176 Heroldsamt, VI W Nr. 93; *Fortgesetzte neue Genealogisch-Historische Nachrichten*, 1771, 116, 550–51). JB's Wylich, appointed commandant of Berlin in 1764, was frequently asked to meet foreign visitors because of his knowledge of French (ADB). His distinguished career in the Prussian army had begun in von Kröcher's infantry regiment, which he had joined as ensign in 1733. He had been appointed major-general for his exceptional courage at Burkersdorf in 1762 and had succeeded to the command of Peter III's infantry Regt. Nr. 13 after that Czar's death in 1763.

[8] The August fair. For JB's visit, see Journ. 7–22 Aug.

[9] Presumably Schönermark, but not further identified.

## Monday 23 July

[MEM. dated Tuesday 24 July.] Yesterday you dined with Lord Marischal who bid you write for Anecdotes of Fletcher.[1] You wrote all afternoon,[2] was hyp'd & walked hard — & it went off as it was very light.

[J.] Lord Marischal dined with us at Froment's. He & I talked of Jacobitism, as how there was something pathetic & generous[3] in it, as it was espousing the cause of a distrest & ancient Royal House. My Lord however owned that they deserved to lose the throne of Britain.[4] I own so too. I am sorry for them. I wish to forget them; and I love from my Soul 'Great George our King'.[5] In the afternoon, I was a little hyp'd; but by walking hard was cleared. How easy is now an attack of this kind!

[1] Lord Marischal was gathering material for Rousseau, whom he had befriended in Neuchâtel while the latter needed pro-

tection from the French and Swiss authorities, and whom he had asked to write a book about Andrew Fletcher of Saltoun (1655–

1716), the great Scottish patriot and republican (see Journ. 3 Dec. and n. 37).

² Whether JB was 'writing for' anecdotes about Fletcher (i.e., requesting information from friends) or bringing up his own journal is unclear.

³ 'Appropriate or natural to one of noble birth' as well as 'gallant, … magnanimous, free from meanness or prejudice' (OED, s.v. 'generous', 2.a).

⁴ Lord Marischal, having supported and advised Prince Charles Edward until 1745, had distrusted him for good reasons since then (see Journ. 6 Dec. and n. 5; also Journ. 18 June n. 6).

⁵ The key phrase in a song extolling the Hanoverian king. First performed in both the Drury Lane and Covent Garden theatres at the time of the Jacobite rising of 1745, the song, later the national anthem of Britain, had been published in the pro-Hanoverian Gent. Mag. (Oct. 1745, xv. 552; W. L. Reed and M. J. Bristow, National Anthems of the World, 7th ed. 1987, p. 198 n. *). JB's strongly stated support of George III marks a change from the Jacobite sentiments he had shared with his Scottish friends the Kellies, who had argued that the Stuarts had not deserved to be ousted from the throne and that they had been succeeded by 'a shabby family' who had embroiled the British in a destructive war in Germany (Journ. 17 Jan. 1763). JB's enthusiasm for George III would be expressed again fulsomely in the extemporaneous fragmentary 'Parliament A Poem'

(Yale MS. M 278), begun on 6 Aug., and would be reinforced by the cordial reception he would receive in Brunswick from the King's sister, the Hanoverian Princess Augusta (see Journ. 13 Aug.). Yet a few months later he would visit Stuart supporters in Rome, albeit cautiously to avoid suspicions of treason. Altogether JB's feelings about the two royal houses would remain ambivalent until his mind was 'settled' by an important conversation with SJ in the Hebrides while they travelled in the footsteps of Prince Charles Edward (see Earlier Years, pp. 213–19; Pat Rogers, Johnson and Boswell: The Transit of Caledonia, 1995, pp. 140–54). There JB would tentatively admit to 'a kind of liking for Jacobitism' (a phrase he would suppress in the published Tour) but would then agree with SJ that the Hanoverians had a right to the throne which they had occupied for as much time as the Stuarts had before them, and that an attempt to restore the latter might provoke a civil war (13 Sept. 1773, Hebrides, pp. 162–63; for the controversy about SJ's possible Jacobitism, see Journ. 15 Dec. and nn. 15, 42), JB in his later years would exhibit 'an almost Oriental' reverence for George III (Hebrides, pp. 163–64 and n. 6; for a summary of JB's changing ideas about Jacobitism, see Gordon Turnbull, 'James Boswell: Biography and the Union', in Cairns Craig, gen. ed., The History of Scottish Literature, Vol. 2: 1660–1800, ed. Andrew Hook, 1987, pp. 161–62).

## Tuesday 24 July

[MEM. dated Wednesday 25 July.] [Y]esterday at 10 You had Soldat françois for des Armes. You din'd Mitchell & was stupid. But after dinner grew gay. He talked that Systems had no effect [—] you said it is all fine sentiments & good habits & youre to write so to Zelide. He talked of Thomson & just brought back all old ideas [—] you resolved to be Scots Baron¹ & in London every spring. At night supt & walked — They said fachés a votre depart — but was prudent. This day resume. Chace libertine fancies.² Happiness upon whole, as Miltons wedded love³ [—] manege. Be bold. Journ all da<y>.

[J.] This morning at ten I had with me a french fencing-master a Soldier in the Prussian service. He was a tall black Gaul & rattled away with his national volubility. I am now quite in the humour of exercises, as will appear from this my Journal.⁴ I dined at Mr. Mitchell's. At table I was stupid. After dinner He & I were left alone, and fell into most agreable conversation of the small effect of Systems of Morality, & on the great importance of early impressing upon the mind just sentiments, which never leave us.⁵ He talked of Thomson whose freind he formerly was in

London.[6] He said that Thomson had more Genius than knowledge, that notwithstanding of his fine imitation of Ovid on the Pythagoraean system, he was an egregious gormandiser of Beefsteaks.[7] He observed that the Drama was not his Province. He was too descriptive. When a sentiment pleased him, he used to extend it with rich luxuriance. His freinds used to prune very freely, & poor Thomson used to suffer. Mr. Mitchell said now & then this is fine but it is misplaced. *Non est hic locus*. Thomson used to sweat so much the first nights of his Plays, that when he came & met his freinds at a tavern in the Piazza, his wig was as if it had been dip'd in an Oil-pot.[8] Mr. Mitchell just recalled my London Ideas, and made me very happy.[9] At night I supped with the family, & then walked with the Ladies.

[1] Either a baron of Exchequer, like Maule (see Mems. 26, 27 July) or, more generally, a Scottish landowner. For the legal right to the venerable title 'baron', which was in use until the Union of Scotland and England in 1707, and JB's decision to adopt it at the German courts, see Journ. 1 Oct. and n. 4.

[2] MS. 'Chace ... *fancies*' scored out in a modern hand.

[3] *Paradise Lost*, iv. 750–52:

Hail wedded love, mysterious law, true source
Of human offspring, sole proprety,
In Paradise of all things common else.

[4] The fencing master has not been identified. JB paid 3 D. (Daalder, Taler) for a month of instruction (Exp. Acct. 23 July, App. 3). As revealed in a brief paragraph written to practise the Dutch language, JB had previously taken fencing lessons with an aged instructor in Utrecht (27 Feb. 1764, *Een Beytie Hollansche*, ed. C. C. Barfoot and K. J. Bostoen, 1995, #16, pp. 34–35).

[5] JB here echoes two key ideas of Adam Smith: his questioning of the ethical 'systems' valued by other philosophers and his emphasis on sympathy as the most significant 'moral sentiment', to be accepted as a guide to conduct (*Theory of Moral Sentiments*, 1759, I. i. 2.2; VI. ii. 16, ed. D. D. Raphael and A. L. Macfie, 1976. JB had admired Smith's lectures at Glasgow University where Smith (1723–90) had served as Professor of Moral Philosophy from 1752 after a year as Professor of Logic, and where JB had studied from 1759 to 1760 (*Earlier Years*, p. 42). For a nuanced appraisal of Smith's influence on JB, see Gordon Turnbull, 'Boswell in Glasgow: Adam Smith, Moral Sentiments, and the Sympathy of Biography', *The Glasgow Enlightenment*, ed. Andrew Hook and Richard B. Sher, 1995, pp. 164–70).

Two weeks earlier JB had written to Belle de Zuylen about his efforts, often unsuccessful, to live by fixed rules and to judge his conduct in terms of right and wrong, propriety (Smith's term) and impropriety. JB had also quoted from a letter (not extant) in which Smith had warned: 'Your great fault is acting upon Systems'. Belle de Zuylen, too, appears to have admired Smith (JB to Belle de Zuylen, 9 July, *Œuvres Charrière*, i. 197; *Holland*, Heinemann p. 299, McGraw-Hill p. 308). JB evidently planned to continue the discussion of Smith's ideas with her but had no opportunity to do so. Later he would seek to interest his future wife in Smith's ideas, sending her a copy of his treatise (From Margaret [Montgomerie] Boswell, 17 Oct. 1769, Yale MS. C 427).

[6] Mitchell had been not only a friend of James Thomson (1700–48) but also co-executor of his estate (Andrew Bisset, *Memoirs and Papers of Sir Andrew Mitchell*, K. B., 1850, ii. 38).

[7] The summary of Mitchell's comments shows JB practising to record an extensive conversation. Thomson had indeed imitated Ovid's lines describing Pythagoras's plea to spare helpless animals and rather take vegetarian nourishment (*Spring*, 1728, ll. 358–70, paraphrasing *Metamorphoses*, xv. 116–26). These lines must have appealed to JB because of his own interest in Pythagoras and vegetarianism (see Mem. dated 9 Sept. and n. 1; Journ. 6 Oct. n. 19).

[8] Thomson's poem *Liberty* (1735–36) had been 'pruned' by his patron, Lord Lyttelton, and the wig incident had occurred on the first night of the tragedy *Agamemnon* in 1738. These details would be noted also by SJ, who would express the same opinion of Thomson's tragedies and blank verse as Mitchell offers here ('James Thomson', *The Lives of the Most Eminent English Poets*, ed. Roger Lonsdale, 2006, iv. 99–100). The

Latin tag 'nec vero hic locus est' ('not the proper occasion') comes from Cicero, *Tuscan Disputation*, IV. i. 1 (Loeb ed., trans. J. E. King, 1966).

⁹ JB, though not acquainted with Thomson, had known his poetry well: one of the drafts of 'October', JB's first extended poem, written in late 1757, was subtitled 'After the manner of Mr. Thomson' (Yale MS. M 265; *Earlier Years*, p. 60). JB had also been interested in the monument planned for Thomson in Westminster Abbey, which he knew about even before it was dedicated in 1762 (To Thomas Sheridan, 9 Dec. 1761; see *Corr*. 9, p. 160 n. 4). And he had subscribed to the new edition of Thomson's works published in the same year, his name appearing as 'James Boswell, Esq; jun. of Auchinleck' among the 'List of the Encouragers' (James Thomson, *The Works of James Thomson, with his last Corrections and Improvements. To which is prefixed, An Account of his Life and Writings. In two volumes …*, 1762). See also Journ. 21 Nov. 1762.

## Wednesday 25 July

[MEM. dated Thursday 26 July.] Yesterday at 7 you entered *Manége* & was quite in foreign Academy. You was *Come*[1] *Burnet* & discovered that all is *circulation du Sang*. So think so.[2] It is needless to mark allways dinner. You was too free at tea. You must learn to be polite. Twill be fine at Edinr. At night you wrote well. Jacob told strange story. You supt & talked latin with Priest[3] [—] you walked — Your'e just Gen. Cochran[4] you'll be in Parlmt — or Baron. Youre free as to Relig — Go on. This day write vers[5] each day proffit travels — write Somelsd & Maasd.[6]

[J,] At seven in the morning I went with young Kirchelsen to the manége of Comte Schafcotz Grand Ecuier du Roi where he has two principal Grooms that give lessons. I put myself under the direction of Mr. Galliard a french German.[7] He was active & lively, & talked with the Authority of a master. I was a little timourous at first. But the exercise warmed my blood, and I got into the true spirit of a Cavalier. I do well to apply thus to the exercises of the Academy. I shall at least receive some benefit. I drank tea at home. I said to Mademoiselle that I would not take her with me to Brunswic as I feared to tire of her in two or three days. This was true; but too free. I must realy learn a little of that restraint which foreigners call politeness, and which after a certain time becomes quite easy. I am much pleased with my Servant Jacob. He is a Bernois a genteel active fellow.[8] I liked this specimen of him upon our journey to Potzdam from Utrecht. He was allways alert & ready to put every thing right. One day the Postilions were at a loss for a machine to carry water in to cool the wheels. Jacob sprung away to the side of a Brook, tore from it's place a young tree that had fixed it's roots in the humid soil, & bringing with it a lump of watry earth, he plashed against the wheels, as a London maid does against the stairs with her moistened mop. There was invention & execution too of the very Epic kind. He is quite sober, has good christian Principles and even generous sentiments. He would fight for his master, & gold could not tempt him to marry a woman he did not like. He had a most extraordinary Adventure before he left Holland. A young officer of the Regiment where his master served, was uncommonly civil to him, & even used him like a freind. He used to invite him of an evening to the Tavern, and give him a Bottle of wine, and show a strange fondness. He at last asked Jacob if he would come and live with him. Jacob began to suspect that the young dog was a man of Italian taste.[9] The Officer however told him 'Je ne suis pas ce que vous m'avez cru'[10] and opening his breast discovered himself to be a Woman. She was of a good family & fortune, but had run away from her freinds. Jacob however, would not marry her, upon any account.[11]

[1] That is, 'Comme', clarified in JB's later admonition to himself to 'take exercise like Burnet' (Mem. dated 27 Aug.).

[2] Although JB had already heard about the importance of circulating blood from Mme de Froment (Journ. 3 July), he here seems to accept this as a new idea.

[3] Not identified.

[4] Gen. James Cochrane was the brother of JB's grandmother Euphemia Cochrane Erskine (?1693–?1721) and so JB's great-uncle. He had been a convinced Hanoverian (Boswelliana, p. 7). JB would remember that at the age of five, he had been given a shilling by the General to pray for King George instead of for King James (Life, 14 July 1763, i. 431, n. 1; Earlier Years, p. 15). For JB he seems to have epitomized stability in life.

[5] Presumably French for 'verses'—JB's first mention of writing the poem about parliament which he would begin a few days later (see Journ. 6 Aug. and App. 1).

[6] François Cornelius van Aerssen, Heer van Sommelsdyck (1725–93), was JB's second cousin once removed, through his paternal grandmother Lady Elizabeth Bruce, daughter of the second Earl of Kincardine. Her mother was Sommelsdyck's great aunt Veronica (Ominous Years, Gen. Chart III, p. 376; Corr. 5, p. 12 n. 1). Aarnoud Joost van der Duyn, Baron Maasdam, a general of cavalry, was Sommelsdyck's brother-in-law. JB wanted to thank both for the hospitality they had shown him in The Hague.

[7] The riding school was in Altkölln on the Breite Strasse, a broad street leading from the palace (Nicolai, i. 118; ii. 719–20). Johann Nepomuc Gotthard, Count von Schaffgotch (1713–75), had been Frederick II's master of the horse since 1744 and was also a Knight of Malta. He was said to be handsome, vain, and rich (Lehndorff, Dreissig Jahre, p. 71; Nachträge, i. 128; Thiébault, iii. 42, 44). His groom, Jacques Galliard (1719–71), was a Huguenot born in Berlin (Kirchenbücher der französischen Kirche zu Berlin, Mrt 7, p. 173).

[8] JB had engaged Jacob Hänni just before leaving The Hague and had recently spent money on improving his tailor-made outfit (Journ. 6 June, Holland, Heinemann p. 266, McGraw-Hill p. 273; Exp. Acct. 23 July, App. 3). Jacob, born in 1735, came from the small town of Toffen, near Bern, where the parents, Abraham and Johanna Hänni, were 'Bürger', solid citizens (K Belp 4, p. 286, AEN Bern). The young man, alternatingly pleasing and irritating to JB, would remain with him almost to the end of the latter's Continental travels (see Journ. 2 Jan. 1766).

[9] Practising sodomy (see 'Italian fashion', Hugh Rawson, A Dictionary of Invective, 1989, p. 213).

[10] MS. 'He at last … cru' scored out by a modern hand.

[11] According to an IGI Record, Jacob would marry a local woman, Anna Streit (b. 1745) on 24 Oct. 1766, after JB's return to England.

## Thursday 26 July

[MEM. dated Friday 27 July.] [Y]esterday at 10 you had long dispute on £1000 with Ladies & made 'em angry — have a care — when abroad learn politeness — afternoon Hubner carried you to Garden — poor Vauxhall — home and resolved devotion. Study & Baron of Exchequer & Laird of Auchinleck allways on guard against Gloom.

[J.] I put my Ladies of the family in a Passion, by affirming that I would not marry any woman whose fortune was less than £10,000.[1] They were seriously shocked, & gave me all the good common arguments against low interested matches. Very well. But my purpose is fixed. My Wife shall have a handsom fortune and that will allways be something sure.[2] However, I need not say so. Let me above all strive to attain easy reserve. In the evening, I went with Hubner and young Kircheisen to the Garden of Corsica, a kind of little Vauxhall, and indeed a Very little one.[3] We supt & drank Cherry wine which I found delicious. At night when I got home, I resolved ever to cultivate sublime devotion, to be a Baron of Exchequer, and a Laird of Auchinleck.

[1] This sum, not the £1000 mentioned in the Mem. dated 27 July, is presumably what JB had in mind. In an earlier flight of fancy, he had even envisaged marrying 'a lady of the highest distinction, with a fortune of a hundred thousand pounds' (To AE, 8–9 May 1762, published in *Letters between the Honourable Andrew Erskine and James Boswell, Esq.*, 1763, Letter XXVIII; *Corr. 9*, pp. 247–49).

[2] JB would still be trying to achieve this goal in 1767, when, under pressure from his father, he would woo Lord Auchinleck's ward Catherine Blair (?1749–98), 'the Princess'. JB would not be overly disappointed, however, when she rejected his proposal, and she would eventually marry Sir William Maxwell of Monreith in 1776 (see To WJT, 30 Mar. and 12 June 1767, and 8 Feb. 1768, *Corr. 6*, pp. 182, 183 n. 16, 187 and n. 2, 222–24). JB would soon pursue Mary Ann Boyd (b. 1752), 'la belle Irlandaise', to the point of travelling to her home in Dublin (To WJT, 24 Aug., 9 Dec. 1768, 3 May 1769, *Corr. 6*, pp. 241–47). But while courting her, he would come to recognize the attraction and merit of his cousin Margaret Montgomerie (1737 or 1738–89), who had been his loyal friend and confidante, and who had accompanied him to Ireland. Although she had only £1000 to her name and Lord Auchinleck did not approve, JB would marry her on 25 Nov. 1769 (To WJT, 3 May 1769, *Corr. 6*, p. 246). For the full saga of JB's courtships, see *Earlier Years*, pp. 322, 329–30, 391–93, 402–09, 418–19, 440–41, 555–56; and *Search of a Wife*, pp. 50–132 passim, 179–236, 257–62 passim, 348–49).

[3] The Korsika, 'near the Arsenal on the water', was on the Werder, one of two small islands embraced by arms of the Spree not far from the Kircheisens' neighbourhood (Nicolai, i. 149, ii. 966). Named after a rich Berlin merchant, who had recently bought it from its bankrupt former owner, it served supper at more than fifty small but well-appointed tables (Lehndorff, *Dreissig Jahre: Nachträge*, i. 407, 433). In contrast, the pleasure gardens at Vauxhall in London could accommodate 1200 visitors (Henry B. Wheatley and Peter Cunningham, *London Past and Present*, 1891, iii. 428).

## Friday 27 July

[MEM. dated Saturday 28 July.] [Y]esterday you dined Mitchel & after it talked of living & how men had different talents — & how King of Prussia & Abbé Jerusalem would have still the same opinions as all had been allready said & truth would remain at bottom well [—] then Court — Home after. This day learn a little restraint. Be grave and gay & not Houst Stewart.[1]

[J.] I dined with Mr. Mitchell, who allways gives me agreable views. He said that in living every man must be his own director; for, our tastes are extremely different. He said if Lawyers had a fixed Sallary, they surely could not drudge as they do. But the little refreshing presents keep them alive.[2] He counselled me much to pursue the law in Scotland as I might by that means attain a usefull and honourable Station. Yet he owned that some People could not follow that Profession. I said nothing but had a secret satisfaction to find that my aversion to the law was not absolutely absurd. At six we got into his Excellency's coach. I told him that the Abbé Jerusalem had wished to dispute with the King of Prussia, on Religion. Indeed said Mr. Mitchell they had better save themselves the trouble; for, the King has heard all the Abbés Arguments, and the Abbé has heard all the King's; and after they have said a great deal, each will retain *his* own opinion. Then, Sir, said I, you think Truth is at the bottom of the well.[3] Yes, said he, and I suppose will remain there some time. We went to *Mont Bijou* & payed our respects at Court. Dull enough.

[1] Houston Stewart (1741–?86) had retained this name, although the name Nicolson was added when he succeeded to the entailed estate of Carnock in 1752. He had been a good friend of JB and AE (for whom see Journ. 30 July n. 4, and *Corr.* 9, p. 56 n. 2), and like them he had contributed to Alexander Donaldson's second *Collection of Original Poems by ... Scotch Gentlemen*, published in 1762 (see To AE, 22 Jan. 1762; Journ. 3 Jan., ?14 and 22 Feb. 1762; *Corr.* 9, p. 192 n. 30). But by the following year JB had been troubled by Stewart's behaviour and no longer found him a desirable model: 'We were too extravagant in the ludicrous style, and I was not happy' (Journ. 29 Apr. 1763). And a few years later he would observe: 'Houstoun was dissipated as ever. You felt calm superiority' (Journ. 15 Mar. 1767).

[2] By English custom, a barrister was not paid directly by his client but depended on honoraria from the solicitor, who then charged the client. Mitchell himself had seen lawyers at work from 1734 to 1738 while a member of the Middle Temple. He had studied law at Leiden from 1730 to 1731 (Namier and Brooke, iii. 143).

[3] Mitchell well knew the King's character and opinions. After winning his confidence, Mitchell had accompanied him on several campaigns between 1756 and 1761. But Mitchell had lost the King's favour in 1762 when British subsidies to Prussia were discontinued (Andrew Bisset, *Memoirs and Papers of Sir Andrew Mitchell*, 2 vols. 1850, i. 355–06, ii. 200–05; Patrick Francis Doran, *Andrew Mitchell and Anglo-Prussian Diplomatic Relations*, 1986, pp. 187–90, 278–89, 296–01, 373). JB's last comment is a proverb dating from classical antiquity that suggests the truth cannot be established with certainty (*The Oxford Dictionary of English Proverbs*, 2nd ed., compiled by William George Smith, rev. by Paul Harvey, p. 674).

## Saturday 28 July

[MEM. dated Sunday 29 July] Yesterday in chaise with Hubner & Conseiller you took tour to *Stols's* fine campagne. Sat under tree eat currans lay in Sun — was easy & genteel & cordial. He a fine young fellow. Sail on river — romantic wood — Spoke english — Found your disease just ill health — resolved to live like B[.] Maule and to keep principles to self[1] — Being allways a freind of Johnson & moderate Christian. This day churches — then Journ — & think œconomy but genteel. <Le>tters. Hague. Perhaps Zelide — See Mitch — and fix Italy[.][2]

[J.] At five in the morning I set out on a party with Heer Hubner & a *Conseiller*.[3] We had a clever chaise and drove by Spando to the *campagne* of Mr. Stoltz who should have been sent *chargé d'affaires* to England. He was a good genteel young fellow; & spoke english not amiss.[4] We eat Currants, we reposed ourselves in the Sun, we dined chearfully. We walked about his Place, which is sweet & romantic. I was more and more convinced that Hypochondria is ill-health,[5] & resolved to live like Baron Maule.[6] We drove back to Berlin by nine.

[1] MS. 'Found ... self' scored out, probably by a modern hand.

[2] JB was evidently already planning the later stages of his tour, which would include Italy and France.

[3] Not identified.

[4] Spandau, about 7.5 miles (c. 12.1 km) from the centre of Berlin, was situated where the Spree meets the Havel and approachable by either land or water. It was one of the oldest towns in the region, dating from the twelfth century (Nicolai, iii. 1018). Stoltz (dates not found) had been one of two possible replacements for Abraham Louis Michel (1712–82), the Prussian representative who had served in London in various capacities from 1747 (*Repertorium*, ii. 297) and who was being recalled at the request of the British government (Frederick II, *Pol. Corr.* xii. 368–69, 397 and n. 1). Stoltz, a close friend of Hübner's, had just been rejected for the peculiar reason that his written French was not good enough (From Ministers Finckenstein and Hertzberg to Frederick II, 4 July 1764, GStAPK, I.HA Rep. 96 Geheimes Zivilkabinett, ältere Periode, Nr. 199 E Bd. 46b). There is no basis for the assumption in *Grand Tour I*, p. 41 n. 1, that he had been Mitchell's candidate. He would die of a fever a few months after this meeting while returning from a pleasure trip to Hamburg and Holland (From Hübner, 28 Jan. 1765).

[5] JB's new insight, that his depression was a physical malady and not just a psychological problem, was in keeping with Dr. Cheyne's theory that both spleen and hypochondria were 'nervous diseases' (title page, *The English Malady*). Cheyne attributed these to unfavourable climate, heavy food, and lack of exercise, to be counteracted by moderate diet and unstrenuous physical exertion (pp. i–ii, 192–204). A similar diagnosis of JB's complaint would be suggested by the twentieth-century physician Dr. William B. Ober in 'Johnson and Boswell: "Vile Melancholy" and "The Hypochondriack"', in *Bottoms Up!: A Pathologist's Essays on Medicine and the Humanities*, [1987], pp. 197–202; for related writings, see Ober, 'Eighteenth-Century Spleen', *Psychology and Literature in the Eighteenth Century*, 1987, pp. 225–53.

[6] See Journ. 10 July n. 4.

## Sunday 29 July

[MEM. dated Monday 30 July] [Y]esterday you went with Hubner & saw old churches. Also Regiment of Cadets noblesse all instructed — General &c. dined in order one read exploits said you wished you had been so elevé.[1] Supt & walked —

[J.] Honest Hubner went with me to look at some of the Lutheran Churches here.[2] I was pleased with their decent Ornaments. I drank tea at home, & talked latin with a fat Lutheran Parson.[3] Then I made a tour in the chaise with Madame and Mademoiselle who looked sweet and chearfull & had her green-silk *Para-sol* and looked like an indian Princess. We walked in the Park with Mesdemoiselles Beemer etc.[4] I then came home as agreably as I went out and very happy I was.

[1] The cadets were housed in a large circular building not far from the Spandau bridge (Nicolai, i. 23, 242–43). They had to belong to the aristocracy, as did all of Frederick II's officers (Vehse, iv. 324–26; MacDonogh, 342–43). Their commanding officer, Maj.-Gen. Johann Jobst Heinrich, Count (Freiherr) von Buddenbrock (1707–81), lived on the premises (*Adres-Calender*, 1764, p. 11). He had been in his present position since 1758 and had just been put in charge also of the *Ritterakademie* ('chivalric academy'), a school which Frederick II wished to revitalize. Previously, from 1732, Buddenbrock had been adjutant to the then Crown Prince Frederick and had belonged to his circle of friends. On Frederick's accession to the throne in 1740, Buddenbrock had been appointed major, had risen to the rank of major-general in 1753, and would be appointed lieutenant-general in 1767, these being the normal stages of advancement in the Prussian army (DBE, p. 192).

[2] At this time Berlin had fifteen Lutheran churches, two of which alternated between Lutheran and Reformed (Calvinist) services (*Adres-Calender*, 1764, pp. 113, 116–27).

[3] Not identified.

[4] The daughters of Friedrich Ehrenreich Behmer (see Journ. 17 July, n. 1), not further identified.

## Monday 30 July

[MEM. dated Tuesday 31 July.] [Y]esterday you rose at five did all exercises well. Was in noble spirits — at tea was Stense & Bemers. You was too Odd & owned Dame marie dont vous etiez amoureux &c. *She* loved you. You repeated english. I fly yet I love you & on Thamess banks where Greenwich &c. They thought it Russian. At night walked trees. This day letter Catt[1] & Sommelsd. & Maasd — & bring up much Journ & prepare Trunk.[2]

[J.] I did my exercises nobly. I was in superb spirits. Mademoiselle Stensen & other young Ladies drank tea at our house.[3] I was very gay. They begged me to repeat to them something in English. I repeated Erskine's beautifull Stanza 'I fly yet I love you my fair'.[4] They thought it Russian. I also repeated Mr. Johnson's verses 'On Thames's banks',[5] etc. and they thought them no less rude. How curious is this! Here are human Beings who don't understand english; and to whom Mr. Samuel Johnson does not exist, and Erskine seems Savage. Mademoiselle Stensen taught me a sweet Song 'Je reconnois les atteintes, qui m'ont autrefois charmés' — etc. It touched me sensibly & made me own cela me fait me souvenir d'une Dame mariée dont J'etois extremement amoureux.[6] I must be on my guard.

[1] JB wrote two drafts of this letter to Catt, asking for an introduction to the King with some urgency since his other possible sponsors—Lord Marischal, Andrew Mitchell, and Alexander Burnett—had failed him. In his first version JB wrote expansively and enthusiastically about his admiration for Frederick, the sight of whom had 'electrified' him (repeating his phrase for Prince Ferdinand of Brunswick-Lüneburg on 27 June) and at whose feet he had almost thrown himself at Charlottenburg (see Journ. 22 July). JB presented himself as a proud Scottish baron who venerated the King as his superior and had been reading the works of the 'philosophe de Sans Souci' every day. JB could not resist expressing his disapproval of the King's rejection of an afterlife in his poem addressed to Field-marshal Keith ('Épitre XVIII: Sur les vaines terreurs de la mort et les frayeurs d'une autre vie', *Œuvres de Frédéric le Grand*, x. 194–203). Nonetheless, JB regretted the possibility of having to leave Prussia without being able to tell his grandchildren he had spoken to 'Frederic le Grand' (an epithet that had been in vogue since the Silesian wars in the 1740s), and he ended by begging for Catt's advice. (For this version, in an English translation, see *Grand Tour I*, Heinemann pp. 41–45, McGraw-Hill pp. 43–46.) In the second draft, giving the same arguments with more brevity and restraint, JB

added that he believed he deserved to be an exception to the King's rule not to receive unknown visitors. Which one of the drafts JB actually sent is not known, but he would later find good use for several of his arguments and phrases in his efforts to persuade Rousseau to meet him (see his letter of 3 Dec., App. 2).

JB would receive a polite reply from Catt but no help, and would persevere on his own (see Journ. 7 Sept. n. 3; 21 Sept.). For his changed view of Frederick II, see Journ. 9 Oct.

[2] JB did not write his letters to Sommelsdyck or Maasdam, but he did pack his trunk for his trip to Brunswick.

[3] Mlle Stensen was a granddaughter of Mme Wreech (d. 1764), one of the few women to inspire romantic feelings in Frederick II as a young man (From Caroline Kircheisen, 2 Feb. 1765; 'Friedrich des Grossen Briefe und Gedichte an Luise Eleonore von Wreech', J. A. Stargardt, Katalog 500, pp. 9–10, 27; see MacDonogh, pp. 84–85. The other ladies were the young Behmer girls (see Mem.).

[4] The lines came from the last stanza of AE's 'A Pastoral Ballad in the Manner of Shenstone', which had appeared in *A Collection of Original Poems by the Rev. Mr. Blacklock and Other Scotch Gentlemen* (pp. 92–94). A dozen other short poems—pastorals, elegies, mock-heroic pieces—by

AE (1740–93) had also been included in this volume. A dozen more, as well as a dozen signed by JB and nineteen others attributed to him by F. A. Pottle, had been published in a second volume two years later (*Lit. Car.* pp. 13–14). AE had joined him and GD (1732–1818; for whom see Journ. 6 Aug. n. 7) in publishing the sarcastic *Critical Strictures on the New Tragedy of 'Elvira'* (Jan. 1763) that panned a new play by David Mallet, originally Malloch (?1705–65; see Journ. 21 and 27 Jan., 28 Feb. 1763), and had also collaborated on the publication of the *Letters between the Honourable Andrew Erskine and James Boswell, Esq.* in Apr. 1763 (*Lit. Car.* pp. 12–24; *Earlier Years*, pp. 64, 103–06, 486–87). JB had considered AE and GD 'companions' and 'literary partners' but had distinguished them from his 'friends' WJT and JJ (Journ. 16 Feb, 7 July). The bulk of the JB–AE correspondence appears in *Corr.* 9.

AE, the third son of the 5th Earl of Kellie, belonged to a large family with Jacobite leanings (see Journ. 23 July n. 5), whose company JB had enjoyed in Scotland and had occasionally found embarrassing in London (Journ. 1 Dec. 1762, 17 Jan. 1763). AE had paid more attention to his writing than to his career with the 71st Regt. of Foot, to which he had been attached from 1759 and on half-pay when the regiment was disbanded later in 1763 (*Army List*, 1759–65 annually). Contact between JB

and AE would diminish once the former travelled on the Continent. AE would compose a farce, *She's Not Him, and He's Not Her*, staged in Edinburgh at the theatre in Canongate in 1764, four 'Town Eclogues' written c. 1763–65, pub. 1773, and several more poems. He would also return to military duty, now in the 24th Regt. of Foot, which he would join briefly in Gibraltar in the summer of 1766, only to return to Britain by early 1767 and resign in 1770 (see AE to JJ, 2 June 1766, *Corr.* 1, pp. 218–19 and n. 10; *Army List*, 1765–69 annually; From Bruce, 23 Feb. 1767, *Corr.* 8, p. 14 and n. 1). From 1770 he would live with his widowed sister Lady Colville (c. 1734–94) in Edinburgh without ever finding a satisfying occupation (see John Kay, 'Biographical Sketches', *A Series of Original Portraits*, 1877, iii. 58–59). JB would meet him occasionally, would lend him money when needed (see Journ. 6 Aug. 1779 and n. 5, 31 Jan. 1780, *Laird*, pp. 127, 178), and would be deeply shocked by the news of his suicide (Journ. 13 and 24 Oct. 1793, *Great Biographer*, pp. 242 n. 9, 245 n. 9).

[5] *London*, ll. 21–24.

[6] The song has not been identified. JB here alludes to his most serious love relationship, in 1762, not described in this journal but confessed to Rousseau toward the end of the year (see Journ. 14 Dec. n. 16 and App. 2).

## Tuesday 31 July

[MEM. dated Wednesday 1 August] [Y]esterday, you was out of order morning. [Y]ou made blood circulate & grew gay. You went with Hubner to Richards & supt — then home, & was reconcil'd after difference with the fair Caroline & heard that you was liked by All. This day — pay Hub. & Leopold their money.[1] Send for great coat. Send to Post & know all — Then in coach visit. Sheenmark, *Brandt*[2] Stense Beemer Hubner &c [—] wait on Schickler & get 15£ in ducats.[3] Send Taylor to Hubner & have Silk suit by Saturday.[4] Resolve stay in all Thursday & bring up Journ. & think & prepare for journey to Brunswic & still keep in mind being Baron & Laird of Auch. & shun wild ideas; for you're[5] Mr. Samuel Johnson's freind.

[J.] This morning I was out of order. But, by making blood circulate, I became quite well. I went with Hubner to the Garden of Richards in the Park, & supt.[6]

[1] 'Leopold' was young Kircheisen. JB did not note the amount nor the reason for these payments in his Expense Account.

[2] MS. 'Brandt' inserted above 'Sheenmark'

[3] Ducats, gold coins usually minted in Holland, were more stable in value than German coins, whose value had been fluctuating in the previous nine years and had

been undermined during the Seven Years' War when inferior coins were circulated. Frederick II had tried to stabilize his realm's currency by decreeing that foreign coins such as ducats and louis d'or be accepted at their prewar value (Edict of 29 Mar., #4; Friedrich von Schrötter, *Das preussische Münzwesen im 18. Jahrhundert*, Acta Borussica [1902–11],

p. 403). But ducats may still have been more acceptable in Brunswick.

[4] Not recorded in Exp. Acct.

[5] MS. 'your'

[6] The Richardsche Kaffeegarten was in the Tiergarten (Lehndorff, 21 June 1757, *Dreissig Jahre*, p. 113 and Index).

## Wednesday 1 August

[MEM. dated Thursday 2 August] Yesterday you dined Mitchel & talked on Travels & how Books & Authours differed. Formey was there & said Benedictus benedicat Bernardus Bernard.[1] Voltaire Je perds les yeux comme Tiresias mais pas pour chercher les secrets de ciel.[2] Then visits &c — supt Mad. *Brandt*. Homme disoit touts sont morts jusque a ce qu'il avoit diné &c. This day *think* your'e too free — youre like Eglint.[3] You take *present* hour you *must* be distinguished Apart wait till time show. In all day Journ & letters father &c[.]

[J.] I dined at Mr. Mitchells, where was Mr. Formey perpetual Secretary to the Academy of Sciences at Berlin. He was facetious, but vain. He talked of his books, & he talked of his lectures.[4] He said quand vous entendez le tambour a neuf heures au soir, vous pouvez dire Formey est dans son lit. He told us that Mr. Gualteri a french Minister here was so hypochondriack that he caused tie his legs together at night, lest he should get up, and do himself some mischief.[5] How strange a distemper is this! When he was gone, Mr. Mitchell & I talked on the difference of sentiment among mankind, and of the infinite number of books which deluge the field of literature. I then got into my Coach, and payed a number of visits to the Ladies of my Acquaintance. In particular I waited on Madame de Brandt, to whom I was presented at Charlottenbourg; having by mistake accosted her daughter who lives with her thinking that it was her daughter who is Lady of honour to the Queen. Madame de Brandt was Lady to one of the Great Officers of the Prussian Court. She has been very handsom, & is still a fine figure. She has a very courtly address and is clever.[6] She asked me to Supper. I accordingly returned & found there another Lady & Gentleman whose names I did not hear and had no inclination to ask.[7] Madame de Brandt told us of a shrewd Saxon[8] who loved his dinner, that when asked after his freinds & neighbours replied shortly. Ils sont touts morts; so kept all the company busy with lamentation, till he had eat as much as he chose; after which he gravely began & told that all the good people were come alive again. I was here quite at my ease; but, too vivacious. I realy beleive that I must for some years yet, now & then give scope to my vivaciousness.

[1] A learned pun starting with 'Benedictus benedicat' ('May the Blessed One give a blessing'), a commonplace grace said before meals (Reginald H. Adams, *The College Graces of Oxford and Cambridge*, 1992, p. 86). Prof. Gordon Williams suggests that possibly Formey was transforming the 'Blessed One' (i.e., Christ) into St. Benedict, who founded the Benedictine Order in c. 525, and was also invoking St. Bernard of Clairvaux, who founded the Cistercian Order in 1115 to reform the Benedictines, whom he regarded

as having lapsed from the rules of their founder. Prof Williams then comments: 'If this is such a witticism, then Formey probably said not "Bernard" but "Bernardat" (or "-et") to form a subjunctive verb from Bernardus to parallel "benedicat" (which he would mentally envision written with a capital): "May Benedict benedict, May Bernard bernard"' (letter of 4 May 1998).

[2] Voltaire's allusion to the blind seer Teiresias may have been inspired by his own weakened eyesight (see Mem. dated 25 Dec. and n. 3).

[3] Eglinton (see Journ. 28 June and n. 6).

[4] Jean-Henri-Samuel Formey (1711–97), Perpetual Secretary of the *Académie royale des sciences et belles lettres* or *Königliche Akademie der Wissenschaften* from 1744, was a prolific writer on philosophy, pedagogy, theology, history, and politics, eventually credited with more than 600 volumes exclusive of the Memoirs of the Academy (Thiébault, v. 67–70). After serving as pastor of the French church of Brandenburg from 1731, then of the French church in Berlin in 1736, he had functioned as Professor of Philosophy at the French college in Berlin from 1737 to 1739 and had been named historiographer of the Academy in that year. He was also a member of the Imperial Russian Academy of Sciences, the Royal Society in London, and other learned societies (*Adres-Calender*, 1764, p. 38).

[5] Samuel Melchisedec Gualteri (d. 1774) had been the minister of the French Huguenot church of Friedrichstadt from 1744 after serving the French Reformed (Calvinist) congregation of Bernau from 1723 and of Magdeburg from 1729 (letter of 24 Jan. 1990 from the Consistorium der französischen Kirche zu Berlin). For his son, who suffered

even more intensely from depression, see Journ. 11 Aug. and n. 11. Presumably Gualteri was known to Formey through the latter's activities at the centre of a large network of Huguenots in Berlin (see the voluminous correspondence, Nachlass Formey, SBB-PK).

[6] Luise (von Kameke) von Brandt (1710–82) was the widow of Christoph Wilhelm von Brandt (1684–1743), who had occupied the positions of *Kammerherr*, *Oberhofmarschall*, and *Oberhofmeister* (chamberlain, chief marshal, and chief major domo) of the Queen Mother, Sophia Dorothea (see *Œuvres de Frédéric le Grand*, xvi. 150 n.; *Beiträge zur Geschichte der Familie von Kameke*, 1892, p. 52; correcting the identification in *Grand Tour I*, Heinemann p. 46 n. 1, McGraw-Hill p. 47 n. 1). Mme von Brandt had been known at court as *Die Schöne* ('The Beauty') in earlier days, and had remained coquettish (Lehndorff, 23 Sept. 1753; 25 June, 24 Aug. 1757, 19 July 1765, *Dreissig Jahre*, p. 111, *Nachträge*, i. 115, 133, 430). She had lived in reduced circumstances during the Seven Years' War but had recently inherited 25,000 Taler from a grateful old servant of her father's (Lehndorff, 1 Jan. 1764, *Dreissig Jahre: Nachträge*, i. 390). JB had mistaken her younger daughter, Elisabeth Friderica Charlotta (1733–99), for the older one, Sophia (1731–82), who lived in the palace with the other ladies of the bedchamber ('dames d'atour', *Adres-Calender*, 1764, p. 6; names and dates from the Birth Register of the Evangelische Zentralarchiv in Berlin kindly transmitted by J. L. H. Thomas of Berwickshire, letter of 4 Feb. 2001).

[7] Not identified.

[8] Not identified.

## Thursday 2 August

[MEM. dated Friday 3 August.] Yesterday was a sad wet day. Your nerves were unstrung. You was gloomy. You din'd Mitchel well — after dinner talked of metaphysics, origin of evil, fate & freewill &c. & concluded that all was stuff & that Man must be kept employed & chearfull [—] This day prepare all for Brunswic Jaunt.

[J.] This was a dreary wet day, and my nerves were soaked in the moist æther, so that I was a little dreary myself. I dined at Mr. Mitchell's, who after dinner talked with me on metaphysics, fate freewill the origin of evil & all those beautifull Themes. In support of freewill, I maintained that Omniscience could not foresee the actions of men & that it was nobler to create a Being with such powers that God knew not how it would act, than to create a mere machine of whose motions he should be certain.[1] Then, said Mr. Mitchell, it is more ingenious to make a child than to make a watch. This pleasantry has a colour, but the question is if a man can make a child; if a man can give a child the spark of celestial fire. In short his Excellency and I ended our conversation with affirming that dark speculations were to be shunned, & man kept busy & chearfull.

[1] JB had been introduced to these themes, and profoundly disturbed by them, at the age of sixteen at his Edinburgh college in the course on metaphysics taught by John Stevenson (d. 1775), who held the Chair of Logic and Metaphysics from 1730 (*Earlier Years*, p. 32; see Sir Alexander Grant, *The Story of the University of Edinburgh During its First Three Hundred Years*, 1884, ii. 328–30). JB's thinking had still been unsettled as recently as 23 May, when he wrote to WJT: 'I have been tormenting myself with abstract questions concerning Liberty and Necessity, the attributes of the Deity, and the origin of evil. I have truly a dark disposition. I must be patient. I may yet become quite clear' (*Corr.* 6, p. 87). In arguing in favour of free will with Mitchell, JB rejects both his boyhood Calvinism with its emphasis on predestination, and the deists' conception of God as creator of the universe according to rational principles that need no further intervention. He is also rejecting the more extreme materialism of Julien Offray de La Mettrie (1709–51), who had proposed in his *L'Homme machine* (1747) that human beings are mechanisms that function without a special deity. La Mettrie, a favourite of Frederick II and member of the Berlin Academy, was presumably known to Mitchell.

## Friday 3 August

[MEM. dated Saturday 4 August.] Yesterday you was baddish — You heard of Lord Baltimore destroying himself in Turkey, a warning against giving way to idle wild schemes. You must be constant to one good woman. At night you was too ludicrous. Jouez sans culottes — lhonneur de les oter, &c.[1] You are losing serious practice. Take up — Buy Parrassol — Write Father Somelsd — Maasd — Take Journ. with you.

[J.] A Swiss Gentleman who dined with us at Froment's, told me that Lord Baltimore[2] was living at Constantinople as a Turk, with his Seraglio arround him. He said that this nobleman was quite the man of english whim. He lived luxuriously, and enflamed his blood, then he grew melancholy & timorous, & was constantly taking medecines. In short he is there leading a strange wild life, useless to his country, uneasy to himself except when raised to a delirium and must soon destroy his constitution.[3] The Swiss very sensibly observed that the greatest kindness My Lord's Freinds could do him, would be to put him aboard a ship, feed him moderately on wholesome food, and make him work hard. By this means he might be restored to health & soundness of mind; after which, they might put his estate into his hands which he then might truly enjoy. Lord B was a Beacon to me. I trembled to think of my wild schemes.[4] At night Madame Muller a young Widow supt with us.[5] I was too ludicrous; but It was in order to kiss the widow, & heartily did I smack her little lips.

[1] MS. 'At night ... oter, &c.' scored out, possibly by JB. He made a separate record of this anecdote about a German lady who asked the classic question about what highlanders wear under their kilts. Assuming that JB was a highlander, she asked whether he practised

with his weapons in the morning without 'culottes' (underwear), whereupon he retorted that he did not, but that if she came to see him, he would gladly take them off ('Boswelliana', M 82).

[2] MS. All but the initial letter scored out by a modern hand, as also later in this entry.

[3] Frederick Calvert, 6th and last Baron Baltimore (1731–71), was spending a year in Constantinople. A descendant of George Calvert (1582–1632), first Baron Baltimore (from 1625), who had been granted the territory of Maryland shortly before his death, Lord Baltimore still owned this large American property. On his return to England, he would publish a prosaic travel book, *Tour of the East in the Years 1763 and 1764*, 1767 (which provides no details about his exotic experiences), as well as other undistinguished miscellaneous writings (see John G. Morris, 'The Lords Baltimore', *Maryland Historical Society Fund Publication* No. 8, 1874, pp. 6–16, 48–58). Continuing his licentious life, he would face trial for rape in 1768 and, though not condemned, would leave England under a cloud. The following year he would arrive in Vienna with a little harem of eight women, two black servants, and a doctor (Count Maximilian von Lam-

berg, *Le Mémorial d'un mondain*, 1774, pp. 110–11, quoted in *Grand Tour 1*, Heinemann pp. 47–48 n. 1, McGraw-Hill pp. 48–49 n. 2, which also gives more details about his scandalous life and unpleasant character). He would die in Naples, leaving the province of Maryland to Henry Harford, his illegitimate young son (Morris, p. 59).

The Swiss gentleman has not been identified.

[4] JB had recurring fantasies about living as a polygamous patriarch (see Journ. 14 Dec.).

[5] Very likely Christiane Louise Müller (born c. 1746), widow at the age of seventeen of the banker Carl Friedrich Müller, whom she had married in obedience to her father, the powerful businessman Johann Ernst Gotzkowsky (for whom see Journ. 30 Aug. and n. 3). Now a mere eighteen years old, she was presumably living with her father in the Brüderstrasse, close to the Kircheisen family, who would mention her in later letters (From Caroline Kircheisen, 2 Feb. 1765; From Henriette Kircheisen, [Feb. 1766]). She would marry Count Jean Baptiste de la Canorgue in 1767 but would soon be widowed again (*Adres-Calender*, 1764, p. 235; Hugo Rachel and Paul Wallich, *Berliner Grosskaufleute*, 2nd ed., ii. 458, 465–66).

## Saturday 4 August

[MEM. dated Sunday 5 August][1] [Y]esterday you din'd Heer President fine, & had Gateaus made. — [w]as quite Spaniard & cordial Gentleman [—] They were touchés to part — call'd Hubner — gave him glass — He saw you to Waggon — cold — wet — a little discontent — resolved just to lie by[2] till Brunswic.

[J.] This day I had fixed to set out for Brunswic. I dined Heer Presidents, and after dinner Madame made fine *Gateaus* (diet cakes) for me to eat upon my journey. Never was a fellow so kindly used as I am here. This little instance of attention shows a true cordiality. I was quite a Spaniard — a gallant Gentleman. I had hesitated much how to travel. I found that hiring a machine[3] or horses would cost me very dear, and I did not chuse to join company with any merchants or merchants clerks. I therefore took places in the *Post wagin*. Heer Hubner saw me mount, & fairly set off. The Post Waggon is a remain of barbarity of manners. It is just a large cart mounted upon very high wheels which jolt prodigiously. It has no covering, and has three or four deal boards laid across it, to serve for seats.[4] In this manner do the Germans travel night & day. It was wet, & I began to fret. However I fell upon an Expedient. I fixed my Attention on the court of Brunswic which I was going to visit, where I shou<ld> be very happy, and therefore all the intermediate time was to be considered as nothing. As I past thro' a wood before I entered Potzdam, a branch struck my eye & hurt me a good deal. It made me muse on the risque I had run of losing the half of one of my senses. I had time in the dark silence of night to ruminate on the great question concerning Providence. Should I now have said that Providence preserved my eye? But I pray you why did Providence permit the branch to strike me? O — that was a natural event: very well — & the degree of force was natural too; so that very naturally I have not lost my right eye. For shame divines how dare you bring in Providence on every trifling occasion. Nec deus intersit nisi dignus vindice nodus[5] — 'Tis true our heavenly Father sees every Sparrow that falls to the Ground. Yes — the Universal eye perceives every thing in the Universe. But surely, the grand and extensive System employs the attention of God, & the Minutiae are not to be considered as part of his care; at least we are not to presume that he interests himself in every little accident.[6] At Potzdam we stopt two hours. I laid myself down upon a timber stair and slept very sound.

[1] MS. 'Mad. K or Mad/ll/M/adam' written in a fine pen to the left of the date, perhaps the beginning of a note to the Kircheisen ladies.
[2] 'To keep quiet, withdraw from observation; to remain inactive, rest' (OED, s.v. 'lie, v.[1]', IV. 21.d).
[3] A coach; see Journ. 12 July n. 4.
[4] For a similar description of this com-

monly used conveyance, see Nugent, ii. 67.
[5] 'Nor must God intervene except in great matters' (Horace, Ars Poetica, l. 191).
[6] For the sparrow image, see Matt. 10: 29–31, and An Essay on Man, Epistle I, ll. 87–88. The passage as a whole echoes Pope's argument in this poem about Providence and God's general laws (Epistle I, ll. 113–16, 145–48).

## Sunday 5 August

[MEM. dated Monday 6 August] [Y]esterday better — well jaded — no Philosophy.

[J.] I was well jaded. I had a Jew and many other Blackguards with me.[1] I past by the name of Heer Sheridán, francois Coufman nag Berlin.[2] I was too tired to speculate.

[1] JB here accepts a stereotype, common in his period, of the Jew as rogue and cheat (Felsenstein, pp. 55–57). Viewed with suspicion as aliens, and expelled repeatedly from German territories from the thirteenth to the fifteenth centuries, Jews had been returning in the last hundred years, subject to restrictions in places of residence, choices of occupation, and special taxes. The Jew seen by JB was very likely one of the poorer Askenazim who had settled in Germany and Holland or had recently immigrated from Poland (Leo Trepp, Geschichte der deutschen Juden, 1996, pp. 42–44, 52–54, 66–67; Moses A. Shulvass, From East to West, 1971, pp. 51–70).
JB had had little opportunity for personal contact with Jews. In England, where they had been expelled by Edward I in 1290, some had returned under Cromwell in the mid-1650s and others under Charles II in

the 1660s (see Cecil Roth, 'The Resettlement of Jews in England', Three Centuries of Anglo-Jewish History, ed. V. D. Lipman, 1961, pp. 1–25; for their subsequent varying experiences, see David S. Katz, The Jews in the History of England, 1485–1850, 1994, pp. 211–72). But hardly any Jews had settled in Scotland by JB's time (see A. Levy, 'The Origins of Scottish Jewry', The Jewish Historical Society of England 19, Transactions, Sessions 1955–59 [1960]: 129–38, 141). JB's reference may have been influenced by Charles Macklin's portrayal of Shylock, which had been acclaimed on the London stage from 1741. JB may have heard of this portrayal in London, even though he seems not to have seen Macklin's performance and would not meet him until 1769 (Felsenstein, pp. 168–80; James Shapiro, Shakespeare and the Jews, 1996, pp. 214–15). Later JB would visit two synagogues in London and give their worshippers a 'sympathetic reconsideration' (Journ. 4 Apr. 1772; see Irma Lustig, 'Boswell and the Descendants of Venerable Abraham', *Studies in English Literature, 1500–1900* 14 [1974]: 436–48).

The 'other Blackguards' are not identified.

[2] Possibly JB used this assumed name and styled himself a merchant because he was embarrassed to travel in a common post wa-

gon. Thomas Sheridan, to whom he would write the following day, seems to have been already on his mind, and he may have remembered that 'Jacques Sheridan' had been the name taken in 1747 by James Sheridan, founder of the family's French branch (Walter Sichel, *Sheridan*, 1909, i. 214–15).

## Monday 6 August

[MEM. dated Tuesday 7 August.] [Y]esterday still well ideas alter — let 'em do so — & alter back again. At night stable — German lass & freem'd Man little fun[1] — Magdebourg &c.

[J.] My ideas alter — very well. Let them alter back again. We stopped some hours at Magdebourg. I felt an unusual glow of feeling at this renowned City so famous for it's dreadfull sack by the Austrian General Thili, of which the King of Prussia speaks in one of his Cantos on the art of war.[2] It is a large City very well fortified and has many good houses. Prince Ferdinand of Brunswic is Governour of it.[3] It was a sweet, warm day. I went & saw the Great church, which is noble. I saw there several relics.[4] I was all devotion, and fit to enter into the Society of blessed spirits. All my former sufferings did me no harm. I heard *Horae* solemnly sung.[5] I was quite happy. Why do I like Wharton indulge the 'lust of praise'?[6] Why seek to please all? Why fear the censure of those whom I despise? Let me boldly pursue my own Plan. I now adored my God with holy confidence and implored his influence to preserve my mind from the clouds of gloom, above all from sad notions of his infinite majesty. I began an Epistle on Parliament to Dempster. I was rich in ideas.[7] I wrote a letter to Mr. Sheridan in which I said that all my extravagancies had been occasioned by my nervous disorder which he himself was also subject to.[8] I wrote well & with vivacity; yet discovered a despondency of making any considerable figure. To make a fair tryal how much I depend on my body, I went to bed in noble glow, & by only sleeping a few hours with my cloaths on, in a soft bed, I was relaxed[9] so as to get up sick & dismal.

[1] MS. 'German ... fun' scored out by a modern hand. The girl and the 'freem'd Man' ('fremder Mann': stranger) appear to have been involved in some sort of joke, practical or otherwise.

[2] Johann Tserclaes, Count of Tilly (1559–1632), Flemish general and commander-in-chief of the Catholic League in the Thirty Years War, had won a great victory over Christian IV of Denmark at Magdeburg on 20 May 1631. Tilly's forces, mainly Austrians, had engaged in an orgy of pillaging and violence that took the lives of an estimated 30,000 inhabitants (Heinrich Rath-

mann, *Geschichte der Stadt Magdeburg*, 4 vols., 1800–06, iv, pt. 2, 266–87, 294). Frederick II had acknowledged Tilly's greatness as military leader but had deplored his brutality (*L'Art de la guerre*, 1751, Chant IV):

Tilly, en combattant pour l'aigle des Césars,
De l'éclat de son nom remplit les champs de Mars;
Mais un nuage sombre en obscurcit la gloire,
Son nom fut effacé du temple de Mémoire;
De Magdebourg sanglant les lamentables voix
Éternisent sa honte, et non pas ses exploits.

[3] Magdeburg was so strongly fortified because it was the most easterly outpost of Prussia (*Provinz Sachsen Anhalt*, ed. Berent Schwineköper, 1987, *Handbuch der Historischen Städten Deutschlands*, xi. 311; Brockhaus, xi. 777). Prince Ferdinand, serving as the King of Prussia's deputy, had been its governor from 1755 to 1757 and was so again from 1763 to 1766.

[4] The cathedral was a monumental building, primarily in Gothic and partly still in romanesque style (*Magdeburg*, Monographien Deutscher Städte, 1912, ii. 48–49). It had been spared by Tilly perhaps because its hoard of treasures had made it a sacred Catholic site. The most famous of its many relics were the cranium and other body parts of St. Maurice, a Roman leader (Mauritius) who had been killed for his Christianizing activities in 298 A.D. after leading the Theban legion over the Alps into the Valais. His remains had been brought to Magdeburg by the Emperor Otto the Great (912–73), who had considered Maurice his patron saint (Rathmann, i. 40, 51; E. Schubert, *Der Dom in Magdeburg*, 1994, p. 45; Gottfried Wentz and Berent Schwineköper, *Das Erzbistum Magdeburg*, 1972, *Die Bistümer der Kirchenprovinz Magdeburg*, i. pt. 1, pp. 216–18, with inventory of the relics acquired from 1166 to 1451, pp. 222–40).

[5] *Horae*, literally 'Hours': one of the seven canonical hours at which religious services were performed. Since JB had arrived in Magdebourg earlier in the day, he presumably attended either one of the afternoon services or Vespers in the evening.

[6] JB was recalling Pope's lines on Philip, Duke of Wharton (1698–1731), in *Moral Essays*, i. 180–81:

Wharton, the scorn and wonder of our days,
Whose ruling Passion was the Lust of Praise.

For the erratic behaviour and astonishing career of the Duke, see Mark Blackett-Ord, *Hell-Fire Duke: The Life of the Duke of Wharton*, 1982.

[7] JB's 'Parliament. An Epistle To George Dempster Esq. Written from Prussia in the year 1764' (M 278) and 'Parliament a Poem To Mr. Dempster, Written from Prussia' (M 279) were parts of a work in progress which brought together lines composed in Holland and Prussia in 1763–64, and would include others composed in Italy in 1765. Written variously in a heroic, serious, or jocular vein, largely in couplets with a few prose paragraphs interspersed, the lines versified several strands of JB's scattered thoughts: his friendship with GD; the glory of Prussia in peace after war; the dreariness of living among the Dutch; the shortcomings of William of Orange (1650–1702), who became William III of England in 1689; loyalty to the present English monarchy; melancholy; overly youthful M.P.'s; and his own ideals if he were to enter Parliament. A brief passage characterizes GD as Republican and JB himself as loyal monarchist. The lines would never be reworked into a coherent whole.

GD, a Scot born in Dundee, Forfarshire, and somewhat older than JB, shared many of his interests. He had supported JB's first printed verses by writing one of the three 'critical recommendatory letters' prefixed to *An Elegy on the Death of an Amiable Young Lady*, 1761. He had collaborated with JB and AE on their *Critical Strictures on the New Tragedy* attacking David Mallet's *Elvira* (see Journ. 30 July n. 4). He had frequently accompanied JB to the theatre in Edinburgh and London (*Earlier Years*, pp. 64, 102). More importantly, GD had chosen a professional path which JB could take as a model. He had begun in the law, being admitted advocate in Edinburgh in 1755, and had moved on to politics, being elected M.P. for the Perth Burghs in 1761 (see *Corr.* 9, p. 56 n. 1). GD would remain in Parliament until 1790, often defending Scottish interests (Namier and Brooke, ii. 313–14). For his political views, see Journ. 3 Dec. and n. 43; *Corr.* 6, p. 40 n. 4.

[8] This letter would not survive.

[9] That is, 'enfeebled'; see Journ. 8 July n. 4.

## Tuesday 7 August

[MEM. dated Wednesday 8 August] Jogged on – arrived at Brunswic — quite Laird of Auchinleck — but not right ballanced — It will come — quarters gold arm resolved break assoc ideas. Great coat &c. & boots — & Presb Kirk each day [—] yesterday Luters Kirk.

Have a care or your'e gone; command passions better.[1]

[J.] I jogged on. I stopped at *Konig's Luters*: having taken an *extra Post* for the last stage, in order to enter Brunswic as a Gentleman.[2] In the Church-yard of *Konig's Luters* I met an old Gentleman in a dark, shabby dress. I asked him if he was a Clergyman. 'Non,' said he; 'Cantor sum.'[3] I went & saw the great church here. It stands high, and is an excellent old building.[4] At night I arrived at Brunswic, & put up where My Lord Marischal & I were, at the *gulden arm*.[5] I was quite the Laird of Auchinleck serious and calm.

[1] MS. 'Have care ... better' scored out along left margin.

[2] The 'Extra Post' was a post-chaise for a single person. As a private conveyance, it was obviously more high-class than the post-wagon JB had taken from Berlin. In Königslutter he was now 15 miles (24.1 km) east of Brunswick.

[3] 'I am the cantor'; that is, '[h]e whose duty it is to lead the singing in a church; a precentor' (OED, s.v. 'cantor', 2).

[4] A Romanesque church with a central tower 190 feet (57.9 m) high, regarded as 'the most beautiful basilica in North Germany' (Gustav Neumann, *Geographisches Lexikon*

*des Deutschen Reichs*, 1883, i. 612). It owed its beauty primarily to Niccoló da Ficarolo (fl. c. 1106–40), sculptor and architect, who had worked also on the cathedral of Ferrara and the major pilgrimage church of Verona ('Nicholaus', *Dict. of Art*, xxiii. 101–02; Martin Gosebruch and Thomas Gädeke, *Königslutter*, 1985).

[5] It had taken JB three days to cover the 143 miles (230.1 km) from Berlin to Brunswick. The Goldene Arm was situated on the Gördelingerstrasse at the corner of Kaffeetwete [*sic*], a good ten minutes' walk from the palace (letter from Dr. M. Garzmann, Director, Stadtarchiv Brunswick, 22 Sept. 1997).

## *Wednesday 8 August*

[MEM. dated Thursday 9 August] [Y]esterday you awaked relaxed but by exercise drove off. Was indolent — drest paid visits, & was invited to court — Officer to Prince Ferd — said toujours lire et ecrire et devot matin ses prierres chapitre &c [—] remember'd Mother her tender care & resolved to be good humoured & by superior strength of mind to make her gay — This is real. Write her so & God will assist you[1] — Then Hered Court — then German Comedy & Ballet — quite fine.[2] Ball court & supper two eclesiastics &c.[3] This day walk an hour — then Feronce then dress & think.

Your'e well & can be with no girls except sure ones.

Have a care or health & purse ruin.[4]

[J.] I payed visits to Feronce, Stanmer and to M. *de Baeswitz* Grand maitre du Duc.[5] I had immediatly an invitation to dine at court. I went before two, & found an agreable reception from every body & was again presented to the reigning family. *Le Baron de Ples aid-de camp* to Prince Ferdinand, is a brave, worthy, amiable young man.[6] He said 'Duc Ferdinand est un digne homme. Il est toujours occupé. Il lit et il ecrit beaucoup. Cest un Prince extremement devot. Tous les matins regulierrement il fait ses prières, et il lit dans la sainte ecriture. Il est toujours poli et il a l'humeur bien egal. Pendant la guêrre Il fit tout ce qu'il pouvoit pour adoucir les misêres inevitables; au lieu que le Roi de Prusse fut sans humanité. Je lai vu passer des pauvres blessés et se tourner les yeux á l'autre coté.'[7] After dinner, I waited on the Hereditary Prince and Princess; then went to a German Comedy,[8] then supt at Court. It was a glorious change after all my Posting fatigues.

[1] One of JB's rare references to his mother, Euphemia (Erskine) Boswell (1718–66), Lady Auchinleck, noteworthy for being so affectionate. Extremely pious, she belonged to an austere sect of Calvinists and also seems to have sympathized with the evangelism of the Methodist George Whitefield (1714–70). She had introduced JB to the grimmer aspects of her religion, notably the doctrine of the eternity of punishment for sinners (see 'Ébauche de ma vie', App. 2, III.A). So opposed was she to worldly amusements that she had cried bitterly on the one occasion when she had been taken to the theatre (see the unfinished first draft of the 'Ébauche de ma vie', Yale MS. L 1108, App. 2, III.B). JB's letter to her would not survive, the only extant one addressed to her being the stiffly formal condolences JB had written at the age of fourteen on the death of her newborn son (17 July 1754, L127, *Catalogue*, i. 159; *Earlier Years*, pp. 11–12, 25–26).

[2] Such entertainment was provided by the troupe of Konrad Ernst Ackermann (1710–71), which had just been recalled to Brunswick for a five-week stay after the success of its first season in 1763 (Heinrich Sievers, *250 Jahre Braunschweigisches Staatstheater, 1690–1940*, 1941, p. 69). The troupe was known for performing German plays (see note 8 below) and for ballets featuring Friedrich Ludwig Schroeder (1744–1816), the twenty-year-old son of Mme Ackermann (1714–92), whose previous marriage to the organist Schroeder had been dissolved (*Deutsches Biographisches Archiv*). The younger Schroeder would soon become 'the most famous actor and theatrical entrepreneur of the 18th century' (ADB, xxx. 506).

[3] Not identified.

[4] MS. 'Your'e ... ones' written along the top of the page; 'Have ... ruin' written along the left margin, both scored out by a modern hand. Evidently JB feared having to pay for costly medical treatments if he contracted a venereal disease again, as he had in London (see Journ. 22 Jan.–27 Feb. 1763).

[5] Henning Adam, Baron von Bassewitz (c. 1731–70), had been named *Oberkammerjunker* (chief chamberlain) in Apr. of this year after serving as *Schlosshauptmann* (captain of the palace guard) from 1762 (*Hof Etat*, p. 2; 3 Alt 552, pp. 28, 32). He would be appointed *Kammerherr* (gentleman-in-waiting) in Aug. 1765, privy counsellor in May 1766 (3 Alt 552, pp. 35, 37), and Brunswickian envoy to the imperial Diet, the legislative assembly of the Holy Roman Empire in Ratisbon, from June 1766 to the end of his life (3 Alt 554; *Fortgesetzte Neue Genealogisch-Historische Nachrichten*, 1762–75, vii. 288, x. 621).

[6] Christian Ludwig Gottlob von Plessen (1738–98) had been named *Kammerjunker* (chamberlain) on 7 Feb. 1763 after serving as *Hofjunker* (court page) from 1760 (Nds.StAWf 39 Slg Part 1; 1 Alt 25 228–228/1). He came from a family with roots in the thirteenth century and with many branches in Mecklenburg. Plessen would be named *Rittmeister der Garde du Corps* (captain in the Duke's cavalry) in 1766 but would resign before 1771 (Nds.StAWf 39 Slg Part 1). He would be married twice, the second time to Angela Ferrario (d. 1822 in Milan), and would die in Mantua (*Die Plessen*, ed. M. Naumann, 2nd. ed. Helmold von Plessen, 1971, p. 102).

Cuno Burchard von Plessen (1701–Oct. 1764), mistakenly identified as JB's 'de Pless' in *Grand Tour I* (Heinemann p. 342, McGraw-Hill p. 348), worked in the service of Hanover from 1724 to 1763 (*Die Plessen*, p. 87). This mistaken identification continued in *Catalogue*, i. 335, iii. 860, and in *Corr. 5*, p. 85.

[7] Prince Ferdinand's humanitarian spirit was well known. When congratulated on his victory at Crefeld in 1758, he deplored the sight of the dead and wounded with the words: 'This is the tenth spectacle of this sort that I have seen in my life. Would to God that it were the last!' (J. W. von Archenholtz, *Geschichte des siebenjährigen Krieges*, 1788, p. 115). Frederick II, in contrast, had the reputation of being harsh and deliberately inspiring fear in his troops (Georg Heinrich von Berenhorst, *Betrachtungen über die Kriegskunst 1797–99*, 3rd. ed. 1827, pp. 194–95; Christopher Duffy, *The Military Life of Frederick the Great*, 1986, p. 245). Yet anecdotes about his kindness to his soldiers and his distress about casualties in battle are also recorded (Duffy, pp. 120, 240).

[8] Not identified. The performance of a German play on this day as well as on 9 and 17 Aug. attests to a new interest in drama written in the native language. Before the war French drama had dominated the Brunswick stage (Karl Hoppe, 'Die deutsche Theaterreform und ihre Krönung', *275 Jahre Theater Braunschweig*, ed. C.-H. Bachmann, G. Frank, 1965, pp. 44–45; see Journ. 27 June n. 9). In 1765, with the support of Gotthold Ephraim Lessing (1729–81), Ackermann's troupe would establish a national theatre in Hamburg (see Fritz Hartmann, *Sechs Bücher Braunschweigischer Theater-Geschichte*, 1905, pp. 190–91).

The plays were performed at the Comödienhaus, a small theatre built in the central location of the Burgplatz in 1749 by the theatre-loving Duke Karl (Ribbentrop, i. 220).

## Thursday 9 August

[MEM. dated Friday 10 August.]¹ [Y]esterday you walked with Feronce & saw *Foir* & said Life like Portraits should be drawn when one is present & not in *Umbra*.² You dined Hered Prince & after dinner spoke Germans³ with Princess & him; & talked of Madll. Kirkheisen was too *young*. Contesse *Echet*⁴ spoke to You. At *Operétte* was gay [—] madll. spoke ill of you in Allemand. You said Je ne puis pas en Anglois, mais Je le pense. Thought to write Johnson & swear everlasting Attachment while alive & shade when dead. One existence only; if mad, who can help? Right *to be* no more.⁵

[J.] I walked with Feronce in the Fair ou J'etois agreablement etourdi.⁶ I dined chez the Hereditary Prince, & talked lively but too young, from my sad timourous education. At night I was very gay at a pretty operétte.⁷ I sat in the Dukes *loge* and was fine with the Ladies of the Court. Was not this quite as I could wish? My mind was clear & firm & fertile. It contained in itself both male and female powers: brilliant fancys were begotten and brilliant fancys were brought forth. I saw my error in suffering so much from the contemplation of others. I can never be them; therefore let me not vainly attempt it, in imagination; therefore let me not envy the gallant and the happy, nor be shocked by the nauseous and the wretched. I must be Mr. Boswell of Auchinleck and no other. Let me make him as perfect as possible. I think were I such a one, I should be happy indeed, were I such another, I should be wretched indeed, without considering that were I realy these People, I could not have the same ideas of their situation, as I now have; for no man has of himself the notion that other People have of him; especially those who know him little. I considered also the absurdity of my reasoning in low spirits. What gloomy nonsense have I often imagined! I recollected my moments of despair when I did not value myself at Sixpence because forsooth I was but an Individual, & an Individual is nothing in the multitude of Beings. Whereas *I* am all to myself. I have but one existence. If it is a mad one, I cannot help it. I must do my best. Amidst all this brilliance, I sent forth my Imagination to the Inner Temple, to the chambers of Mr. Samuel Johnson. I glowed with reverence and affection, and a romantic idea filled my mind. To have a certain support at all times I determined to write to this great man, and beg that he might give me 'a solemn assurance of perpetual freindship' so that I might march under his protection while he lived and after his death imagine that his shade beckoned me to the Skies; Grand! yet enthusiastic Idea!⁸

¹ 'My Lor' written at the top left of the page in a different pen and ink, apparently the start of a letter addressed to Lord Mari-schal.
² For 'Life like Portraits', see Journ. 16

Aug. *In umbra*, literally 'in the shade', fig-uratively 'in the study', may have been sug-gested by the phrase 'studia in umbra edu-cata' by Tacitus, whom JB had been reading in Holland (*Annales*, xiv. 53; Lewis and

Short, 'Umbra', 4; Journ. 8, 24, 27 Sept., 5, 7 Oct., 21 Dec. 1763, *Holland*, Heinemann pp. 19, 31, 37, 39, 42, 94, McGraw-Hill pp. 20, 32, 38, 40, 43, 97; see also To WJT, 23 Sept. 1763, *Corr*. 6, p. 69).

[3] An idiosyncratic usage (see also Mem. dated 2 Sept. and n. 1; Journ. 8 Sept. and n. 2, 6 Oct. and n. 11).

[4] Not identified further.

[5] MS. 'if mad, who' and 'right ... more' scored out by a modern hand. The text is based on a transcription by an earlier Yale editor.

[6] The fair took place on the 'Kohlmarkt' ('coal-market'), where goods of many different types and from many different places were displayed in outdoor stands or in the 'Messe Gewölbe' (vaulted chambers) built into the first floor of the houses used by merchants (Ribbentrop, i. 109). The fair not only contributed to the economic well being of the city but also greatly enlivened its social and cultural activities (Hans Jürgen Querfurth, 'Wirtschafts- und Verkehrsgeschichte', Moderhack, *Braunschweigische Landesgeschichte*, p. 184).

[7] Not identified.

[8] SJ lived at 1, Inner Temple Lane from 1760 to 1765 (Henry B. Wheatley and Peter Cunningham, *London Past and Present*, 1891, ii. 257). JB would write this letter, in a similarly enthusiastic vein, seven weeks later (Journ. 30 Sept. 1764) but send it only in June 1777 (see *Life* iii. 122 n. 2).

## Friday 10 August

[MEM. dated Saturday 11 August] Yesterday you waited on Feronce grew gloomy. But knew disease.[1] Din'd *Cour* grew well. Then Opera. Quite splendid — quite in spirits. Honest Prince Ferd's man showed Cath Church ask his name[2] — At night well. This day write Johnson give some of your wild dreary fancies & conclude you'll be directed steady by Him &c. &c. & so be allways proud — also Sommelsd Maasd Spaen &c. Dine Cour — French Comedy.[3]

Say to Johns as in Pref to Dict. that all all — were empty names to you.[4]

X mem still but one exist. & none knows futurity.[5]

[J.] The little gloom which I now feel of a morning seems a mere trifle. Instead of those thick, heavy clouds which prest me down at Utrecht, I find only thin dusky vapours, and they are soon dispersed. After dining at Court, *De Ples* & I walked in the Piazzas of the Palace, & in the Garden.[6] He asked me what could occasion Melancholy? & with easy composure I gave him a lecture on that distemper. Then he talked of Religion and carried me to see a catholic church.[7] I then went to the opera, which at Brunswic is very noble. The House is large, and the Decorations much finer than in London.[8] The Performers were very good. The Piece was *Enea in Lazona* Æneas in Latium. He who played Turnus was no Eunuch & had a bold manly voice with which he did wonders — one air in which occurr<ed> *rivale* — and another in which occurred *la traditore* struck me prodigiously.[9] I had no notion of being so much affected by music. My Hypochondriack deadness is allmost forgot. How happy am I now. I dined at court, and after this noble Opera I returned to Court & supt elegant & grand.

[1] MS. 'But ... disease' scored out by a modern hand. By 'disease' JB presumably meant his 'gloom' or depression.

[2] The man has not been identified. For the Catholic Church, see n. 7.

[3] Not identified.

[4] MS. 'Say ... you', written at the top of the page, alluding to the end of SJ's Preface: 'I have protracted my work till most of those whom I wished to please have sunk into the grave, and success and miscarriage are empty sounds ...'.

[5] MS. 'X mem ... futurity' written along the left margin.

[6] 'Piazzas' were covered arcades on the ground floor of the main building and its wings (OED, s.v. 'piazza', 2). The garden, behind the left wing, was partly in the formal, geometric French style and partly in the looser, more natural English style (Ribbentrop, i. 189–94). Both JB and Plessen would later recall their walks with pleasure (To Plessen, 15 Oct. 1764, Yale MS. L 1075; From Plessen, 19 Nov. 1766, *Corr. 5*, p. 85).

[7] St. Nicolai, the only Catholic church in Brunswick, was situated near the Steinthor. It had been built in 1710–12 by the architect Korb by order of the great Duke Anton Ulrich (1633–1714), who had converted to Catholicism a year earlier (Wolfgang Kelsch, *Hermann Korb*, 1985, p. 58). Thanks to the prevailing religious tolerance encouraged by J. F. W. Jerusalem, the Catholic minority lived peacefully together with the dominant Lutherans, though Catholics were not allowed to own property; see Ribbentrop, i. 129, ii. 62–64, 88.

[8] Operas were performed in the *Gran Ducal Teatro* at the Hagenmarkt, a former town hall that housed the stage while an extension accommodated 1,100 to 1,200 spectators. The building, opened in 1690, had been converted into the theatre at the behest of Duke Anton Ulrich at the cost of 27,000 Taler to entertain the visitors to the two annual fairs. It was famous for its picturesque 'decorations', a term JB uses in the sense of 'scenery on the stage' (OED, s.v.

'decoration', 2). The elaborately painted stage sets, which could be quickly rolled sideways or hoisted up and down, had been designed by Johann Oswald Harms (1643–1708) and then improved once the court was permanently in residence in Brunswick from 1753 (Horst Richter, *Johann Oswald Harms*, Die Schaubühne: Quellen und Forschungen zur Theatergeschichte, 1963, lviii. 66–76). The opera house itself had also been renovated under Duke Karl I (Yorck Alexander Haase, 'Theater', Moderhack, *Braunschweigische Landesgeschichte*, p. 304; Heinrich Sievers, *250 Jahre Braunschweigisches Staatstheater 1690–1940*, 1941, p. 68).

[9] *Enea nel Lazio* ('Aeneas in Latium') includes several arias in which Turnus complains of Lavinia's treachery (I. end; II. iii; III. vi, Nds.StAWf 46 Alt 456–58; see also Klaus Kindler, *Findbuch zum Bestand Musikalien des herzoglichen Theaters in Braunschweig*, Veröffentlichungen der Niedersächsischen Archivverwaltung 13 [1990], pp. 231, 238). The composer was Tomaso Traetta (1727–79); the librettist, Vittorio Amedeo Cigna-Santi (1725–85; correcting *Grand Tour 1*, Heinemann p. 53 n. 1, McGraw-Hill p. 54 n. 6). It had been performed on 1 Aug. to celebrate the Duke's birthday (Duchess of Brunswick to Frederick of Prussia, 2 Aug. 1764, *Aus den Briefen der Herzogin Philippine Charlotte von Braunschweig*, ed. Hans Droysen, Quellen und Forschungen zur Braunschweigischen Geschichte, 1916, viii. 190).

## Saturday 11 August

[MEM. dated Sunday 12 August.] [Y]esterday you breakfasted Vaneck & Gov. [—] Swiss — then waited on Abbé Jerus. Saw great Library, & resolved to have one. He talked of K Pruss' seising lidee presenté vivement & si la relig Chret etoit presenté bien coloré &c. You Sustained freewill with Spirit. He talked of the Gualteris noire &c. and of German in England whom he relievd mais a la fin se tuoit.[1] Own'd[2] he had sufferd but God helped — You also owned & boasted Heroism. Talk freely to him. Court — French Comedie. This day up early write Johnson free — then Masks at Vaneck's then De Pless & music. Evening Letters.

Think what treasure will be Journal.[3]

[J.] I breakfasted with Sir Joshuah Van Eck's Son[4] and his Swiss Governour.[5] They answered precisely to my ideas. I then waited on M. l'Abbé Jerusalem, who received me with cordial Joy. I found him in his Library.[6] It pleased me, and I resolved to have a very large and good one at Auchinleck.[7] He gave me an exact idea de l'esprit du Roy de Prusse. 'Monsieur il a beaucoup d'imagination. Il se saisit de la premiêrre idée qui se present agreablement, et Je suis sure si la Religion Chretienne lui etoit presentée bien colorée, Il sera tout d'un coup frappé de sa beauté;' 'et peutetre (said I) Il seroit le plus grand Entousiaste, et ecrirait un Poême magnifique au louange de sa foy'.[8] We started fate & freewill. The good Abbé was affraid to doubt of a quality which he had been allways accustomed to attribute to the Divinity to wit an universal Prescience even of the actions of men and would maintain the scholastic notion that certain foreknowledge did not restrain the liberty of acting.[9] I boldly opposed the Prescience and clearly defended my liberty.[10] I beleive I have not yet mentioned in this my Journal, the melancholy story of M. Gualteri who travelled with young Mackenzie of Seaforth. It happened just before I was first at Brunswic. He was a mighty pretty man: but dreadfully melancholy; He supt at the Hereditary Prince's, where he seemed very happy & played charmingly on the flute. That very night he was seised with a dismal fit, got out of bed, & threw himself from a window three stories high. He was not killed, but bruised in the most shocking manner so that he was at this time half putrify'd and in horrid anguish wishing for immediate death yet finding that the cruel ennemy approached him with slow steps. The Abbé said Il a dit qu'il etoit faché que le coup lui avoit manqué, mais a present Je crois qu'il a des pensees plus justes, et que la Religion lui fournit de la consolation.[11] Son frere a l'esprit d'un ange: mais aussi les idêes les plus noires et une impatience extrême. Il venoit ici voir le pauvre malheureux; mais il n'osoit pas rester, au peur qu'il ne feroit la même chose que son frêre'.[12] The Abbé then owned to me that he himself had suffered most severely from the Hypochondria. Il est etonnant (said he) quelle force peut avoir l'imagination, quoique votre raison reste entiêrre, et vous etes convaincu que l'imagination est derangée. He said that he had great satisfaction from having born it with Patience & that God had helped him. He said he was often terrified lest au quelque moment de desespoir l'imagination la fera se tuer.[13] It is impossible to conceive the satisfaction which I had at hearing that this excellent Person had fought with the Dæmon as I have done, & that he had conquered him; for, he told me, Il est passé. I told him freely what I had endured at Utrecht, and how I thought myself a Heroe.[14] When I[15] rose to leave him, he took me cordially by the hand, & said 'Mon cher Monsieur, soyez assuré que mon estime pour vous est bien fixée. C'est ne pas a cause de votre naissance, mais a cause de votre esprit, votre cœur, et votre maniêrre de penser. Vous pouvez aller ou vous voulez, dans les coins de la terre les plus eloignés; Je ne vous oublierai jamais.' This sincere compliment from a learned & amiable Lutheran Abbé who had the honour to educate The Hereditary Prince of Brunswic, gave me uncommon satisfaction.[16] I shall remember it all my life. He agreed to corespond with me.[17] After dining at court I went to the french Comedie.[18] At night Indolence made me think: Why give myself so much labour to write this Journal, in which I realy do not insert much that can be called usefull — Beg your pardon. Does it not contain a faithfull Register of my variations of mind? Does it not contain many ingenious observations & pleasing strokes which can afterwards be enlarged? Well, but I may die. True but I may live, & what a rich treasure for my after days will be this my Journal.

[1] The German suicide has not been identified.

[2] MS. 'oun'd'

[3] MS. 'Think … Journal' written along the left margin.

[4] Sir Joshua Vanneck would be described as 'one of the richest merchants in Europe' in his obituary (*Gent. Mag.* Mar. 1777, xlvii. 147). Dutch by birth, he had come to London in 1722, had made a fortune in commerce, and had been created baronet in 1751. His son was either Gerard William Vanneck (c. 1743–91), later M.P. for Dunwich from 1768 to 1790 (Namier and Brooke, iii. 573), or Joshua Henry Vanneck (1745–1816; *Comp. Bar.* v. 98).

[5] Joel-Gaspard Monod (1717–83) had recently become young Vanneck's tutor after returning from a four-year stay in Guadeloupe. He had been ordained as minister in his native Geneva in 1741 or 1742 and, having gone to Guadeloupe when it was in British hands, had served as pastor to the reformed French church from 1759 and chaplain to the governor from 1760 to 1763 (J. Monod, *Cent-soixante-quinze ans 1793–1968: les Monod et leurs alliés*, 1969, pp. 8–9). He had translated Samuel Richardson's *Sir Charles Grandison* (pub. Leiden 1757, 2nd ed. 1764, see Montet, ii. 186). JB would meet Monod again in Geneva (see Journ. 30 Dec. and n. 3).

[6] Jerusalem's library, in his house at 3 Steinstrasse, was so substantial that the auction after his death would be scheduled at his house for two days, 25 and 26 Jan. 1790 (*Braunschweig und Umgebung*, 1877, p. 141; No. 6, *Braunschweigische Anzeigen*, Jan. 1790). The catalogue would not survive.

[7] At Auchinleck JB would indeed assemble a good library, consisting of 1250 volumes primarily of ancient and modern literature and history (Margaret Boswell, 'Catalogue of the Auchinleck library', Yale MS. C 437.6, c. summer 1783). It included the 'very curious collection of the Classicks and other Books' assembled by JB's father as mentioned in JB's will (*Pride and Negligence*, p. 8).

[8] JB had already heard Andrew Mitchell's doubts about Jerusalem's possible success in converting Frederick II (Journ. 27 July).

[9] Jerusalem, drawing on the Leibnizien concept of 'preexisting harmony', emphasized the harmonious coming together of divine foreknowledge and the human will. He regarded the foreknowledge of an omniscient, benevolent deity as axiomatic but also believed in a feeling that impels human beings freely to choose the good (*Betrachtungen über die vornehmsten Wahrheiten der Religion*, 1768, i. 75, 277–88, 297, 302; Wolfgang Erich Müller, *Johann Friedrich Wilhelm Jerusalem*, 1984, pp. 97–98, 109–13, 174–80).

[10] JB here accepts the notion of free will more confidently than in his recent talk with Andrew Mitchell (see Journ. 2 Aug. and n. 1). Yet a few weeks later JB would be less sure again. Having realized that the conversation with Jerusalem had been inconclusive and that he himself had defended free will too vehemently, JB would concede that some ideas could come to mind involuntarily through the workings of memory (To Jerusalem, c. 16 Nov., Yale MS. L 654). Such religious questions would remain unresolved for JB for the rest of his life and would lead him to several vain attempts to gain reassurances from SJ (see *Life*, 10 Oct. and 26 Oct. 1769, ii. 82, 104; 15 Apr. 1778, iii. 290–91; 20 Mar. 1781, iv. 71; 23 June 1784, iv. 329).

[11] Gualteri would die of his injuries many months after incurring them, as reported in the *Braunschweigische Anzeigen* 74 [14 Sept. 1765], p. 308, where he is identified as P. C. Gualtieri. When Mackenzie, who had returned to Britain, heard of his former tutor's fate, he sent £50 to the father, Samuel Melchisedec, and granted him an annuity of £100 the following year (Sir Andrew Mitchell to Alexander Burnett, 22 Mar. 1765; 17 Feb, 1766; Alexander Burnett to Sir Andrew Mitchell, 4 Mar. 1766, Burnett of Kemnay Archives, Bundle 82).

[12] This brother, Karl Albert Samuel Gualteri, had been continuing in his father's profession as Huguenot clergyman in Berlin (mentioned as 'Gualtieri' in Lehndorff, 4 March, 23 Apr., 22 July 1753, 5 Aug. 1758, *Dreissig Jahre*, pp. 58, 68, 90, 408). Socially ambitious, he would establish his provenance from a noble Italian family and would gain the right—for his father, himself, and his progeny—to prefix his name with 'von' or 'de' (Letter from Frederick II, 14 Oct. 1769, in Jean-Pierre Erman Nachlass #55, *Französische Kirche zu Berlin*).

[13] Jerusalem's son, Karl Wilhelm (1747–72), who was similarly afflicted with depression, would actually commit suicide. He would gain posthumous fame as the model for the hero in Goethe's autobiographical novel *Die Leiden des jungen Werther* (*The Sorrows of Young Werther*, 1774).

[14] JB's intermittent periods of depression while in Utrecht had reached crisis proportions after hearing of the death of his illegitimate son, Charles, at the age of fourteen months (Journ. 24 Mar., *Holland*, Heinemann p. 30 n. 2, McGraw-Hill p. 31 n. 2)

and again when fearing that his father would not permit him further travel. He had then rejoiced on recovering his good spirits (To WJT, 23 Mar., 17 Apr. c. 11 June 1764, *Corr.* 6, pp. 87, 90, 99–100; *Holland,* Heinemann pp. 272–73, McGraw-Hill pp. 281–82).

[15] MS. 'I I', slip of the pen.

[16] Jerusalem had originally come to Brunswick in 1742 to take charge of the Hereditary Prince's education (Müller, p. 4).

[17] No correspondence between Karl Wilhelm Ferdinand and JB is recorded (*Catalogue*).

[18] Not identified.

## Sunday 12 August

[MEM. dated Monday 13 August] [Y]esterday You breakfasted honest Baron de Pless & then went to Duke's Chappel & heard grand sacred Music Flutes Fiddles French horn Organ Trumpets — quite heavn thought of Johnson. Home & wrote — then Princess — & verses laugh'd — then din'd Court — music spoke much to Mad. Buick thought on Auch Kirk. You must think of Zelide [—] then Garden — then Concert then cards. Not invite supper — was mortify'd — 'twas weak. Could not sit up as fretfull & tomorrow ride at six [—] so write Johns fine & long.

[J.] I breakfasted with my worthy Baron de Ples, & then he conducted me to the Duke's Chapel, where I heard a Psalm performed with magnificent music, Eunuchs and other singers from the Opera, an Organ, a french-horn Flutes, fiddles trumpets.[1] It was quite heaven. I adored my God, and I hoped for immortal Joy.[2] It was realy grand to see the the serene family of Brunswic at their devotions. After Chapel was the levee of the Princess Hereditaire, this day being her Birth-day. The Court was in Grand Gala. Unluckily, I did not think of this before I left Berlin, so had only with me two suits of silk cloaths. However I past very well. Upon occasion were presented to the Princess English Verses by *G L. Hertel Lector and Teacher of the English Language at the Julius Charles University in Helmstedt.*[3] But such verses not Sternhold could exceed.[4] He said he had imagined it was very difficult to write Poetry; But, when he tried it now for the first time, he found it very easy. I asked him if he just found a kind of sudden inspiration. He said Yes. I wrote verses to him in his own stile, of which the following was a Stanza.

> Ye Muses nine! on english wings
>     A Poet German sails!
> Now may in Greenland Hams arise
>     And in Westphalia Whales!

As I found him a good creature, I did not present them to him. I have them together with his.[5] We had a prodigious company to dine at court and a most magnificent dinner. I eat by Madame de Boik Gouvernante to the young Princesses, an amiable pleasant old Lady.[6] Grand music played in an apartment adjoining, and round the Table was a vast crowd of Spectators. I confess that I was supremely elevated. I had the utmost pleasure of contrast by considering at this hour is assembled Auchinleck Kirk, and many a whine and many a sad look is found therein — But how shall I support it some time hence?[7] I know not, & let it not disturb me at present.

However, let me firmly resolve to drive off the *veteres Avias*.[8] Let me not encourage the least gloomy idea of Religion; but let me be firm & chearfull. After dinner we walked in the Garden, then had a concert at court, & then grand court in the Duke's Bedchamber where every Sunday he receives the compliments of his Subjects.[9] I played at Whist. I was not invited to Supper, & was weak enough to go home vexed a little. Such is a mind rendered too delicate by fine living. I however recollected that when there was such a crowd the Maréchal might easily forget me.[10]

[1] The chapel was situated in the left wing of the palace (Ribbentrop, i. 193). Duke Karl's permanent orchestra for this year included a conductor, twelve 'instrumentalists', and one male singer, evidently augmented by other singers on this occasion (*Hof Etat*, p. 19). Eunuchs (castrated as young boys to produce high-pitched voices of special timbre and wide range) were evidently still in vogue for church music and operas, showing an Italian influence (*New Grove 2*, s.v. 'castrato'). Duke Karl was spending freely on his chapel, opera, and theatre. His extravagance would increase in the following years and would bring Brunswick close to bankruptcy before he was curbed by the Hereditary Prince and Feronce in 1773 (see Journ. 27 June n. 8; Otto von Heinemann, *Geschichte von Braunschweig und Hannover*, 1892, iii. 290–98).

[2] The association of music and heaven had been established for JB by his first private tutor, the Rev. John Dun, who had promised him beautiful music in the afterlife if he behaved well (see 'Ébauche de ma vie', App. 2, III.A). The Duke's Sunday concert, which inspired JB with hopes of a joyful afterlife, differed greatly from the Calvinist sermons on hell and eternal punishment which had depressed him as a boy. It also differed greatly from the Dissenters 'roaring out the Psalms' which JB had heard recently in a London chapel (Journ. 15 May 1763).

[3] Georg Ludwig Hertell (c. 1700–81) had been appointed lector at the university in 1760 and also gave private English lessons to students at the Collegium Carolinum (Nds.StAWb 37 Alt No. 507). He had learned English during a stay in London after working as a wig maker (J. J. Eschenburg, *Entwurf einer Geschichte des Collegii Carolini*, 1812, p. 73).

The university, a Lutheran institution in Helmstedt about 18.5 miles (c. 29.8 km) from Brunswick, had been inaugurated in 1574 and named after its founder, Duke Julius Charles (1528–89). It had reached its heights in the sixteenth century—Giordano Bruno (1548–1600) had taught there in 1589—but was now beginning to decline ('Helmstedt', *Handbuch*, ii. 220; Ursula Schelm-Spangenberg, 'Schulen und Hochschulen', Moderhack, *Braunschweigische Landesgeschichte*, pp. 264–65).

[4] Thomas Sternhold (d. 1549), the chief early versifier of the Psalms, was notorious for his hackneyed phrasing forced into pedestrian ballad meter. His version, first published in 1549, had been supplemented by other translations and became the Sternhold-Hopkins Psalter (*The Whole Book of Psalms*), 1562, one of the most popular and influential books of its time (Rivkah Zim, *English Metrical Psalms*, 1987, pp. 112–51).

[5] Hertell's verses (Yale MS. M 280) in 28 quatrains include the following ambitious lines (printed in Helmstedt; JB's copy, Yale P 60):

> Awake my Muse! Ye graces all
> Attend! to grace my Lay,
> Inspire me oh allchearing Phoebe!
> To sing this glorious Day.

> Hail happy Morn! that gave the world
> And Brittain such a Treasure,
> A future Mother Brunsvics House
> Beyond all hope and measure.

> My Friends! let us with festive Joy
> This happy Day adorn,
> A Day that brought us so much Bliss
> When AUGUSTA was born ...

JB recorded only the funniest of his own stanzas, the third, in his journal but also wrote three others:

> Renowned Lector of Helmstedt
>     Thy Verses I have seen
> Which prove to me beyond dispute
>     That thou with Phoebe hast been

> The Royal Princess Augusta
>     Thou praised hast so meetly

That she no doubt must have cried out
O Hertell thou singst sweetly.

Great Bard Accept this tax of praise
Let it a trophy be.
Thou singst of Brunswic's *hups Princess
I sing great Bard of thee.

JB added: '*For the information of the english Reader it is necessary to say that in the
German tongue hups signifys beautifull or
pretty' (M 280). By 'hups' JB means *hübsch*,
'pretty'.

Hertell pronounced 'Phoebe' as a single
syllable ('Pheeb') and took her to be a muse.
JB followed suit in his first stanza.

[6] Frederique or Friederike (von Janvier)
von Poigk (d. 1799) had been the *Hofmeis-
terin* in the Duchess's retinue since 1756, and
as such was the second-ranking lady (*Hof
Etat*, p. 20; Nds.StAWf VI Hs 10 Nr. 9;
correcting *Grand Tour I*, Heinemann p. 57
n. 2, McGraw-Hill p. 59 n. 2). She was the
widow of Friedrich Christian von Poigk (d.
1755), a court official with the title *Hofrat*
(Wolfenbütteler Hauptkirche, 1 KB Nr.
1324; Nds.StAWf 31 A Slg, index to 39 Slg).
Later she would be plagued by debts, from
which Feronce would extricate her in 1777,
whereupon she would leave the court with a
pension in 1778 only to fall into debt again
in 1788 ('Mémoire touchant les affaires de
Mad. de Pogck', probably written by Feronce,

10 Aug. 1777; see also From Feronce, 12 Aug
1777 and 5 July 1788, all in Nds.StAWf 71
Alt 119).

[7] Church of Scotland ministers often
irritated JB with their singsong or whine,
known as 'the sough' (see 'Some Account of
Scotland, and the Manners of the Inhabitants', *Gent. Mag.* Aug. 1754, xxiv. 370,
quoted in Mary Margaret Stewart, 'Boswell's
Denominational Dilemma', *PMLA* 76 [Dec.
1961]: 505 n. 9). For JB's painful memories
of the depressing Scottish church services he
had endured in his youth, see his 'Ébauche de
ma vie', App. 2. III.A.

[8] 'Foolish old prejudices', Persius, *Satire*
V, l. 92.

[9] The Duke's bedchamber was on the second floor of the palace, the ground floor
being taken up by the arcades.

[10] Since 1762 the chief marshal had been
Albrecht Edmund, Baron von Münch-
hausen (1729–96; *Hof Etat*, p. 1; see also 3
Alt 552, p. 28). He was distantly related to
Karl Friedrich Hieronymus, Baron von
Münchhausen (1720–97), the famous teller
of tall tales as immortalized in Rudolf Erich
Raspe's *Baron Munchausen's Marvelous Tra-
vels* (1785). For the Münchhausens, see
Gebhard von Lenthe and Hans Mahren-
holtz, *Stammtafeln der Familie von Münch-
hausen*, Schaumburger Studien 28 (1971),
Tafeln I, II, IV, XXV, and XXX).

## Monday 13 August

[MEM. dated Tuesday 14 August] Yesterday you waited on Feronce. He said vos
idées s'arrangeront chacune dans sa cellule &c. The Blanchiseuse was charming &
put blood in motion. You wished to take her *avec*. You met at Court marquis
Cavalcabo. He had relachées nerves & said he was cur'd by *Glace* which digested
as if a man had millstones in his Belly. Mem *this*. Then Sauteurs very well. Ball
Court. Danc'd Princess August. & Queen of Prussia, &c. Home could not sit up.
This day be *firm* & try to write.

[J.] There came into my room this morning the sweetest Girl I ever saw, a
Blanchiseuse eighteen fresh gay. I spoke German to her with unusual ease,
and told her that I would not for the world debauch her to give myself a few
days pleasure; but, if she would go with me to England, and then to
Scotland, I would be very kind to her.[1] She was realy innocent. Her Beauty
thrilled my frame. I thought that I might be an old Patriarch upon occasions
and could not see any harm in taking her with me. She refused to go; but,
promised to come back from time to time.[2] I called on Feronce as I do indeed
allmost every morning, & if I find him not amuse myself with his Books. I
said Je suis embárrassé d'une foule d'idées qui se confondent dans ma tête.
Mais (said he) avec le tems chacune s'arrangera dans sa cellule. This is well.

I met at Court the marquis Cavalcabo, an Italian nobleman of ancient family, not rich, but very knowing, & extremely clever.[3] He told me J'ai ete extremement incommodé d'une faiblesse de l'estomac, et un relachement des nerfs. Mais Je me suis guerit a force de prendre du Glace. Monsieur l'eau qui se mele avec la nouriture la rend molle, et le froid du Glace donne une elasticité aux fibres de l'estomac, et vous digerez comme si vous aviez des Pierres de moulin dans le ventre. His system pleased me much & his vivacious expression made me relish it more. I determined to try it, & he promised to teach me how to make ice.[4] After dinner I was at the noble entertainment of rope-dancing, at which was the Duke and all the Court.[5] I have omitted in this my Journal to mention that one day last week we had a ball at Court, where I danced most agreably. I asked to dance a minuet with the Hereditary Princess. She graciously consented, but we had just made our reverence, when the fiddles struck up a country dance which the Hereditary Prince was to begin. So we were stopt. O I was a mortified Gentleman. This Evening was again a Ball; no sooner did the amiable Princess perceive me, than she came up to me with a smile celestial and said 'Mr. Boswell, let us finish our minuet.' Accordingly I danced with her Royal Highness, who danced extremely well. We made a very fine english minuet; or British if you please; for it was a Scots Gentleman and an English Lady that performed it. What a group of fine ideas had I! I was dancing with a Princess, with the Grand-daughter of King George whose Birth-day I have so often helped to celebrate at old Edinburgh,[6] with the daughter of the Prince of Wales who patronized Thomson and other votaries of Science and the muse:[7] with the Sister of George the Third my Sovereign.[8] I mark this variety to show how my Imagination can enrich an Object; so that I have double pleasure when I am well. It was noble to be in such a frame. I said to the Princess 'Madam I return your Royal Highness a thousand thanks for the honour you have done me. This will serve me to talk of to my Tennants as long as I live.'[9] I was next taken out to dance by the Princess Elizabeth who is to be Queen of Prussia,[10] and by the Princess Dorothea.[11] My spirits bounded; yet was I solemn, and stretched my view to the world of futurity. It was fine to be in the Palace of Brunswic, and see the illustrious family brilliant & gay, & the Prince diverting himself after his scenes of Heroism.[12] I don't know if I have as yet mentioned in this my Journal the Comte Schuvaloff Chambellan to the Empress of Russia. He was a little lively man, had a knowledge of the names of books if not more, and much easiness of manner.[13] He & I were very well. On Sunday night we stood in a window with the Prince Hereditaire who said Il est tres difficile d'unir l'occupation et les plaisirs; and when he had talked of Warriors hazarding so much pour la gloire, he said c'est une folie. He said too J'ai fait une action genereuse á un homme qui etoit mon Ennemi. Il est mort: mais cela Je vous jure, me fait toujours un veritable plaisir. This night again, I did not sup at Court.[14]

[1] MS. 'and told her ... kind to her' deleted by a modern hand.
[2] MS. 'and could not see ... time' deleted by a modern hand. JB made a separate note

of the young woman's address: 'Belle Blanchiseuse Brunsvic: Sandelmans auf der coes-stras in [F]resen hausen' (M 94; see App. 1, II). No such street, a dialectal form of 'Kuh Strasse' ('cow street'), is recorded in Brunswick (Hermann Kleinau, *Geschichtliches Ortsver-zeichnis des Landes Braunschweig*, 2 vols., 1967). Perhaps she came from the Friesenhausen east of Frankfort or from the one east of Fulda in Hessen. For JB's recurring fantasy of being a polygamous Biblical patriarch, see his conversation with Rousseau, Journ. 14 Dec.

³ George Cavalcabò (dates unknown) had been trying for several years to find employment and, more importantly, to regain the lands and title due him as descendant of the marquises of Montferrat, former owners of part of the Viadana in the Duchy of Guastella (*Dizionario Biografico*, xxii. 586–601; GStAPK, I.HA Geheimer Rat, Rep. 9 Allgemeine Verwaltung, K lit n, Fasz. 8). In Vienna in the 1750s he and his brother had tried in vain to win the support of the Emperor, to whom the duchy of Guastella belonged. They had then appealed to Lord Marischal in Neufchâtel, and at his suggestion had sought a place in Prussian service in 1759 only to find Berlin occupied by the Russians and Frederick II absent, whereupon they had spent the war years in Hamburg. In Spring 1763 the Duchess of Brunswick had pleaded Cavalcabò's cause with her brother (Philippine Charlotte, Duchess of Brunswick, to Frederick II of Prussia, 9 Apr. 1763), and in May 1763 Cavalcabò had submitted a plan to Frederick II for an elite school in the hope of being appointed its head (GStAPK, I.HA Geheimer Rat, Rep. 9 Allgemeine Verwaltung, K lit n, Fasz. 8, Bl. 2, 6–9). His appeal to two Prussian Ministers had been rejected by Frederick II, who had scrawled in the margin that he had enough pension-seekers of his own without taking care of foreigners ('Leute die Versorgung mit Pensions, nottig haben, habe ich genug im Lande, ohne dass das auf Ausländer gehen dorfe', marginalia on note from Finck von Finckenstein and Ewald Friedrich von Hertzberg, 16 May 1763, GStAPK, Rep. 9, K lit n, Fasz. 8, Bl. 12). A few months later Calvacabò had unsuccessfully applied for a position in Dresden (To Andrew Mitchell, 8 Sept. 1763, BL Add. MS. 6851, f. 35). He would be last heard of when named director of the Office of the Prussian Lottery in Hamburg, a position he would still hold a year later (Alexander Burnett to Andrew Mitchell, 2 Mar. 1765, MS. 2339, Aberdeen University Library; From Henriette Kircheisen, [Feb. 1766], Yale MS. C 1762).

⁴ For possible methods of making ice, see *Grand Tour I*, Heinemann p. 59 n. 1,

McGraw-Hill pp. 60–61 n. 5. Whether Cavalcabò ever taught JB ice-making is not recorded.

⁵ Italian rope-dancers and other acrobats, newly arrived from Berlin, presented their show starting on 6 Aug. Tickets were on sale at the Goldene Arm coffee-house, JB's inn (*Braunschweigische Anzeigen*, 4 Aug. 1764, p. 258).

⁶ Princess Augusta was the granddaughter of George II (1683–1760), whose birthday had been celebrated on the actual date of his birth, 10 Nov. (*Edinburgh Almanack*, 1760, p. 23). In describing the minuet he danced with the Princess as 'British', JB identifies an important historical moment when 'Scottish' and 'English' blended into a new identity created by the Union of 1707 (see Gordon Turnbull, 'James Boswell: Biography and the Union', in Cairns Craig, gen. ed., *The History of Scottish Literature*, Vol. 2: 1660–1800, ed. Andrew Hook, 1987, pp. 160–61).

⁷ Frederick Louis (1707–51), Prince of Wales, had predeceased his father, George II, and had hence not inherited the throne. In spite of severely limited funds, he had supported the arts. He had provided James Thomson with an annual pension of £100 from 1738 to 1748 (John Walters, *The Royal Griffin*, 1972, pp. 142, 209). He had also paid the debts of John Gay (1685–1732) and had patronized Italian opera at the new Lincoln's Inn Fields Theatre (Walters, pp. 94–96). And he had presumably taken an interest in the sciences in his role as Chancellor of Dublin University, to which he had been named in 1739 (Sir George Young, *Poor Fred, The People's Prince*, 1937, p. 204).

⁸ JB had already thought of possibly profiting from this acquaintance: 'Who knows … but she may recommend me to the King? Who knows what the King may do for a Man recommended by his Sister?' (To WJT, 23 July 1764, *Corr. 6*, p. 106).

⁹ JB would proudly recall this honour in a letter of 16 May 1793 to the Marchioness of Salisbury (Yale MS. L 1125).

¹⁰ JB uses the English spelling, 'Elizabeth', for Princess Elisabeth's name (see also Journ. 21 Aug.). Contrary to his expectations, she did not become queen even though he had recently seen her betrothal to the Prince of Prussia celebrated at Charlottenburg (Journ. 21 July). Her marriage in 1765 would end in divorce four years later, after she repaid the Prince for his infidelity by bearing an illegitimate child in 1767, and she would be forced to live out her days in seclusion in Stettin (ADB, vi. 37–38).

[11] Auguste Dorothea (1749–1810) would remain single after her uncle, Frederick of Prussia, failed in his attempt in 1767 to arrange her marriage to Ernst Ludwig (1745–1804), Hereditary Prince of Saxe-Gotha-Altenburg, and in the same year would prevent her from accepting the suit of William V (1748–1806) of Orange (*Die Erinnerungen der Prinzessin Wilhelmine von Oranien*, ed. G. B. Volz, 1903, vii. 82). She would receive a pension from Frederick and would eventually be named Abbess of Gandersheim in 1778.

[12] When the French occupied Brunswick in Aug. 1757, the Prince had disregarded his father's orders to go to Holland and had joined the Prussian forces commanded by his uncle, Prince Ferdinand. Placed in charge of increasingly large units, he had commanded the entire right flank of the Prussian army at Vellinghausen in 1761 and had been wounded three times, the last time seriously on 30 Aug. 1762 (Savory, pp. 35–36, 171–74, 190–91, 222, 253–54, 267–78, 291, 402–06, 500; Selma Stern, *Karl Wilhelm Ferdinand, Herzog zu Braunschweig und Lüneburg*, Veröffentlichungen der historischen Kommission für Hannover, Oldenburg, Braunschweig 6 [1921]: 11–22). His bravery had been celebrated by Frederick of Prussia, his uncle, in the 'Ode au Prince Héréditaire de Brunswic' (*Œuvres de Frédéric Le Grand*, xii. 22–29).

[13] Andrei Petrovich, Count Shuvalov (1744–89), had successively gained the favour of the Empress Elizabeth, Tsar Peter, and Catherine the Great. Lord Cathcart would describe him as 'busy, important and ambitious' but would find that 'his knowledge is of the general superficial and dictionary kind' (1770, quoted in W. F. Reddaway, *Documents of Catherine the Great*, 1931, p. 347). According to the custom of his society, he had been assigned to the army from childhood, having been appointed sergeant-major in the cavalry at the age of four, cornet at seven, and lieutenant at twelve. In 1757 he had also been prepared for life at court by being named gentleman of the bedchamber and three years later gentleman-in-waiting. His intellectual aspirations would lead him to visit Voltaire at Ferney in 1765 and to support the Moscow Academy in its translation of the *Encyclopédie*, begun in 1767 (Erich Donnert, *Russland im Zeitalter der Aufklärung*, 1984, p. 91). He would serve as Secretary of the Legislative Commission in Moscow from 1767 to 1768, as Director of currency banks in Moscow and Petersburg in 1768, and as chairman of a commission for the preservation of Russian history (*Russkii biograficheskii slovar*, 1911, xxiii. 472–75).

[14] On this day JB finally wrote to Sommelsdyck and inquired about Maasdam (see Mem. dated 26 July and 11 Aug.).

## Tuesday 14 August

[MEM. dated Wednesday 15 August][1] Yesterday you went at six & calld on young Faukner & with Bloem rode brisk to Wolfenbuttel — Old town. Library noble — building rotundo [—] 108 thousand volumes [—] 5000 manuscripts catalogue by Duke Antonius Ulricus' hand — was highly pleas'd. Luther's Inkhorn bruised then Saltzdaal. Garden Parnassus. Tableaux. China. Dind court grand Opera — Russian Shubalof beaucoup d'estime coté de ma femme, supt court. This day up early write Johnson. At 9 M de Quan the Swede then Abbé Jerus. & propose court recommendation.[2]

[J.] This morning at six I went to the Collége de Caroline,[3] to young Faukener son to Sir Everard.[4] He & I & a Mr. de Bloem a German,[5] took horses & went to Wolfenbuttel. As we rode along I was as pleasant & gay as when in my boyish years, & all the horrors that I have since endured, had left no mark on my mind. Well then, may I not be in heaven at last. It was a charming day. Faukener is a genteel pretty, amiable, young fellow. The Country between Brunswic & Wolfenbuttel is very fine. At Wolfenbuttel which is not a bad town, we saw the Palace the ancient residence of the Dukes.[6] We saw the noble Library. The room is a spacious Rotunda and contains 10800 Books and 5000 Manuscripts. This Library was made by the Duke Antonius Ulricus Great Grandfather to the present Duke. There is a Catalogue of it in four thick quarto Volumes written by his own hand. He has also marked with their titles the backs of the manuscripts and of many of the Books.[7] He was a man of learning, in the taste of the times; and has written a Treatise on the Game of Chess,[8] and some other pieces. We saw here Luther's Inkhorn which he threw at the Devil's head when he appeared to him. He hit him with such force that the Inkhorn which is of lead, has a deep dimple in it, & is very much crushed. A very just emblem of the outrageous temper of this Reformer.[9] We next went to Saltzdall, where we saw the Garden in which is a Parnassus adorned with the nine muses, poor enough.[10] But the Palace is noble, and has a Gallery of Pictures which contains many valuable pieces; and a gallery of China the finest thing of the kind that I ever saw. The China is magnificent, and disposed with excellent taste.[11] I rode briskly back to town, was all glowing & gay, and dined at court with pleasure. In the evening I was at the grand Opera[12] where The Russian Comte Shuvaloff invited me to his loge & said 'Allons monsieur mettez vous á coté de ma femme.[13] Je vous assure que J'ai beaucoup d'estime pour vous'. I shook his hand and was pleased.

[1] MS. Several scribbles, followed by the word 'Gerunds', written along the left margin.

[2] For Quant, see Journ. 17 Aug. and n. 3. The recommendations appear to have been to the Duke (see Mem. dated 16 Aug.).

[3] The Collegium Carolinum was located at 41 Bohlweg, near the palace (Isa Schikorsky, *Gelehrsamkeit und Geselligkeit: Abt Johann Friedrich Wilhelm Jerusalem*, 1989, p. 137 and illustr. 34). Founded in 1745 by Jerusalem and named after Duke Karl I, it prepared some students for the university and others for nonacademic careers. Because it taught not only the classics but also practical and scientific subjects, it would come to be regarded as the precursor of the twentieth-century polytechnic (Müller, p. 4; Ursula Schelm-Spangenberg, 'Schulen und Hochschulen', Moderhack, *Braunschweigische Landesgeschichte*, p. 266).

[4] William Augustus Fawkener (1747–1811) had been matriculated at this school earlier in 1764, after being at Eton from 1757 to 1763 (J. J. Eschenburg, 'Matrikel des Collegii,' *Entwurf einer Geschichte des Collegii Carolinum*, 1812, p. 83). He would become clerk to the privy council and would be sent on a secret mission to Russia in 1791.

Sir Everard Fawkener (1693/94–1758), merchant and diplomat, had made his fortune during nine years in his family's textile business in the Levant (Aleppo). Back in London from 1725, he had moved in court circles. Ten years later he had become ambassador to Constantinople, had been knighted, and had successfully negotiated the end of the Russo-Turkish War (1735–39) before returning to England in 1742. From 1745 to at least 1749 he had served as secretary to the Duke of Cumberland, and as reward for service in Flanders had also been appointed postmaster-general jointly with the Earl of Leicester in 1745 (see Norma Perry, 'Sir Everard Fawkener', SVEC 133 [1975]: 24–26, 33–48, 70–72; Archibald Maclachlan, *William Augustus, Duke of Cumberland*, 1876, pp. 130–32).

[5] Friedrich von Blum (d. 1778) had been matriculated at the Collegium Carolinum in 1760 (Eschenburg, p. 80). Later a member of the legal bureaucracy, he would be named *Hofrat an der Justizkanzlei* (counsellor at the court of chancellery) in 1773 (Nds.StAWf 3 Alt 552 S. 52).

[6] Wolfenbüttel was about 4 miles (c. 6.4 km) from Brunswick (Nugent, ii. 215). It had been the seat of the Dukes of Brunswick from the end of the Thirty Years' War, had become a centre of baroque art and culture under Duke Anton Ulrich, and had remained the ducal residence until 1753, when the court moved to the larger town of Brunswick (Moderhack, 'Geschichte der Städte', *Braunschweigische Landesgeschichte*, pp. 154–55, 178). The palace, one of whose wings dated back to 1283, had been restored in the later seventeenth century but had been left

to deteriorate after the court moved away (P. J. Meier and K. Steinacker, *Die Bau- und Kunstdenkmäler des Herzogthums Braunschweig*, 1890–1910, iii. pt. 2, pp. 30–32, 122–23).

[7] The renowned library was based on the extensive collection of Duke August of Brunswick-Lüneburg (1579–1666). It was he and not Duke Anton Ulrich who was the present duke's great grandfather and who was responsible for the book collection, but JB correctly attributes the building with its famous rotunda to Anton Ulrich, who was the present duke's great uncle (Ingrid Recker-Kotulla, 'Baugeschichte der Herzog August Bibliothek,' *Wolfenbütteler Beiträge aus den Schätzen der Herzog August Bibliothek*, vi [1983]: 3–14; Wolfgang Schmitz, *Deutsche Bibliotheksgeschichte*, vi [1984]: 84–86). The catalogue actually consists of six volumes, of which Duke August personally wrote and annotated vols. 1–3 and part of vol. 4. His secretaries compiled the rest of vol. 4 and vol. 5, while vol. 6 lists books purchased after his death (Maria von Katte, 'Herzog August und die Kataloge seiner Bibliothek', *Wolfenbütteler Beiträge*, i. 174–88). The books were shelved by fields of knowledge (e.g., theology, history) and within these by size according to the principle of *elegantia*, with the largest on the bottom.

[8] The Duke's book on chess, *Das Schach- oder König-spiel*, 1606, a folio of 495 pages, was his first significant publication. Under the pseudonym 'Gustavus Selenus', it was printed in Leipzig at the Duke's own expense even though he could ill afford the cost (Marion Faber, 'Schachspiel', *Sammler Fürst Gelehrter*, 1979, pp. 173–75).

[9] The story that Martin Luther (1483–1546) had thrown his inkstand at the devil to avoid being distracted from translating the Bible into German, is associated with the Wartburg near Eisenach, where Luther had sought refuge in 1521 and where an ink blot on the wall supposedly confirms the legend (H. Schwerdt and H. Jäger, *Eisenach und die Wartburg*, 1871, pp. 68–69). How the damaged, lopsided inkstand seen by JB came to Brunswick, and whether it had ever belonged to Luther, has not been ascertained. Luther never visited Wolfenbüttel, whose dukes had remained Catholic until 1568 and had strongly resisted their subjects' efforts to introduce Lutheran teachings into their realm (Hermann Kuhr, 'Kirchengeschichte', Moderhack, *Braunschweigische Landesgeschichte*, pp. 119–20). The inkstand had meanwhile become a significant

relic, along with 'Luther's drinking glass', even though Luther himself had disapproved of venerating such objects (Jörg Jochen Berns, introduction to 'Herzog August— Frömmigkeit und kirchliche Tradition', *Sammler, Fürst, Gelehrter*, p. 344 and #733–35).

[10] Salzdahlum, the ducal summer residence 4 miles (6.4 km) from Brunswick (Nugent, ii. 244), had been built by Anton Ulrich from 1668 to 1697 and was famous for its size and splendour. Dominating the entrance closest to Wolfenbüttel was a small hill called the Parnassus, on which the statues of the nine muses had originally flanked an Athena, and an Apollo had been placed above them as a compliment to the ruler. With the renovations of 1707 these statues had been scattered over the area and the main focus had shifted to several picturesque mock-ruined arches that capped the hillside (Gerhard Gerkens, *Das fürst-liche Lustschloss Salzdahlum*, Quellen und Forschungen zur Braunschweigischen Geschichte, 1974, xxii. 38, 51–54, 57, 127, 139–42). Nugent had found the garden 'in no bad taste' but had considered the statues 'contemptible' (Nugent, iv. 244).

[11] The elaborate palace, which combined Palladian, Dutch, French, and native half-timbered styles, was constructed of wood, much of it painted in vivid colours and made to resemble more precious materials such as marble (Gerkens, pp. 59–60, 70–75). Its greatest treasures were about 600 paintings, primarily Italian and Dutch, housed in the long gallery (Gerkens, pp. 95–114). The collection of china, in separate smaller galleries, included majolica pieces based on designs by Raphael (*Bemerkungen über die Majolika-Sammlung*, 1876). Nugent had thought the paintings 'exceeding fine', singling out works by Rembrandt and Rubens among others, but had declared the china gallery 'in a grotesque taste' (Nugent, iv. 244). The Salzdahlum palace would later be allowed to deteriorate and would be torn down in 1813.

[12] Not identified.

[13] Catherine (Saltykov) Shuvalov (b. 1743) was even younger than her husband. Immensely wealthy, the couple was on the grand tour and, according to Count Lehndorff, was squandering a fortune. When presented to the Queen of Prussia in Berlin on the occasion of Princess Elisabeth of Brunswick's engagement to the Prince of Prussia, the Countess was said to have worn more jewels even than Princess Augusta (Lehndorff, 18 July 1764, *Dreissig Jahre: Nachträge*, i. 405).

## Wednesday 15 August

[MEM. dated Thursday 16 August] Yesterday you was with Abbé Jerus: who said Hered Prince was allways warlike & had esprit inquiet the greatest court not equal to a camp. Obliged to please his father in little things parade &c. vexed. Owned his fear that melanch Imag might make him — horrid thought. Said Je vous estime pour votre manierre de penser votre cœur votre esprit & votre amour de la verité.[1] Promis'd treatise for Prince & correspondence. Give him address. Bid him recommend Duke modest worthy man.

[M]em Relig. allways gay & not Sr. W Max of Monreith. Be firm & stable by Johnson amen.[2]

[J.] I past the morning with my worthy Abbé Jerusalem. He said the Duke was un digne homme, but passionate, et quelquefois il a des accès terribles. I said Le Prince me paroit reveur et même melancolique; Monsieur (said he) Il a toujours aimé la Guêrre, de sa jeunesse il en etoit charmé. Il a l'esprit inquiet. Il lui faut beaucoup d'occupation, et des grands Objets. A present il ne se trouve pas bien. La plus grande Cour n'est pas egale a un Camp.[3] Ainsi il n'est pas si grand homme qu'il a eté. Apres avoir eu tant a faire, il est maintenant tout a fait desœuvré. D'ailleurs il est obligé de plaire au Duc. Il faut qu'il soit regulierement tous les matins a la Parade ainsi sa matinée s'envole insensiblement. Ensuite il faut s'habiller, aller á la Cour, recevoir du monde chez lui, aller aux spectacles, en un mot passer son tems dans une manièrre qu'il trouve au desous de lui. This description pleased my discontented mind. I saw that all ranks must take their portion of evil. I saw the Prince was with his Father, just as I must be with mine. He is obliged to attend the Parade, just as I must be obliged to attend the Day-labourers. The Abbé also told me that the Prince had good principles of Religion, and would never give up Christianity, altho' often carried away by his passions. His highness came lately to the Abbé and complained that[4] by dissipation and keeping company with infidels, he found his principles wavering, and therefore begged that the Abbé would draw up for him a neat summary of the proofs of Christianity which might allways keep his mind settled. The Abbé most kindly promised me a copy of this Summary.[5] He told me that the Dutchess of Brunswic had much of the Genius of her Royal Brother. Formerly, when she read an Infidel Book her imagination was struck *tout d'un coup*, and she was thrown into uncertainty. The Abbé was sent for, solved the Objections and calmed her mind. Now she is more constant and is a true christian, sur tout dans la pratique. At night was french Comedy.[6]

---

[1] Here JB has shifted to Jerusalem's words.

[2] MS. 'Mem … amen' written along the left margin. Why JB was reminded of his Ayrshire neighbour Sir William Maxwell of Monreith is unclear. JB did not much like him. Two years earlier JB had noted that Sir William had deteriorated from 'a genteel, pretty-looking man' to someone who 'looks like an overgrown drover' (Journ. 24 Sept. 1762).

[3] For the Prince's wartime experiences, see Journ. 13 Aug. n. 12.

[4] MS. 'that' squeezed in, possibly a later correction.

[5] JB would still ask for these proofs by letter from Basel (To Jerusalem, 26 Nov. 1764, Yale MS. L 655) but would never receive them. Nor would a copy of them survive among the papers of the Prince or of Jerusalem (Nds.StAWf 1 Alt 22 Nr. 1485).

[6] Not identified.

## Thursday 16 August

[MEM. dated Friday 17 August] Yesterday You wrote all morning dind court Operette supt — fear'd to lose grand ideas — grew better — Thought a man sent to world to gather ideas as flowers in life have em fresh — in books at second hand. They must dry — vices are weeds that rot &c. &c. Drive off prejud. Take Leyden as father had it With Chas. Maitland[1] — Twas as *true* then as now — & make Zelide help you to humour him. [W]rite again letts Brown and Sr. Dav[2] — & write few but correct. More exercise — walk if not dine.

[N]ever sup or youre bad.[3]

See Abb Jerus. & be recommend at court distinguish virt & vices.[4]

[J.] I past the morning at home, in writing. I have attempted to write to Mr. Johnson, every day since I formed the resolution of demanding a charter of his freindship, but have not yet been able to please myself. Want of motion flattened me. I was not much amused at the Operête.[5] At court at supper I cleared up. I came home gay. I had store of delicious ideas. I considered that mankind are sent into the world to gather ideas like flowers. Those who take their ideas from Books have them at second-hand as flowers[6] from a stall in Covent Garden. Whereas those who take them from real life have them fresh from the Garden, pull them themselves. Care is to be taken in gathering these flowers. Vices are weeds[7] pretty enough when fresh, but when faded, have a most terrible stench. Virtues are often beautifull when fresh, & when faded have allways a pleasing odour. Let us lay up our flowers in some order. Let us pull flowers of size & figure, nor fill our repository with trifling ones which have neither colour nor scent. However let us not despise a flower because it is small. The Violet, tho' scarcely perceived among the grass has many sweets.

[1] 'Alexander Boswell, Scotus' had matriculated in law at the University of Leiden on 29 Dec. 1727 (*Album Studiosorum*, p. 915). Charles Maitland of Pittrichie, Aberdeen (c. 1708–51), his close friend since they were in the same Greek class in Edinburgh, may not have been matriculated at Leiden (he is not listed in the Album), but had been with Lord Auchinleck during the latter's five months in Paris on his journey home (Auch. Memoirs, p. 47). Maitland had been admitted to the Faculty of Scots Advocates in 1727, had become sheriff of Edinburgh in 1746, and had served as M.P. for Aberdeen Burghs from 1748 to the end of his life (*Fac. Adv.*, p. 143; Sedgwick, ii. 239).

[2] JB was writing to the Rev. Robert Brown (1728–77), Scottish presbyterian minister at the so-called English Church in Utrecht (see App. 1, n. 7; *Corr. 5*, p. 10 n. 1), and to Sir David Dalrymple (1726–92), later Lord Hailes, his avuncular friend in Edinburgh. Dalrymple's answer of 10 Oct. reveals that JB's letter was about his own future, explaining the circumstances under which he would agree to live in Scotland on his return.

[3] MS. 'Never ... bad' written along the top of the page. JB apparently believed that eating supper would make him feel depressed.

[4] 'See ... vices' written along the left margin.

[5] Not identified.
[6] MS. 'flowers' inserted above the line with a caret.

[7] MS. 'weeds' inserted above the line with a caret.

## Friday 17 August

[MEM. dated Saturday 18 August.] Yesterday you was hyp'd a little went to Feronce said Je suis grand *Tory* said he Vous avez *tort*. Court well. Comedie Allemande — hurt with wavering ideas & obliged to write letts twice over. So let coresps be few & well — nor follow every suggestion to write. This day write Johnson. At 9 — *lunch*[1] at 10 Parade at 11 Cabinet — then Madms. Bloem & Baeswitz and Stanmer. Good man eat & drink more moderate — Sweat full. Temperance is virtue.[2]

[J.] Quantin a Suede an officer in the service of Brunswic was kind enough to entertain me with some music this morning.[3] He plays delightfully on the German flute, & composes very well in a singular taste, with[4] quick transitions from high to low notes very hard to play. He paints too. He is a lively genteel brisk young man. He brought to my mind many ideas of healthy, accomplished foreign Officers. He told me, there were many of my name in Sweden. Some Generations ago, four sons of our family went over to the service of Gustavus Adolphus.[5] I was at the German Comedy in the evening.[6] I was hurt with wavering ideas. I found myself obliged to write my letters twice over. I determined to check fancifull warm inclinations to write, and to have a moderate chosen corespondence.

[1] 'A light meal at any time of day' (OED, s.v. 'lunch', 2.a; 'A slight repast taken … esp. between breakfast and mid-day dinner' (OED, s.v. 'luncheon', 2.a).

[2] MS. 'Temperance … virtue' written along the left margin; below, 'My dear Brother' in a different quill, presumably the beginning of a letter to one of JB's younger brothers, John (1743–c. 1798) or David (1748–1826). Along the right margin, a trial of various letters: 'M, My'; a few letters of Gothic script; 'But rose' and 'ye fair'.

[3] Carl von Quant (Quandt) had been a major in the garde de corps (life guards or household guards) since 1763 (Nds.StAWf 35 Slg; Otto Elster, *Geschichte der stehenden Truppen*, 1901, ii. 335).

[4] MS. 'With' inserted above the line with a caret.

[5] JB would later ascertain that three, not four, earlier Boswells—younger sons of James, the 4th laird (d. 1618)—had gone abroad in the early seventeenth century

('Boswell of Auchinleck', Hyde Collection; Glasgow Testaments, 25 Aug. 1618; *Ayr and Wigton*, i. 192–93; *Earlier Years*, p. 451). Two of their sisters are also said to have joined them (MS. Jasper John Boswell, 'The Parent Tree of the Boswell Family', vol. ii, 1900, unpub.). George, William, and Matthew had apparently served in the Thirty Years' War (*Ominous Years*, Chart II, p. 375), in which many mercenaries had fought for the Protestant cause under Gustavus Adolphus (1594–1632), the brilliant Swedish general known as 'Lion of the North' (Nils Ahnlund, *Gustav Adolf the Great*, 1940, pp. 259–61, 267–80; Michael Roberts, *Gustavus Adolphus*, 2nd. ed. 1992, p. 100). JB would eventually trace some Boswell descendants who had settled in Prussia, and at their request would provide them with an authenticated 'pedigree' or 'diploma' (M 23, c. Feb. 1791, sent to Christoph Leopold and August Ferdinand von Boswell in eastern Prussia, 10 June 1791).

[6] Not identified.

## Saturday 18 August

[MEM. dated Sunday 19 August] [Y]esterday you got up a little baddish —
walk'd round Ramparts — went to Parade — then with Marquis Cavalcabo to
Cabinet de Duc — very well — Then saw Stanmer [—] din'd Hered Princess.
Then Pantomime very clever — Centaur Centinel. Supt court was quite easy.
This day break at 8 du Pless then Chap. Royal then Cathol Church then walk &
try to finish letters to Johnson &c. *Think* on Auchinleck and Father & be prudent.
    Find the soldier & pay him.[1]
    Be moderate or nerves go & mind with em as Kelly and B Drum.[2]


[J.] Hypochondria was at me. I however walked hard round the ramparts,
from whence I had a fine prospect. I then saw the Parade which merits to
be seen. Then the Marquis Cavalcabo and I went & saw the Duke's
Cabinet which is a very valuable one. It is very rich in medals, precious
stones antiques of different kinds and natural curiositys. There is here an
Onyx formed into a cup of which Montfaucon has given a description.[3] I
then waited on the worthy Stanmer, who had fallen from his horse, and
broken an Arm. I dined chez la Princesse Hereditaire; then saw a very
clever Pantomime. Harlequin changed himself into a Centaur and into a
Sentinel both which changes went very well. The Centaur was formed
with two Harlequins.[4] I thought to mark these for my freind Love.[5] I must
here record my romantic consideration. Before I set out from Berlin I took
up thirty ducats from my Banker, by way of Journey-money for my
Brunswic Jaunt, and enough it was for three weeks. But a Rogue of a Taylor
and a Rascal of a Shoemaker came and picked my pocket of seven or eight
of these same pieces, so that I was left bare enough.[6] I did not however
perceive it till I had been a week at Brunswic. When I called on my trusty
Jacob, & told him my case & asked him, Avez vous d'argent? Oui (said he)
J'ai cinq louis monsieur. Eh bien Jacob. Gardez ces cinq louis. Ils payeront
les depenses en retournant á Berlin. Et moi Je mettrai ici trois ducats pour
deux jours en des differents papiers. J'ai assez pour six jours. Quand mes
ducats sont depensés, nous en irons.[7] This plan I followed most exactly. I
was so good an œconomist, that I had money sufficient to keep me three
days longer than the six days, & these three days I stayed. This night I had
an Adventure. I had no chair to bring me home from court, and my Servant
had brought no Lanthern. Indeed he had not come for me at all. So that I
was obliged to trudge home by myself in the dark. It is a regulation at
Brunswic, that if any Person is found on the streets after ten oclock at
night, without a light, the Patrole shall carry him to the Guard.[8] I dreaded
this, and as I was posting along, up came a couple of musqueteers on
Horseback. I tried to escape but in vain. They rode me up to the Wall. I told
them Ich bin ein Heer das von den Hoft comt. Your Servant. The Cavalry
answered 'Er moes met oons geen'.[9] However, after pausing a little, They
asked me where I lodged. Upon which they separated, and one of them
followed me to my Inn, taking special care that I should not run away from
him. I imagined that he was only to tell the people of the house that I was

his prisoner, & then carry me to the Guard; So I offered him money to go away. No — he would not be bribed. I therefore resigned myself to my fate. Happy was I to find that he allowed me to enter my quarters in peace, saying 'das is een Heer, das ich hab op straas gevonden'.[10]

[1] MS. 'Find … him' written along the top of the page, presumably at a later date. Perhaps the payment was to reward the soldier who had accompanied JB and refused a bribe.

[2] MS. 'Be moderate … Drum' written along the left margin. For Kelly, see Journ. 16 Sept. and n. 4. 'B Drum' presumably refers to George Drummond of Blair, the brother of Lady Kames, but the phrase is puzzling, for JB had found him sensible, honest, and friendly, though proud, at an earlier meeting ('Journal of my Jaunt, Harvest 1762', 16 Oct. 1762). For his subsequent career, see Journ. 27 Sept. n. 12.

[3] The collections belonged to one of those 'cabinets de curiosités' that absolute rulers liked to assemble and that mark the beginnings of modern museums. They included the holdings previously kept in Wolfenbüttel and Blankenburg as well as the Duke's new purchases of paintings, sculptures, and antiquities. The prize of the Brunswickian collection was the cup carved out of a single onyx, six inches high and embellished with fertility scenes, which had been described in detail by Bernard de Montfauçon (1655–1741) in his *L'Antiquité expliquée* (5 vols. in 10, 1719, II. i. 180–84 and Pl. LXXVIII; see also Ribbentrop, ii. 286, 296–302). At one time it had been thought to be a relic from Solomon's Temple in Jerusalem but would later be dated 54 A.D. Known as 'the Mantuan vessel' because it had been owned by Isabella d'Este, Margravine of Mantua, it had been captured during a siege of Mantua in 1630 and had come into the Duke of Brunswick's possession through a series of inheritances. It would be taken from Brunswick when the ducal family fled from Napoleon; would be brought back temporarily in 1815; taken away by Duke Karl II (1804–73) when he was ousted in 1830; left among the objects he bequeathed to the city of Geneva; and finally returned by that city in 1874 (notice in the Anton Ulrich Museum, Brunswick, where the vase would remain; see also *Braunschweig und Umgebung*, p. 62).

[4] Pantomimes with magical transformations were the special forte of the Italian impresario Filippo Nicolini (dates of birth and death unknown), who served as 'Grand Maître des Théâtres et Spectacles d'Opera, Comédies, Tragédies et autres' in Brunswick from 1749 to 1771 (Nds.StAWb 2 Alt Nr. 33 3365; Gottlieb Benzin, *Versuch einer Beurtheilung der Pantomimischen Oper des Herrn Nicolini*, 1751, p. 15; Fritz Hartmann, *Sechs Bücher Braunschweigischer Theater-Geschichte*, 1905, p. 161). The pantomimes were performed by a French company in the small Comödienhaus built especially for Nicolini on the Burgplatz (*Braunschweig und Umgebung*, 1877, p. 109; Klaus Kindler, *Findbuch zum Bestand Musikalien des herzoglichen Theaters in Braunschweig*, Veröffentlichungen der Niedersächsischen Archivverwaltung 13 ⌈1990⌉: x).

[5] James Love, the stage name of James Dance (1722–74), was a versatile man of the theatre: comic actor, assistant stage manager of the Canongate Theatre in Edinburgh, as well as writer of plays and pantomimes. JB had considered him his 'second best friend' in 1758, and had continued to have various dealings with him in London, where Love worked at Drury Lane Theatre from 1762 to the end of his life (To WJT, 16 Dec. 1758, *Corr. 6*, p. 15 and n. 7; *Corr. 1*, p. 23 n. 2; *Corr. 9*, p. 8 n. 1). Staging pantomimes had been part of Love's assignment when David Garrick (for whom see Journ. 27 Sept. n. 11) called him to Drury Lane, and Love had featured a harlequin in his two pantomimes: *The Witches; or, Harlequin Cherokee*, which played from 23 Nov. 1762, and *The Rites of Hecate; or, Harlequin from the Moon*, from Dec. 1763 (*Biog. Dict. Actors*, ix. 360). JB had seen *The Witches* on 10 Jan. 1763 and had found it 'but a dull thing'.

[6] Neither the tailor nor the shoemaker has been identified.

[7] This scheme is not recorded in JB's Expense Account. Both louis and ducats were gold coins, a ducat being worth roughly half a louis d'or (Nugent, ii. 60).

[8] Eighteen guards, assigned to five different districts, patrolled the town, nine working before and nine after midnight (Werner Spiess, *Geschichte der Stadt Braunschweig im Nachmittelalter*, 1966, ii. 555).

[9] JB's spelling for *Ich bin ein Herr der von dem Hof kommt*: 'I am a gentleman who has come from the court' and *Er muss mit uns gehn*: 'You must go with us'.

[10] *Das ist ein Herr den ich auf der Strasse gefunden* ⌈*habe*⌉: 'This is a gentleman I found on the street'.

## Sunday 19 August

[MEM. dated Monday 20 August] [Y]esterday You was at Chapel — then walked Du Pless who said *melancholique* [—] din'd Court Lady M. Cooke. At night Ladies complain'd.

[J.] I was again at the Dukes Chapel, but so hyp'd, that I could hardly relish in any degree the noble music. By reason, however, I maintained my devotion, and my immortal hope. *De Ples* and I then walked in Garden. He said he was fort melancolique, et tout d'un coup sans aucune raison. I explained to him that miserable distemper, & bid him ride and be gay. He told me he lived with a *danceuse* an Italian Girl.[1] He said Je ne me marierai jamais. Je serois jaloux comme le Diable. Je ne fierai mon honneur á aucune femme au monde. He had also a religious disposition, was devout, & did not think keeping a Girl any sin. He carried me to the Romish Chapel,[2] where we saw his charmer. This day I saw at court Lady Mary Cooke who came hither from Hannover, chiefly to see the Hereditary Prince, who went away several days ago to meet the King of Prussia in Silesia.[3] This night after supper some of the Ladies of honour complained to me of their not having time enough to themselves, etc. etc. What! is discontent heard to murmur amongst the fair Ladies of a gay court? Well, Life! I call thee sad.

[1] Not further identified. Years later Plessen, having left Brunswick, would marry an Italian in Mantua (see Journ. 8 Aug. n. 6).

[2] For the Catholic church, see Journ. 10 Aug. n. 7.

[3] Lady Mary Coke (1727–1811) was an eccentric widow who travelled widely and was notorious for her 'frenzy for royalty' (From Horace Walpole to Sir Horace Mann, 28 Nov. 1773, *Corres. Walpole*, xxxi. 175). The daughter of John Campbell, 2nd Duke of Argyll, she had endured an unhappy marriage with Edward, Viscount Coke (1719–53), only son of Thomas Coke, 1st Earl of Leicester, a profligate and brutal husband who had refused her a divorce (*Comp. Peer*. i. 370, 377–78; Romney Sedgwick, *The House of Commons 1715–1754*, 1970, i. 564). His death had left her free to live her own life.

Frederick II had left Berlin on 20 Aug. to review his troops in Silesia and would be away until 15 Sept. (Karl Heinrich Siegfried Rödenbeck, *Tagebuch oder Geschichtskalender aus Friedrich's des Grossen Regentenleben*, 1840–42, ii. 242).

## Monday 20 August

[MEM. dated Tuesday 21 August] Yesterday You wrote all forenoon [—] at court Baeswitz said he kept book. Afternoon wrote — supt. Hered[1] Princess. This day finish lett. to Johnson. Send books to Feronce, & get him to coresp. At 11 Abbé Jerus — leave Address — take his vow regard — Call Falkner[2] — Be quite prudent — At one Duke Ferdinand. Pay compliments.

[J.] Baron Baeswitz told me that he kept a regular book of all the Strangers that came to the Brunswic Court. This idea pleased me. He marks their titles, their employments, when they came, how long they stayed.[3] There came this day a Comte of the Empire and some more Strangers.[4] I could see a certain joy in the faces of the Courtiers, quand des Etrangers sont annoncés. No wonder. It furnishes them with new ideas. And indeed I could observe their highnesses also pleased. I wrote all this afternoon. I supt chez la Princésse Hereditaire, where was a very great company. I was vexed with Lady Mary Cooke in whom I found all the absurd distance of manners by which the english Ladies petrify People. She rendered me just as I used to be at Lady Northumberland's. I stood like a pillar of 'dull cold marble' and looked at her without daring to approach. At last I stept up to her, & said. How comes it, Madam, that I can speak to all these foreign Ladies with ease and can scarcely say a word to your Ladyship? 'Sir (said she) We have not the same ease with them'. Some more Syllables feebly muttered in the air, & then our lips were again glewed (not hers to mine & mine to her's, but as if each had been affraid that the other would bite and had got them bound over to the peace.[5] O sad manners! Avaunt.

[1] MS. 'Heered', a slip of the pen.
[2] That is, young William Augustus Fawkener.
[3] Bassewitz's book of strangers would not survive. JB would later maintain a similar record of visitors at Auchinleck (see *Book of Company*).
[4] The count and the other visitors have not been identified.
[5] This tense meeting between JB and Lady Mary Coke and particularly the position of their lips have ironic undertones if she is indeed, as F. A. Pottle speculated, the 'Lady Mirabel' with whom JB carried on flirtatious conversations in the winter of 1763 at Northumberland House (see Journ. 14 Jan., Mem. dated 21 Mar. 1763; for the pros and cons of Pottle's identification, see also *Earlier Years*, pp. 484–85). The phrase 'dull cold marble' comes from Shakespeare's *Henry VIII*, iii. 2. 433.

## Tuesday 21 August

[MEM. dated Wednesday 22 August] Yesterday You had Marquis Cavalcabo with you who said vous avez eté dans une bonne melancholie & owned he had been so. And tout de corp. Heureux est celui qui connoit son corps. You felt just clear new set of ideas. You waited at one on Duke Ferdinand gracious — dind court. Then Opera was too much touched even to couper gorge &c. — supt court — took leave jamais un plus honette homme &c — said Reviendrai en vingt cinq anns — cordial leave of all was quite gay & yet mild. Cavalc — anglois au fond plus legers. This day no gloom love God — circulate blood.

[J.] Cavalcabo payed me a visit. He told me that he had been 'si triste que sil n'avoit eté que Je devois avoir soin de ma belle Sœur et de ses enfants, J'etois capable de me donner un coup de Pistolet.'[1] I told him 'Monsieur en verité J'etois extremement noire. Mais Je pensois questce que ca fait? Que Je souffre ou non, c'est presque egal. Je ne suis qu'un seul Individu.' 'Eh bien Monsieur (dit il) vous etiez justement tombé dans une bonne melancolie.' 'Tout cela vient du corps et peut etre gueri par une Regime. Heureux est celui qui connoit son corps.' I found him the true bon *Catholique*: for he talked with ease of having women, & yet told me of a distemper that he had brought on himself by fasting. This was my last day at Brunswic. I talked at court Je reviendrai en vingt cinq anns, et Je verrais qui seront morts, et qui seront en vie. I dined in a kind of luxurious sorrow. I must not forget to mark that I fell in love with the beauteous Princess Elizabeth. I talked of carrying her off from the Prince of Prussia and so occasioning a second Trojan War. Madame de Boick was my Confidante. I was also smitten by Lady Mary Cooke. Madame de Boick would ask me 'Eh bien Monsieur estce L'angloise ou l'Allemande qui vous plait le plus ce soir?' At the Opera[2] this evening, I was quite ravished. It made me recollect a story of Doctor Colquett's, how at some fine music in London, Dukes & Lords cried they'd dash out their brains against the wainstcoat.[3] I owned to Feronce Je pourrois presque souhaiter qu'on me couperoit la Gorge. Feronce agreed to corespond with me. So did de Ples.[4] I shall have a pretty corespondence in all at Brunswic. I said to Cavalcabo, on parle beaucoup de la legereté et vivacité francoise mais en verité ils ont plus de raison que les Anglois. Ils ont toujours quelques regles. L'anglois n'en a point. 'Monsieur, said he, les françois ont plus d'etourderie, dans l'exterieur; mais ils n'ont pas tant veritablement. Un françois saute et chants devant sa maitresse. Il est pourtant maitre de soimême. Mais l'anglois est tout caprice et avec tout le sang froid du monde il va mettre le feu á la maison.' I was pensive at Court. I had taken leave of the Hereditary Princess. I mused on the life of a Courtier here. Putting myself by strong imagination in every one's place, my gloomy temper found all their situations uneasy even the Duke's. Yet I recalled the best ideas, and felt pleasing regret. I took leave of the Dutchess shortly. I have seen in her room a Portrait of the King of Prussia, the only one for which his Majesty ever sat. It is very like; but it stoops too much.[5] When I took leave of the Duke, I said 'Monseigneur vous avez eu á votre cour[6] des gens plus brillants que moi; mais jamais un plus honnête homme ou un homme plus sensible aux politesses qui fait votre Altésse.' The Duke of Brunswic replied 'Monsieur, Je suis bien aise que vous avez eté content de votre Sejour ici.' I expected still more civilitys than I received because forsooth The Duke spoke to me at Charlottenbourg. I magnify all events in my own favour, & with the wind of vanity blow them up to size immense. I took a tender leave of the Ladies and Gentlemen de la cour & said 'Nestce pas triste que nous ne nous reverrons jamais'.

---

[1] George Cavalcabò's older brother Melchior had died of an illness supposedly brought on by the frustration of not having the claim to the family estates recognized, and had left the care of his wife and four children to George (GStAPK, I.HA Geheimer Rep. 9 K lit n, Fasz. 8, Bl. 12 [M]).

[2] Not identified.

[3] The anecdote has not been identified. The Rev. Edward Colquitt (b. 1716), an early friend of JB's, was a Scottish Episcopal minister in Edinburgh and then rector of Husbands Bosworth, Leicestershire, from 1754 to 1776 (Corr. 9, p. 41 n. 1; David M. Bertie, Scottish Episcopal Clergy 1689–2000, 2000). JB would later remember him as 'a man who had lived much in the world and … eminent for gay sociality' ('Memoirs of James Boswell, Esq.', Eur. Mag. 1791, in Lit. Car., p. xxxii). The 'Doctor' is playful.

[4] JB wrote to both Feronce and Plessen on 15 Oct. Feronce seems not to have replied but Plessen wrote immediately, on 20 Oct., and again on 19 Nov. 1766.

[5] Frederick II usually refused to sit for his portrait, but as a favour to his sister, whom he had visited at Salzdahlum on 18–19 June 1763, he had posed for the Hanoverian court painter Johann Georg Ziesenis (1716–77; correcting Grand Tour I, Heinemann p. 68 n. 3, McGraw-Hill pp. 70–71 n. 4). The portrait seen by JB was not the original, however, but a copy that the painter had made immediately in order to keep the original for himself. The Duchess's 'pseudo-original' would disappear (August Fink, 'Herzogin Philippine Charlotte und das Bildnis Friedrichs des Grossen', Braunschweigisches Jahrbuch 40 [1959]: 117–18).

[6] MS. 'á votre cour' inserted above the line with a caret.

## Wednesday 22 August

[No MEM. for this day]

[J.] I was hypish. I went upon the Parade & saw the Duke once more. I wondered how he could plague himself every morning with making Men march about. I was convinced that all situations are judged of by comparrison so that He who has been Laird of Auchinleck ten years, feels himself as great as he who has been Duke of Brunswic ten years. I then took leave of *Ap Herusalem* as they call him here.[1] I dont know how it is but I am allways gloomy on leaving a room where I have lodged. I could get no *extra Post* which vexed me a little. I however hoped the court would suppose me gone in some company. I mounted the Post-Waggon without the gate, & away we went.

[1] See Journ. 28 June n. 2. JB's rendering of the name may be reflecting its pronunciation.

## Thursday 23 August

[No MEM. for this day]

[J.] Rumbled along.

## Friday 24 August

[No MEM. for this day]

[J.] Why relate that I had Blackguards with me, that I was sorely shaken, that the night air began to grow cold. That I slept at every stage.[1] I had however a very bad custom of running allways to the stable, making a bed of straw or of lint, throwing myself down and making Jacob call me when the horn sounded. This was very dangerous. I might have easily been robbed. The horses might have broke loose, & trampled me to death in the dark.

[1] JB had covered the roughly 127 miles (c. 204.4 km) between Brunswick and Potsdam on his three days' journey but left no record of the stages in either his Expense Account or Reg. Let.

## Saturday 25 August

[MEM. dated Sunday 26 August] From Wednesday to this day was your Journey, hard but healthy. At night you was glad to arrive. Had letters: talk'd to Lord Marischal freely.
    Mr. Voltaire[1]

[J.] This morning I arrived at Potsdam and breakfasted with honest Scott who told me that Lord Marischal & all his family were at Berlin. I took an *extra post* & came briskly to town. I immediatly waited on his Lordship, and found him well. I then went home & was kindly wellcomed by the Ladies. I received a packet of letters, one of which was from M. de Zuylen.[2] I have never mentioned that at Brunswic I received a second letter from Zelide, disclaiming love, but vowing strong freindship, and charging me to write much to her. I did write her a long letter a few days after my arrival at Berlin. I wrote to her with the serious freedom of a freind, convinced her that she could never have me for a lover, and assumed the tone of a Preceptor. Her conduct shows me that she was just titillated by love; for I have had no answer.[3] But, let me not blame her. Let me wait a little. At eight I waited on Lord Marischal told him how I was subject to melancholy & said his Lordship releived me at Utrecht, as the man was releived who fell into a coal pit, & imagined himself fifty fathoms from the bottom, when in reality he was not two feet. My Lord said I must have occupation, and must avoid gloomy or absurd company. It is fine to see his peace of mind.

[1] MS. 'Mr. Voltaire' written in the left margin with a finer quill.
[2] The letter from Belle de Zuylen's father, dated 17 Aug. and answering JB's letter of 30 July, welcomes JB's thought of himself as M. de Zuylen's son-in-law. It also responds obliquely to JB's letter to Belle of 9 July by reporting that she would not forget JB's advice but might not be able to follow it.
[3] Belle's letter to Brunswick has not survived. For JB's long letter to her from Berlin, see Journ. 9 July n. 4.

## Sunday 26 August

[MEM. dated Monday 27 August] Yesterday you dind Burnet well — but was a little restless. Refusd Stoltz and Hub to walk — Twas wrong. 'Twas Eglint.[1] This day after manege buy Earings[2] & then Journ all day — bring up clear & well & finish Epistle to Dempster.[3] Write Father that you'll go to Italy for the same time & expence as France, & will come home & take exercise like Burnet.

[J.] My Lord and all of us dined at Mr. Burnets, where we were exceeding well. My Lord chatted finely, & said I am old enough to remember storys told me by those who lived in the reign of Charles the Second.[4]

[1] Perhaps an allusion to Eglinton's capricious refusal to see JB in London (Journ. 20 Feb. 1763).
[2] Presumably for Caroline Kircheisen. Instead of earrings, he purchased an étui (a needle case or box) for her for 18 écus two days later (Exp. Acct. 29 Aug., App. 3). For the nostalgic little poem JB wrote about her after this time, see App. 1.
[3] That is, his verses on Parliament (see Journ. 6 Aug. and n. 7).
[4] Since Charles II had ruled from 1660 to 1685, Lord Marischal's informants had belonged to the generation before his.

## Monday 27 August

[MEM. dated Tuesday 28 August] Yesterday you din'd & sup'd Home but was too gay. Saw Smith's prints. This day at home[1] [—] Journ All day & see how you can do business & pray return to retenue & study & think on Temple and on Johnson with whom your happy days are to come. Also write Love & Father & Dempster & Davie & Johnston[2] &[3] think to live happy.

[J.] I dined and supped at home. But I was too free, & too merry. I was introduced to Mr. Artinslepen half-brother to Madame la Presidente. He was captain of Cavalry, but was so much wounded, that he quitted the service. He is a changeable, splenetic unhappy man.[4] He was feverish with gayety this night. He hurt me. But, he taught me a German Song.[5] Hubner & I had been this morning to see the Prints of Smidt. He works very well. But engraves only heads.[6] 'Tis pity.

[1] MS. 'h', followed by 3m gap; 'home' is conjectural.

[2] These letters, to family members and close friends, would not survive, if indeed they were really written at this time. Davie was JB's younger brother David, later known as Thomas David or T. D., now aged sixteen. JJ was one of JB's closest friends. Although he was about ten years older than JB, they had been at Edinburgh University at the same time, probably from 1755, and he would remain a lifelong confidant (see *Corr. 1*; Journ. 6 Sept. n. 5; *Earlier Years*, pp. 28–29).

JB did not note that on this day he also wrote to Andrew Mitchell, expressing surprise at his sudden departure from Berlin and asking him to write to Lord Auchinleck to recommend further travels for JB (BL Add. MS. 6858, ff. 11–14). Mitchell had left Berlin for reasons of health. Ailing for several years, he had suffered from exhaustion while on campaign with Frederick II in 1760 and from a dangerous fever while in Magdeburg the following year (Andrew Bisset, *Memoirs and Papers of Sir Andrew Mitchell*, 1850, ii. 347; Patrick Francis Doran, *Andrew Mitchell and Anglo-Prussian Diplomatic Relations*, 1986, pp. 282, 288, 290). In 1766 Mitchell would return to Prussia as Envoy Extraordinary and Minister Plenipotentiary with a modest pension and a knighthood. He would spend his remaining six years in Berlin but would not regain the friendship of Frederick II (D. B. Horn, *British Diplomatic Representatives 1689–1789*, 1932, p. 108; Namier and Brooke, iii. 143).

[3] MS. Damaged by a blot and hole; '&' is conjectural.

[4] JB misheard or misremembered the name, which was Aschersleben. Where and how Friedrich Karl Leopold von Aschersleben (dates unknown) was wounded has not been determined, but he is listed as lieutenant-colonel of cavalry in the Regt. Kyau, in which he had started in 1751 (*Verbesserte und Vollstaendige Liste der Koeniglich-Preussischen Armées* (sic), Amsterdam, 1753, p. 13). The year after meeting JB he would find a brighter future in Brunswick as *Rittmeister* and *Kammerjunker* (cavalry officer and gentleman of the bedchamber), to both of which he was appointed 22 Oct. 1765 (NStAWf 3 Alt Nr. 553, D. 33; see From Henriette Kircheisen, [Feb. 1766], Yale MS. C 1672). He would be appointed *Kammerherr* (chamberlain) in 1773, and *Hofmarschall* (marshal) from 1776 to 1786 (NStAWf 3 Alt Nr. 552, pp. 35, 52, 57; VI Hs 10 Nr 15 Bd 1, p. 166).

[5] Not identified.

[6] Georg Friedrich Schmidt (1712–75), one of the foremost engravers of his day, specialized in prints of important portraits, including Antoine Pesne's head of Frederick II (L. D. Jacoby, *Schmidt's Werke*, 1815, Register and p. 13). He also created prints and drawings on religious, mythological, satiric, and pastoral sujects, which JB evidently did not see (Aloys Apell, *Das Werk von Georg Friedrich Schmidt, Zeichner, Kupferstecher und Radirer* [1886], Index).

## Tuesday 28 August

[MEM. dated Wednesday 29 August] On Sunday Castillon advised you every night to recollect what you had read *penible au commencement. Mais á la fin tres utile*. Yesterday you dined Burnet *tête á tête*. Then went with him in chais to Park. He told you Story of John Tiby Esq; Tis excellent. Mark it. You found him a sollid sensible fellow & much better than yourself. At night you *resolved* to please worthy Father as at Auchinleck month october wood fire coffee & to be retenue. So compose mind — & stay here forthnight[.]

[J.] On Sunday last I complained to the Professor Castillon that my memory was bad. He bid me recollect every evening what I had learnt during the day. 'C'est penible au commencement; mais il deviendra aisé et sera tres utile.' I dined this day tête á tête with Mr. Burnet, after which he carried me in his chaise to the Park, where we had a fine drive. He told me that during the last war Marischal Keith was one day riding out when there came up to him an Englishman who called himself John Tibi Esq: His story is curious; but, I find it too long for my Journal, so shall mark it in another place.[1] Burnet said that Marischal Keith was a noble fellow. He had not much vivacity; But he had what was a great deal better, much knowledge & strong sense. He spoke very slow. His manners were courtly & amiable.[2] I found Burnet a sollid, clear-headed fellow, much better than myself.[3] We past the Afternoon well.

[1] JB's separate account would not survive, but he would allude to it in 1779 in his notes for a projected life of Gen. James Edward Oglethorpe (1696–1785), for which see Yale MS. M 208. The story is curious indeed, for 'John Tebay' had been Oglethorpe's alias when he volunteered his services to Fieldmarshal Keith (Lord Marischal's younger brother) and had accompanied him into battle during the Seven Years' War. It was in Oglethorpe's arms that Keith, mortally wounded at Hochkirch, had died (BL Add. 6836). In the 1730s, Oglethorpe had founded the colony of Georgia and had led his regiment against the Spaniards. He had then served as general in England but had incurred the wrath of the Duke of Cumberland for supposedly lagging in his pursuit of the Jacobite rebels in 1745. Feeling discredited as military commander even though acquitted by a court martial, and further despondent on losing the seat in Parliament which he had held from 1722 to 1754, he had left England and had returned only in about 1761 (R. M. Baine and M. E. Williams, 'Oglethorpe's Missing Years', *Georgia Historical Quarterly* 69 [1985]: 193–210). Eventually he would regain his good reputation, and would become a friend of JB's after personally congratulating him on his *Account of Corsica* (see To WJT, 26 Apr. 1768, *Corr.* 6, pp. 232–33 and n. 5).

[2] James Keith had had a remarkable career as a soldier. Like Lord Marischal, he had joined the Jacobite cause in 1715 and had taken part in several battles (Sheriffmuir, Glenshiel) until forced to escape from Scotland. He had found a post in Spain, had been present at the siege of Gibraltar, but realizing that his advancement after nine years was limited by not belonging to the religion of the country, had moved on to Russia in 1729. There he had served briefly under Czar Peter II (1715–30) and then as bodyguard of the Czarina Anna Ivanovna (1693–1740), distinguishing himself in the war of the Polish succession (1733–35) while fighting the French, and in the ongoing Russo-Turkish war, in which he had been wounded at Ochakov and incidentally had found Emetulla (see Journ. 18 June n. 7). After recuperating with Lord Marischal in Paris, he had returned to become governor of the Ukraine. He had taken a leading part in the war between Russia and Sweden (1741–43), winning the favour of the new czarina, Elisabeth, only to become a victim of court intrigues and to depart surreptitiously in 1747. Within a month he had found employment as field-marshall in Prussia, where he was greatly admired by Frederick II and would come to be considered a heroic figure by the German people (*Oxford DNB*; 'A Discourse on the Death of Marshal Keith read Before the Royal Academy of Science at Berlin', 1760).

[3] On this day Burnett wrote to Andrew Mitchell, now at Spa on his way back to England, that he had found JB spoiled by his stay in Brunswick and eager to embark on further travel. Burnett suggested that Mitchell invite JB to Spa and persuade him to return home (Burnett of Kemnay Archives, Bundle 86).

## Wednesday 29 August

[MEM. dated Thursday 30 August] Yesterday at manége you found that all things seem insipid when lazy. But get on horseback, & they seem gay. You had jaunt to

Trepzel[1] with Castillon who talked of freewill without cause as dernier ressort —
like the Divinity. You dind & danced & was merry. You talked of Utrecht un[2]
*Philosophe est dans un cas que de cacher ses plus belles qualités est son plus grand devoir.*
Home but talked too free *gare geit*[3] grown a goat. See Aristot.[4] This day Journ —
enrich mind with learning. Be sedate.

[J.] At manêge I found that all things seem insipid when a man is sluggish,
& his blood stagnates: But set him on horseback, & make his blood
circulate, and all things seem gay. This is an original principle. I examine
no farther. At eight a Captain of Artillery carried Castillon & his family
and several more and myself by water to Treptow, a Public house allmost
opposite to M. Schickler's Campagne.[5] We din'd & danc'd & were hearty.
But the Company did not please me. Before dinner Castillon & I walked
out, & brought free will on the Carpet.[6] He said he could conceive that
most perfect prescience, without restraining liberty. This is absurd. He said
that God must leave his Creatures free, because they neither can add to or
diminish the happiness of the supreme Creator. I asked if it was possible to
give freewill, as every effect must have it's cause. Sir (said he) I distinguish.
Most effects have, to be sure, their causes. But there are others which
contain their causes within themselves. The Will of God is a *dernier ressort*.
It is not influenced by extraneous force. It now & then is no doubt moved
by circumstances. But it can pronounce merely from it's own determina-
tion. God having been pleased to communicate a portion of his own nature
to man, man has the same will in a certain degree. This we feel to be fact.
The common instance of two eggs proves that we may determine without
a motive. I liked to hear this reasoning. It is just & clear.[7] Castillon
complained of Utrecht. I said. 'Monsieur n'est il pas curieux de supposer un
Philosophe tellement placé que de cacher ses plus belles qualités est son
plus grand devoir? et pourtant vous avez eté dans le cas, á Utrecht.'[8]

[1] Treptow.
[2] MS. 'on', a slip of the pen.
[3] An unidentified Scottish saying about a
greedy, stupid child (Jamieson, s.v. 'gare'
['greedy'], 'geit' ['stupid child']), apparently
referring to JB's awareness of having been too
talkative, or having lacked 'rétinue' with
Castillon.
[4] Possibly the word 'goat' triggered an
association with 'goat-song', etymologically
linked with tragedy (τράγος ['goat'] and
ᾠδή ['ode']), which may have suggested
Aristotle's discussion of tragedy in the
*Poetics*, 1449[a] (OED, s.v. 'tragedy').

[5] For this officer, Captain Henri Durand,
see Journ. 15 Sept. and n. 4. For Schickler's
country house, see Journ. 6 July and n. 4.
[6] MS. '& brought ... Carpet' scored out
by a modern hand.
[7] F. A. Pottle
confronted with identical objects (*Grand
Tour I*, Heinemann p. 75 n. 1, McGraw-Hill
p. 77 n. 6).
[8] Possibly Castillon had been forced to
play down his ideas about free will in the
intellectual climate of Utrecht, where the
dominant Calvinism no doubt favoured
predestination.

## Thursday 30 August

[MEM. dated Friday 31 August][1] [Y]esterday you stayed at home all morning but
was amazed at doing so little. You must learn quickness. You dined not. At 3 went

to Gofbzowski's Garden — played Billiards, saw Porcelaine walked — heard madame sing — supt was charmed with madame. At night madll. said Je vous plaigns de revenir chez vous — vous vous formez — mais il faut etre un peu plus poli. This day *think*. Journ till dinner then out then see Madll. Thiel — Mad. Brant Mad. Rottembourg & pray cultivate acquaint with Lord Marisch. Gen. Keith's Brothr.[2]

[J.] This morning I was hurt to find how little I had done after being employed several hours. I must learn more quickness, acquire more spring in action. I did not dine; but at three went with our Ladies to the Garden of Gotzkofsky a great Banker.[3] Here we had coffee, then walked, then saw the China manufactory;[4] then supped in a very handsom room in his Garden which is very large, & well laid out. He is a gallant German stupid comely cordial. She was a *Danceuse*, & he married her for love. She is a stout good-looking *frow*, but struck me as if she had been the greatest Beauty.[5] I raved 'Ma foi! quelle charmante Dame' etc. etc. & told the Husband 'Vous etes l'homme le plus heureux au monde'. He was pleased, & made us dance a minuet together. She sung well and I was in raptures. So fiery is my Imagination that if an object furnishes only a spark, I am very soon all in flame. As We went home I said 'Si J'avois eté né seulement pour adorer cette Dame, il auroit eté assez.' O can I not tame this turbulence of mind!

[1] MS. 'Friday' written over deleted 'Saturday'. Further additions to the MS: 'her 9bre 'fr', 'M' and other doodling along the left margin, a trial of the quill; more pen strokes at the top of the page above the date; 'John Thom' and then 'unam virginem' in Gothic letters, both written along the right margin.

[2] Neither Mademoiselle Thiel nor Madame Rottembourg (Rothenburg?) has been identified further. They had apparently known James Keith or had known of him while he was Frederick II's trusted field-marshal from 1749 to 1758, and either wished to cultivate their acquaintance with Lord Marischal or urged JB to cultivate it.

[3] Johann Ernst Gotzkowsky (1710–75) lived in a large house with a park-like garden in the Potsdamer Strasse, later called Leipzigerstrasse (Folkwin Wendland, *Berlins Gärten und Parke*, 1979, p. 94). Although better described as an entrepreneurial businessman, he was a 'banker' in that he dealt in bills of exchange, as did other merchants before the state bank was founded in 1765 (M. C. von Niebuhr, *Geschichte der königlichen Bank in Berlin*, 1971, pp. 25–38). He was said to be descended from Polish nobility, but he had started as apprentice in a Berlin grocery store, had become partner in a concern selling small luxury wares that had won him the patronage of Queen Sophie Dorothea and the future Frederick II, and had established a successful jewelry business. Gotzkowsky had become partner in a velvet factory with C. F. Blume (d. 1744), whose daughter Anna Louisa Blume (1725–55) he had married in 1740 and whose share in the factory he had bought after Blume's death. Gotzkowsky had also acquired a silk factory in 1753 and a satin factory in 1758. During the Seven Years' War he had suffered losses, among others from having to dispose of paintings which Frederick II had asked him to purchase for Sanssouci in 1755 but could not afford because the war had depleted his finances (they would be sold to Catherine the Great after the war; see GStAPK, I.HA Geheimer Rat, Rep. 11 Auswärtige Beziehungen, Nr. 171–75 Russland D Interzessionalia, G 1751–65). Gotzkowsky had been able to persuade the Russians occupying Berlin in Oct. 1760 to reduce the huge 'contribution' they demanded of the city, and had himself made some of the payments, as described in his autobiographical *Mémoires d'un négociant patriote*, 1768, pub. anon. as 'Geschichte eines patriotischen Kaufmanns' (in *Schriften des Vereins für die Geschichte der Stadt Berlin* 7 [1873], pp. 1–92; also in his unpublished autobiographical essay, GStAPK, VI. HA Familienarchive und Nachlässe, NL Johann Ernst Gotzkowsky).

Although he appeared prosperous to JB, Gotzkowsky had suffered from bankruptcies in Amsterdam and Hamburg as recently as July 1763, and only in Apr. 1764 had he paid his creditors 50% of what he owed (GStAPK, I. HA Rep. 96 Geheimes Zivilka-binett, ältere Periode, Nr. 74E, Bl. 33). His financial status had now improved, but he would suffer another reverse three years later and, hounded by creditors, would die in poverty (for the history of his complicated financial dealings, see Hugo Rachel and Paul Wallich, *Berliner Grosskaufleute*, 2nd ed., 1967, ii. 442–67).

[4] The factory produced fine, translucent hard-paste chinaware by a secret process that had been developed by the arcanists of Meissen and learned by Prussians when they occupied Meissen during the Seven Years' War. Gotzkowsky had operated the factory under the protection of Frederick II from 1761 until 1763 when, beset by financial troubles, he had persuaded the King to take possession of it. Renamed the Royal Porcelain Manufactory (*Königliche Porzellan Manufaktur*, Berlin's famous KPM), it had remained on Gotzkowsky's premises (Nicolai, ii. 537; Rachel and Wallich, ii. 446–47, 451, 460–63; 'Von Gotzkowsky zur KPM', exhibition at Charlottenburg Palace, Aug.–Nov. 1986).

[5] Gotzkowsky's second wife, Sophie Friederike (Eichmann), whom he had married in 1763, seems not to have been a professional performer even though she liked to dance. His first wife, Anna Louise (Blume), had died in 1755 at the age of thirty (*NDB*, vi. 689; Rachel and Wallich, ii. 444).

## Friday 31 August

[MEM. dated Saturday 1 Septr.] [Y]esterday you dind Burnet who said English mad as *Maddin* guineas & glass great Genius. Home All evening too gay — Sat up till one — but was bad — resolved never so — your'e in fine train and one night may break constitution so go on with regular mind …[1] [S]tay in whole days & bring up Journ — Calm mind. Think old Lairds of Auch better than little tickling pleasure. J— Bruce &c.[2] This day Journ — house all day for once to recover[.]

[J.] I din'd at Burnet's, who said that the young english were realy mad. He gave me an instance of young Maddan of the Guards who was with him at an academy in London. He came in one day, & said 'By the Lord a glass was never broke with Guineas', and immediatly took out some Guineas, & broke a fine mirror.[3]

[1] MS. 'but was bad … mind' scored out either by JB or by a modern hand; three illegible words follow 'mind'.

[2] James Bruce (1719–90) was the overseer at Auchinleck, having succeeded to this post on the death of his father in 1741. He had known JB from his childhood and was very likely the 'gardener' with whom JB had tried to discuss his first experience of sexual arousal (see 'Ébauche de ma vie', Outline 1, App. 2, III.D). He had now become a good friend (see From James Bruce, 10 Jan. 1763, *Corr. 8*, pp. xxxiii–iv and pp. 1–2).

[3] Frederick Madan (1742–80), ensign in the 1st Regt. of Foot Guards from 1759 to 1765, who would become lieutenant and captain from 1765 to 1776, then lieutenant-colonel in the Guards and Paymaster to the British Forces in America. He was 'young' Madan in relation to his older brother, Charles Madan (1739–61), ensign in the 3rd Regt. of Foot Guards from 1756 to his death. Frederick had been high spirited and undisciplined from his youth (Falconer Madan, *The Madan Family*, 1933, pp. 126–27).

## Saturday 1 September

[MEM. dated Sunday 2 Septr.] Yesterday by sitting up you lay till 8 so was bad; but knew it — din'd Rufins. Heard Italian doubt his existence. Thought him blockhead. How changed from Utrecht. Afternoon fine with sweet Madll who is realy the only girl you ever saw constantly agreable [—] You are to practice Germans[1] with her. At night wrote & was quite well.

This day write Lord Marischal & Madame Spaen & M. Sommelsd[2] — Call Hubner & Stoltz & fix day for Campagne & take coach to show your gratitude — *Think* be good.

Every year youre growing better. For shame pay Madll Schonmark monday.[3]

[J.] I dined at Rufins where Nehaus an Italian wanted to shine as a great Philosopher; and accordingly doubted of his existence & of every thing else.[4] I thought him a Blockhead & recollected with wonder my scepticism at Utrecht. In the afternoon I talked much with Mademoiselle Kirkheisen whom I like much. She has good sense, & enough of vivacity, & she is comely. She is the only Girl I ever saw constantly agreable. She has but one fault. She loves too much to *badiner* & thence is now & then a little impolite. She is a mimic, & that is dangerous.

[1] An idiosyncratic usage.

[2] In his letter to Lord Marischal JB announced that he planned to visit Potsdam (see Journ. 5 Sept.). He also asked for introductions to Frederick II and to Rousseau. The letters to Mme de Spaen and Sommelsdyck had to wait another week.

[3] MS. 'Every ... better' written along the left margin in a different quill; 'For shame ... monday' written at the right margin. Why and how much JB had to pay Mlle Schönermark has not been determined.

[4] Giovanni Jacopo Giacomo Casanova (1725–98), Chevalier de Seingalt, was staying at JB's inn at this time and may have been using the German version of his name (Casanova, x. 55–56 and 335 n. 37). Scepticism was not, however, Casanova's usual philosophical position. A twentieth-century commentator, J. Rives Childs, suggests that Casanova did not believe the ideas he was expressing but rather, finding JB pretentious, 'undertook to pull his leg' (*Casanova: A New Perspective*, 1988, p. 177).

## Sunday 2 September

[MEM. dated Monday 3 Septr.] Yesterday you was splenetic a little [—] went & saw Doms kerk & Garnison. [T]hen wrote — but trifled got letter from Johnie was angry but composed self. Then Gottzowsky's english Lady odious. You must be prudent nor marry till 30 — You was too extravag. This day Journ hard. Morn. & bring up much — then write Spaen & Sommelsd. After dinner with Castillon take coach & visit Sheenmark — Rottembourg Thil Brandt. Be not indolent Rose.[1]

Take money both for Castill & Sheen in pocket.[2]

[J.] Spleen prest me down. Young Kirkheisen carried me to the Doom's Kirk where are the tombs of several of the Princes of Brandenburgh; next to the Garnisoon Kirk, & then to a Catholic Chapel.[3] I got a letter from my brother John telling me that he had quitted the Army, & was going to England, to learn to be a Farmer. I was vexed & angry. But, recollecting his Hypochondriack disposition, I resolved to make the best of it, & be as kind to him as possible.[4] At four I went with the family to Gotzkofsky's Garden. Burnet was there — & an english Lady wife to a German merchant in London.[5] She was detestable. We had coffee, & a fine supper, & a dance. I was again too fiery.

[1] Probably James Rose (c. 1737–?1800), second son of James Rose (1699–1762) of Brea, and Margaret Rose, daughter of James Rose of Broadley. He was a cousin of Hugh Rose (1705–72), 17th Laird of Kilravock, and probably the James Rose who graduated A.M. from Marischal College, Aberdeen, 1755, and matriculated at Glasgow University in 1757. A companion of JB's in Utrecht who tutored him in Greek, Rose had admitted to being 'very lazy' (Journ. 22 Mar., *Holland*, Heinemann p. 188, McGraw-Hill p. 192). He was later ordained a Church of England clergyman, and was the 'Rev. Mr. Rose' whom JB met again many years later in London (Journ. 24 Mar. 1794).

[2] MS. 'Take ... pocket' written along the left margin.

[3] The *Domkirche* (Cathedral), in the Lustgarten, served the nearby palace and housed the sarcophagi of the earlier rulers of Prussia. Designed by Johann Boumann the Elder (1706–76) and dedicated in 1750, it had replaced the earlier cathedral demolished by order of Frederick II (Nicolai, i. 76–77; H. H. Möller, *Dome, Kirchen und Klöster in Brandenburg und Berlin*, 1961, pp. 65–66). The *Garnisonskirche* (Garrison Church), the largest church in Berlin, was reserved for the army and held the monuments of important military leaders. A plain Renaissance-style hall, it was built in 1722 after a previous building had been destroyed by a nearby explosion of gunpowder (Nicolai, i. 22; ii.

861; Werner Schwipps, *Die Garnisonkirchen von Berlin und Potsdam*, 1964, pp. 10–22). The Catholic chapel, the only one in Berlin at this time, was at the back of the imperial Austrian embassy in the Leipzigerstrasse. The more elaborate Catholic church of St. Hedwig had been begun in 1747 but would not be consecrated until 1773 (Nicolai, i. 196–97; Möller, p. 47). JB liked to visit houses of worship of different denominations and had attended mass in the Bavarian chapel in London (see *Earlier Years*, p. 46) as well as a Jesuit church in Utrecht (*Holland*, Heinemann p. 174 n. 2, McGraw-Hill p. 179 and n. 1).

[4] JB's younger brother John (1743–c. 1798) had been an ensign from Apr. 1760 and lieutenant from May 1762 ('Commissions in the Army', *Catalogue*, C 401.8, ii. 483). In Oct. 1762 he had suffered the first of the episodes of mental instability that would plague him intermittently for the rest of his life. He had gone on leave from the army on 28 Aug. of the current year and was trying out a new occupation by staying with a farmer, Ralph Foster, near Newcastle. Although he would return to his regiment briefly in 1766, he could never settle on a career and would always remain a worry for JB (see *Earlier Years*, p. 21; Journ. 24 Dec. 1789, *Great Biographer*, p. 25 and n. 2; *Corr. 5*, p. 15 n. 5; *Catalogue*, C 404–08, ii. 484–86).

[5] Not identified.

## Monday 3 September

[No MEM. for this day][1]

[J.] Hubner went with me to see the Royal Library of Berlin. It is large.[2] The manuscripts are numerous. It has received many presents. Amongst others who have added to the Library of Frederic the Great is Walter Hart one of the Canons of Windsor who has here deposited his life of Gustavus Adolphus bound superbly. An Inscription is written on the initial blank leaf: 'Accipe, Princeps illustrissime', etc.[3] I dined with M. le Professeur de Castillon. I talked to him of Hypochondria. He said. 'Monsieur, J'ai beaucoup souffert de cette maladie. Apres la mort de ma premierre femme il y avoit un ann que Je dinois seul, et Je vous jure que pendant ce tems la, Je ne jamais touchais le couteau et la fourchette, sans avoir envie de me tuer.'[4] This was another proof to me that I am not a singular Victim to the dire disease. At night I was the Guest of Stoltz at an ordinary[5] for Supper. I did not like it much. After supper, Hubner and Blancho and some more of us went to a Berlin Bawdy House,[6] which I was curious to see. We found a poor little house, an old Bawd & one whore.[7] I was satisfy'd with what I saw.

[1] Possibly four pages, folded into two leaves, are missing for the memoranda of 4 to 8 Sept. (Yale MS. J 5; see *Catalogue*, i. 5).

[2] The library was housed in a side building of the palace (Nicolai, i. 116; ii. 760–63). Its extensive collection of books was organized into 17 classes, ranging from religion, law and medicine to philosophy, history, and literature. It had been augmented by the library of Ezechial Spanheim (1629–1710), minister of state and scholar, which had been purchased in 1735 by the then ruler Friedrich I, first King of Prussia (Nicolai, ii. 763).

[3] 'Accept, most illustrious prince'. The Rev. Walter Harte (1709–74) had evidently been proud of his *History of the Life of Gustavus Adolphus*, published in two volumes in 1759. His book had however suffered by comparison to William Robertson's *History of Scotland*, 2 vols., published at the same time. SJ thought well of Harte's scholarship but referred to 'defects in his history' due to 'foppery' (*Life* ii. 120). Lord Chesterfield, who had engaged Harte as travelling tutor for his son Philip Stanhope (whom JB would

soon meet in Dresden; see Journ. 10 Oct.), found the book 'full of good matter' but also 'execrable' in style, 'full of Latinisms, Gallicisms, Germanisms, and all isms but Anglicisms' (16 Apr. 1759, *Letters*, ed. Bonamy Dobrée, 1932, v. 2348).

[4] Castillon's first wife, Elisabeth du Frène, had died in 1757. He had married again two years later (DSB, iii. 119–20).

[5] An eating place that serves prix fixe meals (see OED, s.v. 'ordinary', III. 12.b).

[6] MS. 'Hubner ... House' scored out by a modern hand. Blanchot (first name and dates unknown) was at the beginning of a career in diplomacy. He would be assigned to the *Geheime Kanzlei* (privy chancery office) in Berlin in 1768, would serve as secretary of legation in Dresden from 1768 to 1776, would represent Prussia as Resident in Warsaw in 1776, and would hold another diplomatic post in Vienna from 1776 to 1779 (*Adres-Calendar*, 1768–76; *Repertorium*, iii. 335).

[7] MS. 'old Bawd' and 'one whore' scored out by a modern hand. The bawdyhouse and the two women have not been identified.

## Tuesday 4 September

[No MEM. for this day]

[J.] Hubner went with me to the Park, where I saw a Prussian Regiment exercised. The Soldiers seemed in terror. For the least fault they were beat like Dogs. I am, however, doubtfull if such fellows don't make the best Soldiers. Machines are surer Instruments than men. Were I to knock down a Scoundrel, I would rather take a Stick than take a child by the heels to give him a blow with. I also saw a Deserter pass the *Baguette* twelve times. He was much cut. It made me sick to see it.[1] I had Stoltz for my Guest to dine at Rufin's. In the afternoon, I walked four hours with Blancho, who is auprés l'Ambassadeur de Suède.[2] He entertained me much; being a fellow of knowledge and clear expression. He said the french music was a contrast to the french temper. The french are gay. Their music is grave. A frenchman never looks so serious, as when he sings a song. He said the King of Prussia had been sadly debauched in his youth: for he used to go to the common Bawdy houses as well as to divert himself with the Ladies of the Court. He is now (said Blancho) quite impotent.[3] At night Blancho & Hubner drank a glass of wine with me, at my lodgings, and Blancho showed me on the map my route to Geneva, so as to take several German Citys & Courts in my way.

[1] The *baguette* was a hazel switch soaked in water that was used to beat an accused as he ran between two ranks of soldiers. It was the established punishment for deserters, of whom there were many among those who had been forcibly impressed (Christopher

Duffy, *The Army of Frederick the Great*, 1974, p. 63). JB not only sympathized with the man but also gave him 4 Groschen (Exp. Acct., App. 3).

[2] The Swedish Ambassador, Karl Julius, Count von Bohlen (1738–1813), served in

Berlin from Nov. 1763 to June 1766 (*Repertorium*, ii. 378).

[3] MS. 'debauched in', 'for he used ... Bawdy houses', and 'quite impotent' scored out by a modern hand. The reports of Frederick II's sexual experiences would remain difficult to substantiate, but JB's comments show that rumours were already rife. Possibly the young prince had frequented bawdy houses toward the end of his stay at Küstrin, where he had been sent in Nov. 1732 after the Katte affair (for which see Journ. 19 June n. 4) and where he may have contracted venereal disease. While at Küstrin he had also formed a romantic attachment to Eleonore von Wreech (d. 1764), whose daughter, not acknowledged by her husband, was thought by some to have been Frederick's (Robert B. Asprey, *Frederick the Great*, 1986, pp. 83, 113). A few years later, at the estate of Rheinsberg given him by his father as a wedding present, he had flirted with Louise von Brandt, at the time a lady in waiting at his mother's court and now an acquaintance of JB's (see Journ. 1 Aug. and n. 6). His later impotence in sexual relations with his young officers or cadets would be described in detail and quite likely with malicious intent by Voltaire: 'les choses n'allaient pas jusqu'aux dernières extrémités, attendu que le Prince du vivant de son pere, avait été fort maltraité dans ses amours de passade, & non moins mal guéri. Il ne pouvait jouer le premier rôle; il fallait se contenter des seconds' (*Mémoires pour servir à la vie de M. de Voltaire, Écrits par lui-même*, 1784, p. 46). After Frederick's death, other published accounts of his impotence would attribute it to physical damage resulting from the earlier treatment for his venereal disease (Anton Friedrich Büsching, *Über den Charakter Friedrichs II*, 1788, and Johann Georg von Zimmermann, *Fragmente zu Friedrichs Charakter und Lebensgeschichte*, 1790; for later, more considered interpretations of Frederick's sexuality, see Hans Dollinger, *Friedrich II von Preussen: Sein Bild im Wandel von zwei Jahrhunderten*, 1986, pp. 106–07; MacDonogh pp. 105–06).

The talk of the King's impotence inspired JB to a witticism: after hearing from 'a Gentleman', presumably Blanchot, that a female dancer had spent an hour trying to arouse Frederick but 'ne pouvait pas le branler.... Monsieur vous savez que sa Majesté est *inebranlable*' ('Boswelliana', Hyde Collection, p. 83).

## Wednesday 5 September

[No MEM. for this day]

[J.] Some days ago I wrote to My Lord Marischal that Mr. Burnet and I intended this day to have the honour of eating an Olio[1] with his Lordship. At six we set out in a clever chaise. The day was good. My spirits were fine. We talked of Spleen. Burnet said that Mr. Mitchell was sadly distrest with it; that sometimes he would sit without speaking a word, & say Well I could not have thought that this could get so much the better of me. All this was realy owing to his being costive, to prevent which he took every proper method.[2] He had his own Box, which was constantly tied behind the coach, and with Mr. Locke's regularity did he attempt the necessary operation.[3] We found all well at Potzdam. My Lord gave us an Olio which I found excellent. After dinner we went & saw the Garden and House at Sans Souci. I looked with pleasure at the King's study, which is elegant, and has it's Books finely bound, as at Potzdam. In his Bed-chamber I found some verses on a table. We then went to the Gallery, where I saw the noble room and rich pictures with true relish. We then looked at the foundation of the house which the King is going to build for My Lord, which makes his Lordship very happy.[4] At night Macpherson and I drest ourselves in the highland dress, of which Macpherson had two suits, and a fine frolic did we make of it. We wrote a card 'To The Right Honourable George Earl

Marischal of Scotland', 'Two Highland Gentlemen Messrs. Mcdonald & [M]cintosh⁵ beg leave to have the honour of paying their respects to The Earl of Marischal. They ask pardon for troubling him at so untimely an hour.' The direction & the word 'untimely' were excellent. Away we went, & Scott & Burnet behind us, past the centinels & went to My Lord's apartment in the Palace. I asked the Servant in German for My Lord, & delivered the Card. His Lordship made us wellcome. We stood just within his door, bowing much. He cried 'Come in, Gentlemen, come in'. He advanced & immediatly knew us, & asked how Cows sold. He took our joke in good part. We marched home again. Going & coming we were followed on the street; for, we spoke a barbarous language. I did at least; for I made it. We supt on Sowans hearty, & were *canty Chields.*⁶ Burnet had a bed, & in the same room the Highlanders lay on straw. Thus did I talk. Thus was I merry.

¹ 'A spiced meat and vegetable stew of Spanish and Portuguese origin' (OED, s.v. 'olio', 1). JB had written his letter on 2 Sept. (see Mem. for that date).

² MS. 'All this … method' scored out by a modern hand.

³ According to John Locke, '… if a man after his first eating in the morning would presently solicit nature and try whether he could strain himself so as to obtain a stool, he might in time, by a constant application, bring it to be habitual' (*Some Thoughts concerning Education* [1693], §24.4, ed. Ruth W. Grant and Nathan Tarcov, 1996, p. 23). JB, aware of this advice, had planned in Utrecht to 'follow Mr. Locke's prescription of going to stool every day regularly after breakfast' (Journ. 11 Oct. 1763, in *Holland*, Heinemann p. 43 and n. 3, McGraw-Hill p. 45 and n. 7).

⁴ For JB's earlier visit to the palace and gallery, see Journ. 4 July. The house for Lord Marischal, adjoining the park of Sanssouci, would be completed the following year and would consist of one good-sized room and 'a parcell of Rabbit Holes' for the rest (Alexander Burnett to Andrew Mitchell, 5 Oct. 1765, BL Add. MS. 6842). Lord Marischal would spend the remainder of his life there, well cared for by the King.

⁵ MS. 'Messrs…. [M]cintosh' inserted above the line. Part of the joke played by JB and Macpherson was to present themselves as a Macdonald and a Mackintosh, rival members of the Clanchattan (see Journ. 14 July n. 2; see also *Corr.* 9, p. 83 n. 46).

⁶ Scottish terms: 'sowans' = a slightly fermented porridge (see CSD, s.v. 'sowans'); 'canty chields' = cheerful chaps (CSD, s.v. 'canty', 3.1; 'chields').

## Thursday 6 September

[No MEM. for this day]

[J.] I rose stout & well. After breakfast I disputed against the Union. Burnet was my Antagonist. After much warm disputation, I said 'Sir, the love of our country is a sentiment. If you have it not, I cannot give it you by reasoning.'¹ I waited on Lord Marischal. I had written to him from Berlin, complaining of his coldness of manner, which prevented me from enjoying with ease his excellent conversation, telling him what esteem I had for him, & how I had 'old fashioned ideas' which made me have a particular veneration for the 'Representative of the illustrious family of Keith'. I also begged his advice as to my travels.² I found that my letter had pleased him. He was more affable than usual. I owned to him that I was affraid I could not do great things as a Scots Lawyer, & could wish to be in some other employment. As for the Army (said he) it is too late. Then 'My Lord, might I not be employed abroad?' Sir you must begin as Secretary, & if you are not with a man to your mind, you are very unhappy. Then if you should be sent Envoy if you are at a Place, where there is little to do, you are idle & unhappy. If you have much to do, you are harrassed with anxiety. Well then My Lord, I would get into Parliament. No Sir. You would be obliged to stick to a Party right or wrong, thro' thick & thro' thin.[3] Or you must be singular & be thought absurd. My Lord, if you go on, you'll chace me out of existence altogether. What say you to my following the law in Scotland moderately? jogging on between the Parliament House[4] & Auchinleck, and so doing pretty well. Indeed Sir I'm for your jogging on. Your Father will see that you do your best. He has a great liking for you, & you'll do very well together. Then My Lord will you write to him, that in the mean time he may allow me to travel a year. I will. His Lordship then gave me my route by Switzerland Italy & France. I was very happy, quite in the humour of revering the Old Earl. I thought on the Abbey of Holyrood-house. I thought on worthy Johnston.[5] I talked with my Lord against the Union, & how we had lost our spirit. I said You find Scotsmen in the Highlands. But very few south of Tay;[6] I ought to be valued, My Lord, as a rare Scot. He took down from his Book-case, the History of Robert the Bruce in old verse & made me a present of it, writing upon it 'Scotus Scoto.'[7] and saying now you must read this once every year. I had allmost cried before the good old man.[8] We dined with his Lordship. After dinner Burnet & I set out. He was excellent company. His storys flew thick.[9] He insisted that I should sup with him. I did so & merry we were. Yet, my gloomy eye saw the situation of an Envoy in an unpleasing light. I am an unhappy Dog.

[1] The union of Scotland and England had abolished the Scottish Parliament, though separate legal and ecclesiastical systems had been retained. Many Scots including JB resented what they considered a diminution of Scottish rights and the loss of an independent national identity. Earlier, in a conversation with the Kellies in London, JB had expressed his concern at greater length about the loss of loyalty as well as of 'public spirit and national principle' attributable to the confusing political changes in the prior hundred years (Journ. 17 Jan. 1763; see Gordon Turnbull, 'James Boswell: Biography and the Union', in Cairns Craig, gen. ed., The History of Scottish Literature, Vol. 2: 1660–1800, ed. Andrew Hook, 1987, pp. 158–62; and Paul H. Scott, 'Boswell and the National Question', in Boswell in Scotland and Beyond, ed. Thomas Crawford, 1997, pp. 22–32). Two hundred and ninety years later, in 1997, the Scottish people would vote to restore a parliament of their own.

[2] The letter was written on 2 Sept. (Yale MS. L 950).

[3] These were prophetic words. In 1790 JB would hope to gain a Parliamentary seat by attaching himself to James Lowther, 1st Earl of Lonsdale (1736–1802), but would be unable to submit to his patron's demands for complete subservience (Journ. 17 June to 14 July 1790, Great Biographer, pp. 66–93; see also Frank Brady, Boswell's Political Career, 1965, pp. 131–79; Later Years, pp. 391, 407–08, 413). In the event, JB never actually had an opportunity to run for Parliament.

[4] Parliament House, Edinburgh, where the business of the Scottish Court of Session was conducted (see Boswell for the Defence, 1769–1774, ed. W. K. Wimsatt and F. A. Pottle, 1959, App. B, pp. 351–52; Anon., A Pictoral and Descriptive Guide to Edinburgh, 7th ed. rev., n.d., pp. 82–83).

[5] For JB's association of Lord Marischal with the Abbey of Holyroodhouse, see Journ. 3 July. JB's enthusiasm for the Scottish past was shared by JJ, to whom he had written: 'Remember you are to be ready to attend me in the Abbey of Holyroodhouse whenever I write to you. Is not this quite in taste for us? quite romantic and old Scotch?' (17 Aug. 1762, Corr. 1, p. 13).

[6] The Tay, the longest river of Scotland, measuring about 120 miles (c. 193 km), issues from Loch Tay in the west, draining through the greater part of Perthshire, and passing off to the sea at the Firth of Tay between Forfarshire and Fifeshire in the east (OGS, 1901, pp. 1559–60). Although it runs an uneven course, sometimes east-northeast and sometimes south-southeast, JB evidently considered it the separating line between the lowlands and the highlands.

[7] MS. Full stop after 'Scoto', perhaps Lord Marischal's, completing the dedication which JB was transcribing. The phrase means: 'A Scot to a Scot'.

[8] John Barbour's *Brus* (1375) celebrates Robert I (1274–1329), also known as Robert the Bruce, who captured most of Scotland from the English in notable victories against Edward II (1284–1327), especially at Bannockburn in 1314, and eventually won recognition for his country's independence. The inscription must have meant much to JB not only because it came from Lord Marischal but also because JB himself believed that he was descended from Robert the Bruce by way of the royal house of Stuart. JB's mother, Euphemia (Erskine) Boswell, was a descendant of both the Earls of Mar and the Dukes of Lennox (see Journ. 16 Nov.; *Ominous Years*, App. C, Charts I and IV; *Earlier Years*, pp. 8, 11, 453). Lord Marischal would later confirm that the ancestry of the Boswells could be traced to the Bruce, though no farther back (letter of 15 May 1765, see Journ. 16 Nov. and nn. 8–9).

JB would take the book back to Auchinleck, listing it as 'Life & Acts of King Robert the Bruce in Rhyme Black letter' in his 'Catalogue of Books belonging to James Boswell Esq.', 1770 (National Library of Scotland MS. 3285).

[9] Eight of Burnett's anecdotes are recorded in 'Boswelliana'. Several deal with Frederick II.

## Friday 7 September

[No MEM. for this day]

[J.] The civility of Mr. Burnet is very great. I dined with him today, in company with Captain Wake. I don't know if I have as yet mentioned Captain Wake in this my Journal.[1] He is a good Prestonpans man; but has been all his life at sea — & during the last war had the King of Prussia's commission to go out with a Privateer. He took some Swedish Ships. He cannot get the prize-money having carried them into the port of ————[2] where they are retained. He has been two years at Berlin pleading before a court of Justice, in order to recover them.[3]

[1] JB had previously mentioned Wake on 7 July but had not recorded his exploits.

[2] MS. Blank, for the name of the port, which was Cagliari.

[3] Wake had become a Prussian citizen and had commanded the *Emden*, a ship that had been specially built for him. A successful privateer (see Journ. 7 July, n. 1), he had captured a Swedish sailing ship on the northern coast of Spain in 1759 and seven more vessels in the Mediterranean. He had taken these to Cagliari in Sardinia, where they were evidently still being detained. In Sept. 1761 he had left Sardinia for Barcelona, where he had sold the *Emden* which was no longer seaworthy, and had returned to Berlin. He had been litigating with the ministry of foreign affairs ever since (Hans Szymanski, *Brandenburg-Preussen zur See*, 1939, pp. 105–06). Presumably his difficulties stemmed from the fact that he could not produce the captured ships. The outcome of his litigation has not been determined, there being no record in the GStAPK.

After this dinner Burnett expressed his fear, in a letter to Andrew Mitchell, that more travel would only make JB more reluctant to settle down to the career chosen by his father. This letter also clarifies why JB was not able to meet Frederick II: 'He teases me to get him presented to K.P. [the King of Prussia] but I find he makes such absurd Distinctions between Englishmen and Scotchmen ... that I am certain something very ridiculous would happen on that Occasion. He has told me he must be presented as a Scotchman ...' (To Mitchell, 8 Sept., quoted in Susan Burnett, *Without Fanfare*, 1994, p. 119). JB would never know that his friends were deliberately preventing him from having a private interview with the King (see Marlies K. Danziger, 'James Boswell and Frederick of Prussia', *SVEC* 305 [1992]: 1654–57).

## Saturday 8 September

[MEM. dated Sunday 9 Septr.] [Y]esterday you was splenetic — din'd Presid's played cards — At night walked with Stenze &c. then home & talked of death. This day at nine church. Then home & letters & Journ follow Pythag's maxim,[1] & in health & spirits form mind.

[J.] Was splenetic; dined Heer Présidént's; was rude — Madame made me say in Germans[2] the equivalent of lêchez moi le cou.[3] I knew the meaning of it, & yet repeated it several times to an old maiden in the company. At last I said Je le sais tres bien. Bad, bad. At six after playing cards to help away time, I walked *unter linden* with Mademoiselle Stensen & others.[4] I thought them poor Beings. I supt at home. I was still unruly. Something of Houstoun Stewart. Let me take care.

[1] Maxim unidentified. JB learned of Pythagorean doctrines from an eccentric self-educated philosopher, John Williamson (born c. 1717), who was a sheepfarmer from the neighbourhood of Moffat (John Ramsay, *Scotland and Scotsmen*, 1888, ii. 327–28, 334). Pythagoreanism had been a brief stage in JB's search for a satisfying system of belief, following a spell of Methodism and preceding his temporary involvement with Catholicism ('Ébauche de ma vie', Yale MS. L 1107, App. 2, III.A; *Earlier Years*, pp. 33–34, 36, 462).

[2] An idiosyncratic usage.

[3] MS. 'lêchez ... cou' scored out by a modern hand. The usual saying, which is more coarse, refers not to *cou* ('neck') but to *cul* ('arse')—see Robert, 'Cul'. A parallel saying exists in German.

[4] Unter den Linden owed its name to its 1,000 Linden trees. These, together with 1,000 walnut trees, were planted in six rows in a long avenue that began in the square in front of the opera and ran the length of the Dorotheen Stadt, also called Neustadt (Nicolai, i. 168–69, 171–72 and n.**).

## Sunday 9 September

[MEM. dated Monday 10 Septr.] Yesterday you was bad dind Rufin's then walk'd with Officer who said Le Roy a point de Religion point d'humanité &c. At Wood saw fireworks [—] home — was again too free — correct habit. 'Tis to be polite your'e abroad. Begin this day — *Pay Galliard* — & Groom — *Pay Hubner*.[1] See Lord Marish — Be engaged & stay in all day firm to finish.

[J.] It must be the bad weather that overturns me. I am just as much hyp'd as ever. All things displease me. I am even timourous. I dined this day at Rufin's with Prussian officers, & thought them madmen to endure fatigues & risque their lives. Mean thought! One of them a Saxon walked with me after dinner & said Notre Roi n'a ni religion, ni humanité.[2] I said Je suis bien aise de vous entendre parler si librement. He said of the Prince of Prussia C'est un foible Caractère.[3] I called on Hubner, & pitied him & found him insipid. I went with him & some Ladies to the Park, & saw fireworks of magnificent and brilliant structure. Thought of Cannongate-Johnston. Mrs. Bird's Tarts.[4]

[1] In his Expense Account JB recorded 9 écus for one month's riding instruction and 16 Gr. for the grooms, but he did not note a payment for Hübner. On this day JB also paid 1 écu 12 Gr. for half a month's fencing lessons. Moreover, presumably in preparation for the visits he was planning to various German courts, he spent 73 écus 18 Gr. on silk, lining, and a 'riding-coat' for a new outfit (Exp. Acct., App. 3).

[2] The officers have not been identified.

[3] The vagaries of the Prince of Prussia (for whom see Journ. 3 July n. 5) were well known. He had distinguished himself in the war but now indulged in affairs with actresses as well as in boyish pranks such as breaking the windows of acquaintances in the company of his cousins, the two princes of Brunswick (Lehndorff, Feb. 1764, *Dreissig Jahre: Nachträge*, i. 392). His relationship with the precocious Wilhelmine Enke (b. 1752), daughter of a court musician, had made Frederick II insist on his engagement to Princess Elisabeth of Brunswick that had recently been celebrated at Charlottenburg (Journ. 21 July; W. M. von Bissing, *Friedrich Wilhelm II, König von Preussen*, 1967, pp. 12–19).

[4] JB spent 1 écu 12 Gr. at the fireworks (Exp. Acct., App. 3). He had presumably seen similar displays in Edinburgh with his friend JJ. By 'a chain of curious ideas' he had linked his first acquaintance with JJ with their walks through Edinburgh and the pastries they had bought from a Mrs. Bird, who seems to have had a shop in the Canongate (To JJ, 19 July 1763, *Corr. 1*, pp. 91–92; *Grand Tour I*, Heinemann p. 85 n. 1, McGraw-Hill p. 87 n. 4).

## Monday 10 September

[MEM. dated Tuesday 11 Septr.] [Y]esterday you ended Riding. You wrote all day & cured spleen. At night Madll. said She'd write Grand Roi cesse de vaincre — You rag'd on pride & heard with Contempt madn. &c on Content. Poor Beings. This day Scott & My Lord &c[.]

[J.] I took leave of the riding School. I was glad to do so; for I had the spleen. I drove it off by writing all day. At night I supt with the family. Mademoiselle made me a present of a Book to keep an *Album Amicorum* a great custom in Holland & Germany & the northern countrys. You present your book to a freind who writes something in it of his own, or a quotation from some authour & writes his name below; or if he can draw, designs you something. Thus you have a remembrance of your freinds.[1] It is not a bad contrivance; but a little ridiculous. Mademoiselle said she would write in mine. Grand Roi cesse de vaincre, ou Je cesse d'ecrire.[2] She however would not do it as it was not *convenable*. I raged at her being so much pleased with the conceit, & exclaiming. 'C'est noble c'est au dessu de vous. Vous ne comprenez pas la force de votre propre idée, ou si vous le prenez pour un compliment, ou pour un ironique exquise'. I raged in the cause of pride, & said my greatest satisfaction was to have power over others, to have which I would suffer many evils, & I thanked heaven for having given me noble sentiments and the rule over Lands. They talked of contentment. I said it was a poor thing. Indeed, I was too fiery.

[1] Such an album (from Lat. *album*, 'white tablet'), a precursor of the modern autograph album, consisted of blank pages on which pious or sentimental sayings were inscribed, often not by the owner but by friends. This sort of album had originated in Germany (see OED, s.v. 'album') and may have been inspired by collections of the dicta of Luther, Melanchthon, and other Reformation figures (Margaret A. E. Nickson, 'Some sixteenth century albums in the British Library', Jörg-Ulrich Fechner, *Stammbücher als kultur-*

*historische Quellen*, 1981, p. 34). JB's album would not survive.

[2] The first line in Boileau's 'Épitre VIII', addressed to Louis XIV.

## Tuesday 11 September

[MEM. dated Wednesday 12 Septr.] Yesterday after being up all night you was elevated. Woman entered with chocolade & with child — tout d'un coup to bed — Adultery sans penser — was amaz'd[1] — Dind Burnet with Scott & Macpherson had them here at tea. Supt Burnets — & restrained mirth. This day consider *Adventure* as mere accident [—] go on — recover polite restraint — fix mind &c.

[J.] To punish my extravagant Rhodomantading, & to bring up my affairs & compose my spirit, I had sitten up all night.[2] Grievous was it to the flesh, till seven in the morning when my blood took a fine flow. I was quite drunk with brisk spirits and about eight in came a woman with a basket of Chocolade to sell.[3] I toyed with her and found she was with child — Oho! a safe piece — into my closet — habs er ein man. Ja in der Gards bei Potzdam[4] — To bed directly — In a minute — over — I rose cool and astonished — half angry half laughing — I sent her off. Bless me, have I now committed Adultery — Stay a Soldier's Wife is no Wife.[5] Should I now torment myself with speculations on Sin and on losing in one morning the merit of a year's chastity?[6] No; this is womanish. Nay your elegant mystics would not do so, Madame Guion was of opinion that Sin should be forgotten as soon as possible as being an idea too gross for the mind of a Saint, and disturbing the exercise of sweet devotion.[7] Her notion is ingenious. I am sorry that this accident has happened, I know not how. Let it go. I'll think no more of it. Divine Being! pardon the errors of a weak Mortal.[8] Give me more steadiness. Let me grow more perfect. What a curious thing is it to find a strict Philosopher speculating on a recent fault! Well I shall not be proud. I shall be a mild & humble Christian. I was made happy at twelve by a visit of Messrs. Scott and Macpherson. We all dined at Burnet's. Scott had taken it into his head to think of Mademoiselle Kirkheisen for his wedded wife, tho' he had never seen her. I carried him & Macpherson to the President's to drink coffee. The Highlander pleased much. But Scott not at all. Poor fellow! his manners are not taking. I must put his courting project far from him. We supped at Burnet's. Captain Wake was there. He sung

> Wat ye wha I met yestreen
> Coming down the hill my Joe

And some more Scots Sangs.[8] They were a little too free. But, I was master of myself.

[1] MS. 'after about eight ... amaz'd' heavily scored out, possibly by JB. The pregnant woman has not been identified.
[2] MS. 'had sitten' written above 'sat'
[3] Chocolate, made of cacao beans imported from the West Indies or South America, was sold in solid chunks or as paste. It was most often used to make a hot drink, though solid eating chocolate was also known (Peter B. Brown, *In Praise of Hot*

*Liquors: The Study of Chocolate, Coffee and Tea-Drinking 1600–1850*, 1995, pp. 27–34; 'Dietary Liquids', *The Cambridge World History of Food*, ed. Kenneth F. Kiple and Kriemhild Coneè Ornelas, 2000, i. 638). For JB's liking of the drink, see his 'Ten Lines' of 2 Oct. and n. 10).

[4] 'Do you have a husband?' 'Yes, in the guards near Potsdam'.

[5] MS. 'and about … Wife' scored out by a modern hand.

[6] JB had been chaste for slightly more than a year and had evidently kept count of the time. His last reported illicit encounter had been on 1 Aug. 1763, shortly before leaving London for the Continent (Journ. 3 Aug. 1763).

[7] Jeanne Marie (Bouvier) de la Motte-Guyon (1648–1717) was an ardent French mystic who believed that one should concentrate wholly on the divine. True to this belief, she scarcely mentioned sin in her writings, and in one of her best-known works declared: 'Il est de grande conséquence de ne se point inquiéter pour les défauts, parce que l'inquiétude ne vient que d'un orgueil secret et d'un amour de notre excellence [L]a réflexion que nous faisons sur nos fautes produit un chagrin qui est pire que la faute même' (XVIII, 'Des Défauts', *Le Moyen court et autres récits* [1685], ed. Marie Louise Gondal, 1995, p. 94). An English translation had been published in 1703. Mme Guyon had gained a following among Protestant Scots with mystical leanings, especially in Aberdeenshire, notably Alexander (1678–1762), 4th Lord Forbes of Pitsligo, his sons William (d. 1730), 13th Lord Forbes, and James (c. 1689–1710), 15th Lord Forbes, and Dr. James Keith (d. 1726); see G. D. Henderson, *Mystics of the North-East*, 1934, pp. 14–18, 44–51, 56–61, 101 and n. 3. JB would later mention that he had been familiar with her work from his youth (*Hypochondriack* no. LV [Apr. 1782], Bailey, ii. 165), and he would keep a book identified as 'Madam Guion on prayer' in his library (Margaret Boswell, 'Catalogue of the Auchinleck Library', c. summer 1783, Yale MS. C 437.6).

[8] MS. 'Mortal' written over 'Being'

[9] Scots for 'songs' (CSD). 'Wat ye wha', sung to the tune of 'Tartan Screen', had appeared in *Tea-Table Miscellany* (1724).

## Wednesday 12 September

[MEM. dated Thursday 13 Septr.] [Y]esterday you told Madll she said choses picquantes & had not *la vraye* politesse have a care. You dind Wake — heard there two highlanders a stone below your head. D—n your effeminacy — Voltaire owning quelques endroits trop foibles il faut retoucher — Parisen Petit maitre repetoit quelques vers — oui; il faut retoucher — Volt. — Mr. Je puis schier en mes Cotes mais pardieu un autre n'y pissera — Ne croyez pas tout ce que vous lisez. J'ai pourtant lu tous vos ouvrages[1] — Donnez a boire — ou pensez a boire — Mr. vous n'etes pas des gens de demander. Vous devez etre menés á boire. Had Scott &c at supper. This day drive off spleen [—] at 9 Burnet — 10 home [—] 11 Madame & cherish gay gratitude &c. & politeness. 12 Castill — & Book — then Acad. Berl. &c &c[.]

[R]ecover tone & leave Berlin fine &c &c — &c.[2]

[J.] Mademoiselle joked too much with me this morning, & somewhat in the Scots biting way. I was angry with her & said. Vous dites que Je ne suis pas assez poli; et pourtant Je ne jamais dis rien qui paroit rude que ne vous voyez que Je le dis en badinant, ou par etourderie. Mais en verité vous dites des choses piquantes par mechanceté, et cela est de manquer de la vraye politêsse. Burnet & all of us Scots lads dined with honest Wake. Good Biscuits adorned his jolly Board. His dinner was substantial and his Punch strong. I wish he had not mixed three Germans[3] with us, & had not given us a bawdy song. At night Wake and Scott & Macpherson eat Crawfish & drank Rhenish[4] at my lodgings. We were hearty.

103

[1] Burnett contributed this anecdote about a highlander on a mountainside who, unable to sleep, found a stone to place under his head, and whose friend thereupon cried: 'Damn your effeminacy, man. Canna ye sleep without a Stane aneath your head?' (*Boswelliana*, p. 238, corrected against MS. Hyde Collection). JB would include this story in his *Hypochondriack* no. VIII (May 1778); see Bailey, i. 156. JB also recorded the second anecdote, source not identified, more succinctly and less crudely in *Boswelliana*: 'A Gentleman was saying at Voltaire's table. J'ai lu une telle chose. Monsieur said Voltaire Il ne faut pas croire tout ce qu'on a lu. Monsieur replied he J'ai lu pourtant tous vos ouvrages' ('Boswelliana', MS. Hyde Collection, p. 67).

[2] MS. 'recover ... &c &c &c' written along the left margin.

[3] Not identified.

[4] 'Wine produced in the Rhine region', usually white (OED, s.v. 'Rhenish', 2).

## Thursday 13 September

[MEM. dated Friday 14 Septr.] [Y]esterday past morning at Burnet's — din'd Castillon's. Then Academy Berlin — not great. Supt Mad[.] de Brant [—] home & reconciled after coldness. This day at 11. Castill. & *Reid* to see *Cab*.[1] Home 12. 1 Burnet. 3 — then home & write & compose

See Schickler to introduce Castill[.][2]

[J.] The Captains went away. I past the morning with Burnet, who is now Chargé d'Affaires here.[3] I dined chez Castillon. At four he carried me to the Academie Royale de Berlin. The Building is large. Below are the King's Stables and above assemble his Literati, which made a Wag put this Inscription on the Academy 'Musis et mulis'.[4] I saw a poor Collection of natural curiositys except indeed the collection of dried plants of the Levant made by Tournefort.[5] The Academy assembled before five. Formey read a letter from a Physician at Truro in Cornwall concerning some astronomical Phænomenon.[6] He wrote sad latin & when he wanted a word, mixed still worse greek. I was ashamed of him. M. Francheville next read a Dissertation on the art of making Ambergrease, with which I was not greatly edified.[7] After he had done, not a word was said. The Academicians grinned & separated. A Poor Affair this. I then went to Madame de Brandt's where I imagined I was invited. But I had mistaken Tuesday for Thursday, & she punished me by a recital of the fine partie that she had, as it was her daughter's birth-day.[8] How she had a fine supper & a fine Ball & all the Company were drest á la Turque;[9] & how a dress was ready for me. She asked me to stay this evening with her. Much she talked of Gallantry & of The Duke of Portland who was here some years ago.[10] Young Comte Schaffcotz supt with us[11] & after supper we played at 'seek the Pin.' One is sent out of the room till the Pin is hid; & when he enters he must seek it. In proportion as he approaches it one beats harder & harder upon the table, till at last he finds it. Mademoiselle said On s'ennuit beaucoup á Berlin. I beleive it. She said too Mr. Mitchell fut quelquefois fort sombre, et il falloit le laisser á son aise et á la fin il devenoit gaye. Milord Tirconnel aussi qui fut Ambassadeur de la france ici fut fort triste quelquefois; Il avoit une charmante femme qui le rendoit gaye.[12] I past this evening perfectly well.

[1] Presumably the 'cabinet' of 'natural curiosities' that JB would soon visit (see Journ. 14 Sept.). Reid has not been identified.

[2] 'See ... Castill' written along the left

margin. JB evidently planned to make his new friends acquainted with Castillon, who had moved from Utrecht to Berlin only two months earlier (see Journ. 9 July and n. 5).

[3] Burnett would serve in this capacity from Aug. 1764 to June 1766, when Mitchell would return (*Repertorium*, ii. 161).

[4] 'Muses and mules'. The *Académie royale des sciences et belles lettres* or *Königliche Akademie der Wissenschaften*, based on the earlier *Societät der Wissenschaften* founded in 1700 and headed by Leibniz (1646–1716), had been revitalized by Frederick II in the 1740s and was now under his personal control. Displeased when the academicians nominated the dramatist and critic Gotthold Ephraim Lessing (1729–81), Frederick alone thereafter decided on new members, preferring French and Franco-Swiss to Germans, and he had appointed no replacement for Pierre Louis Moreau de Maupertuis (1698–1759), who had presided from 1746 (Adolf Harnack, *Geschichte der königlich Preussischen Akademie der Wissenschaften*, 1900, i. pt. i, pp. 3, 262–89, 469; Angelika Menne-Haritz, 'Die Akademiebewegung' and 'Akademien und Universitäten', in *Panorama*, pp. 68–71).

[5] The *Herbarium* organized according to the principles established by Joseph Pitton de Tournefort (1656–1708), the botanist who had found more than 350 unfamiliar plants while travelling in the Far East (DSB, xiii. 442–44). The collection in Berlin had been brought back by the physician Andreas Gundelsheimer (1668–1715), who had accompanied Tournefort on his travels from 1700 to 1702 (ABBAW I-XIV-25, Bl. 53v–54). Possibly it had been donated to the Academy by Friedrich Wilhelm I in 1717 with other of his collections. From 1724 the *Herbarium* had been used for lectures at the Collegio Medico-Chirurgico, but it had been allowed to deteriorate and was now relegated to part of a room in the library (ABBAW I-XV-22, Bl. 5–7 and I-XV-24, Bl. 18; information from Dr. Wolfgang Knobloch, Director of ABBAW, 10 June 1998).

[6] 'Une Observation du passage de la lune par le disque du Soleil le 1 Avril 1764', submitted by a Dr. Spry (ABBAW, Bestand Preussiche Akademie der Wissenschaften, 1700–1811, I-IV-31, Bl. 240, Sitzungsprotokoll 13.09.1764; information from Dr. Knobloch, 2 Apr. 2003). For this solar eclipse, see also 'Historical Chronicle', *Gent. Mag.* Apr. 1764, xxxiv. 193.

[7] Joseph Dufresne de Francheville (1704–81) was a prolific miscellaneous writer. Born in Dourlens and educated in Paris, he had given up thoughts of an ecclesiastical career to pursue his interests successively in finance, history, and historical fiction. His writings included *Histoire générale et particulière des finances* (1738–40), of which only three of forty projected volumes were completed, the last one also published as *Histoire de la Compagnie des Indes*; followed by *Les premières expéditions de Charlemagne* (1741), and *Relation curieuse de plusieurs pays nouvellement découverts* (1741). Having dedicated his book on Charlemagne to Frederick II, he had obtained employment in Prussia, but only after overcoming the King's displeasure for having written the satiric *L'Espion turc à Francfort* (1741), a continuation of the better known *L'Espion turc dans les cours des princes chrétien*. Francheville's subsequent works included his *Gazette politique* (begun in 1750) and *Bombyx, ou le ver à soie* (1754), a poem in six books about silkworms, whose cultivation was encouraged by Frederick II (Harnack, i. pt. 1, pp. 262–64, 263 n. 4, 326; *Biog. Univ.*, 1816, p. 431).

In his 'Dissertation sur l'origine de l'ambre gris', Francheville offered objections to several theories, including the correct one that ambergris comes from the intestines of sperm whales, but hazarded no explanation of his own (*Mémoires de l'académie royale des sciences et belles-lettres*, 1764, pp. 38–46). He was just founding the *Gazette littéraire de Berlin*, a weekly publication devoted to various arts that contined to 1790 (Jean Sgard, *Dictionnaire des Journeaux*, 1991, i. 571).

[8] The celebration had presumably been for Mme von Brandt's younger daughter, Elisabeth Friderica Charlotta, who had been baptized on 20 Sept. 1733 and whose birthday therefore fell on Tuesday, 11 Sept., whereas the birthday of her sister Sophie, baptized on 24 Aug. 1731, fell in the previous month (record of baptism, Evangelisches Zentralarchiv in Berlin, letters of 26 Oct. 1995, 24 June 1997).

[9] The choice of costumes was no doubt inspired by the presence of the Turkish envoy, Resmi Ahmed, who had been in Berlin from Nov. 1763 to Apr. 1764 and who had created great interest in things Turkish (*Repertorium*, ii. 409; Lehndorff, *Dreissig Jahre*, pp. 465–69; MacDonogh, pp. 326–27).

[10] William Henry Cavendish-Bentinck, 3rd Duke of Portland (1738–1809), had passed through Prussia in Jan. 1758 on his travels to Poland and Russia. At that time he had been styled Marquis of Tichfield (Mrs. Delany to Mrs. Dewes, 17 and 19 Jan. 1758, *The Autobiography and Correspondence*

*of Mary Granville, Mrs. Delany*, 1861, repr. 1974, iii. 472, 474–75, 477–78). Mme von Brandt evidently knew that he had inherited the Portland title in 1762 after his return to England. Member of a distinguished Williamite family and educated at Oxford from 1754 to 1757, he had already been M.P. for Weobley from 1761 to 1762. He would later hold various offices ranging from Lord Chamberlain of the Household, from 1765 to 1766, to Viceroy of Ireland in 1782, to Prime Minister in 1783 and from 1807 to 1809 (*Comp. Peer.* x. 593; *Namier and Brooke*, ii. 84–85).

[11] Karl Wenzel Gotthard von Schaffgotsch (b. 1742), nephew of the master of horse by the same name, would be appointed chamberlain to the Queen in 1765 (Zedlitz-Neukirch, iv. 154). He was known to be an admirer of Mme von Brandt (Lehndorff, 4 Aug. 1757, *Dreissig Jahre: Nachträge*, i. 128). He also appears to have become an admirer of her daughter Sophie. Possibly he was the unknown man for whom Sophie had just capriciously ended a three-year relationship with Ludwig Olivier von Marconnay (1733–1800), a minor Prussian functionary (Kabinettssekretar) and 'the ugliest person one can imagine' (Lehndorff, Aug. 1764, *Dreissig Jahre: Nachträge*, i. 409; see also ii. 216). When Schaffgotsch wished to marry her, however, his disapproving father would enroll him as a knight of Malta, whereupon he would be sent to fight the Turks in

Catherine the Great's first war against them (1768–74); see Lehndorff, 18 July 1769, *Dreissig Jahre: Nachträge*, ii. 159; Kohn, pp. 93–94. Sophie von Brandt would marry Col. Wichard Christian von Platen (1732–82) in 1772 (information from the Evangelisches Zentralarchiv in Berlin, letter of 24 June 1997; J. L. H. Thomas's unpublished 'Stammbaum von Sophie von Brandt', 4 Feb. 2001).

[12] Richard François Talbot, *styled* Earl of Tyrconnel (1710–52), had been the French Minister Plenipotentiary in Berlin from about June 1748 until his early death. A second-generation Jacobite, born and brought up at the court of the titular James III at St. Germain, he had previously joined Nugent's (later FitzJames's) Regt. of Irish Horse in 1721 and had attained the rank of captain by 1728/9. Attempting to join Prince Charles Edward Stuart in 1745, he had been imprisoned at Ostend but had managed to join the Jacobite army in Flanders in 1747 and had been named maréchal de camp in the army of the Low Countries the following year (*Comp. Peer.* xii, pt. 2, 124–25). In spite of his French upbringing, he had struck Lehndorff as having 'all the characteristics of an Englishman' (*Dreissig Jahre*, Mar. 1752, p. 22). Talbot's wife, Madeleine de Lyz Talbot, *styled* Duchess of Tyrconnel, had been a popular hostess during her husband's tenure in Berlin (*Dreissig Jahre*, 15 June 1750 to 23 Mar. 1752, pp. 14, 16, 17, 19, 23).

## Friday 14 September

[MEM. dated Saturday 15 Septr.] [Y]esterday morning you saw Gerard's collection & promis'd him — din'd Burnet. Smit[1] there then Margrave chymist. Got *stone* made by self, promisd — then Castill who said 4 evang only — & no Affections to God. Then Girl breast. Necessity[2] — Care. Just idleness — This day at home till cool — Jaunt Sunday &c much[.][3]

[J.] In the morning Castillon and I went & saw the collection of natural Curiositys of Mr. Gerard: In mettals not amiss.[4] I dined at Burnet's where was Smidt the Engraver. Burnet was hearty. At four Castillon & I went & saw old Margrave the Chymical Professor a very industrious & able man in his Profession.[5] But a strange old fellow. It Thundered & lightened. He cried 'J'aime de voir mon Dieu en flammes'; and he laughed allways when he spoke. Such is man. He must have defects. He may have health and manners: but then he is ignorant. He may have knowledge. But then he is sick or aukward. Margrave showed us glasses of his making, and a composition by which he can imitate all kinds of precious Stones. He gave me a piece like Saphire. His minerals were very compleat. I promised to send him some from Scotland.[6] Castillon went home with me. He said We ought to revere God; but all Affections exercised towards The Supreme Being were only in the fancy of fanatics. He owned that the Gospels were all that he owned as truly christian Scriptures. The Epistles he thought only good pieces which might be of use sometimes. He said the Christian Religion had not added much to morality. What would he be at? He left me at eight. I amused myself with a Street Girl as in London.[7] Idleness — no great harm.

[1] Possibly Schmidt, the engraver, for whom see Mem. dated 27 Aug. n. 6.

[2] 'Then ... Necessity' scored out by a modern hand.

[3] MS. 'Jaunt ... much' inserted above 'home till cool'.

[4] Karl Abraham Gerhard (1738–1821), a promising young mineralogist, was just translating the papers of the French metallurgist Antoine Gabriel Jars (1732–69), whose studies of the major European centres for iron, steel, and coal had begun to be published in 1757 and which would later be collected in *Voyages métallurgique ou recherches sur les mines et forges de fer* (3 vols. 1774–81; ADB). Gerhard had studied medicine but had earned his doctorate with a mineralogical dissertation, *Disquisitio granatorum Silesia atque Bohemiae*, 1760, and had then specialized in mining. Admitted to the *Académie royale* in 1768, he would also be named counsellor for mining, would help to revive the Silesian mining industry, and would found and thereafter direct the academy for mining in Berlin (*NDB*, vi. 274–75; Nicolai, 3rd Sup. iii. 7).

[5] Andreas Sigismund Marggraf (1709–82), head of the Academy's physical-medical class from 1760, was presumably in the Academy's laboratory, opened in 1753 in a separate building where he also lived in a modest apartment (Adolf Harnack, *Geschichte der königlich Preussischen Akademie der Wissenschaften*, 1900, i. pt. i, p. 485). The last great representative of the phlogiston theory, which hypothesized a flammability factor in substances released during combustion, he would be known best for identifying the sugar in beetroot (*DSB*, iii. 119). Like Gerhard's work, his experiments reflected Frederick II's interest in applied rather than pure science (Christoph Meinel, 'Chemie', in *Panorama*, pp. 78–80).

[6] Marggraf's eccentric behaviour is not recorded elsewhere. On this occasion he appears to have been working on crystallization. The 'saphire' has not survived, and there is no evidence that JB sent the promised specimens.

[7] MS. 'I amused ... London' deleted by a modern hand.

## Saturday 15 September

[MEM. dated Sunday 16 Septr.] Yesterday at 8 you went to Stralo — din'd ill — sad society. During[1] dinner you spoke against french. Capt. Durand came &[2] sat by you cest mieux que J'entend des petites impertinences qui passent par ci et par la, que ma Sœur — Mr. Jespere vous n'avez pas trouvé &c — Oui monsr vous avez parlez des françois. Je suis françois et personne parlera comme ça qu'un faquin. Thought on old *David* Auchinleck concerned — Took him to garden faché, impoli — pas badiner[3] — serieux mais Je ne devois pas le dire — He owned error &c & again at supper made harangue [—] good lesson — This day at 9 church — then home — Journ. & compose 3 days.

[J.] Sometime ago I was taken in by Castillon for a dreary dinner at Treptow, of which Captain Durand of the Artillery payed the expence. Castillon & I could not do less than give such another treat, so I could not shun being once more taken in. We went to Stralo & had a sad house. I tired terribly: At dinner I was sulky, & I railed against the french. Durand came & seated himself by me saying 'c'est mieux que J'entends des petites Impertinences qui passent par ci et par la, que ma Sœur.'[4] 'Monsieur (said I) J'espere que vous n'etes pas offensé á ce que J'ai dit.' 'Oui monsieur Vous avez parlé contre les francois. Je suis françois Monsieur et Personne peut parler d'une telle maniêrre contre toute une Nation qu'un faquin'.[5] This last word gave me a blow on the heart. It was a clear affront which could not be put up. I bowed & said Monsieur, Je suis faché Je n'avois pas aucune intention d'etre impertinent. It happened luckily in the middle of dinner; so that I had time to think. I found fear working with me. I recalled old David Laird of Auchinleck my Great Grandfather, & thought he called to me to support the honour of my family,[6] I had also my honour as a Scotsman my character as a man at stake. I must do myself the Justice to say that I was fully determined for the worst. Yet I wished that the affair could be made up, as I was realy in the wrong. I felt myself in the situation which I have often fancied, & which is a very uneasy one. Yet upon my honour so strong is my Metaphysical passion that I was pleased with this opportunity of intimately observing the workings of the human mind. When Dinner was over I took the Captain to a walk behind the house and said 'Monsieur, Je suis bien faché á ce qui est arrivé aujourdhui. J'avois grand tort. Je voudrois si'l est possible eviter une querelle. Mais vous vous etes servi d'une expression qu'un Gentilhomme ne peut pas supporter, et il faut que Jaye de la reparation.' Que voulez vous Monsieur said he. Je suis pret á tout Monsieur said I. Je voudrois que vous avouerez que vous aviez tort de me parler comme vous avez fait. J'avouerai premierrement que J'etois impoli de parler comme J'ai fait contre les françois. By this time one of his Brother Officers and another Gentleman came up to us. To excuse me They said 'Monsieur ne faisoit que badiner.' I replied Pardonnez moi. Non Je ne nierai pas mes sentiments. Monsieur c'etoit mon serieux. J'avoue que J'ai une Antipatie ou si vous voulez un prejugé contre votre nation. J'avoue aussi qu'il ne faut pas le dire dans une compagnie melée. Monsieur, voulez vous avouer que vous aviez tort? He said Monsieur tout ce que vous voulez. Je suis bien faché que je me suis servi d'une telle Expression. Comme Monsieur ne vouloit pas dire que comme françois Je n'etois pas honnêtte homme. Castillon also came & he owned his fault before three or four Gentlemen & Castillon said Tout est fini donc. M. Boswell Vous n'avez rien de plus á demander. However, I was still uneasy. The Affront had been given before all the Company. It was necessary that all the Company should see it repaired. Some went by Land; the rest of us in the Boat. I sat in great uneasiness. We supt all at Durand's very well. After supper I filled up a Bumper of Hock[7] and called to him 'Monsieur le Capitaine. Monsieur Durand. Je repête ici ce que nous avons dit en particulier. Je suis bien faché que J'ai parlé aujourdhui d'une manierre impolie. J'espere que Monsieur dira autant. He replied Monsieur Je suis bien fache que J'ai etois si emporté et que Je vous ai parlé d'une manierre impolie. I cannot remember our very words. I said Monsieur Je voudrois seulement vous faire voir qu'un homme peut parler comme J'ai fait qui est imprudent ou impoli; mais qui n'est pas faquin. 'O Monsieur said he with concern. We drank to each other, and all was fully & genteely settled. When I got home I reflected with a Lucretian Suavity on the mare magnum that I had escaped.[8] In time coming, I shall be more on my guard, & be truly polite.

[1] MS. 'During' written over 'After'
[2] MS. 'came &' inserted before 'sat'
[3] MS. 'badin'
[4] Capt. Henri de Durand, whom JB had met on 29 Aug., was garrisoned outside the Stralau gate. Although he is listed by the name of Heinrich von Durant in the *Adres-Calender* of 1764 (p. 33), he was clearly not German, and since he does not appear in the records of the Huguenot community, he may have been a Frenchman in Prussian service. His sister has not been not identified.
[5] A low-born impertinent wretch: 'homme de la lie du peuple, vil & méprisable' (Antoine Furetière, *Dictionnaire universel*, 1690, repr. 1970, s.v. 'faquin'); 'homme de rien, impertinent, et bas' (*Nouveau Petit Larousse*, 1952, s.v. 'faquin'). With its reference to the lowest of low social class, the term was especially insulting to JB.
[6] In his conception of his family's honour, JB attached particular importance to David Boswell (1640–1713), 6th Laird of Auchinleck, who had been chosen as heir by his uncle, the 5th laird, in preference to

that laird's own daughters. David and his descendants had reestablished the family fortune after hard times, and so JB felt 'an implied obligation' to them (*Life* [15 Jan. 1776], ii. 413–15).
[7] White Rhine wine.
[8] 'Suave, mari magno turbantibua aequora ventis, e terra magnum alterius soectare laborem' ('It is pleasant, when the mighty deep is roused by winds, to stand on shore and watch another man struggling painfully with the waves'). The passage continues: 'not because one really gets pleasure from seeing other people in trouble, but because it is pleasant to see dangers and know that you yourself are free of them' (*De rerum natura*, ii. 1–4, trans. in *Grand Tour I*, Heinemann p. 94 n. 1, McGraw-Hill p. 97 n. 5). But the painful memory of the Durand episode continued to haunt JB, who felt obliged to describe it in an addendum to his confession to Rousseau (31 Dec. 1764, CC *Rousseau*, Letter 3818, xxii. 444–45; trans. in *Grand Tour I*, Heinemann pp. 300–02, McGraw-Hill pp. 309–10).

## Sunday 16 September

[MEM. dated Monday 17 Septr.] [Y]esterday you was at Church a little. Then saw Burnet & referred to him & Wake your quarrel. Din'd with him heard of *Grant*. Votre majesté perdu pucellage.[1] Ma patience me mettroit au tombeau. Supt Kirkheisen [—] talk'd to madame who told you you had been fort choquant — 'tis Kelly [—] once for all then proffit — & be a pretty Scots Gentleman & christian nor make quarrels. This day Journ — 8 Burnet — 10 home in all day. Journ & letters — See Hubner, Shickler compose mind[.]

[J.] At Burnet's I found old Gualteri a fine lively little man who snapped his fingers at every little sally that he gave us. He said Voltaire had all his life assumed characters. When he was at Berlin he played the arrant miser. Now he acts the most generous man alive.[2] When Gualteri was gone, Wake came in & I said Gentlemen I ask you as my Countrymen have I done right or not. I told them the story of my quarrel, and they agreed that I had got into a very ugly scrape; but had brought myself out of it very properly. I dined with Burnet tête á tete. He said if a man owned honestly that he was a Coward he would still esteem him. But, said he, a Coward will fight upon occasions. He has found me several words for my Scots Diction-ary.[3] At night I walked with Wake. I supt at home & after supper told madame my story. She was pleased to find that I had got off so well and bid me by all means avoid being impolite. I asked her if I had been realy so sometimes. She said il faut avouer que vous avez eté quelquefois fort choquant. I explained to her how it proceeded from a flow of vivacious humour. But, that will not do. Lord Kelly has the same.[4] Let me then be master of myself. Let me be mild & agreable.

[1] JB made a separate record of this anecdote about John Grant of Dunlugas, major-general in Prussian service and a favourite aide-de-camp to Frederick II. Grant was reported to have made light of the first Prussian defeat of the Seven Years' War, at the Battle of Kolin on 18 June 1757, with the quip: 'Votre Majeste est dans le cas d'une fille qui vient de perdre son pucellage. C'est la premierre Battaille que Votre Majeste a perdu. Il faut tacher de la reparer' ('Boswelliana', MS. Hyde Collection, p. 55).

Grant had served Elizabeth, Empress of Russia, under James Keith, Lord Marischal's brother, and had followed him to Prussia. Unlike many Scots abroad, Grant was not a Jacobite but had entered foreign military service to further his career. He had seen action in many battles of the Seven Years' War and had become known as a horseman who could deliver dispatches with amazing speed, notably in bringing word of Frederick II's victory over the French at Rossbach to England (Charles Lowe, A Fallen Star or the Scots of Frederick, 1895, pp. 30, 177–79, 188–90, 288, 325; 'Historical Chronicle' for Mon. 28 Nov., Gent. Mag. Nov. 1757, xxvii. 529). Grant had recently been named Governor of Neisse, a fortress in Bohemia on the border of Silesia (Thomas A. Fischer, The Scots in Germany, 1902, pp. 128 and n. 1, 287–88, where Grant is however mistakenly credited with having reported the victory of Leuthen). He would die at Neisse before the end of the year (Alexander Burnett to Andrew Mitchell, 25 Dec. 1764, Burnett of Kemnay Archives, Bundle 82). William Fraser included him among the Grants of Dalvey but, in error, has him still living in the 1770s (The Chiefs of Grant [1883], i. 520–21).

[2] This was Samuel Melchisedec Gualteri

(see Journ. 1 Aug. and n. 5), father of the suicidal tutor whose story JB had heard in Brunswick (Journ. 11 Aug.), but not to be confused with his son Karl Albert Samuel Gualteri, who had left the clergy when ennobled (correcting Grand Tour I, p. 94 n. 2, p. 97 n. 6). The older Gualteri here alludes to Voltaire's financial problems while in Berlin, which had led him to participate in shady financial dealings that finally cost him the friendship of Frederick II. Whether Voltaire was really miserly, or just worried about his finances, is unclear. Thanks to his subsequent investments in property, he could now afford to be generous.

[3] In Holland JB had conceived the ambitious project of compiling this dictionary, with etymologies, to prevent the Scottish language from being forgotten. He had even imagined later ages being grateful to 'vieux Boswell' for allowing them to read the works of their ancestors (French themes, Feb. 1764, Yale MS. M 87). One of more than fifty proposed projects that were never completed, this dictionary would continue to occupy JB (see To Sir John Dalrymple, 18 Apr. 1777; for JB's unfinished projects, see Hebrides, p. 65 n. 2). It would eventually be sold, still in MS, in the auction of James Boswell the Younger's library on 3 June 1825 (see Hitoshi Suwabe, 'Boswell's Dictionary', In Honor of Nobuyuki Higashi, 1995, pp. 47–52).

[4] Thomas Alexander Erskine (1732–81), 6th Earl of Kellie (or Kelly), elder brother of JB's friend AE, was a high-spirited, hard-drinking rake, whom JB would later remember as a 'Mount Vesuvius' (Journ. 18 Oct. 1780; also Journ. 10 Aug. 1769; Earlier Years, p. 64). He was a talented composer, whose works JB would soon hear performed in Kassel (Journ. 26 Oct.).

## Monday 17 September

[MEM. dated Tuesday 18 Septr.] [Y]esterday you breakfasted with Burnet on Pottage & Porter. You went to Gotzkofky's [—] you dined cordial & thanked him for all his politesses and promised to write. Do so. You saw old Officer who had made the Campaigns of Charles 12 & King of Prussia. He said he was better with Charles. He was 89. At 3 you went to Durand's, who was polite. You observed cut on forehead. You thanked him & said Je vous estimerai — He said Il y avoit des fautes d'une coté et de l'autre et Jai fait toute la reparation. J'ai agit comme entre des galants gens comme Je vous crois. At night madame owned humeur changeant. This day prepare all.

[J.] I breakfasted with Burnet on Scots oatmeal Pottage and English Porter. This is[1] one of the best methods that can be taken to render the Union truly firm. I went to take leave of Gotzkofsky. He very kindly kept me to dinner. I saw there an Old Officer of 89 who was Page to Charles the ninth of Sweden, and had made the Campaigns of Charles the Twelfth and of the King of Prussia. There was a tale to brag of. He told me that the Soldiers were much happier under Charles, than under Frederic. He said he had served the latter as Captain ten years, and he had now no greater pension than ten crowns a month. Very hard indeed.[2] I took a cordial farewell of Gotzkofsky, who is indeed what the french call un galant homme. He has shewn me very great civility and in an easy, hearty way, which is not easy to feign. He asked me to write to him. I shall certainly do so. At three I waited on M. Durand and sat half an hour with him. We talked away with genteel ease, as if nothing had happened. I observed a large cut on his forehead which he had got in a duel. I was happy to have avoided any such mark. When I took leave of him, I once more resumed[3] our quarrel; He said to me, Monsieur, pour dire la verité, Il y avoit des fautes de l'une coté, et de l'autre. J'ai fait toute la reparation que Je pouvois, et J'espere que vous etes content. I replied Monsieur, Je vous estimerai toujours. Vous avez agir d'une manierre qui vous fait beaucoup d'honneur. Monsieur (said he) J'ai agit comme on doit faire avec des galants hommes parmi lesquels Je vous crois. Upon my word. This is a fine fellow. I parted from him on the best terms. At night I had a long chat with madame & mademoiselle & owned that I had the misfortune to be changeant in a most unaccountable degree. 'Vous ne saurez croire mademoiselle que quelquefois il m'a fait beaucoup de peine de vous voir le matin, et de vous entendre jouer.' The amiable Ladies were sorry for me, and said that they had observed something about me d'extraordinaire et que Je paroitrois faché un jour faché á ce que J'avois dit l'autre. Madame Kircheisen said Il faut avoir soin, ou vous deviendrez hypochondre. Il faut boire beaucoup d'eau, et prendre beaucoup d'exercise. Mon mari etoit fort melancholique. Il croyoit que tout le monde avoit des plaintes contre lui. Il vouloit rester dans cette salle. Je faisoit porter son lit ici; et Je me suis mit sur la Settée. Alors il disoit 'Je serais mieux sur la Settée,' et nous avons changés. Alors Je faisoit semblant de dormir. Il restoit donc sans fermer l'oeil, il se levoit, il se promenoit par la chambre, il etoit toujours inquiet, il tachoit d'ecrire. Il ne pouvoit pas. Il etoit triste et il se plaignoit amerement. Je me suis levé. Je lui parloit. Je lui donnois des consolations de la Bible. Il se tranquilisoit un peu. Il recommançoit. Alors Je lui dit. Mais, vous me tuerez, et vous même aussi á veiller comme cela, et qu'est ce qu'il deviendra notre famille. Je parlois comme cela pour l'agiter un peu. Alors il etoit faché. Il faisoit des efforts. Il vaincoit son humeur. Il se mit á dormir.[4] This History gave me infinite pleasure. I wish I may have such a wife. Madame la Presidente is between forty & fifty. She is still a handsom Woman. She is of a genteel family. She has excellent common sense & much ease of behaviour. Yet the Bourgeoise appears at times. She is a most estimable mother, and mistress of a family. She is penetrating & she can conceal her sentiments, so that I know her not so perfectly as I have known many a character. Of the Strangers whom I make acquaintance with I shall not draw regular characters. The little Anecdotes which I mark serve to point them out well enough. Madame Kircheisen has an excellent neat descriptive talent. She has often talked to me of the Bel Abbé Bastiani de Breslau who lodged in her house & many pretty little Anecdotes she has of him.[5] She is quite the Scots Lady in one particular. She makes all fine cakes & conserves every morning. I get some good thing or another from her.

[1] MS. 'is is', an inadvertent repetition.

[2] JB wrote 'Charles the ninth' by mistake for 'the eleventh'. The old officer is unidentified. Now 89 years old and so born c. 1665, he could indeed have been page to Charles XI, who had ruled from 1660 to 1697, and he could also have served in the Silesian wars which Frederick II had started as soon as he began to rule in 1740. The campaigns of Charles XII (1682–1718) were legendary and had earned him the epithets 'The Alexander of the North' and 'Madman of the North'. He had repeatedly warred successfully against the Russians, Saxons, and Poles but had been defeated by Peter the Great at Poltova in the Ukraine in 1709 and had eventually died during a siege in Norway. SJ had summarized his career 'to point a moral and adorn a tale' in 'The Vanity of Human Wishes' (ll. 191–222), and Voltaire had written a history of his last years in 1731. That the old officer had so small a pension was presumably owing to Frederick's financial difficulties after the Seven Years' War.

[3] Recapitulated or summarized (OED, s.v. 'resume', 5.b).

[4] Possibly Mme Kircheisen was remembering her husband's behaviour when the Russians occupied Berlin in Oct. 1760. Faced with the demands for a heavy 'contribution', Kircheisen 'was reduced to such a state of nervous prostration that the Russians believed him to be intoxicated and declined to negotiate with him' (W. O. Henderson, *Studies in the Economic Policy of Frederick the Great*, 1963, p. 17). The crisis had been defused by Gotzkowsky, who had paid the Russians from his own funds (Anon. *Geschichte eines Patriotischen Kaufmanns*, Schriften des Vereins für die Geschichte der Stadt Berlin, 1873, vii. 19).

[5] The strikingly tall abbé Giambattista Bastiani (born c. 1712), a wit, *bon vivant*, and libertine, inspired several anecdotes about how he, the son of a mere Venetian tailor, had become the intimate friend of Frederick II and had enjoyed a colourful bisexual life that included both the fathering of illegitimate children and love letters from Frederick himself. A contemporary described him as: 'courtisan et chanoine à quinze mille livres de rentes, partageant son temps entre sa stalle, les boudoirs des dames, et sur-tout les palais des rois, ou les hôtels des grands' (Thiébault, iii. 44–45). Bastiani visited his friend Frederick II in Potsdam almost every year.

## Tuesday 18 September

[MEM. dated Wednesday 19 Septr.] Yesterday you run too much about — Din'd Burnet & was too childish. Visited Gualteri — visite a la Nicodeme — then saw Madame de Brandt, who said after cheval Silva espagnol you was second Ami & said much much. You was quite charmd but saw thro' her. Supt home. This day — go Shickler & ask address to Geneve & if possible credit on Dresden &c & give two months money — Then Steelow & Hubner & Castillon. Then pay President Servants — *Burgess*.[1] Prints put up — Be all ready & fine —

[J.] For the last time I dined at Burnet's. I then payed my visits pour prendre congé, having fixed tomorrow for my day of departure. We went & saw old Gualteri, who said Vous faites une visite á la Nicodeme[2] to Burnet & me. I then sat some time at madame de Brandt's who was mighty civil and said Vous etes le second dont Je regrette infinement le depart. Le Chevalier Silva Espagnol fut le premier. Ah il etoit un aimable homme![3] I said Madame! si J'avois resté ici plus long tems, Je suis sure que vous m'aurrez aimé plus. In short I gave her to understand that I should have been happy as her very humble Servant. She was still a fine woman; & has the most perfect elegance of manners. Her Gallantries have been notorious. Du Roi jusque au Berger a ce qu'on dit.[4] She made me a present of a handsom little Crayon & case. I was realy sorry to leave for ever a Lady who might have greatly formed me. I supt at home for the last night, and upon my word, I felt no small regret and tender melancholy.

[1] The only reference to the fact that on this day JB acquired a 'Bürger-Brief' (certificate of citizenship) in Berlin, made out in the name of the 'Bürgermeister und Rat' (mayor and magistracy) to 'Jacob von Bosvelt' and signed by 'Kircheisen, Pras'. This document, with its largely preprinted text declaring fealty to the King of Prussia and a seal of the city, was no doubt merely a souvenir provided by Kircheisen. JB identified it for his records as: 'Burgess Ticket for the City of Berlin To James Boswell Esquire of Auchinleck Anno 1764'.
On this day JB also paid 30 écus for two months' lodgings as well as 15 écus to Kircheisen's servants (Exp. Acct., App. 3).
[2] At night. Nicodemus was the Pharisee and ruler of the Jews who came to talk with Jesus 'by night' (John, 3:1–21; 7:50–52).
[3] Possibly the de Silva, chamberlain to the Duke of Parma, who had passed through Berlin in June 1763 on his way back from Russia, where he had tried unsuccessfully to make his fortune (Lehndorff, Dreissig Jahre: Nachträge, i. 371).
[4] Mme von Brandt had supposedly attempted to seduce Frederick of Prussia while he was Crown Prince and she was attached to his court at Rheinsberg (14 May, 26 June 1735, Journal Secret du Baron de Seckendorff,

1811, pp. 142, 144). She was also reported to have had intermittent rendez-vous between 1740 and 1744 with Clemens August (1723–61), Archbishop of Bavaria and Elector of Cologne (E. Hegel, Das Erzbistum Köln zwischen Barock und Aufklärung, Geschichte des Erzbistums, Köln 4, 1979, p. 58; M. Braubach, Kurköln. Gestalten und Ereignisse aus zwei Jahrhunderten rheinischer Geschichte, 1949, pp. 306–11). Her name had been linked as well with George II of England while he was in Hanover and with Landgrave Wilhelm of Hessen-Kassel, two rulers whom she had visited consecutively in the summer of 1745 (Braubach, p. 311). Count Schaffgotsch, the master of the horse, had been yet another 'friend and admirer' (Lehndorff, 4 Aug. 1757, Dreissig Jahre: Nachträge, i. 128; see also J. L. H. Thomas, 'Von der Spree zum Tweed', Deutsches Adelsblatt, 15 Nov. 2002, vol. xli, no. 11, p. 288). So notorious was she that, according to an anecdote of 1750, Frederick II exempted her from tax on the jewels she was bringing back to Berlin because these 'had been earned by the sweat of the lady's own body' (quoted in Giles Stephen Holland Fox-Strangeways, Earl of Ilchester, and Elizabeth Langford-Brooke, Life of Sir Charles Hanbury-Williams, 1929, p. 188).

## Wednesday 19 September

[MEM. dated Thursday 20 Septr.] [Y]esterday you had all in order — payed some visits, was quite agitated. Sent away Jacob with Journalière, & took horses. Bid adieu to worthy President & amiable Ladies. Was touched. Young Leopold accompanied. You was quite Laird of Auch. & he Bruce Camp.[1] Had got letts from Gentleman and Doctor. Old ideas — now better [—] rode brisk to Potzdam; found My Lord supt Froment slept Scotts.

[J.] I received a kind letter from worthy Doctor Boswell[2] & one from Mr. Francis Gentleman proposing to dedicate to me a second volume of 'a Trip to the [M]oon'. I answered him immediatly & politely refused his offer. These Letters recalled fully my former days.[3] I felt myself greatly improved. My worthy Lord Marischal offered me to advance me what money I should need for three or four months, if Mr. Schickler made any difficulty, which however was not necessary for my hearty Banker freely gave me what I asked. I run about all morning. I recalled all my scenes of pleasure at Berlin where I was cured of the black Hypochondria. Yet I was glad to go. So much do I love change. I dread that this love may increase. But my warm regard for the Old Auchinleck shall ever fix me. I took cordial leave of my good President before dinner. I did not dine but run about taking leave. I eat a bit of apple-pie at Castillon's. I was not sorry to leave *him*. He is a peevish Being, & if he has knowledge it does himself little good & others far less. It was humbling to see in this man of how little value the possession of knowledge may be. No more of this. At three I came home. I gave every one of the Servants drink-money,[4] and they bid me adieu with regard. Before I quit this house, let me mark some ideas which I shall like to recall. The President's regular employment. The easy uniformity of the family. Three machines.[5] Five good horses. The Court-yard with the Wallnut tree. The Stork. The little temple of ease.[6] Curtzin the neat little maid. I now walked thro' the dining room, with that kind of agreable agitation which I allways feel at quitting a Place where I have been well. My stay here appeared like a dream. Bless me! In two months time have I formed so kind a connection with this family? Well, My agreable talents must be great. I sent away my servant and Baggage by the Journalière to Potzdam.[7] I took leave of the Ladies very tenderly, and set out upon Post Horses. Young Leopold accompanied me half way. I was quite the Laird of Auchinleck; and he was a Bruce Campbell. I rode briskly along to Potzdam, went to Froment's, found there My Lord Marischal & Scott and Macpherson; talked well, supt Froment's. Slept at Scott's.

---

[1] JB had described Bruce Campbell of Milrig and Mayfield (c. 1734–1813), his second cousin, as a 'rough blunt resolute young fellow with much common sense ... very obliging to his friends' (Journ. 18 Oct. 1762; *Ominous Years*, Chart VI, p. 379). When JB became Laird of Auchinleck, he would retain Campbell as agent to help manage the estate (*Corr.* 8, p. 101; *Later Years*, p. 376).

[2] Dr. John Boswell (1710–80), a younger brother of Lord Auchinleck, was JB's favourite uncle. He had studied medicine at Leiden and was now a member of the Royal College of Surgeons in Edinburgh. An easygoing, gregarious man, he had been a freemason since 1742, and it may have been he who introduced JB to the Lodge that JB

joined in 1759 (Allan Mackenzie, *History of the Lodge Canongate Kilwinning No. 2*, 1888, pp. 97, 237–38). Dr. Boswell's letter has not survived.

[3] Gentleman's letter of 16 Mar. had just arrived via London. In his answer, urging Gentleman to find a more celebrated dedicatee, JB pointed out that he has been honoured already in the dedication of Gentleman's *Oroonoko* (1760), adapted from the play *Oroonoko* (1696) by Thomas Southerne (1659–1745), itself adapted from the novel *Oroonoko* (1688) by Aphra Behn (1640–89). Gentleman thereupon addressed a little-known friend, Tindal Thompson, in his dedication of the second volume of his *Trip to the Moon*, a playful satire 'By Sir Humphry Lunatic, Bart.' (Preface 1764,

pub. 1765, see *Catalogue*, i. 243; see also *Corr.* 9, pp. 13–15 nn. 1–3). JB had known Gentleman in 1759 and 1760 in Glasgow, where JB had been sent by his irate father for consorting with Edinburgh theatre people and where Gentleman, a struggling actor, playwright, dramatic critic, and occasional theatre manager, had also recently moved from Edinburgh (*Earlier Years*, pp. 44–45).

[4] A literal rendering of the German *Trinkgeld*. JB spent 15 écus on these gratuities (Exp. Acct., App. 3).

[5] That is, coaches.

[6] A quintessentially German idyll. The stork, a heron-like migratory bird, three feet tall, white with red beak and legs, nests on roofs when it returns in the spring and supposedly signifies good fortune ('Störche, Ciconiidae', Brockhaus, xxi. 185). The 'temple' was presumably a little summer-house or pavillion.

[7] JB spent 2 écus and 16 Groschen for his servant and luggage, 5 écus for the horses for himself, and on the following day an additional 18 Groschen for transporting his trunks (Exp. Acct. 19–20 Sept., App. 3).

## Thursday 20 September

[MEM. dated Friday 21 Septr.] [Y]esterday wrote morning. Din'd Froment's then walk'd Turque said Il vous faut des changements Europe est votre païs. Then played cards — supt Scotts told Storys too many. Heard From[.] say il a perdu Veau — gros et gras jamais amoureux — votre femme[1] Chariot de poste — Go on —

[J.] All the morning was employed in writing. I dined Froment's, & after dinner we all walked. Madame la Turque said to me Vous avez un penchant vers la Melancolie. Il vous faut beaucoup de changements. I said: Quelle donc doit être mon Païs? She replied lEurope. Et qui doit être ma femme? Froment exclaimed Un Chariot de Poste. Very ludicrous & well applied. I supt at Scott's, & told Storys like a Charles Cochrane.[2]

[1] MS. 'feme'

[2] Presumably in 'the humourous style' that JB associated with his maternal uncle,

Charles Cochrane of Ochiltree and Culross (1683–1752); see Journ. 4 Oct 1776, *Extremes*, p. 38.

## Friday 21 September

[MEM. dated Saturday 22 Septr.] Yesterday went in blue Bonnet, saw King on Parade — dind Scott jolly — supt too — was healthy & just Father — This day at 9 Weiligh & ask to see King — Then Hered Prince — then My Lord [—] Letts to Dessau — Gotha & Dourlach — Be compos'd & ask for Strelitz[1] — as also corespond — But that may be asked from Scotland. Prepare all & write evening.

[J.] The whim struck me to put on a blue bonnet, and appear quite a Scots Gentleman. I went in this dress to the parade of the Prince of Prussia. The Prince observed me & asked Scott Qu'estce que ce petit bonnet que porte ce monsieur la? Scott said. C'est le bonnet que portent les Gentilshommes Ecossois.[2] The poor Prince did not like it much, nor could he think that he was a Lord's son who wore it. No matter — I was pleased, and boldly did I march upon the Parade before the Palace, where I again saw the King. But he did not look towards me. However I was pleased to have shewn the first blue Bonnet on the Prussian Parade. I dined heartily at honest Scotts, & supt too. I was healthy & chearfull, & just Father.

[1] The residence of Charlotte Sophia, Princess of Mecklenburg-Strelitz (1744–1818), before her marriage to George III in 1761. Actually, JB would not visit Strelitz, which was north of Berlin and so lay in the wrong direction for him.

[2] This headgear was associated with the highland Scots of ancient and recent times. Earlier in the century it had been observed as part of a highland gentleman's costume ([John Macky], *A Journey Through Scotland*, 1723, p. 194). JB would later, at Coll during their tour of the Hebrides, place 'a large blue bonnet' on SJ's head and relish his friend's appearance as 'an ancient Caledonian', even 'a venerable *sennachie*' ('a Gaelic teller of legendary romances', OED; 17 Oct. 1773, *Life* v. 324–25).

## Saturday 22 September

[MEM. dated Sunday 23 Septr.] [Y]esterday you called on Weiligh who said Jetois fort Hypochondre &c & un General sur chaise percé — croyoit tomber de la tour[1] — dind [F]roment visited Catt — he showed verses — answered 'em. Evening [F]roment's played have a care — This day write Father[2] — See My Lord. Get Lett from Comte d'Anhalt &c[.]

[J.] This morning I called on General Weiligh who told me he had been tres Hypochondre. Said he il faut peu manger; sur tout au soir; car, si on a soupé on a des rêves affreuses et le lendemain quand on s'eveille, on est Je ne sais comment. I see the good General knew it. He said the King a un peu aussi mais il est tant occupé qu'il n'a jamais du tems pour l'encourager. The General said of the Hypochondria, Je ne le trouve pas un temperament malheureux. The Hereditary Prince of Brunswic was now at Potzdam. I waited upon him in the Palace, & talked some time. On the parade I stood by Weiligh, who had promised that if it was possible he would present me to the King. But an opportunity did not present itself. This King is feared like a wild-Beast. I am quite out of conceit with Monarchy. I dined at Froment's. Then Madame & I took a drive in My Lord's coach. We once more talked of Hypochondria, & when I mentioned many gloomy ideas, she said allways 'Il faut etre malade pour penser comme cela'. She is realy right. We payed a visit to Catt & his Lady two poor Beings.[3] At night we all met at Froment's. We played at Pharo. I for the first time. I grew monstrously keen. We supt. Again the Bank went on. I am happily tied up from gaming.[4]

[1] The anecdote of the General and the tower is untraced.

[2] This letter, and one to James Love, are recorded under 'Envoyé' in Reg. Let. Neither one has survived.

[3] Catt had married Ulrike Kuehn, daughter of a Swiss merchant, two years earlier (NDB).

[4] In the card game of faro each player bet against 'the bank' on the order in which pairs of cards were pulled from the deck. So quickly could one gamble away one's fortune that it had been forbidden in France earlier in the century (Richard Seymour, *The Compleat Gamester*, 6th ed. 1739, pp. 122–23).

For JB's being 'tied up', see Journ. 22 July n. 6.

## Sunday 23[1] September

[MEM. dated Monday 24 Septr.] [Y]esterday you saw Lord Marischal for the last time & took a cordial leave — 'You may allways reckon upon me as a most faithfull

Servant' — din'd [F]roment [—] c'est de la totalité de petites choses que la vie est composee. Farewell him — Scott & Macpherson — Hard on Waggon & cold[.]

[J.] Once more I saw the King of Prussia. My Father had proposed to me to pass the winter at Geneva. But I was anxious to go to Italy. Mr. Mitchell wrote in my favour, as did my worthy Lord Marischal. In the mean time I resolved to go to Geneva, but to make a long tour of it, by visiting several of the German Courts. My Lord Marischall approved of this. I past part of the morning with his Lordship, who gave me his good advices with an accuracy & a vivacity that amazed me. He is absolutely free of affectation, which I cannot understand; for, I am sadly plagued with it. He joked with me, & said Well, Colonel! may you not only conquer Portugal, but Africa; and so triumph over the Moors. I took leave of him with a most repectfull and affectionate embrace saying 'My Lord, you may allways reckon upon me as upon a most faithfull Servant.' My heart was big when I took my last adieu of the venerable Scots nobleman. I yet hope to see him again.[2] I allmost cried. At this moment the tears are in my eyes. I dined at Froment's & took leave of my poor Turk with regret. Well, she & I have past curious hours together. Honest Scott said If I come within sixty miles of you, I shall see you. Macpherson & Froment walked with me till I was out at the Gate, & then took leave. All these circumstances mark my being regarded. I mounted the Post Waggon. I found it cold & realy hard enough. Courage.

[1] MS. Dated 24 in error for 23 Sept.
[2] Although JB would not see Lord Marischal again, they would exchange jocular letters until Jan. 1776. At the request of Lord Marischal JB would moreover become Mme de Froment's legal advisor in Scotland. He would hold copies of the papers pertaining to her divorce (Yale MS. C 1324) and would be asked to find investments for the moneys (£500) that Lord Marischal was leaving her unofficially, excluding them from the funds that would go by entail to his Scottish cousin (From Lord Marischal, 10 July, 1 Sept., 12 Sept. 24 Oct. 1767, *Corr. 5*, pp. 185, 211, 217, 244; 12 Sept. 1768, *Corr.* 7, p. 107).

## Monday 24 September

[MEM. dated Tuesday 25 Septr.] Yesterday came to Coswig — asked Vie <veel>[1] troupe — dreaded conspiracy — was taken up — guard — spoke latin — Beest[2] — magistrate — Solvuntur risu tabulo — Then Dessau — Coach court [—] was quite timid — cleaned-up concert supp. This day hunt moderate. Be retenue — Be pious.

[J.] About noon I arrived at Coswig, the residence of the Prince of Zerbst, who is a strange wrong-headed Being. He has got his troops forsooth to the number of 150 foot and 30 horse, and during the last war, he took a fancy that the King of Prussia was coming to attack him. So, he put in readiness his little Battery of Cannon, and led out his 180 to make head against the armys of Frederic. He was not here at present, but at Vienna, as he has a Regiment in the Austrian Service.[3] So I had no opportunity of paying my court to him. The appearance of his little dirty town, his castle and his Sentinels with Sentry boxes painted in Lozenges of different colours like the stockings of

117

Harlequin diverted me a good deal.[4] I walked about & to have a little German talk I asked every Sentry vie veel troepen hebt der Furst?[5] One Soldier whose head resembled that of his Prince had marked me with serious political Attention & dreading that a foreign Spy had got into his Highness's dominions and that a Conspiracy was forming against the state, followed me close & at last when I came to the Grenadier before the Castle-Gate, he laid hold of me charged the Sentry with me, & bringing a Party, conducted me to the Main Guard. I was heartily entertained with this adventure & marched with all the formal composure of a State Prisoner. When I arrived at the Guard, there was a hue & cry arround me, as if I had entered a Kennel of Dogs. I could not explain myself well enough in German & stood for some time like the Stag at Bay. At last a Blackguard dog of a Soldier said, 'Dominus forsitan loquitur latine.'[6] I told this fellow that I was a Stranger a Gentleman of Scotland, and that I had asked the number of his Prince's troops to amuse my curiosity, and that I supposed I had done no harm. He repeated this in German, & most of the troops seemed content. But my foolish fellow of an accuser would see more into the matter, and so away they carried me before the Burgmeester,[7] while I laughed & cried *Beast*.[8] My Interpreter repeated my defence to the Burgmeester & this judicious Magistrate smiled at the fellow and dismist me immediatly.

Solvuntur risu Tabulae, tu missus abibis.[9]
My Lords the Judges laugh, & you're dismiss'd.

This is realy an adventure to tell. My Interpreter told me: Studui Lipsiae.[10] I suppose he has been a very sad Dog. At three I arrived at Dessau, and immediatly drest. I sent immediatly my compliments as M. de Boswell Ecossois to the Maréchal de la Cour begging to have the honour of waiting upon him, & being presented á la Cour. He asked to see me at court at five. Immediatly I had from the Prince an elegant coach, & Footman well laced, & at five I drove to court. This now is quite the thing. My good fortune put me in a flutter, and I became timourous like a Peasant upon whose back is clapped a suit of rich cloaths. The Maréchal spoke no french which was a little aukward.[11] I presented a letter to the Prince Jean George from Count d'Anhalt at Potzdam. I was presented to three Princesses, & to the Prince Albert.[12] I never saw a family that pleased me more. It was one of the grand court days. We had a concert. The reigning Prince was not at home which I regret much, as he has been in England, loves it, speaks the language, & is fond to see the British.[13] Nietschutz his master of horse who was also in England, was now at Dessau, & very kind he was to me, as was also a M. de Bernhorst.[14] I supt at Court where all was very well. The two Princes spoke only German so that I had difficult conversation of it. However, I did so well that I was liked, and I was honoured with the distinction of being offered one of the Prince's horses to go ahunting with, which I most thankfully accepted. I got into true spirits.

[1] MS. Conjectural.
[2] That is, 'Beast'; see n. 8.
[3] Friedrich August (1734–93), Prince of

Anhalt-Zerbst, brother of Catherine the Great (1729–96), was notoriously autocratic and unpredictable in his behaviour. He was proud of his little army, which he had committed to the Austrians during the Seven Years' War and was still keeping in their service, and had come to hate Frederick II, especially after Prussian troops forcibly removed a supposed French spy from Zerbstian protection in 1758. The Prince's first wife having died in 1759, he had just married Friederike Auguste Sophie (1744–1827) of Anhalt-Bernburg in May (Isenburg, i. Tafel 135). A few days after the wedding he had insisted that they leave her family in the middle of the night to return to Coswig, and three months later he had left his realm to settle permanently in Basel. From 1778 to 1781 the Prince would sell his troops to England to use against the new United States (G. A. Stenzel, *Handbuch der Anhaltischen Geschichte*, 1820, pp. 260–67; Vehse, xxxviii. 320–22).

⁴ The castle looked like a toy palace. Its central *corps de logis*, in late-Renaissance style, ended in small picturesque towers, from which wings branched out at right angles. Built in 1555, it had been expanded from 1667 to 1677 to serve as dowager residence for Princess Sophie Auguste (1630–80) of Anhalt-Zerbst, the present ruler's great-grandmother (see *Anhaltische Schlösser* in *Geschichte und Kunst*, ed. Erdmute Alex, 1991, p. 56; Erhard Hirsch, 'Die anhaltischen Residenzschlösser', and Bruno J. Sobotka, 'Coswig, Schloss' in *Burgen, Schlösser, Gutshäuser in Sachsen-Anhalt*, 1994, pp. 72, 281; see also Isenburg, i. Tafel 135).

⁵ JB's Dutch-German for 'How many troops does the Prince have?'

⁶ 'Perhaps my Lord speaks Latin?'

⁷ German 'Bürgermeister', mayor.

⁸ Possibly a phrase used in ombre or a related card game to signify a wrong move and to accept a penalty (Richard Seymour, *The Compleat Gamester*, 8th ed. 1754, pp. 22, 74–76; James Beaufort, *Hoyle's Games Improved*, 1788, p. 125).

⁹ Horace, *Satires*, II. 1. 86.

¹⁰ 'I have studied in Leipzig'.

¹¹ The marshal, one of several, was Wolf Friedrich von Schlegel (d. 1766); see LSAO, A 12b 1 No. 7.

¹² These were the reigning prince's younger siblings: Jean George, also called Hans Jürge (1748–1811); Henriette Katharina Agnes (1744–99); Maria Leopoldine (1746–69); Kasimire (1749–78); and Albert or Albrecht (1750–1811). For JB's letter of introduction to the eldest, see Mem. dated 23 Sept.

¹³ Leopold III Friedrich Franz (1740–1817), known as *Fürst Franz* ('Prince Franz') and later as *Vater Franz*, was the first enlightened and art-loving ruler in a family that was otherwise primarily militaristic. He was so ardent an anglophile that he was planning his summer residence in the style of the English country houses and gardens he had visited in 1763, immediately after the Seven Years' War (*Wörlitz, ein Garten der Aufklärung*, ed. Gerd Biegel, 1992, pp. 23–24, 83–84). Regrettably JB, who yearned to know a great enlightened prince, did not meet him.

¹⁴ Adolf Friedrich von Neitschütz, or Neutschütz (1730–72), had accompanied the Prince on his trip to England (Hirsch, i. 40; ii. 8 n. 145). Georg Heinrich von Berenhorst (1733–1814) was the reigning prince's uncle (see Journ. 1 Oct. and n. 8).

## Tuesday 25 September

[MEM. dated Wednesday 26 Septr.] Yesterday rose at 5 went & was presented to Prince Diederic a fine old cordial German saw his hounds & horses. Then went out on old White — noble forrest. Uniform — Stag — fine chace not too hard. Deer took Elbe — cut in pieces. Prince gave you foot *un marque de distinction*. It must be kept at Auchinleck. Collation. Princesses in Coach. Was quite noble recollected old Edinr. vapours — L. Galloway [—] Toil strung nerves &c. You *must* have daily exercise. Dind in boots.¹ Then visited Comtesse Anhalt. Then Court. Ocredy spoke bawdy — look'd grave — till he said She'd² do like Lobster's claws.

[J.] Like a bold Hunter I rose at five, M. de Bernhorst presented me to Prince Diederic Uncle to the reigning Prince. I found him a tall comely old man of Sixty two. He was formerly Velt Marischal in the Prussian Service.³ He has loved hunting all his life. He now keeps two Packs of good hounds.

He is just one of the old Germans, rough & cordial. He took me by the hand, & showed me his Stables & then we went out. The old Gentleman went in his open chaise to the Rendezvous. The Pack consisted of fifty couple.[4] The Hunters were pretty numerous, and had a genteel uniform of red & blue. There were a great many noble Cornes de chasses the sound of which roused my blood. The forrests of Dessau are magnificent, all of fine oaks some of which are immensely large. I was mounted on a trusty old white, very quiet very sure-footed, & by no means slow. For this day, however, I kept by the young Prince Albert who cut the wood by neat pretty roads which are made in different places. A large Stag was singled out, & away we went after him. It was the first time that I saw this sport and a most noble one it is.[5] Macfarlane would say then it might be a Marquis for most noble is his title.[6] The Chace lasted more than two hours. At last the Stag took the Elbe and was half worried, half drowned, half slain by the Hunter's *Coup de grace*. The Horns then sounded, & we all assembled. The Princesses came out of their coach. I must mark a little Anecdote not quite according to strict decorum; The Prince's Mistress was in a chaise just behind the coach.[7] She did not however come out. After we had payed our respects to Prince Diederic on his Chace, a collation of cold meat, bread & butter & wine was served round. In the mean time the Deer was skinned & the best pieces of vennison laid by. The rest of him was cut to pieces, while the old Prince sat very composedly with his muster roll, and named all the dogs to see if they were all there. I was vexed that they could not answer to their names, especially as there were several english dogs among them.[8] They were then well whipped in,[9] till their hunger increast allmost to fury. The skin & horns were placed above the minced pieces, & then all at once the Pack were let loose, and the moment that they attacked the image of the Deer, the skin & horns were removed, & they were allowed to devour with full freedom. Prince Diederic then presented me with the Stag's foot; saying 'Mon Cher cest une marque de distinction.' This pleased me. It shall be laid up in the musæum at Auchinleck, with an inscription on a plate of gold or silver, telling that Laird James the fourth had it in a present from a German Prince with whom he had the honour of hunting, when upon his travels.[10] We all had oak garlands in our hats, & returned gayly to Dessau. I recollected my old Edinburgh vapours — Lord Galloway — By chace our long-liv'd fathers earn'd their food etc.[11] I resolved to take daily vigourous exercise. We din'd at court in boots as the Ladies were not with us.[12] At three I waited on the Countess d'Anhalt mother to the Count at Potzdam.[13] She has three daughters strong bouncing women. One of them is very clever.[14] In the evening we all met again at court. I must not forget to mention one Personage, Captain Ogrady an Irish Officer in the Saxon service, a good honest light-headed fellow.[15] He keeps a Girl at Dessau, and is very much there. At supper this night he talked a vast deal of bawdy concerning a Mademoiselle Stenix who sat near me. I looked grave, & seemed to give no attention to his discourse, by way of reproving him. At last he said that 'She would go like a pair of Lobster's claws'. This ludicrous idea struck me so much, that I burst out into a fit of laughter, & Master Ogrady was heartily pleased.[16]

[1] MS. 'Dind in boots' an interlineation.

[2] MS. 'Shed'

[3] Prince Dietrich (1702–69) of Anhalt-Dessau was officiating as regent in the absence of the reigning prince, thereby resuming the duties he had carried out from 1751 to 1758 during his nephew's minority. Dietrich had served in the Prussian army with the rank of field marshal (rendered 'Velt Marischal' by JB) from 1747 to 1750 after holding other important commands in Frederick II's Silesian wars (1740–45): as major-general in 1740, as lieutenant-general in 1742, and as general of infantry in 1745 (*Militairisches Pantheon*, pp. 37–38). Forced by ill health to retire from military service, he had devoted himself to landscaping Dessau and encouraging agricultural improvements (Vehse, xxxviii. 201, 206–07; Benno von Knobelsdorff-Brenkenhoff, *Anhalt-Dessau, 1737–1762*, 1987, pp. 53–54).

[4] Pairs of dogs (OED, s.v. 'couple', 1, 4).

[5] Dietrich's favourite sport was the *Parforce* hunt, in which a single mature stag, specially selected, was allowed to run in whatever direction he chose and was pursued by dogs until, tired out, he stood 'at bay' and faced his pursuers. He was then killed by a huntsman and slaughtered in ritual stages (G. Landau, *Beiträge zur Geschichte der Jagd*, 1849, pp. 95–96). Special 'Parforce horns' were used to signal the different stages of the hunt (Georg Karstädt, *Lasst lustig die Hörner erschallen*, 1964, pp. 78, 81, 85). In Britain, stag hunts 'at force' had been introduced by the Normans as a sport reserved primarily for royalty (see OED, s.v. 'force', 22.a). By the eighteenth century, when deforestation had reduced the number of stags, such hunts were rare (Michael Billett, *A History of English Country Sports*, 1994, pp. 82–91). In Scotland, red deer and hares could be hunted, but JB would not record engaging in such sport again until twelve years later, when he would hunt on horseback at Douglas Castle in Lanarkshire (Journ. 22 Oct. 1776).

[6] So splendid was the prey on this occasion that JB thought of Walter Macfarlane of Macfarlane (c. 1700–67), a great antiquarian and a stickler for correct forms of address, who would have called the stag 'Most Honourable', the proper style for a marquis (see *Life* v. 156 n. 3).

[7] Johanne Eleonora Hoffmeier or Hoffmeyer (1739–1816) was Prince Franz's great love, whom he would have married if Frederick II had not objected to another commoner in the family after the father and grandfather had married beneath their rank (see n. 13 and Journ. 1 Oct. n. 7). In 1767 the Prince would marry Princess Luise Henriette Wilhelmine (1750–1811), daughter of Margrave Heinrich Friedrich of Brandenburg-Schwedt, with Frederick's approval. Johanne Eleonora Hoffmeier had borne the Prince a son, Franz Johann Georg (1763–1823), who would be ennobled with the title Graf von Waldersee (Thiele, i. 346). She would be married off to Neitschütz one year after JB saw her (Heese, ii. 7–8, 105; *Deutsches Geschlechterbuch: Genealogisches Handbuch bürgerlicher Familien*, 1936, xcii. 320 n. 3).

[8] Two types of dogs were used: those who found the stag by scent, and those who then pursued him by sight until he stood at bay (Billett, pp. 84–85, 98). In Dessau from 40 to 150 dogs were unleashed on a given day, and their performance was recorded in a special book (LSAO C 10d II). The English ones were bloodhounds that had been imported at great cost (Heese, i. 329–30).

[9] Driven back into the pack by use of a whip (OED, s.v. 'whip in', II. 6.d).

[10] The hoof would not survive but was presumably at Auchinleck when Sir David Dalrymple, at JB's request, sent him a Latin version of the hoped-for inscription on 30 Sept. 1767: 'Æternae Memoriae Theoderici. Anh. Dess. Optimï Principis qui cervum diu cursibus exagitatum, Canibus delamandum praebuit & ut fama egregii facinoris exteris innotesceret. Pedem abscissum Belluae, opima spoliae. Jacobo Boswel Baroni de Auchinleck Laborum simul at victoriae socio. Dono dedit. 1767' ('To the everlasting memory of the most excellent Prince Dietrich of Anhalt-Dessau, who allowed his dogs to tear to pieces a stag that they had pursued in a long chase and, in order that the renown of this achievement might come to the attention of people abroad, bestowed a foot cut from the beast as "spolia opima" on James Boswell, Baron of Auchinleck, the companion of both his toils and triumphs. Given as a gift [by Dalrymple] in 1767'. English translation provided by Robert Warnock.) 'Spolia opima' refers to armour stripped from the vanquished by the victor. Whether JB ever had the inscription engraved and mounted on the hoof is not known.

[11] John Dryden, 'To My Honour'd Kinsman, John Driden' (1700), l. 88. Perhaps JB was quoting a favourite line of Lord Galloway's, for whom see Mem. 27 June n. 4.

[12] Not to change to better footwear to dine was highly informal. Boots were usually worn only outdoors—for riding, hunting, travelling, or military activities (C. Willett Cunnington and Phillis Cunnington, *Handbook of English Costume in the Eighteenth*

*Century*, 1972, p. 81).

[13] Johanne Sophie, *née* Herre (1706–95), Countess of Anhalt-Dessau, was the widow of Wilhelm Gustav, Hereditary Prince of Anhalt-Dessau. She was reported to be the daughter either of a peasant farmer (Bauer, in ADB) or, more likely, of a brewer (Brauer, in G. H. A. Stenzel, *Handbuch der Anhaltischen Geschichte*, 1820, p. 355; Knesche, i. 85). She had lived with Prince Gustav for eleven years and had had nine children, but only on his deathbed in 1737 had he acknowledged this morganatic marriage to Leopold I (1676–1747), his powerful father (Stenzel, p. 355; Knesche, i. 85; for Leopold I, see Journ. 29 Sept. n. 13). The title of countess (*Reichsgräfin*) had been conferred on her and her descendants in 1749 by the Holy Roman Emperor at the suggestion of the next ruler of Dessau, Leopold Maximilian (1700–51); see Vehse, xviii. 200.

[14] Only one of her three daughters, Jo-hanne Sophie (1731–86), later abbess at Mosigkau, has been identified (Heese, ii. 107).

[15] Donogh O'Grady evidently gave JB the impression of being thoughtless or frivolous (OED, s.v. 'light-headed', 2). He had arrived in Dessau on 11 Sept., bringing five horses for the prince as well as twenty-three dogs for Prince Eugene (Leopold Friedrich Franz von Anhalt-Dessau to Friedrich Wilhelm von Erdmannsdorff, 13 Sept. 1764, LSAO, A10 187). Prince Franz had apparently met him in England in 1763 (Hirsch, i. 40; ii. 8 n. 145). By 1765 O'Grady would be master of horse in Dessau (Franz Brückner, 'Geschichte der ehemaligen Sandvorstadt des 16. Jahrhunderts', *Dessauer Kalender*, 1967, p. 52). Mlle Stenix has not been identified.

[16] MS. 'At supper … pleased' crossed out by a single line; within this passage, 'deal … concerning', 'Stenix', and 'She … claws' heavily scored out by a modern hand.

## Wednesday 26 September

[MEM. dated Thursday 27 Septr.] Yesterday morning put papers in order & was well — din'd Court. M. Lestock. Gouv: de Prince spoke well — Le Roy de Prusse venoit un jour. Que faites vous Voltaire? Sire.[1] J'arrange votre linge sale.[2] At 2 waited on Princess Wilhelmine fat and magnificent & hearty [—] then home — then cards there & supt. On y mange bien. At night, fixed route — hesitated at first then *resolved* not in Italy before Christmas but at Turin.[3] So you see courts with full freedom a dozen of em & get acquainted with Princes & form retenue & pass some weeks in Switzerland & see Rousseau & get full advice.[4] This day write [F]roment & bring up Journ.

[J.] I had some conversation with Mr. Lestock who formerly was a Tutor to the Princes. He said their father had a curious whim that he would not allow them to learn any latin.[5] After dinner I waited on Princesse Wilhelmine Aunt to the Prince. She was a large jolly Princess, very high and mighty; but her Pride was of the best kind. It did not shew itself in silent disdain; but in splendid magnificence. Her highness has her master of Horse her grande Maitresse, her Dame d'honneur & in short the true state of a court in a certain degree.[6] I was asked to return at Six. I did so; and found there a little party eight in all. We played at cards till eight when we supped, & exceedingly well. She was very hearty, & conversation went well on. There was just as much restraint as pleased me. Well, I am at present a happy fellow. Where are all my gloomy speculations at Utrecht when I imagined that I knew all the circumstances that could arrive in human life, and that the result was only Insipidity. Castillon gave me no bad answer to this. You know said he all the circumstances of human life, as you know the ingredients of which a dish may be made; but in neither of the cases can you know what will be the effect of a selection & mixture, till you try.

[1] MS. 'Sire' inserted above 'J'arrange'.

[2] JB made a separate record of this famous anecdote: 'When Voltaire was at Berlin he used to be rude to the King of Prussia. The King came into his room one day when he had before him on a table a great parcel of his Majesty's verses, which he no doubt put in order very freely. The King called to him, "Que faites-vous, [M.] Voltaire?" He replied, "Sire, j'arrange votre linge sale"' (*Boswelliana*, p. 227). JB then noted his source: '* M. Lestock cidevant Gouverneur du P. D'Anhalt' (Hyde MS). Whether Voltaire had actually made this quip is not known, but it had soon become public and had irritated Frederick II. Voltaire had blamed his enemy Maupertuis, President of the Prussian Academy, for circulating it in Berlin (see Journ. 9 Oct. n. 2; Christiane Mervaud, *Voltaire et Frédéric II*, SVEC 234 [1985]: 224 and n. 103). For L'Estocq, see n. 5 below.

[3] Turin, which belonged to the Duchy of Savoy, was the first stop after crossing the Alps from Geneva.

[4] JB's first explicit statement in his journal and memoranda concerning his goals in travelling and especially in meeting Rousseau. For the actual meetings, see Journ. 3–5 and 14–15 Dec.

[5] Carl Ludwig von L'Estocq (1725–1807), who had become the Hereditary Prince's tutor in 1750, had been engaged for his knowledge of French, history, geography, and arithmetic as well as for his membership in the Reformed (i.e., Calvinist) Church. Latin had been conspicuously absent from the requirements set by the Prince's father, Leopold Maximilian. L'Estocq had first studied medicine in Leipzig and Halle and had then in 1748 enrolled in the philosophical faculty. Once the Prince had assumed the rule of Dessau at the age of eighteen, during the Seven Years' War, L'Estocq had been sent on various diplomatic missions with the title *Kommissionsrat*. He was now living in Dessau in retirement (typescript copy of his autobiography, 'Selbstbiographie', 1802, LSAO, A10 200, pp. 4–5, 8; Hirsch, ii. 6, n. 121).

[6] Princess Anna Wilhelmine (1715–80), the sister of Prince Dietrich, was unmarried. She would later establish a foundation for single ladies of aristocratic families (Siebigk, p. 258). The members of her personal court have not been identified.

## *Thursday 27 September*

[MEM. dated Friday 28 Septr.] Yesterday you wrote a good deal morning. After dinner saw Prince's room several good pictures and good number of Books. *Rambler* pleased to see him grand old rooms Theatre. Then worthy[1] Nedutsh carried you to see Horses. Fine worthy fellow — Saw also Cattel was quite renewed in old Laird & family ideas Prince gives 600 Daalers to each natural child. Some of them genteel. Do you the same.[2] Was quite well [—] night grande cour. This day Hunting. Be more venturous lay up ideas. Be master of self and fix ideas of Religion. Write a letter to Johnston each court & city & keep them for one packet.[3] Be retenue.

[J.] While I was on bad terms with my worthy Father, I was treated with great kindness by Lord Kames. His Lordship's house was a Home to me.[4] We coresponded while I was in London.[5] But since I have been abroad I have not written to him. This day I wrote him a long letter of which I shall mark the principal passages.

'After a silence of thirteen months you may beleive, My Lord, that Boswell finds some difficulty in beginning a letter to Your Lordship. I feel that my conduct has not been altogether right. I should have written to you before now. Indeed I should. I can make no other Apology than reminding you of the strange nature of man of whose unaccountable conduct I have had so many instances that I am fully confirmed in the beleif of Human Liberty, and that the doctrine of motives is only imaginary.[6] I reserve a detail of my travels for the entertainment of those evenings which I hope to pass with your Lordship in Scotland; when I hope to be better company for you than you have formerly found me. I hope to be company for you in a better stile. I am making a tour thro' the German Courts. I am behaving as my best freinds could wish. Wherever I come I find myself loved. My Dear Lord! is it possible for me not to be flattered when I find that in a day or two I can make Strangers of all kinds regard me? Sure I am this could not be done without external merit. As to my internal worth I am allways certain. To talk philosophically, a man's acquitting himself well or ill depends extremely on the situation in which he is placed. Take me at present as I am. During this portion of my existence in which I am visiting the courts of Germany, I am acting with perfect propriety. I am fullfilling every duty that my Station requires, and when the Sun goes down, I review my day with satisfaction. Place me as a Student in the Temple, as an officer in a Garrison, as a Laird upon his Estate, or as an Advocate in the Court of Session, and I fear my review would not be so pleasing. However, I hope the best. I am every day becoming more temperate in mind. I am every day more convinced that Imagination forms false views of life, and that in all human Affairs there is not as much mystery as a young man is apt to think.[7] Is not this true, My Lord? Speak, thou Sage. For, well thou knowest mortal man.[8]

Is it not amazing to find Voltaire writing still with so much vivacity. I am pretty well informed that he wrote the critical letter on 'The Elements' in the Gazette Literaire de l'Europe. Was there ever such an old Rogue? He gives the french no more idea of your book, than if he had written a love-song or a drinking catch. I must however own that his letter bears hard against[9] your Chapter on Ridicule. For notwithstanding the value which I have for your book, it seemed ridiculous for a minute or two after reading the letter.[10] I beleive I told your Lordship before I left England that I had obtained the freindship of Mr. Samuel Johnson. I look upon this as the happiest incident in my life. The Conversation of that great and good man has formed me to manly Virtue, and kindled in my mind a generous ardour which I trust shall never be extinguished. I hope your Lordship shall one day see Mr. Johnson. His Conversation on Subjects of importance is not more excellent than is his strong humour. Mr. Garrick said to me that he preferred the latter; and Garrick surely knows to judge of humour. Mr. Johnson accompanied me to Harwich, and since I have been abroad, has honoured me with his Corespondence.[11] My Lord, if I should die tomorrow, I have not lived in vain. Pray My Lord what is your Son doing? Will you allow me to say that I think the original plan for him was not a very good one. I think, My Lord, We have honoured trade enough in our Island, by allowing the younger Sons of Gentlemen to follow it, without disparaging their familys. To make merchants of our eldest sons is going too far. Let us not abolish distinctions from which mankind have received more benefit than harm.[12] Since I have been abroad several circumstances have concurred to make me think in a manner more serious than when I had the honour of being with your Lordship. Upon the whole, I think myself a good deal improved. While I thus talk to you without reserve, it would be cruel to laugh or to suspect me of affectation. Pray, My Lord, be kind enough to forget my former extravagant love of Ridicule.[13]

Such was my letter. I think he must be pleased with it, and I expect he will write me a good answer.[14]

After dinner my worthy Neidutsch carried me thro' the Palace which has many noble rooms. I saw a very pretty beginning of a Collection of Pictures which the Prince has made, and a very handsom Library of french, German and English Books. His Highness's English Library is very well chosen. It gave me pleasure to find there Johnson's Dictionary, and my respected freind the Rambler in good attire.[15] We then mounted a couple of the Prince's horses, after having seen his stables in town, & went & saw his Polish & Hungarian Cattel for which he has excellent pasture. They are generally of a blueish colour and resemble the Scots Highland beasts.[16] They are indeed larger; but, like our highlanders they are lean & firm, & when brought to rich feeding make excellent Beef. We saw also the young Horses of which the Prince has a vast many. I was very well amused with these rural sights, and quite in the humour of being a clever farmer at Auchinleck. A Scots Baron cannot do better than travel in Germany. When he goes to Italy & France, he lives with Artificial Men coop'd up in towns & formed in such a manner that nature is quite destroyed. Yet is an art so agreable substituted in its place that these people feel themselves happy, altho' the true manly character is melted into elegant ease. If the Scots Baron were to pass all his life abroad, he would not perceive his Imbecillity more than they do. But, as he must return to his own country, he should not render himself unfit for it. Let him then go & visit the German Courts, where he can acquire french and polite manners, & at the same time be with People who live much in the same stile that he must do at home. He may thus learn to support his character with dignity, & upon his paternal estate may have the felicity of a Prince. Let him make a tour into the delicious countrys of the South, to enrich his mind with a variety of brilliant ideas, & to give his manners a still finer polish. But let him not stay there too long. Let him not remain in the Italian Sun till his Caledonian Iron is melted. At night we had grande cour. A Lady asked me for Le Marquis d'Annandale, whom she had seen at the Hague. I told her with concern his melancholy fate.[17]

[1] MS. 'worth', a slip of the pen.

[2] The generous Prince was not Franz but his grandfather, Leopold I (1676–1747), known as the 'Old Dessauer' (see Journ. 1 Oct. and n. 7). JB's son Charles, born out of wedlock, had died a few months earlier (Journ. 9 Mar., *Holland*, Heinemann p. 173, McGraw-Hill p. 177), but JB evidently expected to have more such children.

[3] The first reference to the plan JB would follow as he continued his tour. He had previously sent his London journal of 1762–63 to JJ and had intended his Dutch journal

for WJT.

[4] Henry Home, Lord Kames (1698–1782), jurist and author, was one of JB's fatherly friends (*Earlier Years*, pp. 75, 86, 94). His nonhereditary title was taken from the name of his estate in southern Berwickshire when he was appointed to the Court of Session, the highest civil court of Scotland, in 1752, and was further due him when he became Lord Commissioner of Justiciary on the highest criminal court of Scotland in 1763. JB had enjoyed staying at Kames's estate from 16 to 26 Oct. 1762 and possibly intended a pun on

'home' even though the Scottish pronunciation of Kames's family name was 'Hume'. While on his harvest jaunt with Kames, JB had come to appreciate his cheerful sociability, dry and whimsical sense of humour, and intellectual accomplishments: 'Lord Kames is a man of uncommon Genius, great Application and extensive knowledge of which his various works are a standing proof' ('Journal of my Jaunt, Harvest 1762', J 2; see also JB's 'Epistle to Miss Home', *Corr. 9*, pp. 116–18, and 119–20 nn. 18–19). Kames had studied Latin as well as civil law, and after passing advocate in 1723, he had supplemented his legal practice by compiling important documents in his *Remarkable Decisions of the Court of Session*, from 1716, to 1728, 1728, and *The Decisions of the Court of Session, from its Institution to the Present Time*, 2 vols., 1741 (two more such volumes would follow in 1766 and 1780). He had also written the philosophical treatise *Principles of Equity*, 1760. Kames had drawn on his knowledge of history and the classics in his *Essays upon Several Subjects Concerning British Antiquities*, 1747. His interest in metaphysics and morality had led him to publish, anonymously, the controversial *Essays on the Principles of Morality and Natural Religion*, 1751, that had involved him in serious difficulties with the local clergy. In a lighter vein, Kames had written an *Introduction to the Art of Thinking*, 1761, that offered younger readers maxims followed by illustrative stories. In his latest, most ambitious work, *Elements of Criticism* (1762, enlarged ed. 1763), Kames had attempted to give a systematic analysis of basic principles governing human thinking and feeling, and had then applied these principles to literary concepts, rhetorical devices, and even to gardening and architecture (see Helen Whitcomb Randall, 'The Critical Theory of Lord Kames', *Smith College Studies in Modern Languages*, Oct. 1940–July 1941, 22. 7 n. 28, 8–11, 23–26).

⁵ Kames had written several letters with advice and warm professions of friendship (5 Dec. 1762, 27 Mar. and 16 July 1763). Very likely he had served as intermediary between JB and Lord Auchinleck, a colleague of Kames's on the bench, when the latter disapproved of JB's rebellious behaviour in London and Edinburgh from 1761 to 1762 (see Richard B. Sher, '"Something that Put Me in Mind of My Father": Boswell and Lord Kames', in *Lustig*, pp. 67–71). JB's answers to Kames would not survive.

⁶ JB here quotes Kames's statement that human actions appear 'strange and surprising' when considered in the mind, but tacitly contradicts Kames's observation concerning 'human liberty'. Kames had rejected the notion of free will on the grounds that human beings do not act 'without or against motive', but that, recognized or not, God's will guides human actions. Kames had written at length about motives, which, he believed, determine the will, which in turn leads to action (*Essays on the Principles of Morality and Natural Religion*, 1751, pp. 159–75; see Arthur E. McGuinness, *Henry Home, Lord Kames*, 1970, p. 48; Ian Simpson Ross, *Lord Kames and the Scotland of his Day*, 1972, pp. 104–05).

⁷ Possibly JB's acknowledgement that he had accepted Kames's advice to let the imagination serve only for 'recreation' and to attend to more serious occupations first (From Lord Kames, 5 Dec. 1762).

⁸ Unidentified quotation.

⁹ Shows 'resentment against' (OED, s.v. 'bear', 16). The resentment was Voltaire's, directed at Kames (see the next note).

¹⁰ A sarcastic review, published anonymously in the appendix to the *Gazette Littéraire* (4 Apr., i. 93–100), had mocked Kames for belabouring the obvious, for extolling low speeches in Shakespeare while criticizing noble lines in Corneille and Racine, and for finding the gardens of Versailles disturbingly artificial. The review had continued with ironic praise of Kames for offering opinions as if they were laws, and had welcomed the arrival from Scotland of rules for all the arts as a sign of human progress (repr. in Theodore Besterman, *Voltaire on Shakespeare*, SVEC 54 [1967]: 85–89). Voltaire may have been irritated by Kames's censure of Corneille for being declamatory rather than expressing passion (*Elements*, chs. 16, 17) just when Voltaire was seeking subscriptions for his new edition of the French dramatist (see Journ. 24 Dec. n. 19; D. Williams, 'Voltaire's War with England', *Voltaire and the English*, SVEC 179 [1979]: 81–82). Voltaire also had been affronted when his *Henriade* (1723), an epic celebrating Henry IV of France, had been faulted by Kames for its 'cold' epic machinery and for allegorical or supernatural beings participating in a narrative of historical events (*Elements*, ch. 22). Although Voltaire had not admitted his authorship of the review, he had praised it as a blow for the French and for good taste in the battle against the English (Voltaire to Charles Augustin Feriol, comte d'Argental, and Jeanne Grâce Bosc Du Bouchet, comtesse d'Argental, c. Jan. 1764, *Corres. Voltaire*, D11645). Voltaire's authorship was an open secret (see David Hume to Hugh Blair, 26 Apr., *Corres. Voltaire*, D11645, Commentary,

n. 1). Yet JB would still seek confirmation while at Ferney (see Journ. 29 Dec.). Kames himself would acknowledge Voltaire as author in a grudging apology added in a footnote in the fifth edition of the *Elements*, 1774 (see Thomas R. Lounsbury, *Shakespeare and Voltaire*, 1902, pp. 244–49, 255).

JB's reference to Kames's chapter on ridicule is puzzling, since the subject of ridicule is not mentioned in the review. Possibly JB no longer clearly remembered the review and merely wanted a jocular introduction to Voltaire's ridicule. Altogether, JB's 'ostensible naïveté' here was, as F. A. Pottle has suggested, 'of course malicious' (*Grand Tour I*, Heinemann p. 108 n. 1, McGraw-Hill p. 111 n. 2).

[11] On the first day of their meeting, JB had been fascinated by SJ's 'conversation' and had decided to record as much of it as he could remember (Journ. 16 May 1763). Their affectionate farewell at Harwich on the day of JB's departure for abroad is described in *Life* i. 472. However, no letter of SJ's written to JB at this time is known. In London on his first visit in 1760, JB had also become friendly with David Garrick (1717–79), the celebrated actor, playwright, and co-manager of the Drury Lane Theatre (Journ. 20 Jan. 1763; see Frank Brady, Introduction, *Corr. 4*, pp. 1–3).

[12] Lord Kames's only son, George Henry Home (1743–1818), embarked on a career in commerce in London after a spell at the University of St. Andrews (Ross, p. 40). After meeting him in London, JB had actually praised him for applying himself 'to his business as a merchant' (Journ. 2 Jan 1763). He however would become a gentleman farmer and would change his name to Home-Drummond in c. 1766 when his mother inherited her brother Blair Drummond's estate (Ross, p. 363; *Oxford DNB*, s.v. 'Home, Henry, Lord Kames'). JB would express his preference for a gentleman by birth—i.e., a member of the upper classes—over a merchant, however wealthy by his own efforts, in similar terms at greater length

in the *Life* (July 1765, i. 491–92).

[13] An allusion to Kames's praise of JB's 'mirth and jollity' coupled with the warning to keep these in check (From Kames, 27 Mar. 1763).

[14] No answer from Kames is recorded, but the correspondence would continue to the year of Kames's death (see *Catalogue*, i. 285–86; ii. 737–38). JB would also compile materials for a biography of Kames (Yale MS. M 135) but would not complete the project because of objections from Kames's son (Sher, p. 73).

[15] The palace was an old building, begun in about 1530 and extended later in the sixteenth century. More recent renovations had been begun in 1748 by Knobelsdorff but had been suspended at the death of Prince Leopold Maximilian in 1751. They would be resumed only three years after JB's visit (Harksen, i. 68–69; Schmetzer, *Dessau: Monographien Deutscher Städte*, 1914, ix. 58). Prince Franz's small 'collection of pictures' included works by Christoph Friedrich Reinhold Lisiewski (1725–94), court painter in Dessau from 1752–72, as well as works by his sister Anna Rosina Lisiewska (1716–83) and other talented members of his family (letter from Erhard Hirsch, 8 June 1981; Thieme-Becker, xxiii. 283–84; see also Journ. 1 Oct. and n. 6). The prince's Anglophilia is confirmed by his 'English Library' with its works by SJ.

[16] Perhaps the Hungarian steppe cattle, which had grey-blue coats (Alderson and Downly, *Rare Breeds*, 1994, pp. 64–65). Highland cattle had shaggy black or dark coats (James E. Handley, *Scottish Farming in the Eighteenth Century*, 1953, p. 224). Possibly they looked blue in a certain light.

[17] George van den Bempdé, 3rd Marquess of Annandale, had become insane in 1742, supposedly in distress over his brother's death two years earlier, and had been declared incapable of managing his affairs by an inquest of Chancery in 1748 (*Comp. Peer.* i. 167–68). The 'Lady' is unidentified.

## Friday 28 September

[MEM. dated Saturday 29 Septr.] Yesterday You had noble Stag chace, rode it all & saw him fairly killed in fair field. Dined Prince Diederic quite hearty Laird — Who said to The Princesse's Servant Myn liever & made him take a glass of wine. In the evening You played at Pharo: With The Princes & a Princess. M ——— held the Bank a clever pretty man. He said. En Allemagne plusieurs Gens & meme des Princes vivent par le jeu. Et on peut faire des tours — you asked comment —

& then told some. He said Mon cher Mr. vous savez ce que vous avez demandé &c. you was stupid. Say today M. Vous avez soupçonné un de meilleurs hommes du monde — mais Je ne puis vous blamer[.]

[J.] Again we went ahunting. We went to another part of the forrest from that where we were last day. We were obliged to wait a long time till the Stag was found. I went into a farmhouse, where I learnt a piece of German Housewifery. The Country People here have in their Gardens a great many Plums of the bluish red kind which we call *Burnets* at Auchinleck. They skin them and take out their stones and then throw them into a great cauldron with a certain quantity of water. They put them over a brisk fire of wood, & keep stirring them till they are sufficiently boiled. They mix no sugar with them as their juice makes them sweet enough, and being well boiled they can be kept a great while. They throw this rustic Jelly into a large tub. They call it *floum moose*.[1] When Butter is dear, they spread it very thick on their brown bread, & a very good relish it makes. I took a hearty Bit of it, for which, Bread & all, I payed a Groshin. At last the Stag was put up, and a glorious chace we had, much better than the first. I acquired venatic courage, took made roads no more, but rushed boldly along with the Heer Overstalmeester, as they called my freind Neitschutz.[2] The Stag did not get to the River. But when run down, he couched three several times, & three several times took another race, & stood at last at Bay. Of all this we had a full view. At last he sunk, the Dogs laid hold of him, and the *coup de grace* laid him dead on the field. Poor Animal! the agitation of sport prevented us from pitying him so much as we ought. All the ceremonies which I mentioned last day, were again performed, and then we returned in triumph. A great parcel of us din'd chez Prince Diederic who made a respectable figure at his own table with his white locks.[3] He was a plain warm-hearted old Man. A servant of Princess Wilhelmine's came to invite us to dinner next day. Bid him in com said the Prince, & when the fellow entered, 'Ah! myn lieber Jan!' said his Highness, & asked him kindly questions. Jan kist the Prince's garment, as is the custom in Germany & was ordered a glass of wine. In the evening at Court, a Brandenburg Gentleman made a Bank of Pharo. The Prince Jean George the Princesse Marie & I played. I lost six ecus. I am allways unlucky at Play, & allways keen.[4] The Brandenburger who was a Chanoine de Halberstat bid me be upon my guard against Play. For said he, il y a en Allemagne beaucoup de Gens même de Princes qui vivent de Jeu: et ils peuvent jouer mille tours.[5] Ah! said I — and a little after il y avoit un Juif á la Haye qui me montroit des tours les plus fins. Said he — Ainsi mon Aimable Monsieur vous savez ce que vous venez de me demander. Non. Monsieur said I Je ne savois pas qu'il etoit possible de faire des tels tours á Pharon. I did not well know how to take this speech of his. It looked as if he suspected me to be an Avanturier. However I took no notice of it, for I did indeed deserve it with my Etourderie. The Chanoine was Etourdi from conceit, altho a real clever young fellow. I told him J'ai dit a ce Juif. Monsieur vos tours sont excellents. Vous pouvez tromper tout le monde. Je n'ose pas les apprendre.

The Chanoine eager to get to the other side of the room yet willing to say a polite thing, replied 'Vous avez raison Monsieur'. Which was as much as saying you are right to fear that you would learn to cheat. By the by, The Pharo & all this Story happened last night.

[1] *Pflaumenmuss*, a kind of plum jam. The local use of 'burnets' cannot now be documented.

[2] 'Venatic': 'employed in … hunting' (OED); 'Overstalmeester': Oberstallmeister, chief master of horse.

[3] Prince Dietrich lived in a small palace that had been built for him in a Palladian-Dutch style in 1760 (Schmetzer, ix. 63).

[4] For faro, see Journ. 22 Sept. n. 4. JB marked his loss with an asterisk in his Expense Account.

[5] The canon has not been identified. He was probably attached to the Liebfrauen-kirche, which had such clergymen living together as a community. The largest church of Halberstadt after the cathedral, it had been converted from Catholicism to Lutheran Protestantism in the 1590s (Peter Findeisen, *Halberstadt Dom, Liebfrauenkirche*, 1995, pp. 9–12). The canon was a 'Brandenburger' because Halberstadt, a town northwest of Dessau that had been an independent bishopric, had been absorbed by Prussia, and this in turn had replaced the older principality of Brandenburg in 1648 (*Zur Geschichte und Kultur des Fürstentums und der Stadt Halberstadt*, 1991, pp. 7–8).

For a further account of this conversation, see Journ. 7 Oct.

## Saturday 29 September

[MEM. dated Sunday 30 Septr] Yesterday You had grand dinner at Princesse Wilhelmine's was presented to Prince Eugene General Saxon an old figure of the last siecle also to the Duke of Courland — a charming Prince. In great Hall. Leopold Prince of Anhalt's Battles marked on the[1] windows. He having commanded 1000 Prussians in the allied army in the war of the Succession. He has his Company of brave Grenadiers painted from the life all in the old great coat of Prussia a curious Spectacle. Also supt cold & danced much — This day Wittemberg [—] solemn Luther. Think on Bellowmillne.[2]

Write Johnston each court & city.[3]

[J.] We assembled in the Palace of the late Prince Maurice which now belongs to the Princesse Wilhelmine.[4] She gave there this day a splendid Entertainment to Prince Charles of Saxony Duke of Courland of which last dignity the Russian Tyrant has deprived him.[5] I was presented to him, & found him a charming Prince, perfectly gay & affable. I admired much a Saxon General who was with him, a Piedmontais, a genteel man about forty, with the most perfect ease of manners that I ever saw, quite master of himself. He had that *Esprit* which is excellent in conversation, talked of l'homme machine, & un Corps bien organisé.[6] He had a most agreable laugh at command. I who am a good Player Myself, could perceive it was made; but it was so nicely managed, that one in a hundred could not see the finesse. I was presented to Prince Eugene another Uncle of the reigning Prince. His name made me think of Sir Roger de Coverley. He was a Saxon General, and a most curious figure, quite a countenance of the last age, venerable and yet queer. Had he been hung up on the side of the room, you would have sworn it was a Portrait by a master long since dead.[7] We had a magnificent dinner. The noblesse of Dessau was assembled. We were in all

Forty seven. Music played in the next room, & by what strange chance[8] I cannot tell, they played among other tunes the Scots Country Dance 'The Campbells is coming oho! oho!'[9] This caused in my mind a most curious mixture of German & Caledonian ideas. I was very healthy and very happy. I had just the same sensations as when a Boy at Culross and Valleyfield.[10] I find it is no impossible matter to be just what one has formerly been. It is no more than having the mind filled with the same ideas. After dinner we had coffee, & chatted an hour or so. Coffee & tea I never drink since I heard the marquis Cavalcabo display their sad effects.[11] In the evening we had a splendid Ball. The Duke of Courland danced the best of any man I ever saw. I danced with all the three Princesses.[12] We had a cold Collation with Wine carried about. In short it was a compleat thing. In the great Hall where we dined & danced was a most singular piece of Antiquity. Leopold Prince of Anhalt Dessau Grandfather to the present Prince was a great warrior. He commanded 10000 Prussians in the allied army under the Duke of Marlbourough in the war of the Succession. The Sieges and Battles which he was at, are marked upon the Windows: not on the glass I hope. No. On the good hard boards. When he came home from the war, he assembled his brave Grenadiers, and has a compleat Company of them painted from the life, with their names under each picture. They are drawn with long blue cloaks, which was formerly the Prussian Uniform, & with their arms and accoutrements.[13] I was pleased with this idea. It has a most singular effect.

---

[1] MS. 'the' written over 'each' inked out by JB.

[2] Bello Mill, jointure land in the barony of Auchinleck, was associated with the Covenanters, a group of determined Presbyterians who had resisted various efforts to impose the Episcopal Church on Scotland. Their leader, Richard Cameron (d. 1680), had been killed near the mill in a skirmish with Stuart forces (Ayr and Wigton, i. pt. 1, 183; Dane Love, History of Auchinleck, 1991, pp. 46, 48; Corr. 8, pp. 98 and n. 1, 227). JB's thoughts of these fierce Protestants may have been triggered by his imminent visit to Luther's town.

[3] 'Write ... city' written along left margin.

[4] Wilhelmine's palace, until recently the residence of her brother Moritz (1712–60), was a two-storey building with a Mansard roof and flanking pavillions. Situated in the Kavalierstrasse, it had been built in 1739 (Harksen, i. 89).

[5] Charles Christian Josef (1733–96), Prince of Saxony and Duke of Courland, had been granted his small duchy on the Baltic by his father, Friedrich August II, Elector of Saxony, who was also King of Poland. Prince Charles had been ousted by Catherine the Great in 1763 after only five years in power,

and now resided in Dresden (Alexander V. Berkis, The History of the Duchy of Courland, 1969, pp. 239–41; Hochfürstl. Sachsen-Gothaischer Hof-Calender). He was a victim of centuries-old conflicting pressures on Courland that were exerted by Poland, to which it had been ceded by the Teutonic Knights in the mid-sixteenth century (see Journ. 27 June n. 1), and by Russia, which had dominated it for the last two centuries. In the recent past it had been ruled by Ernst Johann Biron (1690–1772), the favourite of the Czarina Anna (1693–1740), until a shift of power after her death led to his exile and displacement by Charles. But the latter had been unable to withstand the pro-Biron party and had been forced to leave when Biron returned. Eventually, Biron would be replaced by his son, and both Birons would lose their power to the local nobility. Courland would be officially absorbed into Russia in 1795 (Reinhard Wittram, Baltische Geschichte, 1954, pp. 107–24).

[6] The General from Piedmont has not been further identified. His catch phrases came from two works that popularized the mechanistic view of the universe: Julien Offrey de La Mettrie's L'Homme machine (1747) and Maupertuis' Essai sur la formation des corps organisés (1751, 1754).

[7] Friedrich Heinrich Eugenius of Anhalt-Dessau (1705–81) had a palace of his own on the Kavalierstrasse near his sister Wilhelmina's (Harksen, i. 89). He had entered Saxon service in 1746 as lieutenant-general of infantry, had been named governor of Wittenberg in 1749 and fieldmarshal of cavalry in 1754. Previously he had had a long career on the opposing side. From the age of twelve he had served in the Prussian army like the rest of his family, commanding various cavalry regiments from 1732. He had also participated in Frederick II's first Silesian War in 1740 with the rank of major-general (Siebigk, p. 259). But he had left Prussian service under a cloud in 1742 after losing many of his men in battle (*Militairisches Pantheon*, pp. 51–52). In search of a suitable berth, he had offered his services to the Austrians without success but, according to one story, had been accepted by the Saxons through a ruse of his father's, who had announced his appointment before any decision had been made (Vehse, xxxiii. 340). In Dessau, Eugene appears to have been well respected. Addison's Sir Roger de Coverley was also an amiable eccentric with old-fashioned manners, and furthermore is shown to admire another 'Eugene', Prince Eugene of Savoy (1663–1736), hero of the War of the Spanish Succession (*The Spectator*, No. 269; see also Nos. 2, 106, 107 etc.).

[8] MS. 'chance', an interlineation inserted with a caret

[9] An old melody of unknown origin, predating the well-known verses which refer to the Jacobite uprising of 1715 (Helen Hopekirk, *Seventy Scottish Songs*, 1905, pp. 144–45).

[10] On visits to the area in Fifeshire, on the north shore of the Firth of Forth, where JB's mother, Euphemia Boswell, had grown up. Her mother having died when Euphemia was only two, she had lived at Culross with her father, Lt.-Col. John Erskine (1660–1737), close to her grandmother, Lady Mary (Bruce) Cochrane of Culross Abbey House, and her aunt, Lady Preston (Anne Cochrane), who had married Sir George Preston of Valleyfield House (see Charts IV and V, *Ominous Years*, pp. 377–78). JB felt great affection for the Prestons and their children, and would enjoy his later visits to the region (see Journ. 25 Sept. 1774; 16 Oct. 1778, *Laird*, p. 28 and n. 2).

[11] Cavalcabo's warning, which JB must have heard in Brunswick between 13 and 21 Aug., recalls an old tradition whereby coffee was considered 'enfeebling', causing impotence in men (*The Women's Petition* *against Coffee*, 1674, t.-p. and pp. 3, 6; John Chamberlayne, *The Natural History of Coffee, Thee, Chocolate, Tobacco*, 1682, pp. 4–5). Tea was less suspect but also occasionally linked with illnesses, notably diabetes and the colic (J. Ovington, *An Essay upon the Nature and Qualities of Tea*, 1699, p. 36). JB would not drink tea or coffee for the rest of his stay in German and Swiss territory (see Journ. 30 Dec.). Once back in Britain, he drank both beverages again, and late in life referred to coffee as 'a favourite liquor of mine' (Journ. 3 Sept. 1792, *Great Biographer*, p. 171).

[12] They were 'of gigantic size'. On a visit to Berlin a few weeks earlier, they had danced tirelessly and 'like hussars' (Lehndorff, Oct. 1764, *Dreissig Jahre: Nachträge*, i. 438).

[13] The ball presumably took place in the *Rittersaal* (knights' hall) situated in the south wing of the palace (Harksen, i. 69, 72). Leopold I, called the *Alte Dessauer* ('Old Dessauer') to distinguish him from his five sons who were also in Prussian service, had been the most powerful and militaristic member of the family. He had served brilliantly under three successive Prussian rulers beginning in 1688 with Friedrich I, the father of Friedrich Wilhelm I (K. A. Varnhagen von Ense, 'Fürst Leopold von Anhalt-Dessau', *Preussische Biographische Denkmale*, 1824–30, ii. 301). In the War of the Spanish Succession, during which he had gained the respect of John Churchill, Duke of Marlborough, and the friendship of Prince Eugene of Savoy (Siebigk, p. 235), Leopold had led Prussian troops in the Low Countries and in Italy, and had won the command of the entire Prussian contingent in 1710. He had been named fieldmarshal of Prussia in 1712 and had subsequently become one of three fieldmarshals of the Holy Roman Empire. Still partly loyal to the imperial forces and Austria, he had opposed Frederick II's first war in Silesia, begun in 1740, but had eventually won the decisive battle of Kesselsdorf on 15 Dec. 1745 that had assured Frederick's victory and had ended the second Silesian War (*Militairisches Pantheon*, pp. 20–29). Altogether he had participated in twenty-three battles and twenty-seven sieges (Benno von Knobelsdorff-Brenkenhoff, *Anhalt-Dessau 1737–1762*, p. 13). A stern disciplinarian, he had been merciless in committing his troops to the fray. But he had also been deeply attached to them, especially the grenadiers, some of whom had served under him in the War of Spanish Succession and others who had been recruited in 1719 (*Militairisches Pantheon*, p. 21; Varnhagen von Ense, ii. 301–02). Neither

the wooden panels recording his military engagements nor the portrait gallery of his grenadiers would survive. Other such galleries are known to have been painted, usually by itinerant painters, who would add faces to previously prepared figures (Heidemarie Anderlik, 'Soldatenalltag und Offizierskarrieren', *Preussen: Versuch einer Bilanz*, exhibition catalogue, 1981, i. 182).

## Sunday 30 September

[MEM. dated Monday 1 October.] Yesterday after fatigue of Ball you set out at 7 having risen before 6 & rode brisk to Wittemberg. Old Town sadly ruined by war. Saw old Castle & Church where Luther preached — Was in true solemn humour — kneeled & lay at length on the tomb of Melancthon & wrote to Mr. Samuel Johnson. Saxon Drum myn liever Trummel [—] Saw town university poor — back clever [—] drest — court took leave. This day — give servants &c see Lestock — also leave grands remerciements chez Les Prince<s> et Princesse — Go on.

Be temperate or you'll take fever, temperate like as father.[1]

[J.] After the gay fatigues of the Ball I got up at Six, took Post Horses, and rode four German miles to Wittemberg in Saxony. I found it an old Town sadly ruined by the late war.[2] I saw the Convent where Luther lived,[3] and I went to the old Church in which he first preached the Reformation. It has been miserably shattered by the Bombardments. But the Tomb of Luther is still entire as is that of Melancthon just opposite to it. They are nothing more than two large plates of metal fixed on the floor. They have Inscriptions in raised Letters.

Luther's
Martini Lutheri S. Theologiae D. Corpus H. L. S. E. qui An.

Christi MDXLVI XII.  Cal. Martii Eyslebii in Patria
S. M. O. C. V. An. LXIII. M. II. D. X.
Melancthon's
Philippi Melancthonis S. V. Corpus H. L. S. E. Qui An
Christi MDLX XIII. Cal. Maii in hac Urbe M. O. C. V.
Ann LXIII. M. II. D. II.[4]

I was in a true solemn humour, and a most curious and agreable idea presented itself, which was to write to Mr. Samuel Johnson from the tomb of Melancthon. The Woman who showed the Church was a good obliging Body, and very readily furnished me with Pen and Ink. That my paper might literally rest upon the monument or rather the simple Epitaph of this great & good Man, I laid myself down & wrote in that posture. The good Woman & some more simple Beings gather'd 'round & beheld me with wonder. I dare say they supposed me a little mad. Tombs have been allways the favourite resort of gloomy distracted mortals. I said nothing of hot-headed Luther. I only mentioned the mild Melancthon, and that at his tomb I vowed to Mr. Johnson an eternal attachment. This Letter must surely give him satisfaction. I shall not send it till I see if he gives me a favourable Answer to my two last letters. It is realy an excellent thought.

The letter shall be a valuable Remain.[5] I got a Saxon Drummer to walk with me about the Town, & called him myn lieber Trummel, & took him to my Inn & made him sit down with me, and he and I eat bread & cheese, & drank Brandewyn.[6] What a transition! I am mighty whimsical & even low sometimes. I have had enough of this. Let it be no more. I returned at night to Dessau, as if it had been my home, drest, supt at court, & took leave of the Princes & Princesses. The eldest Princess is a comely black[7] amiable young Lady. The other two are very well. The Prince Jean George is very handsom and very affable. The Prince Albert is a good-looking, blunt, bold little fellow. The Table here was plain but good. The Removes[8] were made by degrees, without obliging us to rise. Half a bottle of Rhenish was placed between two People. You might call for as much more as you pleased. We were served by Footmen which is much better than Pages. A Hussar & a Pole drew my notice.[9] I shall not forget the luscious Vennison with Currant Jelly;[10] The Castle is guarded by a few old Soldiers. This Court is much like the residence of an old British Baron.

[1] MS. 'Be temperate … father' written along the left margin and deleted. The text is taken from a transcription made by earlier Yale editors.

[2] Wittenberg, on the river Elbe, was slightly more than sixteen miles (c. 25.8 km) from Dessau, a German mile being 'better than four English miles' (Nugent, i. 'Of Miles'). The town, dating from the twelfth century, had achieved prestige as the ducal and electoral residence of the ruling house of Wettin (an elector being a prince entitled to elect the emperor of the Holy Roman Empire; see Mem. dated 31 Oct. n. 1). It had also become renowned as the so-called 'cradle of the Reformation' when its university, founded in 1502 by Friedrich the Wise (1463–1525), had attracted prominent teachers such as Martin Luther (1483–1546) and Philipp Melanchthon (1497–1560). The town's importance had waned after 1547, when it was absorbed by Saxony following the defeat in battle of its ruler, Johann Friedrich (1503–54), by the Holy Roman Emperor Charles V (1500–58); see Isenburg, i. Tafel 46; Helmar Junghans, *700 Jahre Wittenberg: Stadt Universität Reformation*, 1995, pp. 37–46. During the Seven Years' War Wittenberg had been occupied by the Prussians, and in Oct. 1760 many of its buildings had been set on fire by Austrian and Württembergian troops trying to dislodge them (Richard Erfurth, *Die Lutherstadt Wittenberg und Ihre Umgebung*, 1927, p. 55). Among the damaged landmarks was the castle (built from 1490 to 1509 for Friedrich the Wise), which had imposing Gothic outer fortifications and sumptuous early

Renaissance rooms (Karlheinz Blaschke, *Wittenberg: die Lutherstadt*, 1981, pp. 6–15).

[3] In Luther's time a house of the Augustinian friars. He had lived there as monk from 1505, as Professor of Theology at the University of Wittenberg from 1512, and then as married man in a small adjoining house with his wife, the former nun Katharina von Bora (1499–1552), and their six children (Erfurth, pp. 36–37; Roger Rössing, *Wittenberg So Wie Es War*, 1993, pp. 20–23). He had been able to remain after the monastery was dissolved in 1522, but his heirs had sold the property to the university in 1564, and by JB's time the house had been made into a wing of the Augusteum, a university building expanded by and named after the Elector August (1526–86) of Saxony; see Fritz Bellmann, Marie-Luise Harksen, and Roland Werner, *Die Denkmale der Lutherstadt Wittenberg*, 1979, pp. 43–44, 62; Oskar Thulin, *Die Lutherstadt Wittenberg und Torgau*, 1932, pp. 29–30).

[4] Luther had often preached in this *Schloss-kirche* (palace church), which had become legendary because on its wooden doors, on 31 Oct. 1517, Luther had supposedly nailed the 95 Theses protesting against the abuses of the Catholic Church. The building had been gutted by the bombardment of 1760 (Rössing, p. 49). The text on the plaque for Luther, in expanded form, reads: MARTINI LUTHERI S. THEOLOGIAE D.[octoris] CORPUS H[oc] L[oco] S[itum] E[st] QUI AN[no] CHRISTI MDXLVI XX CAL[endis] MARTII EISLEBII IN PATRIA S[ua] M[oretem] O[bivit] C[um] V[ixisset] ANN[os] LX

133

III M[enses] II D[ies] X 9 ('Here lies the body of Martin Luther, Doctor of Sacred Theology, who died in Eisleben, his birthplace, 18 Feb. 1546, at the age of sixty-three years, two months, and ten days'). Luther had returned to Eisleben to settle a dispute between two young noblemen in his home district and had died there at the age of sixty-two years and three months. The discrepancy between his actual age at death and the record on the plaque is due to the mistake made during the casting of the bronze plate, on which the digits of the date had been inadvertently transposed (Erfurth, p. 98 n.). JB copied correctly what he saw (Bellmann, Harksen, and Werner, pp. 46–47).

The text on the plaque for Melanchthon reads: 'Here lies the body of Philipp Melancthon, a man of holy life, who died in this city on 19 Apr. 1560, at the age of sixty-three years, two months, and two days' (Erfurth, p. 98).

⁵ Melanchthon (a Grecianized version of his name *Schwartzerdt*, i.e., 'black earth') had been a close friend of Luther's after settling in Wittenberg in 1518 as Professor of Greek. He had become the spokesman for Luther's new ideas, which he explained in his *Loci communes theologicarum* (1521) and summed up in the Augsburg Confession, the official statement of Lutheran beliefs adopted in 1530. His textbooks, commentaries, and translations as well as his reorganization of schools and universities had earned him the sobriquet 'the preceptor of Germany' (Heinz Scheible, *Melanchthon: eine Biographie*, 1997,

pp. 28–51, 144–45; for a concise appraisal in English, see Scheible, 'Melanchthon, Philipp', *The Oxford Encyclopedia of the Reformation*, 1996, iii. 41–45).

In his letter to SJ, JB expressed admiration for Melanchthon's work in reforming the church and also for his mildness and generosity of spirit, calling him 'that great and good man' in a favourite phrase which JB had used recently for SJ in the letter to Kames inserted in Journ. 27 Sept. For subsequent uses of the phrase for SJ, see the note added to the 2nd ed. of the *Life*, 30 Sept. 1769, Yale *Life* MS. Ed., ii. 38; and the 'Advertisement to the Third Edition' of the *Tour to the Hebrides, Life* v. 4). JB would wait until 9 June 1777 to send his letter to SJ, and would eventually include it under that date in the *Life* (iii. 118).

⁶ 'Trummel': JB's version of the German Trommel, 'drum' or Trommler, 'drummer'; brandewyn: brandy-wine, brandy. The Expense Account shows that JB spent 14 Groschen for 'Diner et Brandewyn pour moi et tambour' (29 Sept.). The drummer has not been identified.

⁷ That is, dark haired.

⁸ 'The act of taking away a dish or dishes at a meal in order to put others in their place' (OED, s.v. 'remove' *sb.*, 2.c).

⁹ Neither the hussar nor the Pole has been identified.

¹⁰ For JB's liking for currant jelly, see also his poem with this title in Alexander Donaldson's *A Collection of Original Poems by Scotch Gentlemen*, vol. 2 (1762), p. 88.

## Monday 1 October

[MEM. dated Tuesday 2 Octr.] Yesterday you wrote in Guericke's book Diogene¹ who showed you tableaux de Lizesky & said croyez moi vous etes aime ici! Bien ecrit — you found was the hand — Leave of Princess in Boots. Le Baron Boswell. Set out at 1. Had past a whole week at Dessau & in all not two hours of spleen. Tis manners keep it off. Wet windy day felt preeher, German & Latin — very cold — very tired. Began again lines.

[J.] Monsieur de Guericke who educated the reigning Prince sent me his Album Amicorum which was very splendid.² I wrote thus in it.

'Jamais un Etranger a plus gouté ses voyages que moi. Je voyage en Philosophe. Je n'ai pas la dureté de Diogêne mais Je va comme lui á chercher des hommes, des Gens dignes de soutenir la dignité de la nature humaine, parmi lesquels J'ose nominer M. de Guericke.³ Souvenez vous monsieur d'un bon Ecossois qui a l'honneur d'etre avec une consideration distingué.⁴ Votre tres humble et tres obeissant Serviteur

Boswell d'Auchinleck'.

For Prince Diederic & for the Princess Wilhelmine I wrote the following card. 'Le Baron Boswell pour prende Congé et pour faire ses remerciments tres humbles pour toutes les politesses dont il a eté honoré par son Altesse Serenissimé'. I think proper to take the title of Baron in Germany, as I have just the same right to it as the good Gentry whom I see arround me.[5] Is not this Card in the true stile? I am made for travelling. The Prince was at the hunting. The Princess received me, & I appeared in my travelling dress, quite at my ease. I then went to Guericke's who thanked me for what I had written, but told me 'Je vous montrerai ce qui a ecrit le Prince de Courland, et quoique Vous ecrivez bien, Monsieur, Je crois que vous avouerez que son Altesse ecrit encore mieux'. My curiosity was excited, and I prepared myself to admire a specimen of this Prince's fine Genius. But, what did I find? Nothing but a common-place french sentiment taken from one of their Poets, with a common-place assurance of sincerity &c. Regardez (said my good Guericke) n'est il pas beau? In short I found that it was the fine hand which he admired, and that a Writing-Master would make the best figure in his Album amicorum. He showed me some pretty good pictures which he has got, & some excellent Portraits by the Painter to the Court, Lizisky. His Father was a Painter at Berlin. The Son does remarkably well both large Portraits & miniatures.[6] Gueriche is a sensible, dry cordial man. He said to me, Restez encore quelque tems chez nous. Croyez moi, Vous êtes aimé ici. Let me give this testimony to Dessau. I have past here a full week, during which time I have not had half a day of Hypochondria in all. Let this then be ever a sure consolation for me: for after all my dire gloom at Utrecht I have had much clear joy. The Princes of Dessau have been remarkable for a numerous progeny of natural children. Each of them has a pension of 600 Dollars (£100) and they are educated as Gentlemen.[7] The amiable de Bernhorst is one. He is uncle to the reigning Prince.[8] I shall corespond with him & Neitschutz.[9] At every court where I go I shall establish a corespondence. I began this day a most curious scheme. I would not wish to make my freind Johnston pay postage for frequent letters while I am abroad, yet, to write to him often is agreable, and keeps alive freindship. I shall therefore at every court & city where I reside any time, write him a letter. These Letters I shall direct & seal so that I shall have as little to do with them, as if they were realy sent off. I shall number them, & put them up in a bundle, & when I return to Britain, he & I shall open them, & read them at leisure; and a luxurious entertainment it will be.[10] I had this morning the Coachman groom & footman of the court with me. I gave each of 'em drink-money, & they were humble & thankfull.[11] I have been here like a very Prince. While I drove by in my coach, the People bowed to the earth. My Plan was originally to be at Geneva the end of November, & get to Rome at Christmas, so as to see the splendid Christmas-Eve in St. Peter's Church. But I find that if I follow this plan I shall not be able to see the half of the German Courts that I intended and be hurried to get thro' Switzerland so that I should be in constant Anxiety, and lose seeing many fine courts, and passing many hours with Voltaire and Rousseau, which would be losing many real advantages, of which I may think with pleasure all my life, merely for the solemn satisfaction of a single evening; which too would in all probability not come up to my Expectations. I therefore at once gave up this scheme; and my mind was at ease. I shall go on leisurely, & enjoy fully my tour. At two I mounted the Post-Waggon for Hall.[12] It was sad weather. I had for companion a Felt Preher[13] (Chaplain) to a Prussian Regiment. He & I conversed in Latin and German. He was a clumsy dog, but understood something of Language. This day I resumed my whim of writing ten lines a day.[14]

[TEN LINES A DAY]
October comes, & I resume my Pen
Again to write each day my verses ten
Henceforth 'how many?' let no mortal ask;
He that can count his fingers counts my task.
Why in this month so dreary chuse to sing
When rainy weather[15] damps the muse's wing
When thro' the fading woods rough tempests blow,
Nor leave one garland for a Poet's brow?
Know vain Enquirer that my Genius strong
Amidst all weathers boldly bears along.

[1] MS. 'Diogene' inserted as interlineation.

[2] For such albums, see Journ. 10 Sept. and n. 1.

[3] Friedrich Wilhelm von Guericke (1709–77) had served as the Prince's *Oberhofmeister* (major domo) from 1753 (*Deutsches Geschlechterbuch*, 39. 377) and had accompanied him to the Prussian camp during the war (LSAO, A 9b VII Nr. 2, Bl. 49, 55–57). The Greek Cynic philosopher Diogenes (c. 412–323 B.C.) had dramatized his search for a genuinely honourable person by holding a lamp in daylight.

[4] MS. An inadvertent full stop.

[5] The title *baron*, established in feudal times, was granted by a sovereign and was usually related to land ownership. At the German courts it could be inherited and used by all of a baron's sons. In Scotland the title, also inheritable, was restricted to eldest sons. The Boswells of Auchinleck held their lands under three royal charters, the most important being that of James IV to Thomas Boswell, dated 20 Nov. 1504. This was confirmed by the charter of 16 June 1505, and followed by the charter by James V, dated 12 Feb. 1531–32, granted 'to Jonet Hamiltoun ... and to David Boiswell of Auchinlek, her husband, and the lawful heirs begotten between them heritably, of the lands and barony of Auchinlek' (*Registrum Magni Sigilli Regum Scotorum*, 1306–1668, ii [1882], nos. 2805, 2859; iii [1883], no. 1133). In short, Auchinleck was a barony, and accordingly, JB was entitled to style himself baron upon the death of his father, or rather, would have been, if that rank had not been eliminated with the Anglo-Scottish union of 1707 (information from Prof. Murray Pittock; see Debrett, *Peerage and Baronetage*, 2003, p. 12). In addition, the title was used without right of inheritance by holders of certain important offices, notably by the head of the Court of Exchequer. In this regard, it had been on JB's mind ever since he arrived in German territory (see Mem. dated 25 June).

[6] The prince's collection included 43 paintings by Christoph Friedrich Reinhold Lisiewski (see Journ. 27 Sept. n. 14). His father, Georg Lisiewski (1674–1750 or 51), had specialized in Prussia in portraits of the nobility, generals, and the tall soldiers of Friedrich Wilhelm, and had also painted two of the princes in Dessau. He had been trained in portraiture by Eosander von Gothe, whose servant he had become on first arriving in Berlin from his native Poland (Thieme-Becker, xxiii. 283–84; *Dict. of Art*, s.v. 'Therbusch, Anna Dorothea', xxx. 713). Whether he had also painted the Old Dessauer's grenadiers (see Journ. 29 Sept.) has not been ascertained.

[7] Leopold I, Wilhelm Gustav, and Prince

Franz all fathered children out of wedlock. It was the first of these, the Old Dessauer, who had granted a stipend of 600 Thaler to each of his illegitimate offspring (see Journ. 28 Sept.).

[8] Georg Heinrich von Berenhorst, the Old Dessauer's officially acknowledged son by the middle-class Sophia Eleonora Söldner, was one of the more intellectual members of the family. Like his brothers, he had been trained for a military career in Prussia and had taken part in major battles, especially while serving as adjutant to Prince Heinrich of Prussia in 1757 and to Frederick II in 1759. But he had felt slighted by the latter and had resigned in 1762 with bitter feelings about military life (Rudolf Bahn, *Georg Heinrich von Berenhorst*, 1911, pp. 1–12). Such feelings would still colour his treatise about warfare, *Betrachtungen über die Kriegskunst*, published anonymously in 1797. He had returned to Dessau after the war and would soon accompany Prince Franz on his renewed travels to Italy, France, and England. Later he would supervise the education of the new Hereditary Prince, Friedrich (1769–1814), and write Rousseauistic confessions (*Selbstbekenntnisse*; see Bahn, pp. 12–89; Eberhard Kassel, 'Georg Heinrich von Berenhorst', *Sachsen und Anhalt*, Jahrbuch der Historischen Kommission für die Provinz Sachsen und für Anhalt, 1933, ix. 161–98).

[9] JB would write to Neitschütz a few weeks later, on 16 Nov. (Reg. Let.), but no correspondence would survive. In addition, JB made a separate record of an anecdote he heard from Neitschütz about Frederick II's refusal to reduce the wartime subsidies imposed on Dessau: 'Mon Ami Il faut soutenir des Armees. Je ne suis pas en etat de le faire. Vous savez que Je n'ai rien: Il faut que Je vole.' *Mr. de Neitschutz' ('Boswelliana', Hyde Collection, p. 59; *Boswelliana*, p. 227). For the large subsidies Frederick II exacted from Dessau and his harsh treatment of the inexperienced young Prince Franz, see Benno von Knobelsdorff-Brenkenhoff, *Anhalt-Dessau 1737–1762*, 1987, pp. 68–69).

[10] In the eighteenth century, the recipient, not the sender, paid for the transmission of letters.

On this day JB also wrote directly to JJ to describe his money-saving scheme, first mentioned in his memorandum of 28 Sept. He began to number his letters, preserving the whole series that ended with letter 51 written on 9 Jan. 1766 in Auxerre, France (*Catalogue*, i. 270). The series is published in *Corr. 1* (see especially p. 135 n. 1, and Introduction, pp. xxiii–xxiv).

[11] JB generously gave the coachman three écus, the groom and the footman two écus each (Exp. Acct. 1 Oct., App. 3).

[12] Halle, about 27 miles (43.5 km) from Dessau.

[13] MS. 'Felt Preher' in Gothic letters; the standard German would be 'Feld Prediger'; that is, an army chaplain (not identified further).

[14] JB had previously written such verses in Holland from 25 Sept. 1763 to 28 Feb. 1764 and from 1 Mar. to 16 Apr., omitting only 29 Feb. (*Catalogue*, M 276).

[15] MS. 'the wet season' written above 'rainy weather'.

## Tuesday 2 October

[MEM. dated Wednesday 3 Octr.] Yesterday at 3 you arrived very jaded cold chamber — waked at 6 — Hyp'd — rose exercised — grew better found Kircheisen good fellow Halle old town saw Salt works very simple — orphan House large that's all. Library, tired — but wrote. This day be firm. Say Vous devez rester a Leipsig & be alone.

To a <…> whoring, get a fine woman at lpg will keep you content <…>[1]

[J.] This morning at three I arrived at Halle very jaded. I went to an Inn and was put in to a cold Room. At seven I rose having dozed a little. I was sadly hyp'd. All seemed dismal. But reason remained and assured me that in an hour or two I should be well. I took exercise in my chamber & grew more healthy. At ten I called on M. Kircheisen student here eldest son to my good Landlord at Berlin. He seemed a good, homely fellow.[2] But the male part of this family is nothing like the female. The male seem formed of a much coarser clay. The President indeed makes up for this by his rough warmth. I saw Halle with some curiosity, because Lord Elliock studied here.[3] It is a very old town. I saw the salt-works which are very simple. There is here a Salt-spring from which they draw water from a prodigious depth. They boil it till the saline particles are left at the Bottom. They then take out the salt & form it into large loaves, which they dry & harden in a room well heated by stoves. It is then fit for being transported. This manufactory yeilds the King of Prussia a great deal of money.[4] I should have thought boiling and baking the salt very unwholesom. But it is not so. An old fellow told me here that he had wrought at it I think fifty years. I also saw the Orphan-house, which is immensely large.[5] As also the College Library which is numerous.[6] I saw Halle Students here. I was glad I was not one of them.[7] At night I was alone.[8] Pen & Ink ever amuse me.

[TEN LINES A DAY.]
If Pope good Coffee lov'd as Horace wine,
And sung it's praise in a heroic line,
Tell me, great Critics! can you reasons bring
That hinder me of Chocolade to sing.
Soft as I muse, it's flavour feeds my nose,
And to my brain most comfortably goes.
Husbands! were there no[9] Chocolade for you
What could your loving sighing Ladies do?
And was it not thy Chocolade o White
That lur'd to thee our nobles every night?[10]

[1] 'To a ... content' written along the left margin and heavily scored out, some words illegible. 'lpg' stands for Leipzig, JB's next stop.
[2] Carl Gustav Wilhelm Kircheisen had been studying law at the University of Halle and would soon be admitted to the *Kammergericht* (highest court) in Berlin as *Referendar* (law clerk); see 31 Oct. 1764, GStA PK, I.HA Geheimer Rat, Rep. 9 Allgemeine Verwaltung, Nr. J 7 Fasz. 62, Bl. 47, 48. He would settle in Berlin and accept a position as secretary to the Prince of Prussia (*Adres-Calender*, 1769, p. 82). Two years later he would serve as *Kriegsrat* (counsellor for military affairs) and privy executive secretary to one of the ministers of state. He would continue to live in his father's house next to the St.-Petri-Kirche even after Carl David Kircheisen's death in 1770 (*Adres-Calender*, 1771, p. 111). Later he would rise in the Prussian legal bureaucracy and reorganize the Prussian justiciary. Ennobled in 1798, he would be honoured, on his fiftieth anniversary as jurist in 1821, by a new charitable foundation bearing his name (Zedlitz-Neukirch, iii. 110).
[3] James Veitch of Elliock (1712–93), a colleague of JB's father, had been named Lord of Session with the title Lord Elliock in 1761 and was one of the Scottish *literati*. He had been in Halle as well as in Leiden, where he had studied law in 1733 (*Album Studiosorum*, p. 944; Namier and Brooke, iii. 579). He had stayed in Prussia at the suggestion of Frederick II while the latter was still crown prince and had subsequently corresponded with him (*Scots Mag.* July 1793, p. 361). Veitch had been admitted advocate in 1738, had briefly practised law, and had served as M.P. for Dumfries from 1755 to 1761 before being elevated to the Court of Session (George Brunton and David Haig, *An Historical Account of the Senators of the College of Justice*, 1832, p. 525; Namier and Brooke, iii. 579).
[4] Halle on the Saale was an important centre for salt. Members of a special guild, the *Halloren*, drained the salt from several springs, using the time-honoured procedures observed by JB that would still be demonstrated in the late twentieth and early

twenty-first centuries at the local Halloren-und-Salinen Museum (Johannes Mager, *Kulturgeschichte der Halleschen Salinen*, n.d. [post 1984], pp. 3–41, 57–61). Frederick II benefited because Halle had become a Prussian dependency in 1680.

[5] The orphanage, in tall buildings that covered several streets, was 'the most famous thing in Halle' (Nugent, ii. 249). It had been organized from 1695 to 1700 by August Hermann Francke (1663–1727), a leading Pietist (i.e., a member of a devout Lutheran sect) who had offered both a spiritual and a practical education to the children in his charge. These children helped to make the orphanage and related foundations self-sufficient by producing books and medicines, working the land, baking, brewing, and spinning (Heinz Welsch, 'Die Franckeschen Stiftungen als wirtschaftliches Grossunternehmen', *August Hermann Francke: das humanistische Erbe*, 1965, pp. 28–44). More than 1700 children were cared for between 1758 and 1767 (*Beschreibung des Halleschen Waisenhauses*, 1799, p. 171). At this time the institution was directed by the founder's son, Gotthilf August Francke (1696–1769), and its missionary efforts extended as far as Pennsylvania and India (NDB, v. 325).

[6] The library presumably belonged to the University of Halle, a relatively new institution inaugurated in 1694 that had strong faculties in law, theology, and medicine (Hans Hübner, *Geschichte der Martin-Luther-Universität Halle-Wittenberg*, 1977, pp. 37–48).

[7] Perhaps a reflection of JB's memories of his own university days in Glasgow.

[8] On this day JB bought La Rochefoucauld's *Réflexions ou sentences et maximes*

*morales* (first pub. anon. 1665), for which he paid 16 Groschen (Exp. Acct. 2 Oct., App. 3). JB would soon experiment with writing pithy sayings under the heading 'Maximes á la maniêrre de la Rochefoucault' (M 96, see App. 1; Journ. 15 Oct. n. 2). He would bring the book back to Scotland and note it in his 'Catalogue of Books', 1770.

[9] MS. 'Husbands … no' written over deleted 'Wert not propitious'

[10] Chocolate had been introduced in England in the mid-seventeenth century at about the same time as coffee, which had been celebrated mock-heroically in Pope's *Rape of the Lock* (1714), Canto 3, ll. 105–17. When used for the drink, cacao beans, imported from South America, were ground, mixed with sugar and possibly vanilla and other spices, made frothy by beaten eggs, and diluted by boiling water or wine. Because sugar was expensive and the mixture of ingredients was complicated, hot chocolate was still more a luxury than the coffee and tea that were coming into fashion as non-intoxicating beverages (Peter B. Brown, *In Praise of Hot Liquors*, 1995, pp. 27–30, 34–36).

White's Chocolate House in St. James's Street catered to the highest reaches of society. Founded by Francis White in 1693, it had developed into two clubs, the Old and the Young, which attracted such notable figures as Sir Robert Walpole, the elder Pitt, and the Marquess of Bute. These and other 'nobles' may have been attracted by more than the chocolate since White's was also famous as a centre for gaming (W. B. Boulton, *The History of White's*, 1892, i. 9–11, 67–69, 79–80, 109–13).

## Wednesday 3 October

[MEM. dated Thursday 4 Octr.] [Y]esterday you was baddish & had dreary journey in bad roads to Leipsick found it great city — houses high like Edinburgh same ideas. Found lodging in private.[1] This day Journ till 9 — Then Neidutsch & see at any rate foire & Quaalen — At 11 home & say to Kircheisen Youll not go with him as Lets come & shift it easily to meet at Dresden. Dine at 12 Wappe<ls>[2] [—] fine. Be clean & frisé. Call Gellert & Rabner.[3] Night again Journal.

[J.] I set out at nine, and had a disagreable Journey thro' bad roads to Leipsic, where I arrived at night.[4] I found high houses as in Edinburgh, & had some of my old ideas, when I saw familys living on other's tops.[5] Wappler's the Inn to which I was directed, had no room for me; so I was at a loss. They procured me however quarters in a private house Gabriel's Barber in Peter Straas.[6] As it was fair time the town was full.[7] I was obliged to pay a ducat[8] a day, for lodging for myself & Servant. The People were very civil & of the better sort. I had a damp Alcove to sleep in. But a very handsom Chamber. So I caused Jacob spread my bed on the floor of the chamber, & thus I lay with my cloaths on, a good coverlet above me, & my head reposed on a pillow laid on one of my trunks. This operation however was performed after the good folks of the house were abed; for, I would not shock them by letting them know that I could not bear their dormitory. This is in some degree Benevolence.

[TEN LINES A DAY.]
Of all mankind beneath[9] the northern sky
Without dispute the happiest am I.
Of an old family in the Shire of Ayr
My fate has made me the apparrent heir
Health youth and Gold sufficient I possess
Where one has more five hundred sure have less
Yet, if I all my qualitys must name
Dire Hypochondria mixes with my frame.
Ah my poor mortals are you formed so
That none amongst you is exempt from woe.

[1] MS. 'private', an interlineation above 'in'
[2] MS. Damaged by a hole along the margin; 'Wappels' is visible in a photocopy made by earlier Yale editors. JB means 'Wapplers' (see Journ. for this date).
[3] For Gellert, see Journ. 5 Oct. and n. 9. Gottlieb Wilhelm Rabener (1714–71), a friend of Gellert's, had made a name for himself by writing prose satires (*Sammlung satirischer Schriften*, 1751–55). JB does not refer to him again and seems not to have met him.
[4] Leipzig was about 20 miles (c. 32.2 km) from Halle (Nugent, ii. 215).
[5] Seven or eight storeys were common in the bourgeois houses of Leipzig, about one third of which had been built since the beginning of the century (Brigitte Riese, 'Der bürgerliche Barock', *Leipzig*, ed. Wolfgang Hocquél, 1983, pp. 89–100). In Edinburgh,

houses built on steep inclines, including JB's birthplace at Blair's Land in Parliament Close, could have eight or nine storeys on the downhill side, four on the other (Roger Craik, *James Boswell: The Scottish Perspective*, 1994, pp. 20–21).
[6] Carl Christian Gabriel was a well-established surgeon and barber. His house was in the Petersstrasse, the same street as the inn owned by the heirs of Johann Erasinus Wappler (*Leipziger Adress-Post-und Reise Calender*, 1764, pp. 121, 156).
[7] The fair, the famous 'Leipziger Messe' held three times a year, had begun on 30 Sept. and would continue for fifteen days (Nugent, ii. 227).
[8] For ducats, see Journ. 18 Aug. n. 7.
[9] MS. 'beneath' written above 'that', blotted out by JB.

## Thursday 4 October

[MEM. dated Friday 5 Octr.] Yesterday after sleep on floor bed — saw fair & Saxo<n> troops neat & clean tho' clo<thed> only in 3 years — but froc<ks> [— ] was pleased with fair — din<'d> with Neitschutz Ogrady &c — hearty. Then waited on Gotsched big man good address mighty civil — at once was well with him — & you were among his books — He approved you<r> grammar. A dialect as muc<h as> <Sw>edish — <The>n Baile, f<ine, civi>l, Li<brary> &c. Hom<e all ev. This d>ay a<t 9, Baile. See Lib … &c. Then Gotsched; show Spe … and fix Corrsp mem. Worthy Fathr …>[1]

[J.] Lying on the floor did me much good. I sprung up chearfull. Experience shall ever be my great Guide. I find that to sleep on a very hard bed, prevents my nervous system from being totally unstrung, & so prevents me from being clouded, except when I have eat too much, and so caused obstructions. My room was hung with tapestry adorned with battles well painted. I went & saw the fair where there is a concourse of all nations, even of Turks. Such a scene gives me agreable agitation of ideas. I was pleased to see the Saxon troops all genteel fellows, very neat & clean, though their livery is white, & they are cloath'd only once in three years. They have every year a frock.[2] I then found my worthy Neitschutz who was here to sell some of the Prince's Horses & Ogrady who was here to sell some of his own. It seems he had freighted a ship from Ireland. He talked German with great facility, swore in it, & abused the Germans for not being able to know good cattle[3] when they saw them. There, now, said he, they are all fond of that ugly Animal because he goes with a spring; & that is because he is weak. A right strong nag moves firm and easy. We dined together with some more Germans[4] in a house on the Horse Market, where we were mighty well. I then went and called on the Professor Gotsched one of the most distinguished Literati in this Country. It was he who set agoing the true cultivation of the German Language of which he has given an excellent Grammar. He has also written several Pieces both in Verse and Prose. I found him a big stately comely man, with an ease of manners like a man of the world.[5] Altho' I had no recommendation, he received me with a perfect politeness. We talked of Scotland, of it's language and the difference between it & english. I mentioned to him my Plan of a Scots Dictionary, & promised to show him a Specimen of it.[6] He said the Preface to Johnson's Dictionary was one of the best Pieces he had ever read. Said he: Il connoit le sujet au fond. He advised me to wait upon Mr. Bel Professor of Poetry. I did so, & found him a lively Hungarian, with a degree of french manners.[7] He had a very good Library. I should have mentioned that Gotsched & I were quite easy together in a few minutes; and I was at once among his Books. Both he & Bel promised to be of what service they could to me, during my stay there.

[TEN LINES A DAY.]
Who would not read such Poetry as marks
A mighty Genius fed on Leipsic Larks?
Once were those Larks as gay as Birds could be,
And each fair morning hail'd with tunefull glee.
But now behold them roasted on a Spit,
To fill the Belly of a Northern Wit.
With what delight then must my lines be read,
When one sweet Songster is on others fed.
All this my worthy friends I but divine;
For, 'tis tomorrow that on Larks I dine.[8]

[1] MS. Smudged and partially illegible; the text is lost after 'a<t>' because the bottom of the page has disintegrated. By 'Baile', JB means Bel (see n. 4).

[2] 'A coat with long skirts', part of a military uniform (OED, s.v. 'frock', 5.a and b).

[3] Horses, 'in the language of the stable' (OED, s.v. 'cattle', 4.d).

[4] Not identified.

[5] Johann Christian Gottsched (1700–66) was so large in stature that he had feared being impressed into a Prussian regiment of tall soldiers and had therefore left his native Königsberg, which was in Prussian territory (Werner Rieck, *Johann Christoph Gottsched*, 1972, p. 20). He had lived in Leipzig, which belonged to Saxony, from the age of twenty-four and was now coming to the end of a distinguished academic career, having served as Professor of Poetry from 1729 and Professor of Logic and Metaphysics from 1734. Five times chosen the university's rector in the biannual elections, he was now the senior professor of the philosophical faculty (*Leipziger Adress-Post-und Reisekalender*, 1764, pp. 28, 45). He had worked tirelessly to replace French and Latin with German as a respected scholarly and literary language, particularly through the Deutsche Gesellschaft (German Society) which he had led from about 1727. His grammar, *Grundlegung einer deutschen Sprachkunst* (1748, 3rd ed. 1752, reissued as *Vollständigere und neuerläuterte deutsche Sprachkunst*, 1762), which also taught spelling and etymologies, was influential in stabilizing German usage. His poems included ambitious Pindaric odes, such as the one composed earlier in this year in honour of the ruling prince, Friedrich Christian (1722–63) of Saxony. These were outnumbered by his prose pieces, many dealing with rhetoric and poetry, the most notable being his *Versuch einer Critischen Dichtkunst* (1730, 4th ed. 1751), which recommended the classical rules provided they were used for a genuine imitation of nature. In addition, determined to raise the taste of a new middle-class public, he had encouraged local acting companies to stage serious plays in German instead of low farces. He himself had written pastoral dramas and had translated plays, including the popular *Sterbender Cato* ('Dying Cato', written in 1730, 1st ed. 1732, 10th ed. 1757) based partly on Addison's *Cato*, 1713. He had also published didactic journals similar to the *Spectator* essays, and had summed up his teachings in a series of textbooks for schools and universities (for details about Gottsched's writings, see Rieck, pp. 26–217 *passim*). When JB met him, his reputation was, however, declining, for Lessing had already mocked him for his emphasis on the classical rules (Letter 17, *Briefe, die neueste Literatur betreffend*, 1759; see Daniel Hegeman, 'Boswell's Interviews with Gottsched and Gellert', *JEGP* 46 [1947]: 260–63).

[6] See Journ. 16 Sept. and n. 3.

[7] Karl Andreas Bel (1717–82) was born in Pressburg (after 1918 known as Bratislava), capital of Hungary in his time, and may have acquired his French manners while serving as companion to two young noblemen in Paris in 1740. He had been professor at the University of Leipzig since 1743. By this time he had written at least fifteen Latin treatises on Hungarian and other historical subjects (Adelung-Jöchers, i. 1610–11; Wurzbach, i. 234–35).

[8] Larks, a specialty of Leipzig, could be caught in great number in the autumn. They were served roasted and were thought to be nourishing (Casanova, x. 222, 372 n. 21; also described in Nugent, ii. 229).

## Friday 5 October

[MEM. dated Saturday 6 October] At 10 you went with Bel & saw the Leipsic Library S. Paulini. Inscription over door — ask to take it with you.[1] Great collection old room [—] was venerable & doctus and resolved to add to the number, & have collection self at Auchinleck — Din'd Netschutz &c. At 3 waited on Gelert 20 years sick Hypochond — every night thought to die — every morn. wrote a fable. Said J'aime Pope en Poête mais son Essay sur l'homme pas pour la Philosophie. He said — Ma Poesie est passée Je n'ai plus la force d'esprit. You was gay & talked to him to chear up. He said Je suis bon homme et vous aussi. Then saw Gotsched a little. At 7 went to Bel's who was writing Pref. to Acta Erudit. of which he is the Director. His Father was Luth. Min. in Hung. & he there till 16 — Agreed <to s>end each other literary news. Fine acquisition. Supt <with him>. You ar<e a> villain <if you ever la>ugh <at Ger>mans. <This day dress — 9 Quaalen — 11 Gelert 12 Gotsched, & at night Bread cheese Rhenish. Bell.>[2]

[O]ld monk who remained in college.[3]
[W]rite Temp. & Johnston.[4]

[J.] At ten I went with Bel & saw the University Library. It is in a great old room which was formerly the Cloister *Sancti Paulini*. At the Reformation it was seised. One old monk of a venerable character would not come out. He said he had lived there all his life, and they must allow him to die in peace in his Convent. His request was granted, & he was nourished there till the day of his death. His effigy is preserved in the Library.[5] There is here a very numerous collection of Books arranged according to their Subjects. There is also a number of Portraits of learned men. Every Professor is obliged to give his Portrait to the Library. I was in a true classical humour, quite *doctus*.[6] I resolved to add to the number of Books. I resolved to have a noble Library at Auchinleck.[7] I saw here a Volume of original manuscript Letters of famous learned men in Germany. I saw Luther's Bible, in which the verse of St. James says that the three which bear record in heaven are *one*, is not to be found.[8] Bel sent my name to Gelert a Professor here who appointed me to come to him at three. I dined with Neitschutz, Ogrady &c & merry were we all. I am every day more strong, & less liable to be put out of order by little circumstances. I have seen the time when a dinner would have overturned me quite. Now I defy it. At three I went to Gellert. They call him the Gay of Germany. He has written Fables & little dramatic pieces. I found him to be a poor sickly creature. He said he had been twenty years Hypochondriack. He said that during a part of his life, every night he thought to die, and every morning he wrote a fable. He said Ma Poesie est passée. Je n'ai plus la force d'esprit. He spoke bad latin & worse french; so, I did by best with him in German. I found him a poor mind, with hardly any science. His conversation was like that of an old Lady. You saw nothing of the ruins of a man. Ruins have allways something which mark the original Building. He has just had a tollerable fancy, & a knack of versifying, which has pleased the German Ladies & got him a mushroom reputation. Poor man, he was very lean & very feeble. But seemed a good creature.[9] I did not form my judgment of him, till I had seen him several times, which I did during my stay at Leipsic. I shall not mark them in this my journal. He translated to me in latin one of his fables, and I promised to learn German so as to read him well. Yet alas! how unpersevering am I! where is my Greek? where is my translation of Scots Law?[10] Well all will come about yet. I past the evening at Bels. He was till his sixteenth year in hungary, where his father was Lutheran minister.[11] He read me his Preface to the *Acta Eruditorum* for this year which he was just sending to the Press. The court of Saxe grants him the privilege of being Director of this work, the property of which belongs to the widow of a Bookseller whose family began & carried it on.[12] Bel employs what assistants he pleases, but is despotic Prince to insert or cut out as to him seemeth good. It yeilds him only about £50 a year. I am very fond of Leipsic. The Professors here are easy men of the world. I said I regretted that I had not studied here myself. But, I would go home & marry & send a Son. Give me your hand on that, said Bel. I gave it him that I would send my son to his care. Let me remember this.[13] I supt with him in an easy way with his family. Is not this being treated with much Civility? If I ever laugh at Germans, I am a Villain.

[TEN LINES A DAY.]
Henceforth you ne'er shall in my verses read
On this or that tomorrow I shall feed.
None but the Cook himself & scarcely he
Can tell what dishes shall at table be.
For chance has much to do 'midst roast & boild
Now dishes can't be had, now they are spoil'd.
Now they are rare and of a price so fine
They cant be purchas'd by a Purse like mine.
The Larks of Leipsic have I eat? ah no,
Unless boild beef under[14] that title go.

[1] The inscription, which may date from the opening of the library in 1511, was addressed to readers:

Quisquis huc ingrederis, hospes sive incola frater,
Lecturus sacros gentiliumque libros,
Claudere ne pigeat lectos, interque legendum
Ne quidquam rumpas, commaculesve cave.
Nam locus sacer est, sacra sunt pia dogmata Patrum.
Ne sis sacrilegus, furta dolose cave.

(Gabriel M. Löhr, 'Die Dominikaner an der Leipziger Universität', *Quellen und Forschungen zur Geschichte des Dominikanerordens in Deutschland* 30 [1934]: 80.)

Whoever you are who enter this place, visitor or resident brother,
Intending to read sacred and secular books,
Do not be slow to close them when read, and, while you read,
Be careful not to break or soil anything.
For this place is sacred, sacred are the devoted rules of our Fathers.
Do not commit sacrilege, be careful, thievish fellow, not to steal.'

(Translation kindly provided by Prof. Gordon Williams.)

[2] MS. 'to s>end ... Bell' lost. The text is based on a photocopy made by earlier Yale editors before the paper deteriorated.

[3] MS. 'old monk ... college' written between the dateline and the first line of the memorandum.

[4] MS. 'write ... Johnston' written along the left margin. In his letter to JJ dated 6 Oct., JB congratulated himself for having won a cordial reception from the professors of Leipzig without any letters of introduction, a feat he considered 'a fair tryal of my real Merit' (*Corr. 1*, pp. 136–37). He did not write to WJT on this day.

[5] Bel was university librarian as well as Professor of Poetry. The library, originally part of a Dominican monastery, had been taken over from the monks in May 1540 (Löhr, p. 101). The identity of the recalcitrant monk is unknown, and his 'effigy' has not survived.

During the Seven Years' War the library had served as hospital and as lodgings for prisoners but had now evidently been restored to its proper use. It was listed among the sights recommended to visitors (Emil Friedberg, *Die Universität Leipzig*, 1898, pp. 30–34, 47–48; *Leipziger Adress-Post-und-Reise Calender*, 1764, p. 193).

[6] Learned, erudite (Lewis and Short, s.v. 'Doctus').

[7] For a similar resolve, see Journ. 11 Aug. and n. 7.

[8] The passage—'in heaven: Father, Word, and Holy Spirit; and these three are one ...'—appears in 1 John 5: 7, not in James. Known as the 'Johannine Comma', it is an interpolation, introduced in fourth-century Latin texts, that expands a general reference to 'the spirit, and the water, and the blood' to the more explicit reference to the Trinity (R. Alan Culpepper, *1 John, 2 John, 3 John*, 1985, p. 103; 'John, Letters of', *The Interpreter's Dictionary of the Bible*, 1962, ii. 952). Luther omitted it from his translation because he doubted its authenticity (Hans-Josef Klauck, *Der erste Johannesbrief*, 1991, pp. 306, 309

and n. 888). The King James version of the Bible included it, but later scholars doubted its Biblical origin and accept it only as evidence of subsequent Trinitarian beliefs ('Johannine Comma', NCE, vii. 1004).

[9] Christian Fürchtegott Gellert (1715–69) was Professor of Philosophy at the University of Leipzig from 1751 and lectured also on poetry and rhetoric. He owed his reputation as the German John Gay to his popular fables, first published in newspapers from 1741 to 1751 and then collected as *Fabeln und Erzählungen* ('Fables and Stories', 2 vols. 1746, 1748). Gay (1685–1732) had become popular not only for his *The Beggar's Opera* (1728) but also for his Fables, one volume of which had been first published in England in 1727 and in Amsterdam in 1734, a second volume in 1738, with frequent reprints by 1764 (CBEL, ii. 293). Gellert had also written lively comedies that mingled satire with sentiment, pastoral dramas, and a Richardsonian novel entitled *Die schwedische Gräfin von G.*, 1746, but since 1751 he had produced little except his *Geistliche Oden und Lieder* ('Spiritual Odes and Lyrics'), composed in about 1755 and published in 1757. By the time JB met him he was greatly admired as a writer and lecturer on moral subjects, and had developed a large following, especially among women. For twenty years he had been plagued by illnesses that were more serious than JB could know, but he also suffered from 'hypochondria' (in the eighteenth-century sense of depression), in this instance from feelings of worthlessness intensified by his religious piety (Heidi John, et al., 'Gellerts Leben. Eine Übersicht' in Bernd Witte, ed., *'Ein Lehrer der ganzen Nation': Leben und Werk Gellerts*, 1990, pp. 11–28; Eckhardt Meyer-Krentler, "'… weil sein ganzes Leben eine Moral war". Gellert und Gellerts Legende' in Witte, pp. 238–55; Hans-Jürgen Schings, *Melancholie und Aufklärung*, 1977, pp. 127–30).

[10] Shortly before embarking on his travels, JB had been urged by SJ to study Greek for an hour a day (Journ. 2 Aug. 1763). And Lord Auchinleck, answering JB's letter of 7 Oct., had recommended reading both Greek and Latin authors. He had also heartily approved of JB's plan to study Roman law and to translate John Erskine's *Principles of the Law of Scotland* into Latin (see Mem. dated 17 July and n. 3; From Lord Auchinleck, c. 29 Oct.). This treatise, published in

1754 by John Erskine (1695–1768) of Carnock, who held a chair of Scots law at Edinburgh University, was evidently already known as 'an excellent elementary work' introducing Scottish lawyers to their legal system. It drew on *Justinian's Institutes* and the concepts developed by Samuel von Pufendorf (1632–94) in his philosophy of natural rights (*Oxford DNB*).

[11] Mathias Bel (1684–1749) had been minister of the German Lutheran church as well as rector of a school in Pressburg. Previously he had studied in Halle and had taught at the Francke orphanage from 1704 to 1708. A scholar in his own right, he had translated the Bible into Bohemian, had written extensively on Hungarian history, had been appointed historiographer to the Emperor Charles VI, and had been elected to the academies of St. Petersburg, London, and Berlin (Wurzbach, i. 235–36).

[12] The *Nova Acta eruditorum Lipsiae*, as it was called by this time, was the oldest European learned journal to review scholarly and literary works (Lutz Heydick, *Leipzig: Historischer Führer*, 1990, p. 36). Begun in 1682 and still written entirely in Latin, it was issued every two months and then published in an annual volume. Bel had been its director since the death of Friedrich Otto Mencke (1708–54), whose widow, Johanne Catharine (Langgut) Mencke, had managed to renew the 'privilegium' to publish it. Friedrich Otto Mencke was actually the offspring of not one but two families responsible for the journal. His maternal grandfather, Johann Friedrich Gleditsch (1653–1716), had been the bookseller who sold the original volumes and whose firm, the foremost booksellers of Leipzig, still printed them. His paternal grandfather, Otto Mencke (1644–1707), Professor of Morals and Politics at the University of Leipzig, had founded the journal, and his father (i.e., the son of Otto), Johann Burkhard Mencke (1674–1732), Professor of History, had also continued to edit it. Bel later fell behind schedule and was working on the volume for 1776 when he committed suicide in 1782 (Georg Witkowski, *Geschichte des Literarischen Lebens in Leipzig*, 1909, pp. 185–88).

[13] JB's elder son and heir, Alexander Boswell (1775–1822), would eventually spend some time in Leipzig in the winter of 1795–96, after JB's death, but would not formally enroll in the university.

[14] MS. 'can by' written above 'under'

## Saturday 6 October

[MEM. dated Sunday 7 October] [Y]esterday at 9 you drank Chocolade with worthy Baron[1] Quaalen & resumed your Utrecht Storys — then saw some public Gardens — the dutch taste improved. In one four stone Statues noble. At 11 Gelert. He interpreted one of his fables & you seised fully his sense; you found him a Man of poor reach. No learning & little force no invention. Din'd Quaalen — Rochular[2] MA was there who has given a Johnson in German & french. He <sa>id he'd help you with Scots & would procure you the corespondence of[3] a learned Dane & of Pantopodon Bishop of Bergen. You was rich & eloquent. Then saw with Gotsched *Rat's*[4] or Magistrate's Bibliotheque nob<le> room <goo>d Collect read a passage of <the> Barons letter to Pope took <leave> of Ge<ler>t feeble. Saw Gotsc<hed got list and> promise of aid — Went to <shop[5] that publis>hed Elents[6] curious &c. <Had Bel at> repas. <Was quite sound & well. This day Neidutsch ... all ready, &c.>[7]

[S]wear solemn with drawn sword not to be with woman sine cd nisi swiss lass.[8]


[J.] My old friend at Utrecht The Baron van Quaalen was now studying at Leipsic.[9] I waited upon him this morning, drank Chocolade & talked over our winter's Parties. We then went & saw some Gardens here, which I liked much. One of them is noble & extensive. It has the dutch taste improved. There are in it four large Stone statues of excellent Workmanship.[10] Indeed the best of the kind that I ever saw. One finds here and there choice pieces which are hardly known. Honest Quaalen insisted that I should dine with him. A very good dinner he gave me. We had with us Heer Rogler M.A who has made a surprising progress in the English Language. He has given a Dictionary German and English, which is properly a translation of The Dictionary of Mr. Samuel Johnson, as he says in his title page. But from the unlucky inclination to be voluminous, which is so remarkable in Germans,[11] he has *enriched* it forsooth with 3000 words taken from *others*, so that he has amassed all the rubbish which Mr. Johnson has with so much judicious care kept out of his Book. O quale Caput![12] I gave it him pretty plainly. He was however very obliging, was charmed to hear a specimen of my Scots Dictionary,[13] and mentioned to me a corespondence which may be of great service to me to wit that of M. Rysbrig a learned Dane and remarkable for his talents in Etymology, and the famous Pontopidan Bishop of Bergen of whose son Rysbrig[14] was Tutor. He said I might freely write to both, and might be sure of a good answer from each.[15] I shall not neglect such opportunitys. It has been my wish since I first thought of my Dictionary, to establish corespondences in the northern parts of Europe. I am very lucky hitherto. After dinner Quaalen & I went with Gotsched and saw the magistrates Library. There is a very noble room, and the great collection of books is well arranged. I saw here Anderson's Diplomata Scotiae. My old spirit got up, and I read them some choice passages of the Barons letter to the Pope. They were struck with the noble sentiments of liberty of the old Scots; and they exprest their regret at the shamefull union. I felt true patriot sorrow. O Infamous Rascals who sold the honour of your country to a nation against which our Ancestors supported themselves with so much glory. But, I say no more, only alas poor Scotland![16] I then went to a Sale of the effects of the Comte de Bruhl which was truly a curious sight. There were upwards of 700 Snuff-boxes in gold & many of them rich with Diamonds. There were many fine fire-arms, and a variety of other things of value. The Room seemed like the Shop of three or four rich Jews. These are pretty Remains of a Minister of State. His Sovereign payed for all this magnificent Trumpery.[17] I then went to Mr. Gotsched with whom I had left a Specimen of my Scots Dictionary. He was much pleased with it, and advised me by all means to go on with it, as it would not only be a most agreable present to my Countrymen, but would give much pleasure to the Curious Etymologists of every Nation and therefore he advised me to add to each word it's signification in Latin. This I shall do; as I did in the Specimen. Mr. Gotsched allowed me to search his Etymological Library, and take thence a list of such books as may assist me in compiling my Dictionary.[18] He also promised to corespond with me. At eight I had Bel with me, & gave him Bread & Butter & Cheese and fruit & Wine. I called it *Cæna Pythagorica;*[19] but, I found that our good Professor would have chosen to be of a Sect that lived a little better. We were however very merry, & renewed our literary covenant to send each other mutual accounts of the state of learning in our different countrys. I would gladly know, o my Ennemys! if any young fellow in Britain would have done more at Leipsic.

[TEN LINES A DAY.]

I'm told that Bards have vented many a curse
Against their stars. Because[20] forsooth a Purse
Like that of Charteris heavy to their share
Has never fall'n & so they tear their hair.[21]
O foolish fellows must you still be told
That human happiness is not in gold
Were all the Guineas of Great Britain thrown
Into one chest which I might call my own
Beleive me Boys that Boswell would be seen
As fat as heretofore & just as lean.

---

[1] MS. 'Baon'

[2] Rogler; see n. 12.

[3] MS. Space left for the name, that of the 'learned Dane' Riisbrigh (see n. 15).

[4] 'Raat': German Rat, the town council.

[5] MS. Page damaged by a hole; 'shop' is conjectural.

[6] The bookseller Dyck had published a German translation of Lord Kames's *Elements of Criticism*, entitled *Die Grundsätze der Critik*, in three volumes (1763–66), beginning just one year after the work's original publication (BM Catalogue of Printed Books). JB had noted the name 'Madame Dyck' and also

J. N. Meinhard, the translator, in his list of addresses (M 94; see App. 1, II).

[7] MS. 'Was quite sound … ready, &c.' disfigured by blotches and small holes in the page; 'Neidutch' is followed by an illegible word. The text is based on a transcription by an earlier Yale editor.

[8] MS. 'swear … lass' written along the left margin. The abbreviation 'cd' presumably stands for 'condom' (for which, see Journ. 15 July n. 2). The phrase seems to mean 'no woman without condom except Swiss lass', indicating that JB thought Swiss girls healthier, more likely to be free of infection,

than the street women he was encountering (see 'in Suisse have sweet Girl' (Mem. 11 Oct.).

[9] Josias von Qualen (1742–1819) had studied law at Utrecht from 1762 to 1763. Details about his friendship with JB cannot be ascertained since he is not mentioned in JB's surviving notes written in Holland. Von Qualen was spending two years at the University of Leipzig. He would follow in his father's footsteps by becoming a privy counsellor of Denmark and would head an aristocratic monastery at Itzeho in Danish Holstein from 1808 to 1818 (*Dansk Biografisk Lexikon*, 1899, pp. 318–19).

[10] More than thirty gardens had sprung up in open spaces that had become available on the outskirts of Leipzig after the Thirty Years' War, when the fortifications that had enclosed the town were dismantled (Brigitte Riese, 'Der bürgerliche Barock', *Leipzig*, ed. Wolfgang Hocquél, 1983, pp. 86–87). The garden that particularly impressed JB had been commissioned by Andreas Dietrich Apel (1662–1718), a wealthy merchant and a favourite of August the Strong's (Lutz Heydick, *Leipzig: Historischer Führer*, 1990, pp. 37, 317). The park was laid out in a fanlike shape created by six tree-lined canals. The statues of Mars, Venus, Jupiter, and Juno, on a terrace overlooking the site, were the creations of Balthasar Permoser (1651–1732), the much-admired baroque sculptor (see Paul Benndorf, *Hundert Bilder zur Geschichte Leipzigs*, 1909, p. 55; Gustav Wustmann, 'Apels Garten', *Quellen zur Geschichte Leipzigs*, 1895, p. 519; *Dict. of Art*, xxiv. 460–61).

[11] That is, the German people.

[12] 'What judgment!' JB did not realize that Johann Bartholomäus Rogler (1728–91) had not translated SJ's *Dictionary* but had revised Christian Ludwig's *Dictionary* (3rd ed. 1763), and had 'augmented' it 'with more than 12,000 words, taken out of Samuel Johnson's English Dictionary and Others'. Rogler, a native of Saxony (as revealed in his dedication), was sufficiently well versed in English to produce more than a thousand pages of text, in double columns. He had anglicized his name to John Bartholomew Rogler on the title-page.

[13] See Journ. 16 Sept. n. 3 and 4 Oct.

[14] MS. 'Rysrig'

[15] Børge Riisbrigh (1731–1809) was expert in ancient and modern Greek, Arabic, and other oriental languages. But his chief interest was in philosophy, which he had studied in Leipzig in about 1762, and he would later have a distinguished academic career in this field, earning the sobriquet 'Denmark's Socrates' (*Dansk Biografisk Leksikon*, 1982, p. 223). Erik Pontoppidan (b. 1698) had become Bishop of Bergen in 1747. In writings devoted to Danish history, he had proposed a series of fanciful etymologies in support of his argument that the German language was based on Danish. JB would not take up the correspondence with either of these scholars. Pontoppidan would die in Dec. of this year (*Dansk Biografisk Leksikon*, xi. 436–40).

[16] The library was situated on a separate floor above the armory on the old Neumarkt. Open to the public since 1711, it was recommended to visitors, who could see it on Wednesdays and Saturdays from 2:00 to 4:00 P.M. (*Leipziger Adress-Post-und Reise Calender*, 1764, p. 193). James Anderson (1662–1728), a genealogist and antiquary of Edinburgh with strong Jacobite leanings, had collected facsimiles of medieval charters and other muniments in his *Selectus diplomatum & numismatum Scotiae Thesaurus*, published posthumously in 1739 (*Nouvelle Biographie Générale*, 1857, repr. 1963, i. 524). The barons' letter to Pope John XXII (1249–1334), *Litera Comitium, Baronum, libera tenentium, et totius Communitatis regni Scotiae ad Johannum XXII Pontificatum Romanum apud Abirbrothec*, 6 Apr. 1320 (Pl. 51), famous as the 'Declaration of Arbroath', was a rousing assertion of the Scots' right to self-determination after the Pope excommunicated Robert the Bruce for refusing to accept an unfavourable truce with Edward II (see Journ. 6 Sept. n. 7). JB would use a stirring sentence from this letter as motto for his *Account of Corsica*. The exclamation 'alas poor Scotland' had been attributed to Prince Charles Edward Stuart while he was a fugitive in the Hebrides. JB would later record it on 8 Sept. 1773 as 'O God! poor Scotland' in the journal of his tour of the region with SJ (*Hebrides*, p. 131).

[17] The legendary collection of gold or jewel-encrusted snuffboxes and other valuables had been amassed by Heinrich, Count von Brühl (b. 1700), the 'Maecenas' and all-powerful Saxon statesman who had been Prime Minister from 1746 to his death on 28 Oct. 1763. He owed his wealth to Friedrich August II (1696–1763), Elector of Saxony from 1733, for whom he had secured the crown of Poland with the title August III, Poland having been won earlier by his father, who had carried the double title of Friedrich August I (1670–1733), Elector of Saxony, and August II of Poland, better known as August the Strong (for

these titles, see O. Halecki, *History of Poland*, new ed. 1983, pp. 185–86, 179). Brühl had supervised virtually all aspects of Saxony's political, economic, and cultural life, thereby acquiring so much wealth that he could build his own gallery of paintings and a library in separate buildings next to his sumptuous mansion in Dresden as well as renovating two country houses (Nugent, ii. 265; Aladár von Boroviczény, *Graf von Brühl: der Medici, Richelieu und Rothschild seiner Zeit*, 1930, pp. 358–71, 388–94; Weinart, pp. 321–22). At the end of Apr. 1763 he and his sovereign had returned from Poland, where they had spent the Seven Years' War after the Prussian incursions into Saxony (see Journ. 9 Oct. n. 8). Attempts to discredit Brühl had already begun, but he had been protected until the death of August III, three weeks before his own. Thereafter many of his possessions had been put on sale to repay the huge sums he was said to owe the state (NDB, ii. 660–61; Ludwig Baum, *Heinrich Graf von Brühl als Mensch und Christ*, 1967, pp. 8–19).

A number of Jews in England and in the Netherlands had become prosperous merchants, particularly traders in diamonds and other forms of jewelry (Harold Pollins, *Economic History of the Jews in England*, 1982, pp. 48–50). These stereotypical 'rich' Jews were more likely to be Sephardim, descendants of the group expelled from Spain and Portugal in 1492, than 'poor' Askenazi Jews who were often peddlers and petty traders (see Felsenstein, pp. 51–53; Jonathan I. Israel, *European Jewry in the Age of Mercantilism*, 1989, pp. 249–50). For JB's opinion of Jews, see Journ. 5 Aug. and n. 1.

[18] Gottsched's private scholarly library would be considered 'extraordinary', though primarily for its collection of early German drama (Wolfgang Schmitz, *Deutsche Bibliotheksgeschichte*, 1984, p. 97).

[19] 'A Pythagorean meal', a self-deprecating allusion to the lack of meat, and perhaps also a flattering allusion to Bel's treatise on Pythagoras, *Disputatio de Delectu ingeniorum Pythagorico* (1742); see Adelung-Jöchers, i. 1610–11). The Pythagoreans abstained from eating meat because they believed in the transmigration of souls and hence the kinship of human beings and animals (see Journ. 24 July n. 7, and Mem. 9 Sept. n. 1). As a youngster, JB himself had been influenced by an old 'Pythagorean', the eccentric John Williamson, and had gone through a phase of vegetarianism (see 'Ébauche de ma vie', Yale MS. L 1107, App. 2, III.A; *Earlier Years*, pp. 4, 34).

[20] MS 'Beccauce', a slip of the pen.

[21] Francis Charteris (c. 1665–1732) had accumulated great wealth by gambling and unscrupulous money-lending. Pope had linked 'Chartres, and the Devil' in a passage excoriating unworthy recipients of riches (*Moral Essays*, iii. 17–20; *Oxford DNB*, s.v. 'Charteris, Francis').

## Sunday 7 October

[MEM. dated Monday 8 October] [Y]esterday you breakfasted with worthy Quaalen and took leave at 12 set out good weather.

Spiders webs from Stars.

[J.] I breakfasted with honest Quaalen, who was quite eager to show his regard for me. My worthy Father used now & then to upbraid me that I had no freinds. I must take the liberty to think otherwise upon the evidence of facts. My Father's freinds have been ever ready to oblige him. I have surely more People who would be ready to oblige me. The difference is that my Father formed his freindships very slowly. Whereas I have formed mine quickly. Can I help it, if I find Mankind take an affection for me at once? Besides, my Father's freinds are only rational connections. He has no freinds, for whom he feels that enthusiasm of affection which I feel for Temple or for Johnston.[1] At one I mounted the waggon for Dresden.[2] It was charming weather. For several miles there fell arround us white flakes as of fine thread. My foolish Companions told me that they fell from the *Sterne* (the stars.) I dismounted and picked up a little of the stuff, which I found to be some sort of feild-spider's webs which the wind had carried from the Bushes into the air, & was now falling down again.[3] I know not if we have such webs in Britain. Let me here[4] mark an Anecdote which occurs. After I became acquainted with the Chanoine at Dessau,[5] who had taken me for an avanturier, I told him. Monsieur vous m'avez faché un peu l'autre soir. 'Oui Monsieur (said he) si cela etoit, Je vous demande pardon tres cordialement'. I explained the thing to him; He was sorry, & when we parted, He said to me, 'Monsieur, Je vous aime, et Je vous estime.' So this rub was well smoothed.

[TEN LINES A DAY.]
Wert thou o Tacitus again alive
With me I'd make thee thro' Germania drive[6]
As travelling Governour thou shouldst app
To a Scots Laird as proud as any Peer
But poor enough by day & night to go
on the post Waggons tho' all tempests blow
Upon those waggons in the dead of night
Your bones are shaken & you have no sight
Unless perhaps Postilion you descry
When his well-lighted pipe salutes your eye.

[1] For the distinction JB drew between these close friends, joined by interests as well as affections, and his London companions AE and GD (see Journ. 30 July n. 4).
[2] MS. 'Dresden' written over deleted 'Leipsic'.
[3] Identified correctly by JB, such flakes were gossamer, produced by spiders in a final burst of energy in autumn. The phenomenon would continue into the twenty-first century to be known in German as 'old wives' summer' (Langenscheidt, *New Muret-*

*Sanders Encyclopaedic Dictionary*, 1974, s.v. 'Altweibersommer', 1 and 2).
[4] MS. 'hear'
[5] See Journ. 28 Sept.
[6] In his *Germania* (98 A.D.), Tacitus had described the Semnones (#39) and the Hermunduri (#41), ancient tribes that had inhabited the district JB was now entering (Loeb ed., trans. Maurice Hutton, rev. E. H. Warmington, 1920, pp. 119, 194–95, 198–99). JB had worked his way through the Latin text while in Holland.

## Monday 8 October

[MEM. dated Tuesday 9 Octr.] [Y]esterday had slept in dreadfull mist — awaked all bad — teeth loose [—] danced — better — Day good fine country. Elbe each side hills & vines. Dresden charming call'd Stanhope was wearied went to bed undrest 1st time these 8 nights. This day up early, write journ till 9 — Stan will send — If not call Vattel & see Town. Not in to Stan — S<ee> Kircheisen. Try <for C>onds. Liv<e> spar<e — care. At 8> Wislb[1] sweet la<ss>

[J.] After sleeping all the night in a thick mist on the Postwaggon, I awaked much out of order. My blood was quite stagnated, and my teeth were loose.[2] I was allarmed. When we came to a *Station*, I got down & danced with much vigour, which by degrees brought me to my self.[3] I must realy take care on these Waggons. I now wrap myself up head & all in a great Cloak. But even thus the cold gets at me. Besides, when so wrapped up, I am quite an Egyptian[4] Mummie, and have no use of my arms; so that if the waggon were overturned I should be quite helpless, and probably be bruised & broken. Let me then take care. This day I had a pleasant drive between Meissen and Dresden. We went along the side of the Elbe.[5] On each side of the river were Beautifull rising grounds covered with Vines. Pray may we not have the same in Scotland? Surely our Climate differs little from that of Saxony. I saw too here & there old Castles, *Heerschaften's*[6] houses, seats of Gentlemen. It pleased me. It was Scottish. In Brandenburg[7] I dont remember to have seen any: and I beleive they are extreamly scarce, I got in good time to the beautifull City of Dresden,[8] put up at the Hôtel de Pologne, an excellent house,[9] drest in scarlet & gold, & went immediatly to call on Mr. Stanhope the British Envoy, for whom I had a letter from Mr. Burnet at Berlin.[10] He was not at home. I returned to my Inn, & went comfortably to bed; This was a degree of luxury to me, for I had not been undrest for ten days. I am realy campaigning in Germany. I like it much.

[TEN LINES A DAY]
Without dispute my fancy now must shine
For, it is lighted by good Rhenish wine
Liquor supreme call'd Hock[11] by Britons bold
And which (reverse of Women!) should be old.
Arriv'd at Dresden I am mighty well
The King of Poland's is my good Hotêle
Compleatly tird, what man can be more blest
Than I shall be this night with balmy rest
No King in Europe shall sleep half so sound
For this (as goes the phrase) I shall be bound.

[1] MS. Damaged by small holes; the text is based on a transcription by earlier Yale editors. <C>onds may mean 'condoms'. 'Wislb' has not been identified and is followed by a small break in the paper.

[2] That is, his teeth chattered with the cold.

[3] JB's coach stopped at several stations: Wurtzen, 12 miles (19.3 km) from Leipzig; a place which JB recorded as 'Wirtzburg' (a place name unknown in this region); Stauchitz, about 24 miles (c. 38.6 km) from Wurtzen; and then Meissen, a little more than 15 miles (24.1 km) further (Exp. Acct. 7–8 Oct., App. 3). The total distance between Wurtzen and Meissen was 40 miles, or 64.4 km (Nugent, ii. 412).

[4] MS. 'Eguptian'

[5] The distance between Meissen and Dresden, along the southern bank of the Elbe, was about 12 miles, or 19.3 km (Nugent, ii. 412), while the total distance between Leipzig and Dresden, which JB was covering in one and a half days, was about

52 miles, or 83.7 km (Nugent, ii. 412).

[6] 'Gentlemen'; that is, persons of rank.

[7] An older term for Prussia.

[8] Dresden had prospered since the time that it replaced Wittenberg as electoral residence of Saxony in 1547. Under August the Strong and again under Frederick August II, lavish baroque or rococo mansions had been designed for the elector's family members and courtiers, while substantial houses had been built by a few wealthy bourgeois (Seydewitz, pp. 54–58; Weinart, pp. 226–28; Sieglinde Nickel, 'Die Haupt- und Residenzstadt', *Dresden*, ed. Rudolf Förster, 1984, p. 62). For the effects of the recent war with Prussia, see Journ. 9 Oct. n. 8.

[9] Hester Lynch Piozzi would find it superior to any English inn or tavern when she stayed there more than a decade later (*Observations and Reflections Made in the Course of a Journey through France, Italy, and Germany*, 1789, ii. 326).

[10] Philip Stanhope (1732–68) had come to Dresden as Envoy Extraordinary in July

of this year (Horn, p. 64). See also Journ. 10 Oct. and n. 3.

[11] A popular white wine grown in this region. For the derivation of this name, see Journ. 1 Nov. and n. 6.

## Tuesday 9 October

[MEM. dated Wednesday 10 Octr.] [Y]esterday morning you was in delicious spirits & *sure* that after gloom you can be *quite* well. At 12 Stanhope politely came with coach — stopt at once — you cant go to court — no mourning. Not necessary for 3 days — din'd Table meat brought to each a good custom — & good company. Then stroled 2 hours quite *waff*.[1] But patient — At 6 found Vatel a mighty pretty man — composd book when all wrong in Saxony — tranquil &. his Lady Polonoise — Supt Danish Envoy cards — dishes brought — was quite fine. Voltaire Maupertuis Capitaine de Dragons &c. Esprit differ — de Genie[2] — This day resolve — to be independen<t &> love fine women & proffit of talents yet s<tore.>[3]

[J.][4] This morning I was in delicious spirits. I stood calm in my chamber, while the Sun shone sweet upon me, & was *sure* that after gloom I may be *quite well*. This is a corporeal change. No matter. No Philosophising. Mr. Stanhope sent me his Compliments, & said he'd carry me to court at twelve. He came very politely, & took me in his coach. Scarcely had we gone two yards, when he called out stop—and catching hold of me, said 'you can't go to court.' In short the court of Saxony was in mourning, & I had not a black coat.[5] As I intended staying here only three or four days, Mr. Stanhope said it was not worth my while to make a suit of mourning. But he advised me never to be without a black-coat, as so many accidents may happen. I was set down at my Inn, where I dined at the Table d'Hote. It was in a large room, as in an old Earl's Castle. There was a very good dinner. The *legumes* & lesser dishes were put upon the table. The Soup and the large dishes stood on a Side-board, and the Waiters brought his portion to each of the Company. A very clever method this. There was very good Company, mostly Officers Suiss Brabançons[6] & others who spoke good french. The only Objection to this table is that after dinner one of the Company generally makes a bank at Pharo and this brings on a little gaming. I stroled about & viewed the City. It is finely built of freestone.[7] It gave me great pain to see the ruins made by the Prussian Bombardments. I hated the barbarous Heroe. He was under no necessity to bombard Dresden. It was from mere spite that he did it.[8] I admired the new Catholic Church, which is an elegant Building finely adorned with excellent Statues.[9] I admired the noble Bridge over the Elbe. There is an excellent policy[10] here. Those who are going towards the Catholic Church (for I know not the points of the compass) must walk upon one side of the Bridge, and those who are going from the church upon another. By this means there is no confusion amongst the Passangers. If a blundering fellow takes the side of the Bridge which he should not, the Sentry drives him to his place.[11] I waited this evening on M. Vatel Conseiller privé de la Cour & Authour of The *Principes du Droit des Gens*. I had a recommendation to him from Froment. I found him a mild sensible pretty man. He said he composed his book while Saxony was all in confusion, and he expected to lose all that he had. But, he said Composition preserved him in tranquillity.[12] He presented me to madame Vatel a handsom young Polish Lady.[13] He said he was engaged to pass the evening chez M. l'Envoyé de Danemarc, who was his particular freind; so he begged I might accompany him & Madame Vatel; I did so. The envoy Count Schulembourg was a mighty agreable man.[14] We had four or five more Gentlemen there.[15] We played at Whist and chatted by turns. I was in the very best spirits. Sir James Macdonald could not have made a better figure.[16] I however complained to Vatel that I was ill educated, and had but little knowledge. He said 'Pardonnez moi Monsieur; Vous etes bien instruit.' The Envoy did not let this pass; he looked at me as one looks at one whom one admires, without well knowing for what. Vatel & I talked of learning in general, of the late war in Germany, of fate and freewill, or more properly the origin of evil. He was for the chain of Beings. I stood well against him. We had this evening something curious. The envoy begged pardon for not giving us a formal Supper. We continued to sit as we pleased. The Servants entered, & gave each of us a Napkin. They then brought each a plate of soup. Then each a plate of Ragout, & knife & fork. In short, we had a suite of six or seven dishes, with Bread to each, a plate of genteel dessert, called for wine when we pleased, & drank also good Punch. His Excellency just saved a table and table-cloth. For, it was indeed an excellent Supper. I was much pleased.

⌜TEN LINES A DAY.⌝
Have I not past my freinds this ev'ning well,
In the good company of wise Vatél?
The Danish Envoy was our gracious host
And in my mind he well deserves his post
For very finely were we entertaind
None but a freakish fool could have complain'd.
By turns at whist a sober game we playd
By turns our wit & knowledge we displayed
Besides, my freinds a hearty laugh prepare
The Larks appeard & excellent they were.

---

[1] 'Solitary, without a single acquaintance' (Jamieson, s.v. 'waff').

[2] Presumably the topic of conversation about the different temperaments and talents of Voltaire, who had been Frederick II's court poet and literary advisor in Potsdam from 1750 to 1753, and Maupertuis, the mathematician and astronomer who had been the President of the Royal Academy in Berlin from 1746 to 1759. Their rivalry was well known (Carl Alexander Dill, *Voltaire in Potsdam*, 1991, pp. 57–67). The captain of dragoons has not been identified.

[3] MS. The corner of the page has crumbled, but 'stor' was still visible to F. A. Pottle, who suggested the reading 'store ⌜mind with ideas⌝' (*Grand Tour 1*, Heinemann p. 131 n. 1, McGraw-Hill p. 134 n. 5).

[4] The arrival on this day of 'Hr. v. Boswell, Cavalier aus Schlottland ⌜sic⌝, von Leipzig' was reported on the last page of the *Dressdnische Wöchentliche Frag-und Anzeigen*, 23 Oct., Art. xvii. Both the *von* and the appellation *Cavalier*, 'nobleman', reveal JB in his continuing baronial mode.

[5] The ceremonial mourning for Elector Friedrich Christian, who had died on 17 Dec.

1763, was observed with the utmost seriousness in Saxony. An elaborate dress code, different for the various ranks of society, was prescribed for 54 weeks (published on 19 Oct. and 19 Dec. 1763, *Auserlesener Historischer Kern Dresdnischer Merkwürdigkeiten*, 1763, pp. 78–81, 95).

[6] Natives of the Brabant, a region in the Low Countries that belonged to Austria (C. Ingrao, *The Habsburg Monarchy 1618–1815*, 1994, p. 206). The Swiss officers were very likely following their usual occupation as mercenaries.

[7] That is, limestone (OED, s.v. 'freestone').

[8] Frederick II's cannons and the resulting fires had inflicted heavy damage on Dresden from 14 to 29 July 1760 (Weinart, p. 84). His forces had ferociously bombarded the town, destroying or severely damaging more than 500 buildings, causing more than 3,500 deaths by the end of the year, and creating 'indescribable misery' (Sieglinde Nickel, 'Die Haupt- und Residenzstadt', *Dresden*, ed. Rudolf Förster, 1984, p. 66; Gustav Klemm, *Chronik der Königlich Sächsischen Residenzstadt Dresden*, 1837, pp. 433–41; Seydewitz, p. 85). The Prussians had previously occupied the town in Sept. 1756, thereby beginning the Seven Years' War, and had been driven out in 1758 by the Austrians, who in turn had set fires in the outskirts to help defend the centre of the town. The 'spite' imputed to Frederick II may have been motivated by his fury at meeting such fierce resistance that he had to abandon the siege (see MacDonogh, pp. 295–96).

To appreciate the volte face in JB's view of Frederick II, see Journ. 13 July.

[9] The Catholic court chapel (*Hofkirche*) had been the special interest of Friedrich August II. Begun in 1739 and completed in 1756, it was a splendid late-baroque building designed by the Italian architect Gaetano Chiaveri (1689–1770) and built by Italian workmen. The exterior was decorated with sixty-four large statues of saints and other religious figures, executed by the sculptor Lorenzo Mattielli (c. 1678 or 1684–1748; see Weinart, pp. 53–54; Löffler, pp. 21–22). The interior included Permoser's elaborately carved pulpit and several of his statues. Although Saxony had been predominantly Protestant since the Reformation, its rulers had reverted to Catholicism when August the Strong became a convert in 1697 to make himself eligible for the Polish throne (see Journ. 6 Oct. n. 177; Löffler, p. 11).

[10] MS. 'pollice', 'advantageous procedure' (OED, s.v. 'policy', 4.a).

[11] 'Passangers' in the older sense of a traveller on foot (OED, s.v. 'passenger', 1.b). The massive stone bridge that spanned the Elbe had been constructed between 1727 and 1731 under August the Strong and had been named the Augustus Bridge in his honour. By his edict of 4 Sept. 1733 all traffic had to bear right. In addition, riders, carriages, and persons carrying heavy loads had to use the wide central roadway while ordinary pedestrians were to use the narrower, slightly elevated pathways on either side (Carl Christian Schramm, *Historischer Schauplatz in welchem die merkwürdigsten Brücken ... beschrieben werden*, 1735, pp. 29–30).

[12] Emmerich de Vattel (1714–67), a native of Neuchâtel, had studied philosophy in Basel and Geneva, and had entered diplomatic service in Saxony in 1743, becoming Saxon minister to Bern four years later. In spite of few assignments and only sporadic payments, he had remained in Dresden except for frequent visits to Neuchâtel, and had been named *conseiller privé* to the Elector in 1758. He had published his *Défense du système leibnitien* in 1741, his belletristic *Poliergie, ou Mélange de littérature et de poésies* in 1757, and *Mélanges de littérature, de morale et de politique* in 1760 (*DHBS*, vii. 50). During the Prussian occupation of 1756–58 he had written his ambitious *Droit des gens* (2 vols. 1758), which reflected contemporary events by including a lengthy section on the rights of nations and individuals in war. Its subtitle, *ou principes de la loi naturelle appliqués à la conduite et aux affaires des nations et des souverains*, indicates that he was drawing on the theories of natural law developed by Hugo Grotius (1583–1645), Samuel von Pufendorf and particularly Jean-Jacques Burlamaqui (1694–1748), who had taught at the Geneva academy from 1694 to 1748 (Ulrich A. Cavelti, *Einflüsse der Aufklärung auf die Grundlagen des Schweizerischen Staatskirchenrechts*, 1976, pp. 83–116 and n. 9). Vattel had continued the examination of natural law in his *Questions de droit naturel et observations sur le Traité du droit de la nature de M. le baron de Wolf* in 1762. JB was meeting him after these achievements and shortly before ill health would limit his activities, then cut short his life.

[13] Vattel had married Marie Anne, Baronne de Chêne de Ramelot, in Jan. of this year (Cavelti, p. 85). She was not Polish but belonged to an aristocratic French family that had established itself in Saxony (Albert de Lapradelle, Introduction, *Le Droit des gens*, 1916, vol. 1, pp. iii–vi).

[14] Werner Count von der Schulenburg had come to Saxony as Danish envoy on 9 Sept. 1763 and would remain until 28 Apr. 1768. He had begun his diplomatic career as envoy to Poland in about 1736 and to France in 1738, had then served in Cologne in 1746 and in Poland again in 1763. In addition, he held the title privy counsellor and the rank of major-general, later general of cavalry (*Repertorium*, ii. 34, 37–43, 53, 666).

[15] Not identified.

[16] Sir James Macdonald (1741–66), 8th Bt. Macdonald and 15th Chief of Sleat, had greatly impressed JB in London by his serious intellectual interests, polished man-ners, and self-possession in high society (*Journ.* 26, 29 Nov., 27 Dec. 1762). At Macdonald's invitation JB had visited him at Oxford (*Journ.* 24–25 Apr. 1763) and would later pay him tribute for combining 'the highest reputation at Eton and Oxford, with the patriarchal spirit of a great High-land Chieftain' (*Life* i. 449). To the sorrow of his friends—who included David Hume, Adam Smith, and Lord Lyttelton—Mac-donald would succumb to consumption at the age of twenty five, and would be ho-noured by the sobriquet 'the Marcellus of Scotland' (*Life* iv. 82 n. 1; v. 151–53; for Marcellus, see *Aeneid* vi).

## Wednesday 10 October

[MEM. dated Thursday 11 October] [Y]esterday morning saw the grand Gallery of Pictures. Outside the flemish & dutch School. Inner Italian School. Also room of Pastêlle; din'd Stanhope quite sensible easy & agreable. Abusd K. Prussia din'd well. Secretary queer irish Captain. Irish Col Brown came in. True foreign service. Then on street, amused as in London — wrong low punish — but in Suisse have sweet Girl.[1] This day see Bibliothéque — & raretés [—] at 12 as officer court &c. write J[.] Bruce. Resume *reins*. Let Father force you to be a man.

[J.] I went and saw the grand Gallery of Pictures, which I was told is the noblest in Europe. The Gallery is properly two rooms, one within the other. In the outside room is the Flemish and Dutch school, and in the Inside room the Italian School. There are of both Schools an infinite number of noble Pieces. I was luxuriously entertained for two hours. I also saw a chamber full only of Crayons.[2] I dined at Mr. Stanhope's. He is natural Son to the Earl of Chesterfield; but has received the education of a nobleman and been allways considered, by My Lord his Father in the best light. He is little & young, but much of a Gentleman. He abused the King of Prussia. He talked lightly of the Saxon Court, & said he tired sadly at Dresden.[3] This was not quite the formed man. But, I liked him the better. He shewed me that being employed abroad was not so very mysterious a matter. His Secretary (Mr. *Carrol*, tho' by no means a jolly dog) was an Irish officer of marines.[4] He was an obliging sort of man; but very formal. He was just Mr. Carron at Utrecht in Regimentals.[5] After dinner came in Colonel Brown an Irish officer in the Saxon Service, a very sensible worthy Gentleman.[6] In the evening I must needs go & look at the Dresden Street-walkers, and amuse myself as[7] I used to do in London.[8] Low, low.

[TEN LINES A DAY]
Of Lemonade I know not what you think
But it to me is a delicious drink
Wheneer my Stomach is oercharg'd with meat

Or in my blood there is too great[9] a heat
Or when my nervous system is unstrung
And I appear like one on Gallows hung,
For Lemonade I ask without delay
And cry dear Thomas[10] do make haste I pray.
Thro' all my frame the pleasant liquor flys,
My health restores, & makes my spirits rise.

[1] MS. 'Then ... street' and 'wrong ... Girl' scored out by a modern hand. For JB's assumptions about Swiss girls, see Mem. dated 7 Oct. and n. 8.

[2] The more than 1,300 paintings included 10 Holbeins, 14 Rembrandts, and 39 Rubens among the gallery's Northern painters, as well as 4 Raphaels, 2 da Vincis, 17 Veroneses, and 11 Titians among its Italian masters (see the alphabetical list in Weinart, pp. 239–59). Founded by August the Strong in 1722, the gallery had achieved its reputation for excellence under Friedrich August II, who had purchased various collections, notably from Francesco III (1698–1780) d'Este-Modena, offspring of a dynasty of patrons and collectors (*Dict. of Art*, x. 517–27; *Dizionario Biografico degli Italiani*). The 'crayons' were pastels, chiefly portraits, about 150 of which had been created by Rosalba Carriera (1675–1757), a Venetian painter who had impressed August the Strong in the 1710s and had become a favourite of Friedrich August's (Nugent, ii. 263; Alfred Sensier, 'Notice biographique', *Journal de Rosalba Carriera ... 1720–1721*, 1865, pp. 440–42; Thieme-Becker, vi. 75–77). All the art works were now back in the gallery's spacious rooms above the stables after having been stored for part of the war in the fortress Königstein, which had safer though damper quarters (Seydewitz, pp. 58–61, 64, 85–91).

[3] Stanhope was the son of Philip Dormer (1694–1773), 4th Earl of Chesterfield and Elizabeth du Bouchet (1702–*post* 1773); see Sheila Radice, 'Mademoiselle du Bouchet', *TLS*, 24 July 1937, p. 544). He was the recipient of the admonitory, worldly letters which the Earl had written to give him the social polish and pragmatic views he would need to offset his illegitimate birth. He had been sent to Eton and then on travels on the Continent in the company of the Rev. Walter Harte (for whom see Journ. 3 Sept. n. 3). Between 1751 and 1758 he had held minor diplomatic posts in Paris, Brussels, Bremen, Hamburg, and Ratisbon (Willard Connely, *The True Chesterfield*, 1939, pp. 313, 331–40, 402; *Repertorium*, ii. 144, 148,

152, 153). Thanks to his father's influence, he had also been elected M.P. for Liskeard (1754 to 1761) and for St. Germans (1761 to May 1765; see Namier and Brooke, iii. 464–65). In spite of his discontent, he would remain in Dresden until illness forced him to go on leave in Jan. 1768.

JB had a more favourable impression than did Lord Chesterfield's friends and his subsequent biographers, who reported that Stanhope had been physically clumsy and socially awkward as a boy, later professionally unable to hold his diplomatic posts, and altogether a disappointment to his father (Colin Franklin, *Lord Chesterfield: His Character and 'Characters'*, 1993, pp. 7, 80–82). JB had no inkling that Stanhope had secretly married Eugenia Peters (1730–83), also illegitimate, in 1761 and that they had two young sons, whose existences would remain unknown until his death in Nov. 1768 (Connely, pp. 391, 395, 402–03, 468, 489, 491). Eugenia, left penniless, would arrange for the publication of the *Letters Written by the Earl of Chesterfield to His Son* in 1774, after the Earl's death (see Franklin, pp. 31–38, 143–45).

[4] William Carroll (or O'Carroll) had served as second lieutenant in the marines for two years before coming to Dresden (*Army List*, 1761–63, p. 216). He would be in charge in Dresden after Stanhope's departure in early 1768, and again in Jan. 1770 in the absence of the next envoy (see Horn, pp. 64–65).

[5] Benjamin Caron had been Reader at the presbyterian English Church in Utrecht since 1754 and had tutored JB in French in that city. Caron's father was Norman French, his mother was English, and he had been a wig maker in London (French theme, c. 2 Oct. 1763, Yale MS. M 87; 'Notulen van den kerkraad 1657–1779', ii. 329, Archief van de Engelsche Kerk, HUA 848). In Utrecht he had been giving private lessons to supplement the yearly salary of 70 guilders paid him by the church ('Rekening boek', HUA 849, p. 23). JB had described him as 'un homme tout a fait accomplis', possibly exaggerating

the praise in the knowledge that Caron would read the essay (French theme, c. 2 Oct. 1763).

[6] Col. Anton de Browne had been in Dresden since 1744. He had risen through the ranks, from 'sous-lieutenant' to major in 1749 and to lieutenant-colonel in 1759, all in the grenadier-life guards (letter of 8 Apr. 1997 from Dr. A Miksch, SächsHStA Dresden).

[7] MS. 'I must ... streetwalkers' deleted in a recent ink; 'and amuse myself as' deleted possibly by JB, who noted 'Petite Avanture, 8 Gr' in his Expense Account for 10 Oct. (see App. 3).

[8] See Journ. 13 Apr. and 19 May 1763.

[9] MS. 'strong' written above 'great'

[10] Probably a generic name for a servant.

## Thursday 11 October

[MEM. dated Friday 12 October] Yesterday You saw Library very noble — Luther & Melanct's own hand. Was a little splenetic. Din'd Inn. Then saw musæum. Shamefull prices — trick'd them. Noble musæum. Thought on James Bruce. Then had Girl merely saluberrima lumbis.[1] Then Comedie — then Girl — pocket pick'd oblig'd to own to Servt. Swear never to be with Girl till you see Rousseau. This day court. Prepare Journ. Never be cast down. But ... and go on.[2]

[S]upport Utrecht ch<aracter> command self.[3]

[J.] I went & saw the Elector's Library. It is put up in four different rooms, part of a superb Building called the *Zwinger*. It is numerous, and has a good many Manuscripts; But what can a Man see of a Library from being one day in it? I dined at my Inn. At three I returned to the *Zwinger* and saw the noble Musæum.[4] It made me think of honest James Bruce with whom I have talked of it so often.[5] I must remark that at Dresden Strangers pay monstrously dear for seeing the fine things which is shamefull when they are the property of a Prince. My Valet de Louage told me that I must pay a ducat to the Library-Keeper, and a Florin to his man, which I was fool enough to do; as I would be genteel forsooth. It seems too I must pay at the musæum a Louis to the Principal Keeper, 2 ecus to another, and a Guilder to the Servant. Instead of this I made two Guilders do the business. I know not how I divided it between the Upper-Keeper & the Servant. I forget. But, no matter. The fellows looked strange & I saved six ecus.[6] The Musæum has indeed many great curiositys. But some of it's richest pieces have been sold to repair the ruins of the war. I then walked to the Garden where I saw some fine antiques in Bronze.[7] I went to the french *Comedie* which is very pretty here.[8] I saw the Elector Prince Xavier & several more of the court.[9] I was enlivened with new ideas. Yet again I went with those easy Street Girls — & between their thighs — merely for health. I would not embrace them. First because it was dangerous. Next because I could not think of being so united to miscreants. Both last night & this they picked my pocket of my handkerchief. I was angry at myself. I was obliged to own to my Servant that I had been avec des filles. Man is sometimes low.[10]

[TEN LINES A DAY]
A fool with justice we unlucky call,
And an old fool unluckiest of all.
So in a due proportion with his years

Each Mortal's folly more or less appears.
The inference comes 'Myself I freely own
A fool alas to goodly stature grown.'[11]
For these two ev'nings I must go forsooth
Amongst the Dresden Girls like simple youth
The worthless Gipsies[12] have me vilely trick'd
And of my handkerchiefs my pocket pick'd.

---

[1] 'Most healthy for the loins', an adaptation of the old Latin jingle 'Mingere cum bumbis/Saluberrimum est lumbis', which, in F. A. Pottle's tactful phrasing, 'lauds the healthful effect of breaking wind while emptying the bladder' (*Grand Tour I*, Heinemann p. 132 n. 6, McGraw-Hill p. 136 n. 5).

[2] MS. 'then ... go on' heavily scored out by a modern hand, one word not deciphered.

[3] MS. 'support ... self' written along the left margin; most of the word 'character' lost because of a hole in the page. JB is referring to the upright character—the 'steady and manly principles', the devotion 'to Prudence and to Morality'—that he had tried to adopt in Utrecht (To JJ, 20 Jan. 1764, *Corr. 1*, p. 119; see Courtney, pp. 97–100). For his rules, see his 'Inviolable Plan' (16 Oct. 1763, *Holland*, App. 1).

[4] The Zwinger, a showpiece of baroque architecture, had been designed by the architect Matthäus Daniel Pöppelmann (1662–1736) as a forecourt to a still grander palace that had been planned by August the Strong but had never been built. Named after a garden previously on the site between the outer and inner city walls, and constructed with many interruptions from 1710 to 1732, it consisted of six ornate pavillions linked by long galleries and adorned by sculptures by Permoser (Seydewitz, p. 50; Löffler, pp. 9, 17–43). JB seems not to have noticed the damage to the building inflicted by the occupying Prussians, who had stored their munitions there (Löffler, pp. 43–44). The library, housed in three of the pavillions, held about 140,000 books, some of them won after battles in the seventeenth century, and others, including Leibniz's, purchased as collections. The MSS ranged from Arabian, Persian, and Turkish to Hebrew, Greek, and Roman, as well as European texts ranging from Russian and Polish to French and German (Weinart, pp. 278–87). By 'musæum', also referred to as 'raretés' in the memorandum dated 11 Oct., JB presumably meant the *Kunstkammer* (treasury), founded in the early sixteenth century, which exhibited portraits of Roman emperors, drawings, paintings on glass, carved ivories, Russian icons, inlaid tables, and other *objets d'art* (Weinart, pp. 277–78; Joachim Menzhausen, 'Elector Augustus's Kunstkammer: An Analysis of the Inventory of 1587', Impey and MacGregor, pp. 69–75). JB seems not to have visited the adjacent rooms, devoted to natural curiosities, anatomical specimens, a model of the temple of Solomon, and a huge collection of prints, each room with its own keeper and staff (Weinart, pp. 266–77, 294–302; *Churfürstlicher Sächsischer Hof- und Staats-Calender*, 1765, pp. 52–53).

[5] For Bruce, the overseer of the Auchinleck estate, see Mem. 1 Sept. and n. 2. JB wrote to him on this or the following day (sent 12 Oct., Reg. Let.). But the letter would not survive, and why JB was reminded of him here is not clear. F. A. Pottle has suggested that Bruce may have accompanied Lord Auchinleck on his travels in earlier years (*Grand Tour I*, Heinemann p. 132 n. 1, McGraw-Hill p. 135 n. 9).

[6] The library staff included a chief librarian, a librarian, and two sub-librarians as well as two servants. JB paid the librarian, privy secretary Heinrich Jonathan Clodius, and either Siegmund Ernst Richter or Johann Eckart, manservants (*Churfürstlicher Sächsischer Hof- und Staats-Calender*, 1765, p. 52; the court calendar for 1764 is not extant). JB does not record his payments for the library in his Expense Account but lists two écus for the museum. This was headed by Gottfried Heinrich Duckewitz, *Hof-und Berg-Rat*, and employed its own clockmaker, Johann Gottfried Händschker, as well as a servant, Johann Friedrich Pattist (*Churfürstlicher Sächsischer Hof- und Staats-Calender*, 1765, p. 53). The previous day JB had spent 3 écus and 16 Gr. to see the gallery of paintings (Exp. Acct. 10 Oct., App. 3). The mention of ducats, florins, écus, louis, and guilders shows that coins from several countries were in use concurrently. His calculations were correct: he should have paid one louis (= 5 écus), plus 2 écus, plus 1 guilder (also worth 1 écu), a total of 8 écus, of which he paid only 2.

[7] Roman sculptures, most of them acquired between 1720 and 1730 by August the Strong, were housed in four pavillions of the 'Great Garden' (Grosse Garten) next to the Zwinger (Weinart, pp. 325–35). JB did not see the famous 'Green Vault' with its treasures of gold, silver, jewels, and ivories, displayed in special rooms of the palace and shown only to favoured visitors (Seydewitz, pp. 64–66).

[8] *Comédie* here is a generic term for 'theatre'. The play this day was the tragedy *Hypermnestre* (1758) by Antoine-Marin Lemierre (1723–93), performed by the new French troupe (SächsHStA Dresden, Oberhofmarschalamt O IV Nr. 160; *Premier recueil des pièces de théâtre représentées sur le théâtre electoral à Dresde par les comédiens françois de la cour*, 6 vols. 1765, ii). This troupe, which had been in Dresden since May, was using a small theatre in the Zwinger (*Auserlesener historischer Kern Dressdener Merkwürdigkeiten*, 7 May, p. 35; 11 Oct., p. 78). JB does not mention that he lost 1 écu 12 Gr. at faro, which was permitted after the performance in a small room adjoining the theatre (Exp. Acct. 11 Oct., App. 3; Vehse, xxxiv. 211).

[9] Prince Franz Xaver (1730–1806), in English 'Xavier', was not the Elector but the so-called 'administrator' or regent of Saxony. He had been appointed after the unexpected death of his brother, Friedrich Christian, who had reigned as Elector only from 5 Oct. to 17 Dec. 1763, and whose son, Friedrich August III (1750–1806), was too young to rule (Isenburg, i. Tafel 55). Xaver, continuing the work of Friedrich Christian, was trying to bring stability and order to Saxony after the Seven Years' War by reorganizing the court hierarchy, the bureaucracy, and the army. Although a Catholic himself, he had officially affirmed the rights of the Protestant church in Jan. of this year (Karl Heinrich Pölitz, *Die Regierung Friedrich Augusts, König von Sachsen*, 1830, i. 31–37). Xaver would remain in Saxony only until his nephew could begin his rule at the age of eighteen in 1768 and would then withdraw to his estates in France, styling himself Count of Lusace (ADB).

[10] MS. Ten lines, from 'Yet agai … low' inked out, possibly by JB. In his Expense Account for this date (see App. 3), he once more noted 'Petite Avanture 6 Gr.' (see Journ. 10 Oct. n. 7).

[11] Unidentified quotation

[12] 'Cunning rogue[s]' (OED, s.v. 'gipsy', 2.a), used metaphorically.

## Friday 12 October

[MEM. dated Saturday 13 Octr.] [Y]esterday you was presented at court as officier dans le regt. de Loudon [—] qui Laudhon en Autriche? Non. Mi Lord Loudoun. Many rooms. Frugal court. Din'd M. Stanhope. McKenzie there who spoke fine french. Took leave & found self well established. Carrol said of Servt. That clumsy *material* fellow. Travelled off at 7. Little Minister — spoke french like the end of Boyer's Grammar[1] — would bring an action against you for not eating & drinking.

[J.] Mr. Mackenzie a relation of the Seaforth family who has been a very long time abroad, waited upon me this morning. He was a genteel pretty man & spoke french like a Parisian.[2] He found me adressing to go to court; for, as I was curious to see it I begged Mr. Stanhope to present me as a British officer. I accordingly put a cockade in my hat and tied a crape around my arm & was presented at the Court of Saxony as un officier dans le Regiment de Loudoun. Qui? Laudoun L'Autrichien? Non. Milord Loudoun.[3] It was a great Palace.[4] The Court went from room to room, I believe to visit different Princes. I called it *une chasse de Princes*. Prince Xavier had something the look of Dempster.[5] The Elector was a sweet Prince.[6] His Governour l'Abbé Victôr was a very pretty man.[7] This Court lives at present very sparingly.[8] Three times a week a few Strangers are asked to the table. I was too short a while[9] there to be asked. The Saxon officers wear white cockades. It looks pretty. I hope there's no offence.[10] I was diverted at the conceit of being an officer for a day. I dined at Mr. Stanhope's. The Elector's master of horse was there.[11] He looked at my coat, & said 'Monsieur ce n'est pas un uniforme cela'. I replied — 'Monsieur non — pas proprement dit. Mais chez nous, si vous avez un habit rouge, vous etes officier — c'est assez.'[12] Mackenzie was there. He said the danish Envoy told him. Vous avez ici un Compatriote M. de Boswell. C'est un Homme bien instruit.[13] I smiled in my own mind. Perhaps I was wrong. Perhaps I am realy now well instructed. Secretary Carrol had a particular phraseology. He talked of Mr. Stanhope's Servants. They will do well Sir. Now that heavy *material*[14] fellow there he'll make an excellent Servant. I realy love Stanhope. He & I were mighty well together. We agreed to renew our acquaintance in London.[15] I went to my Inn, put on my travelling dress, paid visits of Congé & at seven mounted the Post-Waggon. I was vexed to find that to return to Gotha I must take Leipsic in my way, & so just return the way that I came.[16] I had for Companion a little German Clergyman who talked french by way of improving himself. Every phrase that he made use of he turned & turned in his mouth as a man would a piece of sugar-candy, seeming to say 'This I have well'. Poor Man he was very angry with me for running to the Stables & not eating & drinking as all Passengers are obliged to do. He said he might raise an Action against me. I suppose actio de non edere nec bibere.[17]

⌈TEN LINES A DAY⌉
Be it remember'd that a generous Scot
One autumn ev'ning for companion got
A little German Clergyman whose nose
With cold grew red as English Captain's cloaths
Be it rememberd that this little Priest
Had a young wife big as himself at least
And as he was no bustler of the trade
He was poor man but very slightly paid.
<H>is dress was simple, & his Spouse's too.
O British Blackcoats[18] were it so with you.

---

[1] Possibly the clergyman spoke in proverbs and clichés, a list of which had been provided by Abel Boyer (1667–1729) near the end of his *New French Grammar* (1748), previously published as *Compleat French-Master for Ladies and Gentlemen* (1694, pp. 405–12) and frequently reprinted (BM Catalogue of Printed Books). Boyer, a French Huguenot who had settled in London in 1689 and was known especially for his bilingual *Dictionnaire royal français et anglais* (1702), had also published editions of his French Grammar without the distinctive ending. JB listed 'Boyer's French Grammar', 1756, in his 'Cat. of Books' without specifying the content of its last pages.

[2] Very likely William Mackenzie (b. 1730), who had studied at the Scots College at Douai and would later become prior of the Scots monastery at Würzburg (*Scots Peer*. vii. 509, identified by F. A. Pottle in an unpublished marginal note in the index to BP). William was a relation of Kenneth Mackenzie of Seaforth, whom JB had met in Brunswick (see Journ. 27 June and n. 5). William Mackenzie's father, Kenneth Mackenzie of Assynt (dates not found), was a cousin of Kenneth Mackenzie's grandfather, William, 5th Earl of Seaforth (d. 1740; *Scots Peer*. vii. 509–12).

[3] The dress code for the period of mourning, summarized in the *Dressdnische Wöchentliche Frag- und Anzeigen* of 6 Nov., made a uniform mandatory for military personnel (Oberhofmarschallamt, 'Règlement', Art. i. 5). JB's Expense Account includes the entry: 'Craipe pour me faire Officier', 9 Gr' (10 Oct.).

The Austrian 'Laudoun' was Gideon Ernst, Baron Laudon or Loudon (1716–90), lieutenant-fieldmarshal in the service of Austria, who had distinguished himself during the Seven Years' War and had been ennobled after the battle of Hochkirch in 1758. He would be named fieldmarshal in 1776. According to one theory, he had had Scottish antecedents, and his name, indeed, should have been spelled 'Laudoun' (Wurzbach, xvi. 66). The more obviously Scottish 'Lord Loudoun' was John Campbell (1705–82), 4th Earl of Loudoun, of Loudoun Castle, Ayrshire, a Representative Peer of Scotland from 1734, who had led a highland regiment against the Jacobites in 1745–46 (*Scots Peer.* v. 509–10), had commanded British forces in America from 1756 to 1758, and had served as second in command of the British troops in Portugal in 1762. JB was well aware of this Loudon because he had accepted JB's brother John as ensign in his 30th Regiment of Foot (see Lord Loudoun to Viscount Barrington, 31 Jan. 1760; Lord Auchinleck to Lord Loudoun, 9 July 1760; John Boswell to Lord Loudoun, 22 Aug. 1760; information supplied to F. A. Pottle by James Fergusson in Feb. 1955 from Loudoun MSS then in the possession of the Marquis of Bute at Dumfries House, Cumnock, Ayrshire).

[4] The palace was a large old building in Renaissance style with an unimpressive exterior but elaborate, well-appointed interiors. Extended several times in the sixteenth century, it was to have been replaced by the projected new palace adjacent to the Zwinger that was never built (see Journ. 11 Oct. n. 4; Weinart, pp. 229–32; Seydewitz, pp. 24–25, 48–49). The princely family, apart from the young Elector Friedrich August III (for whom see n. 6), consisted of his widowed mother, Maria Antonia Walpurgis (1724–80), daughter of the Holy Roman Emperor Karl VII (1697–1745); his uncle Prince Xaver, the Administrator; his three brothers—Karl Maximilian (1752–81); Anton (1755–1836), who would succeed Karl as king; and Maximilian (1759–1838)—as well as two sisters—Marie Amalie (1757–1831) and Marie Anna (1761–1820)—all listed in the *Churfürstlicher Sächsischer Hof- und Staats-Calender*, 1765, p.

A2 (see also Albert, Duke of Saxony, *Die Wettiner in Lebensbildern*, 1995, p. 106, and Isenburg i. Tafel 55). On this very day, the young Elector's mother and brother Karl Maximilian, together with his unmarried aunts Maria Elisabeth (1736–1818) and Maria Kunigunde (1740–1826), daughters of Elector Friedrich August II, had returned to Dresden (*Auserlesener Historischer Kern Dresdnischer Merkwürdig-keiten*, 1764, p. 78; Hofjournal 12 Oct., Oberhofmarschallamt O IV Nr. 160, SächsHStA Dresden).

[5] For GD, see Journ. 6 Aug. and n. 7.

[6] The young Elector was shy and at this time in delicate health (A. L. Herrmann, *Friedrich August, König von Sachsen*, 1827, p. 17). However, he would live to have a full and varied life, rejecting the offer of the Polish throne, fighting first against and then for Napoleon, and becoming King of Saxony as Friedrich August I in 1806 (ADB; Albert, Duke of Saxony, pp. 130–38).

[7] The abbé Joseph Victor (dates not found) had supervised the education of Prince Xaver and his younger brothers before taking charge of Friedrich August ('Die Einricht- und Unterhaltung der Königl Printzen, Xaverii, Hofstaat … 1738–1763', Geh. Cab. Cantzley Loc No. 13, SächsHStA Dresden, 767, fols. 487–92). 'A very pretty man' indeed, he had just been accused of extramarital relations and fathering a child out of wedlock, and would be relieved of his duties by Prince Xaver three weeks after JB's visit (letter from SächsHStA Dresden, 17 Aug. 1984). Ironically, he had been promoted from counsellor of legation to privy counsellor earlier this year ('Avancement', *Dressdnische Wöchentliche Frag- und Anzeigen*, 24 Jan. 1764) but would no longer be listed in the *Churfürstlicher Sächsischer Hof- und Staats-Calender* of 1765.

Victor was rumoured to be a Piedmontese and the illegitimate son of Victor-Amédée II (1666–1732), King of Sardinia (see J.-J. Vernier, *Etude biographique sur le prince Xaver de Saxe*, 1903, pp. 88–89 and p. 88 n. 2; NBG, xlvi. 99).

[8] Prince Xaver was avoiding unnecessary expenses in order to reduce the huge debts left by the Seven Years' War as well as by the earlier extravagances of Friedrich August II and Count Brühl (see Journ. 6 Oct. n. 17). Xaver was thereby continuing the reforms begun by his immediate predecessor, Friedrich Christian (see Albert, Duke of Saxony, pp. 112–14).

[9] MS. 'shortawhile'

[10] White cockades were the sign of the Jacobites, particularly those who had fought

in 1745 (Bruce Seaton, 'Dress of the Jacobite Army', *The Scottish Historical Review* 25 [1928]: 280–81).

[11] Heinrich Gottlieb, Count von Lindenau, who had been promoted to chief master of horse in Nov. 1763 after serving as master of horse during the preceding four years (SächsHStA Dresden, Oberhofmarschallamt KIV, xiii. 237–38; vi. 136), or alternatively either Hans George Wilhelm von Troyff or Hans Heinrich von Könneritz, both serving as master of horse under Lindenau (*Churfürstlicher Sächsischer Hof- und Staats-Calender*, 1765, p. 65).

[12] The red coat was a distinctive part of a British officer's uniform.

[13] Repeating Vattel's remark to JB overheard by the envoy on 9 Oct.

[14] 'Bulky, massive, solid' (OED, s.v. 'material', A. *adj.* 7).

[15] They had no opportunity to meet again in the four remaining years of Stanhope's life.

[16] Dresden was the farthest point east on JB's German travels. Evidently no direct post road southwest ran between Dresden and Gotha (see Johann Peter Nell, 'Neuvermehrte Post-Charte durch gantz Teutschland', 1709, reproduced in *Archiv für deutsche Postgeschichte*, 1976).

[17] 'An action for not eating or drinking'. The clergyman has not been identified.

[18] Clergymen, black coats being characteristic of clerical garb.

## Saturday 13 October

[MEM. dated Sunday 14 October[1]] On this jaunt You have slept immensely. You found Post engaged — sad scrape. Supt on a dozen of Larks. Leipsic exise for em 17000 ecus. Immense. This day try to get off[.]

[J.] Upon this jaunt I sleep immensely. When I came to Leipsic at night, I found the Post for Gotha engaged. This was a sad scrape. However, I made the best of it, and engaged an Extra.[2] I supt on a dozen of Larks. They are remarkably fine in this country, and prodigiously numerous. The Excise or rather the Custom upon Larks at Leipsic comes to 17 000 Ecus a year altho' the duty upon each is a mere trifle I beleive no more than a Pfenning.[3]

[TEN LINES A DAY.]
Your dainty folks who must their palate please
If they are forc'd to dine on bread & cheese
Against a power whom their ill fate they name
In grief & rage most loudly[4] they complain
Yet many an honest fellow who is poor
Would wish to be[5] of Bread & cheese secure
Give him enough of wholesom bread & cheese
He'd ask no more his heart would be at ease
And his most gratefull incense still[6] would rise
For the same food which dainty folks despise.

[1] MS. 'October' omitted in the dateline.
[2] A private coach. For the six stages between Leipzig and Gotha, JB paid 16 écus, considerably more than the price of the ordinary coach (Exp. Acct. 14–16 Oct., App. 3; see also 'Ten Lines', 14 Oct. and n. 4).
[3] MS. JB's slip of the pen for 'Pfennig'. A tax of 6 Pfennig per fifteen birds (that is, .4 Pfennig per bird) had been imposed by the municipal authorities in 1705 (*General-Accis und Consumtions-Ordnung bey der Stadt Leipzig*, Letter of 15 Jan. 1997 from the Stadtgeschichtliches Museum Leipzig). According to another source, the tax was 20 Pfennig per sixty birds (that is, .33 Pfennig per bird). Although the duty was therefore less than JB mentions, the number of birds caught in a good year—404,340 larks in Oct. 1720—

indeed brought a substantial income (Ursula Walter, 'Leipziger Lerchen', *Leipziger Blätter*, 1984, pp. 92–93).

[4] MS. 'bitterly' written above 'loudly'

[5] MS. 'gladly be' written above 'wish to be'

[6] MS. 'still', an interlineation.

## Sunday 14 October

[MEM. dated Monday 15 October] [Y]esterday could have no ordinary Post. Took *Extra* was melancholy a little. Cleared up. At night felt a most terrible cold. Allmost starved. This day push along.

[J.] I thought it would be better to keep myself snug here,[1] without being seen. At twelve I set out. I was somewhat melancholy in the Glasgow stile.[2] At night I was miserably cold.

[TEN LINES A DAY]
As to be usefull ev'ry man should try
My last night's verses let me now apply.
For Application ever should be made
Both of & to — whatever be[3] your trade.
Few of my freinds would willingly be tost
Upon a German Chariot of the Post
Yet I would ever be contented seen
Could I but ever have that rude machine
For now tis hir'd and for an extra sad
I must pay double,[4] tho' 'tis just as bad.

[1] Back in Leipzig, where he had been from 3 to 7 Oct.

[2] That is, lonely and dispirited. So unhappy had JB become at Glasgow University in the autumn of 1759, in spite of the opportunity to study with Adam Smith and other superior faculty members, that he had run away to London after six months (*Earlier Years*, pp. 37–43).

A brief visit to Oxford had also disillusioned him about that university, where he had found the atmosphere oppressive and the calibre of the students disappointing (*Journ.* 23–24 Apr. 1763).

[3] MS. 'is' written below 'be' and not deleted

[4] MS. 'triple' written above 'double'. For the 'Extra Post' from Leipzig to Rippach, a distance of about 17 miles (c. 27.4 km), JB paid not only 3 écus but also 26 Gr. for the coach and postillion, and 4 more Gr. 'Smear Gelt' (*Schmiergeld*) to grease the wheels (see Exp. Acct. 14 Oct., App. 3).

## Monday 15 October

[MEM. dated Tuesday 16 October] [Y]esterday was better; but was obliged to go on very slowly & wait for horses — resolved never more extra — Felt most vulgar inclinations. Depraved taste, corrected it & was vexed. In such cases — you must just view it as disease & cure it.[1]

[J.] I was obliged to go on very slowly, as they sometimes made me wait five hours for horses to my machine.[2] I resolved never again to take an extra. I stroled about in a Village[3] in search of the ugliest woman I could find. I restrained myself. Such inclinations are caused by disease.[4]

[TEN LINES A DAY]
No more my freind your gaping wonder keep
To hear that I on German Post can sleep:
Not with more pleasure does he close his eyes
Who on soft down luxuriously lyes.
For, know the roughly-rumbling Waggon wild
Is just to me as Cradle to a Child
As on the rugged roads I bouncing reel
My firm corporeal strength with Pride I feel
And while my back upon the boards is knock'd
I think 'Twas thus great Hercules was rock'd'.[5]

[1] MS. 'Felt ... cure it' heavily scored out, perhaps by JB, but still barely legible.
[2] While waiting in Rippach, JB wrote to Plessen, recalling their enjoyable meetings in Brunswick (see Journ. 10 Aug. and nn. 6–7) and also asking to have some newly minted silver coins sent from Brunswick for a coin collection that he had started. Writing on brown paper, which he had acquired from the innkeeper and had used for his letter to Plessen, JB also set down the maxims in the manner of La Rochefoucauld which had been inspired by the book he had purchased in Halle (see App. 3; Journ. 2 Oct. n. 8; *Catalogue*, i. 72; *Grand Tour I*, Heinemann p. 136 n. 1, McGraw-Hill p. 140 and n. 2).
[3] Auerstedt, recorded as 'Oversted' by JB and mistakenly as 'Oberstadt' in *Grand Tour I*, p. 138 n. 1). Leaving Rippach, JB travelled 12 miles (19.3 km) to Naumburg, 8 miles (12.9 km) to Auerstedt, and 8 more miles to Buttelstedt (Nugent, ii. 420). On the two-day journey covering the roughly

52 miles (83.7 km) between Leipzig and Erfurt, he paid two or three écus for each stage as well as a few Groschen for costs related to the coach (see Exp. Acct. 14–16 Oct., App. 3).
[4] MS. 'in search ... disease' scored out by a modern hand.
[5] Hercules, the legendary Greek hero who withstood many hardships while travelling to fulfil impossible tasks, had shown his great strength even in his cradle when he strangled two serpents sent by the jealous goddess Hera ('Heracles', OCCL, p. 201). JB would send these 'Ten Lines' to Lord Marischal, complimenting himself on his comparison of a post waggon to a cradle and making the point 'that such rude rocking could lull to sleep none but a Hercules' (To Lord Marischal, 30 Oct.). JB's ironic image of himself in this heroic pose would become a running joke in his subsequent correspondence with Lord Marischal (From Lord Marischal, 18 Nov.; To Lord Marischal, 20 Jan. 1765).

## Tuesday 16 October

[MEM. dated Wednesday 17 October.] Yesterday came to Erford half catholic. Saw Church & great clock. Several convents but poor — Soldiers who when officer past took all off their hats — very pretty — Fine day had good drive to Gotha surrounded with fine Green hills. Castle on airy eminence [—] was well at Inn with good light supper and wrote. This day faites annoncer á la Cour &c[.]

[J.] I came to Erford which is partly Catholic.[1] There are some Convents here; but none very magnificent.[2] I heard afterwards that there is here a Scots Convent.[3] The Blockheads at my Inn told me nothing of it. I saw the great Clock called the *Grosse Susanne*.[4] I saw here some troops of their Prince the Elector of Mayence.[5] They had a singular piece of exercise. When an officer past by the whole ranks pulled off their hats. It had a very good effect. It was a charming day. I arrived in good time at Gotha. I was pleased to see the pretty green hills arround and the Castle on a lofty eminence.[6] I had a good Inn.[7] A light agreable Supper put me in pleasant humour. I read and wrote chearfully.

[TEN LINES A DAY]
My lines this night good freinds I pray you mark
Because my lines are written in the dark.
Thus 'twas resolvd; But when the darkness came
As out the candle went, went out my flame
And my dull Muse a poor terrestial Jade
Just went to sleep[8] like any Kitchen Maid.
So I am then no Night-bird; & I find
I should not Homer be tho' I were blind.
I will not therefore like the Sage of old
My sight to quench a Bason bright to behold.[9]

[1] Erfurt, roughly 13.5 miles (c. 21.7 km) from Buttelstedt, was primarily Catholic. It had lost its independence as a Hanseatic free city during the Thirty Years' War when it was occupied alternatingly by Swedes, who had made it Protestant, and the troops of the Archbishop and Elector of Mainz, who had brought it back to Catholicism. After the war, in 1664, the city was incorporated into that powerful prelate's Catholic domain (Willibald Gutsche, *Geschichte der Stadt Erfurt*, 1986, pp. 141, 144–48). Still, as in other cities including Minden, Protestants could continue to practise their religion.

[2] Benedictine, Dominican, Franciscan, and Augustinian monasteries, all founded in the Middle Ages, continued to exist in Erfurt ([Günter Hoppe], *Historischer Führer, Stätten und Denkmale der Geschichte in Erfurt*, 1977, p. 18).

[3] The *Schottenkloster*, a Benedictine monastery, still had some associations with Scotsmen. It was founded in about 1036, if not earlier, by Irish monks, and had thereafter been led by either Scottish or Irish abbots. Operated as an independent foundation under the protection of the Pope, though supposedly reporting to the Archbishop of Mainz, it was now headed by a Scot, Bonifacius Leslie (1736–68); see Joseph Scholle, *Das Erfurter Schottenkloster*, 1932, pp. 10–14, 20–22, 84; Thomas A. Fisher, *The Scots in Germany*, 1902, p. 219).

[4] The 'great Clock' was not a clock but a bell, nor was it called *die grosse Susanne* but the *Osanna* (for 'Hosanna': 'in praise of God'). Poured in Erfurt in 1474, it was placed in the middle tower of St. Severi, a massive Gothic church next to the cathedral (*Die*

*Kunstdenkmale der Provinz Sachsen: Die Stadt Erfurt*, 1929, i. 508–09). In his use of 'clock' for 'bell', JB may have been influenced by the German *Glocke* and French *cloche* (see his similar reference to 'the famous great clock' of Saint-Pierre in Geneva, Journ. 31 Dec.).

[5] The ruling prince was Emmerich Josef, Baron von Breidbach-Bürresheim (1708–74), Elector and Archbishop of the ecclesiastical court of Mainz (Wolfgang Balzer, *Mainz: Persönlichkeiten der Stadtgeschichte*, 1985, i. 194; see also Journ. 1 Nov. n. 7).

[6] Gotha, 12 miles (19.3 km) from Erfurt, was situated among the gently sloping hills and forests of Thuringia (Keyssler, p. 155). It had been the residence of the dukes of Saxe-Gotha-Altenburg since 1640, when Ernst (1601–75) der Fromme (Ernest the Pious) chose it on becoming ruler of a large part of Thuringia. Soon after his death the territory had been divided among his seven sons, the eldest of whom and his descendants had become rulers of the small duchy of only about 52 square miles (c. 134.7 sq km) that JB was now entering (see Stavan, p. 30; Wettiner, pp. 265–69, 287).

The castle, called Friedenstein ('stone of peace'), overlooked the southern part of the town. It had been built from 1643 to 1654 on the ruins of the castle Grimmenstein, which had been destroyed during the Thirty Years' War. The new palace, in restrained early baroque style, consisted of a large rectangular edifice enclosing an arcaded courtyard and sporting two Italianate corner pavillions surmounted by small towers (Wolfgang Steguweit and Bernd Schäfer, *Schloss Friedenstein*, 1985, pp. 2–13; see also Volkland, ii. 1–9).

[7] The Estril (see Exp. Acct. 20 Oct., App. 3). This was probably one of the inns on the Neumarkt, the town square below the castle (*Gotha: Das Buch einer deutschen Stadt*, ed. Kurt Schmidt, 1938, ii. 69–70).

[8] MS. 'fell asleep' written above 'went to sleep'

[9] Perhaps Teiresias, that 'sage of old', who according to one myth was blinded for having seen Athena naked in a fountain or bath (a 'basin') but was compensated by gifts such as the ability to prophesy (Callimachus,

*Hymn* V, ll. 57–92, 117–28, trans. A. W. Mair, Loeb Classics, 2nd ed. 1954). In another version of this myth, Teiresias was glad to have lost his sight since he gained insight instead (Nonnos, *Dionysiaca*, v. 337–43, trans. W. H. D. Rouse, Loeb Classics, 1940). Possibly JB was contrasting himself with Teiresias when he declared himself not willing to blind himself to increase his gifts. JB quoted Callimachus's poetry in *An Account of Corsica*, 1768, p. 15.

## Wednesday 17 October

[MEM. dated Thursday 18 October.] Yesterday having seen all the world in black was affraid to go to court. But was sent to Maréchal waited on him — very sensible polite man — said twas dueil[1] presque fini & I might well go to court. At 1 & half went — large old Chateau [—] had full ideas of Princess of Wales — A grave court — Great rooms — Guards in the Passages — Presented to Duke & Dutchess old plain People. He talked of *Ma Sœur* like a Scots Gentleman. Prince quiet — Second brisk. Princess ugly jocular foolish. Grace before and after by Page Marechal standing by. Tollerable Table. At 7 Court — Whist. Supper talked with Lady educated with the Queen &c. This day resume. See medals & get Coins.

[J.] Last night I had seen some of the Courtiers, & found them all in mourning.[2] This alarmed me. I sent this morning to the Baron de Keller[3] & M. de Gotter,[4] for whom I had recommendations, but they were both out of town. However, Madame de Gotter opened my letter, so that it was known that I was a Gentleman. I sent to the Baron de Thungen Hofmaréchal,[5] & said that there was a circumstance which rendered it absolutely necessary that I should pay my respects to him, before I durst *me faire annonçer á la cour*. He received me, & I found him a sensible polite man. I told him the circumstance which was the want of mourning: But he told me that it was now allmost over, and that I could be presented without it. We talked of the Duke of Wurtemberg's excessive gallantrys.[6] He said Monsieur c'est un marque d'esprit de ne pas pouvoir gêner ses passions de tout. De le restreindre c'est une affaire du temperament. Mais assurement on peut les menager. He desired to see me at court at one. I came accordingly, and was presented. The Duke and Dutchess were plain Old People. The Duke talked of *Ma Sœur* (The Princess of Wales) just like a good Scots nobleman.[7] The Hereditary Prince was mild & quiet,[8] the other Prince Auguste very brisk. He was just arrived from getting himself installed Knight of the Teutonic Order.[9] The Princess was ugly, but easy & comical.[10] It was a fine old castle. We had a very good dinner. The Grand Passage was lined with honest looking Guards, quite comfortable.[11] After dinner I retired to my Inn. At seven we returned to court, & chatted and played cards. They made a Whist-Party for me.[12] I found the stile of this court easy and cordial. I am allready well with Chambellan Hellmolt a fine fellow like Lord Cassilis,[13] [t]he Grand Ecuier — the Grand Echançon

Forstern — [t]he Baron von Schlegel and my good freind the Maréchal.[14]
The Ladies are also very agreable. At Supper I sat by Mademoiselle de
Bilow, who was educated at Strelitz with the Queen. She was very like Mrs.
Hamilton of Bangour.[15] She had fine eyes. She had much sentiment. She
begged of me to tell the Queen that I had heard her praised by one who had
the best opportunity of knowing her Majesty.

[TEN LINES A DAY]
Come, my dear Muse! my sweet celestial fair!
How is thy Genius in Saxe-Gotha Air?
Here from whence came the mother of our King
Say shalt thou not with double vigour sing?
Shall not the gay green hills that rise arround
Gayer & greener in thy strains be found.
yet let thy strains be such as well may suit
The Scottish Bagpipe of the Earl of Bute.
O Wilkes! thou squinting dog; if thou wert here,
Thou wouldst regard me with malicious sneer[16]

---

[1] MS. 'dueil' written above the line

[2] The Duke's brother, Prince Ludwig
Ernst (b. 1707), had died on 13 Aug. 1763
(noted in the Duke's hand on the page facing
August in the Hochfürstl. Sachsen-Gothaischer
Hof-Calender, 1763; Isenburg, i. Tafel 49; see
also Grand Tour I, Heinemann p. 137 n. 2,
McGraw-Hill p. 141 n. 4). Official mourning
for close relations lasted at least a year (see
Journ. 9 Oct. and n. 5).

[3] Christoph Dietrich von Keller (1699–
1766) had been first minister in Saxe-Gotha-
Altenburg until his retirement on 28 Nov.
1763 (Hess, pp. 81, 165). He had arrived in
1738 as envoy from Württemberg but had
entered the service of Gotha, where he had
functioned as privy counsellor from 1751, as
director of excise from 1757, and as the
Duke's chief advisor and Vorsitzender des
Geheimen Ratskollegium (head of his privy
council) from 1757 to 1760 (Hess, pp. 80–81;
Repertorium, ii. 420). Before the Seven Years'
War Keller had also been a valued member of
the Duchess's inner circle. He had now
returned to the service of Württemberg and
had come to Gotha for a visit on 7 Oct. (see
the Wöchentliche Gothaische Anfragen und
Nachrichten, 12 Oct. 1764).

[4] 'M. de Gotter' is not recorded in the
court calendar of this time. Possibly JB
meant Heinrich Ernst Gotter (1703–72),
Archivar (Master of Rolls) from 1735 as well
as Legation Rat (counsellor of legation) from
1743, Geheimer Assistenzrat (assistant privy
counsellor) from 1759, and head of the

privy council's secretariat from 1752 to
1772 (Hochfürstl. Sachsen-Gothaischer Hof-
Calender, 1764; Hess, pp. 8, 82). He belonged to a respected bourgeois family and
was the father of the poet Gotter (1746–
97); see Rudolf Schlösser, Friedrich Wilhelm
Gotter, 1895, pp. 7–8). If this identification
is correct, 'Mme de Gotter' was Madeleine
(von Wangenheim), who had become Gotter's second wife in 1762 (Schlösser, p. 68).

[5] Siegmund Carl von Thüngen, described
as 'maréchal de la cour de Saxe-Gotha' on
JB's list of addresses (M 94), is identified as
Hofmarschall (marshal) under a Ober-Hof-
marschall (chief marshal) in the Hochfürstl.
Sachsen-Gothaischer Hof-Calender, 1764. His
polite note agreeing to meet JB, and excusing
the 'terrible Derangement' of his lodgings
caused by his moving to new quarters, is preserved among JB's letters as 'Specimen de
Formalité Allemande par le Marechal de la
Cour de Gotha' (From von Thüngen, [17
Oct.], Yale MS. C 2989).

[6] Karl (II) Eugen (1728–93), Duke of
Württemberg, was notorious for his 'erotic
adventures', which had caused his first wife,
Friederike (1732–80), née Brandenburg-
Bayreuth, to leave him in 1756 after eight
years of marriage and which had become
even more scandalous after her departure
(Gerhard Storz, 'Herzog Carl Eugen', Neun-
hundert Jahre aus Württemberg, ed. Robert
Uhland, 1984, pp. 246, 248, 253). Having
assumed power at the age of sixteen after a
seven-year regency, he surpassed the other

absolute rulers in German territories by his self-indulgence in both his private and his public life. He heedlessly oppressed his subjects to achieve the cultural and social brilliance for which his court at Stuttgart had become famous (Hansmartin Decker-Hauff, 'Herzog Karl Eugen von Württemberg', *Die Geschichte Baden-Württembergs*, ed. Reiner Rinker and Wilfried Setzler, 1986, pp. 162–65).

[7] Friedrich III (1699–1772), Duke of Saxe-Gotha-Altenburg, and his duchess, Luise Dorothea (1710–67), *née* Saxe-Meiningen, were neither so old nor so plain as JB assumed, but the Duchess was in ill health and prematurely aged (Stavan, p. 54). Before the Seven Years' War, thanks largely to her, Gotha had been one of the most intellectual courts in Europe. The Duke was in general estimation boring and only moderately intelligent (Stavan, p. 31; Vehse, xxix. 38). The Duchess, on the other hand, was lively, clever, and well read in philosophy as well as literature. She had invited Voltaire to stay in Gotha in 1753 after his departure from Potsdam (Osten, pp. 15–44, 140–42; Stavan, pp. 30–35, 49). During the war the Duke and Duchess had remained on good terms with both the Prussians and the French, who had occupied Gotha alternatingly; on one occasion, the Prussians had sat down to the dinner prepared for the French (Lehndorff, *Dreissig Jahre: Nachträge*, i. 142; Vehse, xxix. 31).

The Duke's favourite sister, Augusta (1719–72), had married Frederick Louis, Prince of Wales, in 1736 (Isenburg, i. Tafel 49).

[8] Ernst Ludwig (1745–1804) was studious and interested in the sciences. He would encourage these in Gotha after succeeding his father in 1772 (Osten, pp. 360–65; R. Ehwald, 'Ernst II. von Sachsen-Gotha-Altenburg', *Mitteilungen der Vereinigung für Gothaische Geschichte und Altertumsforschung*, 1904, pp. 1–44).

[9] August (1747–1806), brother of the foregoing, was witty and given to sarcasm, as he had acknowledged to his mother in his 'Réponse' of 9 Mar., one of the little essays he was composing for her each day (FLB Gotha, Chart. B 1317). On 6 Oct. he had been initiated into the order of the Teutonic Knights (for whom see Journ. 27 June n. 9; see also Osten, pp. 305–06).

[10] Princess Friederike Luise (1741–76) had just been dissuaded from accepting a proposal from the recently widowed Duke d'Orléans (1725–85) because Frederick II of Prussia had objected to her converting to

Catholicism, as her marriage to a French prince would have required (Osten, p. 300; Christophe Levantal, *Ducs et pairs et duchés-pairies laïques à l'époque moderne*, 1996, p. 832). She would remain unmarried.

[11] 'Mons. de Boswell Cavallier aus Englandt' ('nobleman from England') dined at the table of 'Serenissimus' and 'Serenissima', as recorded in the book of the *Fourier*, the official who oversaw the social arrangements of the court ('Fourierbuch', 4. Quartal).

[12] For whist, JB's favourite card game, see Journ. 27 June and n. 16.

[13] Christian Georg (1728–1805) von Helmoldt, *Kammerherr* (chamberlain), was also major of the life guards and had been appointed master of horse in 1763 (*Hochfürstl. Sachsen-Gothaischer Hof-Calender*, 1764; Hess, p. 88). In addition, he had literary aspirations, which would lead him to translate Pope's 'Eloise to Abelard' and several French plays (see Hamberger-Meusel, ii. 90). Sir Thomas Kennedy of Culzean, recognized as 9th Earl of Cassilis by the House of Lords in 1762, was one of JB's Ayrshire neighbours and a cousin of Lord Eglinton (*Scots Peer.* ii. 492 and iii. 456; *Comp. Bar.* iv. 316). He had talked to JB about the pleasures of being in Italy, where he had spent three years (Yale MS. M 108).

[14] The chief master of horse was Johann August von Benkendorf (1715–68), colonel of cavalry, commander of the horse guards, and director of the war commission from 1751 to 1768 (Hess, p. 371; *Hochfürstl. Sachsen-Gothaischer Hof-Calender*, 1764). Friedrich Karl von Forster, until recently chamberlain and privy counsellor of legation, had been named chief steward (Oberschenk) on 1 Mar. (ThStA Gotha, Geh. Arch. UU XXIV. 25). Von Schlegel is listed neither in the court calendar nor in the 'Fourierbuch', and has not been identified.

[15] Augusta Charlotte von Bülow had been appointed lady-in-waiting a year earlier (*Hochfürstl. Sachsen-Gothaischer Hof-Calender*, 1763). For the connection of Strelitz and Queen Charlotte Sophia, wife of George III, see Mem. dated 22 Sept. n. 1. Elizabeth (Dalrymple) Hamilton (c. 1733–79) had attracted JB during his first recorded jaunt (26 Sept., 'Harvest 1761', J 1.1). She was the widowed second wife of William Hamilton (1704–54), a Jacobite poet whose work JB admired (see *The Scottish Antiquary*, 1891, v. 87; 1900, xv. 214; Bailey, ii. 126 and n. 5; *Life* iii. 150).

[16] For George III's mother, Princess Augusta, see n. 7. Her favourite, the Scotsman John Stuart (1713–92), 3rd Earl of Bute,

had served as Prime Minister from May 1762 to Apr. 1763 (James Lee McKelvey, *George III and Lord Bute: The Leicester House Years*, 1973, pp. 21–23, 33–35, 42–43, 48–49). JB's monarchical enthusiasm was not shared, as he knew, by the radical John Wilkes, who had been accused of seditious libel for his article in *North Briton* No. 45 of Apr. 1763, in which he had attacked both Bute and George III . Wilkes had avoided trial by escaping to the Continent on Christmas Eve of that year and had been expelled from Parliament in Jan. (for a detailed account of these events, see Arthur H. Cash, *John Wilkes: The Scandalous Father of Civil Liberty*, 2006, pp. 65–163). JB had been introduced to Wilkes in London (Journ. 24 May 1763) and would later become friendly with him in Italy in spite of the differences in their characters and opinions (Journ. 18, 25 Feb., 6–19 Mar. 1765, see *Grand Tour II*, Heinemann pp. 53–61, McGraw-Hill pp. 50–58).

## Thursday 18 October

[MEM. dated Friday 19 Octr.] [Y]esterday at 12 saw Cabinet of Medals very nobly arranged in cases with the heads of the Emperors in Plaister bronzed. [A]bout 15000 pieces rich in Greek & Latin. 5 Tiberius — an Alexander with his own head — True Antiques round — counterfeit square. Olim non *frappé* ut nunc.[1] Many Modern many British several Scots — At dinner Prince of Philipstal. At 4 waited on La grande maitresse very affected. Elle s'ecoutoit — talk'd of daughter's death. Yet clever. Count Sapia grand Ecuier de la Lithuanie aller en Angleterre. Dieu m'en guarde — en [F]rance pour apprendre notre nouvel devoir &c [2] Then Garden. Then Ball in Domino — very gay & happy. This day at 8 Helmolt Rousseau.[3] At 10 *monnoye* & collect a Bibliothèque — Get *letters* today. Pray remember Caldwell and command till youre coll[4] again.

[J.] At twelve I went & saw the Duke's Cabinet of Medals. It is nobly arranged in cases with drawers in which are divisions for each medal. The heads of the Emperors in Plaister bronzed make a very suitable ornament to the Cabinet. It contains about 15000 pieces. It is very rich in Greek and Latin Medals, & contains some very curious ones. There is here an Alexander the Great with his own head, & five pieces of Tiberius.[5] The Gentleman who has the care of the Cabinet, was very intelligent.[6] He told me that he could discover counterfeit antiques because the veritable antiques were round in the edges as anciently they coined in a different manner from what they do now. I found here also several English coins, & a few old Scots ones.[7] This day the Hereditary Prince of Hesse Philipstall din'd at court.[8] After dinner M. de Schlegel carried me to wait on the *Grande Maîtresse*, who was a woman of beaucoup d'Esprit; but she talked with affected refined grief on the death of her only daughter & had the dissagreable manner to s'*ecouter* as a french author says.[9] It is a sad fault. I have it in some measure. All affected people have it, and as I was ill educated, I am obliged to affect more genteel manners and so have learnt the habit of playing a part.[10] Schlegel & I then went & saw the Garden, which is very well. All the German Princes are very magnificent and at every court you find things worth seeing. I indulged agreable reflections how I should talk of Saxe Gotha to the Princess of Wales, how I should remind her of the pretty *Zee Bergen* near the Palace, the romantic *Thuringer Valken* at a distance, as also the *Insuls Berg*[11] on the top of which is a

Cottage, but as it is very cold, one can go there only in the heat of the summer, and the house must be warmed some days before. At night we had a Ball at court. We were in Dominos, and I pleased myself with the idea of being in Spain.[12] M. le Grand Ecuier was kind enough to lend me a very genteel Domino, white with red Ribbands. We were very happy. I must observe that my Journal serves me not so much as a history as it serves me merely as a Reservoir of ideas. According to the humour which I am in when I read it, I judge of my past adventures, & not from what is realy recorded: If I am in gay spirits, I read an account of so much existence, & I think Sure I have been very happy. If I am gloomy I think sure I have past much uneasy time, or, at best, much insipid time. Thus I think without regard to the real fact as written.

[TEN LINES A DAY]
I wish my Muse thou couldst be more sedate
And at more leisure Poetry create
For, this same rapid rhiming much I fear
May make a very Sloven of my Dear.
May make thee learn to hobble up the hill
Like lumpish Johnie of my Father's Mill
Who trudges slow along the plashy Way
Each foot well loaded with a pound of clay[13]
No mayst thou ever march with bounding strides,
And, like thy Poet equal him that rides.

---

[1] 'Formerly, not struck as now', adapting the phrase 'olim non ... ut nunc', often used in Latin, especially by Horace, 'to contrast present decadence plangently with a golden past' (Prof. Gordon Williams, letter of 4 May 1998).

[2] Count Aleksander Michal Sapieha (1730–93), who belonged to an old Polish-Lithuanian family, had visited Gotha on 9 Oct. ('Fourierbuch', 4. Quartal; Joseph L. Wieczynski, The Modern Encyclopedia of Russian and Soviet History, 1976–90, lii. 216). He had been military commander (hetman) of Lithuania from 1763 but had left his country in fear of arbitrary government when Stanislas Augustus Poniatowsky (1732–98) was elected Stanislas II, King of Poland, on 7 Sept. of the present year (Adam Zamoyski, The Last King of Poland, pp. 98–100). The anecdote of Sapieha's loving liberty but preferring France to England was told to JB by Juliana von Buchwald (for whom see n. 9 below) and is recorded in Boswelliana, p. 232. Subsequently Sapieha would return to Lithuania, where he would become commander-in-chief of the entire militia in 1775 (Wielka Encyklopedia Powszechna PWN, 1962, x. 354).

[3] Jacques Auguste Rousseau (1729–1808 or 09), styled Hofrat (privy counsellor) and Verwalter (curator) of the ducal cabinet of coins and medals (To Formey, 6 June 1763, Nl. Formey, SSB-PK). Born in Berlin, he had come to Gotha to supervise the education of the Hereditary Prince and his brother, and was still attached officially to the former as 'Informator' (Hochfürstl. Sachsen-Gothaischer Hof-Calender, 1751–55, 1757–65). In 1767 Rousseau would become permanent keeper of medals, replacing his aging father-in-law Julius Carl Schläger (for whom see n. 6) as he informed Formey in his letter of 10 Oct. 1766 (Nl. Formey, SSB-PK; see also Behrendt Pick, Das Gothaer Münzkabinett, 1912, p. 6).

[4] Possibly a slip of the pen for 'cool'. The Rev. Samuel Caldwell was an Anglican Irishman in whom JB had confided in The Hague (Journ. 23 Apr., Holland, Heinemann p. 226 and n. 1, McGraw-Hill p. 231 and n. 6). He had advised against 'irregular love' (12 May, p. 243), had recommended cold baths to overcome gloom, and had tried to bolster JB's self-esteem (letter of 18 May, quoted in Holland, Heinemann pp. 241–42, McGraw-Hill pp. 247–48; Journ. 2 June, Holland, Heinemann p. 260, McGraw-Hill p. 267).

[5] The cabinet of coins and medals was situated on the second floor of the palace's east wing (Klebe, p. 54). It had been inaugurated in 1713 and housed several collections acquired during the previous hundred years. Placed between the cabinets designed especially for coins and medals were twelve busts of Roman emperors, which appeared to be bronze but were actually made of plaster (Pick, pp. 1–4). One of the rarest coins was the Alexander, unusual in depicting the bared head of Alexander the Great (356–23 B.C.) rather than a deity or mythological figure (Klebe, pp. 56–57). The five coins of the Emperor Tiberius (42 B.C.–37 A.D.), stepson and later son-in-law of Augustus, attest to the richness of the collection.

[6] Julius Carl Schläger (1706–86) was *Hofrat* (privy counsellor) and 'Antiquarius' in charge of the cabinet of coins and medals, as well as director of the ducal library (*Hochfürstl. Sachsen-Gothaischer Hof-Calender*, 1764). Born in Hanover, he had studied at the University of Helmstedt and had been appointed Professor of Greek and Oriental Philology there in 1736. He owed his position as keeper of medals, which he had held from 1744, to the fact that his long essay on the Alexander medal had come to the attention of Duke Friedrich III (Pick, p. 5; Gerhard Pachnicke, *Gothaer Bibliothekare*, 1958, p. 11). Once in Gotha, Schläger had compiled a useful catalogue of the coin collection (Heinrich Eberhard Paulus, *Über einige Merkwürdigkeiten der Herzoglichen Bibliothek zu Gotha*, 1788, p. 39). Recently he had undertaken the onerous task of replacing in their proper drawers all the medals that had been hidden away during the war (see his complaint in his letter to Formey, 20 Feb. 1763, Nl. Formey, SBB-PK).

[7] A curious medal, struck in Rome, showed Prince Charles Edward Stuart 'with his imaginary royal titles' on one side and his companion Clementina Walkinshaw on the reverse with the inscription 'Clementina Magnae Britanniae e.t.c. Regina' (Keyssler, i. 157). For these personages, see Journ. 6 Dec. n. 5.

[8] Wilhelm (1726–1810), Hereditary Prince of Hessen-Philippsthal, belonged to a collateral branch of the ruling house of Hessen-Kassel, being descended from the younger brother of the great Landgrave Karl (for whom see Journ. 24 Oct. n. 8). In addition, his sister, Charlotte Amalie (1730–1780), was the widow of Duchess Luise Dorothea's uncle, Anton Ulrich (1687–1763) of Sachsen-Meiningen (Isenburg, i. Tafeln 50, 102). Wilhelm had studied in Marburg and Geneva, and was serving in the army of the Netherlands, in which he attained the rank of general (Philippi, p. 164). He would succeed to his small dukedom in 1770 (Isenburg, i. Tafel 102).

[9] Juliana Francisca (von Neuenstein) von Buchwald (1707–89) was in charge of the duchess's household with the title of Oberhofmeisterin (roughly: high stewardess or chief lady-in-waiting, *Hochfürstl. Sachsen-Gothaischer Hof-Calender*, 1764). She was the closest friend of the Duchess and had been a key member of the order of 'les Hermites de bonne humeur' that had amused the court before the Seven Years' War (Vehse, xxix. 32–33). Known for her intellectual interests and her salon, Juliana had gained the friendship of notable men including Frederick of Prussia and Voltaire (Friedrich Wilhelm Gotter, *Zum Andenken der Frau von Buchwald*, Gotha, 1790, pp. 19–45; Osten, pp. 369–84; Rudolf Schlösser, 'Eine Frauengestalt aus dem geistigen Leben des vorigen Jahrhunderts', *Leipziger Zeitung*, Wissenschaftliche Beilage, 2 Feb. 1893, p. 55). The Duchess characterized her as being 'tendre, bonne et ardente amie' but as having more wit than heart, being easily bored, and unleashing torrents of politeness on those she wished to dismiss ('Schilderungen einiger Personen aus der Umgebung der Herzogin Luise Dorothea', FLB Gotha, Chart. B 1678, pp. 3–5). Frau von Buchwald's daughter, Johanna Sophia Louise Friderica, Countess von Werthern (1740–64), had died in Jan. by choking on a bone (Schlösser, p. 55). She had been married for less than two years to Johann George Heinrich (1735–90), Count von Werthern, chamberlain and *Ober-Hofmeister* (chief major domo) of the duchess of Gotha (Lehndorff, 29 July 1766, *Dreissig Jahre: Nachträge*, ii. 26; *Fortgesetzte Neue Genealogisch-Historische Nachrichten*, 1765, Pt. 37, p. 120; for dates of von Werthern, see Kneschke, ix. 543).

[10] For JB's occasional sense of social inferiority, see Journ. 27 June and n. 6.

[11] Three well-known landmarks: 'Seebergen', a wooded upward slope flanked by one of the two Seebergs 2 miles (3.2 km) southeast of Gotha; the Falkenstein (lit. 'falcons' stone'), a picturesque porphyry rock about 12.5 miles (20.1 km) away, but too low at 328 feet (100 m) to be visible 'at a distance', hence possibly 'Thüringer Wald', the famous Thuringian woods as rendered in *Grand Tour I*, Heinemann p. 139 n. 3, McGraw-Hill p. 143 n. 2; and the more distant Inselsberg (3,005 feet, or 915.9 m) notable for its porphyry summit (Karl and

Ingrid Zagora, *Thüringer Wald*, 1977, pp. 342–43, 580; Baedeker, *Northern Germany*, 1925, pp. 255, 271, 277, and *Thüringen*, 1920, pp. 56, 82).

[12] JB associated the masquerade costume —a long gown, hood, and mask—with Spain, where it had originated (OED, s.v. 'domino'). Fifty-one persons attended this ball ('Fourierbuch', 4. Quartal, 18 Oct.). For JB's interest in Spain, see Journ. 23 June and n. 4, and App. 1.

[13] A rare report of a childhood memory, either of a work horse (suggested by F. A. Pottle, *Grand Tour I*, Heinemann p. 140 n. 1,

McGraw-Hill p. 144 n. 3) or of a farm labourer, possibly John Wyllie, who had worked on the Auchinleck estate for many years and whom JB would have observed during summer visits from Edinburgh (see From Bruce, 8 July 1763, *Corr.* 8, p. 5 n. 5; To Bruce, 6 Jan. 1784, *Corr.* 8, p. 78 n. 3). Wyllie is mentioned three times in the *Book of Company* (29 Dec. 1782; 30 Sept., 2 Oct. 1783). The place was presumably Auchinleck Mill on the Lugar Water, the mill of the barony about a mile (c. 1.6 km) from Auchinleck House (*Corr.* 8, p. 2 n. 10).

## Friday 19 October

[MEM. dated Saturday 20 October.] Yesterday You saw the Library. Very large some curious pieces. Was drest in velvet suit of five colours. Princesse said M. Boswell — mais vous etes Beau & bid you put on black Ribband & have other Sword-knot — quite easy — a good Girl. Had just the ideas you intended for Saxe Gotha. This day dress write Johnston — & at 11 Library & mark Anecdotes of Bible & roman designs. Get *Money* from Mint. At one wait on Prince Hered. Ask them all what you shall say to Princess of Wales — & ask Duke to give you a mark that you have seen him well. Twill please her. Ask as favour something that She & he knows. Get Letters, one also for Cassel. Correspond with Thungen. At 5 Be ready. Keep mind composed[.]

[Y]oure to consult Rousseau on diseased mind.[1]

[J.] I went and saw the Duke's Library, which is very large, in excellent order, and contains some curious pieces. There is a french Book entitled La Truantise (ie in old fr: Pauvreté) de l'Ame, where there is an Allegorical picture of a poor soul which comes to receive from the Holy church the Alms of grace. The Soul is painted as a Woman stark naked who presents herself before five or six sturdy Priests and holds a Bag to put their Alms in. The Book is in Manuscript.[2] There is also a German Bible which formerly belonged to the Elector of Bavaria. It is a manuscript written an Age before the Reformation. It is in two volumes. The first contains the Historical Books of the Old Testament. It is probable that there has been another Volume in which the rest of the Old Testament has been written. This first Volume is decorated with paintings in an odd taste, but finely illuminated, & richly gilded in the manner of that Ancient art which is now totally lost. Some of the designs are truly ludicrous. When Adam & Eve perceive that they are naked, God comes in the figure of an old man, with a pair of Breeches for Adam & a Petticoat for Eve. One would allmost imagine that the Painter intended to laugh at the Scriptures; But in those days it was not the mode to mock at the Religion of their country. The Genius which is now employed to suport Infidelity, was then employed to support Piety. The Imagination which now furnishes licentious sallies was then fertile in sacred Emblems. Sometimes Superstition rendered them extravagant and

sometimes weakness made them ridiculous as I have now given an example. The second Volume contains the New Testament complete. It is
illuminated by the same hand as the first Volume, as far as the history of
Our Saviour's passion in the fourteenth Chapter of Saint Mark. It has been
reckoned that the gold employed in illuminating the two Volumes may
amount to the value of a thousand Ducats. It is probable that the ancient
Painter has died when he had got as far as the fourteenth of Mark. The
Duke of Bavaria has however taken care that the work should not be left
imperfect. At the end of this volume the arms of Bavaria are painted, and
there is an Inscription bearing that Otho Henry Duke of Bavaria caused
the remaining part of the sacred Oracles to be adorned by a more modern
Painter Anno 1530–2 — for it took two years to finish it. The Work of the
last Painter has not the advantage to be illuminated with gold in the
ancient manner, as was the work of the former Painter. But, the Modern
has been a much superiour Genius. His Designs are remarkably well
conceived, & executed with accuracy & taste. His colours are fresh and
lively. He has however now & then fallen into little Absurditys. The
Evangelist tells us that when Mary Magdalene found our Saviour after his
Resurrection, she supposed him to be the Gardener: for which reason the
Painter has drawn Christ holding a Spade. Now Mary supposed him to be
the Gardener because he was in a Garden. Had he had a Spade in his hand
it was impossible to doubt of it. But how suppose that Jesus had a Spade?
Upon the whole, this Bible is one of the noblest Books that I have ever
seen.[3] There is here another remarkable Book, 'Magnum Opus continens
Nummismata Imperatorum Romanorum a Jacobo de Strada Mantuano
elaboratum Anno 150.'[4] This Work was executed by order of the Count de
Fugger whose family was in Germany what the family of the Medici was in
Italy. The Work consists of 31 Volumes in each of which is from 300 to 500
leaves. For each leaf the Count de Fugger paid a ducat so that at the least
it must have cost 9300 ducats. It would seem that there have been more
copies of this work, for some of the first volumes are to be found in the
Librarys of Vienna & Dresden.[5] The Library-Keeper at Gotha is a very
learned man, simple quiet and obliging.[6] I was this day drest in a suit of
flowered Velvet of five colours. I had designed to put on this suit first at
Saxe-Gotha. I did so. It is curious; but I had here the very train of ideas
which I expected to have. At night the Princess made me come to the table
where she sat at cards, & said Monsieur Boswell — mais, vous etes beau.
She is a good lively Girl. I am allready treated here with much ease. My
time passes pleasantly on. Between dinner and evening court I read the
Nouvelle Heloise.[7] I write, I think.

[TEN LINES A DAY.]
Two things there are which while I am awake
I'd in most cases rather give than take
What these two things are would the Doctor know
One is advice, the other is a Blow.
The first indeed may sometimes do us good;

So also may the last, if not too rude.
But if I draw with an impartial Pen
The usual tongues & sticks of mortal men,
I fancy Doctor you will hardly say
Boswell, be quiet: You are mad today.

[1] MS. 'youre … mind' written along the left margin. For the cause of JB's feelings of guilt, see 'Ébauche de ma vie', Yale MS. L 1107, App. 2, III.A, and Journ. 14 Dec. and n. 17.

[2] The library, founded in 1642 by Ernst der Fromme and greatly extended by the present duke's father, held about 50,000 volumes at this time (Gerhard Pachnicke, *Gothaer Bibliothekare*, 1958, p. 4; Klebe, pp. 71–72). *La Truandise de l'âme*, a literal translation of Johannes Gerson's *Tractat de mendicitate spirituali*, n.d., was an untitled MS. of 272 folio pages (136 numbered) that had belonged to Philippe de Clèves (fl. 1478). The figure of Poverty appears as a naked winged woman on the opening page (FLB Gotha, Memb. I 118; Friedrich Jacobs and Friedrich August Ukert, *Beiträge zur ältern Litteratur der Herzogl. öffentlichen Bibliothek zu Gotha*, ii [1836], pp. 168–72).

[3] The artists who worked on this magnificent Bible, written in Middle High German, are unknown. The last miniatures, completed in about 1530, had been commissioned by Heinrich Otto (1502–59), Elector Palatine, Duke of Bavaria (Klebe, p. 73). The manuscript had been acquired by Gotha in 1632 when Munich was captured during the Thirty Years War (Jacobs and Ukert, ii. 38 n. 1).

[4] MS. Date left incomplete by JB.

[5] This elaborate multi-volume manuscript,

illustrating coins of the Roman emperors, bears the title *Magnum ac novum Opus Continens descriptionem Vitæ imaginum, numismatum omnium tam Orientalium quam Occidentalium Imperatorum ac Tyrannorum, cum collegis coniugibus liberisque suis, usque ad Carolu V Imperatorem*. The first volume is dated 1550 (FLB Gotha, Chart. A 2175), presumably the year JB meant to record. The artist, Jacopo de Strada (1507–88), had combined his talent for drawing with a knowledge of numismatics. A native of Mantua, he had worked for Johann Jakob Fugger (1516–75) from about 1544 to 1556. Fugger belonged to the sixth generation of a family of merchant princes (see Thieme-Becker, xxxii. 145–46; Günter Ogger, *Kauf dir einen Kaiser: die Geschichte der Fugger*, 1978, with a genealogy on its inside cover). In paying one gold Gulden per page, he had made this 'perhaps the costliest book in the world' (Klebe, p. 55).

[6] Presumably Gottfried Christian Freiesleben (1716–74), who served as second librarian from 1740 to 1774. Called 'overworked and underpaid', he was publishing descriptions of the library's holdings and had written French poems praised by Voltaire (Pachnicke, pp. 10–11).

[7] JB was preparing himself for his hoped-for meeting with Rousseau, whose *Julie, ou la nouvelle Héloïse* had been published in 1761.

## Saturday 20 October

[MEM. dated Sunday 21 October.] Yesterday was again in Library, quite in studious humour. The keeper a good quiet learned man. After dinner took leave — They said Je suis faché. Plain people. Then master of mint ugly dog but civil. Rousseau did good. This day <march.>[1]

[J.] Rousseau gives me an enthusiasm of feeling which I thought was all over with poor melancholy Boswell. Thus agitated my heart expands itself & feels the want of an object to love. Zelide is next my heart. She presents herself to my Imagination with all her advantages. I see the daughter of one of the first nobles of Holland, I see a foreign Lady of Genius science and fortune. I see the Amiable Companion of my winter at Utrecht, who might make an amiable Companion for life. But then again I recollect that She studies Metaphysics and Mathematics. That She despises the common affairs of life, which form the Sum total of terrestrial happiness; that her Imagination is so strong that there is no depending upon her conduct, and that her constitution is naturally bad, and has been rendered worse by an irregular Education. My heart then starts back from such an Alliance, and rests contracted within itself.[2] It is uneasy to be so. Fancy comes kindly to it's releif, and amuses it with pleasing pictures of tender felicity with a Spanish or an English Lady. Thus flows my Existence at present. As to the future part of it, I can as yet say nothing. I may be thrown into Situations which may give me quite a new turn of thinking, make me quite a new man. I have allready experienced this in some degree. Since I parted from Mr. Samuel Johnson at Harwich, what a variety of minds have I had! This day I was in excellent frame I had a cordial regard for the worthy court of Saxe-Gotha. I must remark a curious form here. Before and after dinner, the Marischal posts himself opposite the Duke and Dutchess, and at his side has one of the Pages. The Marischal makes a signal, and the Page says Grace. I think this form very decent: But, I could wish that their Highnesses would not talk, but remain in decent silence.[3] We dined allways in a large old room. There were in it two Alcoves opposite each other. In the one was the Furnace, and in the other a Buffet which by candle-light had an excellent effect. The table here at dinner was excellent. At Supper it was moderate. After dinner I took leave of the Dutchess, who said 'Je suis fachée que vous allez nous quitter. Peutêtre vous reviendrez un jour'. I also took leave of the Ladies of the court. Mademoiselle Slotiem said 'Je crois vous etes liant'. Her Grandmother Madame de Rickslepen educated the Princess of Wales.[4] I am somewhat of a Virtuoso.[5] Wherever I am, I make a collection of the silver specie struck the year in which I have been in the country. I went & waited on the Master of the Mint who had been in [E]ngland, and spoke english tollerably.[6] He supplied me with new coins, & treated me with good Rhenish Wine. He was one of your old staunch Germans. How curious is it to think that every Man is of infinite importance to himself, & yet groupes of Individuals serve only to furnish amusing speculation for me. I then returned and took leave of the Duke, & of the Gentlemen. They were all extremely kind. The Grand Ecuier said 'Vous devez rester plus long tems. Vous savez que vous êtes bienvenu ici'. I went to my Inn, undrest, & wrote till four in the morning. Slept only two hours.

[TEN LINES A DAY.]
Thy bread, Westphalia, thy brown bread I sing,
Bread which might make the dinner of a King.
Tho' one of those whom Englishmen call dogs,
One whose nice palate had been us'd to frogs,
Could not forsooth digest a stuff so coarse,
But call'd it good provision for his horse.
An Etymologist who runs[7] his nose
Into old holes that Time has tried[8] to close
May learn that Niccol was the[9] horse's name.
Hence the Bread's title Bon pour Niccol came.[10]

[1] Conjectural; word squeezed in at the right margin of the MS.

[2] JB had expressed similarly ambivalent feelings about Belle de Zuylen in his letter to her of 9 July; see Journ. of the same date, n. 4.

[3] Although the Duke and Duchess seem not to have taken religious observances seriously, they were practising Lutherans (see Gertraud Zaepernick, 'Die Anfänge der Aufklärung im Herzogtum Sachsen-Gotha-Altenburg und Cyprians Stellung dazu', *Ernst Salomon Cyprian*, 1996, pp. 211–12).

[4] Eleonora Dorothea von Schlotheim had been lady-in-waiting to the Duchess and the young princesses for seven years and would continue to serve at least for six more years (her name is inserted in the Duke's hand in the *Hochfürstl. Sachsen-Gothaischer Hof-Calender* of 1757 and appears annually in print to 1770). Mme de Rüxleben (first name and dates not found) had accompanied Princess Augusta to London in 1736 on the eve of her wedding to the Prince of Wales, but had been sent home in the same year for persuading her mistress to attend German Lutheran services rather than the Anglican ones at which a member of the royal house was expected to worship (John, Lord Hervey, *Some Materials Towards Memoirs of the Reign of George II*, ed. Romney Sedgwick, 1931, ii. 560–61). JB sat at the same table with two sisters of the same name and presumably of the same old aristocratic family, prominent in Thuringia and Hesse, who were ladies-in-waiting at the court of Gotha ('Fourierbuch', 4. Quartal, 19 Oct.; Kneschke, vii. 620–21). Their diminutive stature inspired JB's *bon mot*: 'il faut les prendre comme des Alouettes par la demidouzaine' (*Boswelliana*, p. 232, and M 282).

[5] 'One who has a special interest in, or taste for, the fine arts; a student or collector of antiquities, natural curiosities or rarities' (OED, s.v. 'virtuoso', 2).

[6] The master of the mint, Ludwig Chris-tian Koch (1717–92), had been in London from 1746 to 1750 as part of his professional training. After working with his father, Johann Christian Koch (1680–1742), who had preceded him as master of the mint, he had spent six years on travels with financial support from the Duke, and had observed the mints in various German states, Denmark, and France as well as England. He had been appointed to his present post immediately after his return (Wolfgang Steguweit, *Geschichte der Münzstätte Gotha*, 1987, pp. 113, 121–37).

The mint was housed at two locations close to or within the west wing of the palace: in small buildings at the moat used for smelting, rolling, and cutting the metals, and in rooms on the wing's ground floor used primarily for stamping the impress (Steguweit, pp. 62–63, 125–26). JB would take his collection of German coins with him on his travels, leaving them in his large trunk in Leghorn while he went to Corsica (M 112, see *Catalogue*, i. 76). He brought them back to Auchinleck and made them part of his collection of medals and coins, which would be stored in the ebony cabinet at Auchinleck and eventually moved to Malahide Castle (*Pride and Negligence*, p. 66).

[7] MS. 'pokes' written above 'runs'

[8] MS. 'dark' written above 'old'; 'which' above 'that'; 'wish'd' above 'tried'

[9] MS. 'his' written above 'the'

[10] JB appears to be versifying an anecdote concerning a Frenchman who found pumpernickel, the coarse Westphalian rye bread, so indigestible that it was only 'bon pour' his horse Nickel (Nugent, ii. 80, cited in *Grand Tour I*, Heinemann p. 145 n. 1, McGraw Hill p. 149 n. 8). Another explanation associates a goblin called Nickel with 'Pumpern', flatulence, the supposed effect of eating this bread (Duden, *Das Grosse Wörterbuch*, 1980, v. 2068; Brockhaus, xv. 260). The actual etymology of 'pumpernickel' is unknown (OED).

## Sunday 21 October

[MEM. dated Monday 22 Octr.] Yesterday rose at six after two hours sleep.[1] Found church & candles many good people — had the sweetest flow of blood the gayest fancy; but knew not how. Two miles to Langsaltz. Dismounted from Chariot drest — Sent to Grand Maitre & in a moment court. Made water <&>c.[2] This is business. This is shooting a Princess flying — good decent table all [G]ermans — sat by her by aunt of King — moderate quiet creature [—] took leave had coach. Parson came showed Garden poor — field of skirmish Saxons taken.[3] Was fatigued — went to rest — Prayed God. Was sensible that disease was on you & swore neither to speak Infidelity nor act loosely till youve seen Rousseau. 1 month no hard matter.[4]

[K]eep all papers in little separate parcels.[5]

[J.] I got up at six. I heard the noise of an Organ. I entered the great church.[6] I found there a numerous congregation, a great many well drest people, lustres lighted. This morning Worship had a fine effect. I then mounted my old freind the Post-Waggon. I was in the sweetest spirits, 'Tis strange that want of sleep should produce such an effect. But, so I find it. I drove two miles to Langensalza, where the Waggon was to stop all day. I dismounted, went to my Inn and sent a card to the Grand maitre of the Princesse Frederique of Saxe Gotha Douarrière de Saxe Weissenfels a house now sunk into that of the Elector.[7] I only notified that a Scots Gentleman wished to be presented to the Princess. The Grand Maitre sent immediately to know my rank, & was told I was a Baron: upon which I was asked to come to his house at twelve, & afterwards go to court. I went accordingly to him: he spoke only German. He carried me in a coach to court.[8] I found the Princess very civil. I was quite the man of fashion. I was placed by her Highness. The table was plentifull and the Servants numerous. She is pretty old. She has public table only three days a-week. She has her Dame d'honneur. We had Officers & other honest Germans.[9] I was here quite at my ease in the house of the sister of the Princess of Wales and the Aunt of my King.[10] After dinner I took leave politely, saying I should be happy to tell the Princess of Wales that I had the honour of paying my respects here. I had one of her Highness's coaches to conduct me to my Inn. Was not this a rare adventure? I called this 'Shooting a Princess flying.' I was indeed the Person in motion, and her Highness the person at rest. I was in a moment again in my travelling dress. Her Highness's Chaplain who had dined with us waited upon me, and carried me to take a walk & see the town. It is the dirtiest that I ever saw. Its streets are overflowed with liquid mud: And with difficulty you step along a narrow path on each side. The Chaplain was a laughing fellow tollerably knowing.[11] At six we parted. I was somewhat splenetic & dreary apprehensions as to my conduct distrest me. I swore solemnly neither to talk as an Infidel nor to enjoy a woman before seeing Rousseau. So, I am bound a month at least. I was very heavy-headed from having had no sleep last night; & as I did not know when the Waggon might set out, I threw myself on the bed leaving orders to Jacob to call me. I slept till eleven, & got up unhinged; But a glass of cold water[12] & a walk up & down the room set me to rights. By long study I shall be quite master of Spleen. Between eleven & twelve at night I set out.

[TEN LINES A DAY.]
While metaphysics rack[13] the sickly brain
What mem'ry is can any Sage explain
Can any Sage with any clearness tell
How is produc'd what we perceive so well
If human Souls are of an Essence pure

How fix ideas in[14] them to endure
And If too material canst thou not [M]unroe
The little cells of our ideas show[15]
Ah no — for here we ever ever find
That all Philosophers alike are blind.

[1] MS. 'after ... sleep', an interlineation.

[2] MS. 'made ... <&>c', an interlineation written above 'court'—a rare mention in JB's journal of such physical necessity.

[3] On 14 Feb. 1761 the Saxon army had been badly beaten by Hanoverian troops led by Fieldmarshal August Friedrich von Spörken (1698–1776), for whom see ADB, s.v. 'Spörken'; for the battle, see Ann. Reg. 1761, i. 10.

[4] MS. 'Was sensible ... matter' scored out by a modern hand.

[5] MS. 'keep ... parcels' written along the left margin.

[6] Very likely the Margarethenkirche, a large, austere hall church begun in 1494 and renovated several times since then. The chief church of the town, it occupied one end of the Neumarkt close to several inns (Volkland, ii. 25–27, 69–70; see 16 Oct. n. 7).

[7] Friederike (1715–75), second wife and widow of Johann Adolf of Saxe-Weissenfels (1685–1746), had no surviving male offspring, her five sons having died in childhood. Hence the tiny dukedom, which had belonged to the Saxe-Weissenfels since 1656, had reverted to Saxony after the death of her husband (Isenburg, i. Tafel 57).

[8] The grand maître at this time was von Zeng (first name and dates not found, ment. in Carl Friedrich Göschel, Chronik der Stadt Langensalz, 1844, p. 178). That he took JB to court by coach suggests the Duchess was not in her chief residence, the fortress-like old Dryburg at the centre of town, but in the smaller, more comfortable Friederiken palace on the outskirts (G. and H. Schütz, Chronik der Stadt Langensalza, 1900, pp. 268, 277).

[9] Neither the lady in waiting nor the officers and other Germans at table have been identified.

[10] Like Augusta, Princess of Wales, she was the daughter of Friedrich II of Saxe-Gotha (Isenburg, i. Tafel 49).

[11] Not identified.

[12] MS. Coldwater

[13] MS. 'bruise' above 'rack'

[14] MS. 'impressions on' written above 'ideas in'

[15] By 'cells' JB here means 'compartments' of the brain or 'pigeon-holes' for receiving knowledge (OED, s.v. 'cell', 11.c). Alexander Monro (1697–1767), also known as Monro Primus to distinguish him from his son of the same name and profession, was Professor of Anatomy at Edinburgh University and author of the widely used Anatomy of the Human Bones and Nerves, 3rd ed. 1741 (DSB, ix. 480; Rex E. Wright-St. Clair, 1964, pp. 34–35, 161–63). In this work he gives a detailed description of the bones and nerves—that is, the material aspects of the body—but throws no light on the possible seat of the memory.

JB may have heard Monro at the Select Society of Edinburgh, where he was a popular speaker (H. D. Erlam, 'Alexander Monro, primus', repr. from University of Edinburgh Journal, summer 1954, p. 89). For JB's membership in this elite group, see Journ. 9 Nov. and n. 13. JB's continuing interest in memory is shown in his letters to J. F. W. Jerusalem (c. 16 Nov., see Journ. 11 Aug. n. 10) and to JJ (18 Dec. 1765, Corr. 1, pp. 196–97).

## Monday 22 October

[MEM. dated Tuesday 23 October.] [Y]esterday sad travelling. At night near Helse down Hill — Waggon in hole — could not get out dreadfull rain — Postil went for help — Sat two hours & walk'd — in sad rain — quite campagne[1] [—] quote Blunkett lines.[2] They would have staid like Beasts[3] — Quite in good temper — can do any thing. At last Village sent watcher — to straw.

If you escape this youre strong indeed & may go safe to Suisse coverd —[4]

[J.] Sad travelling. About twelve at night as[5] the Waggon was rumbling down a hill, one of it's wheels fell into a deep hole, & there we stuck fast &

had allmost been overturned. We could not get the horses to pull out the Waggon. Luckily we were within a little of our Station the Village of Helse.[6] The Postilion went to bring help. He returned with a man & a horse. Still it would not do. He went once more. He was an old creature & mighty slow. It was a dreadfull rain. We remained upon the hill more than two hours. It was quite serving a Campaign. The Postilion I do beleive would have allowed us to remain asoaking till day-break. But, at last we walked to the Village, & sent a man to watch our Baggage. I kept my temper. I went to bed and slept pretty sound.

[TEN LINES A DAY.]
Behold Ye Hessians! from the Shire of Ayr
A Laird whom your Moustaches have made stare
While a meer child, nor yet advanc'd to taw,
You in Edina's ancient town he saw
When the[7] Rebellion you came o'er to quell
And send forsooth the monster back to hell.[8]
While Arthur-seat[9] resounded with your drums
I saw you buying Breeches for your Bums.
But with your Breeches you were not more[10] stout
Than the bold Highlanders who went[11] without.

---

[1] MS. 'camagne'
[2] An allusion to 'the blanket of the dark' (*Macbeth*, I. v. 53; see Ten Lines, 23 Oct. and n. 15).
[3] JB appears to be congratulating himself for leaving the scene while the other passengers would have 'stayed like beasts'.
[4] MS. 'If you … coverd' written along the left margin, a reference to a closed wagon, unlike the open one he just left (see Journ. 27 Oct.).
[5] MS. 'as' inserted at the beginning of the line.
[6] For this part of his travels, JB was taking the regional 'Hesse Post' owned by the landgraves of Hessen-Kassel (see Exp. Acct. 21 Oct., App. 3 and n. 62). He had come from Langensalza by way of Mühlhausen, Wanfried, and Bischhausen (Exp. Acct. 22 Oct., App. 3). Helsa was just under 9 miles (14.5 km) from his next destination, Kassel.
[7] MS. 'a' written above 'the'

[8] Approaching Hesse, JB records his childhood memories of the Hessian troops who had come to Scotland to help suppress Prince Charles Edward Stuart's Jacobite uprising. Six thousand men were reported to have arrived in Edinburgh in Feb. 1746 (*Scots Mag.* 1746, viii. 84–85). JB recalls the Hessians even though he was only six years old at the time and so too young even to play with marbles (OED, s.v. 'taw' *v.*[2]). Edina is a poetic version of the Gaelic name for Edinburgh.
[9] The 'lofty romantic mountain' on the outskirts of town was so dear to JB that he had bowed to it ceremoniously on leaving for London in 1762 (see Journ. 15 Nov. 1762).
[10] MS. 'so' written above 'more'
[11] MS. 'As' written above 'Than', 'were' above 'went'. The highlanders were reputed to be bare-bottomed under their kilts but fierce fighters nonetheless.

---

## Tuesday 23 October

[MEM. dated Wednesday 24 Octr.] Up at 7 — out of order affraid of fever [—] drove on to Cassel — Stockholm good — Inn Landgrave from home.[1] 1st cold marischal because maid went with letter [—] wrote all night — feard disease took exercise [—] to bed[2] — This day up — Journ. Swear moderate like Temp[le] &

few letts — Send to La Porte. Get Rousseau.
Get Eloise from Laporte³

[J.] My last night's Adventure had fermented my blood. I dreaded a fever.
We drove thro' a pretty, wild country to Cassel. As I approached it, I
thought of the last war.⁴ It's three divisions situated on Eminent ground
have a good effect. I put up at the Stockholm a very good Inn.⁵ I sent
immediatly to the Grand Maréchal du Rösey.⁶ My Reception was cold: for,
a Girl went with my Card, & he asked if I had no Servant—. One perceives
in trifles the stile of a court as the character of a man. He sent me notice
that the Landgrave was out of town, but that he would let me know when
his Highness returned. I past the evening at home, & wrote a good deal. I
was curious to see the Landgrave. After the King of [F]rance he is the
Prince in Europe who tires the most. My Chairman told Jacob that his
Highness used to say 'Oh! Ik hab lang syde. Der Syde valt meer lang.'⁷ He
said too, that since the Prince changed his Religion he had no peace, and
that he would willingly give up Popery, but his Regence will not allow him.
In short that they will oblige him to be damned. What absurd ideas enter
into the heads of the Vulgar!⁸

[TEN LINES A DAY]
Last night as Waggon down a hill did rowl,
One of it's wheels went⁹ plump into a hole
By this Sad Accident were we stuck¹⁰ fast
While night her thickest darkness cast¹¹
O had her darkness been that Blanket good
For which old Shakespear's stile has been thought rude¹²
Then had I been defended¹³ from the rain,
Then had I honour'd Shakespear's wildest¹⁴ Brain
And against thee great Johnson giv'n my vote
For an expression which kept dry my coat.¹⁵

¹ MS. 'home', an interlineation.
² MS. 'feard … bed' scored out by a
modern hand.
³ MS. 'Get … Laporte' written along the
left margin. Jean-Jacques de la Porte (1721–
78) was one of three pastors of the French
congregation in Kassel (Hochfürstlich-Hessen-
Casselscher Staats- u. Adress-Calender, 1764,
p. 108; dates from his tombstone in the old
cemetery of the Lutherkirche, later moved to
the main cemetery of Kassel; information
from H.-J. Reuter of Kassel). He was a
second-generation French Huguenot, born
in Hameln, where his father had been pastor
(see Die französischen Gemeinden in Kassel,
ed. Hugo Dreusicke, Forschungen zur hessischen Familien- und Heimatkunde 45
[1962], p. 348). Because of his French roots,
he could be expected to have a copy of

Rousseau's novel, which JB had been reading
in Gotha (see Journ. 19 Oct. and n. 7).
⁴ Hessen-Kassel had been drawn into the
Seven Years' War even though Landgrave
Wilhelm VIII (1682–1760) had hoped to
maintain his country's neutrality. He had
had long-standing ties with the British,
which included sending troops in return for
financial subsidies, and so the Austrians had
imposed on him the formal ban (Reich-
sacht) of the Holy Roman Empire, whereupon their allies, the French, had occupied
Kassel in the summers of 1757 and 1758 and
for a longer period from July 1760. It had
become the site of major campaigns in 1761
and 1762, and had been retaken by the
Hanoverians on 1 Nov. 1762, only two days
before the signing of the preliminary peace
treaty between England and France ended

the war (*Ann. Reg.* 1762, p. 234; see Hugo Brunner, *Geschichte der Residenzstadt Cassel*, 1913, pp. 258–84; Both, *Wilhelm VIII*, pp. 108–23).

⁵ The town had spread out over three inclines: the Altstadt and Oberneustadt on one side of the river Fulda, the Unterneustadt on the other side (Gunter Schweikhart, 'Die Stadtentwicklung Kassels bis zum 18. Jahrhundert', *Stadtplanung und Stadtentwicklung in Kassel im 18. Jahrhundert*, 1983, pp. 7–8). JB's inn, owned by J. G. Holtzschue, was situated in the Mittelgasse of the Altstadt (*Hochfürstlich-Hessen-Casselscher Staats- u. Adress-Calender*, 1764, p. 118).

⁶ Alexandre Eugène du Rosey (1705–79), chief marshal (*Oberhofmarschall*) and privy counsellor since 1763, had been in Hessian service as chief chamberlain (*Oberkämmerer*) since 1752 (Wilhelm Strieder, *Grundlage zu einer hessischen Gelehrten-und-Schriftsteller Geschichte*, 1787, repr. 1986, vii. 24 n). Possibly he came from the Valais, Swiss home of the du Roseys (DHBS, v. 558). For Madame de Wintzingerode, see Journ. 24 Oct. and n. 3.

⁷ Friedrich II (1720–85) had become landgrave of Hessen-Kassel on the death of his father in 1760 and had returned to Kassel in Jan. 1763 at the end of the Seven Years' War. His characteristic comment, that time was heavy on his hands (in standard German spelling, 'Ich habe lange Zeit. Die Zeit fällt mir lang'), meant that he was bored. The French King, said to be even more easily bored, was Louis XV (1710–74). The 'chairman', one of the two bearers who carried a one-person sedan chair on poles, has not been identified further.

⁸ Friedrich's conversion to Catholicism and its consequences evidently still puzzled some of his subjects. When it was revealed, his enraged father, a staunch Calvinist, had forced him to sign a stringent formal agreement, the so-called *Assekurationsakte* (1754), which committed him to retaining Calvinism as the state religion of Hesse when he came to rule, in effect relinquishing his princely right to determine the religion of his realm. He had abided by this agreement, and he had joined the Prussian side during the Seven Years' War, chiefly because he admired Frederick II. Although there is no evidence that he himself wished to revert to Protestantism, it is not clear who might have prevented him. Perhaps *regence* refers to the Hessian privy council (*Geheime Rats-Collegio*) and ministry (*Geheime Ministerium*), appointed by Wilhelm VIII to make political, economic, and religious decisions without Friedrich's consent. Or perhaps the term refers to the Protestant powers, including England, Prussia, Sweden, Denmark, and the Netherlands, whom Wilhelm had persuaded to guarantee Hesse's continued Protestantism (Hartwig, pp. 40–59). Any of these quasi-regents might have feared a change that could have undermined their power.

⁹ MS. 'went' written over another, deleted word.

¹⁰ MS. 'misfortune' written above 'sad accident', 'we were all kept' above 'were we stuck'

¹¹ MS. 'monstrous' written above 'darkness cast' but presumably an alternative for 'thickest'

¹² MS. 'call'd' and 'rude' written above 'thought'

¹³ MS. 'we all' written above 'I', 'cover'd' above 'defended'

¹⁴ MS. 'strangest' written above 'wildest'

¹⁵ A witty literalizing of the passage in *Macbeth*, I. v. 50–54:

> Come thick night!
> And pall thee in the dunnest smoke of hell,
> That my keen knife see not the wound it makes;
> Nor Heav'n peep through the blanket of the dark,
> To cry, Hold, hold!

SJ had criticized Shakespeare for introducing low, commonplace diction ('dun', 'knife', 'peeping through a blanket') in this speech, which SJ attributed to Macbeth in *The Rambler* (No. 168, 26 Oct. 1751) but which is actually made by Lady Macbeth.

## Wednesday 24 October

[MEM. dated Thursday 25 Octr.] Yesterday you waited on Gr. Marechal du Rosey old genteel man — found recommend necessary — as he was cold till he heard madame de Winsingerode — Told Avanturier fils du Duc Hamilton quoique pas en equipage point de domestique — seulement une Ridingcoat — On l'equipe on le presentoit — on trouvoit que cetoit ni anglois ni ecossois. Then *La Porte* who came to you at 4. Saw maison de models — singular & pretty [—] cascade noble — Orangerie. Before it Statues some Antiques in bronze — some new in white marble from Italy Venus de Med — parnassus. Boys & grapes. Other Boys sweet — Apes — Parrots &c. Grotto where Landgrave devot — La Porte with him at Bains — received letter [—] gave him — ministre rude — de changer relig[.] & croire fausse — mal — no answer — prepar'd with *dates &c*. David & Peter pieux — mais un &c — mais ils avaient¹ repentis — Oui il faut les imiter dans leur² piete &c. Superstit[.] prayed Virg<in> doublement obligé accorde Bien f<ai>t & pour une telle prierre[.]

[J.] I waited on M. du Rôsey, & found him an elderly Suiss Gentleman mighty polite & genteel. I found that a Recommendation was necessary; for he was cold till I told him that I had a letter for Madame de Winsingerode.³ He told me. Il y a quelque tems que nous avons eté attrapé ici. Il venoit un monsieur, qui s'appelloit fils du Duc Hamilton. Pourtant il n'avoit ni equipage ni Domestique, pas même des habits. Il etoit en Ridingcoat. On l'equippoit. Il etoit presenté á la cour. Il avoit assez bonnes façons; mais aprês son depart on decouvrit qu'il etoit ni Anglois ni Ecossois, mais un Avanturier Etranger qui avoit appri un peu la langue.⁴ I said 'Monsieur Si on reçoit un homme comme cela, on merite d'etre trompé'. I then called on [M]. de La Porte french minister here, Brother to [M]. de La Porte whom I knew at Utrecht.⁵ I found him at dinner. He promised to come to me after dinner. He did so, & proved to be a knowing sagacious man, very plain very obliging, and very deliberate. He resembled somewhat Mr. Clow at Glasgow.⁶ He carried me to see La maison des Modêles which is a singular thing. You have here models of all the Buildings & gardens of the Prince, in particular however of the Grand Waterfall which is not yet completely executed. But there are here many pieces yet unexecuted. The Waterfall must be a Work of prodigious Expence. The Water issues from a hill, & flows down a flight of steps, till it reaches a Bason; from thence it again is conveyed to a flight of steps. In short this Alternation will be carried on a vast way. On each side of the fall are Evergreens, verdant banks, & a serpentine Stair. On the top of the hill or Rock is a large Statue of Hercules, [i]n the inside of which is a stair. The Statue is so large, that a man may stand in the head of it. It was the Grand Uncle of this Landgrave who caused make⁷ the water-fall. His son the King of Sweden came to see him, & was immediatly carried to view the Fall. His father asked him n'est il pas beau? pouvez vous concevoir aucune chose que manque ici? The King replied 'Rien qu'un potence pour celui qui a donné ce plan á votre Altêsse.' This pleasantry however was taken seriously ill by the old Prince & his Majesty of Sweden was obliged to decamp without taking leave.⁸ We then saw the Orangerie. Before it stand some Acient Statues in Bronze four I think on the terrace. There are here also some very pretty figures of white marble, which came from Italy a good time ago but have not been brought hither till very lately, by reason of the war. There were a parcel of sweet little Children & three grand Pieces, a Narcissus, a Venus de Medicis, & a groupe of Boys with grapes.⁹ We then saw the menagerie, which is very well. I remarked in a room ten or a dozen Apes; & in another the various kinds of Parrots.[10] We then viewed some pretty walks on the side of the hill. They are done with taste. I saw here a Grotto. Here it was that the Landgrave used to have his private devotions, before it was discovered that he was Catholic. It was concealed seven years.[11] His Valet de Chambre was much vexed & told him, Monseigneur quand cela sera connu, dans Ce moment Je vous quitte.[12] I was very desirous to know from good Authority the real character of the Landgrave. De La Porte said Monsieur soyez persuadé qu'il est un bon Prince. Il a eu beaucoup des chagrins. On l'a traité fort severement. Il y avoit une Dame d'honneur Angloise qui a contribué beaucoup de faire la separation entre son Altesse, et une Princesse qu'il adoroit.[13] Il ne lui manque que des Gens sensés et habils pour le conduire. Il ne sauroit donner attention á[14] tout; et quelquefois les choses vont assez mal. I then asked him to explain the reason of his Highness's change of Religion. He said 'Il a eté fort mal elevé. Donop qui etoit son Precepteur, avouoit "J'ai besoin d'un Precepteur moi même". C'etoit un joli homme, mais sans des principes sollides. Ainsi Le Prince n'etoit pas fondé d'une maniêrre sur laquelle on pouvoit compter.'[15] I found De La Porte prudently avoided to seem convinced of the real reason of this change, which was indeed his Highness's attachment to a certain Countess of the Catholic Religion who insisted that his Highness should surrender his Soul to her, before she would give him up her body. By this means, I suppose she made matters easy with her conscience, or with her vanity. She either imagined that gaining a Prince to her Communion might attone for her sin of gallantry, or that the rank of her lover might bear her up against the contempt of being a mistress.[16] De La Porte gave me several anecdotes of the Landgrave. He told me he had been with him at the *Bains* in the neighbourhood[17] et que le Prince lui avoit parlé beaucoup. Il a beaucoup etudie la controverse entre les Catholiques et Protestans. Il sait bien l'histoire de l'Eglise, et il faut être bien au fait dans une etude particuliêrre pour pouvoir disputer avec lui. Il a la memoire rempli de dates et de petites Anecdotes et si vous en etes ignorant, il triomphe. Il vous renvoye aussi á Bossuet pour un Explication des Articles difficiles.[18] Si vous savez rien des livres dont il parle, il vous conseille d'etudier sa religion car vous ne le savez pas. C'est ainsi qu'il renvoye les ministres Allemands. Il est pourtant á croire que Son Altesse n'est pas tout á fait fixé dans ses principes et qu'il est même quelquefois faché a ce quil a fait. Il y avoit un certain Ministre qui lui ecrivoit une lettre tres rude. Il me le montroit. C'etoit une piêce grossiêre. Il lui paroit de son changement de Religion sans garder aucune Bienseance. Et il se meloit des affaires politiques avec laquelle il n'avoit assurement rien á faire.[19] Je dis a son Altesse mes sentiments la dessus. Il m'a dit. Monsieur Je ne crois pas tout ce que les Prêtres me disent. Assurement au jour de Jugement les dignes hommes de chaque Religion seront sauves. Et pour mon changement de Religion, ce n'est pas une Affaire de quoi faire un si grand Bruit. Je lui dis hardiment mon Seigneur si on change sa religion pour une autre qu'on croit fausse, Le bon Dieu doit être offensé. Il ne me donnoit point de reponse. Un jour il me frappoit singulierrement. Il me disoit. 'David et Peter furent tous deux pieux mais cependant l'un Commit des adultêres et l'autre trahit son maitre'.[20] Oui Monseigneur Je repondois; mais ils se sont sincerement repenti. Il s'arretoit quelque tems. Alors il disoit. Oui, il faut les imiter dans leur pieté et non dans leur vices. Bon jour Monsieur de la Porte. Et il s'en alloit. Moi—J'etois etonné car il ne m'avoit traité comme cela jamais. Je craignoit de l'avoir offensé. Mais quelques jours après un monsieur de la cour me dit. Mon Seigneur vous aime beaucoup. Alors Je m'imaginoit que son Altêsse avoit eu quelque mouvement de remord que lui avoit fait partir si brusquement. Il a pourtant un Melange de Superstition car il me dit un jour. 'Monsieur ne croyez vous pas que nous pouvons obtenir des graces du ciel par des prierres aux Saints. Je vous raconterai un trait. Un jour Je demandois quelque chose de bon Dieu par l'intercession de la Viêrge Marie; C'etoit quelque chose de consequence; et Je l'obtint'. Je repondis sans ceremonie. Votre Altesse est bien redevable au Dieu, premierrement pour vous avoir accordé ce que vous souhaitiez: en second lieu, pour l'avoir accordé pour une telle prièrre. Is not M. De La Porte a very fine fellow? Indeed he is. He came with me to my Inn & drank a glass of Wine.

[TEN LINES A DAY.]
O Hesse thy Landgraves must be ever nam'd
As Men for changing their religion fam'd
One Landgrave[21] drove *the Reformation* on
Another back to the old church is gone.
A Pious Prince to women much inclin'd
Will still the Clergy most indulgent find
When Landgrave[22] Philip found one wife too few,
Fierce Luther decently allow'd him two[23]
And sure ye popish priests ye cannot miss
To be at least as generous to this.[24]

---

[1] MS. 'avaent'

[2] MS. 'leurs'

[3] Eleanor Maria Dorothea von Wintzingerode (1733–80) was the widow of Achaz Philipp von Wintzingerode (1722–58), a major in the army of Hessen-Kassel (Woringer file of Hessian Officers, MS. Murhard und Landesbibliothek, Kassel). For JB's introduction to her, see Journ. 25 Oct. and n. 13.

[4] The Hamilton whom the impostor had claimed as father was possibly the 5th Duke, James (1702/3–43), who had been known for his connections both with the Jacobites (he had been named Knight of the Thistle in 1722) and with the Hanoverians (he had become Lord of the Bedchamber to George II in 1727). His two sons still living—Archibald (1740–1819), later 9th Duke, and Spenser (1742–91)—were presumably the same age as the impostor (*Scots Peer.* iv. 392–94).

[5] JB had dined with this la Porte, who was serving as a tutor, on 5 Feb. (French theme, Yale MS. M 87).

[6] For Jean-Jacques de la Porte, see Journ. 23 Oct. n. 3. James Clow was Professor of Logic at Glasgow University from 1752 to 1787 (J. D. Mackie, *The University of Glasgow 1451–1951*, 1954, p. 187). JB may have lived in his house while a student in Glasgow from 1759 to 1760 (*Earlier Years*, pp. 43, 466–67).

[7] A Scotticism (see CSD, 'caused').

[8] 'Pour voir la maison de Modêles — 12 Gr.' (Exp. Acct. 24 Oct., App. 3). The house of models, like many other important buildings in Kassel, had been established by the powerful and art-loving Landgrave Karl (1654–1730). Its most spectacular exhibit, completed in 1709, was the long cascade of 220 feet (67.1 m) crowned by the statue of Hercules (Schmincke, pp. 192–94; A. Holt-

meyer, *Die Bau- und Kunstdenkmäler im Regierungsbezirk Cassel*, 1923, vi. pt. 2. 542–43). The model was the work of Johann Heinrich Wachter (d. 1708), an architect as well as modelist (Philippi, pp. 586, 591). The actual complex was situated 4 miles (6.4 km) west of Kassel (Nugent, ii. 371) on a hillside called the Karlsberg (renamed Wilhelmshöhe in 1798 in honour of Landgrave Wilhelm IX, 1743–1820). A remarkable example of baroque garden architecture, it was created between 1701 and 1717 according to the grandiose plans of the Roman architect Giovanni Francesco Guernieri (1665–1745), only one third of which were ever realized (Philippi, p. 588; Karl-Hermann Wegner, *Kassel: Ein Stadtführer*, 1981, p. 48). The actual waterfall, descending for 820 feet (250 m) down 825 steps, each almost 38 feet (11.6 m) wide, ended in a large ornamental basin and was to have been carried still further (W. Döring, *Beschreibung des Kurfürstlichen Landsitzes Wilhelmshöhe*, 1804, repr. in Fritz Lometsch, *Wilhelmshöhe: Natur und Formergeist in dem schönsten Bergpark Europas*, 1961, pp. 81–82). The statue of Hercules, a copy of the famous Farnese Hercules excavated in Rome and here a symbol for the absolute rule of the landgraves, was a colossus of sheet copper standing more than 30 feet (9.1 m) high, created by the goldsmith Johann Jakob Anthoni of Augsburg from 1714 to 1717. It topped a pyramid which, in turn, stood on a huge octagon, the whole dominating the landscape outside Kassel into the twenty-first century (Philippi, p. 588; Wegner, p. 48).

Landgrave Karl was the grandfather, not granduncle, of the present landgrave. Karl's son, Friedrich I (1676–1751), had been elected King of Sweden in 1720 as husband of Ulricke Eleanora (1688–1741) of Sweden, the sister of Charles XII (1682–1718) of that country. Friedrich was not yet king at the time of his visit to Kassel (ADB, vii. 522–24; Philippi, *Das Haus Hessen*, p. 174).

[9] The orangerie, a summer residence for the landgraves, was situated below the palace and overlooked an extensive park known as the Karlsaue, which in turn was almost entirely enclosed by the river Fulda and other waterways. The orangerie itself, built from 1703 to 1710 according to designs by the architect Johann Conrad Giesler (d. 1712), was a low baroque building inspired by the Trianon at Versailles (Philippi, pp. 590–91). Apart from the bronzes, which represented the four parts of the world, and the other pieces mentioned by JB, the sculptures included allegorical figures of the virtues and

images of Roman emperors (Schmincke, pp. 120–21).

[10] The menagerie, situated within the Karlsaue and famous for its monkeys, had been recently renovated and moved to the bottom of the northern hillside (Both, *Friedrich II*, p. 81; Kalbfuss, *Die Karlsaue*, 1972, p. 21).

[11] This grotto, situated high up on the northern hillside, could be reached unobtrusively by the landgrave from the top of the hill, where he owned a small palace that had served as his residence while he was Hereditary Prince (Schmincke, pp. 110–11, 310; Hugo Brunner, 'Geschichte des Bellevueschlosses in Kassel', *Zeitschrift des Vereins für hessische Geschichte* 49 [1916], pp. 238–39). The existence of the grotto and the 'story' of Friedrich's secret prayers here would be doubted by his biographer Wolf von Both, but shown to be plausible by J. H. Reuter, who verified the location of the grotto in 1993 (correcting *Grand Tour I*, Heinemann p. 150 n. 1, McGraw-Hill p. 154 n. 9).

JB's dating of Friedrich's experiences, however, was not accurate. The young man had been drawn to Catholicism as early as 1742, had been converted in 1749, and had kept his secret until 1754; hence his indecision, not his concealment, had lasted for seven years.

[12] The valet, Weissenburg, himself a Catholic, had obviously feared the consequences of revealing Friedrich's conversion. These were dire, for not only had Friedrich been forced to sign the *Assekurationsakte* a few weeks later, but his wife, Princess Mary (1723–72), daughter of George II of England, had immediately left him, taking their three sons with her (Both, *Friedrich II*, p. 15). The valet had remained, presumably because Friedrich had been granted permission to retain a few Catholic servants (*Assekurationsakte* Art. 15; see Hartwig, p. 39). A 'Louis Wissenbourg' was still listed in the *Hochfürstlich-Hessen-Casselscher Staats- u. Adress-Calender* for 1764 (p. 40).

[13] The Englishwoman blamed for undermining the landgrave's marriage of 1740 to Princess Mary had apparently been the flirtatious Lucy Young, Lady Rochford (c. 1723–73), maid of honour to the Princess of Wales (*Corres. Walpole*, xx. 58; see also *Corres. Walpole*, ix. 42 n. 19).

[14] MS. 'A'

[15] August Moritz von Donop (1694–1763) had been Friedrich's tutor from 1732 and had remained a close and loyal advisor until shortly before his death. He belonged to a distinguished military family (Friedrich

Henkel, 'Die von Donop in hessischen Diensten', *Hessenland*, 1892, vi. 248). Although he had lacked polish, he had shown a keen interest in the arts, a trait not mentioned by la Porte (Both, *Friedrich II*, pp. 19–20; see also Both, *Wilhelm VIII*, pp. 136, 236).

[16] MS. Heavily scored out from 'who insisted' to 'By', then crossed out with a double or single line to 'mistress'. The anecdote is recorded also by Lehndorff (*Dreissig Jahre*, p. 419). The lady, not definitively identified, may have been a Countess Hatzfeld, whom Frederick II had named as the cause of Friedrich's 'sottise' (*Pol. Corr.* x. 469).

[17] The baths (not the same as the marble bath JB saw on 26 Oct.) have not been identified.

[18] Jacques Bénigne Bossuet, Bishop of Meaux (1627–1704), French theologian, orator, and polemicist, had defended the Catholic church against the Protestants particularly in his *Exposition de la doctrine catholique* (1671) and in his *Histoire des variations des églises protestants* (1688). In the latter he had criticized the Protestants not only for having left the true church but also for then having split into factions (Aimé Richardt, *Bossuet*, 1992, pp. 119–20, 184–87).

[19] The clergyman has not been identified.

[20] For David's adultery with Bathsheba, see II Sam. 11:2; for Peter's denial of knowing Jesus, Matt. 26:34, 69–74.

[21] MS. A few letters underlined.

[22] MS. 'Landgrave' written above deleted 'potent'.

[23] Philipp (1504–67) the Magnanimous had been a crusader for Protestantism who had also become famous for his bigamy. Driven by intense libido, supposedly caused by a physical abnormality, he had not been satisfied with his wife Christina (1505–49), Princess of Saxony, by whom he had already had seven children and would father three more. Pleading the Old Testament precedent for polygamy, he had persuaded Luther to let him also marry Margarete von der Sale (1522–66), by whom he had seven more sons after 1540 (see Philippi, *Das Haus Hessen*, pp. 63–64; Ernst Vogt, 'Zur Doppelehe Philipps des Grossmütigen', in *Philipp der Grossmütige*, ed. Julius Reinhard Dieterich and Bernhard Müller, 1904, pp. 505–06; Isenburg, i. Tafel 97). He had lost the support of his fellow Protestant princes when his second marriage became known, and later, after military reverses, had spent the years from 1547 to 1552 as prisoner of the Catholic Emperor Charles V (Isenburg, i. Tafel 97). After the death of Christina, Philipp had acknowledged Margarete as his sole wife (Vehse, xxvii. 8–18).

[25] That is, to forgive the present landgrave.

## Thursday 25 October

[MEM. dated Friday 26 Octr.][1] Yesterday you wrote all morning. Before two went to court. Fine old rooms — thought of P. Hesse in Rebellion — Introduc'd — Very grave to keep up his dignity. Good dinner — Ham with pears — at 5 Madame de Winsingerode & the Princesse Charlotte quite affable — quite lively — Then concert very well — Saw Land atiring — & whispring — Then cards — Supt. Grand Ecuier civil — Courtier. L. Hope homme d'esprit.[2] This day 8 Kunst camer.[3] Then La Porte — 10 Tableaux. Then Bains — Then cascade[4] — Then dress [—] afternoon La Porte — Swear few letters — *Think* & be Johnson Temp[le] & Gray. Is not *Britain* noble — restrain Envoy ideas — Auchin & jaunts each year — Gardens Pictures miss Bosville[.][5]

[J.] All the morning I wrote. My method is to make a memorandum every night of what I have seen during the day. By this means I have my materials allways secured. Sometimes I am three, four, five days without journalising. When I have time & spirits, I bring up this my Journal as well as I can in the hasty manner in which I write it.[6] Some years hence I shall perhaps abridge it in a more elegant stile. I take up too much time in writing letters. I am resolved to guard against this. I shall make my corespondence valued by making it scarce. Yet, while I am abroad it is pleasant to have a variety of Corespondents, and it will also be pleasant when I am settled at home. Well then; why make grave proud resolutions of writing little? I was in the wrong; & there's an end on't.[7] At one I went to court. The Palace is an Old Building but large, & the Rooms are magnificent.[8] I was pleased to find here a family Picture of the present house of Brunswic done by          the Landgrave's Painter.[9] I was curious to see the Landgrave who as Prince of Hesse was in Scotland in the year 1745.[10] He appeared at last, and I was presented to him. He scarcely spoke, in order to keep up his dignity. I dined. The table was very good. I took particular notice of a Ham with Pears well boiled in Sugar. It made an excellent dish, & I eat of it very heartily. The Grand Ecuier & some more of the Courtiers were very civil to me.[11] At five I was presented to the Princess Charlotte Cousin of the Landgrave. She was mighty lively & affable.[12] I saw also Madame de Winsingerode for whom I had a letter from mademoiselle de Stang Dame d'honneur á Brunsvic.[13] We had a very good Concert. But, I perceived the Landgrave atiring; for, he was continually calling to him his Courtiers, & whispering to them. Then we returned to the apartment and played Cards. They made a party of Whisk for me.[14] I supt at court.

[TEN LINES A DAY,]
Alas! alas! how often do we find
The merest trifles vex the human mind!
Should I what now disturbs me freely tell
Your cheeks companions would with laughter swell.[15]
[O]ut with it man. Why then, without disguise
Two quires of paper of an equal size
I cannot find; and so my lines must write
On Sheets now great now small — an aukward sight.
Oh! oh! thou goose of geese! Thou fool of fools!
Thou yet shouldst be a conning grammar rules.[16]

---

[1] MS. Along the right margin: 'My Dear Johnston', followed by a gap, then 'Saxe-Gotha', and below this '20 Octr. 1764'; 'Let not' written 1½ inches lower down—all signs of an abandoned beginning of JB's letter to JJ, 20 Oct. (see *Corr. 1*, p. 139). For another indication that JB was short of paper, see the 'Ten Lines' for this day).

[2] Evidently Lord Hope had also passed through Kassel on his travels (see Journ. 27 June nn. 3 and 17).

[3] This and the following phrases refer to what JB planned to do the following day. The beginning of the next Mem., dated 27 Oct., covers what he actually did.

[4] Presumably one of the cascades in the Karlsaue. JB would not have had the time to visit and return from the great waterfall at the Karlsberg, at least 4 miles (6.4 km) from the

centre of the town (see Journ. 24 Oct. n. 8).

[5] Elizabeth Diana Bosville (1748–89) was the daughter of Godfrey Bosville, a Yorkshire squire whom JB considered a kinsman and head of the Boswell clan. JB apparently regarded her as a possible marital prospect, but she would remain unaware of or be unimpressed by his interest and would marry Sir Alexander Macdonald of Sleat (c. 1745–95, *Comp. Bar.* ii. 292; see To WJT, 22 Apr. 1765, *Corr. 6*, p. 135; *Earlier Years*, pp. 284, 374). For her dates, see A. E. B. Macdonald, *Fortunes of a Family*, 1927, pp. 119–21; and *Corr. 6*, p. 114 n. 34.

[6] For JB's practice of recording his experiences, first in the memoranda and then in his journal, see F. A. Pottle, *Grand Tour I*, Heinemann p. 152 n. 1, McGraw-Hill p. 156 n. 3.

[7] On this day, JB in fact sent letters to his father and to his friend AE (Reg. Let.). They have not been recovered.

[8] The palace, on a high point overlooking the town, was an imposing Renaissance building constructed from 1557 to 1562 by the architect Antonius Riemenschneider (dates not found); see Fritz Lometsch, *Kassel in alten Bildern*, 1966, pp. 57–58. Its spacious rooms were embellished with gilt and stucco decorations, and its high ceilings were unsupported by pillars (Schmincke, pp. 97–104).

[9] MS. A blank for the name of the painter. The group portrait (approx. 9' x 12') painted by Johann Heinrich Tischbein the Elder (1722–89) in 1762, shows the Duke and Duchess of Brunswick, their four sons, four daughters, a son-in-law (who had already died), and J. F. W. Jerusalem (see Journ. 28 June and n. 2). JB presumably saw it in the audience chamber (Dorothea Heppe, *Das Schloss der Landgrafen von Hessen in Kassel von 1557 bis 1811*, 1995, p. 24). From the nineteenth century it would hang in the Weissenstein wing of the Wilhelmshöhe palace (see E. von Schenk zu Schweinsberg, rev. by Heinz Biehn, et al., 'Schloss Wilhelmshöhe', 1974, pp. 3–5, 19; reproduced in *Grand Tour I*, Heinemann facing p. 12, McGraw-Hill facing p. 14; see also Heinemann p. ix, McGraw-Hill p. vii).

[10] Friedrich II had actually arrived with his troops in Feb. 1746 (see Journ. 22 Oct. n. 8). Although JB knew of Friedrich's military experience and was learning about his religious concerns, he did not hear of the landgrave's desire at this very time to become an enlightened ruler. He had expressed his principles in his 'Pensées diverses sur les princes' (c. 1760, publ. anon. 1776) and had already put some of them into practice, notably religious tolerance

and reforms in the treatment of the poor and the sick (Otto Berge, 'Wohlfahrtspflege und Medizinalwesen unter Landgraf Friedrich II', *Zeitschrift des Vereins für hessische Geschichte 65–66* [1955–56]: 120–42).

[11] The Master of Horse was Julius Jürgen von Wittorf (1714–1802). He had served in this capacity from 1738 after beginning as page to Friedrich's father in 1728. Wittorf enjoyed the confidence of all members of the ruling family and was frequently sent on diplomatic missions (Both, *Friedrich II*, p. 26; ADB). The other courtiers have not been identified.

[12] Princess Charlotte (1725–82), daughter of Friedrich's uncle, Maximilian (1689–1753), did the honours when a woman's presence was needed at court (Both, *Friedrich II*, pp. 20–21).

[13] JB had not mentioned meeting Mlle von Stangen in Brunswick, where she had served as lady in waiting to Duchess Philippine Charlotte since 1755 (*Hof Etat*). Nor has her letter been recovered, but perhaps it was the 'Lettre de Brunsvic' for which JB paid 3 Gr. on this date (Exp. Acct. 25 Oct., App. 3).

[14] Alternative name for JB's favourite card game (OED, s.v. 'whist', *sb.*[3]; see Journ. 27 June and n. 16). He lost 15 Gr.

[15] MS. 'swell' inserted above 'laughter'.

[16] MS. 'which hurts' written above 'an aukward'. JB was evidently not satisfied with the new paper he bought for 12 Gr. on this day, not even for the drafts he seems to have written before making a fair copy on folio leaves (see Exp. Acct., App. 3; M 281, *Catalogue*, i. 120). His sudden change of subject to himself as 'fool' seems to be a spontaneous comment on what he had just written, the ungrammatical 'which hurts' that does not fit with 'sheets' (l. 8).

## Friday 26 October

[MEM. dated Saturday 27 Octr.] Yesterday at 8 saw Maison de Sciences very rich — tho' not so as [D]resden menagerie by Rosa 13000 Ducats a lie 3 years here.[1] Burning glass a foot under water. Then Gallery Pictures noble Pieces — Still wish to marry Zelide [—] as flemish school [—] stuff — Take care. Then Marble Bath octagon[2] — charming figures — not dine court poor — 6 Comedie Tartuffe not amiss. Kelly — sad & fast. Supt court — Leave cold — Prince whither come you & go you? This day send to *Mint*[3] to Grand Marechal & Mad Winsing — & Post — Break at 8 [—] La Porte — Go on —

[J.] At eight I saw the maison des Sciences, in which are several rooms of curiositys rich but inferior much to the Musæum at Dresden.[4] There is a good many Antiques. A collection of old Musical Instruments, an odd enough conceit.[5] There is a fine picture by Rosa of the Great Landgrave's Menagerie. It is very large, and immensely full, without any Confusion. Rosa lived here three years to paint this picture for which I was told he had 1300 ducats.[6] I saw an exceeding large burning glass, which burns a foot under water.[7] I saw several curious pieces invented by the great Landgrave himself, amongst others a Clock in the form of a Man which at whatever hour you please fires a Pistol & lights a lamp; so that You are awaked in the night, & have a light immediatly.[8] I next saw the Gallery of Pictures, amongst which are some noble pieces, chiefly of the flemish School.[9] I never see a Portrait of a comely Dutchwoman, but I think with kindness of Zelide. What a fancy! I next waited on De la Porte, & saw his Sister, a good hearty Old maiden;[10] then saw the marble Bath which in it's kind is truly *une chose unique*. The Outside has nothing remarkable; but, within there is an Octagon Room with four superb Statues & four pannels richly carved, besides intermediate pieces of marble. The floor is also marble. In the middle is the Bath, an octagon too adorned with other four Statues. In short it is a most magnificent Work.[11] I was not asked today to dine at court. It is not the custom to send to Strangers. They must pay their respects at court, & perhaps they are invited to the table, perhaps not. It is not a true hospitable court, altho' it is however not amiss. At six I went to the Comedie. On entering the house, I was surprised to hear the Orchestre play one of Lord Kelly's Concertos. They however played it very ill. The pretty, slow parts they made a country dance of.[12] The Piece was Tartuffe, & pretty well performed.[13] I was asked by a General who speaks good English 'Why I had not been this morning at Court?' I said I had been seeing fine things. I supt at court. Before Supper I took leave of the Landgrave. He was very Hypochondriack. For most part, he talks too freely. But all he said to me when presented first, was. 'Where do you come from last?' and when I took leave 'Ou allez vous ici?' He seemed gloomy. Cassel has been but so so.

[TEN LINES A DAY]
Whip whip my muse, whip whip nor spare the spur
Up up the hill up up — make no demur
How little of this day is in thy power
A quarter only of a fleeting hour
Whip whip I say as if upon the back
The bony back of a Queensferry Hack[14]
O Pegasus! can horse celestial bear
That with a dirty Hack I thee compare
Forgive me quadruped tis but for once
Or else Apollo make thy Bard a dunce.

[1] '13000 Ducats' corrected to the more plausible '1300' in the Journ. for this day. The 'lie' refers to the number of years Roos had spent in Kassel (see n. 6).
[2] MS. 'octgon'

[3] JB was again collecting specimen coins as in Gotha (see Journ. 20 Oct. and n. 6).
[4] The Kassel museum, also called the *Kunsthaus* ('house of art'), had been inaugurated in 1709 to accommodate the collections

of the art-loving Landgrave Karl that had outgrown their quarters in the stables (Franz Adrian Dreier, 'Die Kunstkammer of the Hessian Landgraves in Kassel', Impey and MacGregor, pp. 104, 107). The building had been named the Ottoneum by Landgrave Moritz (1592–1627) 'The Learned' for his recently deceased favourite son Otto (d. 1617). Constructed between 1603 and 1605 for visiting English actors, it had the distinction of being the first building in German territory specifically designed as theatre. After only eleven years it had been converted to an armoury and then to a garrison church (Christiane Engelbrecht, 'Musik und Theater in Kassel von den Anfängen', *Theater in Kassel*, 1959, pp. 12–16).

[5] To display musical instruments, here in a special room, seems to have been a novelty.

[6] Pride of place, in a room reserved for paintings and stuffed animals, was given to a huge canvas (408 x 722 cm, or 13.4 x 243.7 ft) by Johann Melchior Roos (1659–1731) that depicted lynxes, ostriches, monkeys, exotic birds, a lion, a camel, and other animals belonging to Landgrave Karl's menagerie (Jacob Hoffmeister's *Gesammelte Nachrichten über Künstler und Kunsthandwerker in Hessen*, ed. G. Prior, 1885, pp. 102–03). This menagerie had been sold after the Landgrave's death in 1730 (Schmincke, pp. 187) and so was not the one seen by JB on 24 Oct. Roos's painting had taken even longer than three years to complete, as seen in a local magistrate's complaint to the Landgrave that Roos had been at work for five years but had accomplished little in the last three (30 Aug. 1727, cited in Bernhard Schnackenburg, *Gesamtkatalog Gemäldegalerie Alter Meister Kassel*, 1996, GK 1114, p. 255). Roos, whose whole family had specialized in animal paintings, had come to be known as 'Saturday Roos' because he reputedly worked only on Saturdays, when he needed money for the week's expenses (Hermann Jedding, *Der Tiermaler Joh. Heinr. Roos*, 1955, p. 184). Exactly how much he had actually been paid has not been determined.

[7] The burning glass was one of several measuring more than four feet (1.22 m) in diameter that were displayed in the 'optical room' (Schminke, p. 174). The most famous, about 2.5 feet (.8 m) in diameter, had been constructed by the Saxon physicist Ehrenfried Walther von Tschirnhaus (1651–1708) to produce very high temperatures (Ludolf von Mackensen, *Die naturwissenschaftlichtechnische Sammlung in Kassel*, 1991, p. 128, illustr. 103). Whether the foot refers to

twelve inches or a human foot is unclear.

[8] This clock, designed by Landgrave Karl and constructed between 1715 and 1720, did not represent a man but Pallas Athena (Rudolf Hallo, *Schriften zur Kunstgeschichte in Kassel*, 1983, p. 135). The dial had been placed on Athena's breast and the pistol in her right hand. As soon as the alarm in the clockwork hidden in her stomach stopped, the pistol lit a fuse and thereby put on a light (Schmincke, p. 165; information from Prof. von Mackensen). The pistol bears the name of the armourer Matthias Conrad Pistor (1691–1761). In combining artistic and mechanical skill, this work is typical of the baroque pieces that European rulers of the sixteenth and seventeenth century collected for their 'cabinets of curiosities'.

[9] The gallery had been built from 1749 to 1751 according to plans by François Cuvilliés the Elder (1698–1767) and other architects. It housed Landgrave Wilhelm VIII's extraordinary collection, which included 20 Rembrandts and had been enriched in 1750 by the purchase of 64 paintings from the heirs of Valerius van Reuver in Delft (Hans Vogel, 'Wilhelm VIII. als Kunstsammler' in Both, *Wilhelm VIII*, p. 140).

[10] Presumably Esperance Marguerite de la Porte (1707–70); see *Die französischen Gemeinden in Kassel*, ed. Hugo Dreusicke, Forschungen zur hessischen Familien- und Heimatkunde, 1962, xlv. 348.

[11] This small, sumptuous baroque building, next to the orangerie, had been modelled on an octagonal Roman bath and embellished by medallions, reliefs, mosaics, marble facings, stucco work, columns, and statues. It had been designed and executed from 1720 to 1728 by the architect and sculptor Pierre-Etienne Monot or Monnot (1657–1733), who had based most of his representations on Ovid's *Metamorphoses* (Schmincke, pp. 123–28; Kalbfuss, *Die Karlsaue*, 1972, pp. 23–24). By 'too adorned', JB may have meant 'also adorned' or, more likely—as suggested by F. A. Pottle in his punctuation of this passage—'also octagonal' (Marlies K. Danziger and Hans-Joachim Reuter, *Ein Schotte in Kassel im Jahre 1764*, illustr. 42, p. 72; *Grand Tour I*, Heinemann p. 154, McGraw-Hill, p. 158).

[12] Performances took place in a building dating back to the early seventeenth century that was also used for festive balls. Rebuilding this makeshift theatre had been planned before the Seven Years' War but would begin only in 1773 (Hans Joachim Schaefer, 'Theater und Musik', *Aufklärung und Klassizismus in Hessen-Kassel unter Landgraf Fried-*

rich II, 1979, pp. 113–14). Perhaps Kellie's composition was being played because it was influenced by Johann Stamitz (1717–57), who was popular in this region. Kellie (also spelled 'Kelly') had studied with Stamitz in Mannheim from 1753 to 1756 and had adopted his new dynamic—a slowly intensifying or decreasing loudness—as well as other surprise effects. In later times Kellie would be regarded as 'Scotland's greatest classical composer' of the seventeenth and eighteenth centuries (*New Grove 2*, s.v. 'Kelly, 6th Earl of'; information also from H.-J. Reuter, formerly of the Kassel Symphony Orchestra). The musicians may have played badly because their concert master had just left his post in annoyance when furniture that had been lent to him in Jan. was repossessed (Robert Pessenlehner, 'Die provisorische Opernbühne Landgraf Friedrichs II', *Zeitschrift des Vereins für hessische Geschichte* 75–76 [1964–65]: 426).

[13] Molière's *Tartuffe* (1664) was very likely performed by the landgrave's French troupe, which began its residence in Kassel in this year and performed classical French plays on days not devoted to operas, concerts, or balls (Schaefer, pp. 113–14).

[14] A broken-down horse on the Queensferry Road, the main route from Edinburgh to the northeast of Scotland (Oliphant Smeaton, *The Story of Edinburgh*, 1926, p. 315).

## Saturday 27 October

[MEM. dated Sunday 28 Octr.] Yesterday break La Porte was quite Father, but too lively & he Clow. At 1 set out. Valet de louage one of the Hessians in Scotland — Sad frenchman for Companion. Impudent dog [—] cover'd waggon hard rolling.

[J.] I breakfasted at honest La Porte's; & as I had told him that I never drank tea or coffee, there was Wine & Bread & Butter & Geneva Confections.[1] What kindness! Worthy People. I was quite my Father. At one I set out for Francfort. The Waggon was covered with leather: But it was a monstrous machine. One could see nothing from it's little openings for it had no glasses. It jolted most horridly, & as it was constructed with Iron Bars, when I attempted to sleep, I received most severe raps & was realy in danger of having my head broke. In short it was a trying machine,[2] worse than my good freinds the open Postwaggons, for, upon them I could see the country, feed on the fresh air, & sleep like a mariner on the top of a mast. I am surprised how I neglected to mention that one of my chairmen at Cassel had been in the Hessian troops who were in Scotland in 1745.[3] He talk'd of *Bart* by which he meant to say Perth. I had with me in the waggon a french servant, a Blackguard, impudent dog.[4] Yet at night I supt with him & my Servant. Such is my hardy plan on my German travels. I also lay down with them on the straw. It was terrible. The heat of an Iron Stove rendered the straw musty & the air hot & this joined to the breaths of a good many people by no means of the most clean race rendered the room most abominable. I could not sleep. One sad circumstance in the *Stube* or common room of a German Inn is being obliged to sleep with a tallow candle or a coarse lamp aburning. I had recourse to the *Stall Knecht*[5] & got a place in the Hay loft, where I slept sound tho' cold.

[TEN LINES A DAY.]
Here am I sitting in a German Inn[6]
Where I may pennance do for many a sin
For I am <pe>ster'd with a thousand flies
Who flap <&> buz about my nose & eyes
A lumpish Landlord has the easy chair

Hardly he speaks, but wildly does he stare
In haste to get away I did not dine
And now I've had cold beef & cursed wine
And in five minutes or a little more
I shall be stretch'd on musty straw to snore.

[1] For JB's avoidance of tea and coffee, see Journ. 29 Sept. and n. 11. 'Geneva confections' were presumably preserves made of fruit and sugar (OED, s.v. 'confection', 5.d).

[2] The Hessian coaches were more primitive than those of the competing service run by the princes of Thurn und Taxis, who held a monopoly over most of the postal routes on the Continent (see Wolfgang Behringer, *Thurn und Taxis, die Geschichte ihrer Post und ihrer Unternehmen*, 1990). For JB's route from Werkel and Marburg to Frankfurt, see Exp. Acct. 28 Oct., App. 3 n. 67.

[3] JB again mistakes the date, which was 1746. The sedan chair bearer, different from the one mentioned in the journal of 23 Oct., has also not been identified.

[4] Not identified.

[5] Ostler

[6] At Werkel, 'a little dirty village' (To JJ, 27 Oct., *Corr. 1*, p. 140). JB wrote these verses on a separate page (M 282) and then transcribed them, with the change only from 'Sin' to 'sin', on the gathering of leaves on which he recorded his other 'Ten Lines' (M 281; see *Catalogue*, i. 120).

## Sunday 28 October

[MEM. dated Monday 29 Octr.] Yesterday afternoon Game[1] [—] went out Jacob & you alone very cold came to Marpurg — out of order resign'd to fate.

[J.] In the afternoon we got rid of the Frenchman, & I & Jacob came to Marpurg[2] a large City. I was out of order. I knew not what to make of my existence. I lay down between two feather-beds, & resigned myself to my fate.

[TEN LINES A DAY.]
View me at Warpurg[3] town of goodly size
In which all sorts of curious merchandise
Are to be found, as in Great London! Thee
Where all they can desire mankind may see
Here Strangers too may find you need not doubt
What good mankind might as well be without
Vice of all kinds to ruin rich & poor
The fell attorney & the rav'nous whore[4]
When I came here 'twas dark;—eer break of day
I shall set out; no more then can I say.

[1] Unexplained.

[2] Marburg. It was 39 miles (62.8 km) from Kassel (Nugent, ii. 366).

[3] Marburg. JB did not stay long enough to recognize that it was a university town

(see Nugent, ii. 372).

[4] Two stereotypes: 'fell attorney' perhaps quoted from SJ's *London*, l. 16, 'fell' meaning 'cruel'; a source for 'rav'nous whore' has not been identified.

## Monday 29 October

[MEM. dated Tuesday 30 Octr.] Yesterday was joind by Camerdiener Erf[1] Prins quite a Bruce Campbell & a roaring dog — Better — at night 13 in room besides women & children Heer Baron got bed[.]

[J.] This day[2] we were joined by the *Camer dienar* of the Hereditary Prince of Hesse Cassel, quite a Bruce Campbell, as also a tall roaring dog who had studied law, but was now going into Darmstat Guards.[3] We jogged well on. At night we were layd thirteen in a room besides a danish woman and three children.[4] I could not bear this; so the Post-master gave me his own bed.

[TEN LINES A DAY.]
This is too much my freinds too much indeed
For any man who has but learnt to read
The livelong day fatigue me as you please
But, let me have at night a little ease.
In cover'd Waggon I pursue my way,
Which oft I find most cruel to my clay
For tho' my feet with coldest ice are shod
My head all drowsy now & then must nod
And while I wish to take an easy nap
On the hard wood I get a ruthless rap.

[1] By 'Erf', JB means 'Erb', i.e. 'hereditary'.
[2] JB's twenty-fourth birthday, not mentioned as such.
[3] The *Kammerdiener* (valet) has not been identified. For the Hereditary Prince, see Journ. 31 Oct. and n. 4; for Bruce Campbell, Mem. dated 20 Sept. and n. 1. Darmstadt, south of Frankfurt, belonged to Hessen-Darmstadt, which had been separated from Hessen-Kassel under Philipp the Magnanimous. JB's travel companion was joining the well-disciplined troops for which Hessen-Darmstadt was famous (Nugent, ii. 379) and

with whom the Hereditary Prince, Ludwig (1719–90), had served with the rank of lieutenant-general until forced to resign by his father, Ludwig VIII (1691–1768), who sided with Austria during the Seven Years' War. On succeeding his father as Ludwig IX, the prince would build up his troops to 2,400 men and would create a special settlement for them in Pirmasens, earning the sobriquet 'Drummer of Pirmasens' (Philippi, *Das Haus Hessen*, pp. 114–17, 175).
[4] JB gave the woman a whole écu (Exp. Acct., App. 3).

## Tuesday 30 October

[MEM. dated Wednesday 31 Octr.] Yesterday in bad humour a little with Jacob — correct his freedom by your retenue & learn [—] sung Zwager & Zwester — Arriv<d> [F]rancfort — lett[.] Marisch[.] & money [—] Gratitude — This day see Church Bull[1] — get money — Hanau Prince[2] & Princess &c at Manheim Jour<n.>

[J.] We jogged well on. The roaring dog taught me a comical German Song: *Want du myn Swager wilt werden* &c.[3] About two I arrived at Francfort on the Mayn.[4] I was in bad humour. Jacob asked me why I waited in the Court-yard. I said pour avoir soin du Baggage. He replied with a kind of sneer, 'Oui, pour avoir soin du Baggage'. I was irritated. I wished to turn him off. Yet I considered, He is a most excellent Servant, and a fellow of common sense and activity in his duty cannot have the supple politeness of one who has a kind of genteel Sentiment, & at the same time is negligent and perhaps dishonest. It was certainly true that my staying in the court-yard could do no good, & the *naif* fellow could not help telling me so. I made him understand that he had done no wrong; and he was sorry &

seemed very desirous to do his duty. And now comes a good Anecdote. I had brought with me from Berlin 68 Louis, with which I imagined I might compleat my tour thro' Germany to Geneva. When I had got as far as Dresden, I perceived that my money would run short.[5] I wrote to My Lord Marischal my Situation, begged his Lordship's advice whether I should proceed from Francfort directly to NeufChatêl or should visit the courts of Manheim, Durlach, & Stutgard,[6] and if he thought it proper for me to visit those courts, begged he might send me to Francfort a Bill for 30 Louis. This afternoon I sent to the Post and had the pleasure to receive an obliging letter from his Lordship with the Bill inclosed & besides that an order on Neufchatel for 30 Louis more, in case I should want more.[7] I was filled with Gratitude to the venerable Earl. I felt myself a man of worth to be regarded by him. I stroled with pleasant Etourderie in the streets of Francfort.

⌈TEN LINES A DAY.⌉
Ye who with fortune ever are[8] at stri<fe>
And make a noise about the ills of life
What had you said if ye like me had been
With lubbers stretch'd on straw in all thirteen
Some roaring Germans in a drunken tone
Still rudely Bawl'd vie slaft der Heer Baron[9]
Myself of mighty consequence to make
A Baron's title I forsooth must take
And for my vain indulgence as you hear
I now & then must pay a little dear.[10]

---

[1] The church was St. Bartholomäus, the cathedral in Frankfurt in which the election of the Holy Roman Emperor by four prominent German rulers and three archbishops took place (Walter Kinkel, *Dom Sankt Bartholomäus*, 1986, p. 12). The document that recorded the procedure for electing him as well as other regulations, written in Latin in 44 quarto MS. pages (88 sides), was known as 'the golden bull': 'bull' because its seal (Lat. *bulla*) identified it as an official edict, and 'golden' because this seal was attached to the document in a golden capsule about the size of a large gold coin, such as a taler. Revered as a record of the most basic law of the Holy Roman Empire, it existed in several copies, the most frequently consulted of which was kept in the town hall (the 'Römer') close to the cathedral and was recommended to visitors as Frankfurt's most important sight (Anon., *Einige besonders zu sehenden Merckwürdigkeiten des Heil. Röm. Reichs Wahl- und Handels-Stadt Franckfurt am Mayn*, 1749, pp. ⌈3⌉–6). Since JB does not mention it again in the journal, he may not have gone to see it.
[2] MS. 'Princ' or 'Prine', a slip of the pen.
[3] The lines 'Willst du mein Schwager sein/Heirat meine Schwester!' ('If you want to be my brother-in-law/ Marry my sister!') occur in a jocular song, 'Ich bin ein armer Geigermann' ('I am a poor fiddle player'), which exists in several variations (Gr. VIIb, *Deutsches Volkslied-archiv*, identified by Prof. Morris Brownell). Schwager was a slang term for a rival in seeking a woman or in enjoying her favour (see Jacob and Wilhelm Grimm, *Deutsches Wörterbuch*, 1854–1971, s.v. 'Schwager', ix. 2178).
[4] The river Main, which runs through Frankfurt, is usually mentioned with this town to distinguish it from the other Frankfurt further east, on the Oder.
[5] JB had spent more than 30 louis by the time he left Dresden. This calculation is based on the assumption that an écu or crown (= .25 £ sterling), the unit in which he continued to record his expenses, was worth roughly the same as a louis or only slightly more (£1.02 in 1766, McCusker, p. 9, Table 1.1). JB seems to have equated louis and écus in his Expense Account (see App. 3).
[6] The residence of the Duke of Württemberg, who had engaged JB's interest earlier

(see Journ. 17 Oct. and n. 6).

[7] The order asked 'Monsieur le Conseiller Rougement' at Neuchâtel to make 30 louis available to JB from Lord Marischal's account if needed (for a translation of Lord Marischal's letter, dated 17 Oct., and JB's answer, written on this very day, see *Grand Tour I*, Heinemann pp. 157–59, McGraw-Hill pp. 161–63). François-Antoine III (1713–88) de Rougemont belonged to the eighth generation of a premier family of Neuchâtel and had been named *conseiller d'état* in 1758 (Jacqueline and Pierre-Arnold Borel, *Livre de Raison et chronique de famille: Quartier De Rougemont,*

*1983*, p. 33).

In his letter to Lord Marischal JB included the copy of the 'Ten Lines' of 15 Oct. that depicted him as Hercules in a postwagon (see Journ. 15 Oct. n. 5).

[8] MS. 'are' inserted twice above the line.

[9] JB's rendering of 'Wie schläft der Herr Baron' ('how does the Baron sleep?'). JB had been adopting the baronial title, which he could claim according to the standards of the German courts, at least since his stay in Dessau (see Journ. 1 Oct. and n. 5).

[10] MS. The last four lines squeezed into the bottom of the page in smaller script.

## Wednesday 31 October

[MEM. dated Thursday 1 Novr.] Yesterday you rose with sad headach took chaise & drove to Hanau — Sent an hour too late — heard hints that you had been at Cassel — not well. Was sadly enrhumé had dreadfull headach stood it — dreaded fever — was gloomy with *real* terror — *quelque chose de nouveau*. At night, cleared [—] wrote letters and journ well. Only wait — & years will surely make you a Philosopher — If retenue — young sapling — old tree. This day chaise & Boat Mayence.

You must marry an english Lady as the Spectator show<s>[1]

[J.] The Cold had got into my head. I rose with a sad headach. I took chaise & drove to Hanau with intention to wait on the Landgrave of Hesse Cassel, the Princess Mary of England.[2] Du Rosey had given me a recommendation to the court. I sent it between eleven & twelve to the Maréchal,[3] saying that I was obliged to go next day. He sent his Compliments, & was sorry that it was an hour too late. I had a hint that a Stranger from the court of Cassel could not be very wellcome. I could not retract what I had said as to my departure. So I mist seeing the court here. I was sorry not to see a daughter of George the Second, and the young Landgrave with his danish Princess.[4] I composed myself to Patience. My Headach was dreadfull. It was as severe as I can imagine. I resolved to stand it firm. I did so. Yet, at night I dreaded seriously that I should take a fever, and perhaps die. I was alarmed with *real terror*: quelque chose de nouveau. I cleared up at night. I thought of my own character, and I was revived with this thought: 'A Sapling is not an Oak; But it will most certainly become one. I am the Sapling of a Philosopher, & want only experience. Some years hence I shall undoubtedly be a sollid happy man. But, I must take care to preserve myself, so that time may have fair occasion to exert it's Influence, & form me into a mellow Character.' With this thought I fell asleep.

[TEN LINES A DAY.]
Imperial Stoics I approve you much;
But, greatly fear that there have ne'er been such
I grant you men[5] may easily maintain
That they[6] no evil can perceive in pain
But I have learnt that boldest words are air
As Satire has pronounc'd your vows ye fair.

I cannot think[7] that eer the human frame
Could from all feeling an exemption claim
And therefore Stoics!—with a candid breast
That you existed boldly I contest.

[1] MS. 'You ... sh<ows>' written along the left margin, some of the edge crumbling. The choice of a wife, but not specifically of an English one, is discussed in *The Spectator*, No. 261.

[2] 'Landgrave' is here used in the feminine, a form possibly suggested by French usage. Hanau had been deeded to Princess Mary when she and her sons left Friedrich II of Hessen-Kassel immediately after learning of his conversion to Catholicism (see Journ. 24 Oct. n. 12).

[3] Presumably Count (Freiherr) Georg Friedrich von Verschuer (1722–75), Princess Mary's chamberlain, who was in charge, there being no marshal at the court of Hanau at this time (see Rainer von Hessen, ed., '*Wir Wilhelm von Gottes Gnaden*': *Die Lebenserinnerungen Kurfürst Wilhelms I von Hessen, 1743–1821*, 1996).

[4] His visit to the residence of Friedrich II

had evidently made JB *persona non grata* at the court of Friedrich's estranged wife. Prince Wilhelm (1743–1821) was not yet landgrave but Hereditary Prince. He had married Karoline (1747–1820), second daughter of the King of Denmark, on 12 Sept. in Copenhagen (Isenburg, i. Tafel 100) and had returned to Hanau on 12 Oct. (Erich Meyer, *Maria, Landgräfin von Hessen*, 1894, p. 330). Wilhelm and his brothers would eventually be reconciled with their father, Wilhelm would succeed him as Landgrave Wilhelm IX of Hessen-Kassel in 1785, and he would become Elector as Wilhelm I in 1803 (Martin Ernst von Schlieffen, *Einige Betreffnisse und Erlebungen, 1830–1840*, pp. 201–03).

[5] MS. 'one' written above 'men'
[6] MS. 'He' written above 'they'
[7] MS. 'Beleive I cannot' written above 'I cannot think'

## Thursday 1 November

[MEM. dated Friday 2 Novr.] Yesterday[1] [l]eft Hanau betimes. From Francfort had boat past Hockum[2] to Mayence with young Barnard of Dunkirk, who played Ally Croaker at church at Dusseldorf.[3] At Mayence — All Saints saw two churches — no Elector[.]

[J.] Early this morning I left Hanau, & returned to Francfort where I got into the Boat for Mayence. My headach was better. I met in the boat with Mr. Barnard a Dunkirk Merchant Grand[4] Son to the great Sir John.[5] He was a good lively fellow. We had a pleasant sail of about eight hours. We stopt an hour at a Village, where we dined. We saw in our passage the village of Hockeim, which tho' situated on the banks of the Main, gives name to the best Old Rhenish.[6] When we arrived at Mayence, I heard that the Elector was from home, and would not return for a forthnight. I was sorry at this; as I had a letter for one of his Chambellans, & wished to see an eclesiastical court.[7] Patience was again my kind comforter. Barnard & I went and viewed the town. It contains some very good houses, and it has a certain air very becoming in an eclesiastical Town. It was All-Saints day. We went into two churches, which were both grand.[8] My Soul was elevated to Devotion by the solemn Vespers. Barnard & I supt at my Inn. We had with us a French Traveller.[9] We were hearty.

[TEN LINES A DAY.]
Why mighty Boswell! hesitate so long
Why without cause put off thy daily Song?

Does want of power oblige thee to refuse,
And have twelve hours of winter chill'd thy Muse?
No — but my Pen awav'ring[10] 'twixt two Themes
Like the most puzzled of all Mortals seems
I know not whether in a solemn strain
Loudly to sing of all the Saintly train
[O]r call up Mem'ry's melancholy store
And the sad fate[11] of Lisbon to deplore.[12]

[1] MS. 'Yesterday' inserted above and just before the beginning of the entry.

[2] MS. 'past Hockum' inserted above 'Mayence'. 'Hockum' is JB's spelling for 'Hochheim', for which see n. 6.

[3] MS. 'Dusseldrorp'. 'Ally Croaker' was a popular song about a young Scotsman whose gambling caused him to be rejected by his 'Ally' (for the text, see *The Vocal Library*, London 1824, p. 270). For an anecdote concerning this song, played on an organ in Düsseldorf by Sir John Barnard (for whom see n. 5), and Sir Adam Fergusson (c. 1732–1813) of Kilkerran, an Ayrshire neighbour of JB's see *Boswelliana*, p. 232.

[4] MS. 'Grand' inserted between 'Merchant' and 'Son'.

[5] Sir John Barnard (c. 1685–1764) was a much-admired London merchant. As M.P. for London from 1722 to 1761, he had opposed Robert Walpole but had gained that powerful minister's respect. Barnard had been knighted in 1732, had served as alderman from 1728 to 1758, sheriff in 1735–36, and lord mayor of London in 1737–38 (Namier and Brooke, ii. 49). He had written some popular pamphlets on trade and finance as well as several guides for apprentices. His statue had been erected on the Royal Exchange in 1747 in appreciation for his part in ending a financial panic two years earlier (*Oxford DNB*). The younger Barnard is not further identified.

[6] The village is situated 7.5 miles (12.1 km) from Mainz near the confluence of the Main and the Rhine. The term 'hock', used in Britain for any white Rhine wine, comes from the abbreviation of the German *Hochheimer* (OED, s.v. 'hock', *sb.*[4]), a term that means 'coming from Hochheim'.

[7] The Elector, Baron von Breidbach-Bürresheim, was also the Archbishop of Mainz and primate of Germany, hence one of the most powerful secular as well as religious rulers of the region. He was credited with introducing the spirit of the Enlightenment into his realm, but his court was not particularly splendid. While he was in office from 1763 to his death in 1774, the last six years also as Bishop of Worms, he was known for his good character, simple tastes, and love of hunting (Vehse, xlv. 168–73). JB had been in his territory at Erfurt (see Journ. 16 Oct.). The chamberlain has not been identified.

[8] The two most imposing were the centrally situated Cathedral of St. Martin and St. Stefan, a complex Romanesque building with Gothic side chapels dating from about 1036 A.D., and the almost equally elaborate St. Stefan, a Gothic building begun a few decades later and constructed mainly from 1290 to 1338. This one, the oldest cruciform church in the middle Rhine, was situated closer to the city walls, on the southwest incline of the Stefansberg ([Angela Schumacher], *Stadt Mainz: Altstadt, Kulturdenkmäler in Rheinland-Pfalz*, 1988, ii. pt. 2, pp. 76–79, 116).

[9] See Journ. 2 Nov. and n. 2.

[10] MS. 'a wav'ring'

[11] MS. 'wretched' written over 'sad fate'

[12] This day was both Hallow-e'en and the anniversary of the catastrophic earthquake in Lisbon in 1755. The latter had inspired Voltaire's 'Poème sur le désastre de Lisbonne', 1756, which expressed doubts about a benevolent deity.

## Friday 2 November

[MEM. dated Saturday 3 Novr.][1] Yesterday came from [F]ranc[.] to Worms with frenchman & old Germ[.] Wom[.] who laughd at each other had terrible headach feared fever. Past Worms arriv'd Manheim [—] Prince Friederique[.]

[J.] The French Traveller was Monsieur Bertollon a merchant of fine stuffs at Lyons. He & I & my servant & a German Woman got into an *Extra Post* for Manheim. The Frenchman had a Pomeranian Dog called *Pomer* whom he was mighty fond of. He was a singular frenchman; a great lubberly dog with a head like a British Tar. He sung most outrageously. He was jolly. The German *Frow* was oldish and very fat. When he sung, She was like to choak with laughing, and when she recovered her breath cried *Er is ein lustiger Mensch.*[2] I do not remember to have met with a more ludicrous scene, for the frenchman and the frow mutually laughed at each other. I was highly diverted, tho' my headach still continued. It was a heavy cold. I was in a real fever. I was just transported like a Sack. We dined at Worms. A Jew came into the Parlour. He exchanged German money with me. I gave him some pieces which would pass only in the States which I had left, & he gave me pieces which would pass every where. By way of being generous to the poor Israelite I gave him Six *Batsen.*[3] He went away. I found he had cheated me to the value of some *Batsen.* O Israel! why art thou ever so dishonest?[4] At night we arrived at Manheim, & put up at the *Prince Frederique.*[5] I eat a wine soup[6] & tumbled into bed.

[TEN LINES A DAY.]
A fool is he who little things neglects
For from small causes oft spring great effects
A subject often I must seek in vain
And vex'd exclaim against my barren brain
While gainst my self my enmity grows hot
See on my paper sudden falls a blot
A Blot! — and who'd a better subject seek
I could an hour on as small matters speak
And he shall find that whether wrong or right—
On as small matters I ten lines can write[.][7]

[1] MS. 'major' (not identified) written in the right hand margin between the memoranda dated 2 and 3 Nov.

[2] 'He is a merry fellow'. Bertollon was associated with Cochet and Co. of Lyon, as he informed JB in a brief note of c. 4 Nov. (C 148, *Catalogue*, ii. 418). JB would remember Bertollon as 'a jolly dog' when he later got into touch with him in Lyon (Journ. 2 Jan. 1766).

[3] Worms, a 'free' (i.e., independent) city about 28 miles (45.1 km) from Mainz, belonged to the south-German currency zone where Gulden and Kreuzer were in use, as opposed to Prussia and Saxony of the north- and mid-German currency zone, where Taler and Groschen were the prevailing currency. Although higher-value silver coins such as Gulden and Taler as well as gold coins were accepted throughout the region, smaller coins had to be exchanged, as they were by JB. Batzen were silver coins of small value (1 Batzen equalling 4 Kreuzer), so JB's loss was not great. In any case, he may not have been cheated, for possibly the coins were worth less than their face value so soon after the Seven Years' War, when some 'bad' coins were still in circulation in spite of efforts in the region of the Upper Rhine to improve the official standard of measurement (the *Münz-fuss*) in 1764 (Konrad Schneider, *Die Münz- und Währungspolitik des Oberrheinischen Reichskreises im 18. Jahrhundert*, c. 1995, pp. 178–79; further information kindly provided by letter from Dr. Schneider, 13 Aug. 2001).

[4] JB, though not personally acquainted with Jews, here accepts the stereotype of Jews as petty swindlers (Felsenstein, pp. 51–52; see Journ. 5 Aug. n. 1).

<sup>5</sup> JB had now arrived in the Palatinate (German: 'die Pfalz' or 'Kurpfalz', the latter title in recognition of the ruling Kurfürst or elector). The 'Prinz Friedrich' was located in Square B 2, No. 8, the usual form of street address in Mannheim, where most streets are designated only by blocks from A 1 to U 6 (location confirmed in the land register of 1795 and 1801, MS in the library of the Mannheim Altertumsverein, Sig. C 324 and C 324b, without pagination). The town had developed from a mere village in the later seventeenth century but had been levelled by the French in 1693 during the devastating local war variously called the Palatinate War, the War of the League of Augsburg, the Nine Years War (1689–97), or the War of the First Grand Alliance; it was also called the War of Reunification by the French to justify their attempt to regain areas ceded after 1648, the end of the Thirty-Year War (Rolf Gustav Haebler, *Badische Geschichte*, 1951, repr. 1987, pp. 77, 79; Ragnhild Hatton, *Louis XIV and Europe*, 1976, pp. 295–97). Mannheim had achieved its 'chessboard' pattern of parallel streets cut by others at right angles only after 1700 (Nugent, ii. 393–94; Friedrich Walter, *Bauwerke der Kurfürstenzeit in Mannheim*, 1928, pp. 7–9).

<sup>6</sup> A popular, easily digestible soup, half white wine and half water, seasoned with sugar, cinnamon, and nutmeg (*Saltzburgisches Koch-Buch*, 1719, i. 93).

<sup>7</sup> MS. Lines 5–8 squeezed in at the bottom of the page; the last two lines crowded into the right-hand corner. The blot is not visible on this sheet, but possibly appeared on a separate page used for a first draft.

## Saturday 3 November

[MEM. dated Sunday<sup>1</sup> 4 Novr.] Yesterday sent to Furstenberg — sick — very polite [—] recommended to Harold went to him — fine old man. Talk'd of L. Baltimore & real facts<sup>2</sup> — din'd Inn — Fever gone. At 2<sup>3</sup> nephew Capt Harold genteel clever young fellow. Saw opera rehears'd — home. Chace Price not remember'd till robbd — 3 days out of use could do nothing.<sup>4</sup> This day dress at 8 & from 9 to 11 Journ & 10 lines.

[J.] I sent to the General de Furstenberg a card of recommendation which I had to him from a Monsieur de Franckenberg at Cassel.<sup>5</sup> He returned me an absurd extravagant card, full of respect for a man whom he knew nothing of. He said he was confined to his bed; but referred me to M. Harold Gentleman of the chamber, & Irish by nation. I waited on Harold, & found him a hearty old fellow full of Anecdotes. He has been abroad a great many years. He has been thirty years in the Elector Palatine's service. He taught his Highness to read english.<sup>6</sup> He told me that I could not be presented till Monday, as the Elector was gone a hunting this day, & as tomorrow was his Jour de fête when nobody was presented.<sup>7</sup> I dined at the Ordinary of my Inn. My fever flew out upon my lips.<sup>8</sup> I was a dissagreable figure. I was fretted. At three Mr. Harold's Nephew waited upon me. He had been long in the french Service & was now a Captain in the Elector Palatine's. He was a genteel young fellow, knew a good deal, & talked well tho' with affectation.<sup>9</sup> He carried me to hear the Opera rehearsed.<sup>10</sup> I was well amus'd for some hours, & then returned to my Inn, & read English newspapers which old Harold sent me. While abroad, I am often long without seeing a London Paper. Now & then I come to a Place, where I get a Budget<sup>11</sup> of them. At Dresden I got one. Here I got one. It is curious how Ideas are effaced & renewed. I had not thought of Chace Price since I left England, till I read tonight in the Papers that his house had been robbd.<sup>12</sup> It made me laugh from the queer light in which I viewed it. I had written none<sup>13</sup> for three days, and this night could absolutely do nothing. The nervous fluid was disordered.<sup>14</sup>

[TEN LINES A DAY.]
Thou lech'rous dotard whom a vicious course
Continued long has drain'd of manly force
Canst thou not now contented eat & sleep
But must thou still a handsom mistress keep?[16]
Say art thou not asham'd the girl to tire
With thy fantastic itchings of desire?
How must she laugh when you between her toes
With grave composure thrust your rotten nose!
Or when you slowly lift your naked[17] heel
And her warm armpits curiously[18] feel[.]

---

[1] MS. Written over 'Saturday'.
[2] For Lord Baltimore, see Journ. 3 Aug. and n. 3.
[3] MS. Damaged by a small hole in the page; the time is conjectural.
[4] MS. 'rehears'd' and 'Chace ... nothing' scored out by a modern hand.
[5] Wilhelm Burkhard, Baron von Fürstenberg (1704–66), was Governor of the fortress Mannheim as well as lieutenant-general, colonel of an infantry regiment, and privy counsellor for war. He had interrupted his military career in the Palatinate to serve as major-general in the Hessian forces in 1757 and had returned to Mannheim in 1759 (dates of birth and death from Hans Huth, *Die Kunstdenkmäler des Stadtkreises Mannheim*, 1982, i. 154–55; Oskar Bezzel, *Geschichte des kurpfälzischen Heeres, 1777*, 1925, List of Generals, App.; *Fortgesetzte Neue Genealogisch-Historische Nachrichten* 13 [1763]: 340; 61 [1767]: 621–22). Franckenberg, not mentioned in JB's account of Kassel, was probably Ludwig von Frankenberg (1728–1815), who had helped to educate the three sons of Friedrich II of Hessen-Kassel and who had begun his diplomatic career in 1763, serving as envoy sent from Kassel to Gotha or already entirely in the service of Gotha (correcting the names of Fürstenberg and Frankenberg as given in *Grand Tour I*, Index; see also Philipp Losch, *Kurfürst Wilhelm I, Landgraf von Hessen*, 1923, pp. 42–43, 48).
[6] Stephan von Harold had been a high steward (Truchsess), one of several, since 1751 (listed as 'von Dharold' in the *ChurPfälzischer Hoff- und Staats-Calender*, 1764, p. 11). Previously he had served as second secretary of the Palatinate government and in that capacity had been involved in an unspecified financial scandal in 1738 (Friedrich Walter, *Geschichte Mannheims von den ersten Anfängen*, 1907, i. 475). He had also been interim director of the comédie française

of Mannheim in 1746 (Friedrich Walter, *Geschichte des Theaters und der Musik am kurpfälzischen Hofe*, 1898, pp. 244, 349).
[7] The Elector, Karl Theodor (1724–99) of Palatine-Sulzbach, was about to celebrate his saint's-day in honour of St. Charles Borromeo (1538–84), who had been canonized in 1610 for working to reform the Catholic church from within (NCE, ii. 710–12). The festivities for this, the most elaborate of four annual 'galas', included a grand reception for the local nobility, ministers, and courtiers, followed by a high mass, and ending with a public dinner served by the chamberlains (announced on the page facing 'December', *ChurPfältzischer Hoff- und Staats-Calender*, 1764; see Journ. 5 Nov. n. 8; see also Stefan Mörz, *Haupt- und Residenzstadt*, pp. 46–52). Karl Theodor, who attended mass daily, had been educated by and later relied on the Jesuit Franz Seedorf (1691–1758) for guidance (see Weich, pp. 133–48; Schaab, ii. 183). Karl Theodor's family belonged to a junior branch of the house of Palatine-Wittelsbach that had reconverted from Lutheranism to Catholicism in 1656. He had come to rule the Palatinate on the death of Elector Karl Philipp (1661–1742), the last male descendant of the Palatine-Neuburg line, which had been recatholicized already in 1613 (Isenburg, i. Tafel 35; Weich, pp. 8, 26, 126–27). Although most of the inhabitants of Mannheim had remained Protestants, Catholics and especially Jesuits exerted a strong influence on the court (Schaab, ii. 182–83).
[8] Symptoms of a cold sore; see Mem. dated 5 Nov. and n. 1.
[9] Edmund, Baron von Harold (1737–*post* 1800), born in Limerick, served in the Palatinate army and would attain the rank of *Generalmajor* (lieutenant-colonel). Later he would contribute to the popularity of the Celtic bard Ossian by translating his poems,

*Die Gedichte Ossians, eines alten Celtischen Helden und Barden* ('The Poems of Ossian, by an Ancient Hero and Bard'), 3 vols., 1775, and *Neuentdeckte Gedichte Ossians* ('Newly Discovered Poems of Ossian', 1787). He would also base his drama *Sylmora*, 1802, on Ossian. See Hamberger-Meusel, ii. 40; Karl Goedeke, *Grundriss zur Geschichte der deutschen Dichtung aus den Quellen*, 1898, 2nd ed. vi. 450.

[10] See Journ. 5 Nov. and n. 8.

[11] A bundle (OED, s.v. 'budget', 3).

[12] JB had evidently forgotten that while in Utrecht he had written about Price, describing him as a politician too concerned with being reelected (French theme, 3 Dec. 1763, Yale MS. 87). A Welsh M.P. who represented Leominster from 1759 to 1767 and who would later represent Radnorshire from 1768 to 1777, Price was also a wit and *bon vivant* (Namier and Brooke, iii. 326). JB had met him in London in the company of Lord Eglinton (Journ. 29 May 1763). The burglary of Price's house in Curzon Street, Mayfair, had been reported in the *London Chronicle* of 9 Oct.

[13] A puzzling statement. Possibly JB meant that he had written no letters.

[14] MS. 'The nervous ... disordered' deleted by a modern hand.

[15] The old lecher and his mistress, not identified, are presumably stereotypes rather than particular people.

[16] MS. 'new-par'd' written above 'naked'

[17] MS. 'snug' written above 'warm'; 'delicately' above 'curiously'; 'ludicrously' below it.

## Sunday 4 November

[MEM. dated Monday 5 Novr.] Yesterday to cire lip Scachylon[1] & at home all day — Journ — but was a little low — knew cause — was silent — evening Capt. Arnold[2] came — a very clever fellow. Frenchman tir'd. To bed quiet — This day resume *regulated* Piety. Send to Harrold[3] to know at what hour court — be clear & gay & in true stile of Elector Palatine[.]

[J.] To cure my cold I kept my chamber all day. At five Captain Harold payed me a visit. My fellow traveller of Lyons was in the next room. He used to come to me at night crying, '*Sacre bleu! Je m'ennuis*' He amused me with little particulars.

[TEN LINES A DAY.]
What my old freind Jack *Spleen* & is it you?
It is indeed my boy. Well, how d'ye do?
For many months your face I scarce have seen
Do tell me why do tell me where you've been
I fancy John you're now inclin'd to be
With some old Lady rather than with me
You love to sit amoaping by the fire
And tell in mournfull[4] language how you tire
So lov'd I too. But now — o pleasant change!
With health & gayety abroad I range.

[1] MS. 'cachylon', with the first two letters hidden under an ink blot or deleted, but clearly visible in the Expense Account of 8 Nov., referring to 'a sort of medicine' (Lewis and Short, s.v. 'diachylon'), or 'a sticking plaster' (OED, s.v. 'cachylon'). The preceding 'cire' is a variant of kire, 'cure' (OED, s.v. 'cire').

[2] 'Arnold' inadvertently substituted for 'Harold'

[3] MS. 'HArnold', with 'r' written above 'n', thereby substituting 'Arnold' for 'Harold'. Presumably JB meant 'Arnold' (see Journ. 5 Nov. n. 4).

[4] MS. 'sickly' written above 'mournfull'

## Monday 5 November

[MEM. dated Tuesday 6 Novr.] Yesterday better — fever prevented — went with Harold to[1] court talked of not presenting you *yet* [—] *you*[2] thought to go off in pet tomorrow o fie — evening Opera — hyp'd & did not truly relish. At night did nothing went to bed as at Utrecht. How easily comes change — You *must* fight.

[J.] My cold was much better. It prevented me yesterday from hearing superb mass in the Elector's Chapel. However, by keeping my room, I have shunned a fever. At eleven Harold carried me to court. The Palace is large & elegant. There is a Gallery a Passage round the whole of it prodigiously long.[3] There were a great many People at court. Harold talked of not presenting me till tomorrow. After having allready waited two days, this piqued me not a little; & had I not been presented this day, I should have bluntly set out next morning. However, the Grand Chambellan[4] presented me to the Elector. His Highness asked me from whence I came. He was very swarthy, & very high and mighty.[5] I was presented to the Electrice, who was much painted, & also exceedingly lofty.[6] I saw here the Prince of Nassau Weilbourg. He recalled to my mind the Hague & all it's ideas.[7] At night I was at the Opera. It was indeed superb.[8] I had the ideas of the Palatine court which Sir Adam Fergusson gave me.[9] When I came home, I could neither read nor write. I was truly splenetic, & went to bed. How frail is this existence of mine! how easily changed!

[TEN LINES A DAY.]
Tis my opinion that if all mankind
Were to their chambers by a cold confin'd,
That all mankind most certainly would be
Feeble & dull as melancholy me.
I now am heavy laden with a cold
And I appear like one exceeding old
Gay projects scarcely will a man contrive
Whose head for three days has been like to rive[10]
Yet I tho' sick most steadily resort
To pay my duty at the muses court.

[1] MS. Damaged by a hole; 'to' is conjectural.

[2] MS. 'you' inserted above 'thought'.

[3] The palace was the centrepiece for seven parallel streets, the middle of which led straight to the court of honour. A monumental building, the largest of its kind in Germany and a symbol of absolute rule, it had 1,500 windows, and its northern front, facing the town, measured about 1,475 feet (450 meters). The gallery, enclosing the main pavillion and various wings, consisted of arcades. Begun soon after 1720, when the electors moved their residence from Heidelberg following disputes with the local Cal-

vinists, the palace was the work of the architects Johann Clemens Froimont (fl. early 18th cent.), Guillaume Hauberat (c. 1680–1750), and Alessandro Galli da Bibiena (1686–1748), completed by Nicolas de Pigage (1723–96) in 1760 (see Berthold Roland, *Mannheim*, 1966, pp. 25–31; Friedrich Walter, *Bauwerke der Kurfürstenzeit in Mannheim*, 1928, pp. 18–20).

[4] Hermann Arnold, Baron von Wachtendonck-Germenseel (1694–1768), had been *Obrist-Kämmerer* (chief chamberlain) at the Palatinate court since 1743 (*ChurPfältzischer Hoff- und Staats-Calender*, 1764, p. 17). Previously he had held a diplomatic post in the

Palatinate dependency of Jülich and had served as Palatinate representative at the election of the emperor in 1741 (Mörz, p. 471).

[5] Karl Theodor was so dark-complexioned that JB referred to him as 'the silent Negroe' (To JJ, 9 Nov., *Corr. 1*, p. 143). He presided over a strictly hierarchical court that employed at least 1000 persons (Schaab, ii. 176). Like other absolute monarchs of his time, he favoured splendid displays attesting to his prestige and power, notably grand opera and other musical entertainments (see n. 8 below, and Journ. 7 Nov. n. 11). He had founded an academy of sciences, the Academia Theodoro Palatina, in 1763 to study the history of his realm (Vehse, xxiv. 146; Schaab, ii. 208–09).

When JB met him, Karl Theodor had overcome his earlier subservience to his wife, whose advice he had gladly accepted in the 1750s and whose lovers he had overlooked (Mörz, pp. 45–58; Schaab, ii. 183). By 1758 he, in turn, had taken the first of several mistresses (Karl J. Svoboda, *Prinzessinnen und Favoritinnen*, 1989, pp. 105–30). Motivated by personal interest, Karl Theodor had stayed out of the Seven Years' War except for sending troops to the imperial armies but remained ambitious for himself and his immediate family. On inheriting Bavaria in 1777, he would move his court to Munich and would try to cede some of his new land to Austria in return for imperial titles for his illegitimate son and daughters as well as the title of king for himself. His territorial plan would fail, however, when Frederick II of Prussia opposed them by waging a short war in 1778 (Schaab, ii. 193–96). On the death of his wife (for whom see n. 6), he would marry the young Maria Leopoldine of Austria-Este (1776–1848) in the vain hope of still producing an heir. The French revolutionist armies would invade his realm in 1792 and a few years later bring about its dissolution. He would die in Munich, and the title of King of Bavaria, for which he had long schemed in vain, would be gained by his successor, Maximilian Josef (1756–1825) of Zweibrücken-Birkenfeld (see Schaab, ii. 248–51; Rall, pp. 313–37; Isenburg, i. Tafel 29).

[6] The Electress, Elisabeth Augusta (1721–94), Princess of Sulzbach, was evidently still treated with respect at court. Like her consort, she was very conscious of hierarchy and rank, and she, too, loved spectacles (Mörz, pp. 78–84). A cousin of Karl Theodor's, she had married him with Papal dispensation and had dominated him until 1761, when their longed-for son died in childbirth. Although this event had ended her personal and political influence, she would continue to accompany the Elector until he moved to Munich, after which she would live increasingly separate from him and retire often to her summer palace (Mörz, pp. 58–64, 69–73).

By 'painted', JB meant that she used rouge (OED, s.v. 'paint' *v.*[1], 4.a).

[7] JB had met Karl Christian (1735–88), Prince of Nassau-Weilburg, in the Hague through his kinsman F. C. van Aersen van Sommelsdyck (see From Sommelsdyck, 28 Apr. 1765). The prince had been a major-general in Palatinate service since 1760, after having served in the Netherlands. On inheriting the principality of Weilburg from his father in 1753, he had left it in the hands of an administrator while he pursued his military career (ADB, xv. 313–14).

[8] *Ifigenia in Tauride*, with music by the Neapolitan Giovanni Francesco Maio (1732–70) and libretto by the court poet Mattia Verazi (fl. 1751–92), specially commissioned for the Elector's saint's day (Friedrich Walter, *Geschichte des Theaters und der Musik am kurpfälzischen Hofe*, 1898, p. 135; New Grove 2; Paul Corneilson, 'Die Oper am kurfürstlichen Hof zu Mannheim', *Die Mannheimer Hofkapelle im Zeitalter Carl Theodors*, ed. Ludwig Finscher, 1992, pp. 120–24). It was presumably the work JB had seen in rehearsal on 3 Nov. Performances, offered free of charge, were given on the large proscenium stage in the magnificent opera house that Galli-Bibiena had built into the far end of the palace's west wing. The auditorium and five tiers of loges could seat 2000 spectators. Lighting was provided by 1200 wax candles as well as a large candelabra that could be retracted into the ceiling during performances (Roland, p. 31; Alexandra Glanz, *Alessandro Galli-Bibiena*, 1991, pp. 39, 54–62).

[9] Fergusson had been on the grand tour in 1757–58 (Namier and Brooke, ii. 419).

[10] 'To split' (OED, s.v. 'rive' *v.*[1]).

## Tuesday 6 November

[MEM. dated Wednesday 7 Novr.] Yesterday you told Harrold that his court was not hospitable — & praised Brunswic. At night saw Comedie very well — Actor quite Lord Kames — This day see Jesuits.

[J.] Why do I not talk of the beauty of Manheim? of it's streets *tirés á cordon* & lighted better than any streets that I have seen?[1] I am in bad humour. The court here is insupportable after the polite reception which I have met with at others. No invitation to dine with the Elector. I told Harrold his court was not hospitable, & extolled that of Brunswic. At night I was at the Comedie. There was a comic Actor there the very Image of Lord Kames.[2] He had his size his countenance, his voice his manner. I never saw so strong a likeness.

[TEN LINES A DAY.]
Five Winter days at Manheim shall I be
And in my lines that City sha'n't you see
Shall not th' Elector Palatine be praised
And to the Skies his noble court be rais'd
No faith my freind to be exceeding plain
Such scurvy courts should never have a[3] strain
Raise it? why faith I'd raise it to the skies,
As the bold Eagle made the tortoise rise
That he might let it drop upon the stones
And to a Jelly crush it flesh and bones.[4]

[1] 'Tiré au cordeau': 'as straight as a die' (Robert, s.v. 'Cordeau'); that is, in straight lines. Street lights, installed in 1748, had increased to more than 500 by 1760 (Stefan Mörz, *Haupt- und Residenzstadt: Karl Theodor, sein Hof und Mannheim*, 1998, p. 101).
[2] Neither the play nor the actor has been identified. For Henry Home, Lord Kames, see Journ. 27 Sept. and n. 4. The French troupe performed in a small auditorium on the second storey of the palace's west wing (Elector's order of 22 June 1748 and of 15 Aug. 1755; information from Mr. Dieter Dumas, Director of the Library, Reiss-Museum of Mannheim, 12 Sept. 1998). This troupe, in residence since 1748, had gained the special protection of the Electress. It would remain in Mannheim until 1770, when the Elector would dismiss it because he had developed a taste for German plays

(see Jörg Kreutz, 'Aufklärung und französische Hofkultur im Zeitalter Carl Theodors in Mannheim', *Die Mannheimer Hofkapelle*, pp. 8–9).
[3] MS. 'deserve no tunefull' written above 'should never have a'
[4] MS. 'bruise it's' written over 'crush it'. JB appears to be adapting Aesop's fable about an eagle who is disappointed in a promise made by a tortoise and kills this creature with his talons. Although the revenge in the two versions differs, JB may have recalled the illustration in a popular edition of Aesop that shows a high-flying eagle clutching a hapless tortoise as if ready to drop him (Fable XL, *Fables of Aesop*, ed. Samuel Croxall, 7th ed. 1760). JB's Edinburgh booklist (c. 1770) showed that he later owned the 8th ed. (1766).

## Wednesday 7 November

[MEM. dated Thursday 8 Novr.] Yesterday you visited Eglise de Jesuites, elegantly painted [—] pannels green — Altars porphyry. College not well within. Pere [M]onier François a Bel homme — a Digges [—] walk'd with him in garden, disputed — found myself a Philosopher felt satisfaction yet sorry that we could not agree — M. Harro<ld> un grandeur de ne pas manger — tor<t.>
Should L. Marischal say I'm a venerable Earl He'd lose respect — so is vanity.[1]

[J.] I went & saw the Jesuits church, which is a very elegant Piece. The outside is of white stone, with some fine carving & one or two good Statues.

The inside is very fine both in painting & gilding tho' a little gaudy. Some of the Pannels were green. The Painting is either Crucifixion Pieces, or Pictures in honour of the order. You find here a representation of the holy consolation afforded by the Jesuits and of their conversions in different parts of the Globe. They seem to triumph far & near. There are here some elegant Altarpieces of marble.[2] I then went to see the Jesuits College.[3] I had heard that there was here a French Jesuit Pêre Monier. I asked for him. He came to me immediatly. He was a black[4] handsom Man between thirty & forty. He showed me their Refectoire, but told me that altho' their College had a good outside it was but poor within. He showed me their Garden where he & I walked an hour. He had been in Canada. He was shrewd & lively. He talked cleverly on the Political affairs of Europe. He talked of the error of The French in having banished his order.[5] He said Je ne suis pas faché contre eux. Je les plaigns. Mais bientot ils ouvreront les yeux. Ils verront les terribles consequences. Ils verront la chute de Literature. Non pas absolument que les Jesuites le soutenoient tout a fait; mais ils donnoient de l'emulation.[6] A present les autres Colleges tomberont en negligence. He asked me if I was Catholic. I told him non. Mais J'espere Je ne serais pas danné pour cela./ striking him gently on the shoulder/[7] Croyez vous en verité que Je serais damné.[8] He replied 'Monsieur c'est dure, mais, il faut absolument que [Je][9] le croye. Vous n'avez point l'excuse d'un pauvre Paysan. Vous êtes eclairé.' I Smiled modestly. He immediatly entered on the favourite subject of Jesuits, the Catholic Controversy. He run on with arguments which I do not conceive any Protestant truly attached to his Religion as the only means of Salvation could answer.[10] I told Pêre [M]onier that I was of no sect. That I took my faith from Jesus that I endeavoured to adore God with fervency; that I found my devotion excited by grand worship, & that I was happy to worship in a Romish Church. I said my notions of God made me not fear him as cruel. The Pére said 'Je suis reêllement faché que vous n'etes pas Catholique'. He was so agreable, I allmost regretted that I could not make him happy by thinking as he did: But, I took him by the hand, & said 'Monsieur J'aurrais le plaisir de vous rencontrer au Ciel'. I asked Captain Harold today, why the Court here did not ask Strangers to dine. He said 'Monsieur, C'est une grandeur qui a notre cour de ne pas avoir beaucoup d'etrangers á sa table'. Monsr. said I. Si l'Electeur croit ce la, il se trompe diablement. Car Je trouverai toujours plus de grandeur á une Cour ou il y a une superbe table, qu'á une cour ou il n'y en a point. In the evening We had what is called the académie de musique. It was very full, and the music was excellent.[11] I quitted this court quite discontented.

[TEN LINES A DAY.]
Yes — be it bruis'd — It is a Stranger's prayer
And let th'Elector it's destruction share
Burn't be his palace to the very ground
And let no vestige where it stood[12] be found.
For Hospitality ne'er enter'd there

But studied grandeur to make Blockheads stare
At noon his highness with dark face appear'd
And much he wanted to be greatly feard.
His cringing Courtiers played the shamefull farce
But I still seem'd to bid him kiss my A—

[1] MS. 'Should ... vanity' written in three lines along the left margin.

[2] This church, close to the palace, had been commissioned in 1733 but consecrated only in 1760. Its exterior, with its well-ordered frontal façade of portals and pilasters, had been the last achievement of the theatre architect Galli-Bibiena. The interior, gleaming with green and white marble, stucco, and gilt, had been completed under the supervision of Franz Wilhelm Rabaliatti (1716–82); see Glanz, pp. 39, 51–54; Hans Huth, 'Jesuitenkirche Mannheim', Schnell, Kunstführer Nr. 1084, 1977, p. 6. Its stucco and many of its frescoes were the work of the noted Bavarian artist Egid Quirin Asam (1692–1750). Those on the ceiling showed the works and miracles of the Jesuit missionary Saint Francis Xavier (1506–52), those on the cupola, the life and transfiguration of the founder of the order, Saint Ignatius of Loyola (1491–1556); and those high up in the lantern, personifications of the four continents suggesting the range of the Jesuits' missionary activity (Friedrich Walter, Bauwerke der Kurfürstenzeit, 1928, pp. 44–45; Gerhard Hojer, Cosmas und Egid Quirin Asam: Führer zu ihren Kunstwerken, 1986). The high altar and six side altars were each embellished with statues and bas reliefs. The church as a whole would continue to be admired as the most important baroque building of southwest Germany (Huth, pp. 8–14).

[3] In the Kalte Gasse next to the church. The college, also designed by Galli-Bibiena, had been built from 1730 to 1734 with financial support from the Elector Karl Philipp and was the first achievement of the Jesuits in Mannheim (see Weich, pp. 37–53; Glanz, pp. 48–49).

[4] Dark-complexioned or dark-haired.

[5] The Jesuits, whose power and influence had provoked increasing hostility in several countries, had been accused of financial malfeasance and other misdeeds, whereupon they had been expelled from Portugal in 1759 and from France in 1762. The order would be totally suppressed by the Pope in 1773 and would be officially revived only in 1814 (see William V. Bangert, A History of the Society of Jesus, 2nd ed. 1986, pp. 372–

83; Alec Mellor, Histoire de l'anticléricalisme français, new ed. 1978, pp. 66–76, 426). 'Monier' is not listed among the faculty of the college (see Weich, pp. 225–26) and may have been present in Mannheim only temporarily. Presumably he was the François le Moine (b. 1711), formerly Prefect at the Jesuit college in Reims, who held the position of Professor of Rhetoric and was confessor at the Jesuit college in Worms (inscribed as 'Franciscus Moyne' in the catalogue of Jesuits in the Upper Rhine, Archiv der Oberdeutschen Provinz SJ, Munich, Kataloge 1764–65 and 1766–67, Rhen. sup., fasc. 7, p. 27). Very likely he was also the 'P. Monet' or 'Moinette' who had just complained to the Elector and Electress that the German Jesuits of Mannheim had not offered the French Jesuits the friendly treatment that they deserved (Letter of Elie Fréron to Franz Joseph Terasse Desbillons, 8 Sept. 1764, cited in Weich, pp. 187–89, 230 n. 146).

[6] Long famous as educators, the Jesuits had promoted the study of classical texts, had organized performances of Latin plays, and had encouraged their students with prizes (Weich, pp. 80–86; Bangert, pp. 306–07). Their reviews in the Journal de Trévoux (pub. 1701–62) had also encouraged literature and other learning (Robert R. Palmer, 'The French Jesuits in the Age of Enlightenment', American Historical Review 45 [1939]: 44–57).

[7] MS. Slashes to set off JB's gestures.

[8] MS. 'danné'. The doctrine of the eternity of punishment—eternal damnation—had been the first great idea ('ma premierre grande idée') inculcated in JB as a child, thanks to his mother's strict Calvinism ('Ébauche de ma vie', Yale MS. L 1107, App. 2, III.A).

[9] MS. 'Je' inadvertently omitted.

[10] The controversy about the extent to which salvation depended on divine grace, free will, or predestination had raged since the late sixteenth century and had pitted the Jesuits, who acknowledged the importance of free will as well as grace, against the more austere Jansenists, who regarded grace as primary (see Weich, pp. 11–12; 'Jesuits', NCE, vii. 906–07).

[11] The académies de musique—concerts held in the Knights' Hall of the palace once a week in the winter season—contributed to Mannheim's reputation for musical excellence (see Bärbel Pelker, 'Musikalische Akademien am Hof Carl Theodors in Mannheim', and 'Theateraufführungen und Musikalische Akademien am Hof Carl Theodors in Mannheim: eine Chronik der Jahre 1742–1777', *Die Mannheimer Hofkapelle im Zeitalter Carl Theodors*, ed. Ludwig Finscher, 1992, pp. 51–53, 233–34; *New Grove 2*, s.v. 'Mannheim').

[12] MS. 'where it stood no vestige be there' written over 'no vestige … found'

## Thursday 8 November

[MEM. dated Friday 9 Novr.] Yesterday took extra & set out at 11 — was baddish [—] dreary wet day [—] thought family going into Edinr.[1] Arrived at Carlsrus — good Inn — supt well.

[J.] My ill humour continued. I was angry at myself. I saw my weakness. In such cases one must open.[2] I said to Jacob. Je n'aimerois pas d'aller en Suisse en cette humeur. Ah (said he) Quand Monsieur verra les Paÿsans avec des grandes culottes et des longues barbes, l'humeur passera bien vite. It was a dreary day. I stopt at an Inn opposite to which was a Convent of Capuchins. I heard them at mass.[3] It made me solemn. After passing some very bad road, I arrived at Carlsruhe the residence of the Court of Baden Durlach.[4] I put up at the *Darmstater Hof* a very good Inn.[5] I supt well, & recovered my good humour.

[TEN LINES A DAY.]
Mason I know you love the great Sublime
And hold in much contempt the[6] sons of Rhime
And in your writings I confess I find
Both what can rouse & what can melt my mind[7]
But when your page I as a Critic turn
Great affectation clearly I discern
Yes I discover in your crowded page
Flowers heapd on flowers to please a gaudy age
Yet worse—not flowers from nature's garden brought
But such as art with gum & care has wrought.

[1] Lord Auchinleck still used the house in Blair's Land, Parliament Close, Edinburgh, in which JB had been born. The family usually returned there from Auchinleck in Nov. (see *Earlier Years*, pp. 26, 38, and 464 n. to p. 38; Roger Craik, *James Boswell: The Scottish Perspective*, 1994, p. 20).
[2] So written in MS; possibly 'be' omitted before 'open'
[3] JB presumably heard this mass outside the walls of the monastery, which was located on two quadrants (N 5 and N 6) at the Heidelberg Gate. The Capuchins, a contemplative order founded by St. Bruno in 1084 (NCE, iii. 162–63), had come to Mannheim in 1685 at the invitation of the Elector Johann Wilhelm (1658–1716) and had fled four years later when French troops sacked the town during the Palatinate War (see Journ. 2 Nov. n. 5). The monks had been able to return in 1698 and had built their monastery from 1703 to 1706, with expansions in 1724. They would remain in Mannheim until their community was disbanded in 1838 (Walther Hümmerich, *Anfänge des kapuzinischen Klosterbaues*, Mainz, 1987, pp. 439–41).
[4] The town had become the margraval residence in 1715 when Karl Wilhelm (1679–1738) of Baden-Durlach, the grandfather of

the currently reigning margrave, built a new palace on a plain near his hillside seat of Durlach. He had made the palace the centre from which thirty-two avenues radiated in a fan-like pattern. The new town had been named 'Karl's Ruhe' ('Karl's Repose') in honour of its founder (Gerda Franziska Kircher, *Das Karlsruher Schloss als Residenz und Musensitz*, Veröffentlichungen der Kommission für Geschichtliche Landeskunde in Baden-Württemberg, Reihe B Forschungen 8 [1959], pp. 4–5).

5 The Darmstädter Hof, at No. 2 Kreuzstrasse, was in a central location close to the palace (*Wegweiser für die Grossherzogliche Residenzstadt Karlsruhe*, 1818, p. 6). It had been in business since at least 1752 (K. G. Fecht, *Geschichte der Haupt- und Residenzstadt Karlsruhe*, 1887, p. 220).

6 MS. 'us' written above 'the'

7 In his popular dramas William Mason (1725–97) had shaped native British sources —Saxon in *Elfrida* (1752) and Celtic in *Caractacus* (1759)—into classical tragedies. They were written in unrhymed verse and in 'the grand or lofty style' that SJ had considered the defining characteristic of the sublime (*Dict. SJ*). WJT had been enthusiastic about *Elfrida*, especially its choral odes, in his letter of 22 July 1758 (*Corr.* 6, p. 5 and n. 2) and had made a present of his copy of Mason's 'Dramatick Poems' to JB, who promised to take it on his travels (From WJT, 24 July 1763; To WJT, 3 Aug. 1763, *Corr.* 6, pp. 50–51, 60). This may have been the *Elfrida and Caractacus*, 1759, mentioned in the 'Catalogue of Books Belonging to James Boswell, Esq.', c. 1770, an index to his library in Edinburgh (Lincoln, App. II).

## Friday 9 November

[MEM. dated Saturday 10 Novr.] Yesterday¹ Madame Schenck² not in town — Sent to Grand Echanson — might come to court [—] came & saw you very polite — at 12 coach — was hyp'd — but went — Prince sensible amiable talk'd much english — you said you had been in club with Hume & Robertson. Brother genteel — Good court. At night supt marechal's table — fool — [F]ontaines fables. Je me tiens trop aux realites. This day dress — 9 medals &c.

Be prudent — swear not letter till Stutgard.³

[J.] The Baron de Thungen Maréchal of the Court of Gotha had given me a letter for his Sister Madame de Schmidbourg.⁴ She was not in town; so, I was here without any Recommendation. I sent a card to Monsieur de Steten *Overschenk* Grand Echanson. He returned me for answer that he would mention me to the Marcgrave, & that he did not doubt but what I would be received at court. A little after He sent to me that the marcgrave would be glad to see me, and that a Coach would come at twelve, to carry me to court. A little after Monsieur de Steten payed me a visit. He was a Colonel in the Marcgrave's service. He was a frank, polite, honest man.⁵ At twelve I had a coach & Servant from the court. I was a little hyp'd, but took resolution. I was presented to the Prince Brother who has a Regiment in the Dutch Service a silent genteel man,⁶ & to the Prince Eugene Uncle to the marcgrave á la mode de Bretagne that is to say Cousin to his Father. This Prince is in the Sardinian Service.⁷ Just before dinner the marcgrave entered. I was presented to him. He had a reserved, modest, amiable address. Mr. de Steten acted as maréchal, & carried his cane, with which he gave two distinct knocks on the floor, then the company said a silent grace, then we sat down to table which was very well served. After table the maréchal again Gives his strokes, grace is said, the Prince retires a moment, coffee is ready, he returns and talks as long as he chuses. He told me he had been in England twice. He spoke english remarkably well.⁸ He talked of

Lord Wemys,[9] Sir James Stewart,[10] Lord Dunmore[11] all Scots Bravo, & my Lord March too.[12] His Highness knew well the present literature of Scotland. I talked to him of the Select Society, of my having been a member of it, of the same Society with Hume & Robertson &c.[13] He was attentive to every little anecdote. I found that I was truly agreable to him. M. de Steten said to me. Monsieur — le Marcgrave ne soupe pas en compagnie: Mais, si [vous][14] voulez venir á la table du Maréchal vous nous ferez beaucoup d'honneur. At eight I went to the Maréchal's table, where I found Steten, the Grand Ecuier[15] and a good jovial Company. I was placed at the head of the table. Much Respect was payed me. There was here a major a Suede as like Sir Joseph Yorke as a natural face can be to an artificial. Nature had given them both a good countenance. The Major's was better than the Ambassador's and was not rendered ridiculous by affected airs.[16] I was mightily amused with two young Courtiers who wanted to be smart before me. One of them said Vous avez lu les Fables de la Fontaine.[17] The other replied mincingly. Non. Je m'attache trop aux realités.

[TEN LINES A DAY.]
Heroes of Gallantry! your limits know
Nor on your Neighbour's grounds to trespass go.
Ye gaudy idle train! ye lordly few
The World of Bus'ness is no world for you,
Amongst yourselves be wicked as you please,
But, let dull mortals live in sober ease.
Cursd with the sickly Appetite of change
Thro' Westminster you may with freedom range
And may at times go roving in the strand
But, beyond Temple Bar is Holy Land.[18]

[1] MS. 'Yesterday' inserted above 'Madame'

[2] See n. 4.

[3] MS. 'Be ... Stutgard' written along the left margin, 'gard' inserted above 'Stut'. For JB's plan to go to Stuttgart, see Journ. 10 Oct. and n. 5. The letter was very likely the sarcastic expression of thanks to an unnamed dignitary for 'the courtesies' JB had—or rather had not—received in Mannheim. F. A. Pottle suggests that it was written on 8 Nov. on the way to Karlsruhe, addressed to the chief chamberlain, Hermann Arnold von Wachtendonck, but never sent. For the text of the letter, see Yale MS. L 1264 and Grand Tour I, Heinemann pp. 168–70, McGraw-Hill pp. 172–74.

[4] The 'Madame Schenck' of the Mem. dated 10 Nov. Her husband was Johann Christoph Friderich Schenk von Schmidburg (d. 1779), Geheimer Regierungsrat (privy counsellor) of Baden-Durlach (Markgräflich Baden-Durlachischer Calender, 1767, p. 21; a

Calender for 1764 is not available). He had been received into l'Ordre de Fidelité, the highest honour the margrave could bestow, in Apr. 1763 (GLA Karlsruhe 47/1.801; for the Order, see Journ. 16 Nov. and n. 5). For Thüngen, see Journ. 17 Oct. and n. 5.

[5] Eberhard Friedrich, Baron von Stetten (1724–83), chief wine steward ('Oberschenk'), was also lieutenant-colonel of a company of grenadiers in the small army of Baden-Durlach (Markgräflich Baden-Durlachischer Calender, 1767, p. 23). He had been received into l'Ordre de Fidelité on 29 Jan. 1764 (GLA Karlsruhe 47/1.723). He would be appointed marshal in 1775 and chief marshal in 1779 (Karl Wilhelm von Drais, Geschichte der Regierung und Bildung von Baden unter Carl Friedrich, 1818, ii. 114).

[6] Wilhelm Ludwig (1732–88) of Baden-Durlach, the margrave's younger brother, was Lt.-Gen. of Infantry in the service of Holland and also governor of Arnheim. He had married Wilhelmine Christine (Schort-

mann), a commoner, in 1760 and owned an estate near Karlsruhe (Lauts, p. 303).

[7] The use of 'uncle' for a parent's male cousin would continue to be called 'in the style of the Bretagne' in France in later centuries (Littré, s.v. 'mode', 2). Prince Karl Wilhelm Eugen (1713–83) had been one of the margrave's guardians during his minority (Lauts, p. 45). As lieutenant-general in the Sardinian army, Eugen had fought on the side of the Austrian and other imperial forces against the French and Spanish in Northern Italy during the campaigns of 1742 to 1749 (Markgräflich Baden-Durlachischer Calender, 1767, p. 16; GLA Karlsruhe 47/1.681). He had again served on the imperial side in the Seven Years' War (N/ Lauts 15/5).

[8] Karl Friedrich (1728–1811) was an enlightened prince par excellence, eager to improve his realm and interested in intellectual pursuits. He had impressed a newly arrived member of his court as 'un des Princes des plus éclairés et des plus respectables, qui aient jamais existé, un vrai et tendre Pere de Sa famille, de Sa cour, et de Sa Patrie, un protecteur zelé et genereux des Arts et des Sciences' (Friedrich Samuel Schmidt to Formey, 24 Sept. 1765, Nl. Formey, SBB-PK; for Schmidt, see Journ. 10 Nov. n. 9). So hospitable was the margrave that he instructed his guards to announce important strangers on their arrival so that they could be invited to dine (Lauts, p. 92). He had visited England from Nov. 1747 to Jan. 1748, and again from May to Aug. 1751 (Lauts, pp. 55–56, 77–78). Towards the end of his first stay he had been elected 'fellow' of the Royal Society by virtue of his royal rank (Journal Book of the Royal Society, JBO 1745–1748, xx. 371) and considered himself a 'patron' of the society (hand-written note on his printed list of members, GLA Karlsruhe FA 47/1.678; N/Lauts 16/1).

The Scots remembered by the margrave (see nn. 9–12) were supporters of the Stuarts, with whose cause he no doubt sympathized in keeping with his position as reigning prince.

[9] David Wemyss (1721–87), Lord Elcho, styled Lord Wemyss, had lived on the Continent since being attainted for his part in the Jacobite uprising of 1745. In the early 1740s he had travelled back and forth among Italy, France, and Scotland, hesitant about aligning himself openly with Prince Charles Edward Stuart. He had joined the Prince in his ill-fated attempt to regain the British throne, accompanying him as far as Derby and even to Culloden, and had barely escaped just before the executions of those Jacobites who had surrendered to the Duke of Cumberland (Elcho fols. 83–122). Wemyss had lost the right to the family title but styled himself 'Lord Wemyss' after the death of his father in 1756 (correcting Grand Tour I, index, Heinemann p. 352, McGraw-Hill p. 356, which lists him as James Wemyss, 4th E. of Wemyss; see also Journ. 16 Nov. n. 6; Comp. Peer. xii. 471–72; Scots Peer. viii. 509).

Wemyss had been introduced to the margrave in 1760 by his brother-in-law, Sir James Steuart (for whom see the next note), had offered the margrave his services (To Karl Friedrich, 1 Jan. 1762), and had embarked on an amiable correspondence with both the margrave and the margravine that would last at least to 1787 (Elcho fols. 249, 260; GLA Karlsruhe FA 5 Corr. 42/35–73; 39/247–52).

[10] Sir James Steuart (1712–80), later Denham, had been in Paris on a Jacobite mission in 1745 and so had avoided the battles in Scotland. Nonetheless he had been attainted in 1748 and had remained on the Continent. He had matriculated at the University of Tübingen in 1758 and had completed his 'Dissertation upon the Doctrine and Principles of Money Applied to the German Coin' in 1761. He had also written enough of his magisterial Inquiry into the Principles of Political Œconomy by 1759 to send a copy of the first two volumes, about 300 pages, to his friend Lady Mary Wortley Montagu on 11 Aug. 1759 and a second copy, with a fulsome dedication, to the margrave on 31 Aug. of the same year (MS in the Badische Landesbibliothek, Karlsruhe). In 1763 Steuart had been allowed to return to Scotland, where he had continued his scholarly work while living quietly on his estate. His Inquiry would be published in 1767, and he would be officially pardoned in 1771 (Andrew S. Skinner, 'Biographical Sketch', in Sir James Steuart, An Inquiry into the Principles of Political Œconomy, 2 vols. 1966, i. xxxi–xlii; ii. 741–42; Oxford DNB).

[11] John Murray (1732–1809), 4th Earl of Dunmore, had accompanied his father, William Murray (1696–1756), the 3rd Earl, during Charles Edward Stuart's campaign and had been page of honour to the prince at Holyrood Palace in 1745. Murray appears to have received a pardon, possibly when it was granted to his father, who however had remained in prison until his death (see Scots. Peer. iii. 387–88; Bruce Gordon Seaton and Jean Gordon Arnot, The Prisoners of the '45,

1928, pp. 30–31). Recruited for the British army, John Murray, *styled* Lord Fincastle at the time, had served in the 3rd Regt. of Foot-Guards as ensign from 1749 and as lieutenant from 1755 to his retirement three years later (*Army List*, 1755–56). He had married Lady Charlotte Stewart, daughter of the Earl of Galloway, in 1759 and had been elected Representative Peer of Scotland, sitting with Parliament in 1761. He would later fill prominent administrative positions as Governor of New York in 1769, of Virginia in the 1770s, and of the Bahamas from 1787 to 1796 (*Scots Peer.* iii. 387–89).

[12] See Journ. 28 June and n. 6 for Lord March. He was Lord Wemyss's cousin (Wemyss to Margravine Karoline Luise, 24 Aug. 1774, GLA Karlsruhe FA 5A Corr. 15).

[13] The Select Society, which flourished from 1754 to 1764 and had 160 members at its height, brought together intellectually ambitious Scots, many only in their thirties. They prided themselves on their debates, which could be on any topic except revealed religion and Jacobitism (Roger L. Emerson, 'The Social Composition of Enlightened Scotland: The Select Society of Edinburgh, 1754–1764', *SVEC* 114 [1973]: 294–322). Lord Auchinleck had been admitted in 1755. JB had been listed as 'proposed' for 1761 but not recorded as 'admitted' (Emerson, pp.

326, 328). Nonetheless, he would declare himself 'admitted member' in his 'Memoirs of James Boswell, Esq.' (*The European Review*, May 1791, p. 324, repr. in *Lit. Car.* p. xxxii). David Hume and the historian William Robertson (1721–93) were among its most distinguished members.

[14] MS. 'vous' inadvertently omitted.

[15] The chief master of the horse was Friedrich August von Üxküll (1720–88). He was also privy counsellor and member of l'Ordre de Fidelité since 3 Nov. 1762 (*Markgräflich Baden-Durlachischer Calender*, p. 21; GLA Karlsruhe 47/1.828).

[16] The Swedish major has not been identified. For Yorke, see Journ. 14 July and n. 5.

[17] The Fables of Jean de la Fontaine (1621–95), originally published in 1668 and 1678, were popular at the court of Baden-Durlach. The margravine translated several to practise her English (GLA Karlsruhe FA 5A/31).

[18] The Temple Bar was an ornamental gateway to the City of London and hence to the territory of merchants as opposed to upper-class wits or 'gallants'. Designed by Sir Christopher Wren in 1672 to commemorate the great fire of 1666, it was situated at the merging of the Strand and Fleet Street (Peter Cunningham rev. by Henry B. Wheatley, *London Past and Present*, 1891, iii. 358).

## Saturday 10 November

[MEM. dated Sunday 11 Novr.] Yesterday At ten you saw medals & Library & Curiositys. Din'd better — after dinner talk'd much with marcgrave on the old preachers like Latimer & many other matters. Then walk'd in wood very fine [—] home & read Eloise [—] you are here truly quiet — with the advantages of a court — you can study & so improve. You resolv'd *not* to [g]o to Stutgard as 'tis 6[1] days & expence. Stay here 5 days more. Bring up Journ — clear. Be in Library every day. Pay great court to marcgrave. Give him just eloges and try for his order[2] — Prepare for Rousseau[.]

Keep your valet if necessary — get habit of living as grand Seigneur & do so in London[.][3]

Ask Schmidt as to Stutgard's being out of road to Suisse.[4]

Go to Bade-Bade.[5] —

[J.] At ten this morning Monsieur de Schmidt Suisse, Conseiller de la Cour waited upon me & carried me to the marcgrave's Library.[6] I saw a very pretty collection. But, one half of his Highness's Books are at Basle, where he has a Palace.[7] M. Molter the Library-keeper was very civil. He has travelled in Italy. He has a good deal of learning & some genius. He is just finishing the third volume of a German miscellany. He has in it odes of his own, & pieces which he has translated from the english.[8] Schmidt proves to be a mighty knowing little man, especially in antiquities. He has gained several Prizes before the academy.[9] He has the charge of the marcgrave's Cabinet. He told me his Highness said *Ce monsieur me fait beaucoup de Joye. C'est un vraye Philosophe.* He had given orders to Schmidt to show me all he could, and to Molter to give me out what books I pleased, and to send me a parcel of London Newspapers. I saw a collection of Curiositys some of which were valuable enough. But, the Cabinet of medals is noble. We began this day to look at the ancient medals.[10] Schmidt knows them perfectly. Were I a couple of months with him, I should be a tollerable Antiquary. It is a pleasing Study. This day I was presented to the Prince Christoph an Austrian General Brother to Prince Eugene. He was a plain hearty cock.[11] I talked with the Marcgrave on the gloomy religion of Holland. On the old method of preaching such as that of Bishop Latimer, & the strange method of talking to the Allmighty of trifles, like the *auld* Scots *Gospel-*ministers.[12] It has been still sad weather here. This afternoon it cleared up. I went & saw the Stables which are excellent. I walked in the wood & *Faisanderie* beautifull & wild.[13] The Baron de Munzisheim a genteel, lively young Gentilhomme de la Chambre lent me the Nouvelle Heloise & Emile.[14] I read two or three hours in the evening. I am perfectly happy here. I improve & am rationally amused. I came hither with intention to stay three days, & then go to Stutgard. I will not go to Stutgard. I will remain five or six days more here. I did not go this night to the maréchal's table.

[TEN LINES A DAY.]
O ye who wou'd[15] show us your poetic strength
By writing poems of prodigious length
A simple fool you now & then may meet
But think not Masters! such as me to cheat
True in such[16] works much merit may be found
If you intend to sell them by the pound.
Yet[17] the Decision is of modern date
Which worth poetic judges by the weight
Upon you then I let my drollery loose
A nightingale is lighter than a goose.

[1] MS. Illegible number; '6' is conjectural.
[2] L'Ordre de Fidelité; see Journ. 16 Nov. and n. 5.
[3] MS. 'Keep ... London' written at the top of the sheet
[4] MS. 'Ask ... Suisse' written along the left margin.
[5] MS. 'Go ... to Bade-Bade' written along the crease of the page below 'road to Suisse'. JB was informing himself about the next stage of his travels. Stuttgart lay southeast of Karlsruhe whereas Baden-Baden was on the direct route south, taking him to Switzerland by way of Rastatt and Strasbourg.

[6] The library and other margraval collections occupied a separate building, three storeys high, next to the east wing of the palace. This annex had been begun in 1761 and would be completed only in 1768 ([Eugen Huhn], *Karlsruhe und seine Umgebungen,* 1843, p. 92; *Carl Friedrich und seine Zeit,* 1981, pp. 67, 211).
[7] Basel had been neutral territory and the margraves' refuge from war since the early seventeenth century. Friedrich VI (1616–77) of Baden-Durlach had bought a house there in 1638 to escape from the Thirty Years' War. His successor, Friedrich

Magnus (1647–1709), had stayed there from 1688 to 1697 while the French occupied, burnt, and pillaged Baden-Durlach, along with Mannheim and other places in the region, during the so-called War of Reunification or Palatinate War (see Journ. 2 Nov. n. 5; Eduard Vehse, *Süddeutsche Fürstenhöfe*, 1921, ii. 253). The books as well as valuable paintings, coins, and antiquities had been sent to Basel for safekeeping in 1688. The next ruler, Karl Wilhelm, had lived in Basel for several years after 1733 while French forces again occupied Karlsruhe during one of the wars of the Polish succession. Even though foreigners were not permitted to buy land in Basel and a local citizen had to live in the house during the margrave's absence, the Council had circumvented its own rules in the 1730s by declaring the margraves non-foreigners because of their long association with the town (Peter Ochs, *Geschichte der Stadt und Landschaft Basel*, 1786–97, vi. 651, vii. 170, 555–59).

⁸ Friedrich Valentin Molter (1722–1808), librarian and privy counsellor, had translated Francesco Algarotti's *Il Congresso di Citera*, 1747, and was in the process of translating Jean-François Marmontel's *Contes moraux*, 1762–70 (Karl Goedeke, *Grundriss der Deutschen Dichtung*, 1916, iv. pt. 1, p. 579). Molter's 'miscellany', the *Carlsruher Beyträge zu den schönen Wissenschaften*, was also published over time: vols. i–ii in 1760, vol. iii nos. 1–2 in 1763, and nos. 3–5 in 1764; no. 6 would be published in 1765. Most of Molter's odes in these volumes were tributes to the margrave and his family or effusions on classical subjects. Molter's translations included William Robertson's *Life of Maria Stuart* taken from the *Gentleman's Magazine* of 1759, Hume's life of James I, and two tragedies by James Thomson. That German rather than French was used in the miscellany indicates the new interest in the native language that was shared by the margrave, who would have founded a German society if he had not been too busy with his new society for political economics (*Ökonomisch-Politische Gesellschaft*); see his journal, 17 Nov., 'Ein Tagebuch des Markgrafen Karl Friedrich vom Jahre 1764', ed. Karl Obser, *Neues Archiv für die Geschichte der Stadt Heidelberg* 9 (1911): 243–44.

⁹ Friedrich Samuel Schmidt (1737–96), a native of Bern, had just come to Karlsruhe as director of the margraval collections. A man of wide interests, he had begun as a theologian but had accepted appointment in 1762 as Honorary Professor of Archaeology in Basel (DHBS, vi. 36–37; Lauts, p. 218). One week after meeting JB, he was officially named Baden-Durlachian privy counsellor and counsellor of legation for French affairs as well as director of the library, of the cabinet of coins and medals, of antiquities and of specimens of natural history (Karl Friedrich's 'Tagebuch' [journal], 17 Nov., p. 241). Schmidt had won prizes for his Egyptological essays in 1754 and then annually from 1757 to 1763 from the French *Académie royale des Inscriptions et Belles Lettres*, which specialized in philology and history (Voss, pp. 72 and n. 175, 204; Antoine-François Delandine, *Couronnes académiques*, 1787, i. 73–80). He would turn to diplomacy in 1769 and would hold the post of the margrave's resident minister consecutively in Frankfurt (a 'free', that is, independent city), Bavaria, Hessen-Kassel, the Palatinate, and other nearby principalities (Lauts, p. 218; *Repertorium*, iii. 9, 11, 21, 197, 252). On being ennobled, he would add 'de Rossan' to his name (letter to Margrave Karl Friedrich, 4 July 1769, GLA Karlsruhe FA 46/6867).

¹⁰ For the cabinet of curiosities, see Journ. 14 Nov. n. 11. The collection of antique coins and medals, begun in 1660 by Margrave Friedrich VI, had just been brought back from Basel (see n. 7; Friedrich Wielandt, *Münzkunde und Münzkabinette am Oberrhein*, 1951, pp. 31–34). The catalogue of 1781 would list 54 Greek and about 80 Roman coins in gold as well as more than a hundred in silver ('Index numismatum antiquorum', MS in GLA Karlsruhe 47/2.021).

¹¹ Christoph (1717–89), Prince of Baden-Durlach was a younger brother of Karl Wilhelm Eugen and so another of Karl Friedrich's uncles 'according to the style of Bretagne' (see Journ. 9 Nov. n. 7). He had served in the imperial Austrian army during the Seven Years' War until a leg wound forced him to retire in 1761. He had begun his long military career in the army of Württemberg during the war against the Turks in 1738 and had then served Austria in the Silesian and subsequent wars, holding various ranks from colonel in 1741 and lieutenant-fieldmarshal in 1752 to colonel of ordnance in 1758. In recognition of this service the Austrians would retrospectively grant him the title of fieldmarshal in 1769 (*Markgräflich Baden-Durlachischer Calender*, p. 16; GLA Karlsruhe N/Lauts 15/4). Christoph would later incur debts which he would ask Margrave Karl Friedrich to pay (Lauts, pp. 303–04).

¹² Hugh Latimer (c. 1485–1555), Bishop

213

of Worcester and Protestant martyr, was known for 'his humour, and gibing drollery', combined with his ability to speak 'immediately from the heart' (William Gilpin, *The Life of Hugh Latimer*, 1755, p. 105). He had preached the Reformation in England and had been burnt at the stake by Mary I (1516–58), the 'Bloody Mary' who had reintroduced Catholicism into England after the deaths of Henry VIII and Edward VI (1537–53), and just before Elizabeth I (1533–1603) had restored Protestantism to Britain. JB's talk of Protestant preachers presumably appealed to the margrave, who, according to Lauts (pp. 44–45), had been brought up by a devout Lutheran grandmother, Magdalena Wilhelmina of Württemburg (1677–1742).

[13] The pheasant preserve, which had existed even before the palace was built in 1715, had been joined to the garden in the rear. It was the margrave's favourite walk (Gustav Rommel, 'Geschichte des Karlsruher Fasanengartens', *Die Pyramide*, 1 Feb. 1925, Nr. 5, pp. 36–38; 8 Feb. 1925, No. 6, p. 44).

[14] Karl Wilhelm von Münzesheim (dates not found) was a favourite of the margrave, who had offered him financial support for his studies at the University of Strasbourg in 1755–56 and had then brought him back to Karlsruhe (Lauts, pp. 140, 476; GLA Karlsruhe FA 5 Corr. 35/122–37). For his first name, correcting *Grand Tour I*, see Lauts, Index, p. 476. In 1767 Münzesheim would be appointed *Kammer-Junker* (chamberlain), a position also held by his brother, Friedrich August (see *Markgräflich Baden-Durlachischer Calendar*, pp. 23–24). In 1774 he would serve as *Reisemarschall* in an important position in charge of travel arrangements (see GLA Karlsruhe 56/453; Lauts, pp. 91, 140). He was rumoured to be an illegitimate descendant of Margrave Friedrich VI and the daughter of one of his officers (Vehse, *Süddeutsche Fürstenhöfe*, 1921, ii. 253; Isenburg, i. Tafel 85).

[15] MS. 'wou'd' inserted above and between 'who' and 'show'

[16] MS. 'your' written above 'such'

[17] MS. 'But' and 'Tho' written above 'Yet', presumably possible alternatives for 'Yet'

## Sunday 11 November

[MEM. dated Monday 12 Novr.] Yesterday Morning went & saw *Decoy* for the first time — curious & simple; was wet to skin. Then saw more Medals. Schmidt very intelligent & obliging — at dinner grand company — Ambassadors from the court of Ratstat to enquire after Princes. Margrave could not talk. Then payed visits — Past evening at Assemblé chez M. le President de finances talked long time. [S]upt court.

[J.] Last night I had resolved to go this morning & see the Prince's Decoy. It rained immensely: However I went a foot attended by trusty Jacob, my Domestique de la Cour, and old Seyfert my *Leyn Lacquay* my valet de Louage a good steady quiet fellow. A Valet de Louage is of no use here; But it is the mode to have one. So I must peacably pay a florin a day on that account.[1] I saw the Decoy, & some Ducks taken. It is mighty simple. They take a vast number here. It shocked me to see the keeper twist about the necks of the ducks, & toss them upon the grass to tumble in agonies till dead.[2] When I got back again, I was wet to the skin. I drest went & had another college on medals. Then to table. This was a grand court-day the Servants were richly drest. There were many more covers.[3] We had two Ambassadors from the Court of Ratstat to enquire after the young Princes who have the smallpox.[4] The Marcgrave was taken up today with public People. I had no conversation with him. I entered the Chapel of the court.[5] It is handsom. I payed some visits, past the evening at an Assemblée chez M. de Gemingen President de la chambre de finances.[6] Supt maréchal's table. It is taken kind in me to go there.

[TEN LINES A DAY.]
Why mighty Johnson! Innovator's huff,
And call the english language rich enough
Tho' in your Lexicon we cannot see,
A phrase like that of [F]rance[7] *Je m ennui*
I *tire* I *weary* you have got 'tis true
But all your *tires* & *wearys* will not do.
In England chiefly th'*ennui* is found[8]
For which the Johns[9] have hang'd themselves & drown'd
Tho' at this word then mighty Johnson storms,
Let it adopted be in all the forms.[10]

[1] Seyffert, JB's temporary local valet, was 'Pesant. Soigneux, intelligent. Honnet' ('Liste des Valets de Place', Yale MS. M 115). He was paid 5 écus 15 Gr. for nine days' service (Exp. Acct. 16 Nov., App. 3).

[2] So complete was the listing of the court hierarchy that even the *Entenfänger* ('duck catcher'), Christian Gerhardt zu Rintheim, was named in the *Markgräflich Baden-Durlachischer Calender*, 1767, p. 53. To see the decoy, JB paid 1 écu 17 Gr. (Exp. Acct. 11 Nov.).

[3] Place settings.

[4] The envoys from the neighbouring Baden-Baden—Joseph, Baron von Freyberg, and Carl, Baron von Tettenborn (d. 1794) —held the position of *Kammer-Junker* (chamberlain), and beyond that, Tettinborn was a *Jagd-Junker* (gentleman of the hunt) as well as lieutenant in the corps of hussars (*Marggräflich Baden-Badischer Staats- und Addresse-Calender*, 1766, pp. 3, 4; Friedrich von Weech, *Badische Biographien*, 1875, ii. 340; see Journ. 18 Nov.). The young patients were either two or all three of the margrave's sons: Karl Ludwig (1755–1801), Friedrich (1756–1817), and Ludwig (1763–1830); see Isenburg, i. Tafel 86.

[5] A small chapel, at the far end of the palace's east wing (Huhn, p. 111).

[6] Reinhard von Gemmingen (1698–

1773) was not only President of the Chamber of Finance (*Kammer-Präsident*) but also privy counsellor ('*geheimer Rat*'), and had been member of l'Ordre de Fidelité since 1732 (*Markgräflich Baden-Durlachischer Calender*, p. 16; GLA Karlsruhe 47/1.718). He came from a respected family dating back to the ninth century (E[dmund] von der Becke-Klüchtzner, *Stammtafeln des Adels des Grossherzogthums Baden*, 1886, p. 145). Now near the end of his long, distinguished career, he had served as chief minister from 1748 to 1755 and was still third in command in the government (Lauts, p. 86).

[7] MS. 'as is the french' written above 'like that of [F]rance'

[8] SJ had not included *ennui* in his *Dictionary*, and in his Preface he had fulminated against foreign words in English as 'the great pest of speech'. JB's interest in the term may have been aroused by his recent attack of spleen (see 'Ten Lines', 4 Nov.), or perhaps by his fellow traveller from Lyon (see Journ. 4 Nov.). For a study of this concept in JB's time, see Patricia Meyer Spacks, *Boredom*, 1995, pp. 31–59).

[9] 'Fellows', 'chaps' (see OED, s.v. 'john', 1.b; 'johnny', 1.a).

[10] MS. Last four lines squeezed together and barely legible.

## Monday 12 November

[MEM. dated Tuesday 13 Novr.] [Y]esterday morning medals & Books — after dinner Prince spoke with you long time — came on freewill was clear strong & lively. Books — Molt read some of his Ode. This day be better — but be retenue — Prepare for Rousseau[.]

[J.] I have quite the disposition for travelling. When I find a court agreeable, I wish to remain there for life. I would be attaché. Were I but so fixed, O how tired would I be. I must however learn to keep my Place at

Auchinleck. It is my duty as I am born a Laird. Were all the German Princes to go & live in the delicious Spain, their familys would fall, & I would find no courts. This day I talked with the Prince on Fate and Freewill. I was clear and lively and strong. His Highness talked with me today a long time. My morning was past among the medals and Books. My evening in reading Rousseau, and supping at the Marischal's Table.

⌈TEN LINES A DAY.⌉
Tis worth your while to read these numbers ten,
Which you will find like Sir John Falstaff's men.
To hear him talking of his muster Roll,
Must tickle ev'ry man who has a Soul.
My[1] clumsy aukward hobling Verses read,
And if your'e grave extinguish'd be your Breed.
Press'd were his greasy[2] Ragamuffins rough;
And my conceits I'm sure are forc'd enough.
Of strong[3] resemblance yet one knot I'll tie
He robb'd the Gibbet, Grubstreet robb'd have I.[4]

[1] MS. 'These' written above 'My'
[2] MS. 'lousy' written above 'greasy'
[3] MS. 'our' written above 'strong'
[4] The lines merge two echoes from *1 Henry IV*: Falstaff calling his men 'rag-of-muffins' (V. iii. 37) and being told the men look as if he had 'unloaded all the gibbets' (IV. ii. 36). For Grub Street, the area in London associated with impoverished hack writers and so crude writing, see Pat Rogers, *Grub Street: Studies in a Subculture*, 1972.

## Tuesday 13 November

⌈MEM. dated Wednesday 14 Novr.⌉ Yesterday again medals &c. Thus goes the morning. At dinner talked of Newmarket. After dinner, long time with Prince told him how you made acquaintance with Johnson — told how you could *take off*[1] twelve or thirteen people but gave it up — as below your character — & as it made ennemys. Afternoon visited a Counsellor ⌈—⌉ some Ladies there.[2]

At night was in fine frame; but had drank too much Rhenish. Was echauffé. Was restless, was allarmed lest drinking inclination should return. Went to bed soon. This day you are to wait on Madame la Margrave.

⌈J.⌉ It is needless for me to mention every day the medals and the Maréchal's table. I had much conversation today with the Prince. I told him how I obtained the acquaintance of Mr. Samuel Johnson. I told him how I had formerly been an excellent mimic:[3] But that I had given it up absolutely, as it debased my Character, and procured me ennemys. During dinner we had talked much of Newmarket. I amused them mightily with Anecdotes of that Place.[4] After table, Mr. Tanner Honorary Professor of English at Strasbourg payed his Respects. He had been four and twenty years in England, had learned the language extremely substantially; but spoke with a most croaking accent.[5] He talked of having seen Mr. Garrick at Strasbourg.[6] This evening I drank too much Rhenish at Supper. I was heated. I was alarmed lest my inclination for drinking should return. Why fear thus?

[EXTRA MEM. undated, c. 14 November][7]
Write ten lines thus — For once let me commit rape on muse. Strange — as if one should fall in love with his wife — I know not if a rape is capital in the court of Parnassus. But if there is a benefit of *Clergy* [i]f I write ten lines I *must* escape[.][8]

[TEN LINES A DAY.]
Yeild yeild, sweet Muse! You cannot now escape.
For, if you yeild not, I commit a rape.
Pleasant conceit indeed! that one should chuse
In prime of youth to ravish his own muse.
It would not now surprise me should I hear
A husband fairly[9] call his Wife my Dear.
Yes, yes, thou yeildest thou resignst thy charms.
O I allready feel thee in my arms.
Thy love in words I ask thee not t'express:
Thy burning blushes plain enough say yes.

---

[1] Mimic (OED, s.v. 'take' v., 85.j), see n. 3.

[2] MS. A line across the page suggests that the entry ends here and the rest is an afterthought. Neither the counsellor nor the ladies have been identified.

[3] JB had boasted about his gift for mimicry in his early pamphlet 'Observations, Good or Bad ... on Squire Foote's *Dramatic Entertainment* intitled "The Minor"', 1760 (see *Earlier Years*, p. 63). He had also imitated David Hume ('Journal of My Jaunt Harvest 1762', 9 Nov. 1762, Yale MS. J 2, quoted in *Earlier Years*, p. 93). Lord Auchinleck had warned him against this practice, calling mimicry 'the lowest and meanest kind of wit' (From Lord Auchinleck, 30 May 1763, Yale MS. C 214).

[4] JB had seen the horse races at Newmarket with Lord Eglinton in 1760 and had used one anecdote in *The Cub at Newmarket, a Tale*, pub. 1762. Left alone in the Jockey Club, he had overcome his embarrassment about being there without acquaintances, and about being teased by some witty members, by writing doggerel verses that turned the situation to his own advantage (see *Earlier Years*, p. 61).

[5] Bartholomew Tanner had just been appointed as the first professor of English at the University of Strasbourg (Voss, p. 129). A copy of his inaugural lecture, 'A Discourse, showing the influence, which the Living Languages, particularly the English

have on the cultivation of Arts and Sciences', dated 27 Jan. and printed in both English and French, remains among JB's papers (Yale P 161). The establishment of this professorship in 1763, to strengthen the university's developing school of diplomacy, attests to the importance that English had gained during the Seven Years' War (Voss, pp. 130, 162–64).

[6] David Garrick had visited Strasbourg in Oct. while returning from Italy (see Garrick to James Clutterbuck, 31 Oct. 1764, *The Letters of David Garrick*, ed. David M. Little and George M. Kahrl, 1963, ii. 425–26).

[7] A prose draft of these and the following day's 'Ten Lines', on an undated page the same size as the other memoranda but written horizontally. Evidently, JB wrote brief preliminary prose drafts for some of his verses.

[8] A facetious treatment of a topic that would continue to interest JB as late as his *No Abolition of Slavery* (1791). Rape was indeed punishable by death in the eighteenth century (Paul Tabori, *The Social History of Rape*, 1971, pp. 63, 69). The 'benefit of clergy'—that is, the clergymen's privilege of avoiding trial by a secular court (OED, s.v. 'clergy', 6.a)—had however been rescinded for cases of rape by the Act of 18 Elizabeth I c.7 in 1575/76 (G. R. Elton, *The Parliaments of England 1559–1581*, 1986, pp. 63–66).

[9] MS. 'boldly' written above 'fairly'

## Wednesday 14 November

[MEM. dated Thursday 15 Novr.] [M]orning Professor Tanner here.[1] Yesterday you visited the young Prince's Preceptor. His name is *Ring*, & he has written a book concerning Rings which signifying eternity, must make his fame so. Ask it from him. Medals again — After dinner, talk'd long with Prince on Religion, & gave him your free notions. He stayed very long. Then had audience of Madame the margrave comely easy lively — wishd to have such a wife — fine cabinet of flemish school. Pieces of her own elegant. Said of her chamber of raritys — Vous pouvez ajouter á remplir — Vous avez promi de revenir — De promettre á deux cest plus fort — Minsischein with you till supper sad Infidel — brush'd him.[2] This day ride — ask about *order* how install'd & what dues. Consult if Stutgard. Send back Rousseau — newspapers &c. After dinner, propose *order*. Take leave of all & pass ev. home. Friday certain Ratstat[3]— dont waver go on.

[SPECIAL MEM. undated, written about 15 Nov.]

### Memorandum.

Try Address ordre de Fidelité. If you obtain this, youre fine man indeed — Go well to work — Be minister in Address — Show verses — talk of your family — Express your real attachment & regard — your wish to be really well with such a Prince & as an old Scots Laird to have the honour of bearing his order — & propose boldly to return from Paris to be installed — what gay prospects[.]

[J.] Munzisheim had carried me yesterday to visit a Conseiller de la Cour, where were two Ladies who sung.[4] This morning Professor Tanner waited upon me. I was quite a genteel Literatus. I payed a visit to the young Prince's Preceptor, a knowing sharp little man; but somewhat of a German Wit. His name is *Ring* and he has written a Treatise concerning *Rings*: and as a Ring is the Image of Eternity, so his name must be immortal. His Wife was a poor pale little insipid good Being.[5] I was amused to see Munzisheim place himself by her, & coquet it with all the attention & all the airs of vanity which I have displayed to the finest Women. It was pleasing & ridiculous. How finely varied are tastes! She however sung a very tender German Song; the words by the brave Kleist, who was killed in the King of Prussia's wars: *Sie fliehet fort* &c.[6] I then went with Schmidt, & saw a new Building which does honour to this court. Below is a Cabinet for natural Curiositys nobly contrived. This belongs to Madame the Marcgrave. Above is the Marcgrave's Library. I must have a draught of both of these rooms.[7] After dinner, his Highness and I talked of Religion. I gave him freely my notions. I maintained the Religion of Jesus as displayed in the four Gospels. I maintained that it was intrinsically good. I talked with vehemence against David Hume and other Infidels who destroyed our principles and put nothing firm in their Place. His Highness said it was the most difficult thing to know if the Bible was realy the word of God. He seemed to be a moderate Sceptic.[8] We talked very long this day. I had sent my respects to Madame the Marcgrave by M. Schmidt begging to be allowed the honour of waiting on her Highness. She was gracious enough to fix this afternoon for that honour. I mounted accordingly, & found her comely, clever, easy, lively.[9] I wished to have such a Wife. She shewed me a very fine cabinet of small pieces of the Flemish School. She shewed me a Venus in Crayon of her own painting. It was extremely fine as also a little Portrait of his Highness which she had taken from the life.[10] They were both excellent. I talked of her Cabinet of Curiositys. She said, 'vous pouvez assister de le remplir. Le marcgrave m'a dit que vous avez promi de retourner ici'. Madame J'aurrais cette honeur assurement — Eh bien vous l'avez promi á moi. De promettre á deux est plus fort qu'a un.[11] The Marcgrave entered and seemed pleased to see her Highness so much admired. One would scarcely beleive that a Princess could paint so. A young Courtier past the evening at my lodging. He owned himself an Infidel, & a materialist, without any notion of futurity.[12] I talked to him with firm vivacity, I shewed him how inferiour he was to me. And that if he reasoned right from his principles, he should steal my Louis d'ors if he could conceal the theft.

[TEN LINES A DAY.]
This rape of mine is something strange & new
Apollo tell me is it so to you?
If for this daring crime a mortal[13] dies
T'will make a cause celebre in the skies.
Come Mercury & touch me with thy Wand
Parnassian Statutes make me understand
Tell me the nature of your justice courts
And let me read a volume of reports
If there I benefit of Clergy see
These lines I'll show and instantly be[14] free.

[1] MS. 'morning ... here' inserted above 'Yesterday ... visited', an afterthought.

[2] 'Moved off abruptly' (OED, s.v. 'brush', V. 3).

[3] Rastatt, in Baden-Baden; see Journ. 17 Nov.

[4] The counsellor and the two ladies have not been identified.

[5] Friedrich Domenikus Ring (1726–1809) had been appointed tutor to the princes in 1759 on the recommendation of his former teacher, the noted historiographer Schöpflin (for whom see Journ 21 Nov. and n. 12; Voss, p. 151 and n. 75). Ring's treatise Die Ringe had been published in Erlangen in 1757. He would subsequently translate sacred and secular texts from the French and Latin into German, including a biography and a collection of works on rhetoric by Schöpflin (Hamberger-Meusel, iii. 269–70; Johann L. Fries, 'Friedrich Dominikus Ring', Die Pyramide 8 [22 Feb. 1925]: 58–59). His wife, Karoline Christine (Wieland), was the daughter of a privy counsellor of Baden-Durlach (Fries, p. 56).

[6] Ewald Christian von Kleist (b. 1715) had died on 12 Aug. 1759 after the battle of Kunersdorf, in which he had continued to fight in spite of a mortal wound. A copy of his Werke (1761) was in JB's library (Lincoln, App. III). 'Sie fliehet fort' comes from the opening of Kleist's idyll 'Amynt', which JB translated into French (see Yale MS. M 283, App. 1, VI) and also recorded in the original German with musical notation (C 1674; MS now defective). The composer, unidentified, is not one of the three whose settings are known to have been written before 1764 (see Grand Tour I, Heinemann pp. 174–75 n. 2, McGraw-Hill p. 179 n. 1; Max Friedländer, Das deutsche Lied im achtzehnten Jahrhundert, 1902, ii. 85).

[7] JB had evidently forgotten that he had already mentioned being in this building (see Journ. 10 Nov. and n. 6). Whether or not he ever made, or ordered, a sketch of it, or asked to have one made, is not known.

[8] Karl Friedrich's scepticism appears to have been confined to such theoretical questioning. In his journal, he privately gave

219

thanks to God and asked for divine guidance (31 Dec. 1764, 'Tagebuch', p. 246). During his early years as ruler, moreover, he had actively encouraged Lutheranism in his realm, insisting on a Bible for every family, no matter how poor (N/Lauts 16/8). Still, true to the ideals of the Enlightenment on which he prided himself, he also favoured religious tolerance. He permitted Catholics and Jews to practise their religion in Baden-Durlach, as had his predecessor Margrave Karl Wilhelm, and would continue to do so after inheriting the neighbouring Catholic Baden-Baden in 1771 (see Journ. 17 Nov. and n. 5; *Carl Friedrich und seine Zeit*, 1981, p. 52).

[9] The Margravine, Karoline Luise (1723–83), occupied a suite on the upper floor of the east wing since the west wing, intended for the margraval private quarters, would be completed only in 1776 (Lauts, p. 288). The rooms used by the margravine were situated at the bend of the gently sloping wing, not in the central corps de logis, which housed the rulers' apartments in most palaces. The Karlsruhe residence as a whole was unusual in being relatively modest, designed for comfort rather than ostentatious display. Its style, a restrained rococo verging on the 'noble simplicity' of the classical, had been suggested in the plan submitted by Balthasar Neumann (1687–1753) and developed by Friedrich von Kesslau (dates not found) and Louis Philippe De La Guêpière (dates not found); see Gerda Franziska Kircher, *Das Karlsruher Schloss als Residenz und Musensitz*, Veröffentlichungen der Kommission für Geschichtliche Landeskunde in Baden-Württemberg, Reihe B Forschungen 8, 1959, pp. 1–12).

[10] The Margravine prided herself on her collection of small, choice paintings, which she not only enjoyed but also used to study artistic techniques. She had added 158 works between 1759 and 1763 (*Carl Friedrich und seine Zeit*, pp. 60–65; Lauts, pp. 155–98). Thanks to instruction from the Swiss artist Jean-Etienne Liotard (1702–89), who specialized in pastel sketches and portraits, she herself had been able to produce accomplished pastels in her favourite red chalk crayon (Lauts, p. 159). Among these were the Venus and the 'little portrait' of the margrave singled out by JB (reproduced in *Grand Tour I,* Heinemann facing p. 176, McGraw-Hill facing p. 180).

[11] Karoline Luise had even greater intellectual interests than her husband. She had been expanding the cabinet of natural curiosities since 1760 and, reflecting the spirit of the French *Encyclopédie*, was trying to create an exhaustive collection of botanical, mineralogical, as well as metallurgical specimens (Lauts, pp. 213–18; *Carl Friedrich und seine Zeit*, pp. 66–71). In enlisting JB's help, the Margravine revealed the same eagerness to expand her holdings as demonstrated in her vast correspondence with scholars, booksellers, and other collectors. A few weeks after this date she would write to JB, reminding him to send her specimens of fossils, marine plants, and shells from Italy and Scotland (From Karoline Luise, c. 9 Dec., Yale MS. C 55). He would reply from Turin that he had found only inferior shells so far but hoped for better specimens in Verona (15 Jan. 1765). Whether he would ever send any is not recorded.

[12] The courtier was von Münzesheim (see Mem. dated 15 Nov.).

[13] MS. 'If' inserted over deleted 'But'; 'Poet' written above 'mortal'

[14] MS. 'get' written above 'be'

## Thursday 15 November

[MEM. dated Friday 16 Novr.] Yesterday morning Minsichein furnish'd horses & you went to Dourlach & saw old tower. Then round Carlsruh, sad cold better of exercise. After dinner felt self hoarse & a little hip'd, & began to imagine the margrave not so kind — o weak man — talk'd with him on trees — on generation — If souls are put in each time — then saw Mad[.] la margrave's pictures. Then Presidents & had music; home & could do nothing. This day chace Spleen. Ride dress — Send all to court. Talk to [M] — of *Order* with eloquence. At night papers in order. —

[J.] A sad cold has again taken possession of my head. Munzisheim gave me one of his horses, and he & I went to Durlach. It is not a bad old town. It has some trade. It is lighted with lamps hung on ropes across the street. The

Palace has been immensely large. We mounted a hill on which stands an old Castle. From hence we had a most extensive view.[1] During dinner today, I talked with the Prince on planting. I had seen his new Garden for all sorts of fruit trees. It will be very noble. I was a little hyp'd today, & began to imagine the Marcgrave not so kind. Despicable weakness! I however talked with him on the human soul. He observed that we were absolutely ignorant how it was produced. When the act of generation is performed,[2] said he, is there some power ready to put in a Soul at the Critical minute; and to take it out again if the Experiment fails?[3] We laughed very heartily at this speculative pleasantry and I regained my good humour. I then waited once more on Madame the Marcgrave, and saw her pictures to great advantage. I then went to President Gemingen's and heard some music. Then went home; but could do nothing made my excuse this evening to the Marischal's table.

[TEN LINES A DAY.]
If Manheim's haughty coldness made me fret,
And only serv'd my Satire's edge to whet,
If it's stiff swarthy Prince provok'd my muse
Him & his Court most freely to abuse
If in the boiling fury of my ire
I was so cruel as to wish for fire,
To wish occasion might again return
That the Palatinat the french might burn
While Nero-like their monarch might descry
The flamy smoke ascending to the Sky.[4]

[1] Durlach, a small town 2.5 miles (4 km) to the north, had been the residence of the margraves of Baden-Durlach from 1565 to 1715. It had lost its importance and prosperity after Karl Wilhelm created his new palace and well-planned town in Karlsruhe. The old Durlach palace, consisting of the customary impressive corps de logis flanked by two wings at right angles, was so large that, according to legend, four-horse carriages could be driven up a ramp into the dining room on the second floor (Karl Gustav Fecht, *Die Geschichte der Stadt Durlach*, 1869, repr. 1969, p. 657). The hill, 464 metres (1522.3 feet) above the town's market place and 862 metres (2828.1 feet) above sea level, offers a superb view of the surrounding countryside, from Mannheim to the north to Strasbourg to the south. The 'old castle' must have been the medieval watchtower, presumed to have been a Roman lookout, that gave the hill its name of Turmberg (Fecht, pp. 642–44).

[2] MS. 'When ... performed' scored out by a modern hand.

[3] These speculations were presumably inspired by Voltaire's sceptical questioning of what human beings actually know about the nature of the soul. The first version of his *Dictionnaire philosophique* with its article 'Ame' had been published in June of this year (*Dictionnaire philosophique portatif*, see Bengesco No. 400, i. 412; *Dict. Voltaire*, p. 11). Voltaire had visited Karlsruhe in Aug. 1758 (Lauts, pp. 130–32).

[4] For the sacking of Mannheim by the French, see Journ. 8 Nov. n. 3. The story of Nero's exulting in the fires he had set to destroy the buildings of Rome is recounted by Suetonius (*The Lives of the Caesars*, vi. 38, Loeb ed., trans. J. C. Rolfe, 1959–64). JB's sentence, begun in these verses, is continued in the next 'Ten Lines'.

## Friday 16 November

[MEM. dated Saturday 17 Novr.] [Y]esterday Minsischein again gave you horse. 'Twas charming day & you was lively, heard that Monseigneur lov'd the Girls —

large [—] snug — but, without pains. Gave good price. After dinner took leave of Prince (after having said Les Hollandois portent des peruques & des habits comme des hardes) then said to Prince you could not express — He said Je ne puis vous demander de rester a peur de vous ennuyer — you then talked of order. J'ai un faveur Je ne sais si J'ose le dire — was quite free & clear. Nous verrons — renewed subject — asked genealogie — then visits — danc'd — then ask'd Minsch, assur'd to have it. This day go on.

[EXTRA MEM. Undated]:[1] Never sit up as *il echauffe* [—] wash head with brandy. Swear today conduct — yet have it to conscious self. Remember your'e Candidate for *Fidelitas*
Get habit of *retenue* Courts are your bladders — By & by you may swim without 'em —
If principles dissappear then return[2]

[J.] Munzesheim again carried me out to ride. It was charming weather. I was lively. I was amused to hear Mon Seigneur[3] aime les filles. Il aime quelque chose de grande et fraiche qu'il peut avoir sans se donner de la peine; car, il est modeste. And now let me record my talents as a Courtier. From my earliest years I have respected the Great. In the Groves of Auchinleck I have indulged pleasing hopes of Ambition. Since I have been in Germany it has been my ardent wish to find a Prince of merit who might take a real regard for me, and with whose enobling freindship I might be honoured all my life. I pleased myself with thinking that among the variety of Princes whom I intended to visit, Such a one might be found. After having been at a number of courts, I had allmost given up my idea. At the last court but one, my utmost wish has been fullfilled. I have found a grave a knowing and a worthy Prince. He has seen my merit. He has shewn me every mark of distinction. He has talked a great deal with me. Some days ago, I said to him 'Is it possible Sir that after I am gone from this I may give you any mark of my Gratitude?' He answered 'I shall write to you sometimes; I shall be very glad to receive your letters.'[4] The Prince of Baden Durlach has an order to give. He creates Knights of the order of Fidelity. They wear a star and a ribband hanging from their necks.[5] My Lord Wemys has this order.[6] I fixed my inclination upon it. I was determined if possible, to obtain it. When the Prince honoured me so far as to grant me his Corespondence, I thought he would surely grant me his order. I asked him once en passant if only Counts could have it. He said It is enough to be a good Gentleman. Munzesheim had told me that the Prince was a little nice[7] in giving it. This being my last day here, I was presented to take leave. The Prince said I cannot ask you to stay longer as I am affraid you would tire. I said by no means; but I was a little hurried at present, & would return again & pass a longer time. I then took courage & said Sir I have a favour to ask of you, a very great favour. I don't know whether I should mention it. I was quite the Courtier; for I appeared modest and embarrassed, when in reality I was perfectly unconcerned. He said What Sir? I replied your Highness told me that a good Gentleman might have your Highness's order. Sir might I presume to ask you that if I bring you proof of my being a very good Gentleman I may obtain the order. He paused — I looked at him steadily. — He answered I shall think of it. I said Sir you have allready been so good to me that I flatter myself that I have the merit for obtaining such a favour. As to my rank I can assure you that I am a very old Gentleman (some days ago I had given his Highness a history of my family) & it may sound strange, but, Sir, I can count kindred with my Sovereign from my being related to the family of Lennox, & the Royal family of Stewart.[8] Sir, I am one of your old proud Scots. If you grant me this favour, you will make me happy for life, in adding honour to my family, & I shall be proud to wear in my own country the order of fidelity of such a Prince. He seemed pleased. I said I hope Sir you do not take amiss my having mentioned this. I was anxious to obtain it & I thought it was [a] pity to want what I valued so highly for want of boldness to ask it. He said let me have your Genealogy attested — and when you return we shall see.[9] O I shall have it. I took leave of his Highness with much respect. I then went to President Gemingen's where I heard Music and danced & was gay. I have a weakness of mind which is scarcely credible. Here amidst music & dancing I am as chearfull as if nothing had ever vexed me. My mind is like an air-pump which receives and ejects ideas with wonderfull facility.[10] Munzisheim went home with me a little. I told him in confidence my proceedings with his Sovereign as to the Order. He told me I would obtain it when I returned.[11] I bid him speak plain. He assured me that I might depend upon having it. I supt at the Marischal's table, where I am much liked. It has been observed that the Grand Ecuier has spoken more to me than to any Stranger. He is silent & backward. I have put him at his ease, led him on to talk of horses of which I am by the by compleatly ignorant. But I had address enough to make that conversation go well on. After supper, I took leave of them all very kindly, & said messieurs Je serois bien faché de sortir de cette chambre, si je pensois que Je n'y reviendrais pas. And upon my word I thought so. Jacob is a most excellent fellow. I had mentioned to him my wish to have the order. He wished it as much as I did, & to obtain it said he would walk a certain length, give a certain sum of money, or do some other extravagant thing which I do not remember. When I told him tonight that I was to have it, the fellow was quite overjoyed. I piqued his vanity by saying Vous aurrez une maitre avec une Etoile.

[TEN LINES A DAY.]
At Carlsruhe how diff'rent is my strain
Here my good humour fully I regain.
Here flow my hours in elegant content
And not a day is without pleasure spent.
T'is true no gaudy pleasures here are found
Tis true I cannot run a giddy round
Tis true I can no splendid opera hear
Nor at french Comedy In lace appear
Nor in a crowded concert take my seat
Music to hear & handsom Girls to meet[.]

¹ Without heading, written horizontally and upside down on the same sheet as the note from Bertollon (Yale MS. C 148; see Journ. 2 Nov. n. 2). On the reverse is the extra Mem., undated, of c. 14 Nov.

² The bladder of a sheep, ox, or other animal could be inflated and used as a flotation device (OED, s.v. 'bladder', 3). Shakespeare's *Henry VIII*, a phrase from which JB quoted (see Journ 20 Aug. and n. 5), has the line 'Little wanton Boyes that swim on bladders' (*Henry VIII*, iii. 33. 359, cited by OED). JB evidently means that he sees his experience in the courts as preliminary practice for later life, lived with the social self-assurance he seeks to acquire.

³ MS. 'MonSeigneur', referring to the margrave. Before and after his marriage Karl Friedrich had indulged in occasional affairs with young women of the lower-classes, and would later support an illegitimate son (Lauts, pp. 60, 96, 140–41). The preceding margrave, Karl Wilhelm, had carried his amorous inclinations much further. He had enjoyed his Dutch 'tulip girls', for whom 24 small rooms had been created in his palace's central tower, quite as much as the tulips they had been brought to cultivate in his gardens (Katrin Boskamp-Priever, 'Der Schlossturm', explanatory flyer written for the reopening of the renovated tower, Badisches Landesmuseum Karlsruhe, 1994).

⁴ JB would respond to this offer in a grateful letter of 25 Nov. (see *Grand Tour I*, Heinemann pp. 201–02, McGraw-Hill pp. 205–06), to which he would receive a reply in English dated 9 Dec. (MS. draft in GLA Karlsruhe FA 5, Corr. 23 #39, see *Grand Tour I*, Heinemann p. 266, McGraw-Hill p. 273; see also Journ. 22 Dec. n. 9). But he would receive no answers to his subsequent letters of 15 Jan. from Turin, 11 May from Rome, and 1 Sept. 1765 from Siena nor of 6 Feb. 1766 from Calais (drafts or copies at Yale, MS. L 21–25, originals of JB's letters from Basel, Rome, and Siena in GLA Karlsruhe FA 5 Corr. 23 #40–41). Ironically, the margrave would write an affectionate letter as late as 24 May 1768, regretting the lack of news from JB and urging him to write (#42). The fact that this letter is addressed to 'Sir Boswell of Auchinleck' suggests that JB's claim to aristocratic standing had been recognized, but JB would never know, for it, too, would never be sent to him. Whether the correspondence with JB was stopped deliberately, as F. A. Pottle suspects, and if so by whom, has remained a mystery (*Earlier Years*, pp. 279–80).

⁵ The members of this prestigious order are listed before the margraval household in the annual court calendar. The order had been founded by Margrave Karl Wilhelm on 17 June 1715, the day the first stones were laid for his new palace in Karlsruhe, and was intended to promote loyalty, friendship, and harmonious companionship. Originally limited to eight 'knights', the order would include sixty-six by 1767 (*Markgräflich Baden-Durlachischer Calender*). Membership was restricted to those who could demonstrate both their aristocratic descent and good character—in the English version of its laws and statutes, those 'of a good and Noble Equestrian [*sic*] Family, leading an upright, righteous life' (in the German version 'gute Adelige Rittermässigen Herkommens und recht-schaffenden Wandels'); see GLA Karlsruhe 47/1.642, 645. Its special insignia consisted of four double overlapping Cs, in honour of its founder (*Carl Friedrich und seine Zeit*, p. 113).

⁶ Lord Wemyss had been received into the order on 3 July 1761 (mistakenly dated 1760 in his journal; see Elcho, pp. 249, 253). He had identified himself 'David de Wemyss Comte de Wemyss, Vicomte & Baron d'Elcho, Chevalier Baronet & Pair d'Ecosse' on the obligatory family tree he had submitted. In a letter expressing his gratitude, Wemyss had declared that his acceptance would be 'tres avantageux en Angleterre' (Wemyss to Margrave Karl Friedrich, 15 July 1761, GLA Karlsruhe 47/1.839). Later he would ask the Margravine to intercede with the King of England to grant a pardon for him, or at least to provide a pension for the young woman he hoped to marry if his finances allowed (19 July and 14 Nov. 1774, GLA Karlsruhe 5A Corr. 15). Although his atteinder would never be reversed, he would marry the twenty-year-old Mlle Üxküll (1756–77, first name not reported), daughter of a Baron von Üxküll of Baden-Durlach and niece of the master of the horse whom JB met in Karlsruhe (see Journ. 9 Nov. n. 15). She would die in childbirth in 1777, only a year after her marriage (for her dates on her tombstone at Bôle, see Evan Charteris, 'Memoir', in David, Lord Elcho, *A Short Account of the Affairs of Scotland*, 1907, pp. 215–16; see also *Comp. Peer.* xii. 472; Wemyss to Margrave Karl Friedrich, 15 Sept. 1776 and 1 Jan 1778, GLA Karlsruhe, FA 5 Corr. 42 #57, 59; To Margravine Karoline Luise, GLA Karlsruhe FA 5A Corr. 15).

⁷ In several senses: 'reluctant', 'fastidiously careful', 'difficult to satisfy' (OED, s.v. 'nice', 5 and 7).

[8] JB's mother, Euphemia Erskine, was descended from the Lennoxes through her great-grandmother, Mary (d. 1644), second wife of John Erskine (1562–1634), Earl of Mar. Lady Erskine was the daughter of Esmé Stuart, 1st Duke of Lennox (c. 1542–83), who, in turn, was second cousin to James VI (1566–1625) of Scotland (from 1603 James I of England). Through this branch JB could claim kinship not only with the exiled Stuarts but also with the Hanoverians, since Sophie, Electress of Hanover, had won the British throne for her son George I as descendant of James VI (see Journ. 25 June n. 2). In addition, JB's father was related to the Stuarts in being descended from Princess Mary Stuart (d. 1488), who was Lady Hamilton, eldest daughter of James II (1430–60), and sister of James III (1451–88) of Scotland (see Chart I, 'Boswell's Connexions with the Royal Line of Stuart', and Chart IV, 'Boswell's Maternal Line: The Erskine and Douglas Connexions', in *Ominous Years*, pp. 374 and 377; *Earlier Years*, pp. 8, 452–53).

[9] JB would try to gain support for his claim from Lord Marischal, to whom he wrote on this very day and from whom he would receive a copy of a letter recommending him to the Margrave as being 'de bone et anciene [*sic*] Noblesse'. Lord Marischal would doubt, however, that JB could trace his genealogy further back than to Robert the Bruce (From Lord Marischal, 15 May 1765, Yale MS. C 1952). Unhappily, JB would have no opportunity to present this letter to the Margrave.

[10] The air pump, here used as an image of rapid input and output, is more usually associated with strength. Such a pump, a major invention in the mid-seventeenth century, drew air out of an enclosed vessel and created a vacuum that was capable of withstanding great force (Carlo M. Cipolla and Derek Birdsall, *The Technology of Man*, 1979, 142–43, 146, 148–49).

[11] JB would still plan to return to Karlsruhe the following year (To Karl Friedrich of Baden-Durlach, 1 Sept. 1765, Yale MS. L 24). But the lack of replies to his letters would discourage him (To Karl Friedrich, 6 Feb. 1766, Yale MS. L 25). In any case he would cut short his return journey on hearing of the death of his mother in Jan. 1766 (*Earlier Years*, pp. 274–75).

## Saturday 17 November

[MEM. dated Sunday 18 Novr.] Yesterday had sat up all night. Discharged all in sweet composure. Set out like Lord Marischal. Italian Courier like Lord Galloway run with you to Village [—] gave him silver. Bad morning cold & sick — walk'd — better. Ratstat — announced [—] presented Marc — too free quite Body. Comedy allemand tird sadly — was like to sleep — Supt court — This day send letter on Hesse verses.[1] Freyberg is worthy fellow — After mass Journal — After dinner much Journ. compose[.]

[J.] I had sitten[2] up all night to journalise. As usual I felt myself immediatly bettered by it. I discharged my Bill. Last night I chose to make a figure, & gave to my Coachman & Domestique de la Cour each a Louis for the common Purse of the servants and each a ducat to himself.[3] I had given them besides a Bottle of wine a day. So that I have payd pretty well for my state. I set out composed & mild like My Lord Marischal. The Prince's Italian *Coureur* who resembled Lord Galloway, ran before my chaise a good way. I gave him what silver I had.[4] The Rogue knew how to flatter M. le Baron. I drove to Ratstat the Residence of the Marcgrave de Baden-Baden the elder branch of the Baden family. As he has no heirs, upon his death my worthy Marcgrave of Baden-Durlach will be the first of the family and will obtain an accession of Country equal to what he has at present.[5] ∴[6] My Landlord gave me no very favourable account of his Sovereign. He said he was very extravagant, & was allways borrowing money, & was owing to Butchers & Bakers & the Servants of the court.[7] I caused myself be[8] announced. The Fourier came & told me in latin that I should be wellcome, & had a coach for me before Six.[9] I went, & found a very elegant Palace in the outside, & pretty well within.[10] The Prince was a neat little lively old fellow, quite easy & free. It was impossible to be bashfull before him. The Courtiers were very gracious. At six we went to a little Theatre in the Palace, and saw a German Play. One scene was ludicrous enough. A sort of Drawcansir made a row of lubberly fellows stand behind each other & each take the left foot of his neighbour under his arm. Thus ranged he bastinadoed them, & made them hop off the stage in a groupe.[11] As I understood very little of the play, & had been a night out of bed, drowsiness overpowered me and I fell sound asleep by the side of a very pretty young Lady. We had a splendid Supper.

⌜TEN LINES A DAY.⌝
Rich pleasures I have had, & may again
If in this world I any time remain.
At twenty four I would not be so wise
As all amusement sternly to despise
No; tho' a decent character I play
It still shall be my study to be gay.
Mistake me not; I am not one of those
Call'd dreadfull Bucks[12] or despicable Beaux.
In moderation I my senses please
And to my mind secure a chearfull ease.

[1] For the 'Hesse verses', see Journ. 19 Nov. and n. 7.

[2] Scottish form of the past participle of 'sit' (OED, s.v. 'sitten').

[3] See Exp. Acct. 16 Nov., App. 3.

[4] Very likely Frederico Baduano, the only Italian among the four couriers ('Läufer') listed in the Markgräflich Baden-Durlachischer Calendar, 1767, p. 28. JB estimated the worth of the 'silver' at one écu (Exp. Acct. 16 Nov., App. 3). For Lord Galloway, see Mem. dated 27 June n. 4.

[5] The margraves of Baden-Baden belonged to one of several branches descended from the dukes of Zähringen, who had ruled a wide territory from Baden-Durlach to Bern in the early thirteenth century. They had fought on the imperial side in the Thirty Years' War and had reintroduced Catholicism into their territory in 1634 (Rentsch, pp. 6–7), but the union of their territory with Baden-Durlach, which was Lutheran, was inevitable under the circumstances mentioned by JB and would be confirmed by a family compact signed in 1765 after six-year-long negotiations. It would take effect in 1771 on the death of August Georg, the last male margrave of Baden-Baden, though it would be fully accepted by Karl Friedrich's new Catholic subjects only in 1789 after

years of legal challenges (see Hans Georg Zier, 'Karl Friedrich, Markgraf, Kurfürst und Grossherzog von Baden', Die Geschichte Baden-Württembergs, ed. Reiner Rinker and Wilfried Setzler, 1986, pp. 180–81).

[6] MS. Three dots in triangular formation, possibly a masonic symbol. This may allude to Margrave Karl Friedrich's membership in the masonic order, to which he had been admitted while in England (see the list compiled by the Musée de la Grande Loge de France, Paris; see also Eugen Lennhoff and Oskar Posner, Internationales Freimaurer-lexikon, 1932, p. 117; for Karl Friedrich's visits to England, see Journ. 9 Nov. n. 8). If this interpretation is correct, JB here signals his awareness of a fellow mason while still observing the code of silence required of freemasons. JB had been initiated into the Canongate Kilwinning Lodge No. 2 in Edinburgh in 1759 and had served as Junior Warden in 1761 (Allan Mackenzie, History of the Lodge Canongate Kilwinning No. 2, 1888, pp. 85, 245). Possibly their common experience as freemasons had strengthened the bond between him and the Margrave. A similar unspoken bond may have existed between JB and Carl David Kircheisen, who had joined the first lodge in Berlin, 'Aux trois Globes', at its inception in 1740. Prince Ferdinand of

Brunswick-Lüneburg, who had spoken so warmly to JB in Brunswick, also belonged to the 'Trois Globes' in Berlin and was organizing a new lodge, 'St. Charles de l'Indissoluble Fraternité', in Brunswick at the very time JB met him (*Geschichte der Grossen National-Mutterloge zu den drei Weltkugeln*, 1903, pp. 10–12; F. H. A. Lachmann, *Geschichte der Freimaurerei in Braunschweig*, 1844, pp. 22–29; see also Marlies K. Danziger, 'Le Jeune Boswell en voyage et ses rapports avec la Franc-Maçonnerie', *Franc-Maçonnerie: Avenir d'une tradition*, Musée de Beaux Arts de Tours, 1997, pp. 58–60).

[7] August Georg (1706–71) had been ruling prince for only three years and was ill-prepared for his position. He had been destined for the Church but had been released from his vows by papal dispensation so as to marry and provide Catholic offspring on succeeding his brother Ludwig Georg (1702–61), whose only son had died in 1733 (ADB; *Richard Dold, Maria Viktoria, die letzte Markgräfin von Baden-Baden*, 1938, p. 6). In 1735 August Georg had married Maria Viktoria (von Aremberg; 1714–93), but their only son had died in infancy. Meanwhile August Georg had embarked on a military career, serving on the imperial side and also commanding two infantry regiments for the United Provinces. During the Seven Years' War he had been named Lt.-Gen. Fieldmarshal for the Circle of Swabia, which included the area of Württemberg, Baden-Durlach, and Baden-Baden (Nugent, ii. 10; *Marggräflich-Baden-Badischer Staats- und Adresse-Calender*, 1766, p. 1).

August Georg and his wife had moved to Rastatt from their previous residence in Baden-Baden in 1762. By the time JB met him, his affairs were in such disorder that complaints about his debts and non-payment of salaries were widespread. Six weeks earlier his niece Elisabeth (for whom see Journ. 18 Nov. n. 7) had secretly asked Karl Friedrich of Baden-Durlach for money to cover her debts and ongoing expenses (Lauts, p. 263).

[8] A Scottish idiom (CSD, s.v. 'cause').

[9] For 'fourier', see Journ. 17 Oct. n. 11.

[10] This large baroque edifice, modelled on Versailles, had an impressive *corps de logis* crowned by a gilt statue of a lightning-throwing Jupiter, a symbol of absolute power. It had been commissioned, after Baden-Baden was laid waste by the French in the Palatinate War, to provide a fitting residence for Margrave Ludwig Wilhelm (1655–1707) —'Turkish Louis'—on his return from his remarkable victories over the Turks at Nissa in 1689 and at Slankamen in 1691 (Rentsch, pp. 7–8, 11). Built from 1700 to 1706 according to plans by the Italian architect Domenico Egidio Rossi (dates not found), the palace had been embellished with fine stucco work and painted ceilings created by Bolognese artists. These had been dismissed after Ludwig Wilhelm's death by his widow, Auguste Sybille (1675–1733), who had engaged her favourite architect, Johann Michael Rohrer (1683–1732), to complete the work (see Wolfgang Hug, *Geschichte Badens*, 1992, pp. 159–60; Gerhard Peters, 'Das Rastatter Schloss', *Heimatsblätter 'Vom Bodensee zum Main'*, No. 27, 1925, pp. 3–72; Rentsch, pp. 4–17).

[11] This farce, not further identified, was the sort of low entertainment that Gottsched, among others, had been trying to banish from the stage (see Journ. 4 Oct. n. 5). Drawcansir is the boastful, bellicose knight who arrives in the last act of *The Rehearsal* (1671) and 'kills 'em all on both sides' (stage direction, ed. Montague Summers, 1914, p. 69). The play, by George Villiers, 2nd Duke of Buckingham (1628–87), and others, parodies Dryden's heroic drama *The Conquest of Granada* (prod. 1670–71).

[12] 'A gay, dashing fellow' (OED, s.v. 'buck', 2.b).

## Sunday 18 November

[MEM. dated Monday 19 Novr.] [Y]esterday morning went to the Prince's Chapel & heard mass good music — well painted — was in good frame, & relish'd full the contrast between the Romish Church & *Auch Kirk*. Then Court din'd well. Then saw Billiards — margrave well with Princes — Quite Christophe. They hearty here — Played Pharo & lost louis — Was immed. hyp'd as Kirk makes sad. Immed effects. Avoid & continue promise till you're 40. Evening — concert — [M]arg. B Dour[1] s'amuse des affaires [—] les autres s'amuse des amusements — evening past well. This day Gala — Prince Dour: Princess mass — relish cour. Send books to Munzis[.] & letter. Take leave at night.

[J.] I went to the Prince's Chapel. The Roof is very finely painted. He is a Catholic Prince, so we had mass. There were seven masses at a time.[2] The music was excellent. I was very devout, and fully relished the Contrast between *Affleck Kirk* and the Romish worship.[3] Then went to court where I met with the two ambassadors whom I had seen at Carlsruhe M. de Freyberg Chambellan a kind honest fellow, & M. de Tetbourn officer of Hussars a tall, well-made worthy young fellow.[4] We had a most excellent dinner, after which coffee; then the Ladies retired, & the Prince & all we Gentlemen went to the Billiard-room where we had Billiards & Pharo; & now & then a glass of wine was served to the Princes. The two Princes Uncles of Baden Durlach were here. They come often. They love this court much better than their own. They have much more merriment, & much more ease. The Marcgrave calls them mes chers Princes. Today He called to one of them 'Christophe' quite familiar.[5] I lost a Louis at Pharo. Cards make me allways melancholy. It is an instantaneous effect like a Presbyterian Sermon. Lest I may have forgotten it in it's place, I now record that when at Berlin I made a most extraordinary experiment. I composed a discourse against fornication quite like an old Scots minister. I said to myself what damned stuff is this! and was clearly convinced that I said what was certainly true. I then read it aloud with the Presbyterian tone, & upon my word frightened myself. Ought not this to prevent me from being any more rendered dismal by a *Domine?*[6] No. for, as My Lord Marischal said a sermon is to me like a dolefull tune which I cannot resist. In the evening we had a Concert & Cards. There is at this court the Marcgrave's niece the Princess Elizabeth, a good civil Princess.[7] The Prince has a particular regard for a madame de Weyfelt; and censorious People go the length to say that there is love between them. She is not handsom; but the idea of her being a mistress to the Prince made me think of her with a kind of desire & even imagine her very well.[8] There is here a mademoiselle de Geismar a charming Creature tall, handsom, good humoured, the only Beauty I ever met with who had no caprice.[9] I sat by her at Supper, & gay we were.

[TEN LINES A DAY.]
At Carlsruhe a worthy Prince I find
Of generous heart and cultivated mind.
Who not contented just to strut in state
And make lac'd Courtiers on his orders wait,
Rules his dominions with attentive care,
Resolved that Justice shall inhabit there.
While other Princes ignorant and vain
Their wretched Subjects[10] of their substance drain
Bid gaudy domes of costly pleasure rise
And with loud concerts drown the widows cries.[11]

[1] MS. 'Girl de', deleted by JB between 'Dour' and 'amuse'. JB evidently began to record an anecdote about Karl Friedrich's enjoying 'affairs' with local girls (see Journ. 16 Nov. and n. 3) before setting down the bon mot that the margrave amused himself with business affairs while others amused themselves with amusements. The witticism

is also recorded in *Boswelliana* (p. 233), where JB attributed it to 'Krimberg' (i.e., Grünberg).

[2] This chapel, adjacent to the left wing of the palace, had been added by Rohrer from 1719 to 1723 for Auguste Sybille, who had arranged for a special staircase, the 'holy stairs', from her private quarters directly into the choir of the chapel. The baroque ceiling painting, by an unknown artist, depicts the Empress Helena's vision of the Holy Cross (Rentsch, pp. 43–50; Gerhard Peters, 'Das Rastatter Schloss', pp. 73–83 and Pl. 43). Seven masses were celebrated because there were seven altars (see Mem. dated 20 Nov.).

[3] JB had expressed similar feelings about presbyterian and Catholic worship in his journal of 24 June (Journ. 24 June and n. 4).

[4] See Journ. 11 Nov. and n. 4.

[5] For Christoph, the youngest of Karl Friedrich's three 'uncles', see Journ. 10 Nov. and n. 11. The other visitor was presumably Karl Wilhelm Eugen, who had a particular interest in Rastatt (see n. 7 below).

[6] This mock sermon, composed after his 'fornication' of 11 Sept., was not mentioned in the journal entry for that date, but evidently still haunted JB (see *Grand Tour I*, Heinemann p. 181 n. 1, McGraw-Hill p. 185 n. 3). By 'domine' he means a parson (OED, s.v. 'domine' *sb.*, 2).

[7] Elisabeth Auguste Franciske Eleonore (1726–89) was the daughter of Ludwig Georg (1702–61), the preceding Margrave of Baden-Baden and brother of the present ruler. She was unmarried but would reject the advances of Karl Wilhelm Eugen of Baden-Durlach

even though he had converted to Catholicism in the hope of marrying her and thereby preventing Baden-Baden's reversion to Baden-Durlach (Lauts, pp. 262–63). Later she would marry her major domo, Baron Michael Wenzel von Althann (b. 1743), in a secret ceremony on 2 Feb. 1775, as attested to by the officiating priest in a document dated 2 Jan. 1790 that would remain hidden in Margrave Karl Friedrich's files (GLA Karlsruhe, 46/4353).

[8] Mme de Weveld was possibly the wife of Lothar, Baron von Weveld, Imperial chamberlain and privy counsellor of Baden-Baden as well as of Trier (*Marggräflich Baden-Badischer Calender*, 1766, p. 2).

[9] Either Elisabetha, Baroness von Geismar zum Riepen, *styled* Mossbach von Lindenfels, or her sister Charlotte, both listed as ladies-in-waiting in the *Marggräflich Baden-Badischer Calender*, 1766, p. 13 (see JB's enthusiastic description to JJ, 22 Nov., *Corr. 1*, p. 144). Their father, Lothar Franz von Geismar zum Riepen, *styled* Mosbach von Lindenfels, was a privy counsellor and held the important position of president of administration (Regierungspräsident) of Baden-Baden (*Marggräflich Baden-Badischer Calender*, p. 2; *Markgräflich Baden-Durlachischer Calender*, 1767, p. 21. He had been received into l'Ordre de Fidelité in Nov. 1763 (GLA Karlsruhe, 47/1. 716).

[10] MS. 'People' written above 'Subjects'

[11] The last four lines again indirectly disparage Carl Theodor of the Palatinate, whose Mannheim was famous for its concerts.

## Monday 19 November

[MEM. dated Tuesday 20 Nov.] Yesterday at 10 Grand Mass. Seven Altars at once — Superb Music — After all woe was fully content. Ten lines — O fanatics dispute not if this will bring me to heav'n. I'm there allready. Then Guns discharg'd pretty troops — Then court to Princesse. Grand dinner — Billiards &c. Music court. The whole day employed. But not very proffitably — But 'tis *forming manners* at a most free court. This day set out at six. You have much to write. This night at Stras. 5 hours Journ, next day much. See Schoefling & Gaio. Pray prepare mind for Suisse[.]

Enter not Suisse — till Germ journalised.[1]

[J.] This being St. Elizabeth's day, is kept splendidly on the Princess's account. In the morning the troops paraded, & a fine figure they made. At ten we had grand mass with music still more noble than what we had yesterday. After all former woe I was fully content. The troops discharged. We had a grand dinner being all in Gala & having first payed our respects to the Princess. After dinner a fire broke out in the Guard-room, & to extinguish this amused us some time. We then went to the Billiard-room. Krimberg (Grand Maitre to madame La Marcgrave who is allways indisposed) is a very agreable fellow.[2] He made very nicely the distinction between *Temperament et Humeur*. Le Temperament est une certaine constitution du corps. Il influ beaucoup sur l'humeur. Mais il ne le fait pas tout. Car on peut avoir un mauvais temperament, et une bonne humeur si on a eu une bonne Education. Voyez les françois. Il y en a quelques uns sans doute qui sont naturellement inquiets. Cependant vous les voyez touts de bonne humeur. He was for a little more ease in the German Courts which he approves of as the great resource for the *Noblesse* which is truly the case. He told me that in a court where there is good order on ne s'ennuit jamais. This Court is the easiest that I have yet seen. They don't[3] embarrass themselves by taking a ceremonious care of you. They[4] leave you to your own choice. You have all sort of good things, & when you chat with them, they are polite & obliging. I see that if I had nothing else in view but to pass time, I might stay half a year here without any fear of strange looks or signs. It would give them pleasure. Yesterday I saw the Prince's treasure. He has a number of antiques of a size for seals & rings. I observed two Pillars of about a foot & a half each, all surrounded with these antiques. He has a variety of very valuable things. But his glory is to possess the third diamond in Europe after that of the King of France & that of the Emperor[5] comes that of the Marcgrave of Baden-Baden. It is very large. It is fixed in a hat.[6] This day was entirely filled up at court. One might say not very profitably; But I answer I am forming my manners. I should have mentioned that I left some of my verses with the marcgrave of Baden Durlach.[7] This night I took leave here. I remember Mr. Brown told me that I should see a prodigious difference between the Protestant and Popish towns of Baden.[8] I could not perceive it.

[TEN LINES A DAY.]
Charles Fred'ric calmly wise his force computes,
And to his force his Undertaking[9] suits
Charles Fredric form'd to taste superior joys
His precious moments usefully employs
Active and steady he his course pursues
Nor full of projects knows not which to chuse,
Yet blest with serious talents & with gay
He jogs not still on[10] one continued way
No in his Highness conduct[11] we admiring see
The regulation of variety.[12]

[1] MS. 'Enter ... journalised' written along the left margin; 'Germ': 'Germany'.

[2] Carl, Baron von Grünberg (d. 1794) was *Geheimer Rat* (privy counsellor) and *Obrist-Lieutenant* (lieutenant-colonel) of the army of the Circle of the Upper Rhine as well as *Obrist-Hofmeister* (chief major domo) of the ruling Margravine (*Marggräflich Baden-*

*Badischer Staats- und Addresse Calender*, 1766, p. 2). He had been received into l'Ordre de Fidelité of Baden-Durlach in Feb. of this year (GLA Karlsruhe, 47/1.732). The Margravine (1714–93), known chiefly for her intense piety and devotion to the Catholic Church, was not interested in sociability (Dold, p. 10).

[3] MS. 'do'nt'

[4] MS. 'The', a slip of the pen.

[5] MS. 'Emperor' inserted above the line with a caret.

[6] The Baden-Baden diamond is not mentioned in later inventories of the Rastatt jewels, nor is there evidence that it was the third-largest diamond in Europe in JB's time. The first and second largest belonged to Louis XV (1710–74) and Maria Theresa (1717–80) of Austria (Edwin W. Streeter, *The Great Diamonds of the World*, 2nd ed. 1882, pp. 169–83).

[7] JB had left Karl Friedrich copies of three of his Ten Lines with only minor changes in capital letters and punctuation. Two, written in Kassel and no doubt the 'Hesse verses' mentioned in the Mem. dated 18 Nov., were presumably chosen for their appeal to the Landgrave: 'O Hesse' because they dealt with landgraves Philipp and Friedrich's changes of religion, and 'Heroes of Gallantry' because they focused on high life in London. JB had appropriately entitled the latter 'London Verses' and had signed them 'James Boswell of Auchinleck in the County of Ayr Scot-

land'. He had also left his lines 'Should some smart fopling', which he had written in Holland (dated 24 Oct. 1763), and which again recalled high life in London. All three Ten Lines would remain in the correspondence not of the Margrave but, for unknown reasons, of the Margravine, placed unindexed at the end of a file (GLA Karlsruhe FA 5A Corr. 31). JB may have remembered leaving these copies because he was composing the tribute to Karl Friedrich in his Ten Lines dated 18 and 19 Nov.

[8] For Robert Brown (1728–77), pastor of the English (presbyterian) church in Utrecht, see 'Abregé d'un Voyage en Allemagne', App. 1, n. 6.

[9] MS. 'operations' written above undeleted 'undertaking'

[10] MS. 'in' above undeleted 'on'; possibly an allusion to Autolycus's song 'Jog on', *The Winter's Tale*, IV. iii. 133–37.

[11] MS. 'conduct' written above 'Highness'

[12] Possibly JB wrote this appreciation of Karl Friedrich's sensible restraint after having seen the looser ways of Georg August of Rastatt.

## Tuesday 20 November

[MEM. dated Wednesay 21 Novr.] Yesterday set out in good time & drove to Strasbourg — Wrote all night — *Write* better [—] you are too free with Servant. Check — This day Gaio — & Scheofling. See Cathedral & town. Go on Journ — resume regulated conduct, or you fall back to Lainshaw.[1]

Learn order in affairs [—] mem worthy Father —[2]

[J.] Set out early & drove to Strasbourg;[3] was amused to find myself in the dominions of the french King, & to see on Bills posted up 'De Par Le Roi'.[4] My Inn was L'Esprit.[5] I wrote all the evening.[6]

[TEN LINES A DAY.]
Behold him try to trace the wond'rous plan
Which Heaven may have had in forming[7] man.
For notwithstanding all that Pope has said
And finely sung, by wicked St. John's aid
If we have sense & candour we must own
Man is as yet exceedingly unknown.
Fancy may form a few ingenious dreams
And such a system mighty pleasing seems
But when we the wit with a judgment cool
We think it's authour should be sent to school.[8]

[1] The estate of JB's cousins, the Montgomeries of Lainshaw, about 17 miles (c. 27.4 km) northwest of Auchinleck (*Earlier*

*Years*, pp. 401–02) and at this time the epitome of a disorderly household for JB. He knew four of the five unruly boys: Walter, later Sir Walter Montgomerie-Cuninghame (?1755–1814); Alexander (d. 1784); David (?1759–1814); and James (?1761–1837); but not the youngest, Henry Drumlanrig (?1763–90), who had been an infant when JB left for the Continent. They were the children of Capt. Alexander Montgomerie-Cuninghame (d. 1770), first husband of Elizabeth Montgomerie (d. 1776) of Lainshaw, who was the elder sister of JB's future wife Margaret (*Book of Company*, p. 187). The boys would become 'high-spirited, reckless, and improvident' (*Later Years*, p. 166), but JB would take an interest in their well-being and later support them financially even when he himself was short of money (*Great Biographer*, p. 21 n. 5).

² 'Learn … Father—' written along the left margin.

³ 24 miles (38.6 km) from Rastatt (Nugent, ii. 435).

⁴ 'In the name of the King'. Strasbourg had been part of France since 1681, when it was forced into a 'voluntary union' that was confirmed by the Peace of Ryswick of 1697 (Ragnhild Hatton, *Louis XIV and Europe*, 1976, pp. 296–97). Previously it had been a free and independent city but had suffered from pressure by the imperial Austrian forces on the one hand and the French on the

other. After the Palatinate War which had also engulfed Mannheim, Baden-Durlach and Baden-Baden (see Journ. 2 Nov., n. 5; 10 Nov., n. 7) and which the French had called the War of Reunification, the others had regained their independence, but Strasbourg had, in effect, capitulated to the French (Livet, iii. 165–92).

⁵ At No. 15 quai Saint-Thomas, facing the old port (Livet, iii. 557).

⁶ Presumably the half-sheet with notes on the sublime, plans for the *Hypochondriack*, and references to various friends (see App. 1).

⁷ MS. 'informing', a slip of the pen.

⁸ These verses criticize Pope's *Essay on Man* (1733–34), which was based partly on the ideas of his friend Henry St. John Bolingbroke (1678–1751). Like JB here, Pope had emphasized the limitations of human knowledge, but he had then sketched an orderly hierarchical universe according to the classical scheme of the great chain of being. Bolingbroke was known not only for his philosophical bent and his activities as Queen Anne's minister during the War of the Spanish Succession but also for being a lifelong rake (Sydney Wayne Jackman, *Man of Mercury*, 1965, pp. 20–21).

## Wednesday 21 November

[MEM. dated Thursday 22 Novr.] [Y]esterday you waited on young Gaio genteel, lively. Armstrong's freind. Physique sur Morale — s'élève comme un aigle. Dind sweet Lady — Docteur shrewd materialist. Then Schoeflin quite Kames. Lhistoire des fables dont vous ne devez etre ignorant. At night wrote — For curiosity enjoy'd the air — no breach of oath — but swear again.¹ This day dress — then Schoev.² in chaise — then Gaio & Garrick's lines — get his. Prepare — 1st grand idea hell³ — Pronoun Possess *His*[.]⁴

[J.] I waited on young M. Gaio, fils du Preteur Royal. M. Tanner had desired me to present his compliments. M. Gaio was a genteel black little man, much of the Gentleman and the man of the World, quite *fait*⁵ as the French say. His Father had been employed to take care of the provisions of the french army, & he had resided much at Cassel where he formed a freindship with Doctor Armstrong Physician to the Army. He corresponds with him. He described the Doctor with great justness. C'est un Homme Hypochondre, chez qui la physique influ beaucoup sur la morale. Avant diner il est tout abattu. Mais quand il a eu un Bouteille de bon vin il commence de se sentir; il etend les ailes il s'eleve comme un Aigle. Quand il etoit comme cela, Je le mena dans ma voiture hors de Cassel. Nous nous sommes mis sur l'herbe á notre aise, et il haranguoit d'une manierre la plus vive, avec un feu celeste. The Doctor has given a fine character of M. Gaio in his Epistle called Day.⁶ Mr. Garrick had past lately some time at

Strasbourg and had been much with M. Gaio who he Said had stolen his Villa at Hampton for M. Gaio's is much the same.[7] M. Gaio spoke good english, tho' his accent was foreign. He has studied that language much. He observed that the English put the Pronoun possessive in the Gender of the Possessor & not in that of the thing possessed as, His mare, Her horse which is very clear whereas in all other languages the Pronoun Possessive takes the Gender of the thing possessed. Garrick had owned that this was a perfection in our tongue which he had not before attended to. I explained it to M. Gaio, & shewed him that we had but one Pronoun possessive *my* which changes not it's termination. As for *His* it is only the Genetive of *He* & *Her* is also the Genetive[;] the *s* is not added on account of the harsh pronunciation.[8] I found myself mightly well with Gaio. He asked me to dine with him. He presented me to his Lady a young pretty sweet creature without any airs.[9] She charmed me by calling her Husband allways *Mon bon Ami*. We had with us also M. le Docteur a Physician, a great Admirer of Dr. Pringles, on account of his knowledge, judgment and vivacity of Style.[10] He had studied man as a machine & said L'homme depend de la position ou il se trouve. We had an agreable freindly dinner, after which M le Docteur gave me some arguments for Materialism which I could not answer.[11] M. Gaio sent for Le Professeur Scheofling Historiographe du Roi. He is of the country of Baden-Durlach and has lately written an elegant latin History of the Principality of Baden. It consists of five or six volumes & is elegantly printed at Carlsruhe. This Gentleman was a tall figure, full of knowledge, healthy and lively. We went to his house, and saw his Library, which is immensely rich in history & Antiquities.[12] He said 'Vos Sceptics disent Pourquoi etudiez tant les faits de l'Histoire. Peutêtre ils ne sont pas vrayes. A cela Je reponds. Messieurs Supposons quils soient des fables: ils sont des fables dont tout le monde parle, et dont vous ne devez etre ignorants. En parlant ainsi Je leur ferme la bouche, et Je m'epargne toute la peine de leur expliquer la force de la foi historique. This was putting the matter in a new light, with great justice.[13] M. Gaio was kind enough to offer me his Coach while I remained at Strasbourg: But I did not put him to that trouble.

[TEN LINES A DAY.]
Those men no doubt in ev'ry age have err'd
Who have to bus'ness idle sport preferr'd
And yet when I consult my books I find
That men to sport have ever been inclin'd
How lives the Man of Nature on his hill?
The Savage mortal[14] ignorant of ill;
Tho' firm his limbs and vigourous his hands,
No art he knows no bus'ness understands
Amongst his tribe there is not even found
The Art most simple how to till the Ground.

[1] Presumably an allusion to his vow not to 'enjoy a woman before seeing Rousseau' (Journ. 21 Oct.).

[2] MS. 'dress Schoev' deleted by JB with thick ink strokes.

[3] Preparing for his interview with Rous-

seau, JB was planning to discuss his first ideas of hell as inculcated by his mother and Calvinist teacher (see 'Ébauche de ma vie', Yale MS. L 1107, App. 2, III.A).

[4] MS. 'Pronoun … His' written along the left margin, part of the discussion about pronoun endings recorded in the journal.

[5] Arrived at full development, mature (Robert, s.v. 'fait, faite', 2).

[6] Félix-Louis de Gayot (1733–69) had studied law at the University of Strasbourg and was now one of the city's six 'sénateurs nobles' (Ingeborg Streitberger, Der Königliche Prätor von Strassburg, 1685–1789, 1961, p. 204; Jacques Hart, Listes du grand sénat de Strasbourg … du XIIIe siècle à 1789, 1963, pp. 368–70, 436). He owed his prominent social position in Strasbourg to his father, François-Marie de Gayot (1699–1776), the official representative of the King with the title of Royal Praetor. Starting in 1757, Gayot senior had been in charge of procuring supplies for part of the French army, notably before and after the battle of Rossbach in 1757, and had remained successfully in his post despite complaints that he cared more about the local merchants than about the French troops (Charles Nicolas Dublanchy, Une Intendance d'armée au XVIIIe siècle [1905], pp. 187, 204–05). Félix-Louis had assisted his father as commissary from 1754, had served with the French armies on the lower Rhine from 1757 to 1759, and after a leave for reasons of health had been stationed in Kassel while the French forces occupied the town (see Journ. 23 Oct. n. 4; Livet, iii. 295–96). It was he, not his father, who had become friendly with Dr. John Armstrong (1709–79) in the summer of 1760 (see his letter of 1 Jan. 1767, Corr. 5, pp. 103–04). Armstrong, a minor poet and essayist who had published his poem The Art of Preserving Health in 1744, had accepted the appointment as Physician to the Forces in Germany in Mar. 1760 after he could not obtain a licence to practise medicine in London, where his Scottish medical degree was not recognized by the College of Physicians (see Gent. Mag. xxx. 155; William J. Maloney, George and John Armstrong of Castleton, 1954, pp. 13–14, 43 and n. 11; and Donald Bruce, Radical Doctor Smollett, 1964, p. 26). While in French-occupied Kassel, he had presumably been free to develop his friendship with Gayot because of the Anglo-French agreement, dating from 1743, to respect the neutrality of military hospitals (see n. 10).

Armstrong's Day: an Epistle to John Wilkes (1761), a rambling poem that confirms the report of Armstrong's gourmet tastes, praises the younger Gayot for being 'good and amiable' as well as 'generous and plain, the friend of humankind' (concluding section). These lines are particularly appreciative in that they were written in wartime about an enemy. The poem had been published in fragmentary form by Wilkes without its author's knowledge (Maloney, p. 38; L. M. Knapp, 'Dr. John Armstrong, Littérateur,' PMLA 59 [1944]: 1039–41).

[7] JB had met David Garrick (1717–79) in London in 1760 and again in 1763 when the latter was already an acclaimed actor, a successful dramatist, and the manager of the Drury Lane Theatre. JB not only admired Garrick but also appreciated his spontaneous kindness, beginning a lifelong friendship (Frank Brady, 'Introduction to the Boswell-Garrick Correspondence', Corr. 4, pp. 1–20). Garrick's country house, situated on the Thames, was a three-storey building of pale yellow brick to which the architect Robert Adam (1728–92) had added a white arcade and portico as well as stone pilasters (Carola Oman, David Garrick, 1958, pp. 188–91). Purchased by Garrick in 1754, it was modelled on much larger mansions such as Chiswick, owned by his friend the Earl of Burlington, and Chatsworth, owned by another friend, the Duke of Devonshire (George Winchester Stone Jr. and George M. Kahrl, David Garrick, 1979, pp. 362, 382).

[8] JB did not realize that the form of the feminine pronoun without an 's' is not related to the sound but is derived from the Old English (see Grand Tour I, Heinemann p. 184 n. 1, McGraw-Hill p. 188 n. 3).

[9] Not identified further.

[10] Sir John Pringle (1707–82) had been physician to the British army in Flanders from 1742 to 1748, except for service with the Duke of Cumberland's forces at Culloden, and his personal experience had taught him the dangers of unhygienic conditions. In combatting these, he would come to be regarded as the 'founder of modern military medicine' (Oxford DNB [DNB Archive]). It was he who had inspired the agreement of the British and French to consider military hospitals as neutral 'sanctuaries of the sick' (see Andrew Kippis, 'The Life of the Author', Six Discourses by Sir John Pringle, Bart., 1783, pp. viii–ix, xxix). His Observations on the Diseases of the Army, 1752, and other writings were admired on the Continent. In London, he was elected Fellow of the Royal Society in 1763 and would serve as its President from 1772 to 1778 (Oxford DNB). A longtime friend of Lord Auchinleck's,

Pringle would become a firm but kindly mentor to JB (see his many letters and JB's 'Memoirs of Sir John Pringle, for use in Dr. Kippis's life of Pringle', M 217).

[11] Gayot's doctor friend has not been identified. Evidently he had adopted the materialism made fashionable in La Mettrie's *L'Homme machine* (1747).

[12] Jean-Daniel Schöpflin (1694–1771), at this time the most distinguished scholar at the University of Strasbourg, had been professor of history and rhetoric since 1720 and royal historiographer to Louis XV since 1740. Born in Sulzburg, Baden-Durlach, he had attended school and the university in Basel from 1705 to 1711 and had studied in Strasbourg, where he had then been named *professor historiarum et eloquentiae* at the early age of twenty six (ADB). He remained in Strasbourg in spite of invitations, at different times, to teach in St. Petersburg, London, Upsala, Vienna, and Leiden. Meanwhile he had been elected to numerous learned societies, including the Royal Society in London and the Académie des Inscriptions in Paris. Thanks to his stature and influence, his university had preserved some of the prerogatives of its Lutheran professors in spite of pressure from the Catholic authorities, and Strasbourg had become a major centre of Enlightenment thought (see Bernard Vogler, 'L'Université de Strasbourg au milieu du XVIIIe siècle', *Strasbourg, Schoepflin et l'Europe au XVIIIe siècle*, ed. Bernard Vogler and Jürgen Voss, 1996, pp. 11–16; Voss, pp. 191–222). Recently Schöpflin had been the guiding spirit behind Karl Theodor's new academy, and although he had declined to move to Mannheim, was serving as its honorary president (see Journ. 5 Nov. n. 5; Voss, pp. 207–15).

Schöpflin was now seeing through the press the last volumes of his monumental history of the dynasties of Baden-Baden and Baden-Durlach, *Historia Zaringo-Badensis* (Zaringo referring to the barons of Zähringen, from whom, the book demonstrated, the margraves of Baden-Durlach and Baden-Baden could proudly trace their descent). The handsome quarto volumes—four of text and three of archival documentation, published from 1762 to 1766—had benefitted from the advice of both the Margrave and the Margravine of Baden-Durlach (W. Mez, 'Johann Daniel Schöpflin', *Die Pyramide*, 18 Sept. 1921, No. 38, pp. 308–09; Voss, pp. 272–79; *Carl Friedrich und Seine Zeit*, p. 212). Schöpflin had chosen Latin for this and his previous work, a learned history of the Alsace entitled *Alsatia Illustrata* (2 vols. 1751, 1761). But for a wider reading public, Johann Christian Sachs's German translation of the *Historia Zaringo-Badensis*, entitled *Einleitung in die Geschichte der Marggravschaft und des marggrävlichen altfürstlichen Hauses Baden*, 5 vols, 1764–73, began to appear even before the publication of Schöpflin's later volumes (Mez, p. 308).

Schöpflin's library—more than 11,000 volumes at his death—was open to students. He would bequeath it, along with his collection of antiquities, to the magistracy of Strasbourg in return for a small annuity, ensuring its continued use by the public and the university (ADB; Georges Livet, 'Les Relations de Schoepflin avec les notables en Alsace', *Strasbourg, Schoepflin et l'Europe*, p. 36).

[13] After this visit, Schöpflin would write to Margrave Karl Friedrich that JB was 'un jeune homme qui ira loin' (letter of 29 Nov., see *Johann Daniel Schoepflins Brieflicher Verkehr mit Gönnern, Freunden und Schülern*, ed. Richard Fester, Litterarischer Verein in Stuttgart, 1906, p. 172).

[14] MS. 'man' inserted above 'mortal', 'yet' inserted after 'mortal'

## Thursday 22 November

[MEM. dated Friday 23 Novr] [Y]esterday you waited on Schoefling. A Student & Governour gave you the Spleen. There needs no more. Gaio visited you. Dined with him. M. l'Abbé. M. le Docteur all charming. After dinner he said Madame bonne, tranquille. He quite fine fellow *male* á Petersburg — L'Imperatrice accorda le manege — le premier francois qui pensoit qu'il pouvoit apprendre quelque chose hors de son païs elevé a souffrir — Son oncle Porcelaine cassé — Levoit le par le bras donnez burgogne [—] crois — a eu peur — Pere tout le Vin 30 ans — mon vin est bu.[1] Then Comedy not grande chose — had seen Cathedral, & answerd Garrick — Send him them or keep them for London — maintain dignity & youll be with Armstr — Johns Garrick. This day all pack'd — no haste — set out — read. Retenue but chearfull [—] never own changes. Plan Rousseau[.]

[J.] I went & saw the Cathedral, which is one of the noblest pieces of Gothic Architecture that I ever beheld.[2] Mr. Garrick had written verses expressing his Indignation at seeing little Shops built round it. M. Gaio shewed me the verses, & I answered them.[3] I entered a little, and heard solemn service.[4] I then waited on Scheofling. He is realy an able man, & his attachment to the Marcgrave of Baden Durlach makes me regard him particularly. A Student & his Governour entered.[5] I became a little splenetic. There needs no more to turn the course of my ideas. Gaio payed me a visit, & then carried me home to his house where I din'd. We had M. l'Abbé[6] uncle to Madame Gaio, & our good freind M. Le Docteur. We were gay and chearfull. I should have mentioned yesterday, that Madame Gaio made me a present of a Collection of Prints representing the Rejoycings of Strasbourg on the arrival of the King. I could not carry them with me. She promised to give me them as I returned to Carlsruhe, or to send them for me to England.[7] This day after dinner M. Gaio showed me a genteel room, saying, Tenez— quand vous retournez ici voici votre chambre.[8] Il vaut mieux que l'Esprit. Ou vous serez la, ou á ma Campagne. Was there ever more Civility?[9] And he had not a crum of the usual flattery. He is a noble fellow. He told me I had a french air, & that I would undoubtedly speak good french. He bid me speak slow to avoid the hissing pronunciation of the British. He told me he had been early accustomed to suffer, & so had acquired calm[10] fortitude of mind. He told us several good Storys. I past the evening at the Comedie which is not very brilliant here. I was pleased with one Song, 'Maudit Amour', &c.[11] I was sorry not to find there the Marischal Contades who was the french General at the Battle of Minden. He is at present Commander here.[12]

[TEN LINES A DAY.]
When he had done no good, I've lost a day
An ancient Roman nobly us'd to say[13]
And I confess with sorrow and with shame
That of this ev'ning I must say the same.
Instead of turning some rich Classic Page
Or journalising with vivacious rage
Grossly I've talk'd with a french wicked smart
On th'operations of the Paphian Art[14]
And have a Judge's grave attention paid
While he Parisian Lechery display'd.[15]

[1] Snatches of the dinner conversation, ending with two anecdotes recorded in *Boswelliana*. When young Gayot's uncle saw a servant breaking a valuable china tea set, he told another servant: 'Ecoutez, donnez un verre du vin de Bourgogne á François, je crois qu'il a eu peur'. When Gayot's father heard that a huge cask of especially good Rhine wine had burst, he merely said, 'Eh bien, mon vin est bu' (*Boswelliana*, p. 234, correcting Rogers' 'en' to MS. 'eu' and Rogers' 'lu' to MS. 'bu').
[2] The cathedral with its three-aisled nave, great portals, and rose window is noteworthy for the delicacy of its Gothic style. Most of it had been built from 1252 to 1365, while its distinctively tall and slender north tower, designed by Ulrich von Ensingen (d. 1419) with help from his son Matthäus Ensinger (c. 1390–1463), had been completed in 1439 (the complementary second tower, though discussed at various times, was never built). Earlier parts, dating from 1176 to 1245, are in romanesque or transitional style, and a few remnants of a still earlier medieval buil-

ding remain in spite of successive fires (Julius Euting, *A Descriptive Guide to the City of Strassburg and Its Cathedral*, 1896, pp. 10–30; Hans Reinhardt, *La Cathédrale de Strasbourg*, 1972, p. 249.

[3] For Garrick's lines 'Upon Seeing Strasbourg Cathedral Extempore by a Stranger (David Garrick, Esq.)' (C 1335) and JB's reply (M 284), see App. 1 (also *Grand Tour I*, Heinemann pp. 186–87, McGraw-Hill p. 191, and *Corr. 4*, App. I). Garrick had termed the small shops that had sprung up close to the Cathedral 'a disgrace', an 'impious act' perpetrated by 'Goths' who reveal 'their want of virtue, taste and righteousness'. He was referring to the shoddy shacks which nestled against the sides of the building, and which would be replaced by less disreputable Gothic-style stalls in 1772 (*Strassburg und seine Bauten*, 1894, p. 154). In his reply, JB defended the 'honest bus'ness' of the shopkeepers and insisted on their reverence for the 'majestic pile'. But he changed his mind when he actually saw the site the following day, as he acknowledged to the Margrave of Baden-Durlach, to whom he sent a copy of Garrick's verses and his own, now with the title 'Answer of The Shop-keepers round Strasbourg Cathedral' (letter of 25 Nov., GLA Karlsruhe, FA 5A, Corr. 23). On his return to England JB would also send a copy of his verses to Garrick, as planned, and receive an appreciative reply (see From Garrick, 25 Nov. 1767, *Corr. 4*, p. 22).

[4] A Catholic service. The cathedral, which had been Lutheran from the 1520s, had been reclaimed by the Catholic church when Strasbourg was absorbed by the French in 1681 (see P. A. Granddidier, *Essais historiques et topographiques sur l'église cathédrale de Strasbourg*, 1782, pp. 81, 278; Livet, iii. 190).

[5] Not identified.

[6] Not identified.

[7] *Représentation des fêtes données pour la convalescence du roi*, engraved by J. M. Weis, celebrated Louis XV's triumphal entry into Strasbourg on 5 Oct. 1744 after recovering from smallpox at Metz (*Grand Tour I*, Heinemann pp. 185–86 n. 2, McGraw-Hill p. 190 n. 7). The King's five-day stay in Strasbourg had been the first visit to the town undertaken by a French monarch since 1681 (Livet, iii. 497–501). The Gayots would try to send Weis's sumptuously printed volume to JB by way of Paris, with a second copy to be transmitted to Dr. Armstrong (From Gayot, 7 Jan. and 5 Feb. 1766; *Corr. 5*, pp. 103–04 and n. 4). But JB seems not to have received these volumes, which do not appear in the lists of

his library at Edinburgh or Auchinleck, nor would he write to Armstrong at this time.

[8] Gayot was living in the older part of the family's large town house, the hôtel Gayot, an elegant building dating from 1740 and extended fourteen years later according to plans by the respected architect Joseph Massol (c. 1706–71); see Thieme-Becker, xxiv. 222; 'Massol', *Nouveau dictionnaire de biographie alsacienne 26* [1982]: 2550). It was situated between the rue Brûlée and the promenade du Broglie (Livet, iii. 477). Félix would succeed his father as praetor of Strasbourg in 1768 but would succumb to consumption the following year (Ingeborg Streitberger, *Der Königliche Prätor von Strassburg, 1685–1789*, 1961, pp. 202–05; Livet, iii. 295).

[9] More than a year after his visit JB would gratefully recall Gayot's hospitality and apologize for his delay in writing (To Gayot, 1 Dec. 1765). Gayot would continue the correspondence in letters of 7 Jan. and 5 Feb. 1766 and 1 Jan. 1767 (see *Corr. 5*, p. 103).

[10] MS. The pagination changes inadvertently, from 773 to 734, on the inside page of a small sheet folded once, then continues with the new numbering.

[11] In Act II of *Le Peintre amoureux de son modèle* (1757), libretto by M. Louis Anséaume (1721–84), music by Egidio Duni (1708–75). French plays, popular in Strasbourg, were performed with the permission of the commandant of the garrison as well as of the magistracy (Gonthier-Louis Fink, 'Strasbourg, carrefour des Lumières', *Strasbourg, Schoepflin, et l'Europe*, p. 294).

[12] Contades had commanded the French forces at Minden together with Broglie and had blamed his defeat on Broglie's inadequate attack on Prince Ferdinand of Brunswick and his troops (see Journ. 24 June and n. 3). Disgruntled, Contades had left the army, whereupon he had been appointed commandant of the garrison of Alsace in 1762. He had chosen Strasbourg as his residence and would remain, much appreciated, until the French Revolution, which he would barely survive (DBF, ix. 523–24).

[13] The Emperor Titus Vespasiamus would reproach himself by saying he had lost a day if he had not benefited someone ('Amici, diem perdidi', Suetonius, *Lives of the Caesars*, viii. 1, Loeb ed., trans. J. C. Rolfe, 1959–64).

[14] The art of love as epitomized in the 'Paphian Aphrodite'. According to legend, Paphos, in Cyprus, was the place where the goddess Aphrodite had come up from the sea ('Cyprus', OCCL, p. 129).

[15] MS. Five asterisks mark the end of this set of Ten Lines.

## Friday 23 November

[MEM. dated Saturday 24 Novr.] Yesterday Postilion [—] had engaged frenchman. Impertinent — would not take him — Expedient. Joli Garçon Engraver mild instruit[1] lively. At night too much of Girls[2] &c. This day Go on to Basle be well.

[J.] I said last night to Jacob. Allons partions pour une fois sans être á la hate. We did so today. My rogue of a Coachman had engaged a frenchman to go in my machine, & to pay him twelve livres to Bâle. I was very angry & wanted to keep him out; But hearing that he had not payed the Coachman, I took him in on condition that he should pay me ten livres, & give the coachman nothing.[3] He was a very genteel, clever young fellow an engraver,[4] who had past three years[5] in Holland. He was knowing & lively [—] modest for a frenchman. We had a good day's journey to          [.][6]

[1] Educated (Robert, s.v. 'instruit').
[2] MS. 'At night ... Girls' deleted by a modern hand.
[3] A *livre* ('*livre tournois*', English: pound), the French monetary unit used in Strasbourg, was worth a third of an écu (René Pomeau, 'Note sur les monnaies', *Écraser l'Infâme*, 1994; John J. McCusker, p. 88, Table 2.22). This valuation is corroborated by JB's insertion of '24£' next to the '8 écus' he noted as his coach fare (Exp. Acct. 24 Nov., App. 3). The distance between Strasbourg and Basel was 18 miles, or 29 km (Keyssler, iv. 65).
[4] Charles-Ange Boily (b. 1739/40), an engraver specializing in book illustrations, was leaving Holland to try to establish himself in Switzerland. He was bringing with him eight advance copies of Rousseau's *Lettres écrites de la montagne* from the Dutch

publisher Marc-Michel Rey (1720–80), a Huguenot born in Geneva who had settled in Amsterdam in 1744 and was becoming the leading publisher of Rousseau as well as of Voltaire and other *philosophes* (see Elizabeth L. Eisenstein, 'The Libraire-Philosophe', *Le Livre et l'Historien*, 1997, pp. 544–46; for the *Lettres de la montagne*, see Journ. 24 Dec. n. 24). Boily was supposed to do a crayon portrait of Rousseau to be used for engraving but, lacking time to go to Môtiers, would send the books through others (From Rey to Rousseau, 5 Nov., Letter 3625; From Rousseau to Henri Laliaud, 9 Dec., *CC Rousseau*, Letter 3726, xxii. 15–16, 19 n. g, 202).
[5] MS. 'in', written below 'years' at the bottom of the page.
[6] MS. Space left for their destination: Basel.

## Saturday 24 November

[MEM. dated Sunday 25 Novr.] [Y]esterday fine journey — very gay. Jacob dull did not dance in Switzerland — Arrived Bale. Singular Hote, very eloquent — Voltaire '*un demi* Poulet n'est pas un poulet.' Walk'd out. Supt with him very merry. This day journ. well. Resolve to stay till [M]ond evening — So as to see a curious old learned town [—] write from Erasm tomb.[1] Swear — Journ clear & Rousseau. Send Emile.[2]

[J.] We were very gay. M. Boili my frenchman made a very just distinction between his Nation & the British. Les Anglois ses croyent au dessus des autres et il les meprise souverainement. Les françois ne meprisent pas les autres. Mais c'est certain qu'ils ses croyent au desus des toutes les Nations. He taught[3] me a Song. He was a materialist too forsooth.[4] He made scarcely any distinction between Master & Servant. He had no judgment to know when to speak & when to hold his tongue. We now entered Switzerland. They are a phlegmatic Nation. Jacob shewed no signs of lively joy at the sight of his country.[5] We arrived at Basel & put up at the Three Kings finely situated on the bank of the Rhine. Imhof our Landlord was a most original fellow. He was prodigiously fluent in the praises of his town which he said deserved to be seen at great length so that I should stay with him several days. He went out & took a turn with us, expatiating on all that he saw. We supped at his Table d'hote where He harangued on the number of People & on the distinguished Savants who had been in his house. He said 'Voltaire vint ici. Il se mit au lit. Je demandais de son Domestique. Votre maitre veut il souper quelquechose? Je ne sais pas. C'est selon. Peutêtre oui, peutêtre non. Moi Je fis faire un bonne soupe et appreter un Poulet. M. Voltaire s'eveille, Il demande á souper. Je lui sers la soupe, Il la prenne. Il la rejette, puis il la reprenne. C'est une excellent Soupe. Il est entré un Monsieur á qui J'avois donné la moitié du Poulet. Je sers l'autre moitié á M. Voltaire. Il le prenne. —Il le rejette. Puis il le reprenne. C'est un excellent Poulet. Il se fache quil n a pas un Poulet entier et il dit toujours un demi poulet n'est pas un Poulet — un demi Poulet n'est pas un Poulet. Enfin il fut fort content de ma Maison.' There goes a Specimen Eloquentiae Imhoffianae. He amused me much, & I concluded him to be either a very honest fellow, or a very great Rogue.[6] I had a most excellent Bed-chamber.

[1] Evidently JB planned to write from this tomb, in the cathedral of Basel, as he had from Melanchthon's (see Journ. 30 Sept.).

[2] Presumably 'send for' *Émile*, another preparation for the meeting with Rousseau.

[3] MS. 'talked'

[4] See Journ. 27 Nov. and n. 2.

[5] Jacob Hänni, whom Boswell had engaged in Holland because he spoke French and German, came from the neighbourhood of Bern (see Journ. 25 July n. 8, 29 Nov. n. 6).

[6] Johann Christoph Imhof (1705–86) was the enterprising proprietor of the Drei Könige, which was said to be the most expensive inn in Switzerland at this time (Pierre Grellet, *Les Aventures de Casanova en Suisse*, 1919, pp. 143–45; *Basel anno 1760: nach den Tagebüchern der ungarischen Grafen Joseph und Samuel Teleki*, ed. O. Spiess, 1936, p. 36).

## Sunday 25 November

[MEM. dated Monday 26 Novr.] Yesterday you read the Savoyard's Creed & was struck. At 12 went & saw Dance of Death. *Glaubens* but several times renewed — so french card.[1] After dinner Arsenal — very clean many arms of the Duke of Burgundy the windows painted with all famous men. Among the rest Samuel with an immense sabre — I suppose to hew Agag.[2] Waited on Wohleb too lively animal spirits. Foreigner — you'd be damn'd [—] J. Christ. Bâle Clock 3 quarters forward absurd custom.[3] Bertoli[4] accounted bad Dial — why not change? Some say. Ennemys betray [—] they put forward — or by *miracle*. Some during the Council — to meet sooner your mistresses — 10 years — custom half a year ago debated in Council — gravely affraid that it might ruin their Republic, might hurt workmen to rise 4 — This day coup de pein. 8 — Library & Tomb Erasm & maison ville — no *cabinet*. Pay frenchman 8 Bats.[5] Prepare — set out tonight — & Journ at Inne — Send Emile — &c.

Send to Post for lett from Cazenove.[6]

[J.] I read with attention Rousseau's Creed of the Savoyard. I was struck with it's clearness, it's Simplicity and it's Piety.[7] I went & saw the famous *Dance of Death* which has been called the work of Holbens, as that Painter was of this City, but it was in reality painted by *Jean Klauber*. It is very old but has been so often mended that like William the Lion's chair at Aberdeen it has very little remaining of the first work. I bought a book of the Designs & Inscriptions. It is in a cover'd Gallery with rails in front that the *Death's Dance* is placed. Malicious Boys now & then get at it with stones, and spoil it.[8] I dined with our Hote who raged Il faut vivre — nous n'emportons rien d'ici. I then went & saw the Arsenal which contains a great many arms kept in the best order. They shone like a Looking-Glass. There are here many arms taken from the Duke of Burgundy.[9] I then waited on M. Wohleb, President de la Chambre de Justice.[10] I had been recommended to him by Professor Gotsched at Leipsic. I found him a German Suiss Literatus full of animal spirits. I put him at his ease, & he talked away with much volubility. He told me a most curious anecdote. The Clock of the City of Basel is about an hour before all the Clocks in the Country & indeed before the Sun himself by which they are regulated so that when a Stranger sets out from Basel at noon, after travelling a league he finds it noon still. Various are the causes assigned for this particularity of the Basel Clock. Some say that there was a Conspiracy of the Citizens to rise in arms at a certain hour, and that the magistrates having had notice of it, advanced the Clock an hour, so that some of the Conspirators came to the Rendezvous too late, & others too soon & in short were all in confusion. Some again maintain that the Ennemy was at their gates, & were to be let in at a certain time by some wicked malecontents; but that a miracle was wrought in the favour of Basel, & the Clock advanced an hour. This tradition is highly natural. It flatters their vanity & pleases their superstition to suppose such an Interposition of Providence. No less a man than the late famous mathematician Bernoilli set himself to account for this strange mensuration of time. He supposed that they had taken a Dial which was not just, to regulate the Clock of the Cathedral by. By this means the Cathedral Clock has been put wrong, and the others have followed. But this account will not suffice: for if the Dial for the Cathedral Clock had been bad, it would have been corrected by the others. Wohleb said that most probably the Clock had been advanced during the Council of Basel that the Ecclesiastics might meet an hour sooner, perhaps with design to be an hour sooner with their mistresses. As the Council lasted ten years the irregularity of the Clock became a custom.[11] I asked if they did not think to correct this absurd custom. A grave Gentleman[12] of Authority in the City gravely replied that not a year ago the affair had been debated in Council, and [s]ome of the members had maintained that the Clock should not be changed, as it might perhaps bring ruin upon their Republic.[13] Is it possible that such darkness can remain in an age so enlighten'd? Wohleb said that the Servants and Workmen would lye longer abed by the change; as to rise at five would appear terrible altho' they realy rise at present at that hour by the name of six. I must give a specimen of Wohleb's wit. When in England he said 'You english dont love the foreigners; & yet had it not been for a foreigner you would be damned. You own there is no salvation but thro' Jesus Christ — Yes sure — Well, Jesus Christ was a Foreigner. Ha! ha!' This is wit like Kennicot's.[14]

[1] 'Glaubens': Klauber; 'french card': possibly the figure of a French cardinal added to the original figures in the 'Dance of Death' (for which see n. 8).

[2] To fulfil God's command, Samuel had killed Agag, king of the Amalekites, who had opposed the Israelites during their journey from Egypt and had been temporarily spared by Saul (1 Sam. 15:33).

[3] Actually, the clocks were set a full hour in advance (see Journ. for this day).

[4] Bernoulli (see n. 11).

[5] Why JB was paying Bertollon is not indicated in his Expense Account.

[6] MS. 'Send ... Cazenove' written along the right margin. Cazenove, Clavière et fils, bankers in Geneva, were receiving letters for JB (see Journ. 6 Dec.).

[7] 'La Profession de foi du Vicaire Savoyard', a long interpolated section in Book IV of Émile, expresses a belief in a benevolent God governing all things and also affirms the importance of each individual's 'inner light' and conscience. This profoundly personal credo, a kind of emotional deism, is attributed to a curate from the Savoy but also represents Rousseau's own ideas (see Journ. 3 Dec. and n. 24; OC Rousseau, iv. 565–35; May, pp. 98–105; Eigeldinger, 'Profession de foi', and Charles Porset, 'Profession de foi du Vicaire Savoyard' in Dict. de Rousseau, pp. 751–56). JB's praise marks a change from his attitude a few months earlier, when the 'Savoyard's Creed' had shaken his faith (To WJT, 22 May, Corr. 6, p. 98 and n. 5).

[8] Thirty-seven allegorical images, all but two showing Death dancing with different representatives of society (though no French cardinal), had been painted on the churchyard wall of the former Dominican monastery. This mural was sometimes attributed to Hans Holbein the Younger (c. 1497–1543) because he had made famous engravings of The Dance of Death (pub. in 1530). He could be considered 'of this city', although born in Augsburg, because he had settled in Basel in 1715 and had worked there for many years, having been admitted as master in the painters' guild in 1519 (Rowlands, pp. 60–63). But the mural had actually been created from 1437 to 1741, and had then been repainted in 1568 by Hans Hug Klauber or Kluber (1535/36–78). It had been restored at least three times since then. It was however now in disrepair, the Council having refused in 1760 to have it restored again. JB's book was very likely Johann Jacob Merian's popular Todten-Tantz (1621), which provided woodcuts of the figures and accompanying verses, and which had appeared in at least 12 editions (François Maurer, Die Kunstdenkmäler des Kantons Basel-Stadt, v. 294–99; Stephan Cosacchi, Makabertanz, 1965, pp. 762–63 and n. 42). JB paid 20 Batsen to see the mural (Exp. Acct. 26 Nov., App. 3).

The chair attributed to William the Lion (1143–1214) was one of several 'of curious and rude workmanship' that stood in Trinity Hall in Aberdeen (William Kennedy, Annals of Aberdeen, 1818, ii. 242). William, the Scottish king who had regained his country's independence from Richard I of England, had granted the first recorded charters to the burgesses of Aberdeen (Kennedy, i. 5–11).

[9] At the battles of Grandson and Morat in 1476, where the forces of Charles the Bold (1433–77), Duke of Burgundy, had been routed by the armies of the Swiss confederates in a remarkable victory of republican burghers over French noblemen who had long exerted power over them (Florens Deuchler, Die Burgunderbeute, 1963, pp. 15–18, 20–22, 44–46).

[10] Emanuel Wolleb (1706–88) was a Schultheiss, the highest judicial official in Basel. He also wrote philosophical, moral, and satirical essays, some of which were collected in the Helvetische Patriot (2 vols. and supplement, 1755–57; DHBS, vii. 376). A dedication to Gottsched appeared in the first volume.

[11] Most of Wolleb's explanations, though fanciful, had been proposed by earlier chroniclers. The foiling of traitors inside and outside the city had been associated with attacks by the Austrians at some time between 1256 and 1273 (J. Stumpf, Schweitzer Chronik, 3rd ed., 1606, fol. 717; Theodor Zwinger, Methodus apodemica, 1577, p. 185). A miraculous intervention to confuse would-be traitors had been surmised by Christian Wurstisen, Beschreibung des Münsters zu Basel, 1587 (see Beiträge zur vaterländischen Geschichte 12 [1888]: 421–23). The theory of a faulty dial in the cathedral's original sun clock had been advanced by Johann Bernoulli (1667–1748), member of a well-known family of mathematicians, and also accepted later by his son Daniel (1700–82), who would

241

argue for changing the time in a strong letter to the Council dated 11 Nov. 1774. The frequent link with the third reforming Council of Basel (1431–49), for which about 800 clerics had assembled to oppose the heresy of the Hussites (a Bohemian and Moravian group trying to reform the Church) and to assist the Greeks who were threatened by the Turks, usually had an anti-clerical bias by suggesting that its participants wished to escape boredom, eat earlier, or flee from a feared attack. For all these explanations, see M. Fallet-Scheurer, 'Die Zeitmessung im alten Basel', *Basler Zeitschrift für Geschichte und Altertumskunde* 15 (1916): 297–305. Wolleb's supposition that the clerics advanced the time to meet their mistresses at an earlier hour was less commonly expressed but fits his salacious interests (see Journ. 26 Nov.). In the twentieth century the special time in Basel would be attributed to the medieval practice of designating noon and midnight as 'one' (*hora prima*) at the beginning of the twelve-hour sequence for church services, a model that had been retained because it satisfied both the Church and the bourgeois society of the city (Fallet-Scheurer, pp. 312–14, 341–42).

[12] Not identified.

[13] Basel, which had been a bishop's see until 1521, had become an independent republic governed by its great and small councils (the *Grosse Rat* of 180 members and *Kleine Rat* of 64 members) while also belonging to the confederacy of thirteen Swiss cantons which it had joined in 1501 ('Bâle', DHBS, i. 532; Josef Rosen, *Chronik von Basel*, 1971, pp. 91–104). No discussion about changing the time was recorded in the council minutes in the year prior to JB's visit. When the debates of 1774–78 would lead to a change in 1779, this indeed would cause such dissatisfaction and confusion about working hours that it would be re-scinded a few weeks later. Only in 1798 would the time be changed permanently in the aftermath of the French Revolution (Fallet-Scheurer, pp. 342–51).

[14] Wolleb had been in England from about 1733 to 1735 (*Die Matrikel der Universität Basel*, ed. Hans Georg Wackernagel, Max Triet, and Pius Marrer, 1975, iv. 467). Benjamin Kennicott (1718–83), D.D. was a Biblical scholar at Oxford who devoted his life to collating Hebrew texts for a new edition of the Bible (*Oxford DNB*). Possibly Kennicott was known for dullness and JB was being sarcastic (suggested by F. A. Pottle in an unpublished annotation).

## Monday 26 November

[MEM. dated Tuesday 27 Novr.] Yesterday at 8 Wohleb came to you. Instructed fille: etes-vous en humeur?[1] mais vous ne devez pas souvent[2] être en humeur false. Went & saw a Cabinet of Pictures. Some good — then saw maison de ville Holbens Passion wrote of it. Then Erasmus's Tomb in Cathedral[3] — Stone Pulpit. Carving of Priest indecent with Nun. On *Pont Rhin* Chapel above door beneath pict of Virgin ornament of womans thighs & all displayd. Strange. At two College Library. Many rich pieces of Holbens — a whole book of designs moræ encom done for a Schoolmaster & in his hand at Erasm's Picture uxorem duceret.[4] Erasm *will*[5] [—] 5[6] set out — This day resume. At night swear immed much Journ prepare all.

[J.] Basel makes me think of my worthy Father, as Erasmus & Frobenius lived here.[7] Wohleb waited upon me. We talked of Rousseau's idea of teaching nothing to a child before twelve or fourteen, because before that age, a child has no inclination to learn, and he should never be forced.[8] Mais (said Wohleb) un enfant peut avoir de l'inclination á apprendre, á meilleure heure. Par example J'ai une fille. Je disois toujours 'etes vous en humeur?' — Si elle disoit oui. Je l'enseignois quelque chose, si non — Je la laissoit — I asked him if he took no method to force her inclination. 'J'avoue J'ai lui dit il ne faut que vous soyez souvent pas en humeur.' Ah Monsieur (said I) vous gatez tout. I went & saw a private collection of Pictures; some of which were good.[9] I then saw at the maison de Ville a picture by Holbens, the sufferings of Christ in eight pieces. I wrote a description of it.[10] I then saw the Cathedral Church one of the venerable Gothic Buildings. The Pulpit is of Stone curiously carved.[11] In those times when this church was built, Superstition run[12] high, but morals were at a very low ebb. There is carved in this church a monk in most gross Copulation with a Nun. Wohleb also showed me an old Popish Chappel on the *Pont du Rhin*. Above the door was a niche in which was formerly placed a statue of the Virgin, & under this niche, by way of ornament was carved a Woman's thighs wide open & all her nakedness fully displayed. It has appeared so indecent, that they have effaced it a little, yet still the *ipsa res* appears.[13] At two we went & saw the College Library, Which is very numerous, & has a good many manuscripts. I asked for a manuscript [A]nacreon. But, o strange Penury! There was here neither manuscript nor printed Anacreon.[14] But this Library has a vast treasure in possessing a great many Capital Pieces of Holbens. Amongst others, a Suite of Christ's Sufferings better done than in the town-hall, particularly where our Saviour is bound & scourged. In the Town-Hall he is a poor shrinking figure, like a real malefactor. Here he preserves his dignity amidst all the ignominious treatment of his foes.[15] There is here a large book of Drawings by Holbens. They ought to be engraved. As also a moriæ encomium of Erasmus, which belonged to a Schoolmaster who used to have Holbens often at his house; and he to amuse himself made most excellent designs on the margin.[16] There are Plates done after them to embellish several printed editions — Poh! what language is this! A printed Edition. One might as well say a written Manuscript. But I journalise in haste: so let errors be pardoned. At five I set out for Soleure.

[1] MS. 'Instructed … humeur' scored out by a modern hand.

[2] MS. 'pas souvent pas'

[3] This tomb, not mentioned in the Journal, was marked by a red marble tablet with a laudatory inscription by Bonifacius Amerbach (1496?–1562) and a tondo showing Erasmus in profile. Such markers were no longer permitted in the Reformation, but an exception was made for Erasmus, who had lived in Basel while it was Catholic and had died there after it became Lutheran (for details on Erasmus, see n. 7 below; also François Maurer-Kuhn in *Das Basler Münster*, 1982, p. 33). The tablet was affixed to a pillar in the nave and would remain there until the 1850s (Hans Reinhardt, *Das Basler Münster*, 1961, pp. 40–41). Its location prevented JB from writing on top of it, as he had on Melanchthon's tomb.

[4] 'Would take a wife', Erasmus's famous quip. When told that the youthful scholar drawn by Holbein in the margin of the *Encomium moriæ* (*In Praise of Folly*, Paris, 1511) was meant to be him, Erasmus had exclaimed that if he still looked like that, he would find himself a wife (Lewis and Short,

'Uxor'; *Erasmi Roterodami Encomium Moriæ*, ed. Heinrich Alfred Schmid, 1931, i. S3; ii. 30 n. 1; Rowlands, p. 18). For the *Encomium moriæ* and the schoolmaster who owned the copy with the Holbein sketches, see n. 16.

[5] The will, one of the treasures of the Basel University Library, is a brief document written on both sides of a single sheet of parchment (Mscr ANIII 15 Bl. 96).

[6] MS. The number is partly obscured by an ink blot and is given here in light of JB's journal entry.

[7] Desiderius Erasmus (1466?–1536), originally known as Gerhard Gerhards or Geert Geerts, had left his native Rotterdam and, after travelling widely, had lived in Basel from 1521 to 1529 and again in the last two years of his life. By his writings, including a large correspondence, he had made Basel the centre of humanism (see Léon-E. Halkin, *Érasme parmi nous*, 1987, pp. 239–40, 440). Johann Froben (Frobenius, c. 1460–1527), his close friend, had been the printer of his works as well of Luther's and Holbein's (Rowlands, pp. 57–58). Lord Auchinleck liked to read Erasmus on Sundays to avoid idleness and gloom (From Lord Auchinleck, c. 26 Oct. 1763, Yale MS. C

223; 2 Apr. 1764, Yale MS. C 225).

[8] True to his belief that human beings are good by nature but easily corrupted by society, Rousseau had suggested that for a child's first education, no attempt should be made to teach virtue or truth, but every effort should be made to keep the heart free of vice and the mind free of error ('garantir le cœur du vice et l'esprit d'erreur'). If then taught from the age of twelve, the youngster might become a 'prodigy' (*Émile*, Bk. II, *OC Rousseau*, iv. 320–24).

[9] Very likely the valuable collection of books, manuscripts, and art objects assembled by the jurist Remigius Faesch (1595–1667), which had remained in his house on the Petersplatz and was being overseen, as stipulated in his will, by the male descendant of each generation who was a 'doctor juris'. The collection would be taken over by the University Library in 1823 and would be absorbed by the municipal museum of art (the Kunstmuseum) in 1849 (see Andreas Heusler, *Geschichte der öffentlichen Bibliothek der Universität Basel*, 1896, pp. 53–70; Martin Steinmann, *Die Handschriften der Universitätsbibliothek Basel*, 1982, p. 27).

[10] The famous Passion Altarpiece (c. 1520) commissioned by the Council, perhaps for the chapel of the town hall. JB took notes on each of the eight scenes, which were painted on four panels unified by a decorative framework (M 98, see App. 1).

[11] The large cathedral overlooking the Rhine had been built in six stages from about 1000 to the second half of the fifteenth century, partly in late Romanesque and partly in early Gothic style. A fire in 1258 and an earthquake in 1356 had led to changes and expansions that included fifty side chapels. The architects included Ulrich von Ensingen, who had also worked on the cathedrals of Strasbourg and Bern, and other members of his family (see Journ. 30 Nov. and n. 9). After the Reformation took hold in Basel in the 1520s and many of the cathedral's treasures were destroyed in the night of violence (the *Bildersturm*, 'picture-storm') of 1529, the building, stripped of ornaments, came to be used for Lutheran worship (François Maurer-Kuhn, 'Das Münster von Basel', *Schweizerische Kunstführer*, rev. ed. 1986, pp. [2]–6, 11, and *Das Münster von Basel*, p. 17). The stone pulpit of 1486 is decorated with unusual carvings suggesting upward surging flames (see

Maurer-Kuhn, 'Das Münster von Basel', p. 11). It is attributed to Hans von Nussdorf (d. 1503), who worked in Basel from 1472 (DHBS).

[12] Presumably used here as past tense.

[13] MS. 'by way … Woman's' and 'It has … appears' crossed out by a single line; 'thighs … displayed' heavily scored out by a modern hand (*ipsa res*: 'the thing itself'). The indecent carvings in this tiny chapel, situated in the middle of a wooden bridge across the Rhine, together with those in the Cathedral reveal the pervasive anti-Catholic feelings of this stronghold of the Protestant Reformation.

[14] JB inscribed himself in the guest book of the library as 'Jacobus Boswell Baro de Auchinleck in Scotia' (AN II 30, Bl 228r). He hoped to find a manuscript of Anacreon for Sir David Dalrymple's planned edition of Greek lyrics, having had no success in this search at the University of Leiden (From Dalrymple, 28 July 1763, Yale MS. C 1428; repr. *Holland*, Heinemann p. 94 n. 1, McGraw-Hill p. 96 n. 8).

[15] The library was in a separate building called The Mosquito ('die Mücke'), which it had occupied since 1671, ten years after the Council's purchase of the remarkable Amerbach Cabinet had required new space. This collection, strong in the works of Holbein, had been assembled by Basilius Amerbach (1533–91), whose father, the jurist Bonifacius Amerbach, had been a friend and heir of Erasmus (see Heusler, pp. 17–19; *Das Amerbach-Kabinett*, ed. Christian Müller, 1991, pp. 8–9). The powerful figure of Christ in the Flagellation belongs to a cycle of five paintings known as 'Scenes from the Passion', which however may have been painted by Hans Dig (b. 1503), rather than by Holbein (see Rowlands, pp. 23–24, 230).

[16] The 240 drawings by Holbein in the Amerbach collection are authentic. Notable among these are his marginal drawings in the Basel edition of Erasmus's *In Praise of Folly* (1515), added one year after the volume's publication by Froben and created at the request of the schoolmaster Oswald Geisshüssler (1488–1552), called Myconius (*Erasmi Roterodami Encomium Moriae*, ed. Heinrich Alfred Schmid, facs. ed., 1931, ii. 15–19). The volume had been purchased by Basilius Amerbach in 1578 (Heinrich Alfred Schmid, *Die Werke Hans Holbeins in Basel*, 1930, p. 13).

## Tuesday 27 November

[MEM. dated Wednesday 28 Novr.] Yesterday set out by times — good journey.

Grand mountains & Rocks. Castles on them — Arrivd Soleure — sent to M. de Barthes de Marmoriêrre. He came politely askd to manger — Boily said vous etes plus fait que moi — plus de jugement [—] was proud of this — Jacob again settling accounts called francs florins[1] chid him — He said Monsieur peut faire une erreur comme cela — very angry at him — Take care. Be on quite decent footing with the frank fellow. Dont joke with him but very rarely — & Be active like My Lord Marischal. This day in boots see Fortificat & Jesuits church — Then home & dress — dine Amb. Then Cheval [A]regger — night Journ.

[J.] Boili my Strasbourg french Companion lyes down at night and rises in the morning with a full persuasion of the materiality of his Soul. What a poor Being is he to think thus![2] He still accompanies me. We lay last night at a little Village.[3] This day we travelled along excellent road. We had on all hands Grand mountains & Rocks & now & then a Castle.[4] I must not omit the dress of a Suiss Country Girl. She has a Petticoat, & short gown fixed on the fore part with Buttons or Clasps; a little straw hat stuck on her head & her hair plaited threefold, & hanging at full length. If her hair is not long enough, she adds a piece of black ribband[5] for it seems indispensibly necessary that a Suiss Girl have a queue down to her heels. At Soleure I put up at the *Couronne*.[6] I sent a letter of recommendation from M. de Schmidt at Carlsruhe to M. de Barthês de Marmorière Secretaire de l'Ambassade de France. He politely waited upon me, & we chatted easily. He was a little man, well-bred & clever, a proof of which is that he is the only Secretary of his nation not chosen by the Ambassador, but sent out by the King.[7] He invited me to *manger demain chez l'Ambassadeur*.[8] Boili reenter'd. We were of the same age. But (said he) Vous etes beaucoup plus fait que moi. It is true. It gives me pride & pleasure. I shall be every day more so.

[1] Two different currencies, both originally in gold but now chiefly in silver. The franc, used in some of the Swiss cantons as well as in France, was valued at about 9d or 10d by British money changers in the eighteenth century (DHBS, iii. 160; OED, s.v. 'franc', b). A florin, widely used in German and Swiss territories, was the equivalent of half a crown [2s 6d], and so worth more than a franc (DHBS, supplement, p. 72).

[2] The idea that the soul was merely part of the body was being popularized by the French materialist philosophers La Mettrie and d'Holbach. JB as usual upheld the traditional Christian belief in the soul as a separate spiritual entity.

[3] Not identified.

[4] The castles Alt-Falkenstein and Neu-Bechburg in the Jura mountains were visible from the main route from Basel to Solothurn, a distance of 28 miles, or 45.1 km (Paul Ludwig Feser, *Reisen im schönen alten Solothurn*, 1989, pp. 56, 62; Nugent, ii. 385).

[5] MS. 'ribband' inserted with a caret. For an illustration, see DHBS vi, facing p. 256).

[6] The best inn, at the centre of the town.

[7] Antoine Barthès (or Barthez) de Marmorières (1736–1811), diplomat and minor writer, had been in Solothurn for the past two years after serving as counsel to the Parliament in Toulouse. He had come as secretary to Henri de Latis, Marquis d'Entraigues, *chargé d'affaires* in 1762–63 in the absence of an ambassador, and it was Entraigues who had received a special appointment directly from the King (see *Recueil des instructions données aux ambassadeurs et ministres de France du traité de Westphalie jusqu'á la révolution française*, ed. Georges Livet, 1983, XXX, Suisse: i. 341, 351). Barthès, energetic from the start, had read a paper on the agriculture and population of Solothurn at the local Economics Society a few days after his arrival (StASo, BN 5.1, 'Arbeiten des Kantor Hermann', Dossier Nr. 2). He would serve as *chargé d'affaires* from 1765 to 1767

and again in 1768 (*Receuil*, XXX: i. 341). In that capacity, he would offer refuge to Rousseau in 1765 when the latter, driven from Môtiers, was on his way to England (*Confessions*, Bk. XII, *OC Rousseau*, i. 653; see Journ. 3 Dec. n. 32). On retiring from the French diplomatic service with a pension in 1768, Barthès would obtain a '*lettre de naturalité*' from the Swiss canton of St. Gallen, where he was born while his parents were travelling. Using his French and Swiss connections, he would find minor positions in various royal households. During the Revolution he would retire to his 'patrie suisse', only to claim to be an emigré from France in 1797 and to receive a pension from the Directoire (Arch. inéd. du Min. des Aff.

étrangères, Dossiers personnels, vol. 4, cited by Jacques Voisine in his 'Indexe des noms de personne', Rousseau's *Confessions*, 1964, 949–50). Barthès would publish a tragedy, *La mort de Louis XVI* (1793), and two fictional works on Biblical subjects, *Einathan ou les âges de l'homme*, supposedly translated from the Chaldean (1802), and *Moïse en Egypte* (1802); see NBG, iii. 631; DBF, v. 690.
   [8] Solothurn had been the residence of the French ambassadors to the Swiss confederacy since diplomatic relations between France and the Swiss were established in 1530. The ambassadorial presence had encouraged the building of elegant houses and had contributed to the town's patrician atmosphere (Loertscher, p. 3; Sigrist, pp. 62–72).

## Wednesday 28 November

[MEM. dated Thursday 29 Novr.] [Y]esterday at 8 walk'd to Jesuits Church fine building front by Kings of France — then ramparts — marble — just any hard Stone — Environs pretty — Francisc[.] church.[1] Cathed[.] — one Column standing [—] noble church a building. 12 French Ambassador's tall pretty man — quite formé — Cheval Aregger long in Spain — 5 years in Algiers — home with you — 5 Madame de Role. Quite easy, home 2 hours 8 Ambassadors — Indigestion a little hyp'd. Took leave home — too late up. Swiss cantons revolution Soleure french & spanish party — better hated nobly by english than as serpents by Suiss. This day set out — Bern. Journal.
   [N]ot uncommon Suiss Peasant on his[2] rustic mountain: K. France kiss his Backside.[3]

[J.] Soleure pleases me because it is the first Place I have come to mentioned by Mr. Addison in his Travels. I just take a contrary route[4] from his. He began at Marseilles and ended at Soleure, & the other Suiss Towns with a little of Germany. I begin at Soleure and shall end at Marseilles. I saw Soleure with a kind of Classical pleasure, when I thought 'the Spectator has been here'. I had Addison's Travels with me.[5] I shall compare his Remarks with every place which I visit. I walked out this morning early. I saw the Jesuits Church which was a building when Mr. Addison was here. As he was here more than Sixty years ago the Church does not seem new. The front of it was built by the munificence of Louis 14 & Louis 15 as an Inscription bears.[6] Where the old Cathedral stood they are now building a magnificent Church. When Mr. Addison was here there was a church a building. When Mr. Boswell is here, he finds the same thing. There is a stroke of real vanity. Mr. Addison mentions two tuscan Pillars which stood at the ascent to the Cathedral. One of them is still standing.[7] I mounted a Tower & saw the Town. It is not large. I took a walk on the Ramparts. Mr. Addison says 'the whole fortification of Soleure is faced with marble. It is indeed faced with a hard stone which may be called marble, but which is so coarse that the term marble should hardly be given to it'.[8] At twelve I waited on M. de Barthês. He complained much of his Situation. He said that Soleure was divided in Politics. The french Party hates the Spanish; & they live ill together. He complained much of the Suiss, who he said had lost their morals & had no longer their attachment to the French nation. He called them a dull mean People. He said: 'Nous voudrons être noblement haïs par les Anglois plutot que par ces Suisses qui nous haïssent comme des Serpens!' He said Un de ces Paÿsans sur sa rude montagne vous diroit que le Roi de France peut lui lecher le cu. I must say this in English. The Suiss are now very little in the interest of [F]rance. The Vulgar are taught to despise that renowned monarchy: so that it is common enough for a Peasant on his rude mountain to bid the King of France kiss his Backside.[9] I was presented to the Ambassador, M. Buisson de Bodeville a tall lean man, quite french, quite formé.[10] He had the most finished smoothness of manners. I am a Physiognomist.[11] I am sure he is a good sort of man. I found here the Chevalier Aregger, to whom I had Compliments from My Lord Marischal. He has been long in the service of Spain. He was once taken by the Algerines, & lived as a Slave for five years, till they lowered his price, and his freinds ransom'd him.[12] He now lives at Soleure. We had here a large Company of the Chiefs of the Canton & others. There was here a genteel young man a Genevois, M. Buisson.[13] He & I chatted a good time together. He gave me a letter to a M. Huber at Geneva.[14] I said 'Monsieur vous etes bien changé á Genêve. Si Jean Calvin reviendroit Il ne vous reconnoitroit pas'. 'Non (said he) ma fois, il aurroit mauvais Jeu.'[15] Aregger carried me to a Partie chez une madame de Rhole.[16] I stayed there some time, & then went home & wrote two hours.[17] At eight I returned to the Ambassador's. He had asked me, faites vous quelque Sejour ici? 'Non. Monseigneur. Je pars demain'. Vous reviendrez á souper pourtant. We had an elegant dinner. Our Supper was very genteel. The Ambassador was quite agreable. M. le Chevalier his nephew[18] & I were well together. I imagined myself in Paris. I have talents to appear well in that brilliant Capital.

---

[1] The church, belonging to the Franciscan monastery that had been established in Solothurn in 1289, had been built from 1426 to 1436 to replace an earlier one destroyed by fire (Loertscher, p. 17).

[2] MS. 'his' inserted above 'on rustic'

[3] MS. 'not uncommon ... Backside' written along the left margin in smaller, neater script.

[4] MS. 'rout'

[5] Joseph Addison (1672–1719) had embarked on a four-year tour of the Continent starting in France and Italy in the autumn of 1699 and had reached Switzerland in 1701 (Oxford DNB). He had described these travels in the later parts of his Remarks on Several Parts of Italy, &c. in the Years 1701, 1702, 1703, a brief but informative account that had been published in 1705, revised in 1718, and issued in several further editions

(The Hague, 1718; others, 1726, 1733, 1736, 1745; Glasgow 1755; in French 1722; see CBEL, ii. 604). JB had admired Addison and the Spectator papers ever since being introduced to them by his first tutor, John Dun (see 'Ébauche de ma vie', Yale MS. L 1107, App. 2, III.A). These essays, written by Addison and Richard Steele (1672–1729) and first published six times a week from 1711–12, continued in 1714, had been collected into volumes published in 1712–15 and frequently thereafter (CBEL, ii. 603). While in London, JB had read The Spectator with WJT 'with infinite pleasure' and had modelled himself on Addison (see Journ. 10, 13, 23 Apr. 1763). He had also enjoyed following in the footsteps of Addison's persona, Mr. Spectator (Journ. 11 Dec. 1762, 8 Jan., 29 May, 28 June 1763).

[6] The Jesuit church, much admired for its

baroque style, had been built from 1678 to 1702 with advice from the Jesuit architects Christoph Vogler (1629–73) and Franz Demess (dates not found). Its façade, built into the street near the side-entrance of the Couronne, bears the inscription LUDOVICI MAGNI REGIS CHRISTIANISSIMI MUNIFICENTIAE MONUMENTUM ('A monument to the munificence of the great, most Christian Kings Louis'), acknowledging Louis XIV's generous grants of 3,000 *livres* in 1676 and again in 1678, and further grants from Louis XV. The Jesuits had received permission to settle in Solothurn in 1668 and would remain until their order was dissolved in 1773 (Benno Schubiger, *Die Jesuitenkirche in Solothurn*, 1987, pp. 25–29).

⁷ The Cathedral of St. Ursus, begun in 1762 to replace an earlier Romanesque-Gothic edifice, was an imposing basilica combining late baroque and neoclassical elements. Built according to the plans of Gaetano Matteo Pisoni (1713–82) of Ancona, it would be completed in 1773 (Loertscher, pp. 5–6; Max Dörflinger and Dieter Butters, *Solothurn*, 1972, p. 50; Thieme-Becker, xxvii. 108). The cathedral held a commanding position at the top of a series of steps facing the Couronne. The pillars had been described by Addison as 'Tuscan' in proportion but taken from 'an old heathen Temple, dedicated to Hermes' (*Remarks on Several Parts of Italy*, 1753, p. 276). The close proximity of the Franciscan monastery, Jesuit church, and cathedral, all within three blocks of each other, attests to the strong Catholic presence in Solothurn, which had retained the old religion in spite of the Reformation.

⁸ The town had been fortified since Roman times and was also protected by several massive round towers dating from the Middle Ages. Later fortifications, encircling the town and built according to the model established by the French military engineer Vauban (1633–1707), used an off-white polished limestone known as 'Solothurn marble' (Loertscher, pp. 4–5). Many other buildings in Solothurn were made of the same material.

⁹ The two parties consisted of the supporters of Solothurn's mercenary regiments in French and in Spanish service (correcting *Grand Tour I*, Heinemann p. 205 n. 2, McGraw-Hill p. 209–10 n. 8). Antagonism between the two groups had been inflamed by recent crises, notably an attempt to honour the newly appointed Inspector-General of the Swiss troops in French service, Lt.-Gen. Pierre-Joseph-Victor Besenval (1721–91), which had led to protests by the pro-Spanish party. Further hostility had been created by the revelation of a seemingly conspiratorial letter of Besenval's, which had caused his ouster from the local Council (Dec. 1763–Jan. 1764), and by the Council's delay, as recently as 3–6 Nov., in accepting new regulations for the regiments in French service (Eugen von Arb, *Solothurn's Politik im Zeitalter Ludwigs XV*, *Jahrbuch für Solothurnische Geschichte* 43 [1970], pp. 149–58, 163–64; Sigrist, pp. 61, 104–10; Jean-Jacques Fiechter, *Le Baron Pierre-Victor de Besenval*, 1993, pp. 53–55). Clearly Barthès realized that the local patricians, though wooed with pensions and other gifts, were no longer reliably pro-French. The English, traditional enemies of the French and Spaniards, had been on the opposing side as recently as the Seven Years' War.

¹⁰ Mature, polished (Robert, s.v. 'Formé'). Pierre Buisson, Chevalier de Beautéville (1703–92), was a career army officer only recently appointed to his diplomatic post. From 1735, while captain in the Regiment de Normandie, he had participated in many battles and sieges, including the occupation of Bavaria during the War of the Austrian Succession (1740–48), in which the French had opposed Maria Theresa (1717–80) of Austria in her claims to succeed to the Hapsburg possessions of her father, Charles VI (1685–1740), last of the Austrian Holy Roman Emperors (DBF, vii. 650). After recovering from wounds in 1743–44, de Beautéville had been appointed assistant marshal in charge of billeting troops by the famous Maréchal de Saxe (1696–1750) while the latter commanded the French forces occupying Flanders. Various responsible military assignments had followed, notably in 1757 the task of surveying places to be fortified throughout southern France. In 1760, having attained the rank of lieutenant-general, he had been seconded to the Spanish army, where he had remained during the last years of the Seven Years' War. These varied military experiences had well prepared him to renegotiate the regulations for the Swiss troops in French service and had been the reason for his appointment as ambassador even though his origins were bourgeois (see *Receuil* XXX: i. 355–56; Sigrist, pp. 65).

De Beautéville had arrived in Solothurn in Oct. 1763 and, after a customary delay, had been ceremoniously welcomed the following year (see Solothurn *Ratsmanual*, 1763, p. 1085; 'Discours de son Excellence Monseigneur le Chevalier de Beauteville', 15 Oct. 1764, StASo, Hv 138; Sigrist, p.

66). JB's meetings with him and young Buisson presumably took place at the ambassador's palace, known as la Cour, which was the centre of the town's social and diplomatic activities (Grellet, pp. 29–30). A large horseshoe-shaped building, it had been rebuilt after a fire in 1717. Its plain exterior encased splendidly decorated interiors appropriate for the French embassy (Doerflinger and Butters, p. 25; Loertscher, p. 15).

[11] 'One who judges of the temper or future of fortune by the features of the face' (*Dict. SJ*, s.v. 'Physiognomist'). The term was evidently in use before it was popularized by Kaspar Lavater (1741–1801) later in the century.

[12] Jean-Victor-Laurent Arreger von Wildensteg (1699–1770), correcting 'Wildenstag' in *Grand Tour I* index. A military officer and member of a distinguished Solothurn family, he had been in Spanish service from 1728 after six years in French service. In 1732, returning from a leave to rejoin his regiment in Africa, he had been captured by pirates, who had turned him over to the Algerians, who in turn had incarcerated and then consigned him to a chain gang. Only after protracted negotiations about his ransom had he been released, in 1738, through the combined efforts of his family and Spanish, Swiss, and French missionaries (J. J. Amiet, *Geschichte des Lorenz Arreger*, 1920, pp. 3–86). On his return, he had taken the place of his recently deceased brother Pierre d'Arreger (1691–1737) as Col. of the Regt. Arreger (DHBS, i. 426; Vallière, pp. 460–61).

[13] Jean-Jacques Buisson (1732–1809), whose family, originally from Lyon, had established a branch in Geneva in the late sixteenth century (Galiffe, ii. 517). Young Buisson was de Beautéville's nephew, as JB notes later in this entry.

[14] For Jean Huber, see Journ. 26 Dec. and n. 7.

[15] John Calvin (1509–64), leading Protestant theologian, had formulated his austere moral and social code when he took up residence in Geneva in 1536, and except during his exile from 1538 to 1541 had dominated that city's religous, political, and social life. JB was no doubt interested in Calvin because he had inspired JB's earliest religious educators (see 'Ébauche de ma vie', App. 2, III.A).

[16] Presumably a relation of Arreger, who had married Maria Helena Jakobea von Roll (1724–1803) in 1745 (Ludwig Rochus Schmidlin, *Genealogie der Freiherren von Roll*, 1914, p. 185). The von Rolls were a powerful patrician family in Solothurn who belonged to the pro-French faction (Sigrist, p. 61). The von Roll house was diagonally across from JB's inn. His hostess was very likely Maria Anna Ludovica von Roll (1737–1825), who had been drawn into a brief romantic intrigue with Casanova just after her marriage in 1760 to the much older Urs Viktor Joseph von Roll (1711–86); see Pierre Grellet, *Les Aventures de Casanova en Suisse*, 1919, pp. 50–51; Casanova, vi. ch. 4, pp. 99 104 and n. 22. Her husband had served as ensign, then captain, in various companies of the Swiss guard in the service of France, and on his return had been active in municipal affairs as the town's *Stadthauptmann* (governor) from 1750 to 1757, in the Chamber of Commerce in 1755 and 1757, in the consistory in 1757–59, on the municipal court in 1758–59, and on the Economic Council in 1761 (StASo, Aemterbesatzung 1501–1798, p. 28; Schmidlin, pp. 157, 198–99).

[17] To JJ, JB wrote of attending 'a card assembly', presumably at Mme von Roll's, as well as 'kissing (but no more) a comely healthy maid at my inn' (28 Nov., *Corr. 1*, p. 146).

[18] That is, de Beautéville and young Buisson.

## Thursday 29 November

[MEM. dated Friday 30 Novr.] Yesterday had sitten up till 3 — rose five — pleasant journey to Berne. Jacob rejoiced. Faucon din'd — a return of distemper — walk'd in Arcades quite gone [—] Home immediatly to work. Cur'd? yes. Good houses here fine stone without. Good Wood within. This day after sound sleep dress [—] receive M.  [1] See Arsenal & Library & great walks[.]

─────────────────────────────────────────────[2]

Send packets to Schmidt & to Sinner & ask to see Library. Prepare for Rousseau. Be compos'd. Recall Utrecht contemplations — then ask him *how o how* to behave with the daughter of your respected freind — the wife of the amiable — Put the case of her menacer de lui dire.[3] In short pass some rich days at [M]ôtié[.][4]

[J.] [A]t five I set out & had a pleasant drive to Berne.[5] Jacob rejoyced not a little to find himself in his own Capital within two miles of which he was born.[6] I put up at the *Faucon*.[7] Berne is a pretty Town. The Houses are excellent; good Stone without, & wood within. They are very warm. This town has a singular convenience in having on each side of the principal Streets spacious Piazzas, so that one can traverse the whole Town in the worst weather without suffering any inconvenience.[8] This afternoon I had a return of my gloom. I walked out & was very uneasy. I returned to my Inn, journalised and recovered.

[1] MS. gap, presumably for 'Lombach' (see next journal entry and n. 6).
[2] MS. A horizontal line separates this half from the bottom of the page.
[3] For the details about his adulterous affair, which JB here was planning to discuss with Rousseau, see 'Ébauche de ma vie', Yale MS. L 1107, App. 2, III.A; Journ. 14 Dec.; and *Earlier Years*, pp. 78–79.
[4] Môtiers, the village in which Rousseau had sought refuge (see Journ. 3 Dec.).
[5] A distance of 12 miles (19.3 km) from Solothurn (Nugent, ii. 367).

[6] Toffen, identified on the receipt of 4 Jan. 1766 (A 53), which Jacob Hänni would sign for the wages due to him from JB. Toffen was a small village named for the *tufa* stone found in its vicinity ('Toffen', DHBS, vi. 624–65).
[7] 'Der Falken', in the Marktgasse in the centre of the town (Paul Hofer, *Die Stadt Bern*, Die Kunstdenkmäler des Kantons Bern, 1952, i. 36 n. 6).
[8] 'Piazzas': covered arcades in the inner city that extended for 4 miles, or 6.4 km ('Bern Stadtplan', pamphlet [c. 1990]).

## Friday 30 November

[MEM. dated Saturday 1 December.] [Y]esterday met Lombach. Old Utrecht Companion went with him & saw Arsenal — many arms Duke of Burgundy's Life Guards Guns Ivory inlaid. Many coats of mail — He who founded the City[1] — Tell & his son & Apple[2] — Many Bears proud of that animal have him in all quarters. Two alive by wall — Old Church by the[3] same Architect as at Strasbourg. But, fell from hence & was kill'd. Saw Sinner & Library no Anac[.] — the foolish Englishman. Perhaps *Grady*.[4] Saw Gruner worthy slow man carried you to several Societys. Supt with Lombach — At night table hote sent for money — in bad humour, but genius of Addison.[5] Jacob's mother &c fine sight. This day calm — At Inn Journ — Neufchatel — prepare Rousseau. Serious delicate.

[J.] Whom should I meet today but Lombach my Utrecht acquaintance. For a moment he recalled to me some dreary ideas.[6] He carried me to see the Arsenal where there are arms for 100.000 men, notwithstanding that every Peasant is obliged to have his arms in good order. Such a groupe of mortal engines made me feel some horror. But let me not now philosophise. The Arms here are not so bright as at Basel. There are here a vast many Suits of Armour; as also many a figure of the Bear, the Crest of this Canton, from which it takes it's name. *Berne* in German is a Bear. The Bernois have a prodigious Affection for this Animal. They have figures of him in all quarters, & in different attitudes. They have two live Bears in a fossé by the fortifications of their town.[7] I hope no good Catholic will be offended with me for saying that the Bear appeared to me like the Tutelar Saint of this People. I was amused with the History of a Gigantic figure in wood, which stood in one of their Churches, as the Representation of some Holy Person or other. At the Reformation instead of destroying this figure amongst other remains of Idolatry, they mounted him upon one of their gates, & made him represent Goliah of Gath, and upon a well just opposite to the Gate they have placed a figure of David ready to sling at him.[8] Lombach dined with me at my Inn, after which we went and saw the great church an old Gothic Building by the same Architect who built the Cathedral at Strasbourg: But the Tower here is not built; for, the Architect fell from one of the Corners, & was killed on the Spot.[9] We then waited on M. Sinner Library Keeper, to whom I had a letter from Schmidt. He carried us to the Library which is noble, but, has no manuscript Anacreon, tho rich in Manuscripts. Sinner has given one Volume of a Catalogue of them in an excellent form. He gives of each Manuscript the Title the size and when he can, the year in which it was written, as also the Persons to whom it has belonged. This is curious and usefull.[10] In the Catalogues of other Librarys the simple title of a manuscript is given, & a man knows not, whether it can be of use to him or not, without going to see it. In the Catalogue of the King of France's Library I find 'Anacreontis Odae' but I can have no notion whether it is a manuscript of the 15th Century or of fifty years ago.[11] I must here remark that in this & all the principal Librarys that I have seen abroad they have shewn me a present of Books sent them by a certain unknown whimsical Englishman. He is no doubt a most prodigious Whig, for he has sent Milton's Prose Works (which I suppose he preferrs to his Poetry) Toland's life of [M]ilton[,] Algernon Sydney's works and several other such dainty pieces of British Republican Writing. The Books are bound in red morocco, and adorned with gilded Stamps of the Cap of Liberty, Pitchforks, Swords and I know not what other terrible Instruments of fury. I am surprised that he has not thought of introducing the Scaffold the Block and the Ax. He might have adorned a whole Board with a Representation of the Murder of King Charles.[12] He has however a stamp of Great Britain, as she is usually seen[13] upon Our halfpence: to render her however compleat he has subjoined this sensible & sublime Inscription 'O Fair Britannia! hail!' Lest Sydney[,] Milton & Toland should not be strong enough in the good cause, our Enthusiast has now & then added notes of his own, & quotations from others like himself. He has taken care to copy an apt Passage in the Poetry of Mr. Richard Glover.[14] In short he has made me laugh very heartily. As Jacob's freinds are only two leagues from this, he had written to them to come & meet him. This day his mother his Sister & three Brothers arrived.[15] He entertained them well. He insisted that I should shew myself to them. I did so, & was highly pleased to see this picture of family affection. Gruner an old Dutch Suiss Colonel to whom I had a letter from Schmidt carried me to two Societys at Berne like those at the Hague.[16] I past there some hours dully enough. Then Lombach carried me to sup with him at an Inn, where were some handsom female merchants;[17] for it was now the fair of Berne.

[1] By tradition, Duke Berchtold V von Zähringen (d. 1218), member of the Zaringoline from which the margraves of Baden-Durlach and Baden-Baden also traced their descent (see Journ. 21 Nov. n. 12). A suit of armour weighing more than 50 lbs (22.7 kg) was once thought to have been Berchtold's, though it was actually made c. 1450 ('Trajansaal: Waffen und Rüstungen', Historisches Museum, Bern).

[2] Two almost life-size figures (c. 1590) representing William Tell and his son. According to the legend as recorded among others by Gilles 'Aegidius' Tschudi in his *Chronicon Helveticum* (comp. in the 1550s, rev. 1569–70), Tell had successfully shot an apple from his young son's head with a bow and arrow at the behest of the despotic Austrian bailiff Gessler and had later killed this tyrant. For these deeds, Tell had become a symbol of Swiss freedom (Jean-François Bergier, *Guillaume Tell*, 1988, pp. 15–21; DHBS, iii. 402). The statues, made of painted wood by an unknown Bernese wood carver, had come into the possession of the arsenal in the late seventeenth century (J. R. von Salis, 'Ursprung, Gestalt und Wirkung des Schweizerischen Mythos von Tell', *Tell: Werden und Wandern eines Mythos*, 1973, pp. 24–28, 48).

[3] MS. 'byhe'

[4] Not knowing the identity of the 'foolish' Englishman (for whom see n. 14), JB suspected that this was the 'good, honest, light-headed' Captain O'Grady whom he had met in Dessau and Leipzig (see Journ. 25 Sept. and 4 Oct.).

[5] Perhaps JB was cheered by continuing to read Addison's *Remarks on Several Parts of Italy* (see Journ. 28 Nov. and n. 5). JB made a point of seeing all of the sights in Bern described by Addison, notably the cathedral, arsenal, and library.

[6] Niklaus Lombach (1733–83), an officer in the service of Holland, belonged to a patrician family in Bern (Louis de Tscharner, *La Grande Société de Berne, 1759–1909*, 1909, p. 135). JB had met him on 24 and 29 May (*Holland*, Heinemann pp. 252, 256, McGraw-Hill pp. 258, 263). For his 'dreary' spell, see To WJT, 22 May (*Corr. 6*, pp. 97–98).

[7] The arms in the arsenal included swords, maces, shields, more than 100 halbards and battle axes, and close to 60 javelins. Some of these were booty from the battles of Grandson and Morat, of which Bern had received a larger share than Basel (see Journ. 25 Nov. and n. 9; Florens Deuchler, *Die Burgunderbeute*, 1963, pp. 46–52). JB would see a similar arsenal of 'mortal engines' in Venice and

would later write eloquently about 'the horrid irrationality of war' (*Hypochondriack* no. III, Dec. 1777, Bailey, i. 120). The ubiquitous bear appeared on the earliest known seal of the city, dated 1224, and the possible derivation of the city's name from 'Bären' ('bears') was widely accepted (see *The New Encyclopædia Britannica*, 1998, ii. 143). But the name was more likely inspired by the legendary Dietrich von Bern (DHBS, ii. 79). Bears would still be on display in two pits outside the city walls in the twenty-first century.

[8] A wooden figure of St. Christopher, standing almost 30 feet (9.4 m) high inside the 'Christophel' Gate, had at one time been renamed Goliath, and a fountain with a David figure had been aligned with it (Hofer, i. 249). The St. Christopher statue had never been intended for a church, however, but had been created specifically for the gate (Eduard von Rodt, *Bernische Stadtgeschichte*, 1886, pp. 67–68). Its monumental head and feet, the only remains, would survive to be displayed in the Historische Museum of Bern in the twenty-first century.

[9] The cathedral, begun in 1421, is regarded as the greatest example of the late Gothic in Switzerland (Hans R. Hahnloser, 'La Collégiale de Berne', *post* 1950, p. 4). Its chief architect, Matthäus Ensinger (c. 1390–1463), had worked on the building from 1420 to 1466, bringing the tower up to the height of the side aisles. He had previously worked on the Strasbourg cathedral under his father, Ulrich von Ensingen [*sic*] (see Journ. 22 Nov. and n. 2). Far from having fallen to his death, Matthäus Ensinger had gone on to design the cathedral of Ulm and had died there (Luc Mojon, *Der Münsterbaumeister Matthäus Ensinger*, Berner Schriften zur Kunst, 1967, x. 1–4, 11). Work on the lower part of the tower in Bern had commenced c. 1481, after his death, and work on the upper part had been suspended in 1592 because of structural weaknesses. The tower would not be completed until the end of the nineteenth century (see Luc Mojon, *Das Berner Münster*, Die Kunstdenkmäler des Kantons Bern, 1960, iv. 2–4, 11, 14, 49).

[10] Johann Rudolf Sinner von Ballaigues (1730–87) was the respected chief librarian of the municipal library. A Bernese patrician whose family dated from the fifteenth century, Sinner had been named to his position at the age of eighteen, not because of favouritism as had been claimed, but because other candidates had dropped out (P. Decker, 'Johann-Rudolf Sinner von Ballaigues', *RHV*

22 ⌈1914⌉: 33–38). He had read widely and had travelled to Holland, London, and Paris. His marriage in 1756 to Louise-Émilie de Gingins had brought him the domain of Ballaigues. The first volume of his *Catalogus Codicum MSS Bibliothecae Bernensis annotationibus criticis*, a remarkably complete descriptive catalogue of more than 650 pages, had been published in 1760; two more volumes would appear in 1772. Sinner's catalogue of printed books (over a thousand pages long) in the library of Bern had just appeared (Decker, p. 40; Adolf Burri, *Johann Rudolf Sinner von Ballaigues*, 1913, pp. 74–80). JB's reference to Anacreon indicates that he was continuing to search for Anacreon MSS for Sir David Dalrymple.

Sinner had also already published his *Historia onjurationis quae in urbe Berna feliciter suppressa est*, 1750, describing with eyewitness reports a recently attempted insurrection in Bern against the ruling councils of Sixteen and Two Hundred ('le Conseils des Seizes' and 'le Conseil des Deux-Cents'). He had also compiled an anthology of French verse, *Extraits de quelques poésies du moyen âge* (1759), and in that same year had translated Congreve's *Way of the World* with the title *Train du monde*. His translation of Persius's satires into French would be published in 1765, and his imitation of Goethe's *Werther*, with the title *Malheurs de l'amour*, in 1775. On retiring from the library to become bailiff of Erlach, he would publish anonymously, in 1779, his ambitious compendium *Voyage historique et littéraire dans la Suisse occidentale* (Decker, pp. 40–42; BM Catalogue of Printed Books).

[11] The catalogue of the Greek MSS in the library of Louis XV (the second volume of the ambitious ten-volume catalogue that included printed books as well as manuscripts) had been published in 1740; the project as a whole had taken from 1733 to 1753 and remained incomplete (Henri Omont, *Le Catalogue imprimé de la bibliothèque du roi au XVIIIe siècle*, 1895, p. 3).

[12] JB assumed that the donor, with his republican sentiments, would condone the execution of Charles I, and showed his own monarchist sentiments by calling this 'murder'.

[13] MS. 'pourtrayed' inserted above 'seen' with a different pen.

[14] The eccentric donor was the wealthy Thomas Hollis (1720–74), who wished to popularize his republican views but insisted on anonymity. From a philanthropic family of Dissenters and a lawyer by training, he was steeped particularly in the writings of Milton. Hollis had come to respect the republicanism of the protestant Swiss during six years of travels on the Continent, first in 1748 and then from 1750, and had donated close to 300 magnificently bound folio volumes to the public library of Bern. His first shipment had arrived in 1758, a second as recently as Aug. of the present year, with more to come. Included in his second shipment were John Toland's *Life of Milton* (1699) and Algernon Sidney's *Discourses Concerning Government*, edited by Hollis himself in 1761 and 1763 respectively (Francis Blackburne, *Memoirs of Thomas Hollis, Esq.* 1780, i. 6, 26, 68–69, 186, 242–49, ii. 740–42). The quotation from Richard Glover (1712–85) came from his *London, or the Progress of Commerce*, 1739, a copy of which Hollis also gave to the city of Bern (W. H. Bond, *Thomas Hollis of Lincoln's Inn*, 1990, p. 26). Some of his books were embellished with the prefatory engraving of Britannia and the other images mentioned by JB as well as with the invocation 'fair Britannia', Hollis's favourite quotation from Mark Akenside's *Odes* (I. viii, 1744 ed., see Bond, p. 17). But JB exaggerates: the delicate gilt decorations, stamped on the outside, and Hollis's small neat handwriting in some of the volumes, do not suggest violence; the 'instruments of fury' do not include pitchforks but Neptune's or Britannia's trident; in any case, olive branches, lyres, and other images of peace abound. Hollis had also donated books to the libraries of Leiden, Berlin, Wolfenbüttel, Leipzig, and Basel, where JB could have seen them, as well as to the libraries of Geneva, Zurich, and most generously, following a family tradition, to Harvard College (Bond, pp. 80, 108, 113–15; Blackburne, pp. 126–27).

[15] By 'friends', JB meant 'family'. For Jacob's mother, Johanna Hänni, see 25 July n. 8. His other relations and friends have not been identified.

[16] David Gruner (1722–1805), younger son of a wealthy Bernese banker and merchant, had served in Holland until his retirement as lieutenant-colonel in 1751 and had just been elected to the city's Great Council (DHBS, iii. 652). He presumably took JB to the prestigious *Grande Société*, founded in 1759, to which both he and Sinner belonged (DHBS, iii. 651–52; Louis de Tscharner, *La Grande Société de Berne, 1759–1909*, 1909, pp. 47–49, 53, 68, 130, 135). The second society, not identified, may have been one of the several clubs frequented by pipe smokers at a time when the use of tobacco was frowned upon in Bern (Tscharner, p. 49).

[17] Not identified.

## Saturday 1 December

[MEM. dated Sunday 2 December] Yesterday set out early [—] good Coach. Good day. Indolent — drove to Neufchatel — Thought of Lord Marischal. Sent to Col. Chaillet — Allready asked to supper — Heavy a little. This day dress. Then Chaillet — Be moderate. Then Church — Ask for Rousseau & Prepare but be quiet. Consult how to have Letts & money.

[J.] Betimes I set out in a good Coach & in agreable Indolence drove to Neufchatel.[1] I sent to Colonel Chaillet a letter which My Lord Marischal had given me to him.[2] He asked me to sup with him. But I had allready eaten heartily of excellent Trout.[3]

[1] A small town on a lake with the same name, the capital of a principality of about 32,000 inhabitants. By vote of its citizens, Neuchâtel had chosen to join Prussia in 1707, when its own ruling house had died out, with the understanding that it would retain its time-honoured government and customs. Frederick II was its titular head and Lord Marischal his appointed governor, but the real power was held by its wealthy citizens and Calvinist clergy (Eigeldinger, pp. 31–42).

[2] Jean-Frédéric Chaillet (1709–78) had been an officer in the service of Sardinia until his retirement with the rank of lieutenant-colonel in 1748. He had been a member of the ruling Conseil d'Etat from 1752 and had become a good friend of Lord Marischal while the latter was in residence. Chaillet had chosen exile in support of a local clergyman who had been ousted for questioning the eternity of punishments, a doctrine fiercely upheld by the entrenched Calvinists, and had returned only recently (see Eigeldinger, 'Chaillet', Dict. de Rousseau, pp. 714, 130; CC Rousseau, xii. 200 note h). For Lord Marischal's letter to Chaillet, written on about 23 Sept., see Journ. 7 Dec.

[3] On the way to Neuchâtel JB had stopped at Walperswil, where he had spent 15 Batsen, presumably for the trout (see 'Walberstswwiel', Exp. Acct. 1 Dec., App. 3; Dictionnaire géographique de la Suisse, vi. 410).

## Sunday 2 December

[MEM. dated Monday 3 December] Yesterday morning bad with supper — waited on Chaillet in bed — fine hearty brave sensible man — Din'd Inn — Boule[1] — Neufchatel. Headach [—] Afternoon with Madm Chaill. Company, Whist. This day great day.[2] Write Geneva[3] — Go to Rousseau — Mem old Auchinleck — Father.[4]

[J.] I waited on Colonel Chaillet whom I found to be a sensible, hearty, brave old fellow.[5] I dined at my Inn the Treize Cantons with my Landlord Meuron.[6] I was a little hyp'd. At four Madame Chaillet carried me to a Company, where we played Cards.[7]

[1] Possibly the game of boule, a favourite men's pastime similar to marbles but played with large balls on the ground.

[2] Because he was on the way to see Rousseau.

[3] Not recorded in Reg. Let.

[4] MS. The rest of the entry is defective: 'Not van for stars. Be', in an incomplete line at the bottom of the page; 'The great point is to hit<...>' followed by truncated, incomprehensible words written along the left margin.

[5] Lord Marischal had described him, in similar terms, as 'a brave, honest hearted man' (From Lord Marischal, 17 Oct., Yale MS. C 1950).

[6] Abram Meuron (fichier général, AEN).

[7] Elisabeth (de Chambrier) Chaillet (1728–1815) belonged to one of the foremost families of Neuchâtel (CC Rousseau,

xii. 200 note h; OC *Charrière*, iv. 911). At
the card game, JB lost one écu (inserted as

'oubli' in Exp. Acct. 3 Dec., App. 3).

## Monday 3 December

[MEM. dated Tuesday 4 Decr.][1] [Y]esterday early [—] let Jacob go see his
freinds. Set out on little horse with sack [—] met *Abram Francois* who lent spur &
whip — wild mountains stopt Bro — / — [M]otié. Landlady look'd odd — drest
[—] sent letter — return for answer — walk'd out to prepare. Answer — affraid
[—] went curious — easy voulez vous promener? Sa santé medecins — Jaime mes
livres ils m'ont sauvé la vie — mais les maux qui m'ont attiré vient ensemble. Roi
de Prusse force — meme revange étoffe faire quelque chose — Espagn grands ames
— Passions dures [—] Eclesiastiques nouvel explic de quelq incomprehen. Mais
la Jerusalem pas une piêre. Vous les avez mis — tenez otez cela cela — ne vous
tenez pour le soutenir mais nous voulons etre employés. Chimêre Je vis. Un autre
chim pas mien. Ma Gouvern dit meil leur hum seul — obliged to quit sat too late.
This day Send to know. Go & ask — & come & go easy —

[J.] I let Jacob go for a week to see his Relations which made him very
happy. One great Object which I have ever had in view since ever I left
Britain has been to obtain the Acquaintance and if possible the regard of
Rousseau.[2] I was informed that he lived in a wild Valley five leagues from
Neufchatel.[3] I set out early this morning mounted on a little horse with a
*Reysesac*[4] which held some shirts. I was joined by *Abraham François* a
merchant here.[5] My horse was lazy: he lent me a spur & a whip, & on we
jogged very cordially. He taught me a french Song 'Sous le nom de l'amitié
Phillis Je vous adore' to a minuet tune.[6] I amused my self with him; & this
amusement formed an excellent Contrast to the great object which occupied my mind. We had a fine hard road amidst mountains covered with
snow. We stopped at Bro the half-way Inn. M. Sando the Landlord had a
handsom daughter, very lively & very talkative, or rather chatty, to give
the young Lady a lighter word.[7] She told us Monsieur Rousseau vient
souvent passer quelques jours ici avec sa Gouvernante Mademoiselle
Vasseur.[8] Cest lhomme le plus aimable. Il a une belle Physionomie. Mais il
n'aime pas qu'on vienne le regarder comme un Homme á deux têtes. Mon
Dieu! la curiosité des Gens est bien grande. Il y a tant tant du monde qui
vient pour le voire; et souvent il ne veut pas le recevoir. Il est malade et il
ne veut pas etre incommodé. Voila un Clue[9] ou Je suis allé avec lui et
Mademoiselle Vasseur — nous y avons diné. Il se promene dans ses lieux
sauvages toute une journée. Des Messieurs qui sont venus ici m'ont
demandé mille questions. Et sa Gouvernante est elle jeune? est elle jolie?
All this chat of mademoiselle helped to frighten me. There was here a
Stone-cutter who had wrought for Voltaire. The most stupid of Human
Beings will remember some Anecdote or other of a Great man whom he
has had occasion to see. This Stone cutter told me: Monsieur il y avoit un
Cheval á tirer un Char á Fernier,[10] et M. Voltaire disoit toujours Pauvre
Cheval! vous etes maigre, vous etes comme moi. Any trifle of such a
Genius has a value. *Abraham François* & I drank a glass of good wine, &

pursued our journey. We passed one Place exactly like Gillikranky,[11] & another where [a] groupe of broken rocks seemed every moment ready to tumble down upon us. It will most certainly tumble e'er long. M. Rousseau lives in the Village of Motiers. A league on this side of it Abraham parted from me after I had returned him his whip & his spur. I advanced with a kind of pleasing trepidation. I wished that I might not see Rousseau till the moment that I had permission to wait upon him. I perceived a white house with green window-boards. He mentions such a one in Emile.[12] I imagined it might perhaps be his, & turned away my eyes from it. I rode calmly down the street, and put up at the *maison de Village*. This Inn is kept by Madame Grande Pierre a Widow, and her two daughters fat motherly maidens.[13] The eldest received me. I told her 'Jai donné permission á mon Domestique d'aller voir ses Amis et Parents. Je suis donc seul. Il faut que vous ayez bien soin de moi.' Said she 'nous ferions notre mieux'. I asked for M. Rousseau. I found he kept himself very quiet here as My Landlady had little or nothing to chatter concerning him. I had heard all that could be said as to his being difficult of access. My Lord Marischal had given me a card with compliments to him, which I was sure would procure me admission.[14] Colonel Chaillet had given me a letter to the Chatelin M. Martinet the principal Justice of the Place who could introduce me without difficulty.[15] But my romantic Genius which will never be extinguished, made me eager to put my own merit to the severest tryal. I had therefore prepared a letter to M. Rousseau, in which I informed him that an ancient Scots Gentleman[16] of twenty four, was come hither with the hopes of seeing him. I assured him that I deserved his regard, that I was ready to stand the test of his penetration. Towards the end of my letter I shewed him that I had a heart & a soul. I have here given no idea of my letter; It can neither be abridged nor transposed, for, it is realy a Master-Piece. I shall ever preserve it as a Proof that my soul can be sublime.[17] I drest & dined & sent my letter chez M. Rousseau ordering the maid to leave it, & say she'd return for the answer; so that I might give him time to consider a little, lest perhaps he might be ill and suddenly refuse to see me. I was filled with anxiety. Is not this romantic madness? Was I not sure of admittance by my Recommendations? Could I not see him as any other Gentleman would do? no: I am above the Vulgar crowd. I would have my merit fairly tried by this Great Judge of human nature. I must have things in my own way.[18] If my bold Attempt succeeds the recollection of it will be grand so long as I live. But, perhaps, I may appear to him so vain, or so extraordinary, that he may be shocked by such a character and may not admit me. I shall then be in a pretty situation; for, I shall be ashamed to present my recommendations. But, why all this doubt & uneasiness? It is the effect of my melancholy timidity. What! can the Author of Eloisa be offended at the enthusiasm of an ingenuous mind? But if he does admit me, I shall have a very difficult character to support; for, I have written to him with unusual elevation and given him an idea of me which I shall hardly come up to. To prepare myself for the great Interview I walked out alone. I stroled pensive by the side of the River Ruse[19] in a beautifull Wild Valley surrounded by immense mountains, some covered with frowning rocks, others with clustering Pines, and others with glittering snow. The fresh, healthfull air and the romantic Prospect arround me gave me a vigorous and solemn tone. I recalled all my former ideas of J. J. Rousseau, the admiration with which he is regarded over all Europe, his Heloise, his Emile, in short a crowd of great thoughts. This half hour was one of the most remarkable that I ever past. I returned to my Inn, and the maid delivered to me a card with the following Answer from M. Rousseau.

'Je suis malade, souffrant, hors d'etat de recevoir des visites. Cependant Je ne puis me refuser à celle de Monsieur Boswell, pourvu que par egard pour mon etat il veuille bien la faire courte.'

My sensibility dreaded the word *courte*. But, I took courage, and went immediatly. I found at the street door Mademoiselle Vasseur waiting for me. She was a little lively neat french Girl and did not increase my fear.[20] She conducted me up a darkish stair, then opened a door: I expected 'now I shall see him' — But it was not so. I entered a room which serves for Vestibule & for Kitchen. My Fancy formed many many a Portrait of the wild Philosopher. At length his door opened & I beheld him a genteel black man in the dress of an Armenian.[21] I entered saying 'Bien bien de graces.' After the first looks and bows were over, He said voulez vous vous asseoir? ou voulez vous que nous promenions dans la Chambre?[22] I chose the last and happy I was to escape being formally placed upon a chair. I asked him how he was. Tres mal. Mais J'ai quitté les medecins.[23] Oui oui vous ne les aimez pas. As it is impossible for me to relate exactly our conversation I shall not endeavour at order but give sentences as I recollect them. Monsieur vous avez un grand plaisir á penser de vos livres. 'Je les aime. Mais ils m'ont causé tant de maux dont le souvenir revient quand Je pense de mes livres, que Je ne sais — Mes livres m'ont sauvé la vie. Le Parlement de Paris.[24] Si une Societè pourroit être disgracié, elle le seroit — Je pourrois leur rendre fort disgraciê seulement en mettant sur[25] une coté leur edit contre moi et sur l'autre le droit de Gens et de l'equité.[26] Mais J'ai des raisons pour ne le pas faire á present' — Peutêtre nous l'aurrons un jour? Peutêtre. I was drest in a coat & waistcoat scarlet with Gold lace, Buckskin Breeches & Boots. Above all I wore a Greatcoat of Green Camlet lined with Fox-skin fur, with the collar & Cuffs of the same fur. I held under my arm a hat with a sollid gold lace, at least with the air of being sollid. I had it last winter at the Hague.[27] I had a free air & spoke well & when M. Rousseau said what touched me more than ordinary, I seised his hand, I thumped him on the shoulder. I was without restraint. When I found that I realy pleased him, I said 'Savez vous Monsieur que Je vous suis recommandé par un homme que vous estimez beaucoup.' 'Ah! Milord Marischal.' Oui, Monsieur. Milord m'a donné un Billet pour m'introduire chez vous. 'Et vous ne vouliez pas vous en servir?' Non, Monsieur. Je voulois avoir une preuve de mes merites. 'Monsieur il n'y aurroit eté aucune merite d'entrer avec un Billet de Milord Marischal. Tout ce que vient de lui me sera toujours bien reçu.[28] Il est mon Protecteur, mon Pere, J'ose dire mon Ami.'[29] One circumstance embarrassed me a little. I had forgotten to bring with me from Neufchatêl My Lord's Billet. But a generous consciousness of Innocence & honesty gives a freedom which cannot be counterfeited. I told M. Rousseau En verité J'ai oubli de porter avec moi ce Billet: mais, vous me croyez. 'Oui assurement. Il y a eu plusieurs qui voloient me rendre service selon leur façon. Milord Marischal l'a fait Selon la mienne. Il est le seul homme sur la terre a qui Je dois des obligations.[30] Quand Je parle des Rois, J[e] metts á cotè le Roi de Prusse. C'est un Roi tout a fait unique. Cette force qu'il a.[31] Monsieur cela est la grande affaire d'avoir la force — meme du Revenge — il y a toujours d'etoffe de quoi vous pouvez faire quelque chose. Mais quand il n'y a point de force mais tout est petit, tout fricassé il n'y a point d'esperance. Par exemple Les François c'est une vile nation.' Les Espagnols Monsieur[?][32] 'Oui En[33] Espagne vous trouverez des grands Ames.' 'Et dans les montagnes d'Ecosse. Mais depuis notre maudite union Ah —'[34] 'Vous vous êtes perdu.' 'O Oui. Mais Milord m'a fait le plus grand plaisir. Je vous le raconterais. Il vous appelle Jean Jaques par affection. Il me dit un jour Jean Jaques est l'homme le plus reconnoissant. Il vouloit ecrire la vie de mon frère.[35] Mais Je l'ai prié[36] d'ecrire plutot la vie de M. Fletcher of Saltoun et il m'a promi de le faire.[37] Oui monsieur Je le ferais avec les plus grands soins et plaisir. Je sais que Je deplairais aux Anglois. Mais n'importe. Voulez vous me fournir des Anecdotes sur les Caractêres de ceux qui firent cette traité d'union, sur les circonstances qu'on ne trouve pas dans les Historiens.'[38] Oui, monsieur, mais avec la chaleur d'un ancien Ecossois. 'Oui Faites comme cela.[39] Les Eclesiastiques — quand un de ces Messieurs donne une nouvelle explication de quelque chose incomprehensible, en le laissant aussi incomprehensible que jamais, alors on crie "Voici un grand Homme." "Mais, Monsieur, ils vous disent qu'on ne doit negliger aucun point de la Theologie, qu'on doit regarder comme sacrée chaque pîerre de la Jerusalem mystique, de ce Batiment de Dieu." "Oui. Mais ils y ont ajouté des pierres. Tenez, otez ceci; otez cela. Vous voyez le Batiment est tres complet: et ne vous tenez la pour le soutenir. Mais nous voulons être necessaires." Ah! — Monsieur vous ne voyez pas l'ourse dont vous avez entendu parler. Monsieur Je n'aime pas le monde. Je vis ici dans un monde de chimêres et Je ne puis souffrir le monde comme il est.' 'Mais quand vous trouvez des hommes chimeriques, est ce que vous ne les aimez pas? Mais ils n'ont pas les mêmes chimêres que moi. Votre Pais Monsieur est fait pour la liberté. J'aime vos manîerres. Vous et moi nous pouvons nous promener ici sans parler. Deux François ne peuvent pas faire le même. Les hommes me degoutent. Aussi ma Gouvernante dit que les jours que J'ai eté seul, Je suis en beaucoup meilleur humeur que quand J'ai eté en compagnie.' 'On a ecrit beaucoup contre vous Monsieur.' 'Ils ne m'ont pas compri. M. Vernet á Genêve. Cest un Archi-Jesuite voici ce que Je puis dire de lui.'[40] Monsieur, est ce que vous ne me trouvez pas comme Je vous ai dit? 'Monsieur Je ne puis pas encore juger mais toutes les Apparences sont pour vous.' Je craigns que Je n'ai resté trop long tems. Demain J'aurrais l'honneur de revenir. 'O Je ne sais.' 'Monsieur Je me tiendrais tranquille ici dans le Village. Si vous pouvez me voir Je serais charmé; Si non Je ne ferais aucune plainte. Mylord Marischal il a une connoissance parfaite du Cœur de l'homme tant dans la Solitude que dans la Societé. Je suis accablé des visites de Gens desœuvrés'. 'Et que font ils?'[41] 'Ils font des Complimens. Je reçois aussi une quantité prodigieuse de lettres: Et chacun croit quil est le Sœul'. 'Vous serez bien surpris Monsieur qu'un Homme qui n'a pas l'honneur de vous etre connu prenne la liberté de vous ecrire.' 'Non Je ne suis point surpris. Car J'ai eu une telle lettre hier, avant hier, et bien de fois.'[42] 'Monsieur votre Serviteur tres humble. Quoi voulez vous aller plus loin?' Je ne va pas avec vous. Je va me promener dans le passage. Adieu.

I had great satisfaction after finding that I could support the character which I had given of myself, after finding that I should most certainly be regarded by the illustrious Rousseau. I had a strange kind of feeling after having at last seen the Authour of whom I had thought so much. I sat down immediatly and wrote to Dempster.[43] I sat up too late.

[1] MS. 'major' written with a different pen at the top of the right margin.

[2] JB had contemplated this goal even before leaving Britain, when WJT had suggested their travelling together on the Continent, and had fantasized about meeting two of the most famous men of their time: 'Voltair, Rousseau, immortal names! we might enjoy the benifit of their conversation'. That the young men's plan did not materialize was probably owing to the financial problems of WJT's father (see From WJT, ?Spring 1759, Corr. 6, pp. 17–18 and n. 5, and Introduction, pp. xxxviii–xxxix).

[3] The Val de Travers, on a picturesque plateau behind the first range of the Jura mountains above Lake Neuchâtel. The valley, which owes its name to its position transverse to the Jura, is about 15 miles (24.1 km) from the town of Neuchâtel. A league was the equivalent of about 3 miles (c. 4.8 km).

[4] A phonetic spelling for 'Reisesack', German for a large knapsack. For the cost of maintaining the horse, see Exp. Acct. 5, 6 Dec., App. 3.

[5] Not further identified.

[6] The melody, said to be by Adolph Blaise (d. 1772), is given in La Clé du Caveau, n.d., c. 1825. The lyrics have been attributed to Jean-Joseph Vadé (1720–57); see Grand Tour I, Heinemann p. 210 n. 4, McGraw-Hill p. 215 n. 1.

[7] Jean Louis Sandoz (1709–1800), landlord of La Couronne at Brot-Dessous, and his daughter Suzanna-Marguerite Sandoz (?1747–1816). Rousseau, finding her reading Fénelon's philosophical novel Télémaque (1699), had sent her his Nouvelle Héloïse, but her mother had promptly confiscated it (Karl Johann Christian von Zinzendorf,

Journal, 10 Sept., quoted in CC Rousseau, A332, xxi. 332).

[8] Thérèse Levasseur or Le Vasseur (1721–1801) was Rousseau's housekeeper, former mistress, and loyal companion. He had met her in 1745 or 1746 while she was a servant in a Paris hotel. She was now in her forties, and although her relationship with Rousseau was no longer sexual, she controlled who could meet the great man (Charly Guyot, 'Esquisse pour un portrait: Thérèse Levasseur', MN n.s. 49 [1962]: 159–70).

[9] MS. 'Clus', alternative term for 'creux' (Robert, s.v. 'clu', 'creux'). They had gone to the Creux du Vent, a remarkable rock with an excavated hole that produced a wind strong enough to blow a visitor's hat into the air (Zinzendorf, Journ. 7 Sept., in CC Rousseau, A332, xxi. 329).

[10] 'A cart at Ferney' (Grand Tour I, Heinemann p. 211, McGraw-Hill p. 216); alternatively, 'a cart with manure: un char á fumier' (G. R. de Beer to F. A. Pottle, 2 Jan. 1951; see Robert, s.v. 'fumier'). The stonecutter has not been identified.

[11] The extremely narrow pass of Killiecrankie in Perthshire (see OGS, p. 926). JB had almost certainly gone through this pass on 12 May 1761 while travelling from Dunkeld to Blair Atholl on the Northern Circuit with his father (see 'Journal of North Circuit', Yale MS. J 1).

[12] Rousseau's lodging was midway down the Grande Rue, the main street of Môtiers (population c. 350; see Eigeldinger, p. 74 and n. 2). The house described in Bk. IV of Émile had become a symbol of the simple life in an idyllic landscape that Rousseau had popularized (see OC Rousseau, iv. 686–87; CC Rousseau, A334 note g, xxii. 370).

[13] The inn was part of the Maison des Six

Communes, so called because it served as village hall for the six communities of the Val de Travers. The building, with its five rounded arches sheltering an arcade on the ground floor, held a prominent place at the end of the Grande Rue (Jean Courvoisier, *Les Monuments d'art et d'histoire du canton de Neuchâtel*, 1968, iii. 74–75). Marguerite-Marie Grandpierre was the widow of Jean-Auguste Grandpierre, who had been inn-keeper there since 1741. Although she was threatened with bankruptcy in 1759, she and her unmarried daughters—Jeanne-Elisabeth (b. 1724) and Marguerite-Esabeau (b. 1726) —would maintain the inn until June 1765 (Schnegg, 29 Jan. and 8 Mar. 1955; CC *Rousseau*, A334 note h, xxii. 370.

[14] A brief, undated note, possibly written on 23 Sept., in which Lord Marischal had wished JB 'bon voyage' and had asked about Rousseau's health.

[15] Jacques-Frédéric Martinet (1713–89) was the most important personage in the district, combining the offices of prefect, magistrate, justice of the peace, and prose-cutor. It was to his care that Lord Marischal had recommended Rousseau after offering him a place of refuge from the French, Ber-nese, and Genevan authorities (see n. 24).

[16] That is, 'a gentleman of ancient Scot-tish family'.

[17] JB had actually written three drafts of this letter, one in Brot before hearing of Rousseau's dislike of visitors, the others to arouse his interest (see App. 2). In the final version JB presented himself as 'un ancien Gentilhomme Ecossois' and boldly declared himself to be 'un Homme d'une merite singulierre ... un Homme qui a un Cœur sensible, un Esprit vif et melancolique'. He described the impact of Rousseau's writings in the impassioned tones of St. Preux, the hero of *La Nouvelle Héloïse*: 'Vos ecrits, Monsieur, m'ont attendri le Cœur, m'ont elevé l'Ame, m'ont allumé l'Imagination'. Continuing in this heightened language, he urged Rousseau to see him: 'Ouvrez donc votre Porte, Monsieur, a un Homme qui ose vous assurer qu'il merite d'y entrer. Ayez de la confiance dans un Etranger singulier'. And he boldly asked Rousseau to be alone at their first meeting (quoted from the letter JB actually sent, now at BPUN; see App. 2). In calling this letter 'sublime', JB refers both to the noble sentiments and to the elevated style.

[18] Apart from disdaining to use a custo-mary letter of introduction and insisting on his unique individuality (both Rousseauesque stances), JB had a less high-minded motive for his approach, as he would admit to Rous-seau later in their meeting.

[19] The river Areuse (JB's 'Ruse') runs through nearly all of the Val de Travers and then flows down into Lake Neuchâtel. Rousseau had described the same scene a year earlier as 'plus Sauvage que riante' (To the Maréchal-Duc de Luxembourg, 28 Jan. 1763, CC *Rousseau*, Letter 2457, xv. 113).

[20] At age forty-three, she was not as young as this description suggests.

[21] 'Black man': dark complexioned or dark haired. The 'Armenian' dress was a caftan-like garment which Rousseau habitually wore at Môtiers for comfort and for ease in trea-ting his medical problem (for which see n. 23). He had begun to wear this garment occasionally from 1756 to 1762 while at Montmorency (*Confessions*, Bk. XII, OC *Rousseau*, i. 601; Cranston, *The Solitary Self*, pp. 39–40).

[22] Rousseau and Thérèse Levasseur occu-pied the upper floor of a run-down house belonging to Mme Julie-Anne-Marie Boy de la Tour (1715–80), the niece of Rous-seau's friend Daniel Roguin (1691–1771) of Yverdon (Eigeldinger, 'Môtiers', *Dict. de Rousseau*, p. 628). Rousseau's 'chambre' in-cluded in its primitive furnishings two arm chairs and twelve straw-bottomed chairs, along with some bookshelves, a wooden plank used as desk, and a curtained-off bed (François Matthey, 'La Maison et l'apparte-ment de Rousseau á Môtiers' in the 'Cata-logue de l'exposition permanente', *Musée J.-J. Rousseau a Môtiers*, 3rd ed. 1986, pp. 10–11).

[23] Rousseau, who suffered from a urinary obstruction, had dispensed with doctors as early as 1753 when his health had suddenly improved without their help (*Confessions*, Bk. VIII, OC *Rousseau*, i. 389). Only once more, in 1761, had he allowed a surgeon to introduce a probe to lessen a particularly severe pain, and had then learned that al-though his condition was incurable, he was not mortally ill (*Confessions*, Bk. XI, OC *Rousseau*, i. 571–72 and 1554–55 n. 3). More recently Rousseau had become embittered about medical 'charlatans', whom he blamed for the death of his friend and patron the Maréchal-Duc de Luxembourg just after the death of the Maréchal-Duc's four-year-old grandson (*Confessions*, Bks. XI–XII, OC *Rousseau*, i. 550–51, 668, 1543 nn. 1 and 2).

[24] Rousseau's recent problems had begun soon after the publication in May 1762 of *Émile*, primarily because of the ideas he had expressed through the Savoyard Vicar. The Paris Parlement had ordered him arrested

on 9 June and the book burned by the public executioner two days later, for supposedly attacking the divinity of Christ and the Christian religion as well as the authority of the sovereign ('Arrest de la Cour de Parlement', *CC Rousseau*, A254, xi. 262–70). The Petit Conseil of Geneva had condemned *Émile* on 19 June for criticizing its civil government, and had ordered the public hangman to burn it together with the just-published *Contrat Social*. In Amsterdam the publication of *Émile* had been prohibited on 23 June. In Bern the book had been condemned on 8 July, just after Rousseau was officially banished from Yverdon (which belonged to the canton of Bern). In France, finally, another blow had come on 20 Aug. from the pastoral letter (*mandement*) issued by Christophe de Beaumont (1703–81), Archbishop of Paris (Eigeldinger, p. 63; T. L. Aminot, 'Condamnations', 'Berne', *Dict. de Rousseau*, pp. 151–52, 76. For the relevant documents, see *CC Rousseau*, xi. A253–55, A264–68; xii. A27378). Warned about these condemnations, Rousseau had fled from French soil in Montmorency on 9 June, and from Yverdon a month later (Eigeldinger, p. 19). Under these circumstances, his claim that his books had saved his life was paradoxical, but perhaps he meant that they had given him a *raison d'être*.

[25] MS. 'sure', as also eight words later in the sentence.

[26] Probably *De jure naturae et gentium* (1672) by Samuel von Pufendorf, translated and abridged by Jean Barbeyrac (1674–1747) with the title *Droit de la nature et des gens*. Pufendorf had maintained that 'a state or ruler may not injure a private subject because both are under the same common law of nature', and that a ruler may not 'brand an honest Person with Disgrace and Ignominy' (*De jure*, Bk. VII, ch. viii, quoted here from *Of the Law of Nature and Nations* [rev. ed. 1710], trans. Basil Kennet). Rousseau had read Barbeyrac's two-volume abridgement of 1718 while staying with Mme de Warens (1699–1762), his first protectress (see *Confessions*, Bk. III, *OC Rousseau*, i. 110, 1283 n. 5; *Dict. de Rousseau*, p. 773). He was drawing on the natural-rights philosophy developed not only by Pufendorf but also by Grotius and Burlamaqui, all of whom he admired (see 'Burlamaqui, Jean-Jacques', and 'Grotius, Hugo', *Dict. de Rousseau*, pp. 120–22, 399–94).

[27] JB had referred to his suit of 'scarlet and gold' in his letter to WJT of 25 Sept. 1763 (*Corr.* 6, p. 74). He had planned to wear it for 'the great day of Count Nassau's dinner'

in Utrecht on 14 Oct. ('Notes for Journal in Holland', 14 Oct. 1763, *Holland*, Heinemann p. 45, McGraw-Hill p. 46). The hat is mentioned on a list of the clothes found by François Mazerac on entering JB's employment (Sept. 1763, Yale MS. C 1994).

SJ in his *Dictionary* had described 'camlet' as a 'kind of stuff originally made by a mixture of silk and camel's hair; it is now made with wool and silk' (*Dict. SJ*, s.v. 'camelot/camlet'). According to OED, the name was 'originally applied to some beautiful and costly eastern fabric, afterwards to imitations and substitutes'; it may never have referred to camel hair (OED, s.v. 'camlet'). This and other parts of his outfit JB may have purchased on Lord Marischal's advice concerning appropriate dress for the German court. The colourful garments and costly materials reflect the high fashion of the French and English aristocracy (From Lord Marischal, 25 May 1764, Yale MS. C 1945; see Daniel Roche, *The Culture of Clothing: Dress and Fashion in the 'Ancien Regime'*, trans. Jean Birrell, 1994, p. 198; Jane Ashelford, *The Art of Dress: Clothes and Society 1500–1914*, 1996, pp. 135–40). Yet the fact that the gold lace on JB's hat had only 'the air of being sollid' suggests his limited financial resources. Altogether, his attire reveals both his social aspirations and his naive misconception about what would impress Rousseau.

JB would wear this ensemble, including the green fur-trimmed greatcoat, for the portrait that he would order from George Willison in Rome (Journ. 6, 7 May 1765, *Earlier Years*, pp. 221–22; the portrait, bequeathed to the National Portrait Gallery of Scotland in 1913, is reproduced on the front jackets of *Earlier Years* and of David Daiches, *James Boswell and his World*, 1976).

[28] MS. 'receu'

[29] Rousseau had owed his asylum in Neuchâtel to Lord Marischal, who had obtained the necessary permission from Frederick of Prussia (Cuthell, ii. 129–32). The father-son image, which had appealed to both Lord Marischal and Rousseau, would be used most eloquently in Rousseau's tribute recalling his visits to Lord Marischal in Neuchâtel: 'Que de larmes d'attendrissement j'ai souvent versé … en pensant aux bontés paternelles, aux vertus aimables, à la douce philosophie de ce respectable v[i]eillard. Je l'appellois mon pere, il m'appelloit son enfant. Ces doux noms rendent en partie l'idée de l'attachement qui nous unissait, mais ils ne rendent pas encore celle du besoin que nous avions l'un de l'autre …' (*Confessions*, Bk. XII, *OC Rousseau*, i. 597).

[30] Rousseau's pride was so well known that to provide him with the support he needed, Lord Marischal had sent him not money, but rather corn, wine, and wood (Cuthell, ii. 132–34, 140). Lord Marischal had carried his benevolence so far as to invite Rousseau to join him in Scotland in a little 'republic', together with David Hume, who would be returning to Scotland after serving as unofficial private secretary to the British ambassador in Paris (Lord Marischal to Rousseau, 2 Oct. 1762, *CC Rousseau*, Letter 2204, xiii. 149; Cranston, *The Solitary Self*, p. 38; Ernest Campbell Mossner, *The Life of David Hume*, 1980, pp. 434–35, 494–95). This quixotic scheme would never be tested by reality because Lord Marischal would leave Scotland before Rousseau's arrival in England in Jan. 1766.

[31] Rousseau's feelings about Frederick II were ambivalent. Although praising him here for his energy, Rousseau had criticized him for his military aggression, for having relinquished the sceptre for the sword (Rousseau to Frederick II, 30 Oct. 1762, *CC Rousseau*, xix. 106–07; see also 'Frédéric II', *Dict. de Rousseau*, pp. 358–59).

[32] From here on, the punctuation and sense are ambiguous because of the sparcity of JB's quotation marks. Omitted opening or closing quotation marks are added without comment where the sense is clear (see Editorial Procedures), but for this sentence about the Spaniards, quotation marks are lacking entirely, although these words were probably uttered by JB.

For a more conservative transcription, leaving JB's quotation marks without closure, see *CC Rousseau*, App. 334, xxii. 351–55.

[33] MS. 'En' corrected from 'In'

[34] For JB's objection to the Union of Scotland and England, see Journ. 6 Sept. and n. 1.

[35] For Fieldmarshal Keith's career, see Journ. 28 Aug. n. 2.

[36] MS. Illegible final letter deleted on 'prié'

[37] In proposing Fletcher of Saltoun as alternative to James Keith, Lord Marischal was honouring a proud, fiercely independent Scot whose colourful life was also worthy of Rousseau's attention. Fletcher, a convinced anti-royalist, had spent time in the Netherlands and France from 1668 to 1677 and had joined the Duke of Monmouth in his rebellion against James II in 1685. Killing a fellow supporter of Monmouth's in a private quarrel had forced Fletcher to leave England again before Monmouth's defeat, and his part in the Monmouth affair had led to his being convicted for treason. Fletcher had

thereupon spent several more years on the Continent, partly in fighting on the side of the Hungarians against the Turks. Back in England by 1689 in the train of William of Orange, he had become a spokesman for Scottish rights. He had written pamphlets favouring the use of militia (e.g., *A Discourse Concerning Militia's* [*sic*] *and Standing Armies*, 1697, revised in 1698 as *A Discourse of Government with Relation to Militia's*). He had also urged economic improvements such as support of the newly formed Scottish trading company in Panama (in *Two Discourses Concerning the Affairs of Scotland*, 1698). Above all, as member of the Scottish parliament from 1703 to 1707 he had strongly opposed the Union, notably in his *Speeches as a Member of Parliament*, 1703. These political activities had earned him the sobriquet 'The Patriot' (*Oxford DNB*, s.v. 'Fletcher, Andrew, of Saltoun'; P. H. Scott, *Andrew Fletcher and the Treaty of Union*, 1994, pp. 75–208). JB, who greatly admired Fletcher, would hope that Rousseau's projected biography would 'do immortal honour to Scotland and to true Scotsmen' (To Lord Marischal, 20 Jan. 1765, Yale MS. L 953, written from Turin).

[38] From 'Oui monsieur' to 'les Historiens', JB has tried to capture Rousseau's voice in direct quotation, though without quotation marks.

To provide Rousseau with material, Lord Marischal had already asked JB to gather interesting anecdotes (Mem. dated 24 July and n. 1; see From Lord Marischal to Rousseau, 21 Aug., *CC Rousseau*, Letter 3459, xxi. 53–54). Rousseau would hear on 8 Dec. that documents pertaining to Fletcher were being translated (From Lord Marischal to Rousseau, *CC Rousseau*, Letter 3713, xxii. 184–85), and would receive these by the end of the month (*CC Rousseau*, summary of Letter 3822, xxii. 350; see also Letter 3900, 8 Jan. 1765, xxiii. 145). Faced with more urgent problems, however, Rousseau would not actually write this biography, and several of Fletcher's notebooks would remain in the hands of Rousseau's friend and literary heir Pierre-Alexandre Du Peyrou (1729–94) until after Rousseau's death (see Du Peyrou to René-Louis, Marquis de Girardin, *CC Rousseau*, Letter 7334bis, 29 Oct. 1778, xl. 72).

[39] MS. Before 'Les Ecclesiastiques', JB mistakenly introduces another opening quotation mark (omitted here for sense), even though he is continuing with Rousseau's words. In a concise paragraph, JB offers Rousseau's sarcastic comments on the two chief religious points of view of his time: one re-

presented by the Catholic clergy, who insist on adding explanations, however incomprehensible, and win undeserved praise ('voici un grand homme'); the other expressed by what F. A. Pottle calls the 'Reformers' (obviously Protestants), who wish to destroy the Catholics' additions yet remain important. These two voices (indicated by double quotation marks) are introduced within Rousseau's larger speech, which is then continued by his question about his bear-like demeanour and ends only with 'le monde comme il est'. For a helpful interpretation of this complicated passage, primarily by supplying missing quotation marks, see *Grand Tour I*, Heinemann p. 218 n. 2, McGraw-Hill p. 223 and n. 7.

[40] Since two Genevan theologians with roughly similar names had recently attacked Rousseau, the one singled out by Rousseau cannot be identified with certainty. Both had turned on Rousseau after having admired him and maintaining friendly relations with him in the 1750s. JB's spelling of Vernet, suggesting a two-syllable pronounciation, points to Jacob Vernet (1698–1789), a Calvinist who had held a chair in literature in Geneva from 1739 to 1756 and then a chair in theology. He is said to have privately disapproved of Rousseau's receiving communion in Môtiers on 29 Aug. 1762 without fully subscribing to orthodox Calvinist beliefs (see Journ. 5 Dec. n. 5; *Grand Tour I*, Heinemann p. 219 n. 1, McGraw-Hill p. 224 n. 8). But his many writings on moral and religious topics, notably his anti-Voltairian 'Lettre écrite de Genève à M. de Voltaire' in 1757, include few explicit criticisms of Rousseau (Montet, ii. 609–10). And his generally liberal attitudes make the term 'arch-Jesuit' inappropriate.

A more likely antagonist is Jacob Vernes (1728–91), pronounced as one syllable, who had served as pastor in Céligny in the republic of Geneva from 1761. Although he had been an admiring correspondent of Rousseau's from 1754 to 1761 and had included Rousseau's writings in his anthology *Choix littéraire* (24 vols., 1755–60), Vernes had been the first to attack Rousseau personally and publicly after the French Parlement and the Petit-Conseil of Geneva had condemned

*Émile* (Paul Waeber, 'Autour du Voyageur sentimental' (1786), François Vernes dans la fougue de ses vingt ans', *Revue du Vieux Genève*, 1986, p. 69). He had become progressively more hostile in his *Lettres sur le christianisme de J.-J. Rousseau, Dialogues sur le christianisme de J.-J. Rousseau*, and *Réponse à quelques lettres de J.-J. Rousseau*, all published in 1763, in which he had objected particularly to Rousseau's questioning of miracles in the Savoyard Vicar's 'Profession de foi' (Montet, ii. 606; J.-D. Candaux, 'Vernes, Jacob', *Dict. de Rousseau*, p. 915). As recently as Oct., Rousseau, in turn, had mockingly likened Vernes and his fellow ministers to Jesuits, who urged others to do what they would not do themselves (*Lettres écrites de la montagne*, Letter 2, OC *Rousseau*, iv. 751 and 1605, n. 5).

[41] MS. This short question, set off with ambiguous quotation marks, is presumably JB's.

[42] Rousseau had expressed a similar complaint in his letter to 'Henriette' (not otherwise identified, 4 Nov., CC *Rousseau*, Letter 3621, xxii. 8). He may have been irritated by the letters from Jacob Benezet (1711?–88) expatiating on religion (?Dec., Letter 3690, xxii. 144–46; see p. 370, note p) and from Mademoiselle Allard concerning the pedagogical ideas in *Émile* (13 Nov., Letter 3642, xxii. 48–51).

[43] For GD, see Journ. 6 Aug. n. 7. JB wrote to him exultantly of having met 'the Wild Philosopher'. That GD was the first of JB's friends to receive a report of this momentous meeting was presumably due to his interest in Rousseau's political ideas. In a discussion with SJ about the *Discours sur l'inégalité* (1755), GD had approved of Rousseau's emphasis on personal merit while SJ had insisted on the greater importance of rank and money in society (Journ. 20 July 1763, recounted with the same date in *Life* i. 439–41). Earlier, GD had proved his friendship by responding to JB's desperate plea, during his first unhappy days in Holland, to come from Paris to Brussels, and had not taken it amiss when JB had not gone to Brussels after all (16–23 Aug., *Holland*, Heinemann pp. 7–13, McGraw-Hill pp. 7–13; To WJT, 2 Sept. 1763, *Corr.* 6, p. 65).

## Tuesday 4 December

[MEM. dated Wednesday 5 December] Had been too late up — wrote — walked — went to his door. Madll out. Din'd table d'hote — waited on Chatelin hearty cordial — Home — 5 — Rousseau — gay Abbe St. Pièrre tout independant alloit son chemin. Les hommes grands Enfans. Alloit tout droite — sans passion que la passion[1] de la raison — en des Bagatelles — portoit montre a un bouton. Madame Je vous ennuye mais vous amusez Je reste. — Creatures[2] de Louis 14 fit chasser de l'academie — Alloit le voir — il m'amuse — Je ne le sais malgré. Il a eu de l'interet — il agi ainsi. Ses fils — point de secret — Professions utiles pas Peruquier — Pendant que la Nature fourniroit des cheveux. Bon sens. Mais mauvais stile. Longue diffus mais venoit á bout. Les femmes l'aimoit. Il fut respecté. Il faisoit du bien justement[3] parceque cetoit de faire du bien.[4]

[MEM. dated *Second* Wednesday 5 Decr.] Votre album donc est Album — donnoit Paix Perpetuelle. Me chargoit d'envoyer Memoires de Fletcher — anec-dotes de l'Union — Personnes particuliers — Je le ferois avec le plus grand soin et plaisir. J'ai vu des montagnards Ecossois en [F]rance — J'aime les ecossois pas parceque Mi lord est un — *mais* parceque il les a loué. Told him sad ridicule of Scotch — Parliament. Il faut être fou de Membre — respecté á la fin. Vous me genez. C'est ma nature. Je ne puis[5] m'empecher. Usez envers moi sans facon. — Allez vous en — [M]adll:[6] Je ne le quitterais pour étre Reine de France — Vous pouvez venir matin & Soir. She your freind. Supt Chatel. This day — Be serious with Rousseau — Learn.

[J.] After taking a walk in the Vallon I went to the door of M. Rousseau. Mademoiselle Vasseur was abroad, & I could not get in. I met her on the street, & she said 'M. Rousseau vous fera dire l'aprés midi á quelle heure il peut vous voir.' I dined at the table d'hote with a M. du Rhé a Parisian son to a rich Financier but obliged to fly on account of lettres de cachet which were taken out against him by his Sister's influence who is married to a man in power, and wants to have all the fortune of her father. This same Du Rhé is however a sad dog. He has spent a vast deal of money upon women, and upon absurd plans for the young Pretender. He is a kind of Authour, writes you a criticism in the Journal Encyclopedique, and even composes you a system of education on a plan entirely new. This last has not yet seen the light.[7] Small will be the light which it will impart — 'Not light, but rather darkness visible'.[8] M. Du Rhé lives snug at Motiers & eats in the Inn, when some good freind does not invite him. My other Companion was M. de Turo who has an estate in the neighbourhood, has travelled a good deal, has a good deal of knowledge, and is a tall stout young fellow. But with the whim of an English Oddity he lives constantly in this Inn. The Inhabitants of the Village have named him their Governour an Office of *small* Authority but of consequence enough to make M. de Turo hold his head extremely high.[9] I have seen him grant a *pass* to a Beggar with great dignity. He generally keeps a parcel of dogs, & goes a hunting on the hills. Scandal says that he is intimately connected with my youngest Landlady. Perhaps I have done him an injury in the spelling of his name. Perhaps he writes it Thurot, and possibly may be a near Relation of the gallant Captain Thurot who during the last war awed and dismayed the coasts of Caledonia.[10] After dinner I waited on M. Martinet the Chatelin a knowing hearty fellow. He engaged me to sup with him. At five I went to M. Rousseau, whom I found more gay than he had been yesterday. We joked on Mademoiselle Vasseur for keeping him under lock and key. She to defend herself said he had another door to get out.[11] Said he 'Ah Mademoiselle vous dites tout'. He gave me the character of the Abbe de St. Piérre un homme qui faisoit du bien seulement parceque il le trouvoit bon de faire du bien, un Homme sans enthousiasme. On peut dire qu'il avoit la passion de la raison. On le voyoit á porter de memoires et il disoit, on se mocquera de moi pour cela; Je serai siflé pour cela. Cela ne lui faisoit rien. Il suivoit toujours ses principes même dans des Bagatelles. Par example Il portoit sa montre pendu á un Bouton de son habit, parce que c'etoit plus commode. Comme il ne pouvoit pas se marier il avoit des maitresses et il n'en faisoit point un secret. Il avoit plusieurs fils. Ils ne vouloit pas leur laisser suivre que des Professions reéllement utiles. Par example il ne vouloit laisser aucun de ses fils etre Peruquier, Parceque, dit il, pendant que la nature nous fournira des cheveux de faire des Peruques c'est toujours une Profession incertaine. Il ne se soucioit point des opinions des hommes. Il disoit qu'ils etoient des grands enfans. Il avoit resté long tems chez une Dame. Il lui dit Madame Je voye que Je vous Ennuis mais cela ne me fait rien. Vous m'amusez. Un creature de Louis quatorze le fit chasser de l'Academie pour un discours qu'il y donnoit. Il alloit toujours voir cet homme. Il disoit il a agi selon son intéret. Je ne lui sai mauvais grê. Il m'amuse. Il ne doit pas etre offensé contre moi. Je dois etre offensé contre lui; mais Je ne le suis pas. Enfin il alloit toujours chez cet Academicien jusques a ce qu'il l'empechoit parceque il lui etoit disagreable de voir un homme á qui il avoit eté un ennemi. Il avoit beaucoup de bon sens; mais un mauvais stile. Il etoit longue et diffus mais il venoit toujours au bout. Les femmes l'aimoient. Il alloit son chemin tout independant. Il etoit respecté. Si vous serez membre de Parliament il faut etre comme l'Abbé de St. Pierre.[12] Il faut suivre vos principes. 'Mais il faut donc etre bien instruit.' 'Ah il faut avoir la tête bien meublé.' Mais Monsieur un Membre qui agit en veritable honette Homme, est regardé comme fou. 'Eh bien, il faut etre un fou de membre, et croyez moi on respectera un tel Homme s'il reste ferme dans ses principes. Un Homme qui change á tout moment c'est autre chose.' He talked of his 'Projet d'un Paix perpetuelle tire de l'Abbé de St. Pierre.' I frankly owned that I had not read it. 'Non' said he — then took one down from his Book-case & gave it me.[13] I asked him smilingly if he would not put his name on it. He laughed heartily at me. I talked to him of the German *Album* & how I had been forced to take one; but that except what was written by the Person who gave it me, there was nothing in it. Said he 'Votre *Album* donc est *Album*'.[14] There was a Sally for you. A Precious Pearl. A Pun made by Rousseau. He said J'ai vu des montagnards Ecossois en France. J'aime les Ecossois; pas parceque MyLord Marischal en est un; mais parceque il les loue. Vous me genez. C'est ma nature. Je ne saurrois l'empecher — 'Mais usez envers moi sans façon — Allez vous en.' Mademoiselle allways accompanys me to the door. She said J'ai eté vingt deux ans avec M. Rousseau. Je ne changerois ma place pour etre Reine de France. Je tache de proffiter des bons conseils qu'il me donne. S'il vient de mourir il faut me retirer dans un Couvent.[15] She is a very good girl, and deserves to be esteemed for her constancy to a man so valuable. His Simplicity is beautifull. He consulted Mademoiselle & her mother on the merits of his Heloise & his Émile.[16] I supt with the Chatelin.[17] He said nous sommes seuls, afin de parler d'autre chose que de MyLord Marischal. We were hearty.

[1] MS. 'la passion' written over a deleted illegible word.

[2] MS. 'Creatures' written above deleted 'parti sans'

[3] MS. 'jusquement'

[4] MS. 'bien./turn', presumably because a second entry for 5 Dec. follows on the reverse.

[5] MS. 'suis'

[6] A succinct introduction to Thérèse Levasseur's words.

[7] Joseph-Marie-Anne Durey de Morsan (1717–95) had arrived in Môtiers in Sept. 1763 and had enjoyed the sympathy of Rousseau, who was however beginning to doubt Durey's abilities and motives (Eigeldinger, pp. 298–300). He had been imprisoned for fourteen months, starting in Aug. 1759, at the instigation of his wealthy father, Pierre Durey d'Harnoncourt (1682–1765), who had been enraged by Durey's excessive debts and had used the legal device of a *lettre de cachet*, which permitted indefinite imprisonment without due process. The sister, Louise-Bernarde (b. 1720), was married to Jean-Louis Berthier de Sauvigny, a government official (*intendant*) in Grenoble at this time. She believed Durey guilty of trying to poison his father and remained relentlessly hostile (CC *Rousseau*, Sept. 1763, Letter 2915, xvii. 243, Note Explicatif; Eigeldinger, p. 301). Before and after his incarceration Durey had indulged in several liaisons, had fathered illegitimate children, and had supposedly transmitted his venereal disease to the young woman whom, at his father's behest, he had married in 1746, but from whom he had later been legally separated (Jeroom Vercruysse, 'Joseph Marie Durey de Morsan, chroniqueur de Ferney', SVEC 230 [1985]: 324). One of his 'absurd plans', influenced by an Irishman named O'Leary (not further identified), had been to serve as proxy for Prince Charles Edward in an arranged marriage to the daughter of the King of Morocco, a scheme or story perhaps suggested by the prince's known liaison, from c. 1747 to 1750, with Marie-Anne-Louise Jablonowska (1701–73), Princesse de Talmond, whom he had dubbed the 'Reine de Maroc' (see David Daiches, *Charles Edward Stuart*, 1973, pp. 263, 268–69, 285). Voltaire, into whose vicinity Durey would move in 1765, would mention this plan in a letter to Durey's sister in which he tried to reconcile her with Durey (Voltaire to Louise

Bernarde Berthier de Sauvigny, 30 Jan. 1769, *Corres. Voltaire*, D15454).

Durey's work as author consisted of anonymous publications: a translation of the *Testament politique du cardinal J. Alberoni*, 1753; *Histoire du prétendant*, 1756, based on an eyewitness report of Charles Edward Stuart's Scottish campaign; a summary of *Émile* in the *Journal encyclopédique* (vol. i, 1 and 15 Jan. 1763); and a summary of the *Contrat Social* for the *Journal de jurisprudence* (Jan.–Feb. 1763), DBF, xii. 759; see Vercruysse, pp. 326, 330–31. Durey's pedagogical ideas can be judged by his letter to David Hume of 17 June 1764 (National Library of Scotland, MS. 23156, pp. 285–287v.). Durey favoured an unstrenuous gentlemanly education (little reading or memorizing but practice in dancing and riding). His educational 'system' would be shown to Rousseau a few months later, only to be declared without merit (Rousseau to François-Henri d'Ivernois, 15, 17 Aug. 1765, CC *Rousseau*, Letters 4584, 4587, xxvi. 219, 223–24).

[8] Milton, *Paradise Lost*, i. 63, slightly changing Milton's 'No light ....'

[9] Very likely Charles Auguste Du Terreaux (1725–79); see CC *Rousseau*, Letter 2055, xii. 146 note e. Formerly an officer in Spain, he was now the 'lieutenant' of the Val de Travers (Eigeldinger, p. 76; CC *Rousseau*, A334, xxii. 370 note u). He was rebuilding a house opposite Rousseau's and was disliked by his neighbours, including Rousseau (Eigeldinger, p. 353 n. 1).

[10] François Thurot (1727–60) had become a legendary figure for his exploits in successfully attacking British shipping, particularly between the coasts of Scotland and Ireland, and in the Hebrides. His last exploit, a raid on the Irish coast at Carrickfergus in Feb. 1760, had ended with his being abandoned by two accompanying French ships and fatally shot. He had been buried at sea, but his body had been washed ashore on the Mull of Galloway, and he had been given honourable burial on Scottish soil by JB's Ayrshire neighbour, Sir William Maxwell of Monreith ('A Succinct Account of M. Thurots Late Expedition', *Gent. Mag.* Mar. 1760, xxx. 107–10; BU, 1826, xlv. 593–94; A. T. Q. Stewart, *A Deeper Silence: The Hidden Origins of the United Irish Movement*, 1993, pp. 13–17).

[11] A door next to the kitchen led down extra stairs to the barn and fields (Maurice Boy de la Tour, 'A Propos du séjour de Jean-Jacques Rousseau à Môtiers', *MN* 49 [1912]: 190–91).

[12] Charles Irenée Castel (1658–1743), abbé de Saint-Pierre, was a political philosopher known for his rationalism and utopian vision. Rousseau had met him in old age in Paris and had spent the years 1756 to 1758 in summarizing his prolix writings (Sven Stelling-Michaud, 'Introductions sur l'abbé de Saint-Pierre', in *OC Rousseau*, vol. iii, pp. cxx–cxxiv). In referring to Saint-Pierre as a man who liked 'to do good' (*faire du bien*), Rousseau was alluding to the term *bienfaisance*, which Saint-Pierre was credited with coining for a special sort of unsentimental charity (Littré, s.v. 'bienfaisance'; 'Mémoire pour diminuer le nombre des procès', 1725; *Columbia Encyclopedia*, 2nd ed. 1950, p. 1738). In describing Saint-Pierre's idiosyncracies, Rousseau was drawing on his research for a projected biography of Saint-Pierre. The abbé's habit of jotting down notes (*mémoires*); his unfashionable dangling of his watch from a button instead of around his neck, or attached to a belt, or, in newest style, tucked into a waistcoat pocket (Eric Bruton, *The History of Clocks and Watches*, 1979, p. 112); his weekly rendezvous with servant-girls to counteract the celibacy imposed by his religious vows; his advice to his many illegitimate sons to avoid useless professions such as wig-making; and his view of men as children—all were recorded in Rousseau's 'Fragments et notes sur l'abbé de Saint-Pierre' (*OC Rousseau*, iii. 658, 661–62). The lady whom Saint-Pierre had persisted in visiting was the Duchess d'Aiguillon (1700–72), identified by Jacob Wegelin and Jean-Gaspard Schulthess, who had also visited Rousseau in Môtiers, and who believed that Rousseau's idiosyncratic attire had been partly inspired by Saint-Pierre's disregard of fashion (see 'Caractère de M. Rousseau en 1763', in Jochen Schlobach, 'Un Reportage sur Rousseau', *Dix-huitième Siècle*, 1984, xvi. 221). The 'creature' blamed for Saint-Pierre's expulsion from the Académie française and subject to his annoying visits was identified by Rousseau as Louis de Courcillon, abbé de Dangeau ('Note sur l'exclusion de l'abbé de Saint-Pierre de l'académie française', *OC Rousseau*, iii. 669).

Omitted by Rousseau or JB was the generally accepted explanation that Saint-Pierre had been ousted by other academicians for his *Polysynodie, ou la pluralité des Conseils* (London, 1718; Amsterdam, 1719), in which he had suggested replacing single royal advisors by several councils, thereby insulting the memory of Louis XIV, founder of the Academy (see Stelling-Michaud in *OC Rousseau*, iii. 1559). That so many particulars in this journal entry can be corroborated is evidence of JB's remarkable memory for details and accuracy of reporting.

[13] In this work Saint-Pierre had proposed a league of European princes to resolve conflicts by peaceful means and had extolled commerce as a unifying force. Rousseau's summary, *Extrait du projet de paix perpétuelle de Monsieur l'abbé de Saint-Pierre*, had been published in 1759 and was, together with his summary of the *Polysynodie*, the only part of his Saint-Pierre project that he actually completed. JB's copy is listed in the catalogue of his library.

[14] 'Album' could mean 'blank' as well as 'white' (OED, s.v. 'album'). For JB's experience with albums, see Journ. 10 Sept. and 1 Oct.

[15] Socially and financially insecure, Thérèse Levasseur was understandably worried because Rousseau may not have told her of the will he had made in her favour in 1763 ('Testament de Jean Jaques [*sic*] Rousseau Citoyen de Geneve', *OC Rousseau*, i. 1224–25). Subsequently, she would accompany Rousseau to England, and on their return to France he would marry her in 1768. On his death in 1777, she would not enter a convent but within a year would live with a low-born valet, John- or Jean-Henry Bally (1745–1805), leading to ugly rumours that she had caused Rousseau's suicide but inspiring a spirited defence by Isabelle de Charrière (Belle de Zuylen) in her 'Plainte et défense de Thérèse Levasseur', 1789 (see *OC Charrière*, x. 171–76). During the Revolution, Thérèse Levasseur would contribute to Rousseau's fame by allowing the transfer of his ashes to the Pantheon and donating the MS of his *Confessions* to the French nation, but she would end her days in obscurity and virtual poverty (Charly Guyot, 'Esquisse pour un portrait: Thérèse Levasseur', *MN* 49 [1962]: 170, 173–79).

[16] Rousseau would recall reading the first two parts of *La Nouvelle Héloïse* in 1756, five years before its publication, to Thérèse, who had joined him in shedding tears of sentiment, and to her mother, who had 'understood nothing' and had given only conventional praise (*Confessions*, Bk. IX, *OC Rousseau*, i. 436). There is no record of a comparable scene or discussion about *Émile*, begun some time between 1754 and 1757 (see *Dict. de Rousseau*, s.v. 'Émile', 'Julie ou la Nouvelle

Héloïse', '[Levasseur] Renou (Renoux, Renoulx, Renould), Marie').

[17] Although he had the title 'chatelain', Martinet did not live in the chateau, which was already half in ruins at this time, but in the house next to Rousseau's (Jean Courvoisier, *Les Monuments d'art et d'histoire du Canton de Neuchâtel*, 1968, p. 77; *Confessions*, Bk. XII, *OC Rousseau*, i. 635). A few days after this meeting, Martinet would be named 'conseiller d'état' of Neuchâtel (AEN).

## Wednesday 5 December

[MEM. dated 6 December] Yesterday morning waited on [M]adll De Vasseur who said Je ne quitterois [M]. Rousseau pour être Reine de la [F]rance. Talk'd ma mère & mois disames lheloise aurra grande reputation. Good Being — Saw him 'Mon Cher Monsieur Je suis faché de ne pas pouvoir m'entretenir avec vous' — Told Relig. chang Cath & vouloit être moine en [F]rance. 'Quelle folie.' Jetois aussi Cath. Alors Je retournais a Geneve et fut Protest — Alors aux Cath — Je ne suis plus — mais vivoit bien avec eux — Mais etes vous Chretien? Oui Je me pique de l'être. Il n y a rien qui peut soutenir l'homme que l'evangile. Je le sens, [t]outes les objections — Cela ne me fait rien. Non. Je suis trop foible — Il peuvent être des choses au dessus de moi, ou peutètre celui que les a fait se trompoit. Cela ne me fait rien — Je dis Dieu Le Pere Dieu le fils &c. Cest Dieu. Mais dites moi avez vous eu la melancholie?

[MEM. dated Second Thursday 6 Decr.] Je ne suis pas nee mel — mais serein — Des malheurs m'en ont donnés. Mais moi qui a fait tant de mal — Commencez votre existence. Dieu est bon parcequ'il est juste. Faites du bien. Vous acquiterez tout le mal. Pensez le Matin Allons. Je m'en vais acquiter autant, Six Ans bien passes acquit se que vous avez fait. Mais Des Cloitres &c. — Touts les mommerie des hommes — Si vous jugez selon les hommes vous serez racheté[1] toujours, mais[2] vous ne savez s'ils croyent ce qu'ils disent — Interet Bienséance &c. Voulez vous avoir soin — Je ne puis — Je ne suis bon que pour moi. Mais Je reviens — Je ne promette de vous voir — Soufrant — un pot de chamb a chaque moment — oui vous me verrez — Tableaux. Left him *Ebauche*.[3] Duré & De Tureau, set out rain wind — grand thought. Bro — Sando's establishment. Handsom Girl & *you* sung. Julie [—] was melancholy —

[J.] When I waited upon M. Rousseau this morning, he said Mon Cher Monsieur Je suis faché de ne pas pouvoir m'entretenir avec vous comme Je souhaitrois. I took care to wave such excuses, & immediatly set conversation agoing. I told him how I had turned Roman Catholic & had intended to hide myself in a Convent in France.[4] He said Quelle folie! J'etois aussi Catholique dans ma Jeunesse. Je changeois; — ensuite Je rechangois. Je m'en retournois á Genêve, et Jétois recu Protestant. Je m'en allois chez les Catholiques, et Je leur disois Je ne suis plus un de vous, et Je vivois bien avec eux.[5] I stopped him in the middle of the room & I said to him 'Mais dites moi sincerement: "etes vous Chrétien?"' I looked at him with a searching eye. His countenance was no less animated. Each stood steady and watched the other's looks. He struck his breast and replied 'Oui. — Je me pique de l'étre.'[6] 'Monsieur il n'y a rien que peut soutenir l'Ame que l'Evangile. Je le sens. Toutes des Objections ne me font rien. Je suis foible. Il peuvent étre des choses au dessus de moi, ou peutetre celui qui les a fait se trompoit. Je dis Dieu le Pere, Dieu le fils, Dieu le Saint Esprit.'[7] — Mais dites moi avez vous de la melancolie? 'Je suis née serein. Je n'ai pas naturellement de la melancholie. Mes malheurs m'en ont donné.' — Mais moi Je lai severement — et comment puis Je être content moi qui a tant fait du mal. 'Commencez de nouveau votre existence. Dieu est bon, parceque il est juste — Faites du bien. Vous acquiterez tout le mal. Pensez le matin Allons Je m'en vais acquiter autant du mal — Six ans bien passés acquiteront tout le mal que vous avez fait.'[8] 'Mais que pensez[9] vous de Cloitres de Penitences et de toutes ces remedes?' Touts les mommeries des hommes. Ne prenez point les jugements des hommes ou vous serez balloté toujours d'une coté á lautre. Ne reposez vous sur les jugements des autres, premierrement parce que ils peuvent se tromper[10] aussi bien que vous; dailleurs vous ne savez si les hommes vous disent leur sentimens reels; l'interet, ou la bienseance[11] peut les engager de vous parler d'une autre maniêrre qu'ils ne pensent. 'Monsieur, voulez vous avoir soin de moi?' 'Je ne puis. Je ne suis bon que pour moi.' 'Mais Je reviendrai.' 'Je ne promette pas de vous voir. Je suis souffrant — un pot de chambre á chaque moment.' 'Oui vous me verrez.' 'Adieu. Bon Voyage.' About six I set out.[12] The night was such as Lady Randolph describes

— it was dark December: Wind and rain
Had beat all night.[13]

I was firm and bold and among the wild rocks had grand thought. About nine I arrived at *Bro* where Master Sando & his family took all care of me. I eat biscuits & drank wine. I became gay with the good folks arround me, and Mademoiselle and I sung the Story of Heloise in verse to an old french tune

Quand le fier Baron d'Etange
Sortoit du Païs de Vaud &c.[14]

I was quite in the Highlands of Scotland. She was a Lochaber Lass.[15] Tho the Song is written in a ludicrous stile, the recollection of the events made me cry.[16] The Sandos are a numerous family; About five hundred. Just a Clan. In a Village on one of the Suiss mountains. This Tribe has a fund lodged for the support of their poor Brethren.[17] I was quite the gay & great man.

---

[1] MS. 'racheté' written over inked out word, now illegible.

[2] MS. 'mo'

[3] The only reference before his meetings with Rousseau to the 'Ébauche de ma vie', in which JB tried to bring his personal problems still more specifically to Rousseau's attention. For this document (Yale MS. L 1107), see App. 2, III.A; see also Journ. 14 Dec. n. 10.

[4] JB's most explicit statement in the journal concerning his conversion to Catholicism, about which, according to F. A. Pottle, he was usually quite secretive. For Pottle's highly conjectural chronology of the experiences leading to this step—JB's involvement with an actress presumed to be Catholic and meetings with a priest in Edinburgh, a few months at Glasgow University at his father's behest, and abrupt departure for London in early Mar. 1760— see *Earlier Years*, pp. 40–41, 44–46. Pottle surmises that Boswell made his 'act of submission' to the Church later in Mar., either in his own or a priest's lodgings. Professing Catholicism, though no longer prosecuted as a criminal offence, still incurred severe civil penalties (for which see *Earlier Years*, pp. 45–47, 569–70; *The Encyclopedia of the Laws of Scotland*, 1926–35, xiii, #37–46, pp. 54–58). If JB had persisted, his conversion, even without entering a monastery, would have ended his professional and social prospects in Scotland. In confessing this youthful expe-

rience to Rousseau, JB does not mention that within a month he was wooed back to the worldly pleasures of London under the influence of Lord Eglinton (see Journ. 28 June n. 6, and 'Ébauche de ma vie', App. 2. III.A).

[5] Rousseau, whose mother had died soon after his birth, had been brought up as a Calvinist in Geneva, where his father, a Huguenot, had left him to the care of relations and teachers. He had also been exposed to a moderate Calvinism at a 'presbytery' at Bossey, near Geneva, from 1722 to 1724. He had become a convert to Catholicism under the influence of Mme de Warens, his 'maman' by choice, who had offered him shelter at Annecy and a few years later her love. He had actually entered a seminary in Annecy in 1729 and had remained Catholic during his subsequent stays in Turin, Paris, the French provinces, and Venice. However, he had reconverted to Calvinism in Geneva in 1754 (May, pp. 7–11, 193–94; Cranston, *Jean-Jacques: The Early Life*, pp. 47–48). His change of religion, by his own report, had been owing to a revival of his republican feelings and his desire to return to the church of his father (*Confessions*, Bk. VIII, *OC Rousseau*, i. 392).

[6] MS. Here JB briefly interjects his agreement. This and the following passage are confusing because of the omission of closing quotation marks.

Rousseau is repeating the declaration he had made in answering the charges against *Émile*. Elsewhere, in his letter to Christophe de Beaumont, Archbishop of Paris, he insisted: 'Monseigneur, je suis Chrétien, et sincerement Chrétien, selon la doctrine de l'Evangile' (*OC Rousseau*, iv. 960). And in his just completed *Lettres écrites de la montagne* he again expressed his love of the Gospels and Jesus Christ while decrying the would-be Christians who only profess to offer religious instruction (*OC Rousseau*, iii. 767–68; see also A. Rosenberg, 'Christianisme', *Dict. de Rousseau*, pp. 138–39).

In Môtiers Rousseau had made a point of taking holy communion on 29 Aug. 1762 after convincing the local minister of his sincerity (Eigeldinger, pp. 19, 67–69, 143). In keeping with his Savoyard Vicar's belief that one should comply with the outward forms of worship adopted by one's society while worshipping according to one's own reason and inner sentiment, he had deliberately not discussed points of dogma with the minister (*Confessions*, Bk. XII, *OC Rousseau*, i. 604–05; *Émile*, Bk. IV, *OC Rousseau*, iv. 628).

[7] In invoking the Trinity, Rousseau was affirming the orthodox creed accepted by Catholic and most Protestant churches. For different views of the Trinity, see Journ. 30 Dec. and n. 4.

[8] A succinct statement of Rousseau's characteristic idea that human beings are naturally good, not subject to original sin, although they are capable of evil (P. Hoffmann, 'Mal' and 'Péché Originel' in *Dict. de Rousseau*, pp. 579–81, 706). He also firmly believed that human beings could redeem themselves by good works.

[9] MS. 'penez'.

[10] MS. 'sestromper'

[11] MS. 'bienseaance'

[12] JB here glosses over the roughly five hours between leaving Rousseau and setting out for Brot and Neuchâtel. Contrary to his usual detailed record-keeping, he does not mention the massive amount of writing he accomplished in this time for the 'Ébauche de ma vie', including its drafts and discarded (but preserved) pages (see App. 2, III.A–F).

[13] From the popular melodramatic play *Douglas* (I. i. 229–30), which JB considered a 'beautiful and pathetick tragedy' (*Life*, 28 July 1763, i. 456). JB was acquainted with the author, the Scottish clergyman and playwright John Home (1722–1808); see Journ. 9, 22 Apr. 1763. JB had seen a performance on 5 Mar. 1762 ('Journal in Edinburgh', Yale MS. J 1.2, p. 6).

[14] An anonymous versified 'romance', added to some editions of *La Nouvelle Héloïse*, including the one of 1763. The tune has been identified as that of 'Que ne suis-je la fougère' (see *CC Rousseau*, A334, xxii. 370 note z). The Baron d'Etange is the heroine's father, whose absence makes the action possible. Vaud is the name of the province in which the baron and his daughter Julie live as well as of the setting for the love affair that develops between her and her tutor St. Preux.

[15] For the young woman, Suzanna-Marguerite Sandoz, see Journ. 3 Dec. and n. 7; for Lochaber, see Journ. 13 July n. 2.

[16] 'Ludicrous': 'jocular' (OED, s.v. 'ludicrous', 1). The breezy style can be seen in the following excerpt:

Quand le fier baron d'Etange
Quitta le Pays de Vaud
Pour conduire sa phalange
Contre les Impériaux,
Sa fille encore innocente
N'avoit pas senti son cœur,
Mais la baronne imprudente
Lui fournit un précepteur.
C'étoit un fort joli Suisse

Philosophe de vingt ans
Qui donnoit à sa novice
Tous les premiers élémens.
De morale et de physique
Il raisonnoit savamment.
Aussitôt l'amour le pique:
De maître, il devient amant.

Text supplied by Schnegg, 8 Mar. 1955, from
an MS entitled 'Chanson de Mr Rousseau',
1782.

[17] The charitable trust, known as 'le
Fonds Sandoz', had been started in the early
sixteenth century at Le Locle, a village in
the mountains a few miles above Neuchâtel.
The trust helped poorer members of the
Sandoz family in the eighteenth century
and would remain active until new regulations were adopted in 1922 (Marc Sandoz,
'Étude sur l'histoire de la famille Sandoz',
Jahrbuch 1978, Schweizerische Gesellschaft
für Familienforschung, pp. 82–91).

## Thursday 6 December

[MEM. dated 7 Decr.] Yesterday rose baddish but cur'd immed — Rode brisk —
Neufchat — drest. Sent Chaill — *Friday* — At 3 he came — L. [M]*arisch.* Gazette
Holl [—] York Pretre — Ah toutes nos esperances perdues — Aye me sacrifié
pour ce Bougre de race — Le Pere ne valoit 6 sous et le fils dix mille fois moins. An.
45 — 10 mille hommes — habilem &c pour 10 mill Caval. et habil montagnards
— pour 20 mille et un million — Chargé Prince [—] Il Se laissoit entrainé,
Milord quittoit ecriv en ecosse ne hazardez — c'est un fou — Lui faux manifest
disoit marischal approuvoit — Trop peu dargent [—] menacoit trahir —
Envoyoit a Bale entrei a Neufchat — Milord ecriva au Roi — envoyoit l'amitié
Milord — non comment puisJe[1] quand vous avez fait cela — cela — cela — non
Je ne veux me deshonorer — Reponse non niant faits — mais promettant mieux
— jamais voir — M– [S]ombrun. Cartes — soupé — ennui á la mort — mais
soutenoit. Lettres de Pere nobles — Sr. Dav piquant [—] Johnie absurd. &c. This
day house — wait on [M]ad Sando. Secure 3 or 4 days Journ. Boldly insist on
business. Scotland & happy.

[J.] The morning was gloomy to me as usual. But a good ride to Neufchatel
set me to rights. I had engaged to dine chez Col. Chaillet either this day or
Friday I knew not which. Rousseau said jestingly dinez chez lui tous les
deux. I sent & learnt that it was Friday I had fixed. At three he came to me.
He told me MyLord Marischal was no longer attached to the House of
Stewart. One night at Neufchatel he was playing at Picquet.[2] They brought
a Gazette d'Hollande ou il lisoit que le Duc de York étoit devenu Cardinal.
Il jettoit ses cartes. Il disoit: Ah! voici toutes nos esperances perdues. Ah!
Je me suis sacrifié pour ce Bougre de race! Le Pere ne valoit 6 sols; le fils ainé
deux mille fois moins et voici celui sur qui nous comptions un peu se fait
Prêtre.[3] MyLord meprise le Prince Charles. Dans l'année 45 on demandoit
de la cour de [F]rance 10 mille hommes, habillements pour 10 mille de
Cavalerie, habillements pour 20 mille montagnards, des Armes et un
million. Sans cela les hommes de bon sens ne vouloient faire l'invasion
d'Ecosse. Le Prince avoit promi d'etre ferme, mais il se laissoit entrainer et
s'en alloit comme nous savons. MyLord Ecrivit á ses amis. Ne hazardez rien.
C'est un fou. Le Prince pourtant se servoit du nom de MyLord, jusque a ce
qu'ils envoyerent[4] un Exprès qui leur apportoit ses vrayes sentiments. Après
la Rébellion Le Prince venoit á Bale d'ou il ecrivoit á MyLord de le

271

procurer un Endroit sure dans le païs de Neufchatel. MyLord repondoit qu'il ecrirait directement au Roi de Prusse, et qu'il ne restera pas luimême. Le Prince lui demandoit son Amitié. MyLord repondit 'Je ne veux pas me deshonorer. PuisJe etre l'Ami d'un Homme qui a fait cela cela et cela et il lui donnoit un liste de choses honteuses qu'il avoit fait. Le Prince lui ecrivoit une Reponse ou il ne nioit pas les faits mais promettoit de se mieux comporter pour l'avenir. MyLord ne vouloit jamais le voir. Quand il pensoit que ses Partisans en Angleterre lui envoyoient trop peu d'argent, il menaçoit de donner des informations contre eux; s'ils ne vouloient pas lui donner davantage.[5] What a sad Picture of the Descendant of *Centum Sex Proavi*.[6] At five we went Chez le Capitaine Sonbrun where we played at cards & supt.[7] I had an ennui á la mort, but bore it. I found here Mr. Bowyer an english Sea Captain an amiable, spirited young fellow.[8] I received this night from Geneva a Pacquet of fourteen letters from Messieurs Cazenove Clariêre et fils to whose care all my corespondents have written for some time.[9] I had not heard from my Father for three months, & was very uncertain if he would allow me to go to Italy. His Letter this night was most kind. He agreed to my going to Italy for four months, and wrote to me as to a man. I was penetrated with his goodness. I had a letter from Sir David Dalrymple in which he scourged me with humourous severity till I was allmost angry;[10] and a letter from my Brother John proposing to turn English Clergyman. This vexed me greatly. I wrote to him that he might remain a curate in a little village, & that I would by no means agree to, till he assured me that he could play well enough upon the fiddle to gain him a comfortable livelihood.[11]

[1] JB's spacing of this phrase, presumably to reflect its pronunciation as a single syllable, is hereafter given without further comment as JB wrote it.

[2] A card game for two players using only 32 cards, seven or higher, scoring by complicated rules as soon as the hand of each player is revealed. The game had become popular in 'the best of companies' (Richard Seymour, *The Compleat Gamester*, 8th ed. 1754, pp. vii, 108). Picquet had been regarded 'as the most aristocratic of games', but would die out 'of everyday play by the end of the First World War' (David Parlett, *The Oxford Guide to Card Games*, 1990, p. 175).

[3] The conservative *Gazette d'Hollande*, also known as the *Gazette d'Amsterdam*, reported political events from 1691 to 1796 (Pierre Rétat, *Gazette d'Amsterdam: miroir de l'Europe au XVIIIe siècle*, 2001, p. 4; see the CD-Rom, Voltaire Foundation, Oxford, 2002). However, the title may also refer to other gazettes published in various Dutch towns (Rétat, p. 4).

Henry Benedict, Maria Clement, Duke of York (1725–1807), the younger brother of Prince Charles Edward Stuart, had been born and bred in Rome, and had followed a vocation in the Catholic Church after the Jacobites' defeat at Culloden. Various gazettes had reported his early positions in the church hierarchy: Cardinal Deacon in *'s Gravenhaegse Courant*, No. 90, 8 July 1747; then Cardinal Priest in *'s Gravenhaegse Courant*, No. 117, 7 Sept. 1748; *Leydse Vrydagse Courant*, No. 117, 7 Sept. 1748; *Amsterdamse Donderdaegse Courant*, No. 122, 21 Sept. 1748. He had become Arch-priest and Prefect of the Vatican in 1751, chamberlain (*Camerlengo*) to Pope Benedict XIV just before that pontiff's death in 1758 and then to the new Pope, Clement XIII (1693–1769); and he was elevated to the post of Archbishop of Corinth in 1758, to Cardinal Bishop at Frascati three years later (Brian Fothergill, *The Cardinal King*, 1758, pp. 62–83; Alice Shield, *Henry Stuart, Cardinal York*, 1908, pp. 145, 169–74; see also NCE, iii. 104–06). However, Chaillet seems to have conflated Lord Marischal's dismay on hearing of Henry Stuart's nominations as Catholic prelate in 1747–48, which had made him ineligible for the English crown, and Lord Marischal's later conversation when both he and Chaillet were in Neuchâtel starting in Sept. 1754. In any case, that Lord Marischal, with his many Jacobite contacts, had not heard the news about Cardinal York before coming to Neuchâtel, is unlikely.

[4] MS. 'envoyoyerent'

[5] For Lord Marischal's ambivalent feelings about the Stuarts, see Journ. 23 July and n. 4. Chaillet's report makes clear that Lord Marischal had been disillusioned specifically by Prince Charles Edward and for definite reasons: the Prince's ignoring Lord Marischal's advice in 1745, his misusing Lord Marischal's name, and particularly his threatening to publish the names of English Jacobites in 1754. This threat had led Lord Marischal to break entirely with the prince just before leaving Paris for his new post in Neuchâtel (Cuthell, i. 294; see also McLynn, who argues that the Prince had not meant the threat seriously, pp. 429–31). Chaillet, simplifying the Prince's itinerary after his escape from Scotland in 1746, omits his stay in France until expelled in Dec. 1748, frequent moves thereafter to escape notice and possible assassination while in Avignon, Venice, Lorraine, and Flanders, as well as his secret returns to Paris and London. The Prince had reached Basel only in Sept. 1754 and had stayed there until June 1756 (see McLynn, pp. 362–68, 380–81, 397–99, 433–39). His shameful actions, beyond those already specified, had ranged from capricious dismissals of loyal followers to heavy drinking and love affairs. From 1752 to 1760 he had lived with Clementina Walkinshaw (1720–1802), a young Scotswoman of good family whom he had invited to join him on the Continent, with whom he had had a daughter in 1753, and whom he had subjected to displays of drunkenness and rudeness (see Cuthell, ii. 19–20; McLynn, pp. 415–29; C. Leo Berry, *The Young Pretender's Mistress*, 1977, pp. 46–58).

[6] 'One hundred and six ancestors', a fanciful list of legendary and historic kings of Scotland beginning with Fergus I in c. 3641 B.C. and ending with James V (1513–42). The list was published in *Scots Mag.* [No. 106], 1740 (see also *Grand Tour I*, Heinemann p. 232 n. 1, McGraw-Hill p. 237 n. 1). The phrase was inscribed above the royal arms on the gate of Edinburgh castle as part of the motto about what the '106 proavi' had left unconquered to their descendants (James Grant, *Old and New Edinburgh*, 1882, ii. 73).

[7] Monet or Monnet de Sombrun had served as captain of cavalry in Holland. Originally French, he had been granted the right to residency in Neuchâtel five months

earlier and would remain in that town until 1769 (Schnegg, 29 Jan. 1955). JB does not identify the card game but records a loss of 2 écus (Exp. Acct. 6 Dec., App. 3).

[8] George Bowyer (1739–99) had served in the navy as lieutenant from 1758, commander from 1761, and captain in 1762 while in charge of a frigate. He would enter Parliament in 1784 and occasionally speak in support of the navy. Eventually he would rise to the rank of rear-admiral in 1793, vice-admiral in 1794, and admiral in 1799 (Namier and Brooke, ii. 109). JB described him as having 'the true grave composure of a John Bull' (To JJ, 9 Dec., *Corr. 1*, p. 148).

[9] Splitgerber and Daum informed him that they had forwarded letters sent to them in Berlin (16 Oct.). James Love (for whom see Journ. 18 Aug. n. 5) was sending a letter of introduction, dated 11 Oct., to his brother Nathaniel Dance (1735–1811), later Sir Nathaniel Dance-Holland, who was preparing for a career as portrait painter in Rome and whom JB would meet there several times (Mems. dated 17 Feb., 13 Apr., 24 May 1765). Mme de Spaen, writing from Bellevue, mentioned a 'portrait' written of her by Belle de Zuylen (19 Oct.). Alexander Burnett regretted that he had not found a Spanish gun for JB (20 Oct.) and enclosed a letter from Andrew Mitchell at Spa about keeping Lord Auchinleck abreast of JB's wishes to travel (29 Sept.). Plessen sent coins from Brunswick (20 Oct.). Charles de Guiffardière, a friend from Utrecht, criticized JB's use of French in his recent letter (22 Nov.). Sommelsdyck gave news from The Hague (see From Sommelsdyck, 23 Nov., Yale MS. C 2506). JB would take these letters with him on his further travels, thereby assuring their survival.

[10] The letter from Lord Auchinleck has not been recovered, but here JB offers a moment of unusual warmth and appreciation for his father. Dalrymple was answering a letter of JB's, written in Berlin on 1 Sept., that had set forth his conditions for living in Edinburgh on his return from abroad. Dalrymple agreed that JB should not be just an idle young laird and accepted JB's preference for Anglican worship, but disapproved of JB's plan to live on his own and to travel to London once a year in the manner of Sterne's fictional Tristram Shandy (for JB's admiration of Laurence Sterne and *The Life and Opinions of Tristram Shandy, Gentleman* [1759–67], see *Corr. 9*, p. 30 n. 1, and p. 109 n. 34). Dalrymple made clear that he had not shown the letter to Lord Auchinleck and urged JB 'to form and execute some plan of usefulness' (From Dal-

rymple, 10 Oct., Yale MS. C 1432).
  [11] For John Boswell's earlier decision to
work with a farmer, see Journ. 2 Sept. and n.
4. Evidently his new career plan seemed as
unsatisfactory to JB as John's earlier one. JB
himself had actually tried to play the violin a
few years earlier and had found it too

difficult (see To GD, 19 Nov. 1761, *Corr.* 9,
p. 132 and n. 1; To Rousseau, 31 Dec. 1764,
Yale MS. L 1113, *CC Rousseau*, Letter 3818,
xxii. 344). A receipt, undated, survives for
John's purchase of violin bow, strings, and
bridges in Edinburgh (Yale Gen. MSS. 89,
Series XVII, Box 170).

## Friday 7 December

[MEM. dated 8 Decr.] [Y]esterday slept till near 11 — Capt Bowyer visited you
quite english — Monsieur Suis bien aise & faché de trouver un si aimable Compat
— Je me croyois le plus Sage — Dind Col. Chaillet — A great crowd — Immense
feast, 3 hours at table. Then Partie & Ball. In good enough humour but a little hyp'd
& ruminating madness — This day go immed & visit *Pergo*[1] — Capt. Bowyer then
Col Chaillet — to show attachment. Have a care lest Laird of Auch. grow false like
*Gairlies*.[2] See Mad. *Sando*. Tomorrow early Colombier stay an hour [—] give letter
& seeds we take out[3] — Send Chaillet his louis.[4]

Be Suiss in Italy — make Blue suit with gold Brandenbur.[5]

[J.] Captain Bowyer came & saw me. We spoke french. I said: Monsieur Je
suis bien aise et faché au méme tems de trouver ici un si aimable
Compatriote. Je me piquois d'etre le plus sage de touts nos voyageurs. Mais
vous etes au moins aussi sage que moi. I dined at Colonel Chaillets where
we had a great company & an immense dinner. We were three hours at
table. My Lord Marischal had given me a bill upon Colonel Chaillet. Thus

'Monsieur.
'Il vous plaira payer á M. de Boswell un Bon Poisson cuit á la Suisse; avec
un Bouteille de votre meilleur vin pour votre Serviteur

                                                                    M———'

There is gayeté d'esprit for you. In the evening I went to a private Ball,
where I was tollerably pleased.

  [1] Jean-Frédéric Perregaux (1744–1808)
had studied commerce and banking in Holland and England, and had returned from
London three months earlier (Jean Lhomer
[*sic*], *Lé Banquier Perregaux*, 1926, p. 4 and n.
1; *CC Rousseau*, xxi. 104, 106 note q). His
family had been residents of Neuchâtel since
the fifteenth century. He would leave for
Paris in 1765 and become a respected banker,
heading the newly created French bank.
During the French Revolution he would have
important financial dealings with British
clients (Lüthy, ii. 718–21; Geoffrey de Bel-
laigue, 'Jean-Frederic Perregaux, the Englishman's Best Friend', *Arti Decorative in Europa*,
1986, no. 29–30, pp. 80–90).

  [2] During his harvest jaunt of 1762, JB had
met John Stewart, Viscount Garlies (1736–
1808), the eldest son of Lord Galloway, while
staying at Galloway House on 25–26 Sept.
and had met him again on 28 Sept. as well as
in London on 7 and 19 Dec. (for Garlies, see
also *Scots Peer.* iv. 161–64). JB may have
considered Garlies 'false' because of his
political manoeuvres, whether in spending
large sums to win the parliamentary seat of
Morpeth (which he held 1761–68) contrary
to his father's wishes, or in readily changing
sides from supporting Bute in the peace
negotiations near the end the Seven Years'
War to backing the opposing party when Bute
resigned (see Namier and Brooke, iii. 481).

[3] JB was taking the seeds that Lord Marischal had enclosed with his letter of c. 9 Sept. Lord Marischal liked to send these and similar simple gifts to his friends (e.g., melon seeds and tobacco to Frederick of Prussia from Neuchâtel; see *Œuvres de Frédéric le Grand*, n.d. [1760–61], xx. 281–82).

[4] No such sum is recorded in JB's Expense Account, which does however show that JB gave 6 Batzen to Chaillet's servant (Exp.

Acct. 8 Dec., App. 3).

[5] MS. 'From 'Be Suiss' to 'Brandebur' written along the left margin. 'Brandenburgs' (usually pl.) were 'ornamental facings' on the breast of an officer's coat. The term was first used for the decorations on the uniforms worn by officers of the Elector of Brandenburg, later Friedrich I, King of Prussia (1657–1713), OED, s.v. 'Brandenburg'.

## Saturday 8 December

[MEM. dated Sunday 9 Decr.] [Y]esterday waited on Mad. la Col Sando smart & clever made her talk & got her confession of faith did wrong to tell faults of Zelide. At 3 visited madl Prevost compos'd & polite — Saw Portrait of Zelide — recalled her at night saw one of her letters — talkd of fables sanglantes. D'Hermanches Ami genereux — saw her a hairbraind girl glad not to have her. What is her Genius? 'Tis like playing on a fiddle.

[J.] I waited on Madame la Colonelle Sando whose Husband I had seen at the Hague. She was a smart clever woman. I delivered her My Lord Marischal's Compliments. She was very frank with me, & gave me her confession of faith without reserve. It was much that of Rousseau.[1] After dinner she carried me to wait of[2] Mademoiselle Prevost whom I was very desirous to see, as she had in some measure educated Zelide, having been with her from eight to thirteen, & carried her to Geneva. She was a polite old maiden, & praised much her fair freind.[3] I was in the wrong in talking too freely of Zelide's faults both to madame Sando, & Mademoiselle Prevost. I saw here a Portrait of Zelide which brought her full to my mind, & with unusual grace.[4] I loved her. I called on Captain Bowyer, and sat some time there, & past the evening at Colonel Chaillet's where I found Mademoiselle Prevost who shewed me a Letter from Zelide in which she talked of her having written des fables sanglantes,[5] & called the Libertine d'Hermanches son Ami genereux.[6] I saw her to be a vapourish unprincipled girl. I was happy not to be connected with her. I supt here very jolly. Chaillet recounted his acts of severity in military discipline. He made us all shudder.

[1] Marie-Frédérique-Anne (Bada) Sandoz (1717–92) divided her time between her native Holland and Neuchâtel, where she presided over a literary salon. Lord Marischal had declared her 'worth the whole toune of Geneva, men, women, and children' (From Lord Marischal, 17 Oct., Yale MS. C 1950). She and her friends greatly admired Rousseau's religious ideas as expressed by his Savoyard vicar, and one of her friends proclaimed enthusiastically that she combined the best traits of Rousseau's St. Preux, Julie, and Claire, the chief characters in *La nouvelle Héloïse* (see Eduard Bodemann, *Julie von Bondeli und ihr Freundeskreis*, 1874, pp. 297–98). Her husband, not mentioned in JB's surviving notes from Holland, was Claude-François Sandoz (1715–90; first names as given by Schnegg, 29 Jan. 1955, and Armand du Pasquier, MN n.s. 20 [1933]: 145). Sandoz held the titles of colonel of infantry, major, and captain of the elite regiment of Swiss Guards in the service of the United Provinces, which had been formed in 1748 to add glamour to military ceremonies (AEN; Vallière, p. 573).

This identification of both husband and wife corrects *Grand Tour I*, index.

[2] 'Wait of': 'call on, pay one's respects to' (CSD, s.v. 'wait').

[3] Jeanne-Louise Prevost (1721–85) had been Belle de Zuylen's governess from 1748 to 1753 and had accompanied her to Geneva and Paris in about 1750 (Courtney, pp. 40–43). A Genevan by birth, Mme Prevost was now living in Neuchâtel with a woman friend (OC Charrière, i. 627).

[4] The 'portrait' was presumably one of two mentioned in Mlle Prevost's letters but not recovered: an unknown artist's, showing Belle de Zuylen aged fifteen, or a self-portrait, showing her looking grave (To Belle de Zuylen, Letter 32, 10 Mar. 1755, and Letter 58, 28 Dec. 1758, OC Charrière, i. 67, 116, 537 n. 3).

[5] 'Outrageous stories' (see Littré, s.v. 'sanglant', 7: 'très offensant, très outrageux'). Several of Belle's short stories were being passed around at this time, but those referred to here are not further identified (From Baroness von Spaen, 23 Jan. 1765, Yale MS. C 2519; Belle de Zuylen to Baron Adolf Werner C. W. van Pallandt, 21 Oct.; see Courtney, p. 131). The best known, 'Le Noble', had been published anonymously in Amsterdam in 1763 in the Journal étranger, combiné avec L'Année littéraire and reprinted a few months later in a separate volume, which had been withdrawn almost immediately at the insistence of her parents. It satirized dull, strait-laced aristocrats and described a young girl's interest in love with unusual frankness (see Courtney, pp. 120–21). JB retained a copy in his library in Edinburgh (Lincoln, p. 290).

[6] David-Louis, baron de Constant de Rebecque (1722–85), styled Constant d'Hermenches, of a prominent family in Lausanne, had served in his father's Swiss regiment in the Netherlands from 1736, first as ensign, then as captain in 1742 and as his father's adjutant from 1743. D'Hermenches now cut a dashing figure with a black headband over his forehead covering a wound he had incurred at the battle of Fontenoy in 1745. He had been married since 1744 but spent little time with his wife and children, who lived in Lausanne (see Journ. 21 Dec. and n. 10). He had also fathered a daughter out of wedlock in 1753. Doubtful about his chances for advancement in Holland, he would enter the service of France in a few months' time (Courtney, pp. 60–61; 'Constant, Constant de Rebecque', Recueil de Généalogies Vaudoises, 1950, iii. 213–15).

Belle de Zuylen had met him at a ball in Feb. 1760 and had begun a secret correspondence with him when they met again two years later. Their letters had become intimate and self-revelatory by 1763 as d'Hermenches expressed his frustrations about his career while she sought advice about her various suitors (Courtney, pp. 74–80, 142–48). In what Courtney calls 'the most celebrated of all her letters' she frankly stated that she had been warned about his libertinage, was well aware of his insinuating ways, but intended to retain a relationship that pleased her while she remained virtuous and loyal to whatever husband she would choose (Belle de Zuylen to d'Hermenches, 25 July, Letter 107, OC Charrière, i. 217–17). By this time she had already turned down a cousin, Frederik Christiaan Hendrick van Tuyll Serooskerken (1742–1805), and Baron Christian von Brömbse (1742–1808), a nobleman from Holstein. She was not seriously interested in JB—who had left five weeks earlier— despite moments of warmth and attraction between them, and she had just asked Count Anhalt to give up his plan of wooing her in person (From D. J. van Tuyll, Heer van Zuylen, 11 Dec., Yale MS. C 3175; see Journ. 3 July n. 6). She was beginning to consider a new marital prospect, for whom see Journ. 26 Dec. n. 5.

## Sunday 9 December

[MEM. dated Monday 10 Decr.] Yesterday had been up late, lay long — Home all day writing. Col. Chaill came — many storys. This day pack neat prepare seeds for Colombier.

[J.] I had taken leave of[1] this People last night, with intention to go today; But, Jacob did not arrive as he had promised; so I past the day at home close writing. Chaillet however came & sat an hour with me, and told me many tales of his political prowess while in the Sardinian Service. He has been a bold active pushing fellow. At night Jacob arrived.

[1] MS. 'of' inserted after 'leave'

## Monday 10 December

[MEM. dated 11 Decr.] [Y]esterday at 1 walk'd to Colombier. Maison du Village Sœur de Lisette jolie fraiche aimable — Said she'd go to Scotland — Sent for Ibrahim — came, little brown Turk — Je suis vapoureux — Stepan the old Calmuc — Ibrahim — Nous avons eté par tout. Á la fin nous avons tombé ici dans un trou. Waited on Madlle. Morel — pas brillant soft sweet uniform — Brother Col: jolly — supt well quite at ease — Gave bed — tir'd a little[,] the *whole* ev'ning dreaded visits in Scotland. This day, see Chateau.

[J.] At twelve I walked out two leagues to Colombier, leaving orders for a chaise to take me up next morning.[1] I went to the Maison de Village kept by the Father of Madame Froment's Lisette. Her Sister Caton served me up a good Suiss dinner.[2] I asked her 'Voulez vous aller en Ecosse?' She said: 'Oui Monsieur. Je ne veux rester ici.' She pleased me. Ibrahim the Turk whom My Lord Marischal educated with Ameté came to see me. He was to be a Painter, but became Hypochondriack & has a Pension from My Lord. He was a little dark dog, laugh'd immoderately & said Je suis vapoureux. But talked not amiss. Old Stepan the Calmuc whom My Lord had also from his Brother Marischal Keith, was here. He was long My Lord's Valet de Chambre, but drank so, that he was no longer to be trusted & now has also a Pension. Innumerable are the instances of My Lord's Goodness. Ibrahim looked at Stepan & said 'Nous avons beaucoup voyagé. Nous avons roule le Globe, et á la fin nous sommes tombé ici dans un trou'.[3] I then waited on Mademoiselle Morel to whom My Lord Marischal had given me a letter. She was not very young, but was soft mild chearfull & uniform, & attached to My Lord like a Scots Lass.[4] Her Brother who had been a Colonel in the Sardinian Service was jolly and civil.[5] I was just in a Country family in our own good Island. To sit all the evening here seemed severe. I dreaded the idea of the visits[6] which I must yet make in Scotland. They insisted that I should stay in their house.

[1] Colombier was a small village 6.5 km (4 miles) west of Neuchâtel (Baedeker, *Die Schweiz*, p. 267). JB's walk must have taken him along Lake Neuchâtel, then uphill along an impressive avenue of trees planted in 1657 to mark the visit of the previous ruler, Henri II (1595–1663) de Longueville (DHBS, ii. 547).

[2] The local inn in the 'maison de village' was run by Johannes Otz, who was also a master butcher. His daughters Elisabeth (Lisette) and Catarina (Caton, b. 1737) were two of seven children (Jean Grellet, 'L'ancien hotel de Commune de Colombier', *MN* 25 [1888]: 144–48; AEB, K Oberbalm 3). Lisette had evidently worked for Mme de Froment while the latter resided at the chateau at Colombier (see Journ. 3 July n. 12).

[3] Ibrahim and Stepan had been captured by Marshal Keith in the Russian campaign against the Turks in 1737, and had been passed on to his brother as servants (see Journ. 18 June n. 7, 3 Dec. n. 37; Cuthell, i. 175, 185–86). Ibrahim was possibly a Tartar (Cuthell, i. 186). He had also claimed to be a 'mussulman of the race of the grand lama'; that is, a Moslem descended from the high priest of Tibet or Mongolia (OED, s.v. 'lama'). Joking about this origin, Lord Marischal had dubbed him a 'great almoner' and had put him in charge of distributing charitable gifts (J.-H. Bonhôte, 'Un Gouverneur de Neuchâtel, Milord Marischal', *MN* 1 [1864]: 47). He had become a Christian convert and, taking the name Georges-Abraham Ibrahim, would live out his days at Colombier (Schnegg, 8 Mar. 1955). An orchard close to the chateau would still be known as 'the garden of Ibrahim' two centuries later (Marlies K. Danziger's personal

visit, 6 June 1990). Stepan's background was so unfamiliar that Lord Wemyss described him as a 'Calmouc Tartar', thereby merging the names of two separate though related groups originally from western Mongolia (Elcho, p. 58; see 'Kalmuk', *The Encyclopaedia of Islam*, new ed. 1978, iv. 512). During his visit, JB found Stepan 'a most sober man' (To Lord Marischal, 20 Jan. 1765).

[4] Either Marie-Françoise Morel (1722–82) or her younger sister Marie Louise Morel (1723–1818). They were the daughters of François Morel (1685–1765) of Colombier, an officer in Spanish service (Schnegg, 29 Jan. 1955). Lord Marischal often sent Mlle Morel his 'compliments' at the end of his letters to other friends (e.g., From Lord Marischal, 18 Nov., Yale MS. C 1951; To Samuel Meuron [1703–77], the administrator, then public prosecutor, of Neuchâtel, AEN, 'Correspondance' #51, 1764). JB, repeating the words of his journal, would soon assure Lord Marischal that 'Mademoiselle Morel is very amiable and is attached to your Lordship like a Scots Lass' (To Lord Marischal, 20 Jan. 1765, Yale MS. L 953).

[5] François Morel (1725–1805) was now a lieutenant-colonel of the Neuchâtel militia (Schnegg, 29 Jan. 1955; *OC Charrière*, ii. 642).

[6] MS. 'visists'

## Tuesday 11 December

[MEM. dated 12 Decr.] Yesterday went to Inn — ask'd *Caton* if serious to go in a year. Oui — on m'a maltraité chez Milord Wemys. Je me suis marié par chagrin. Je n'aimoit jamais mon Mari. Il depensoit son bien. Il s'en alloit. Je puis avoir ma divorce. A fine fresh amiable Suiss lass pleas'd. You said: vous comprenez ce que Je veux — Oui Monsr[.] disposera de moi — Je vous crois le plus digne homme. Eh bien Je ne m'engage pas, mais si cela se peut Je vous ecrirai et a Madame la Colonêlle. Quite Adventure [—] drove to Yverdun Sr J. Kinloch campagne. This day B. Brakel in white — Be Marischal.

[J] I went to the Inn & found Caton. Etiez vous serieuse quand vous disiez que vous irez avec moi en Ecosse? 'Oui Monsieur. Jetois chez M——— une jeune fille; <…> me forçer. J'echappois[1] — Je me suis marié par chagrin. Je n'aimois jamais mon mari — Il depensoit son bien. Il s'en alloit. Je puis avoir un divorçe.[2] Je voudrois être loin. J'irois avec un Monsieur a qui Je serois attaché. Je vous crois parfait digne homme.' 'Mais[3] vous comprenez sur quel pied vous serez avec moi. Je ne voudrois pas vous tromper.' 'Oui. Monsieur disposera de moi comme il veut'. She had two pretty children & was a fine fresh Suiss Lass. I said Eh bien. Je ne m'engage pas; mais si Je le trouve apropos, Je vous ecrirai. Mademoiselle Morel carried me to see the Chateau of Colombier where My Lord Marischal lived. It is a large old Building & inspired me with Scottish ideas.[4] At eleven I set out, and had a good drive to Yverdun.[5] I sent a card to Sir James Kinloch, who was still at his Country seat.[6] My Inn at the maison de Village was very bad. Two hours before supper the maid brought me Bread & Cheese and a bottle of wine. I was somewhat surprised and asked the meaning of this. She said 'C'est pour gouter. Est ce que vous ne voulez pas gouter?'[7] I found to *gouter* was a custom in Switzerland, where they eat from morning to night. I complied with the rule & did as others do.

[1] MS. 'Jetois … J'echappois' scored out by a modern hand. The passage, except for a single word preceding 'me forçer', is still decipherable. The long dash following 'M' stands for the name. As revealed in the memorandum for this day, the seducer had been David Elcho, *styled* Lord Wemyss (correcting *Grand Tour 1* index). He had pur-

chased an estate close to Lord Marischal at the latter's suggestion, and thanks to him had obtained the necessary papers to reside there ('Lettre de naturalité' in 1754, permission to 'prendre bourgeoisie' in Neuchâtel in 1760, AEN, *Actes de Chancellerie*, vol. 26, fols. 340–42, 546–47). Presumably he had met Caton soon after Nov. 1758 during his first stay in his new house (Elcho, p. 240). Caton's accusation confirms his reputation as a libertine. He had fathered at least two illegitimate daughters during his travels in Italy (Evan Charteris, 'Memoir of David Elcho', *A Short Account of the Affairs of Scotland in the Years 1744, 1745, 1746 by David Elcho*, 1907, pp. 129, 140). Wemyss also however hoped to marry wealth and, undaunted by several rejections, would later express an interest in Belle de Zuylen, who would hear that he was 'fort libertin' and had brought another illegitimate daughter to stay with him (D'Hermenches to Belle de Zuylen, 25 May 1770, OC *Charrière*, ii. 188 and 556 n. 1; G. R. de Beer, 'Lord Wemyss à Cotendard', *MN* n.s. 37 [1950]: 183–86). In spite of this report and without having met Wemyss, Belle would threaten to accept his proposal, thereby gaining her father's permission to marry her brothers' tutor, Charles-Emmanuel de Charrière (1735–1808), the man she really wanted (see Courtney, pp. 264–72).

[2] No record of Catherine Otz's marriage has been found in Neuchâtel or Colombier, nor is her divorce traceable without her husband's name (letter from AEB, 17 Apr. 1991).

[3] MS. 'Je ... divorce', 'J'irois ... attaché', 'Mais' scored out by a modern hand.

[4] The chateau, in a commanding position overlooking the lake, was built around a quadrangle and looked like a fortified Scottish house. Begun in the fourteenth century, it had been repaired in the sixteenth century and had been renovated again by Lord Marischal, who preferred it to the chateau in Neuchâtel (Cuthell, ii. 8, 14; DHBS, ii. 547–48).

[5] A distance of about 30 km, or 18.6 miles (Baedeker, *Die Schweiz*, p. 266).

[6] For Sir James Kinloch, see Journ. 13 Dec. n. 2; for his country seat at Giez, see Journ. 16 Dec. and n. 1).

[7] To have a light meal between dinner and supper (Littré, s.v. 'goûter', 2).

## Wednesday 12 December

[MEM. dated Thursday 13 Decr.] [Y]esterday morning waited on Baron de Brackel reserved handsom manly figure between 40 & 50. Quite man of world. Letter from Madll Kinloch [M]adame de Brackel, tall, beautifull, easy, gay; din'd well: quite man of fashion — [M]adame de *Copie* & Husband quiet mortals — Cards easy Society. Supt well — Talk'd free — own'd former Mimicry. But had given it up. To bed in calm spirits. Had heard of Ld. [M]arischal's changeable disposition. It consol'd me. This day see linnen for shirts &c.

[J.] I waited on the Baron de Brackel [—] Son in law to Sir James Kinloch. I found him a man about fifty a good manly figure grave, reserv'd polite, quite a man of the world. He insisted that I should come & live in his house.[1] He had been much with Lord Marischal,[2] & he told me that My Lord could not stay long in a Place without taking a dislike to it, & that he was of a most changeable disposition. This consoled me. He gave me a letter from Mademoiselle Kinloch at Utrecht. It was simple & gay, and amused me.[3] I was presented to Madame de Brackel a tall handsom charming Woman. They had a Child of some months old a fine Boy.[4] We dined genteely. After dinner came Madame De Copé another sister & her Husband [—] good quiet People.[5] Company came, & Cards employed the evening. I found myself in an excellent family, supt & was pleased.

[1] Frédéric-Casimir de Brackel (1715–79), married to Louise ('Lisette') Madeleine Kinloch (1733–1814) since 1757, was the brother-in-law of Catherine (Kinloch) Brown (b.

1736) and the Rev. Robert Brown of Utrecht. The Baron had left his native Courland as a political refugee in 1727 and had settled in Yverdon (see Wagner, p. 200; for his earlier life, see Journ. 18 Dec. and n. 8). His house in Clendy-dessus was on the outskirts of the town (*CC Rousseau*, Letter 2083, 17 Aug. 1762, xii. 199 note b). By 'live', JB means 'stay with'.

² Brackel had developed a warm friendship with Lord Marischal while the latter was governor of Neuchâtel and was continuing it by an amiable correspondence (see Dossier F. C. de Brackel, MS. BPUN, 1595; *CC Rousseau*, Letter 2083, 17 Aug. 1762, xii. 199 note b).

³ The letter, signed 'Nanette', was from Anne, also called Anne-Susanne (1742–1813), with whom JB had become friendly in Utrecht (French theme, c. 2–3 Nov. 1763, Yale MS. M 87, quoted in *Holland*, Heinemann pp. 58–59, McGraw-Hill pp. 59–60). Nanette, the younger sister of Catherine Brown, gave news of their mutual friends and was especially laudatory about Belle de Zuylen, whose poem 'Heureux moineaux' she enclosed in copy (see Yale MS. C 1662, *Catalogue*, ii. 739). Nanette would marry JB's friend Jean-Christophe-Guillaume de Rham (1733–1812) in 1774, and they would settle

near her family in Yverdon twelve years later. Her first name is confirmed by her husband's family records (Pierre de Rham, *La Famille de Rham*, 1965, pp. 109–10, 114, where de Rham refers to Jean-Christophe-Guillaume de Rham's wife as 'Anne [dite Nanette] Kinlock') and by a list of persons appearing before the notary François Amiet, 4 Sept. 1789 (ACV, not. Grandson), correcting the identification 'Marguerite Susanne' in Wagner (p. 200), as accepted by G. R. de Beer ('Sir James Kinloch à Giez', *RHV* 59 [1951]: 65) as well as *Holland* (Heinemann p. 410, McGraw-Hill p. 419), *Grand Tour I* (Heinemann p. 244 n. 1, McGraw-Hill p. 250 n. 7), *Catalogue*, ii. 739, and *Corr. 5*, p. 10 n. 6. For Marguerite Susanne, see Journ. 16 Dec. and n. 9.

⁴ Lisette de Brackel had given birth to a son, Henri Frédéric, six months earlier. He was the de Brackels' third child, of the seven they would have by 1771 (ACV, 'Brackel', Eb141¹² p. 151; Wagner, p. 200).

⁵ Rose-Marguerite de Coppet (1735–89), the third daughter of Sir James Kinloch, had been married since 1756 to Charles-Louis de Coppet (1730–95) of Yverdon (ACV, Eb59² p. 418). They had two of their four children by this time (Wagner, pp. 200, 261).

## Thursday 13 December

[MEM. dated Friday 14 Decr.] [Y]esterday Madame de Brackel chose Shirts for you. Proud to receive civilitys from so fine a woman. Beautifull Picture of family felicity. Was in rage against [P]arisian corruption of manners; resolv'd to support conjugal virtue. At 12 Sr. J[.] Kinloch waited on you. Honest East Lothian Gentleman. Was just his man to talk of farming — Rushes to destroy — Soot — perhaps only that of wood — try coals. Din'd well — Waited on Baillif with M. Brackel. — Cards chez———. Supt chearfull — M Brackel [—] talk'd of Paris & rude Londres. This day ¹ mountain Rousseau.

[J.] I lay down last night in calm easy spirits, & I got up this morning in the same happy frame. Madame de Brackel chose Suiss linnen & employed a proper Semstress to make shirts for me. Allready was I upon an easy footing here. I was proud to receive civilitys from so fine a woman. I saw here a beautifull picture of family felicity. I was in an honest rage against Corruption of manners, & I resolved to do my best to support conjugal virtue. At twelve Sir James Kinloch waited upon me. He has been 30 years in this country; but remains the old Scotsman, just an East Lothian Suiss Laird.² He is a most excellent farmer. I contrived to make conversation go well on upon Country Affairs. He said that here Lime cost them about half a crown a Boll.³ I complained to him that we had at Auchinleck a fine grass field destroyed by rushes which made it necessary to plow it up every two or three years. He told me of an infallible remedy which he had found in an old french Book of Husbandry. To lay upon the field a sufficient quantity of Soot. He said he had tried it, & found it succeed. He said that perhaps the soot of coals would not have the same effect as that of wood; but I might try.[4] He dined with us; after which M. de Brackel presented me au Chateau to The Baillif a most sensible knowing respected man.[5] We past the evening at cards chez ———— & supt at home.

[1] MS. Blank, presumably for the name, 'Lapidosa' (see Journ. 14 Dec. n. 8).

[2] Sir James Kinloch (1705–78) was the eldest son of a well-established family in Gilmerton. As a young man he had been entrapped by a woman who had claimed him as her legal husband according to Scottish custom after he had declared his affection (even though he had been drunk). Undeterred by her demands, he had married Margaret Foulis, daughter of William Foulis of Woodhall, in Apr. 1730. But the threat of prosecution for bigamy had caused him to leave Scotland almost immediately, and his wife was presumed to have died soon afterwards (see Comp. Bar. iv. 346–47; G. R. de Beer, 'Sir James Kinloch à Giez', RHV 59 [1951]. 62). In Oct. 1731 Sir James had married Anne Marguerite Wild of Bern, with whom he had eleven children, and two years later he had been received bourgeois in Giez (Notaires de Grandson, no. 2, Amiet, register 1718–1736, p. 158). He would leave the succession to his father's title to a younger brother while enjoying friendly relations with various family members, who visited him in Giez (de Beer, p. 62). Yet his first wife lived on in Scotland, as was known to Lord Auchinleck, who had warned JB not to mention the 'macula natalium' (birth stain, illegitimacy) of Kinloch's daughter Catherine Brown in Utrecht (From Lord Auchinleck, c. 10 Dec. 1763, Yale MS. C 224; CC Rousseau, xii. 199 note b). JB's meeting with Sir James was raucous and enjoyable: 'I talked braid Scots with him, & sung him Sherrifmuir & made him as merry, as if I had poured a bottle of whisky down his throat' (To JJ, 19 Dec., Corr. 1, p. 150 and n. 3). The song chosen by JB, about the final battle of the 1715 rising, suggests that Sir James had Jacobite sympathies.

[3] Lime was widely used also in Scotland to reduce the acidity of the soil (T. M. Devine, The Transformation of Rural Scotland, c. 1994, p. 54). A boll was a dry measure in cubic inches, consisting of six 'imperial bushels'— that is, six times 2218.19 cubic inches (OED, s.v. 'boll' and 'bushel')—but varying somewhat according to what was being measured (see the Glossary, Corr. 8, App. 3, p. 235).

[4] Rushes—marsh grasses that choked the good grass usable for pasturage—were difficult to root out and presented a perennial problem in Ayrshire (William Fullarton, General View of the Agriculture of Ayr, 1793, pp. 31–32). How such rushes could be eliminated by soot, the residue left from the burning of wood or coal, is not clear. The old French book on agriculture has not been identified, nor is there any evidence that JB would try its system on his own estate when, twenty years later, rushes would have to be cleared from Barnsdale Park and lime would be spread as usual (From Bruce, 6 Dec. 1783, Corr. 8, p. 73).

[5] Victor de Gingins (1708–76), seigneur de Moiry, had been elected bailiff of Yverdon in 1758 and would serve in that position for one more year ('Journal of Pillichody', BP Yverdon, fol. 144). He also had literary interests, having written a historical novel, Bacha de Bude (1762), and several political memoirs (DHBS, iii. 418). And he evidently liked to tell anecdotes, one of which, about Voltaire, is quoted in Boswelliana, p. 235.

## Friday 14 December

[MEM. dated Saturday 15 Decr.] Yesterday set out at 8 — past monstrous mountain 13[1] hours & half — alighted [M]otiers. Madll. Vasseur — Je demanderais. Entrez — 'Je suis accablé des maux des chagrins et de tristesse. Sond toujours. Chacun croit que Je dois m'occuper de lui — J'ai lu votre memoire — vous avez eté fariné — ne voyez jamais un Prêtre — mais est il possible que Je soye quelque chose? Oui — la grande difficulté est qui vous le croyez si difficile —

Retournez l'après Midi — mais mettez votre montre sur la table — Pour combien de tems —? un quart heure — answerd[2] vingt minutes [—] allez — non obstant pain laughd [—] quite charming Incident [—] din'd Inn old room & Company walk'd out [—] all water. 4 Rousseau. J'ai qu'un moment. Il faut le bien employer — Est-il possible de vivre parmi les hommes singulier; oui — Je lai fait [—] mais être bien avec eux[?] Ah si vous voulez etre loup il faut hurler — Je fais fort peu de cas des livres — meme vos propres — oui Barbouillage.[3] Ah — vous hourlez — Balloté — ou avons nous donc de fixe — (struck head) mais vous n'aurrez medité si bien si vous n'aviez lu — Non J'aurrais me dite mieux si J'avois commencé plutot. Moral incertain 30 femmes [—] vous faites Madll. sortir. — [M]ais oui — Ah vous aurrez des Jalousie des perfidies des Infidelités — mais dans l'orient — alors vous avez de l'esclavage — et ces femmes font rien que du mal au lieu que les notre font beaucoup travaillent beaucoup. Mais Patriarchs. Mais les loix de votre Societé — non non — il ne faut vous choisir un loix d'ici un autre dela. Il faut prendre celles de votre Societe — remplissez vos devoirs en Citoyen & vous serez respecté si vous tenez ferme. Pour votre dame, quand vous retournez — dites — Cela est contre ma conscience [—] elle vous louera — si non elle est meprisable. Mais si elle menace de dire 1st elle ne le fera. 2. ne faites un mal pour un bien. Mais — pour expier mal — Ah. <...>[4] d'expiation du mal est le bien. Mais est on meilleur [—] oui quand nous sommes spirituelles — J'ai deja vecu comme cela — au lieu que les viles passions du corps.

Histoire — amusements — Loix d'[E]cosse oui ces sont vos outils [—] etes vous gourmand — Je voulois briguer —[5]

To study music.[6]


[J.] At eight I got on Horseback & had for my Guide a Smith called Dupuis. I said Depuis quand avez vous[7] eu ce nom? I past the Mountain Lapidosa which is monstrously steep & in a great measure covered with snow.[8] I was going to Rousseau which consideration levelled the roughest mountains. I arrived at Motiers before noon. I alighted at Rousseau's door. Up & I went & found Mademoiselle Vasseur who told me 'Il est tres malade.' Mais PuisJe le voir un instant? 'Je verrais. Entrez Monsieur.' I found him sitting in great pain. 'Je suis accable de maux de chagrins, et de tristésse. J'ai un Sond.[9] Chacun croit que Je dois m'occuper á lui.' Cela est tres naturel. Et netes vous bien aise de trouver que vous pouvez tant aider les autres? 'Mais'. I had left with him when I was last here what I called 'une Ebauche de ma vie', in which I gave him the important incidents of my History & my melancholy apprehensions & begged his advice & freindship. It was an interesting Piece.[10] He said. 'J'ai lu votre memoire. Vous avez eté enfariné. Ne voyez jamais un Pretre.'[11] Mais est il possible que Je puisse encore etre quelque chose? 'Oui. La grande difficulté c'est que vous le croyez si difficile. Revenez l'aprés midi; mais mettez votre montre sur la table.' Pour combien du tems? 'Un quart d'heure, pas davantage.' Vingt minutes. 'Allez vous en — ha — ha —' notwithstanding the pain he was in he was touched with my singular sally & laughed most realy. He had a gay look immediatly. I dined in my old Room with the two Boarders.[12] After dinner I walked out. There had fallen much rain, & the Vallon was all overflowed. Nature looked somewhat different from the time that I was first here. I was sorry that such a scene was subject to any change. At four I went to M. Rousseau. 'Je n'ai qu'un moment. Il faut le bien employer.' Est il possible de vivre parmi les hommes et d'etre singulier? 'Oui Je l'ai fait.' Mais d'etre bien avec eux? 'Ah si vous voulez etre Loup il faut hurler.[13] Je fais fort peu de cas de livres.' Même de vos propres Livres? 'O des Barbouillages.' Ah vous hurlez. 'Quand Je me fiois aux livres Jetois balloté comme vous[. Q]uoique c'etoit plutot par des conversations que vous avez eté balloté — Je n'avois rien de fixé ici (striking his head) avant que Je commençois á mediter.' Mais vous n'aurrez medité si bien si vous n'eussiez lu. 'Non! J'aurrois mieux medité si J'avois commencé plustot.' Mais par example Je n'aurrois jamais eu les idées agreables que J'aye de la religion Chretiénne si Je n'avois lu la Profession de foi du Savoyard. Mais en verité Je ne voye pas aucun Systeme certain. Le moral me paroit incertain. Par example: Je voudrois avoir trente femmes. Ne pourrois Je pas avoir cela — 'Non.—' Pourquoi? 'Ha! ha! Si Mademoiselle n'etoit pas ici Je vous donnerois une raison tres suffisante pourquoi.' Mais. Voyez vous, si Je suis riche. Je prends une nombre de filles. Je fais des enfants avec elles. La Propagation donc est augmenté. Je leur donne des dotes et Je les marie aux bons Paisans qui les prennent tres volontiers. Ainsi elles deviennent des Epouses á la même age qu'elles aurroient fait si elles eussent restés viêrges, et moi J'ai eu l'avantage de jouir d'une grande varieté de femmes.[14] 'Ah! vous aurrez des jalousies, des infidelités des perfidies.' Mais ne PuisJe faire comme dans l'orient? 'La les femmes sont renfermés [—] il faut donc avoir de l'esclavage et faites attention que leurs femmes ne font rien que du mal; au lieu que les notres font beaucoup du bien, travaillent beaucoup.' Mais Je voudrois faire comme les ançiens Patriarchs des braves Gens dont Je respecte la memoire. 'Mais n'etes vous Citoyen? Il ne faut pas prendre un loi ci et un loi la: Il faut prendre les loix de votre Soçieté; Remplissez vos devoirs en Citoyen, et vous serez respecté, si vous vous tenez ferme.[15] Je ne le dirois pas; mais Je le ferois. Et pour votre dame — Quand vous retournez en Ecosse vous direz "Madame cela est contre ma conscience et Je ne le ferai plus." Elle vous louera; si non elle est meprisable.'[16] Mais si sa passion soit encore forte et elle menace de dire á son mari ce qui est passé, si Je refuse de continuer notre amour. 'Premierrement elle ne le dira pas. En second lieu il ne faut pas faire un mal pour un bien.' Oui. Je puis pourtant supposer des circonstances fort embarrassantes. — Et dites moi comment puisJe faire expiation pour le mal que J'ai commi. 'Ah Monsieur il n y a point d'expiation pour le mal que le bien.' A beautifull thought this. Nevertheless I maintained my doctrine of satisfaction by Punishment. Yes I must ever think that immutable Justice requires attonement to be made for transgressions, and this attonement is to be made by suffering. This is the universal idea of all nations, & seems to be a leading principle of Christianity.[17] I gave myself full scope; for, since I left England I have not had any body to whom I could lay open entirely my mind till I found M. Rousseau. I asked him quand Je serais en [F]rance & en Italie ne puisJe pas jouir de leur gallanterie ou les maris ne prennent pas mal que vous faites

283

l'amour á leur femmes. Même ne seraiJepas plus heureux d'etre d'une nation comme cela? 'Ils sont des cadavres. Voulez vous etre un Cadavre?' He was right. Mais dites moi, un homme qui est vertueux a-t-il[18] veritablement des avantages est il reellement mieux qu'un homme livré a la sensualité? 'Sans doute. Nous sommes des etres spirituelles et quand notre ame sera echappé de ce prison de ce chair l'homme vertueux[19] se trouvera bien. Il verra avec plaisir les nobles emplois des esprits heureux. Il dira J'ai deja vecu comme cela. Au lieu que ceux qui ne connoissent que les viles Passions qui viennent du corps, seront mecontens de voir des plaisirs qu'ils ne savent gouter.'[20] Ma foi Je ne sais comment faire dans ce monde. Je ne sais si Je dois me donner á quelque Profession ou non. 'Il faut avoir un grand Plan.' Mais les Etudes dont on fait tant de cas. L'histoire par example. 'Ces sont des Amusements.' Mon Pere veut que Je plaide devant une cour de Justice en Ecosse. Il est certain que Je fais bien de contenter mon Pere. Il n'est pas certain que Je fais bien si Je suis mes inclinations legêres. Il faut donc que Je m'applique á l'etude des loix d'Ecosse. 'Assurement ces sont vos outils. Si vous voulez etre menusier, il vous faut un Rabaud.' Je suis mal avec mon Pere. Je ne suis pas á mon aise. 'Pour cela il faut avoir quelque amusement commun.' Nous plantons ensemble. 'Cela est trop serieux. Il faut un Amusement que vous mette sur un pied plus egal, par example de tirer á la chasse alors on manque, on badine, mais avec decence, Il y a une liberté sans y penser. Quand on s'est une fois engagé dans une Profession, il faut y continuer quoique on voye ce qu'il paroit une meilleure, car, si on est changeant on ne peut rien faire.'[21] (I should have observed that when I pushed the conversation on women Mademoiselle went out, & M. Rousseau said 'voyez, vous faites sortir Mademoiselle.' She was now returned) He stopped, & looked at me in a singular manner. 'Etes vous gourmand?' Oui. 'J'en suis faché.' Ha! ha! Je badinois parceque vous etes pour la gourmandise dans vos ouvrages.[22] Je sais ce que vous allez dire c'est justement ce que Je souhaitois. Je voulois briguer votre soupe. J'avois grande envie de manger avec vous. 'Eh bien si vous n'etes pas Gourmand, voulez vous diner ici demain. Mais Je vous avertis que vous serez mal'. Non Je ne serai pas mal. Mais Je suis au dessus de toutes ces choses la. 'Venez á midi, alors nous aurrons du tems á causer.' Bien de remerciments. 'Bon Soir.' Mademoiselle carried me to the house of a poor woman with a great many children whom M. Rousseau aids with his charity. I contributed my part.[23] I was not pleased to hear Mademoiselle repeat to the Poor Woman just the common consolatory sayings. She should have said something singular.

---

[1] MS. '13' written inadvertently for '3' (see the beginning of the journal for this date).
[2] MS. 'answerd' squeezed in before 'vingt minutes'
[3] MS. 'Barbouillage' inserted above the line.
[4] MS. Half a line deleted by JB
[5] MS. 'Histoire … briguer —' written along the left margin.
[6] MS. These three words inserted upside

down between the date and the first line. Rousseau had devoted almost as much time to music as to literature and had declared his love of music as consuming a passion as love itself (Confessions, Bk. V, OC Rousseau, i. 219). His writings included 360 articles on musical theory and practice, which he had contributed to the Encyclopédie in 1749 and had expanded for his ambitious dictionary of music, finally completed in this year and published in 1767 (Eigeldinger, 'Dictionnaire de musique', and R. Court, 'Musique', *Dict. de Rousseau*, pp. 213–16, 634–40).

[7] MS. 'vou'

[8] Not a mountain, 'Lapidouze' was a pasturage and farm named for the family Pidoux who had previously owned this property (see Daniel Roguin to Rousseau, 20 Sept. 1763, CC *Rousseau*, Letter 2927, xvii. 259 note e). Situated at the top of an extremely steep ascent, it may have appeared like a mountain to JB. His route from Yverdon must have taken him first along Lake Neuchâtel in the direction of Grandson, then from Fiez up to Lapidouze, from which he must have ridden further to Mauborget before descending to Môtiers. (Most of this route is noted in *Earlier Years*, pp. 502–03, correcting *Grand Tour I*, Heinemann p. 246 n. 1, McGraw-Hill p. 252 n. 2).

[9] Rousseau had been trying out probes of various sizes for more than twenty years to widen his urinary tract (see the draft on his medical condition, c. 1763, 'Documents biographiques', and *Confessions*, Bk. VIII, OC *Rousseau*, i. 365, 1225).

[10] See App. 2. An 'interesting piece' indeed, this frank and informative autobiographical account focuses on JB's family, education, religious training, sexual awakening, experience with women, and concerns about his identity and character. F. A. Pottle considered it so revealing a document that he placed it, in translation, at the beginning of *Earlier Years*.

[11] Rousseau's characteristic suspicion of priests. He had recently argued that as religions grow older, they lose sight of their original doctrines: 'Quand on perd de vue les devoirs de l'homme pour ne s'occuper que des opinions des Prêtres et de leurs frivoles disputes, on ne demande plus d'un Chrétien s'il craint Dieu, mais s'il est orthodoxe' (*Lettre à Beaumont*, OC *Rousseau*, iv. 974).

[12] That is, De Terreaux and Durey de Morsan.

[13] 'Il faut hurler avec les loups', an old proverb, means that one must accommodate oneself to the manners and opinions of those one lives with (Littré, s.v. 'hurler', 4).

[14] For a similar fantasy of JB's, see Journ. 3 Aug. and n. 4.

[15] For Rousseau, to be a citizen meant living according to high standards of civic virtue. Citizenship was not a natural state to be taken for granted but a status that required education and a sense of responsibility. And ideally, laws were an expression of the general will of a society, to be respected as such

even though they were subject to corruption in later ages ('Discours sur l'origine de l'inégalité'; see also A. Prontera, 'Citoyen', and N. Bonhôte, 'Lois', *Dict. de Rousseau*, pp. 140–41, 560–63). Rousseau had acted in accordance with these ideas when, having reassumed his citizenship of Geneva in 1755 in a fit of republican enthusiasm, he had at least outwardly accepted the forms of worship prescribed by its laws (*Confessions*, Bk. VIII, OC *Rousseau*, i. 392).

[16] Rousseau here finally addresses the subject that JB had specifically wanted to discuss and had described in the 'Ébauche de ma vie'. At issue was the married woman about whom he had thought nostalgically in Berlin (see Journ. 30 July and n. 6). F. A. Pottle inferred that she was Jean Heron, who had been only sixteen when she married Patrick Heron of Kirroughtrie (c. 1732–1803), a man of means but of no particular attraction to her. JB had visited her during his harvest jaunt of 1761 and had been drawn into an affair with her in Dec. of that year (see *Corr.* 9, pp. 118 n. 1, 310, and 311 n. 8); for JB's 'An Epistle to Miss Home', see *Corr.* 9, pp. 116–18. He presumably felt guilty not only because he had committed adultery but also because she was the daughter of Lord Kames, his old friend and benefactor (see Journ. 27 Sept. and nn. 4–5). JB would indeed disengage himself from her on his return to Scotland, and a few years later her husband would divorce her for being unfaithful to him with an army officer. At that point her father would disown her and send her to France (*Earlier Years*, pp. 78–79). Twenty-five years later JB would record Lady Kames's description of her daughter's disgrace and departure in his 'Materials for Writing the Life of Lord Kames' (M 135, 29 Nov. 1782).

In urging JB to follow his conscience, Rousseau was restating the Savoyard vicar's eloquent assertion that the individual conscience is a trustworthy, divinely inspired moral guide: 'Conscience! conscience! Instinct divin, immortelle et céleste voix; guide assuré d'un être ignorant et borné, mais intelligent et libre: juge infaillible du bien et du mal, qui rend l'homme semblable à Dieu, c'est toi qui fais l'excellence de sa nature et la moralité de ses actions ...' (*Émile*, Bk. IV, OC *Rousseau*, iv. 600–01).

[17] The Christian doctrine of 'satisfaction by punishment', most fundamentally exemplified in Christ's sacrifice for the sins of mankind, was a topic JB had also hoped to bring up with Rousseau (see 'Topics to Discuss with Rousseau', App. 2). Here JB focuses

on the human need for atonement, which he recognized as being widely accepted in traditional Catholic and Protestant teaching. The term 'satisfaction' had come to refer to the last of the three stages of penance (following confession and contrition), one of the sacraments that had been emphasized by the medieval church, notably by Peter Lombard (?1100–60 or 64) and Thomas Aquinas (?1225–74). After the Reformation the need for expiation for one's sins had been stressed particularly by Calvin ('Satisfaction', *Encyclopædia of Religion and Ethics*, 1979–81, xi. 207–10; Timothy Gorringe, *God's Just Vengeance*, c. 1996, pp. 118–30, 136–40). JB's views show the lasting influence of his education in the Calvinist Scottish Presbyterianism which had depressed him in childhood (see his 'Ébauche de ma vie', Yale MS. L 1107, App. 2, III.A). That Rousseau, in contrast, did not approve of such expiation is in keeping with his fundamental belief in human goodness and his rejection of the doctrine of original sin (Lettre à Beaumont, *OC Rousseau*, iv. 939–40; see also P. Hoffmann, 'Péché originel', *Dict. de Rousseau*, pp. 706–07).

[18] MS. 'verteux at il'

[19] MS. 'verteux'

[20] These remarks about life in an undefined hereafter, rare in Rousseau, suggest that he thought of an afterlife not greatly different from life on earth and that, as explained by the Savoyard Vicar, after death one will compare what one has done with what one should have done (*Émile*, Bk. IV, *OC Rousseau*, iv. 589–605; see also 'Paradis', *Dict. de Rousseau*, p. 683).

[21] In a similar conversation with SJ, JB had expressed his regret about not being at ease with his father and his fear of being forced to study law. SJ had commented sensibly on the age-old struggle between father and son —'one aims at power and the other at independence'—and had approved of Lord Auchinleck's wish to have JB learn 'as much law as is necessary for a man of property', though he had also acknowledged the limits of a father's power by quoting the old proverb about leading a horse to water (14 July 1763, *Life* i. 426–27).

[22] Rousseau had considered 'gourmandise', which he believed to be a natural appetite, preferable to vanity, which depends on the opinion of others, though he actually favoured frugality (*Émile*, Bk. II, *OC Rousseau*, iv. 409–10). And he had described a delicious meal consisting of unusual local dairy and cereal dishes in *La Nouvelle Héloïse* (Part 4, Letter 10, *OC Rousseau*, ii. 452).

[23] JB gave her one écu (Exp. Acct. 14 Dec., App. 3). She is tentatively identified by R. A. Leigh as belonging to the Jeanrenaud family (To Rousseau, 1 Jan. 1765, *CC Rousseau*, Letter 3826, xxiii. 9). JB would inquire about 'la bonne femme avec tant d'enfans' in his letter to Thérèse Levasseur dated 31 Dec. (*CC Rousseau*, Letter 3819, xxii. 347).

## Saturday 15 December

[MEM. dated Sunday 16 Decr.] [Y]esterday morning rode to St. Sulpice & saw the source of the [R]*use* immensely wild — Rocks in courses, like walls — & cover'd with Pines. Retreat of Rousseau. He walks till he is all in a sweat, to have the pleasure of being cool there. Then saw Cour de Justice — amus'd to hear[1] Justice of Peace talking french. Then M. Rousseau. Je n'aime pas les Allegories — quoique votre nation les aiment beaucoup. Gave him Johnson's character — J'aimerois cet hommela — Je l'estimerois. Si Je pouvois ebranler ses principes, Je ne le ferois pas. Je voudrois le voir: mais du loin — de peur qu'il ne me rosseroit — Told him Tirer le Taurreau — Said he Cet homme me detesteroit. Il diroit — Voici un Corrupteur — un qui vient ici *tirer le Taurreau*. Din'd Kitchen neat — 1 Soup — 2 Beef & 2 veal boild [—] 3 Cabbage Turnip Carrot. 4 Cold Pork — 5 Trout.[2] Desert [—] Chesnuts & Pears ston'd. Red & white wines. Estce que Je puis prendre encore? *Rouss*[.] avez vous le bras assez longue? Voulez vous que Je vous donne de ceci? Non Mr. Je puis le donner a moi-même. Par vanite on fait ses honneurs pour ne pas laisser oublier quon est maitre — Je voudrois chacun son maitre & Personne seroit comme maitre de la maison. Que chacun demande ce qu'il veut — si on l'aye[3] qu'on le donne — si non il faut se contenter. Voila la vraye Hopitalité. En Angletêrre silentieux pour être respecté.[4] *Rouss*[.] En [F]rance rien de morne — affectent aisance — comme Je ne craigns de perdre mon respect — un amour propre plus profond — Eh-bien — n'avez vous pas cela? Oui J'avoue J'aime qu'on me respecte — Mais vous etes si simple — Vous n'avez pas la même idee de vous qu'ont les autres. Je comptais de vous voir comme cela — M. Rousseau. On diroit [—] Il ne se fait assez respecté. Poh — mais en Ecosse cette familiarite aigre ne puisJe me battre [—] Non — cela n'est pas permis. Ces sont des Niaiseries et la vie nous est donne pour des choses importantes. N'y donnez attention. On se lassera de parler comme ce la á un Homme qui ne repond pas. On vous appellera Rousseau Jean Jacques. Ah — Peutetre cela est bon — Oui mais on vous dira Pourquoi toutes ces fantaisies [—] vivez dans la Societé comme un Autre. Moi J'ai des inclinations despotiques — e.g.[5] — avec les fermiers sur mes terres. Poh. Mais un Vieillard[6] cheveux blancs n'avez vous pas eu un respect pour le Vieillesse[7] — Oui meme — Jai ete souvent affable aisé — oui vous vous avez oubli et devenu Homme — mais J'etois faché apres. Je pensois hier de m'offrir d'etre votre Ambassadeur aux Corses. Son Excellence. Voulez vous etre Roi de Corse — ma foi! — non cest au dessu de mes forces. J'ai refusé d'etre Roi[8] — Aimez-vous les Chats? Non — Jetois sure de cela. Cest ma preuve d'un Caractére. Voici le despotisme des hommes [—] Ils n'aiment pas le Chat parceque le Chat est libre et ne veut jamais etre esclave. Il fera rien par vos ordres comme les autres animaus — ni un Poulet non plus. Un Poulet feroit si vous pouriez le faire comprendre — Mais un Chat vous comprendra tres bien et il ne fera pas vos ordres — Mais cest ingrat perfide — Non — tout cela n'est pas vraye. Un Chat est un Animal tres capable d'attachement et il fera tout par Amitié. Jai un Chat il a ete eleve avec mon Chien — Ils jouent ensemble. Le Chat lui donne un coup. Il lui donne sa pate (He described the playing of his dog & cat with exquisite eloquence as a fine Painter does a Small piece). Put meat on a trencher & made his dog dance round it [—] sung elegantly — Voici le Ballet — Le Festin nest pas magnifique: mais il est gay —[9] stroked his dog & fed him — Il n'est pas beaucoup respecté mais il est bien servi. Si vous entrez dans une Compagnie de Jeunes Gens á boire qui vous meprisent? Cela me decontenancera — Je suis naturellement timide — Jai eté souvent abbatu par la raillerie des dames &c. Une Compagnie de ces Jeunes Gens me seroit disagreable. Je m'en irois. Eglise Anglicane pour moi. Oui tres belle Religion mais pas l'Evangile tout simple — une autre. Mais cette simplicité au commencement e.g.[10] aussi Paul dit qu'il est mieux de ne se marier pas que de vous marier — Paul — mais ce nest pas l'Evangile — Vous n'aimez donc[11] Paul. Je respecte — Mais Je crois qu'il a aidé de vous troubler la tête — Il seroit Eclesiastique Anglican<e>. Allez vous en. Pas encore — vingt cinq minutes. Mais Je ne puis pas vous les donner. Je vous donnerais autant — Quoi mon tems.[12] Les Rois et tous les grand peuvent ils donner mon tems — *I.*[13] Mais J'aurrois eu 25 — demain 25 apres demain — Je ne les prends pas — Je vous les donne — Ah — vous ne prenez pas mon argent. Vous me le donnez — (repeated satire [—] Ils disent qu'ils vous le donnent) — [M]adll. parlez — J'ai une bonne amie — mais vous vous liguez ensemble — Non point de ligue (Madll. Je dirais directement quand l'heure sonne. Il faut que J'ai l'air apres manger [—] walk'd on his gallery. Mimic autrefois. Mauvaise qualité attache aux petitesses. Quand Je voyois un charactere singulier il faut l'ajouter á ma collection. Laughed from heart — Vous etes un drole de corps. Phisionomie [—] grand Connaisseur. *Rouss*[.] Cela varie selon les differentes nations comme l'accent le ton. Johnson Jacobite. Il ne devoit accepter Pensions. Je ne bois á la santé du Roi Jacques avec le vin qui me fournit le Roi George — Mais vous ne devez parler avec la substance qui vous donne ce vin. Voltaire ne vous aime pas — C'est naturel. Oui on n'aime pas ceux á qui on a fait beaucoup du mal. Sa conversation est tres agreable encore plus que ses livres — Vous avez vu le Dictionnaire Philosophique. Je ne l'aime pas. Je ne suis point intolerant mais il merite du (something like punishment). Il montre un mepris cela est contre les personnes. Vous etes Sots de croîre cela. Quon raisonne contre les opinions — mais qu'on ne se mocque pas des personnes. Cela n'est point bon. Les Chemins sont mauvais — vous serez tard. Non Je marche ou il est mauvais — et le dernier lieu est bon — Savez vous que Je serais bon avocat devant une Cour de Justice. Oui mais Je suis fache que vous avez les talents de soutenir une mauvaise cause. Avez vous des commissions pour l'Italié[?] Lett — a Parme quelques jolies airs de l'Opera. Homme vous appelle [—] Adieu (Prest me in his arms & kist me several several times & I saw St. Preux attendri). O I shall never forget that I have been thus. Vous etes un Galant Homme — *I*.[14] Vous avez eu beaucoup de bonté pour moi. Je le merité. Oui Vous etes malign mais cest une Malignité … agreable — une malignité qui ne me deplaise[15] pas. Ecrivez moi l'etat de votre santé. Et vous m'ecriverez — Je ne sais comment — Oui vous m'ecriverez en Ecosse — O assurement, même á Paris. Bravo! Si Je vis vingt anns — vous m'ecriverez vingt anns. Adieu si vous vivez sept anns Je reviendrais dans la Suisse pour vous voir — Faites cela nous serons des anciennes connoissances. — Adieu. Encore un mot: Dites moi PuisJe m'assurer quel …[16] Je vous suis attaché par le fils le plus mince par une poile (seising a hair) oui resouvenez vous qu'il y des points ou nos âmes sont liee. C'est assez — moi qui suis melancholique, qui me crois quelquefois[17] un etre meprisable, un etre qui est bon pour rien et qui pense de sortir de la vie et[18] penser que Je suis lié avec M. Rousseau me soutiendra toujours. Je vivrai tous mes jours — o, faites cela.[19] Adieu — Adieu Madll. Vous m'avez promi de me donner des nouvelles de la santé de M. Rousseau — oui — Il vous estime beaucoup — Je connois des hommes pendant 22 ans que Je suis [—] Je luis dis Mr. cest un homme qui a une Physionomie honnete. Je suis sure vous en serez content. Je vous enverrais quoi? Collet de Garnauds. Return'd Inn Landlady. Il me semble que vous pleurez. Je suis pourtant fache de quitter M. Rousseau. Rode by. Madll. encore ecrivez chez nous — Good journey home — supt grave. This day fix Journ quiet tomorrow 2 Louis for ruffles.—[20]

[J] At seven in the morning I got on horseback & rode about a league to St. Sulpice where I saw the source of the *Ruse* the river which runs thro' the Vall de Travers. It is a prodigious romantic Place. I could not determine whether the water gushes in an immediate spring from the rock, or only issues out here having pierced the mountain upon which is a lake. The water comes forth with great violence.[21] All arround here I saw mountains & rocks as at Hartfell in Annandale.[22] Some of the rocks were in great courses like huge Stone walls along which grew the towring Pines which we call Pitch firs,[23] & which are much handsomer than the firs of Scotland.

I was full of fine spirits. Gods! Am I now then realy the freind of Rousseau. What a rich assemblage of ideas! I relish my felicity truly in such a scene as this. Shall I not truly relish it at Auchinleck? I was quite gay, my fancy was youthfull, & vented it's gladness in sportive sallies. I supposed myself in the rude world. I supposed a parcel of young fellows saying 'Come, Boswell, youll dine with us today?' No Gentlemen excuse me I'm engaged. I dine today with Rousseau. My tone, my air, my native Pride when I pronounced this! Temple! You would have given half a guinea to see me at that moment. I returned to my Inn where I found the Court of Justice of the Vallon assembled. I entered & was amused to hear a Justice of Peace and honest Farmers and a Country minister all talking french.[24] I then went to M. Rousseau. 'Jespere votre santé est meilleure aujourdhui.' 'O. N'en parlez pas.' He seemed unusually gay. Before dinner we are all so if not made to wait too long. A keen appetite gives a vivacity to the whole frame. I said Vous ne parlez point des devoirs d'un enfant envers ses Parens. Vous ne dites rien du Pere de votre Emile. 'O! il n'en avoit point. Il n'existoit pas.' It is however a real pity that M. Rousseau has not treated of the duties between Parents & Children.[25] It is an important & a delicate subject & deserves to be illustrated by a Sage of so clear a Judgment and so elegant a Soul. He praised the Spectator. He said 'On y trouve des Allegories.[26] Je ne les aime pas les Allegories; quoique votre nation les aime beaucoup.' I gave him very fully the character of Mr. Johnson. He said with force J'aimerois cet homme. Je l'estimerois. Si Je pouvois[27] ebranler ses prinçipes, Je ne le ferois pas. Je voudrois le voir, mais du loin, de peur qu il ne me rosseroit. I told him how averse Mr. Johnson was to write & how he had his levee. 'Ah! (said he) Je comprens c'est un homme qui aime á declamer.' I told him Mr. Johnson's Bon mot upon the Innovators. That Truth is a Cow which will yeild them no more milk, & so they are gone to milk the Bull. He said 'Il me detesteroit. Il diroit Voiçi un Corrupteur, un Homme qui vient ici tirer le Taurreau.'[28] I had diverted myself by pretending to help Mademoiselle Vasseur to make the Soup. We din'd in the Kitchen which was neat & chearfull. There was something singularly agreable in this scene. Here was Rousseau in all his Simplicity with his Armenian dress which I have surely mentioned before now. His long coat & Nightcap made him look easy & well. Our dinner was as follows: 1 A dish of excellent Soup. 2 A Bouilli of Beef & Veal. 3 Cabbage Turnip & Carrot. 4 Cold Pork. 5 Pickled Trout which he jestingly called *Tongue*. 6 Some little dish which I forget. The Desert consisted of stoned Pears & of Chesnuts. We had red & white wines. It was a simple good Repas.[29] We were quite at our ease. I sometimes forgot myself & became ceremonious. Voulez vous que Je vous donne de ceci? 'Non Monsieur. Je puis le donner á moimême.' Est il permi de prendre encore de cela[?] 'Avez vous le bras assez longue? Par vanité on fait les honneurs de sa maison afin qu'on n'oublie pas qui est maitre. Je voudrois que chacun soit son maitre, et que Personne se presente comme maitre de la maison. Que chacun demande ce qu'il veut, si on l'a qu'on le donne, si non, il faut se contenter. Voici la vraye Hopitalité.' En Angleterre c'est tout different [—] on ne veut pas l'aisance. On est roid et silentieux pour être respecté. 'En [F]rance vous ne trouvez rien de morne parmi les gens de distinction. Ils affectent même la plus grande aisance, comme s'ils vouloient dire: "Nous ne craignons pas de perdre notre dignité." Cela est un amour propre plus rafiné.' Eh bien! n'avez vous pas cela. 'Oui J'avoue J'aime d'etre respecté, mais pour des choses importantes.' Vous etes si simple. Je comptois de vous trouvois tout autre. Le grand Rousseau. Mais vous n'avez pas la même idée de vous qu'ont les autres. Je comptois de vous trouver sur une haute chaise á parler avec une authorité grave. 'A prononçer des Oracles? ha! ha! ha!' Oui et que Je vous craindrois beaucoup. Réellement on trouveroit á redire votre simplicité. On diroit M. Rousseau ne se fait pas assez respecter. Je vous assure pourtant qu'en Ecosse il faut prendre un ton different pour eviter une familiarité terrible qui regne dans ce païs. Ma fois Je ne saurrois le souffrir. Pour le prevenir ne puisJe pas me battre avec le premier qui me traite comme cela, et ainsi être en paix toute ma vie? 'Non; cela n'est[30] pas permi. Ces sont des niaiseries pour lesquelles il ne faut pas risquer la vie. La vie nous est donné pour des choses importantes. Ne faites pas attention a ce qu'ils disent. Ils se lasseront de parler á un Homme qui ne repond pas.' Si vous etiez en Ecosse, on vous appelleroit d'abord Rousseau, Jean Jacques, comment va-t-il?[31] tout familierement. 'Peutêtre cela est bon.' Mais on vous diroit Poh! Jean Jacques, pourquoi toutes ces fantaisies — Vous etes un joli homme d'avoir tant de pretentions. Allons, allons, venez vivre dans la societé comme les autres. Et ils vous diroient cela avec un aigreur que Je ne puis pas vous montrer moi. 'Ah. Cela est mauvais.' There he felt the thistle, when it was applied to himself on the tender part. It was just as if I had said 'Howt Johnie Rousseau man, whatfor hae ye sae mony figmagairies?[32] Ye're a bony man indeed to mauk sicana wark; set ye up canna ye just live like ither fowk?' It was the best idea could be given in the polite french language of the rude Scots sarcastical vivacity.[33] J'ai des inclinations despotiques moi. Je suis comme un vieux Seigneur sur nos terres, et Je me fais respecter par les fermiers.[34] 'Mais quand vous voyez un Vieillard avec des Cheveux blancs — et vous un jeune homme, ne sentez vous quelque chose? ne respectez vous pas la vieillesse?' Oui. J'ai eté même souvent fort affable, J'ai causé avec des fermiers tout librement. 'Oui, vous vous etes oublié et devenu homme.' Mais J'etois faché aprês. Je pensois: Je me suis avili. 'Ha! ha! ha!' Hier Je pensois de vous demander une grace, de me presenter pour être votre ambassadeur aux Corses. Voulez vous me faire son Excellence? Avez vous besoin d'un Ambassadeur? Je vous offre mes service. M. Boswell Ambassadeur extraordinaire de M. Rousseau á l'Isle de Corse.[35] 'Voulez vous etre Roi de Corse?' Ma fois! ha! ha! non. C'est au dessus de mes forces (with a low bow.) Pourtant Je puis dire 'J'ai refusé d'etre Roi.' — 'Aimez vous les Chats?' Non.[36] 'J'etois sure de cela. C'est ma preuve d'un Caractère. Voici le despotisme des hommes. Ils n'aiment pas le Chat, parce qu'il est libre, et ne veut jamais être Esclave. Il fera rien par vos ordres comme les autres Animaux.' Ni un Poulet non plus. 'Un Poulet les feroit si vous pourrez les faire comprendre. Mais un Chat vous comprendra tres bien et il ne les fera pas.' Mais un Chat est ingrat, perfide. 'Non: tout cela n'est pas vraye. Un Chat est un Animal tres capable d'attachement, et il fera tout par amitié. J'ai ici un Chat. Il a eté elevé avec mon Chien. Ils jouent ensemble. Le Chat donne au Chien un coup avec sa queue. Le Chien lui donne sa pate.[37] (He described the playing of his dog & cat with exquisite eloquence, as a fine Painter draws a small Piece.) He put some victuals on a trencher, & made his dog dance round it. He sung to him a lively air with a sweet voice & great taste. Voici le Ballet. Le festin n'est pas magnifique, mais il est joli pourtant.[38] I think the Dog's name was Sultan. He stroaked him & fed him, & with an arch air said 'Il n'est pas beaucoup respecté, mais il est bien servi.'[39] Si vous entrerez dans une Compagnie de jeunes Gens á boire qui se mocqueront de vous. Seriez vous au dessus de cela? 'Cela me decontenanceroit. Je suis naturellement timide. J'ai eté souvent abbattu par la raillerie des Dames par example. Un Compagnie de ces Jeunes Gens me seroit dissagreable. Je m'en irois.' I was comforted to find that my sensibility is not despicable weakness. L'Eglise Anglicane pour moi. 'Oui sans doute c'est une trés belle Religion, mais ce n'est pas l'Evangile, qui est tout simple. C'est une autre.' L'Evangile etoit simple au commencement, comme il etoit rigide; comme Paul dit qu'il est mieux ne se pas marier, que de se marier.[40] 'Paul. Mais ce n'est pas l'Evangile.' Vous n'aimez donc Paul? 'Je le respecte. Mais Je crois qu'il a contribué á vous troubler la tête. Il aurroit eté Eclesiastique Anglican.'[41] M. Johnson est Jacobite, mais il a un Pension de 300 livres sterling du Roi. 'Il ne devoit pas accepter un Pension.' Il dit qu'il ne boit pas á la santé du Roi Jacques, avec le vin que lui donne le Roi George. 'Mais Vous ne devez parler contre le Roi George avec le substance que vous donne ce vin.'[42] *Mademoiselle* said: Allez vous voir[43] M. de Voltaire Monsieur? 'Assurement'. Monsieur de Voltaire ne vous aime pas: C'est naturel. 'Oui on n'aime pas ceux á qui on a fait beaucoup de mal.[44] Sa conversation est tres agreable, encore plus que ses livres.' Vous avez vu le Dictionnaire Philosophique? 'Oui.' Eh bien? 'Je ne l'aime pas. Je ne suis point intollerant, mais il merite (I forget his expression here) Qu'on raisonne contre les opinions, mais de montrer du mepris, de dire vous etes sots de croire ceci, cela est contre les personnes.[45] Allez vous en.' Pas encore. Je pars á trois heures. J'ai encore vingt cinq minutes. 'Mais Je ne puis pas vous donner vingt cinq minutes' Je vous donnerois plus que cela. 'Quoi! mon tems! tous les Rois ne peuvent pas me donner mon tems.' Mais si J'avois resté demain J'aurrois eu vingt cinq minutes, et après demain vingt cinq minutes. Je ne prends pas ces vingt cinq minutes. Je vous les donne. 'Ah! vous ne prenez pas mon argent, Vous me le donnez — Then repeated part of a french satire ending with *Ce qu'ils ne vous prennent pas ils disent qu'ils vous le donnent.*'[46] Mademoiselle parlez. J'ai une bonne Amie ici. 'Mais vous vous liguez ensemble.' Non. Point de ligues. *Mademoiselle* said: Messieurs Je vous avertirai directement quand l'heure sonne. 'Allons, il faut que J'aye de l'air après manger.' We walked out to a gallery pendent upon his wall.[47] J'etois grand copiste autrefois. Je pouvois imiter toutes les personnes que Je voyois.[48] Mais Je ne le fais plus. 'C'est une mauvaise qualité, car il fait que nous attachons aux petitesses des caractêres'. C'est vraye mais reellement mon art etoit noble. Je copiois en si grande perfection. J'etois comme un Virtuoso. Quand Je voyois un caractére singulier, Je disois 'Il faut l'ajouter á ma collection.' He laughed with all his nerves 'Vous etes un Drole de corps' Je suis Physionomiste moi.[49] Je vous assure J'ai etudié cet art avec beaucoup de soin, et Je puis compter sur mes jugements. He seemed to agree to this. 'Mais Je crois que les traits du Visage varient dans des differentes nations comme l'accent et le ton qui signifient des Affections differentes dans des nations differentes.' This observation struck me as new & most ingenious. Mais avec le tems on apprend de les interpreter. 'Les Chemins sont mauvais. Vous serez tard.' Je me promene ou il est mauvais, et le dernier lieu est bon. Savez vous que Je serai bon avocat devant une cour de Justice. 'Oui. Mais Je suis faché que vous avez les talents pour soutenir une mauvaise cause.' Avez vous des ordres pour Italie. 'Je vous enverrai á Genêve une lettre: pour Parme.'[50] Pourrois Je vous envoyer quelque chose? 'Quelques jolies airs de l'opera' Bon. O J'ai eu tant á parler que J'ai negligé de vous prier de me jouer une air. 'C'est trop tard.' *Mademoiselle*: Monsieur, L'homme vous appelle pour partir. M. Rousseau embraced me. He was quite St. Preux attendri. He kist me several times, & held me in his arms with elegant cordiality. O! I shall never forget that I have been thus. 'Adieu vous êtes un gallant homme.' Vous avez eu beaucoup de bonté pour moi. Je le merite.[51] 'Oui; Vous êtes malign mais c'est une malignité agreable, une malignité qui ne me deplait pas. Ecrivez moi l'etat de votre santé.' Et vous m'ecriverez? 'Je ne sais comment.' Oui vous m'ecriverez en Ecosse. 'Assurement: Même á Paris.' Bravo! si Je vivrai vingt anns vous m'ecriverez pendant ces vingt anns? 'Oui.' Adieu si vous vivrez sept anns Je reviendrai d'Ecosse en Suisse pour vous voir. 'Faites cela. Nous serons des anciennes connoissances.' Encore un mot. PuisJe m'assurer que Je vous suis attaché par un fil le plus mince? par un poile? (seising a hair of my head). 'Oui; Souvenez vous toujours qu'il y a des points ou nos ames sont lieés.' C'est assez. Moi qui suis melancholique, qui me crois souvent un être meprisable, un être qui est bon pour rien, qui doit sortir de la vie, de penser que Je suis lié avec M. Rousseau me soutiendra toujours. Adieu. Bravo. Je vivrai tous mes jours. 'Sans doute il faut faire cela.[52] Adieu.'

Mademoiselle accompanied me to the outer door. Before dinner She told me M. Rousseau vous estime beaucoup. La premiêrre fois que vous etes venu Je lui disois: Ce Monsieur a une Physionomie honétte. Je suis sure que vous en serez content. I said Mademoiselle peut bien juger. Oui. Said She: J'ai assez vu des Etrangers pendant les vingt deux ans que Je suis avec M. Rousseau, et Je vous assure que J'en ai renvoyé beaucoup seulement parce que leur maniêrre de parler me deplaisoit. I said Vous m'avez promi de me donner de vos nouvelles de tems en tems. Oui Monsieur. Et dites moi qu[ ]est ce que Je puis vous envoyer de Genêve. Dites sans façon. 'Eh bien donc si vous voulez, un Collet de Grenauds.'[53] We shook hands cordialy, & away I went to my Inn. My eldest Landlady looked at me & said 'Monsieur, il me semble que vous pleurez'. This I retain as a true Elogium of my Humanity. I replied. Je suis pourtant faché de quitter M. Rousseau. Je vous reverrai sept anns d'ici. I got a horseback & rode by the house of M. Rousseau. Mademoiselle waited for me at the door & cried 'Bon Voyage: ecrivez chez nous.' Good Creature. I rode gravely to Yverdun contemplating how this day will appear to my mind some years hence. I was received cordially by my gallant Baron and my Amiable Madame de Brackel: Yet did my spirits sink pretty low; No wonder after such a high flow.

[1] MS. written above deleted 'see'

[2] MS. Raised numbers added above each dish, e.g., '1' above 'soup', '2' above 'beef' and again above 'veal', etc. After 'Trout' the phrase 'Pears ston'd' is deleted by JB but inserted a few words later.

[3] MS. 'la ye'

[4] The first of several comments by JB (not signalled as such), interspersed with Rousseau's.

[5] MS. 'eg'

[6] MS. 'Veillard', JB's frequent way of spelling 'Vieillard'

[7] MS. 'Veillesse'

[8] MS. 'Rois', ending hidden by ink blot.

[9] MS. 'mais ... gay' and one illegible word, scored out by JB.

[10] MS. 'eg.'

[11] MS. 'dont'

[12] MS. 'Quoi mon tems' inserted above the line.

[13] MS. By the 'I', JB signals himself as speaker.

[14] MS. Again, the 'I' represents JB.

[15] MS. 'qui ne me d...' inked out, followed by a single illegible word, rewritten as 'qui ne me deplaise' at the end of the sentence; 'se' of 'deplaise' written over 't' of 'deplait'

[16] MS. One word deleted.

[17] MS. 'quelquefois' written above 'qui me crois'

[18] MS. 'et qui pense ... vie et' an interlineation in smaller script and a different ink.

[19] MS. 'Je vivrai ... faites cela' another interlineation written in the same small script and ink as the previous one.

[20] Not mentioned in the Expense Account. JB did however pay 3 écus for stiffened cuffs ('manchettes d'entoilage', Exp. Acct. 15 Dec., App. 3).

[21] Just outside St. Sulpice, a village at the far western end of the valley, the waters of the Areuse emerge from the rocks.

[22] One of the highest points in the southern highlands, at 2,651 feet (808 m), Hartfell belonged to the district of Annandale in Dumfriesshire. It was only 6¼ miles (10.1 km) from Moffat, the spa where JB had stayed on two occasions as a youth (OGS, pp. 52, 808; Earlier Years, pp. 22, 33).

[23] Silver fir trees (Pinus [Picea] foliis folitariis emarginatis) were also called 'pitch trees' because they produce pitch (John Evelyn,

Silva, 1662, ed. of 1776, p. 256). They could grow to about 55 metres, or 180.4 feet (Alan Mitchell, The Trees of Britain and Northern Europe, c. 1978, p. 100).

[24] Court was held at the Maison des Six Communes in a room so large and cold that it would be divided into two in 1778 (Jean Courvoisier, Les Monuments d'art et d'histoire du canton de Neuchâtel, 1968, iii. 73). The justice of peace has not been identified.

[25] Rousseau had deliberately made Émile an orphan so that he would give his full attention to his tutor (Émile, Bk. 1, OC Rousseau, iv. 267).

[26] Rousseau had read The Spectator (1711–14) with pleasure in 1729 or 1730 while staying with Mme de Warens. For such allegories—some moral, some witty—see Nos. 159, 275, and 281.

[27] MS. 'v' for 'pouvois' written over 'rr' for 'pourrois'

[28] In his journal in London JB had recorded this witticism, about David Hume 'and all other sceptical innovators', with the introductory comment: 'finding mankind already in possession of truth, they could not gratify their vanity by supporting her, and so they have taken to error. "Sir", said he, "Truth is a cow ..."' (Journ. 22 July 1763). JB had repeated it in his journal letter to AE, 'A Minced Pye of Savoury Ingredients ...' (5–22 July 1763, Yale MS. L 528), though without mentioning Hume. He would share it again with Pasquale Paoli (for whom see n. 35 below) in Oct. 1765, would record it, with the final note 'I was present', in his 'Boswelliana' (Yale MS. M 39; Boswelliana, p. 212), and would include it in the Life (21 July 1763, i. 444; see Yale Life MS. Ed., i. 444 n.).

[29] The menu confirms Rousseau's report that few fruits and vegetables were available in the valley, fowl and game were lacking, and beef was inferior since most was sent to Neuchâtel or Geneva, but that trout was plentiful and the wines grown near the town of Neuchâtel were good (To the Maréchal-Duc de Luxembourg, 28 Jan. 1763, CC Rousseau, Letter 2457, xv. 120). JB would proudly recall dining with Rousseau when he described his first invitation to dinner with SJ in the Life (11 Apr. 1773, ii. 215).

[30] MS. 'n'est n'est'

[31] MS. 'vat il'

[32] JB's spelling for 'Figmalieries', meaning 'whims', or for 'Whigmaleeries', meaning 'a whim, crotchet; a foolish fancy' (*Scots Dialect Dictionary*, ed. Alexander Warrack, 1911, pp. 173, 671).

[33] For an earlier comment on the informality of the Scots by Denis de Froment, see *Journ.* 21 July. JB himself had chafed at the coarse manners and raillery of his 'plain hamely' friends, the Erskines, who had arrived in London at a time when he was 'studying polite reserved behaviour' (*Journ.* 1 Dec. 1762). For JB's shifting, ambivalent attitudes about the Scottish language and manners, see Pat Rogers, 'Boswell and the Scotticism', *Johnson and Boswell: The Transit of Caledonia*, 1995, pp. 171–91.

[34] About 800 people lived on the Auchinleck lands. JB had already begun to learn about the management of the estate with its more than 24,000 acres and would continue to relish a patriarchal role before and after becoming laird in 1782 (*Corr.* 8, p. xxxii and App. 1).

[35] JB's suggestion was a result of his hearing, in his first meeting with Rousseau, that the latter had been asked to propose a new set of laws for Corsica (see To GD, 3 Dec., Yale MS. L 418). The time for such laws was propitious because, after being ruled by the Genoese since the fourteenth century and being partially occupied by the French from 1739 to 1741 and now since 1747, Corsica had gained considerable independence owing to the efforts of Pasquale Paoli (1725–1807), who had been elected 'General of the Nation' —that is, head of the army and the government—in 1755 (Pierre Antonetti, *Histoire de la Corse*, 1973, pp. 305–57). Rousseau had praised the Corsicans in the *Contrat social* (Bk. II, ch. 10) for having struggled gallantly for independence and now being ready for sound laws (*OC Rousseau*, iii. 391). Inspired by this praise, another Corsican patriot, Mathieu Buttafoco (1731–1806), a captain in French service, had approached Rousseau with the request to write a new constitution (Buttafoco to Rousseau, 31 Aug., *CC Rousseau*, Letter 3475, xxi. 85–88). Though enthusiastic at first, Rousseau had decided against the journey for reasons of health (To Buttafoco, 15 Oct., *CC Rousseau*, Letter 3573, xxi. 258; Du Peyrou to Rousseau, 20 Nov., *CC Rousseau*, Letter 3662, xxii. 86; see also 'Buttafoco', *Dict. de Rousseau*, pp. 122–23). JB's offer to serve as his envoy marked the beginning of the Corsican adventure on which he would embark in Oct. 1765. Once on the island, he would come to know and admire General Paoli, whose noble bearing and firm rule he would idealize in *An Account of Corsica*, 1768 (for a twenty-first century edition of which see *An Account of Corsica, the Journal of a Tour to that Island; and Memoirs of Pascal Paoli*, ed. James T. Boulton and T. O. McLoughlin, 2006). Paoli's hopes of achieving full independence for Corsica would be dashed, however, when the Genoese, still nominal rulers of Corsica, ceded the island to France in 1768 (Antonetti, pp. 365–75). Forced into exile, Paoli would settle in London, where he would become a close friend of JB's and SJ's (see Joseph Foladare, *Boswell's Paoli*, 1979, pp. 97–110; Moray McLaren, *Corsica Boswell*, 1966, pp. 159–79; *Oxford DNB*, s.v. 'Paoli, [Filippo Antonio] Pasquale'). Rousseau, in his joke about JB as king, may have had in mind Theodore I, actually Baron Theodor von Neuhof (1686 or 1694–1756), an adventurer who was proclaimed King of Corsica and reigned briefly in 1736, with further attempts in 1738 and 1743 (Antonetti, pp. 322–27; *Oxford DNB*, s.v. 'Paoli').

[36] For JB's acknowledgement of his 'antipathy' to cats, which made him uneasy even in the presence of SJ's cat Hodge, see *Life* iv. 197 and *Earlier Years*, p. 171 n. 1.

[37] As he had explained to his visitors J. Wegelin and J.-G. Schulthess, Rousseau had taught his cat and dog to live amicably together because he wished to have peace in his household ('Caractère de M. Rousseau en 1763', in Jochen Schlobach, 'Un Reportage sur Rousseau', *Dixhuitième Siècle* 16 [1984]: 223).

[38] MS. 'Voici ... pourtant' written above 'a sweet voice'

[39] MS. 'pas' inserted between 'est' and 'beaucoup'. Sultan would accompany Rousseau on his subsequent travels. In London, according to an anecdote reported by David Hume, concern for the dog, who disliked being left alone, nearly prevented Rousseau from going to the theatre where the King and Queen of England expected to see him (*Grand Tour I*, Heinemann p. 255 n. 1, McGraw-Hill p. 261 n. 5).

[40] 1 Cor. 7:9.

[41] The Apostle Paul (d. 67 or 64 A.D.) had founded a number of churches in the course of his wide-ranging missionary journeys, and so Rousseau may have regarded him as the representative of the established, institutionalized church, at one remove from the Jesus of the Gospel. St. Paul had also first formulated the doctrine of original sin (Rom. 5:12–19; see 'Péché originel', *Dict. de Rousseau*, pp. 706–07; 'Original Sin' and

'Paul, Apostle, St.', NCE, x. 777; xi. 1–2, 272). Possibly Rousseau meant that the Pauline doctrine had played a part in JB's Calvinist education.

[42] This is the earliest known version of JB's claim about SJ's being a Jacobite yet accepting a Hanoverian pension—a subject not mentioned in the London journal of 1762–63. The pension had been offered by George III's government in 1762 as a gesture of good will in spite of SJ's definition of 'Pension', which included the phrase 'pay given to a state hireling for treason to his country' (*Dict. SJ*; see W. Jackson Bate, *Samuel Johnson*, 1977, pp. 353–56). Rousseau had not accepted a pension from Louis XIV or Frederick of Prussia (see Cranston, *Jean-Jacques: The Early Life*, pp. 266–67). So determined was Rousseau not to incur any obligation that he would first refuse and then only half-heartedly agree to a pension from George III's Privy Purse arranged by David Hume in 1766–67, and thereafter cause so many delays that only after his death in 1778 did a small sum finally reach Thérèse Levasseur (see R. A. Leigh, 'Rousseau's English Pension', *Studies in Eighteenth-Century French Literature*, 1975, pp. 110–20).

JB's bald assertion that SJ was a Jacobite leaves unanswered the question of whether SJ indeed had 'a proclivity towards Jacobitism', as suggested by J. C. D. Clark (*Samuel Johnson: Literature, Religion, and English Cultural Politics from the Restoration to Romanticism*, 1994, pp. 150, 159–68, 197) and Howard Erskine-Hill ('Johnson the Jacobite?', *Age of Johnson*, 1996, vii. 3–26), or whether JB was embellishing a point, as argued by Donald Greene (*The Politics of Samuel Johnson*, 1960, pp. 15–16, 41–43, 298–99 n. 37, and especially the Introduction to the 2nd ed., pp. xxix–xliii; see also John Cannon, *Samuel Johnson and the Politics of Hanoverian England*, 1994, pp. 36–38, for a balanced review of the arguments on both sides). In his fuller discussion in the *Life*, JB would recall SJ's insistence that he had accepted the pension only as a reward for his 'literary merit', but would acknowledge that SJ at times indulged in 'an affectation of more Jacobitism than he really had' and that he had admitted he might not have granted victory to Charles Edward Stuart's army at Culloden even if he could have (14 July 1763, *Life* i. 430; see Yale *Life* MS. Ed., i. 300 n. 9). JB, expressing his own opinion, would find 'nothing inconsistent or humiliating' in SJ's accepting the pension (20 June 1762, Yale *Life* MS. Ed., i. 260–61).

[43] MS. 'voir' inserted after 'vous'

[44] Although they had met only once, if at all, and Rousseau had at first written appreciatively to Voltaire, older and more famous than he, tension between the two had been building over the years. Rousseau had written a disapproving letter, dated 18 Aug. 1756, about Voltaire's questioning of providence in his poem on the Lisbon earthquake, and had been irritated three years later by the unauthorized publication of this letter, for which he blamed Voltaire (*CC Rousseau*, Letter 424, iv. 37–52 and 54 n. 1). Rousseau had also objected to the theatrical performances and upper-class tastes that Voltaire was fostering at Les Delices. Having expressed these views in his *Lettre á d'Alembert sur les spectacles* (1758), Rousseau had explicitly accused Voltaire of turning the Genevans against him (17 June 1760, *CC Rousseau*, Letter 1019, vii. 136). Counterattacking, Voltaire had mocked both Rousseau the man and his writing in 1761 in *Lettres sur La Nouvelle Héloïse*, ostensibly written by the Marquis de Ximenes. In 1762 Rousseau had assumed that Voltaire had influenced the Genevan Council in its condemnation of *Émile*, the *Contrat social*, and his person (see Journ. 3 Dec., n. 25; Jean Orieux, *Voltaire ou la royauté de l'esprit*, 1966, pp. 553–56, 613). Voltaire, in turn, had concluded that Rousseau had been responsible for the Genevan Council's banning of all theatrical performances, including his private ones (see 'Voltaire' and 'Lettre á Voltaire', *Dict. de Rousseau*, pp. 516–17, 931–32). For Voltaire's further sniping in a series of minor writings, see R. Trousson, 'Voltaire', *Dict. de Rousseau*, p. 932.

[45] For Voltaire's *Dictionnaire philosophique*, see Journ. 15 Nov. n. 3.

[46] An unidentified quotation.

[47] A covered balcony, which ran along the side of Rousseau's apartment at right angles to the main street. It was closed off by wooden planks at either end but open on the side. In bad weather it provided shelter for a walk (F. Matthey, 'La Maison et l'appartement de Rousseau á Môtiers', in 'Catalogue de l'exposition permanente', Musée J.-J. Rousseau á Môtiers, 3rd ed., 1986).

[48] For JB's earlier references to being a good mimic, see Journ. 13 Nov. and n. 3.

[49] JB had proudly mentioned his ability to read character in a face when meeting the French ambassador at Solothurn (see Journ. 28 Nov. and n. 11).

[50] Rousseau was sending JB a letter of introduction to Alexandre Deleyre (1726–97), an admirer who had become a friend. In Paris from 1750 to 1759, he had served as

intermediary between Diderot and Rousseau, and had informed the latter about the progress of the *Encyclopédie*. A breach with Rousseau, who had disapproved of Deleyre's marriage, had recently been healed, and Rousseau had just asked him to write the preface to the complete works to be published in Neuchâtel or even perhaps in Môtiers (Rousseau to Du Peyrou, 29 Nov., *CC Rousseau*, Letter 3682, xxii. 130; see 'Deleyre', *Dict. de Rousseau*, pp. 197–98; Cranston, *The Noble Savage*, pp. 170–71, 249; Cranston, *The Solitary Self*, p. 96). Deleyre was now librarian to Prince Ferdinand (1751–1802), son of Philip, Duke of Parma (1720–65). JB would find a warm reception when he called on Deleyre in Parma on 29–30 Jan. 1765 and again for a few days from 1 Aug. 1765 (*Grand Tour II*, Heinemann pp. 48–49, 117–19, McGraw-Hill pp. 45–47, 111–13).

[51] A return to the boast about his 'singular merit' that JB had dared to use in his first letter to Rousseau. The phrase had evidently stayed with Rousseau, who quoted the phrase '*d'un merite singulier*' and acknowledged that he had been curious to meet a young man so convinced of his own merit (Rousseau to Deleyre, 20 Dec., *CC Rousseau*, Letter 3753, xxii. 253–55).

[52] JB here quotes Rousseau's advice to live every day as fully as one can and not to allow one's life to be spoiled by imaginary ills or untrustworthy medical prognoses: 'Vis selon la nature, sois patient, et chasse les médecins, tu n'éviteras pas la mort, mais tu ne la sentiras qu'une fois, tandis qu'ils la portent chaque jour dans ton imagination troublée, et que leur art mensoger au lieu de prolonger tes jours t'en ôte la joüissance' (*Émile*, Bk. II, *OC Rousseau*, iv. 306). In his reply Rousseau acknowledges JB's allusion without further comment.

[53] JB would send her a necklace of garnets from Geneva as 'un petit souvenir d'un brave Ecossois a qui vous avez trouvé "une Physionomie honette"' (JB to Thérèse Levasseur, 31 Dec., *CC Rousseau*, Letter 3819, xxii. 346–47).

## Sunday 16 December

[MEM. dated 17 Decr.] Yesterday went in Baron's chaise, with Madame de Copé, to Gi[1] the Campagne of M. Kinloch — saw two other sisters — din'd well — sung — sung old Scots Sungs.[2] Kinloch quite Scots amus'd to see a Suiss Laird. Lady Colstoun his sister[3] — You'll please his freinds to talk of him with moderation. Brackel maintaind Cat not free — dressé &c. Home drest. Chateau Baillif — Rousseau [—] Parlmt Paris — furieux — paragraphe — Berne — Toulouse &c.[4] Non. Mr. L'ambass á Solure fera ses plaints, & vous serez rendu. Non il ne faut pas le faire. Il repondoit — Non Je ne le ferais pas et il se peut que Je sentirais un jour que Je vous suis obligé á present — Je ne le sens pas — Eh bien Je me rappelle a ce tems — Geneve — percé le cœur. Tout triste — ordre de Berne. J'ecris il est malade &c. 2 ordre — Je lui dis avec menagement etes vous bien. Oui mais trop de monde. Je crois Vous serez plus tranquille á Motiêrs. J'avais premierrement loue la maison ou il est — Avec ses regards percant [—] Je crois Je vous comprends — Oui — vous me comprenez. Il partit ce jour. Il avoit les larmes aux yeux. Il dit ces sont des larmes de joye de[5] vous avoir connu. Je lui demand — Comment possible même homme ecrire l'inegalite et le Devin du village — Je suis malade.[6] J'ai d'humeur. Je pensois noire — J'etois trois mois dans un forret sans voir personne — Alors l'inegalité. Apres trois semaines avec des gens aimables *Devin*. Etes vous St. Preux. Le fond de l'histoire est vraye. Je ne puis vous dire plus a present. Je vous dirais un jour — Je suis Jeune homme avec Curé. Sa Profession de foi est vraye — J'ai donné dans mon expression mais Je n'ai pas ajouté une idée [—] Votre Emile pensez vous qu'on pourroit l'executer — O seulement autant qu'on pourroit & trouvoit convenable. At-il fait du bien? Il aurroit peu faire. Mais il ne la pas fait. Grande partie pour gloire. Les femmes sa passion dominante. Il ne croit crime d'avoir maitresse. Mais, il a dit loix — Oui mais il est etre seul[—] point de patrie point de loix &c — non obeissant a sa mere Geneve — supt & played *Vaut rien*. This day write much — & tomorrow too — engage chaise, & sure off Wednesday.

[J] I went in the Baron's chaise with Madame de Copé to Gi[7] the Campagne of Sir James Kinloch. We found there the Baron who had gone before us on Horseback. Madame Packoton a daughter of Sir James, who is separated from a bad Husband,[8] & Mademoiselle Susétte the youngest daughter next to my freind at Utrecht.[9] We din'd well & sung merrily. I gave Sir James some old Scots tunes which he also hummed as well as he could and seemed highly recreated. I could scarcely think myself out of Scotland: Yet the manner of keeping Sunday marked well the difference. The Baron opposed M. Rousseau's system as to the Cat 'car (said he) C'est tres sure qu' il est un animal ingrat, et pour sa liberté. J'ai vu un Chat qui etoit dressé et qui etoit aussi servile qu'un etre puisse devenir. M. Rousseau est singulier. Je l'ai entendu dire qu'il n'avoit point lu pendant vingt anns. Mais il a cité des auteurs qui ont ecrit depuis ce tems la.' In short the Baron is not much his freind. He seems a Disciple of Voltaire. At four we returned, drest and went to the *Chateau*, as is the Custom here every Sunday. I found a very handsom company at Cards. Fourteen in all made the Company for Supper. The Baillif talked a great deal to me, of Rousseau. 'Qand il entendoit le Decret du Parliament de Paris, il etoit furieux. Quand il vint ici il vouloit mettre une Paragraphe sanglante dans la Gazette de Berne ou il comparoit Paris a Toulouse.[10] Je lui dis savez vous les consequences? L'Ambassadeur de France[11] á Soleure fera ses plaintes, et vous serez rendu. Non. Vous ne le mettrez pas.' Il repondit: 'Non, Je ne le ferai pas. Il se peut que Je sentirai un jour que Je vous suis obligé; á present Je ne le sens pas.' Le decret de Genêve lui perçoit le cœur. Il etoit tout á fait triste. Il venoit içi un ordre de Berne pour le faire sortir de notre canton.[12] J'ecrivois qu'il etoit malade. Je voulois gagner du tems. Il vint une seconde ordre. Alors Je le lui communiquois avec menagement. Etes vous bien ici? 'Oui mais Je vois trop du monde.' Je crois vous serez plus tranquille á [M]otiers. Il me fixa avec ses regards perçans. 'Je crois Je vous comprends.' Oui Vous me comprenez. J'avois auparavant engagé la maison ou il est. Il partit ce même jour. Il vint nous prendre congé. Il avoit les larmes aux yeux. Il disoit 'Ces sont des larmes de joye pour vous avoir connu.' The Baillif gave me more anecdotes of him. Mais comment est il possible que le même homme aye peu ecrire l'Essai sur l'inegalité, et Le Devin du Village? Je suis malade. J'ai d'humeur, et alors Je pense noire. Jecrivois l'inegalité dans un forret ou Je n'avois vu personne pendant trois mois.[13] J'etois trois semaines dans une Soçieté fort gaye, alors J'ecrivois 'le Devin du Village'.[14] Etes vous St. Preux? 'Le fond de l'histoire est vraye. Je ne puis vous dire plus á present. Je vous dirai un jour.' Il m'avouoit que c'etoit lui qui etoit le jeune homme chez le Curé Savoyard, dont la Profession de Foi est reêle.[15] M. Rousseau m'a dit qu'il l'avoit mit dans ses expressions, mais qu'il n'avoit pas ajouté une seule idée. Les femmes font sa passion dominante. On voit quand il parle de cela quel feu il a dans les yeux. Il ne le croit pas une crime d'avoir une maitresse. Il parle pour les loix de Citoyens. Mais il se regarde comme un être separé. Il dit qu'on doit executer autant de son Emile qu'il trouvera convenable. I asked the Baillif 'Pensez vous qu'il a fait du bien.' He answered Il aurroit pu le faire: mais il ne l'a pas fait. Il a ecrit en grande partie pour gloire. We supt very well; Then returned to the Hall, & played at *Vaut rien*, the same with *Tres ace* in Scotland.[16] This is a most chearfull country. The Baillif did not scruple to skip with the best of us, and retained his dignity as much as if he had carefully preserved it in stiff & formal gravity.

[1] That is, 'Giez'; see n. 7 below.

[2] Variant of 'songs' (OED, s.v. 'song').

[3] Jenny (Kinloch) Broun was the second wife of George Broun of Coalston (d. 1776), Lord of Justiciary and colleague of Lord Auchinleck's on the Court of Session (*Fac. Adv.*, pp. 21–22). She owed her title to her husband's position. Lord Auchinleck had mentioned her to JB in his letter of c. 10 Dec. 1763).

[4] MS. 'Toulouse &c' inserted above the line.

[5] MS. Written over deleted 'pour'

[6] MS. 'Je suis malade' inserted.

[7] That is, 'Giez'. Giez was about 2 miles (3.2 km) from Yverdon, in the foothills of the Jura.

[8] Marianne Barbille (Kinloch) Paccotton (1732–1820) had just been granted a divorce from her husband, Capt. Louis-Sebastien Paccotton (1729–c. 1783), bourgeois of Yverdon, who had become too intimate with a Genevan lady of good family (ACV, 'Kinloch', Fichier personnes: époques bernoises et helvétique, 1536–1799; AEB, B III 689, pp. 68–70). With proof of her husband's adultery, she had been granted a divorce by the Consistory in Bern (*Loix consistoriales de la ville et republique de Berne*, 1746). For Paccotton's flirtation with Mme Turetin, see the unpublished 'Journal de Jean-Georges Pillichody', BP Yverdon, p. 118.

[9] Suzette, a younger sister of Nanette (for whom see Journ. 12 Dec. n. 3) was Suzanne Kinloch, born in 1745, and recorded as Susanne-Marguerite Kinloch among the family members appearing before a notary in 1789 (correcting the assumption by Wagner that this Kinloch 'died young'; see Journ. 12 Dec. n. 3).

[10] For the decree of the Parlement of Paris, see Journ. 3 Dec. n. 24. The *Gazette de Berne*, officially entitled *Nouvelles de divers endroits*, had been publishing news from abroad since 1689 (Sgard, i. 458). The Parliament of Toulouse had become notorious for its condemnation of Jean Calas (1698–1762), a French Calvinist merchant, who was assumed to have murdered his son Marc Antoine (1732–61) to prevent his becoming a Catholic convert. The son had probably committed suicide, but Jean Calas had been brutally tortured and executed, a victim of the religious persecution of the Calvinists who had remained in the region after the Revocation of the Edict of Nantes (1685) had severely limited the rights of non-Catholics (see José Cubero, *L'Affaire Calas*, 1993, pp. 57–173). Rousseau, considering himself persecuted by the authorities of Paris, Berne, and Geneva (see Journ. 3 Dec. n. 24), had identified himself with Calas (see To Paul-Claude Moultou, 7 June 1762, CC *Rousseau*, Letter 1835, xi. 36).

[11] MS. 'Françe'. The French ambassador at the time was Anne-Théodore de Chavigny (b. 1687), who had held the post since 1753 and had just received his recall (*Repertorium*, ii. 128; *Recueil des instructions aux ambassadeurs*, *Suisse*, ed. Georges Livet, 1983, i. 313–14).

[12] For the decrees of Geneva and Bern (which had jurisdiction over Yverdon), see Journ. 3 Dec. n. 25. Rousseau had been able to stay in Yverdon only from 14 June to 8 July 1762 (MS. annotation in A. Crottet, *Histoire et annales de la ville d'Yverdon*, 1859, pp. 475–76), or 9 July (Eigeldinger, p. 19).

[13] The *Discours sur l'origine de l'inégalité parmi les hommes*, written in 1754, was a serious, controversial essay that gave an unexpected answer to the question posed by the Academy of Dijon about how inequality originated in society and whether this is authorized by natural law. Far from agreeing with the unspoken assumption that humanity had improved with increased civilization, Rousseau traced the stages of human evolution from primitive isolation to simple, harmonious social living close to nature—a state he admired—to an increasingly corrupt society in which ownership of property led to inequalities and the rich oppressed the poor (see Cranston, *Jean-Jacques: The Early Life*, pp. 292–309). His essay did not win the Academy's prize, and many readers, including

SJ, rejected its reasoning, at least partly because they assumed that Rousseau was extolling the life of savages (see *Life*, 20 July 1763, i. 439–40; Journ. 3 Dec. n. 43).

Rousseau had written the *Discours* in the late autumn of 1753 and had indeed brooded about the topic, first during a week's stay in the woods of Saint Germain and then in the Bois de Boulogne in Paris. But he had not been isolated, since even in Saint Germain Thérèse Levasseur and two other women had cooked and cared for him (see *Confessions*, Bk VIII, OC *Rousseau*, i. 388 and 1452 n. 4; Cranston, *Jean-Jacques: The Early Life*, p. 293).

[14] *Le Devin du village*, composed in the spring and summer of 1752, was a light-hearted *intermède* with simple lyrics and catchy tunes about rustic lovers reunited by a village soothsayer (*New Grove 2*). A great success when presented before the King at Fontainebleau, it became Rousseau's most popular work (see Cranston, *Jean-Jacques: The Early Life*, pp. 263–66). Rousseau himself was aware of the paradox of writing such different works as the *Discours* and the *Devin du village* so close to each other (see *Chrono-*

*logie de J.-J. Rousseau*, OC *Rousseau*, i. cvii; *Confessions*, Bk. VIII, OC *Rousseau*, i. 375–79).

[15] Rousseau acknowledged that he had modeled his Savoyard vicar on the abbé Jean-Claude Gaime (1692–1761), who had offered sound moral advice at a time, between 1729 and 1731, when Rousseau had been driven by excessive social ambitions. Gaime, a peasant by family background, had had the advantage of studying at a seminary in Annecy and at the University of Turin, and had become a tutor in an aristocratic household in Turin. But he had remained poor, simple, and high-principled (see *Confessions*, Bk. III, OC *Rousseau*, i. 91, 118–19, 1289–90 n. 2; Cranston, *Jean-Jacques: The Early Life*, p. 62; 'Gaime', *Dict. de Rousseau*, p. 371). Rousseau seems to have drawn also on another priest, Jean-Baptiste Gâtier or Gattier (1703–60), a man of feeling who had eased Rousseau's unhappiness at the seminary in Annecy (see 'Gâtier', *Dict. de Rousseau*, p. 372).

[16] The game, correctly spelled *Tres-acre*, was a form of tag played by six people (Alice Bertha Gomme, *Traditional Games of England, Scotland and Ireland*, 1964, ii. 307),

## Monday 17 December

[MEM. Tuesday 18 Decr.] [Y]esterday wrote all morning & so was hyp'd. Dullish at dinner — Evening great Company. Baron case tete en Hollande.[1] Madll. Martin sweet Creature — Supt — Idle day. This day at 7 walk till sweat south of the Town. Then Journalise [—] visit after dinner Madll. Martin & Baillif. Shun affectation at all times. Swear ... run no risque by women.[2]

[J] I wrote all morning, & grew vapourish,[3] & was dull. After dinner the Baron said si J'eus resté en Hollande Je me serois cassé la tête.[4] At night we had a great company at cards. So many supt. Among others the freind of Mademoiselle Kinloch at Utrecht Mademoiselle Martin[5] a sweet Creature.

[1] MS. 'Baron ... Hollande' inserted above 'Company'
[2] MS. 'Swear ... women' heavily deleted by a modern hand; text tentatively established by an earlier Yale editor.

[3] In low spirits (OED, s.v. 'vapourish', 2).
[4] 'Je' presumably refers to JB; that is, Brackel meant JB would have been bored stiff if he had remained in Holland.
[5] Not identified.

## Tuesday 18 December

[MEM. Wednesday 19 Decr.] Yesterday stopt a day longer — walk'd to Chambollan — thought 'I am just educating for a Periodical Writer.' After dinner President. Then home told Lady Dutch women round — Husband with wife in wax cloath rolling like a Barrel. Supt Mr. Dufoin gay hearty.

[J] I should have gone this morning, but was prevailed with to stay for a Partie at supper chez M. Du foin a Parisian a hearty fellow who is employed to furnish the Suiss Cantons with Salt. His Wife is plump & lively tho' vapourish even to the seeing of visions in the night.[1] I took a walk to Chambellon the Campagne of The Baron.[2] I thought 'I am just educating for a Periodical Writer, I am storing my mind with Anecdotes *quas mox depromere possim.*'[3] Joseph the Coachman shewed me the house. I found the rooms small; one however was locked, which the Judicious Joseph willing to support the honour of his master, would make me beleive was superb. I made our family very merry with this. After dinner the Baron went with me to the Chateau where I took leave in form of the Baillif. We returned home where I found a Mrs. Irwine who had attended the Princess of Wales.[4] I was in a whimsical frame & talking of Holland said that the women in that country were perfectly round, and as the Dutch are very frugal it is very common to see a man rolling his wife before him thro' the streets like a Barrel[;] as they are also very cleanly he wraps Mevrow in a wax-cloth coverlet. What a ludicrous conceit! We supt well at M. du Foin's. The Baillif was there. We had also a Madame de Lus of Neufchatel a genteel pretty sort of woman who writes verses. She is a great admirer of Rousseau. She had a pretty little daughter whom they called in jest Madame Jean Jacques.[5] I took leave of this People with regret. They are virtuous,[6] hospitable and gay. When we got home we were regaled with a glass of choice *Liqueur*. The Baron was formerly in the french service in the Regiment of the great Marechal de Saxe[7] with whom he was very intimate. I found he had been a wild Rogue. He gave me some anecdotes of his life at Paris, & talked of intriguing with a kept Girl when the *Payeur* was absent. It is curious to see a man after a life of libertine conduct turned a grave father of a family.[8]

---

[1] Pierre Perrinet de Faugnes (d. 1773) held the post of 'receveur général des sels du Roy de France' and as such was in charge of distributing salt and collecting the taxes imposed on it by the French, who held a monopoly on it in Switzerland. De Faugnes, evidently interested in local history, had just published his *Examen des eaux potables de la ville d'Yverdon*, first presented to the prestigious Economic Society of Bern (Daniel Roguin to Rousseau, 6 Nov., *CC Rousseau*, Letter 3626, xxii. 19 and note e). He was a popular figure in Yverdon, where his death in Paris shortly after his retirement would evoke genuine sorrow (A. Crottet, *Histoire et annales de la ville d'Yverdon*, 1859, 23 Nov. 1773, MS. annotation facing p. 489). His wife, Suzanne-Jacqueline (Poupardin d'Amanzy) de Faugnes, was an ardent admirer of Rousseau (*CC Rousseau*, xiv. 82–83 note d; see From Rousseau to Julie-Anne-Marie Boy de la Tour, end of Nov. 1770, *CC Rousseau*, Letter 6815, xxxviii. 150 note f).

[2] Chamblon, about 2 miles (c. 3.2 km)

above Yverdon on a hill neighbouring Giez (for Giez, see Journ. 16 Dec. n. 7). Brackel had bought this country house in May 1763 (ACV, Be22; f. 2 à 27).

[3] 'Condo et compono quae mox depromere possim': 'I am putting by and setting in order the stores on which I may some day draw' (Horace, *Epistles*, I. i. 12, Loeb ed., trans. H. R. Fairclough, 1961).

[4] Presumably Anne (Barry) Irwine (d. 1767), second wife of John Irwine (1728–88), daughter of 'the celebrated physician' Sir Edward Barry of Dublin (Nathaniel William Wraxall, *Memoirs*, 1884, iii. 93). Her husband had recently interrupted his military career. He had risen through the ranks from ensign in 1736 to colonel in 1761, all in the 5th Regt. of Foot, then to colonel and major-general in the 74th Regt. of Foot in 1761–62, and would be appointed Governor of Gibraltar in 1765 (see *Oxford DNB* and, for his seat for East Grinstead from 1762 to 83, Namier and Brooke, ii. 667–68). Although Mrs. Irwine had no offi-

cial position in the royal household, her husband's popularity in court circles might have given her entrée to the Dowager Princess of Wales (see *The Letters of David Hume*, ed. J. Y. T. Greig, 1932, i. 393, n. 5). She would die in Gibraltar in 1767 (*Oxford DNB*).

Possibly JB confused this Mrs. Irwine with Anne (Scarborough), Viscountess Irvine (d. 1766), who was Lady of the Bedchamber to the Princess of Wales (*Court and City Register*, 1751, p. 101) and was still listed as such when Princess Augusta, widowed, assumed the title Princess Dowager of Wales (*Edinburgh Almanack*, 1757, p. 31; *Court and City Register*, 1760, p. 100, then annually to 1765, p. 102). She was the widow of Henry Ingram, Viscount Irvine (1691–1761). There is, however, no evidence that Lady Irvine travelled abroad, and JB is unlikely to have omitted her title of nobility.

⁵ Marianne-Françoise (Warney) de Luze (1728–96) came from a prominent family in Yverdon, where her father, Samuel-Nicolas Warney, was a member of the 'Council of 24'. Her husband, Jean Jacques de Luze (1728–79), was a wealthy textile manufacturer, and they lived in a handsome house, le Bied, close to the château of Colombier. Her admiration for Rousseau had been expressed in her first letter to him, informing him that she had sent the chairs he had requested for Motiers ([22 July 1762], *CC Rousseau*, Letter 2023, xii. 83–84 and 'Notes explicatives' 1). She had become a good friend of Rousseau's, as seen in her verses—three jocular couplets complimenting Rousseau—which inspired three reciprocating couplets and a few bars of music composed by Rousseau (Yale MS. C 2421).

Mme de Luze was taking her eldest daughter, Marianne Marguerite (1749–1820), to Geneva in search of better teachers for her (Daniel Roguin to Rousseau, 25 Nov., *CC Rousseau*, Letter 3674, xxii. 118 note l; see Frédéric de Luze, *Généalogie de la famille DeLuze*, 1947, Table VI).

⁶ MS. 'virtous'

⁷ MS. 'rechal de Saxe' scored out by a modern hand.

⁸ Brackel had joined the forces of Maurice, comte de Saxe (1696–1750), during the latter's brief rule of the duchy of Courland (1726 to 1727). Taking advantage of a vacancy in the succession of that duchy, de Saxe (one of the roughly 355 illegitimate children of August the Strong of Saxony) had persuaded the Diet of Courland to elect him, but had been ousted soon by Russians and replaced by Ernst Biron (see Journ. 29 Sept. n. 5; Alexander Berkis, *The History of the Duchy of Courland*, 1969, pp. 213–15, 220). Brackel had gone into exile and had joined de Saxe in Paris, where both had led libertine existences (see Daniel Roguin to Rousseau, 17 Aug. 1762, *CC Rousseau*, Letter 2083, xii. 199 note b). In the 1740s they had fought in the service of France during the war of the Austrian Succession, and de Saxe had won fame in 1745 for his victory over the British at Fontenoy. Already named marshal of France in 1744, he had been granted Louis XIV's highest military title, marshal general, in 1747 (see Jon [sic] Manchip White, *Marshal of France: The Life and Times of Maurice, Comte de Saxe*, 1962, pp. 10, 61–70, 134, 200).

## Wednesday 19 December

[MEM. dated Thursday 20 Decr.] Yesterday kept snug all day writing except taking a walk with le Baron [—] was at night too merry. There is a difference between intemperance of mirth & a chearfull glass of gladness — took leave with cordial kindness — This day set out for Lausanne — recall Dr. Pringle & old ideas.[1]

[J] No machine[2] was to be had; So I was obliged to stay another day. I kept snug from morning to night, except taking a walk with the Baron whose system I combated. He is an old Chieftain in Courland; But he lives in Switzerland & is even inclin'd to sell the estate of his fathers.[3] At night I was too jocular. There is a great difference between Intemperance of mirth & a chearfull glass of Gladness.[4]

[1] For Pringle, see Journ. 21 Nov. n. 10. It was Pringle who had suggested to Lord Auchinleck that JB go to Lausanne, but the latter

had balked because he had 'formed some strange disagreeable idea of it' (To JJ, 21 Dec., *Corr. 1*, p. 151). Lausanne was reputed not to be favoured by young Britons, possibly because, being ruled by Bern, it was mistakenly thought to be German-speaking (see G. R. de Beer, *Gibbon and His World*, 1968, p. 18). This assumption is disproved by the Scots and Englishmen JB met there.

[2] That is, the 'journalière' (see Journ. 12 July n. 4).

[3] The Baron belonged to a branch of the Brackel family that had settled in Courland in 1609. For his departure from there, see Journ. 12 Dec. n. 1. He still owned three estates—Solwen, Berghof, and Daudzewas—

which had become the property of his father, Casimir Christoph Brackel (1686–1742), on his third marriage, this one to the widowed Eva Elisabeth von Plettenberg. The baron would sell them in 1768 (see Maximilian Gritzner, *Der Adel der russischen Ostseeprovinzen*, J. *Siebmacher's Grosses Wappenbuch*, vol. 25, 1898, repr. 1980, p. 252).

[4] Addison had expressed his preference for 'cheerfulness of mind', which tends to be enduring, over mirth, which tends to be momentary (*The Spectator*, No. 381).

## Thursday 20 December

[MEM. Friday 21 Decr.] Yesterday took leave of Baron, & set out for Lausanne — sad roads sickish — Jok'd too much with Jacob — At night supt too free, was harrassed with unclean thoughts — Again enjoyed air.[1] Swear so no more & live more spare. This day See Madm. D'Hermanches &c.

[J] I had last night taken leave of my amiable Landlady. This morning the *brave Baron* was ready to give me the parting embrace, and very cordial it was. I had sad roads to Lausanne where I arrived in the evening.

[1] MS. 'with unclean … air' scored out by a modern hand.

[2] The roads, after leaving Lake Neuchâtel, traverse a plain and some of the Jura mountains until they reach Lausanne, built on a hillside overlooking Lake Geneva. The distance from Yverdon is about 37 km, or 23 miles (Baedeker, *Die Schweiz*, p. 266).

## Friday 21 December

[MEM. Saturday 22 December] Yesterday morning waited on young Murray quite a Scots Boy: heard of Graham & who is this but Garthmore. Quickly called on him overjoyed — walk'd with him happy to see that an Advocate *could* become a fine fellow. He said A man to pass his life writing d–mnd papers &c. Young lawyers like Prussian Soldiers bred to it — seen no other — their amusement — not call'em off [—] eat & drink & return to work as a horse after corn [—] din'd table d'hote — waited at campagne on Prince de Wirtemberg. Aimable — ses enfants Rousseau &c. Priest had been in China — Graham & *Cercle* full of English — ideas altered. Shakespear force of our imagination — jump over space that frenchman trembles[1] — Supt — charming M. Dillon.

[J] I was curious to know what British were here. Amongst others they named me Monsieur *Graam* Ecossois. I went & called upon young nephew to Lord Elibank[2] who gave me full particulars as to Lausanne; and who should this *Graam* be, but young Graham of Garthmore. I flew to see him and happy we were to meet. He was quite gay. It pleased me to see that an Advocate *may* be made a fine fellow. He raged against the Scots Parliament House and a man's passing his whole life in writing d–mn'd *Papers*.[3] I said an Advocate like a Prussian Soldier must be bred to his Business and know no better. The Amusements of Lawyers are not the elegant exercise of Genius and the fine arts, which would unfit them for their dry business. Their entertainment consists in sollid eating & drinking and in rude and boisterous merriment, after which they return to their work like a Horse after his Corn. While Graham and I walked to Lausanne I was as far from being an Advocate as from being a Captain of a man of War. Graham had passed the winter in [F]rance, & was full of that charming country. He seemed not a little pleased at the licking which the Gazette Literaire has given to Lord Kames whom he called the most unequal tempered man alive.[4] Graham was engaged at dinner: So I dined at the table d'hote of my Inn,[5] after which I took a walk to the Campagne of the Prince Louis Eugene de Wurtemberg Stutgard, a man of a character singularly amiable. He married a Comtesse which was an unpardonable degradation. He lives here in a sweet retirement.[6] I sent in my Compliments, & begged to have the honour of paying him my respects. He received me, & I was charmed with him. He has been in the French service some time, and has got that exquisite ease peculiar to the lively nation. He is a man of parts & of letters. He admires Rousseau, and in a great measure follows his plan of education. The Princess agrees to it, and their two daughters will be examples of the new System. I had heard of this, and said Je serois bien aise de voir un enfant elevé selon le plan de M. Rousseau. Said the Prince 'Je puis vous en montrer.' He then caused bring the two young Ladies the eldest of whom he has called Sophie, and a stout lass she was. The other was more delicate; but they both seemed healthy and gay.[7] It was truly a romantic Scene. The Chaplain had been in China, & was a dry matter-of-fact fellow.[8] I past an hour here with uncommon satisfaction. The Princess was a mild agreable little woman. This was quite an Adventure. I shall perhaps write to this Prince. I then went with Graham to what is called Le Cêrcle, where I found about fifteen english playing at whist, and making a great deal of noise.[9] They rendered me Hypish. I should have mentioned that I went and pay'd a visit to Madame d'Hermanches Lady of Colonel Constant at the Hague.[10] She received me very politely. I supt with Graham at his Landlord's, where lived also the two Mr. Grenvilles quite Englishmen.[11] A mademoiselle Dillon supt with us. She was acquainted with M. Rousseau. She was languishing and amiable.[12] I sat by her and enlivened myself by talking with her. Lausanne is a fine airy, agreable Place where the Society is easy & gay. So Graham assured me.

[1] Part of a continuing discussion about the relative merits of Shakespeare and French classical drama (see Journ. 27 Dec. n. 20).

[2] Alexander Murray (1747–1820) of Blackbarony, Peebles, may have been only a visitor in Lausanne. He had been accepted into the 3rd regiment of foot guards as ensign in 1763. In that capacity he would become imbroiled with the Wilkes riots in May 1768, accused but then acquitted of murdering a rioter. After attaining the rank of lieutenant and captain in 1769 but advancing no fur-

ther, he would retire from the army in 1776 and enter Parliament, where he would represent Peeblesshire from 1783 to 1784 and serve as lord-lieutenant from 1794 to 1820 (Namier and Brooke, iii. 183). He would succeed to the title of Lord Elibank as 7th Lord in 1785 (Comp. Peer. v. 48).

His uncle, Patrick, 5th Lord Elibank (1703–78), was one of the Scottish literati, a friend of Lord Kames and David Hume as well as a patron of the historian Robertson and the playwright John Home, and one of the founders of the Select Society of Edinburgh (see John Ramsay of Ochtertyre, *Scotland and Scotsmen*, 1888, i. 319–21; *Letters of David Hume*, ed. J. Y. T. Greig, 1932, i. 84 n. 2). Elibank had been admitted to the Faculty of Advocates in 1722, had then joined the army as ensign in 1737 and had been promoted to lieutenant-colonel in Wynyard's marines two years later, participating in the siege of Carthagena in 1740. Having left the army on his return, he was welcomed in legal as well as literary circles. JB had met him in London, shortly before Elibank's trip through Holland and France with James Macpherson (Journ. 26, 29 Nov. 1762 and 1 May 1763; for Macpherson, see Journ. 27 Dec. n. 32). SJ, meeting him in Edinburgh in 1773, would respect his wide reading and good sense (*Life* v. 386–87 and App. D, v. 570–71).

³ William Graham (?1733–75), eldest son of Nicol Graham (1724–75) of Gartmore, had passed advocate in 1756 and practised law in Edinburgh (*Fac. Adv.* p. 87; see answer to his petition to Court of Session dated 15 Jan. 1765, ESTC N43110). JB had recently seen him in London (Journ. 18 June 1763). Graham had been travelling on the Continent as far as Turkey (JB being surprised that he was not still there). JB found him 'a fine bold Highlander learned lively cordial' (To JJ, 1 Dec., *Corr. 1*, p. 151 and n. 2).

'The proceedings in the Court of Session were carried on very largely in writing, advocates having to present their cases and arguments by way of minutes, representations, informations, memorials, replies, etc.—often in printed form—for the judges to consider' (*Boswell for the Defence, 1769–1774*, ed. W. K. Wimsatt and F. A. Pottle, 1959, App. B, p. 352).

⁴ See Journ. 27 Sept. and n. 10.

⁵ The Lion d'Or, a well-known inn on the fashionable rue de Bourg (Exp. Acct. 21 Dec.; see William de Charrière de Sévery, 'Notes sur quelques maisons de la rue de Bourg', *RHV* 15 [1907]: 184).

⁶ Prince Ludwig Eugen (1731–95) of Württemberg-Stuttgart had arrived in the neighbourhood of Lausanne in Jan. 1763, and in Apr. of the present year had moved his family to Montriond, the house occupied by Voltaire from 1755 to 1759 (G.-A. Bridel and E. Bach, *Lausanne: Promenades Historiques et Archéoliques*, 1931, p. 70). In 1762 the Prince had married Sophie Albertine von Beichlingen (1728–1807), a countess and lady-in-waiting at the Saxon-Polish court. He thereby incurred the displeasure of his brothers, one of whom was the luxury loving Karl Eugen, and forfeited his children's rights to the succession of Württemberg. But the couple was conspicuously happy, and enlivened the social scene of Lausanne (see Pierre Morren, *La vie Lausannoise au XVIIIe siècle*, 1970, pp. 314–16).

⁷ The Prince had embarked on a military career at the age of twelve under the protection of Frederick of Prussia, and after acquiring a taste for French culture during two years of travel had entered the service of France in 1749. That same year he had been promoted from brigadier to majorgeneral (*maréchal de camp*) and in the following ten years had distinguished himself in various battles, notably in the siege of Minorca (1757). He had also frequented the court of Louis XV in Paris and Versailles, where he had gained in polish and had led a somewhat licentious life. In 1760, midway through the Seven Years' War, the Prince had suddenly left the French to volunteer for the Austrians, on whose side he had been wounded that same year in battle against the Prussians at Torgau. In another sudden change of mind in 1762, he had left military life altogether and had gone to Dresden, where he had married his countess and left all court circles behind him. In marrying for love without regard to rank, choosing a simple life of retirement, and focusing on the education of his daughters, he had been inspired by his admiration for Rousseau (see To Rousseau, 25 Sept. 1763, *CC Rousseau*, Letter 2935, xvii. 273–74 and 'Notes explicatives', pp. 274–76; O. Schanzenbach, 'Ein Rousseaujünger im Hause Württemberg', *Festgabe des Eberhard-Ludwigs-Gymnasiums*, Stuttgart, 1902, pp. 1–15). By the time of JB's visit, the Prince had been corresponding regularly with Rousseau about the development and proper treatment of little Antoinette-Sophie ('Sophie', named for the beloved of Rousseau's Émile), born 17 June 1763. She was being brought up in accordance with Rousseau's theory that young children should be toughened (see Prince of Württemberg to Rousseau, 4 Oct. 1763 and 17 Nov. 1764, *CC Rousseau*, Letter 2955, xviii. 13–16, and Letter 3652, xxii. 66–69; *Émile* Bk. I, *OC Rousseau*, iv. 260, 276–78, 292–93; see also Schanzenbach, pp. 22–24, 29–37). She proved to be less robust than when JB saw her at the age of eighteen months, for she died in 1775. The other daughter, Wilhelmine Frédérique, was born on 3 July, as the proud father informed Rousseau that very day (*CC Rousseau*, Letter 3381, xx. 248).

⁸ Not identified.

⁹ 'Le Cercle' was an exclusive club, foun-

ded in 1761, that occupied three rooms at No. 29 of the rue de Bourg. Apart from good company, it provided newspapers and card games but no games of chance. Its members, fixed at eighty, were drawn from respected Lausanne families and duly recommended foreigners. Graham was among those accepted as honorary members in June of this year (ACV, P Charrière Cb1, 'Cercle de Bourg, Procès-verbaux 1761–1803', pp. 1– 3, 5, 15; W. de Charrière de Sévery, 'Le Cercle de la rue de Bourg', RHV 22 [1914]: 251–54; Morren, pp. 120–21). Edward Gibbon (1737–94), who had studied in Lausanne from 1753 to 1758, had played whist and picquet there during his second visit from Aug. 1763 to Apr. of the present year, a few months before JB's stay (see Le Journal de Gibbon à Lausanne, ed. Georges Bonnard, 1945, p. 172, also pp. 25, 50, 60, 143, 146, 172). He would settle in Lausanne in 1783 to write the last two volumes of his History of the Decline and Fall of the Roman Empire (pub. 1788); see G. R. de Beer, Gibbon and His World, 1968, pp. 18–28, 52–58, 91–103).

¹⁰ Anne Louise Jeanne Françoise (de Seigneux) d'Hermenches (1715–72), seven years older than her husband, had moved from The Hague with her son Guillaume-Anne (b. 1750) and daughter Constance-Louise (b. 1755). Her father, Jean-Samuel Seigneux (1688–1760 [DHBS] or 1766, RHV 3 [1895]: 214 n. 1), had been mayor (bourgmestre) of Lausanne. At this time she lived in an elegant house at 28 rue de Bourg (William de Charrière de Sévery, 'Notes sur quelques maisons de la rue de Bourg', RHV 15 [1907]: 8–9; Morren, p. 569). Often ailing, she appeared 'insipid' and ineffectual to d'Hermenches, who would ask for a divorce in 1770 and would obtain it in 1772, two months before her death (BCU/D, Fonds Constant II, Box 1; see also Courtney, pp. 61, 273; 'Repertoire', OC Charrière, i. 625–26).

¹¹ James Grenville (1742–1825) and Richard Grenville (1742–1823), twins, who had also recently been accepted as honorary members of 'Le Cercle'. They belonged to a distinguished family of statesmen and political leaders who had represented Buckingham and Buckinghamshire in the House of Commons for several generations. Both young Grenvilles had been educated at Eton from 1754 to 1758 (Eton College Register 1753–1790, ed. Richard Athur Austen-Leigh, 1921, pp. 228–29). James had attended Christ Church, Oxford, in 1759 and had entered Lincoln Inn in 1760. Richard had chosen an army career, starting as ensign in the 1st regiment of foot guards in 1759 and serving since late 1760 as captain of the 24th regiment of foot guards (Army List, 1765–66). He would join the 2nd regiment of foot guards as captain and lieutenant-colonel in 1772 and would advance to colonel in 1779, major-general in 1782, colonel of the 23rd regiment of foot guards from 1786, lieutenant-general in 1796, and general in 1801. Following their family's tradition, both young men would be elected to Parliament, James representing Thirsk from 1765 to 1768, Buckingham from 1770 to 1790, and Buckinghamshire from 1790 to 1797, and Richard representing Buckingham from 1774 to 1780.

¹² Presumably Jeanne-Marie-Anne d'Illens (1742–83), younger daughter of Marc-Guérard and Henriette (Roguin) d'Illens. Rousseau, who knew her through his friend Daniel Roguin (1691–1771) of Yverdon, would comment favourably on her character and beauty in his Confessions (Bk. 12, OC Rousseau, i. 590, 1564 n. 4). She would marry Georges-Augustin Roguin (1718–88), a distant relation, in 1766 (see Daniel Roguin to Rousseau, 6 Aug. 1762, CC Rousseau, Letter 2063, xii. 60 note c).

## Saturday 22 December

[MEM. dated Sunday 23 Decr.] Yesterday had slept only two hours — set out a little after four, realy sick — Walk'd & grew better — din'd at Nion with french Officers.¹ Came to Geneva at five. 3. Rois. Cazenove came with letts from Prince Rousseau Temple Erskine &c. — Supt table d'hote & defended Rousseau. Distrest with horrid wishes — did as in Ezechiel's punishment to show where that goes² — This day renew resolutions. At nine church — & communicate Temp. neuf.³ Then home & letters — Think Zelide — Worthy de Zuylen — all well no harm. Bring up Journ. Send letts. Keep calm try this.

See L. Stanhope as Sr. D's freind.⁴

Borrou Burrow Borough⁵

[J] I had a good day's drive to Geneva. Curious were my thoughts on entering this seat of Calvinism.[6] I put up aux Trois Rois.[7] I sent immediatly to Cazenove Clavière[8] & fils for my letters. Young Cazenove brought me a good Packet which made me a very happy man. I had letters from The Margraave of Baaden Durlach, from Rousseau from Temple and from Erskine.[9] What a groupe of ideas! I supt at the table d'hote where was a Monsieur de la Sale[10] a Parisian with whom I chatted agreably.

[1] Nyon was about 22 km (13.7 miles) from Lausanne and the same distance from Geneva (Baedeker, *Die Schweiz*, p. 299). The French officers have not been identified.

[2] That is, the Old Testament prophet Ezekiel, who forcefully denounced sexual misconduct (Ezekiel 23). JB's allusion to this passage attests to his feelings of guilt about his 'horrid wishes', but the exact point of his invocation of Ezekiel is obscure. Specific acts of self-punishment and penitence are recounted in Ezekiel 3–5.

[3] Also known as the Temple de la Fusterie, the Temple Neuf was the first Protestant church built in Geneva since the Reformation. Inaugurated in 1714, it was needed for the influx of Huguenots who had come to Geneva after the Revocation of the Edict of Nantes. It was unadorned, avoiding all resemblance to the Gothic churches that continued to be used for Protestant worship (Camille Martin, *Le Temple-Neuf de Genève*, 1910, pp. 3–18). Although JB evidently intended to go to this church, in a working-class street close to his inn, he went instead to the Eglise de Saint Germain (see Journ. 23 Dec. and n. 3).

[4] MS. 'See ... friend' written along the left margin. Sir David Dalrymple had urged JB to visit Geneva 'because Earl Stanhope & his family, deserving people and my friends, are there at present' (From Dalyrymple, 16 June 1763, Yale MS. C 1422). For Stanhope, see Journ. 29 Dec. and n. 21.

[5] MS. Three words written in a different pen in the right margin, possibly JB's experiment with the British spelling for 'bourg' as in rue de Bourg (for which see Journ. 21 Dec. n. 5).

[6] Geneva was the place where John Calvin had settled in 1536 and where, except for his exile from 1538 to 1541, he had preached his austere Protestantism (see Alister E. McGrath, *A Life of John Calvin*, 1990, pp. 95–103). JB's first thoughts on entering Geneva had concerned Calvin's 'gloomy orthodoxy' and his own 'Scots Presbyterian ideas', which had been shaped by Calvin's teachings (To JJ, 15 Jan. 1765, *Corr. 1*, p. 152).

[7] A large establishment in the lower town facing the Rhône (*Plan Billon, 1726*, repr. 1986, i. pl. 51–52). It dated from 1675 ([Jean-Daniel] Blavignac, *Histoire des Enseignes, d'Hôtelleries, d'Auberges et de Cabarets*, 1878, p. 460).

[8] MS. Possibly 'Clarière', although JB's 'v' and 'r' are sometimes indistinguishable. The firm of Cazenove, Clavière et fils had been founded by David Cazenove (1711–82), whose family came from the Provence, and Jean-Jacques Clavière (1703?–76), whose family originated in the Dauphiné. Both families had left France in the late seventeenth century after the Revocation of the Edict of Nantes and had become respected citizens of Geneva (see [Arthur Cazenove], *Quatres siècles*, 1908, pp. 104, 120–29, 144–45; 'Clavière', Galiffe, vi. 232–33). The original partnership had lasted from 1743 to 1748, and a new association now included Clavière's son or sons. One of these, Etienne (1735–93), would be exiled for political reasons in 1782 and would establish himself in Paris, where he would become minister of finance in 1792 but commit suicide one year later, after the fall of the political party which he had supported (Galiffe, vi. 234; From Rousseau, 20 Dec., CC *Rousseau*, Letter 3754, xxii. 255–56 note c). 'Young Cazenove' was probably Paul (b. 1739), son of David's brother Jean Cazenove (1698–1745) and Elisabeth (Bessonet), who had banking connections (CC *Rousseau*, xxii. App. 334, note xx; see also Lüthy, ii. 106, 474).

[9] Karl Friedrich of Baden-Durlach acknowledged receiving JB's verses about Strasbourg Cathedral (see Journ. 22 Nov. and n. 4). Rousseau sent the promised letter of introduction to Deleyre (see Journ. 15 Dec. and n. 50). In two letters dated 13 and 25 Nov., WJT, responding to several of JB's, declared Frederick of Prussia a tyrant rather than the hero JB had admired in Potsdam (To WJT, 23 July, *Corr. 6*, p. 105), encouraged JB to think seriously about Zélide (see Journ. 26 Dec. and n. 6), and revealed the serious financial problems facing the Temple family as a result of the bankruptcy

of his father, William Temple Sr. (see *Corr.* 6, pp. xxxviii–xxxix). For the letters of the Margrave, Rousseau (in English trans.), and WJT (in excerpts), see *Grand Tour I*, Heinemann pp. 266–71, McGraw-Hill pp. 273–

78, and for the full text of WJT's letters of 13 and 25 Nov., see *Corr.* 6, pp. 118–22. AE's letter has not been recovered (Reg. Let.).

[10] Not identified further.

## Sunday 23 December

[MEM. dated Monday 24 Decr.] Yesterday slept till near nine; rose easy & well & wrote good letter to Erskine.[1] Din'd Inn — At two went with Cazenove[2] to Eglise St. Germain. True Geneva Church. Precentor with black wig like Dupont. Probationer areading — Old woman would not give seat — quite the illbred Scots Presbyterians. Le Coint preach'd. Good sermon — Then walk'd on Bastion then Madm. Gaussin too free with Scots woman — then Societé foolish — Cards on Sunday among true calvinists — then home too long letters. This day — Caz — Chapuis. Prepare note of hints & like Temple go see Voltaire.

[J] I slept till near nine. I got up in fine spirits, & sung & was gay even at the seat of Presbyterianism on a Sunday. At two [a]nother young Cazenove came & conducted me to the Eglise de St. Germain, as I wished to see a true Geneva Kirk.[3] I found a large dusky building, a Precentor with a black wig like M. Dupont, a Probationer (a Proposant) a-reading the Bible to the Congregation, in short a perfect Puritanical Picture.[4] Cazenove would have put me into a good seat; but a fat old woman would not give up her place. She made me smile with her obstinate rudeness. She was just a *Scots Gracy*[5] *auld wife*. A M. Le Coint preached a good sensible discourse.[6] After church we walked on the Bastion Bourgeois an excellent airy place where the Genevois and Genevoises assemble.[7] We then waited on M. Gaussin a Banker of this City whose wife is a hearty Aberdeenshire Woman,[8] and then we went to a Society of young Folks where were Cazenove's Sisters.[9] It was rather foolish: But I was amused to see Cardplaying on a Sunday at Geneva and a minister rampaging amongst them. O John Calvin where art thou now?

[1] JB's answer to AE's letter mentioned in the previous day's journal has also not been recovered (Reg. Let.).

[2] MS. 'with Cazenove' inserted.

[3] The other young Cazenove may have been Charles-Louis (1738–1812), son of David Cazenove (for whom see Journ. 22 Dec. n. 8), one of the founders of the firm (Galiffe, iv. 77). The church of Saint Germain, in the old town, had been built c. 1435 in 'flamboyant' savoyard Gothic (a 'sober' style in spite of its name), replacing an earlier church destroyed by fire, and had offered Catholic services until the Reformation was preached there in 1535, followed by its closing. It had served as artillery magazine for almost 200 years but had been reconsecrated in 1750, and was now used for

Protestant services while the cathedral (for which see Journ. 25 Dec. and n. 6) was being renovated. Saint Germain would be returned permanently to the Catholic church in 1803 (see Edmond Ganter, *Histoire de Saint-Germain* [1973], pp. 6–9).

[4] The precentor and probationer have not been identified. Pierre Loumeau Dupont (1699–1786) was one of two ministers in Edinburgh in that town's French church, which had been founded in 1685 by his Huguenot father, Francis Loumeau Dupont (d. 1726). The latter, having fled from his native France, had received permission from the Privy Council to preach to the French Protestants in Edinburgh (information provided by Mr. John Hamilton of Edinburgh to F. A. Pottle, 5 Sept. 1938; for Dupont, see

also Journ. 31 Dec. n. 8).

[5] 'Devout, religious' (Jamieson, s.v. 'Gracie', 2.

[6] Gédéon Le Cointe (1714–82) was a Protestant minister with literary aspirations. A native of Geneva, he had been ordained in 1738 and had spent some time in England. On his return, after failing to be elected to the chair of *belles lettres* in 1756, he had been named Professor of Oriental Languages (Hebrew) the following year. His appointment, authorized by the *Vénérable Compagnie des Pasteurs*, was to the Academy, as the institution of higher learning in Geneva, founded by Calvin in 1559, was called until 1872 (Borgeaud, i. 48–49, 521, 642; *Le Livre du recteur*, ed. Suzanne Stelling-Michaud, 1975, iv. 292). From 1757 Le Cointe had also served as pastor. His writings consisted of several theological, moral, and historical works, including a sermon commemorating the Revocation of the Edict of Nantes (London 1746), *Lettre sur le prix de la vie* inspired by Maupertuis' *Essai de philosophie morale* (1750), and *Harangue de Démosthènes sur les immunités* (Leiden 1750), a translation into French. A selection of his sermons would be published posthumously in 1783 (Borgeaud, i. 642; Montet, ii. 47–48).

[7] The Bastion, below the fortifications of the old town, was a wide walk shaded by rows of trees.

[8] Paul Gaussen (b. pre-1725) of Bourdigny dealt in textiles as well as banking (Lüthy, ii. 107 and n. 49). He belonged to an old Genevan family, originally French, with British connections in London, where his brother, Jean-Pierre Gaussen (1723–88), was a director of the English company of the Levant as well as of the Bank of England from 1761 (*CC Rousseau*, xxxii. 41 note c; Lüthy, ii. 81). Paul's wife, Jane (Forbes), was born in Aberdeenshire in 1728 (film of Church of Scotland parish records, Skene, IGI; Galiffe, iii. 226). Also present was her niece Christian Forbes, born in 1747 in Skene, who would marry James Callendar of Craigforth in ?1768 (IGI; 'Britanniques', Card Catalogue in Rare Book Room, BPU Geneva). Frederic-Guillaume Maurice (1750–1826), son of Professor Antoine Maurice (for whom see Journ. 27 Dec. n. 8), would recall this meeting in an enthusiastic letter to JB dated 25 Feb. 1765 (Yale MS. C 1983).

[9] If the identification of the 'other' young Cazenove is correct (in Journ. 23 Dec. n. 3), these were the as-yet-unmarried daughters of David Cazenove: Marie (b. 1742) and Charlotte-Marie (b. 1743).

## Monday 24 December

[MEM. dated Tuesday 25 Decr.] [Y]esterday called on Bankers & got money, was in fine, sollid frame. At 12 went in coach to Ferney fine drive — elegant house — sent letter. Saw Lady & Gentlemen. Then Voltaire — quite his Print. Lecosse beaucoup de genie. Hume vraye[1] Philosophe. Historien en Phil. pour la premiêrre fois. Roberts — lit [M]*arie* et Gowrie [—] nous n'a dit rien que nous ne savions.[2] Glasgow Editions tres belles. Acad. de Peint. mais notre pas le païs. Non — il faut avoir chaud aux pieds — Elem. de Crit. Oui, Monsr. Kames &c ne connoit beaucoup françois. Ce qu'il me paroit. Tour des isles — Je ne vous empecherais pas — mais Je resterais ici. Jesuite entered — Sir a young Man learning english. A young man of sixty. A broken Soldier of the Company of Jesus. Madm Deny — & [M]adm. Dupuis niece to Corneille. Voltaire suit blue velvet & Wig — old — want teeth: sore eyes.[3] Had groupe of ideas. He smiled & was compos'd. Did not dine with us. Good dinner — Talk'd lively. Oblig'd to come away soon. Was too free with Jacob but humane to take him into coach & so grew free — Romantic afternoon. Past evening chez M. Constant abus'd Rouss. Scelerat &c — Une idiot said Bete d'esprit — Cheval — Beuf — plutot Serpent. M. Pictet[4] said his wife watch'd him & he was calm & Philosophic in danger.

[J]After calling on my bankers Cazenove, Claviere[5] & fils from whom I received payment of a Bill granted me by Splitzerber & Daum, and on Chappuis & fils to whom I was addressed by Messrs. Herries & Cochrane,[6]

I took a coach for Ferney the seat of the illustrious M. de Voltaire. I was in true spirits; the earth was covered with Snow; I surveyed wild nature with a noble eye. I called up all the grand ideas which I have ever entertained of Voltaire. The first object that struck me was his Church with this Inscription 'Deo erexit Voltaire MDCC        '.[7] His Chateau was handsom. I was received by two or three Footmen who shewed me into a very elegant Room.[8] I sent by one of them a letter to M. de Voltaire which I had from Colonel Constant at the Hague.[9] He returned & told me M. de Voltaire est tres fache d'etre incommodé. Il est au lit. I was affraid that I should not see him. Some Ladies and Gentlemen entered, and I was entertained for some time. At last M. de Voltaire opened the door of his apartment, and stepped forth. I surveyed him with eager attention, & found him just as his Print had made me conceive him. He received me with dignity & that air of the world which a Frenchman acquires in such perfection. He had a Slate-blue fine freeze great-coat nightgown, & a three-knotted wig.[10] He sat erect upon his chair, & simpered when he spoke. He was not in spirits nor I neither. All I presented was the 'foolish face of wondering praise'.[11] We talked of Scotland. He said the Glasgow Editions were 'tres belles'. I said Ils ont aussi etabli la une Academie de Peinture, mais cela n'a pas reussit.[12] Notre Ecosse n'est pas un Païs pour cela. He replied with a keen archness 'Non: pour bien peindre il faut avoir chaud aux pieds. On peind guères quand on a froid aux pieds.' Another would have given a long dissertation on the coldness of our Climate. M. de Voltaire gave the very essence of raillery in half a[13] dozen words. I mentioned the severe Criticism which the Gazette Literaire has given upon Lord Kames's Elements. I imagined it to be done by Voltaire, but would not ask him. He repeated me several of the bons mots in it with an air that confirmed me in my idea of his having written this Criticism. He called My Lord allways Ce Monsieur Kames.[14] I told him that Mr. Johnson and I intended to make a tour thro' the Hebrides the northern Isles of Scotland. He smiled & cried. 'Eh bien: mais Je resterai ici. Vous me laisserez rester içi?' Sans doute. 'Eh bien, donc, allez. Je n'ai point d'objections.'[15] I asked him if he still spoke english. He replied. 'Non. Pour parler anglois il faut mettre la langue entre les dents, et J'ai perdu mes dents'.[16] He was curious to hear Anecdotes from Berlin. He asked who was our minister there. I said We had only a Chargé d'Affaires. 'Ah!' (said he) 'un Chargé d'affaires est gueres charge'.[17] He said Hume was Un vraye Philosophe.[18] As we talked there entered Pêre Adan[19] a french Jesuit who is protected in the house of Voltaire what a curious Idea. He was a lively old man with white hair. Voltaire cried in english 'There Sir is a young man, a Scholar who is learning your language, a broken Soldier of the Company of Jesus.' Ah said Pere Adan a young man of Sixty. M. de Voltaire did not dine with us. Madame De Nis his niece does the honours of his house very well.[20] She understands english. She was remarkably good to me. I sat by her and we talked much. I became lively & most agreable. We had a company of about twelve. The family consists of seven. The niece of the great Corneille lives here. She is married to a M. Dupuis.[21] The gates of Geneva shut at five, so I was obliged to hasten away after dinner without seeing any more of M. de Voltaire. At Geneva I called for M. Constant Pictet for whom I had a letter from his Sister in law Madame d'Hermanches. I found his Lady who asked me to stay the evening.[22] There was a company here at cards. I saw a specimen of Genevoises, & compared them with Rousseau's drawings of them. Constant the Husband was lively without wit & polite without being agreable.[23] There were a good many men here who railed against Rousseau on account of his 'Lettres ecrites de la montagne'. Their fury was a high farce to my philosophic mind. One of them was arrant idiot enough to say of the illustrious Authour 'C'est une Bête d'esprit, un Cheval d'esprit, un Bœuf d'esprit.' 'Plutot un Serpent' said a foolish female with a lisping tone.[24] Powers of Absurdity! did your influence ever extend farther? I said ma fois! Il faut que Je sors de ce monde. Quoi les dames peuvent elles parler contre l'Auteur de la nouvelle Heloise! Pictét a Professor of Law Father to Madame Constant, was an Acquaintance of Lord Erskine's.[25] He said he had seen Voltaire morning & evening during a severe sickness, & Madame Pictet his Wife had watched him, and he was toujours tranquille. I supt here.

[1] MS. 'vraye' written over deleted 'veritable'

[2] The Scottish historian William Robertson (1721–93) had described the intrigues carried on during the 1560s by Mary Queen of Scots and the Scottish nobles who opposed her, but he had not discussed the part played by William (c. 1543–84), 1st Earl of Gowrie, *styled* 4th Lord Ruthven until 1581 (see Robertson's *History of Scotland*, Bk. V, 2nd ed. 1759, i. 374–75; *Scots Peer.*, iv. 263; *Oxford DNB*, s.v. 'Ruthven, William, fourth lord Ruthven and first earl of Gowrie'). In 1567 Gowrie had been one of two nobles who had guarded the Queen while she was imprisoned in an isolated house at Lochleven and may have made unwanted amorous advances to her, but he had also joined the disaffected lords who forced her to abdicate her crown in favour of her infant son, the future James VI of Scotland (Claude Nau, *The History of Mary Stewart*, ed. Joseph Stevenson S.J., 1883, pp. 58–64). In 1582 Gowrie had conspired against James VI, had been pardoned only to conspire again, and had finally been beheaded (briefly recounted in Robertson, Bk. vi, *The History of Scotland*, ii. 77–92). JB's keen interest in Mary had already been manifested in his associations with Holyrood House (see Journ. 3 July and n. 3), and would soon inspire him to order a portrait of her in Rome (see Journ. 4, 7 Apr. 1765). Voltaire had described the royal house of Scotland as dogged by three hundred years of misfortunes (*Le Siècle de Louis XIV*, pub. 1752 and 1756, rev. 1767, ch. xv).

Robertson's *History* was in Voltaire's library (*Cat. Ferney*, 'List', no. 2540).

[3] An inflammation ('fluxion') of the eyes that made Voltaire fear he was losing his eyesight (To Philippe Antoine de Claris, Marquis de Florian, 29 Nov., *Corres. Voltaire*, D12214; see also To Sébastien Roch Nicolas Chamfort, and To Jean François de La Harpe, both of 25 May, *Corres. Voltaire*, D11890–91).

[4] MS. 'Pietet'

[5] MS. Possibly 'Clariere'

[6] For Splitgerber and Daum, JB's bankers in Berlin, see Journ. 5 July n. 5. Jacob Chappuis (1705–72) and his sons François (d. 1777) and/or Paul (1737–1809) were merchants and bankers in Geneva (Galiffe, ii. 109). For the firm of Herries Cochrane & Co., JB's bankers in London, see *Corr. 5*, p. 32 n. 1.

[7] MS. Space left at the end of the line for the rest of the date, LXI; that is, 1761. Voltaire had bought the property at Ferney, on the French side of Lake Geneva about 3.5 miles (5.6 km) from the city, at the end of Nov. 1758 and had moved there from *Les Délices* in Sept. 1760 (Baedeker, *Die Schweiz*, p. 296; *Ferney-Voltaire: Pages d'Histoire*, i. 37–38). One of his many improvements had been to use the materials of the old parish church just outside his property to build a more dignified church slightly to the south. The inscription on the pediment read 'Built for God by Voltaire M DCC LXI', a dedication unusual in not invoking a saint but God Himself. As reported by Richard

Twiss (1747–1821), Voltaire liked to say that he would rather build a church for the master than for the servants (28 Sept. 1768, quoted in *Voltaire's British Visitors*, ed. G. R. de Beer and André-Michel Rousseau, SVEC 49 [1967]: 129). Charles Burney would hear the same explanation when he visited Ferney in 1770 (*Dr. Charles Burney's Continental Travels*, ed. Cedric Howard Glover, 1927, p. 16).

[8] Presumably the oval *salon* (drawing room). The chateau, remodeled according to Voltaire's plan, was smaller than its name suggests. Apart from the drawing room, the ground floor consisted of a vestibule, dining room, library, billiard room, and anteroom as well as the bedrooms of Voltaire, his valet, and Mme Denis (for whom see n. 20 below). Rooms for other members of the household and a few guests were available on the next floor, while attics under the roof were used by servants (B. R. [Bruno Racle], 'A propos du chateau de Voltaire', *Ferney-Voltaire*, p. 41). The footmen have not been identified.

[9] JB had asked for this letter when he met d'Hermenches in The Hague on 4 June and had sent a reminder four days later. However, he had neglected to thank d'Hermenches, in spite of Belle de Zuylen's urging of 19 June (see C. P. Courtney, 'James Boswell's Introduction to Voltaire: An Unpublished Letter from Boswell to D'Hermenches', *Notes and Queries* n.s. 32/2 [June 1985]: 224–25). JB would finally express his appreciation on 31 Dec. in a letter that also mentions his visit to Mme d'Hermenches in Lausanne.

D'Hermenches had come to know Voltaire by taking part in his plays in a little theatre at Lausanne in 1756–58 after they were banned in Geneva (Jean-Daniel Candaux, 'Voltaire contre Genève: les stratégies d'un combat pour le théâtre', *Voltaire et ses combats*, ed. Ulla Kölving and Christine Mervaud, 1994). Voltaire would refer to d'Hermenches's abilities as an actor in recommending him to the duc de Richelieu (1696–1788), grand marshal of France and grandnephew of the great Richelieu, when d'Hermenches transferred from the Dutch to the French army in 1765 (Philippe Godet, *Madame de Charrière et ses amis*, 1906, i. 38 n. 2).

[10] The best known print of Voltaire, which serves as a frontispiece in most editions of his works, is modeled on a pastel created in 1736 by Maurice Quentin de la Tour (1704–88), for which see Gustave Desnoiresterres, *Iconographie Voltairienne*, 1879, p. 9, and Charles Wirz, 'Inventaire de l'Institut et Musée Voltaire', 1962, xx. 236–39). By 'greatcoat nightgown', JB means a lounging robe cut like a greatcoat. A porcelain figurine representing Voltaire in this garb is shown in the illustration in *Grand Tour I*, Heinemann facing p. 272, McGraw-Hill facing p. 280. The 'three-knotted wig' probably consisted of three tails of hair—two longer and a shorter one between them, each ending with a knot (for an approximation, see the article 'perruque à deux queues' in the article 'Perruque Barbier, Perruques', *Encyclopédie*, 1765, xii. 411, 415, and Pl. VII, Figs. 5, 6, Pl. VIII, Figs. 1–2).

[11] 'And wonder with a foolish face of praise', Pope, *Prologue* to the *Satires*, l. 212.

[12] The Glasgow Editions, published by the brothers Robert Foulis (1707–76) and Andrew Foulis (1712–75), were known for their handsome typography, excellent paper, and fine bindings as well as careful editing. The brothers had specialized in Greek and Latin classics, producing a famous 'immaculate' Horace (1744) with scarcely a flaw, and a splendid Homer (1756, 1758) in 4 folio vols. (*Oxford DNB* [DNB Archive], s.v. 'Foulis, Robert'). Beginning in 1741, the Foulis press had also produced Shakespeare plays and other standard English texts. The firm would print JB's *Account of Corsica* in 1768 (see David Murray, *Robert & Andrew Foulis and the Glasgow Press*, 1913, pp. 22–29, 47–48). Robert Foulis, who had become Glasgow University Printer in 1743, had founded the Glasgow Academy 'of painting, engraving, moulding, modelling and drawing' after his return from the Continent in 1753 (Murray, pp. 57–89). Only moderately successful by 1763, the Academy would be closed in 1776 (Murray, pp. 90–93, 99; George Eyre-Todd, *History of Glasgow*, 1934, pp. 192–94).

[13] MS. 'halfa'

[14] For this anonymous review with its ironic praise of Kames, see Journ. 27 Sept. and n. 10.

[15] At the Turk's Head coffee-house on 20 July 1763, SJ had expressed the wish to visit the Hebrides, possibly with JB after his return from abroad (*Life*, i. 450). This scheme would be realized in 1773. JB would begin his *Journal of a Tour to the Hebrides with Samuel Johnson, LL.D.*, by recalling Voltaire's unenthusiastic reaction to the plan.

[16] Voltaire had learned the language during his stay in England from May 1726 to Oct. 1728. He had gone there after his clash with a nobleman had led to his detention in the Bastille and release only on condition that he leave the country (Pomeau, *Voltaire*,

i. 158–62). During his first months in England, Voltaire had enjoyed the hospitality of Sir Everard Fawkener, a wealthy, gentlemanly merchant, later diplomat, whom he had met in Paris in 1725 and in whose country house at Wandsworth, near London, he had steeped himself in English (Pomeau, *Voltaire* i. 168–74; for Fawkener, father of the youth JB had met in Brunswick, see Journ. 14 Aug. n. 4). Voltaire acknowledged, however, that he could not pronounce the language and had difficulty understanding it in conversation even after eighteen months in the country (Advertisement to the Reader, prefixed to his first English publication, his *Essay upon the civil wars in France and Essay upon the epick poetry*, 1729). Yet Voltaire had used English in fifteen essays written by 1728 and published in London as *Letters Concerning the English Nation* in 1732 (in French trans. in 1733 and with an additional essay as *Lettres philosophiques* in 1734; see David Williams, 'Voltaire and the English Language', Introduction to 'An Essay on Epic Poetry', OC *Voltaire*, vol. 3B, 1996, pp. 141–49).

[17] Idiomatically, 'n'est guère'. JB is referring to Alexander Burnett, who had replaced Andrew Mitchell when that minister had left Prussia in late August (see Journ. 27 Aug. n. 2). Voltaire was punning on 'chargé' in the sense of 'being in charge of' and 'laden down' (Robert, s.v. 'chargé').

[18] David Hume (1711–76) had already published his major philosophical work, *A Treatise of Human Nature*, 3 vols. 1739–40; the first part was reworked as *Philosophical Essays Concerning Human Understanding*, 1748, the last part as *An Enquiry Concerning the Principles of Morals*, 1751, and the whole republished with the title *Enquiry Concerning Human Understanding*, 4 vols., 1760. A French translation, *Œuvres philosophiques*, was published in Amsterdam in 4 vols., 1758–60, and in 5 vols., 1759–64 (see CBEL, ii. 949–50).

[19] Antoine Adam (1705–87), whose name is consistently misspelled as 'Adan' in these pages, had entered the Jesuit order at his birthplace of Nancy in 1723 and had taught at various places, including Dijon and Metz, before being transferred to Ornex, near Ferney, in 1758. Voltaire, who had first met Adam on a visit to Colmar in 1754, had found him again in the vicinity of Ferney and had invited him to join the Voltaire household. That had happened about a year after the expulsion of the Jesuits from France, soon after the sale of their property at Ornex. When JB arrived a few months later, Adam was still officiating at the local church of Ferney (*Ferney-Voltaire*, p. 323; *Inventaire Voltaire*, pp. 18–20).

[20] Louise or Marie-Louise (Mignot) Denis (1712–90), eldest daughter of Voltaire's sister Marguerite-Catherine Arouet (1686–1726), was married from 1738 to Nicolas-Charles Denis, captain in a French regiment and then in the commissariat from 1738 to his death in 1744 ('Arouet', 'Denis, Marie Louise Mignot, Mme', *Inventaire Voltaire*, pp. 96, 381). She had become Voltaire's companion in the 1740s and had been his mistress in a relationship long suspected, though confirmed only much later with the publication of his passionate letters (Theodore Besterman, *Lettres d'amour de Voltaire à sa nièce*, 1957, translated as *Voltaire's Love Letters to his Niece*, 1958; Besterman, *Voltaire*, 1969, pp. 262–67). She would remain with Voltaire, except for a year's 'exile' in Paris in 1768–69, to the end of his life in 1778. Eventually, she would sell the Ferney estate in 1779 and that same year marry François Duvivier (?1725–*post* 1791)—see 'Madame Denis', *Ferney-Voltaire*, p. 323; CC *Rousseau*, iii. 44 note d; 74 note e.

[21] Marie-Françoise Corneille (b. 1744) was a collateral descendant of the great Pierre Corneille (1606–84), being the granddaughter of the dramatist's cousin also named Pierre Corneille. In 1760 Voltaire, having heard that her family was impoverished, had brought her, at age seventeen, to Ferney, where he had supervised her education and had become fond of her. Her arrival had also inspired him to undertake the ambitious project of editing the works of Corneille, the *Théâtre de Corneille, avec des commentaires*, 12 vols, for which he had obtained the support of the Académie française and which he had just completed. In addition, he had arranged her marriage in 1763 to Claude Dupuits de la Chaux (dates not found), an amiable gentleman who lived in the neighbourhood (see *Corres. Voltaire*, D10939). For this match, Voltaire had granted Marie a substantial dowry from the proceeds of his Corneille commentaries as well as a further 20,000 livres. He would continue to offer her financial support each year as needed (David Williams, 'Voltaire and Marie Corneille', in *Commentaires sur Corneille*, 1974, pp. 27–49).

[22] Françoise Charlotte (Pictet de) Constant (1734–66), married since 1757 and now the mother of four children, was Voltaire's favourite 'Lolotte'. She had been his neighbour while she lived with her parents next to Les Délices, Voltaire's residence on the

outskirts of Geneva (Jean-Daniel Candaux, *Histoire de la Famille Pictet, 1474–1974*, 1974, i. 182–84).

[23] François-Marc-Samuel Constant de Rebecque (1729–1800), the youngest brother of Belle de Zuylen's friend d'Hermenches, had been an officer in his father's regiment in the service of Holland until he was discharged in 1757 ('Constant', *Recueil de Généalogies Vaudoises*, 1950, iii. 222). He had literary aspirations and was a friend of Voltaire's (see Candaux, i. 184). That JB called him 'Constant Pictet' shows that he had added his wife's family name to his own, but he would revert to his family name after her early death and would call himself Samuel Constant in his published works. These included several books for young readers as well as *Dernières pensées du roi de Prusse, écrites de sa main* (1787); two epistolary novels about Swiss life: *Camille ou Lettres de deux filles de ce siècle* (1784) and *Laure de Germosan ou Lettres de quelques personnes de Suisse* (1786); a collection of dramatic pieces entitled *Recueil de pièces dialoguées ou Guenilles dramatiques ramassées dans une petite ville de la Suisse* (1787); and a translation of William Godwin's *Adventures of Caleb Williams* (1795), completed one year after its original publication (see Montet, i. 190–91). Constant was the uncle of Benjamin Constant (1767–1830), who would surpass him in literary fame.

[24] For the arrival of advance copies on Swiss soil, see Journ. 23 Nov. This major polemical work, which had occupied Rousseau in Môtiers from Oct. 1763 to May of the present year, was a vigorous defence of *Émile* and the *Contrat Social*. Rousseau argued that these had not undermined either the government or the religion of Geneva and so had been unjustly condemned by its twenty-five member Petit Conseil of patricians (Letters I–VI). He then attacked the Council for subverting the original principles of the Genevan republic by assuming powers it had never been granted (Letters VII–IX). The impetus for the book had come from bourgeois Genevans friendly to Rousseau, the so-called *représentants*, whose efforts to annul the condemnations of Rousseau's works had been rejected by the Council (the so-called *négatifs*). Rousseau's friend Jacques-François Deluc (1698–1780) had thereupon urged Rousseau to write in support of his defenders and also to answer the *Lettres de la campagne*, a justification of the Council's actions published anonymously in Sept. 1763 but known to be by the *procureur général* Jean-Robert Tronchin (1710–93). Rousseau,

who predictably objected to government by the few, had used both rational argument and barbed comments to criticize the Genevans, thus causing their fury (See 'Lettres de la Montagne,' *OC Rousseau*, iii, pp. clxii–clxxv and 687–897; Cranston, *The Solitary Self*, pp. 73–74, 77, 79; J. Terasse, '*Lettres de la Montagne*', *Dict. de Rousseau*, pp. 522–28).

Rousseau's book would be condemned in The Hague on 21 Jan. 1765, and in Paris on 19 Mar. 1765 (see '*Lettres de la Montagne*', *Dict. de Rousseau*, p. 522; Cranston, *The Solitary Self*, pp. 100–101). In Neuchâtel, in spite of support from Col. Chaillet and the local Conseil d'Etat representing Frederic II, the clergy would also try—unsuccessfully— to have the *Lettres* banned, but would succeed in stirring up the local populace. The result was the so-called 'lapidation', the stoning of Rousseau's house by a few unruly villagers in the late evening of 6 Sept. 1765, which in turn would cause Rousseau's hasty departure from Môtiers and his flight to England (see Eigeldinger, pp. 350–58; Cranston, *The Solitary Self*, pp. 110–33).

[25] Pierre Pictet (1703–68), admitted advocate in Geneva and recipient of a doctorate of law from the University of Valencia in 1723, had been professor of law at the Geneva Academy from 1739 to 1757. He had also served on the *Conseil des Deux Cents* in 1734 and the *Petit Conseil* in 1749. Pictet had retired from his academic position soon after his wife, Marguerite, *née* Cramer (1711–74), inherited considerable wealth from her father, Pierre Cramer de Brandis (d. 1756) —see Candaux, *Histoire de la Famille Pictet*, i. 177–81; *Livre du Recteur*, ii. 182–83; Choisy, p. 324. At that time the Pictets had built a new house next to *Les Délices* and had become good friends of Voltaire's (Candaux, i. 181–83). Mme Pictet was related to Voltaire's publishers, Gabriel Cramer (1723–93) and Philibert Cramer (1727–79), whose grandfathers were brothers (see Galiffe, iii. 151–52; Lucien Cramer, *Une Famille genevoise: Les Cramer, leurs relations avec Voltaire, Rousseau, et Benjamin Franklin*, 1952, p. 13).

Lord Erskine was presumably Thomas (c. 1706–66), eldest son of John, 6th Earl of Mar (d. 1732), still styled Lord Erskine even though he had been deprived of his title after his father's attainder. He had been abroad with Lord Mar and from 1724 had been in charge of a company in an Irish regiment serving France. Thanks to an uncle who had repurchased the Erskine family's forfeited estates for him, Thomas Erskine had been able to return to England, where he had served as captain in a company of foot from 1729 to 1734 as well as sitting for several different constituencies in Parliament: for Stirling Burghs from 1728 to 1734, for Stirlingshire in 1747, and for Clackmannanshire from 1747 to 1754 (Sedgwick, ii.17; *Oxford DNB* [DNB Archive], s.v. 'Erskine, John, 6th or 11th Earl of Mar of the Erskine line').

## Tuesday 25 December

[MEM. dated Wednesday 26 Decr.] Yesterday Except a moment in St. Pièrre good Cath Church[1] — wrote all day & fasted fairly. Wrote to Madm De Nis — sent letter & had answer. All goes well with you. Quite great man. At night low lasciviousness, have a care — Swear with drawn sword never *pleasure* — but with a woman's aid.[2] In Turin & all Italy you find enough — But venture not except with perfect sure people. This day dress immed — Visit Bon-tems. Maurice. Huber. Finish letters by degrees — Some on Alps — Garnet necklace[3] [—] Guineas to Chaillet.[4] Be calm.

[W]rite short & neat to Lady Northumberland.[5]

[J] Altho' this was Christmas day, I fairly fasted, nor stirred out of doors except a moment to the Eglise de St. Pièrre which was formerly a Catholic Church, & is a handsom Building.[6] Worship was over, but I heard a Voluntary upon the Organ. I was in supreme Spirits, and a noble idea arose in my mind. I wrote a very lively letter to Madame De Nis, begging to be allowed to sleep a night under the roof of M. de Voltaire. I sent it by an Express, and Voltaire wrote the answer in the Person of his niece making me very wellcome. My felicity this night was abundant. My letter with the answer to it are most carefully preserved.[7]

[1] A reference to Saint-Pierre before the Reformation (see n. 6 below).

[2] MS. 'Swear ... aid' scored out by JB. A rare reference to masturbation. JB had recently recalled his having experienced such boyhood sexual pleasure while climbing a tree at Auchinleck (5 Dec., 'Ébauche de ma vie', Outline I, L 1109, not included in the final version left with Rousseau, here in App. 2, III.D).

[3] The garnet necklace requested by Thérèse Levasseur (see Journ. 15 Dec.). JB would finally purchase a 'collier de grenats pour Mademoiselle' on 1 Jan. 1765, for the sum of 8 écus (Exp. Acct., App. 3).

[4] Payment not further explained and not recorded in the Expense Account.

[5] MS. 'Write ... Northumberland' written along the left margin. JB was heeding WJT's appeal for help for his family's financial problems (see Journ. 22 Dec. n. 9) by asking Lady Northumberland to find a commission at full pay for WJT's brother Robert (1747–83). The latter had become a first lieutenant in the 85th Regt. of Foot in 1763, at the early age of sixteen, only to be put on half pay in the same year when the war ended

and his regiment was disbanded (see *Corr.* 6, p. 38 n. 9). JB had befriended him when they shared WJT's chambers at the Inner Temple in 1762 and had considered him 'a handsome, spirited young dog' (Journ. 31 May 63).

JB had just written to Andrew Mitchell, by this time back in Britain, with the same plea for help for young Temple (To Mitchell, 26 Dec., BL Add. MS. 6858, ff. 15–17).

[6] This imposing cathedral, at the heart of the old town, had been converted to a Protestant place of worship by plebiscite on 21 May 1536, the official beginning of the Reformation in Geneva. Calvin, who had arrived in Geneva a few weeks later, had made it his pulpit. The cruciform building, erected from 1160 to 1232 partly in romanesque but largely in Gothic style, had recently received a Greco-Roman entrance, designed by Jacques-Germain Soufflot (1713–80), architect of the Pantheon in Paris (Daniel Buscarlet, *Saint-Pierre: Cathedrale de Genève* [1949], pp. 1–13; Peter Meyer, *Schweizerische Münster und Kathedralen des Mittelalters*, 1945, pp. 33–34).

[7] JB had begged to spend the night at Ferney on his next visit, to avoid having to return to Geneva so early as to miss talking with Voltaire, and had declared himself willing to sleep on two chairs in a garret (see this letter and Voltaire's answer in *Grand Tour I*, Heinemann pp. 276–79, McGraw-Hill pp. 283–86). Voltaire's note, written in his handwriting, is identified by JB as 'Answer by Monsieur de Voltaire, in the character of his niece' (C 3044, *Catalogue*, iii. 1009).

## Wednesday 26 December

[MEM. dated 27 December] Yesterday went with young Cazenove & visited Huber an ingenious fellow, but raging against Rousseau. Then Madame Bontems [—] jolly clever eloquent. Rousseau — Je ne le critique — Je ne puis pas le suivre. Il est au dessus de moi. Din'd Inn — was lively. Roi de Prusse considéré[1] des sujets des materiaux — 3 with mad Gauss chez Mad. Palard, splenetic — Russe ici n[°]ose voir des anglois. Supt Inn. Prince de Turenne 10 anns[2] with Ramsay mange cuisse droite. This day call Buisson[3] Maurice Chais.[4] 11 home. Prepare & be rich at Voltaire's — Letts at night tomorrow — never engage.

[J] The worthy M. De Zuylen has written me a kind but misterious letter. I have answered him with warmth, & prest him to be explicite. I have also sent inclosed a letter to my fair Zelide.[5] What are now her ideas I know not. She has not written me a line since the letter which I received from her at Brunswic, altho' I wrote to her a long letter from Berlin, in a severe tone, & one from Dessau in a tone more mild. This will undoubtedly clear up matters. Temple is charmed with her character, & advises me to marry her; but he does not know her well enough.[6] Time must try all. I went with young Cazenove to see a M. Hubér a man of great variety of talents, in particular an amazing art of cutting paper. He was too rough. He raged against Rousseau, & when I talked of his adoring his God, he cried, 'ou est Son Dieu?'[7] We then waited on Madame Bontems sister to Mademoiselle Prevost.[8] She was a jolly, talking woman. She had known Zelide, & said 'Elle a toujours suivi les pensées de sa petite tête. A present elle est devenu si savante et si philosophe, que reéllement Je ne saurrois la suivre.' I din'd at our Table d'hote, after which Madame Gaussin introduced me chez Madame Palard a German Lady very amiable but very vapourish.[9] She gave me a curious anecdote. 'Il ya ici un jeune Russe de bonne famille a qui son Père a absolument defendu de voir les Anglois. Son Gouverneur n'ose pas le mener dans des Societés ou sont ces Messieurs.' This is most excellent; so rude are the young english, that the very Russians shun them. I supt at the table d'hote. M. de la Sale[10] said he had been much with the Chevalier Ramsay who was governour to the Prince de Turenne who when young 'avoit de l'esprit.[11] J'etois á manger chez lui. Il me servoit du Poulet. Je voulois que son Altesse soyoit servi premierrement. Il dit non Monsieur Cela est la cuisse droite et Je ne mange jamais que de la cuisse gauche. Il y avoit une finesse la.'

[1] MS. 's' deleted at the end of 'consideré'
[2] MS. '10 anns' inserted above 'Turenne'
[3] Presumably the young Buisson whom JB had met in Solothurn (Journ. 28 Nov. and n. 13). JB makes no further reference to him and apparently did not meet him in Geneva.
[4] See Journ. 31 Dec. and n. 10.

[5] Diederik Jacob van Tuyll van Serooskerken, Herr van Zuylen, with whom JB had been corresponding about Belle, had mentioned a new suitor whom she was seriously considering, but who was not to be named (From De Zuylen, 11 Dec., Yale MS. C 3176). This was the comte de Bellegarde (1720–90), whom she had met in July (Courtney, pp. 82–89, 138–41, 152–54). Bellegarde's Catholicism made him unsuitable in the eyes of her Calvinist parents, however, and Belle would remain unmarried for the time being. In his answer to M. de Zuylen, JB expressed his own renewed interest in Belle, and in the enclosed letter to her, which he asked her father not to open, he again urged her to clarify her feelings for him (25 Dec., OC Charrière, Letter 174, i. 363; for English translations, see Holland, Heinemann pp. 316–19, McGraw Hill pp. 325–29).

[6] WJT had extolled 'the adorable Zelide' and had teased JB about his 'matrimonial schemes' (letters of 13 and 25 Nov., Corr. 6, pp. 119, 121).

[7] Jean Huber (1721–86), a Genevan artist, was a master of coupure, the special decorative art form whereby scissors were used to create silhouettes of human figures, elaborate landscapes, and other images. It had become a popular entertainment in good society. Huber was known especially for cutting out silhouettes of Voltaire at great speed even with his hands behind his back (Garry Apgar, L'Art singulier de Jean Huber, 1995, pp. 22–37). Huber also produced oil paintings—landscapes and portraits —and would gain further fame by his depictions of Voltaire in private life commissioned by Catherine the Great and disseminated in prints. In addition, Huber composed music, gave bardic recitations, and enjoyed falconry (G. Jean Aubry, 'Jean Huber ou le Démon de Genève: Un Original du XVIIIe Siècle', Revue de Paris 43/3 [1936]: 594–95). He would impress William Beckford as 'a Genius so wild, so irregular, so various' as to be 'a Camelion' (To Sir Edward Thurlow, Spring 1778, quoted in Gary Apgar, 'The Life and Work of Jean Huber', Ph.D. diss., Yale, 1988, p. 18).

Huber's hostility to Rousseau was presumably caused by his close association with Voltaire, whom he had known since 1754, and also by his own social background. His family, merchants from Schaffhausen who had come to Geneva in 1654, had benefitted from the financial schemes of John Law (1671–1729), and since 1752 Huber had been a member of the Conseil des Deux Cents and so of the Genevan establishment (see Apgar, 'Chronologie', L'Art singulier, pp. 209–11).

[8] Jeanne Renée (Prevost) Bontems (1729–82) had been married to François-Louis Bontems (1721–1815) since 1748, and had had six children by 1756 (Galiffe, ii. 361; vii. 21). For Jeanne-Louise Prevost, see Journ. 8 Dec. and n. 3.

[9] Madeleine (Schuhmacher) Pallard had married Jean-Jacques Pallard (1701–76) in Vienna in 1740. A bourgeois of Geneva, he had formerly been a jeweller in Dresden and Vienna (Basel anno 1760: nach den Tagebüchern der ungarischen Grafen Teleki, ed. O. Spiess, 1936, p. 174). She had had ten children between 1741 and 1759 (Recueil genealogique Suisse, 1st ser. 1902, i. 423–27).

[10] Not identified.

[11] Andrew Michael Ramsay (1686–1743), a Scottish Jacobite, Catholic convert, and freemason, had become famous as the author of the imaginary philosophical travels entitled Les Voyages de Cyrus (1727), published in English in the same year as Travels of Cyrus. An admirer of Fénelon and secretary to Mme Guyon, he had been tutor to several boys including the very young Prince Charles Edward in Rome from c. 1718 to 1724 (see George D. Henderson, Chevalier Ramsay, 1952, pp. 31–50, 97–122, 166–71). The precocious youth mentioned by de la Sale was Godefroi Charles, 6th Duke of Turenne (1728–92), whose education Ramsay had overseen from 1732 to 1741 and who had troubled him with his 'youthful unruly passions' (Henderson, p. 190). He was a great-nephew of the famous Marshal Turenne (1611–75) who had successfully led the French forces in the Thirty Years War and whose biography Ramsay had published in 1735 (Henderson, pp. 153, 156–71).

## Thursday 27 December

[MEM. dated Friday 28 Decr.] Yesterday waited on Proff Maurice. Talk'd of Dupont Rousseau much. Was not able to manage vivacity. Then went to Fierney.[1] Earth cover'd with snow. Arriv'd heard that Voltaire himself had written you card. Chev Bouffler painting Madm. Rillet. Din'd well. Then Salle.[2] Some singing some guitar some Shuttlecock — some chatting. All fine. In Pere Adan's room. Before 8 Voltaire — much talk. All supper. Then for self Roi d'[A]ngleterre — Pere Adan voulez vous me donner du vin. Avec plaisir. Quoi! vous donnez la coupe aux Laicques. M. Voltaire said Vous avez le meilleur Gouvernement — Sil devient mauvais — jettez le dans la mêr. C'est pour cela que vous y etes entouré. Vous etes les esclaves des Loix — The [F]rench are the slaves of men.[3] In [F]rance every man is either an anvil or[4] a hammer, he is beat or must be beaten[5] — yet it is a light a genteel hammer. Yes, a pocket hammer. We are too mean[6] for our Governours to cut off our heads. We are on the earth [—] they trample us. This day, mem — great Voltaire. Send Jacob to stop coach & stay here till Saturday & write letters & get more treasure. Get him to write to you in english. Show verses.

Garnet necclace — Go not till Wednesday.[7]

[J] I waited on Professor Maurice the freind of honest M. Dupont, who lived in the house of his Grandfather. I had no recommendation to him, but entered freely, and told him my connection with M. Dupont, & immediatly was well with him.[8] He was a man of knowledge of rough sense, & of that sort of fancy which sound men have in abundance. He received me well. My ideas were somewhat presbyterian; but of the best kind. I was too lively, & was not master of my vivacity. I then went to Ferney, where I was received with complacency & complimented on my letter. I found here Le Chevalier de Bouffler a fine lively young fellow and mighty ingenious.[9] He was painting in crayon a Madame Rillet a most frolicsom little dutch Genevoise.[10] There was here a M. Rieu a Genevois a heavy knowing fellow.[11] M. de Voltaire came out to us a little while, but did not dine with us. After dinner we returned to the drawing room, where (if I may revive an old phrase) *every man soaped his own beard.*[12] Some sat snug by the fire, Some chatted, some sung, some played the guitar, some played at Shuttlecock.[13] All was full. The Canvas was covered. My Hypochondria began to muse. I was dull to find how much this resembled any other house in the Country, and I had heavy *ennui.* At six I went to Pere Adan's room which was just neat & orderly as I could fancy. I know not how it is; but I realy have often observed that what I have experienced has only coresponded to imaginations allready in my mind. Can Præexistence be true? Pere Adan has learnt english in a year's time. He read & translated a Paper of the Spectator with surprising ease.[14] He & Rieu entertained me with the praises of M. de Voltaire's good actions in private life, how he entertains his freinds, and strangers of distinction, how he has about fifty people in his Chateau, as his servants marry & have children, and how the Village upon his manor is well taken care of.[15] Between seven & eight we had a message that Voltaire was in the drawing room. He allways appears about this time anight, pulls his bell, & cries 'Cherchez Le Pere Adan.' The good Father is ready immediatly, & they play at chess together.[16] I stood by M. de Voltaire & put him in tune. He spoke sometimes english and sometimes french. He gave me a sharp reproof for speaking fast.[17] 'Mais vous autres vous parlez si vite.' Nous trouvons que les François font le même. 'Pas moi au moins. Je parle lentement. C'est ce que fais moi' & this

317

he said with a most keen tone. He got into great spirits. I would not go to supper, & so I had this great man for about an hour & a half at a most interesting tête á tête. I have written some particulars of it to Temple, & as our Conversation was very long, I shall draw it up fully in a separate paper.[18] When the Company returned M. de Voltaire retired. They looked at me with complacency & without envy. Madame De Nis insisted that I should sup; I agreed to this, and a genteel table was served for me in the drawing room where I eat & drank chearfully with the gay company arround me. I was very lively & said 'Je suis tout magnifique. Je mange seul comme le Roi d'Angleterre.' In short this was a rich evening.

[The following are the only surviving notes of the conversation with Voltaire, recorded on 27 Dec., and separately catalogued as Yale MS. J 6.1.]

Shakespear often two good lines never six — A madman by G d — A Buffoon at Bartholomew fair.[19] No Play of his own all old Storys.[20] Chess — I shall lose by God[21] by all the Saints in Paradise. Ah here I am riding on a black ram like a whore as I am.[22] Falstaff from the Spaniards.[23] 'I[']ll tell you why we admire Shakespear.' Because you have no taste.[24] But Sir — Et penitus toto divisos orbe Britannos[25] — All Europe is against you. So, you are wrong. — But this is because we have the most grand Imagination. — The most wild — Pope drives[26] a chaise with a couple of neat trim nags: But, Dryden a coach & six with Postilions & all[27] — Repeated well some passages of Dryden. 'What is memory? Where lodge our ideas?' As Thomson says, where sleep the winds when it is calm. Thomson was a great Painter.[28] Milton many Beauties & many faults as there is nothing perfect in this damn'd[29] world. His Imitators are unintelligible. But when he writes well, he is quite clear.[30] What think you of our Comedy? a great deal of wit, a great deal of plot & a great deal of Bawdy-Houses.[31] What think you of Fingal[?][32] Why it is like a Psalm of David. But there are noble passages in it. The Homer of Scotland.[33] There are in both. You speak good english.[34] O no[35] I have scraps of latin for the Vicar.' Addison is a great Genius. His character shines in his writings.[36] Dr. Clarke was a metaphysical Clock. A proud Priest. He thought he had all by demonstration; and he who thinks so is a madman.[37] Johnson is a most orthodox man but very learned has much genius & much worth. He is then a dog. A superstitious Dog. No worthy man was ever superstitious.[38] He said the K. of Prussia wrote like your Footboy &c. He is a sensible man.[39] Will you go and see the Pretender at Rome? 'No. It is High Treason.'[40] I promise you I shall not tell your King of you I shall not betray you. You would see a Bigot: a poor Being — 'His son is worse. He is drunk every day. He kicks women & he ought to be kicked.'[41] Homer was the only man who took it into his head to write twelve thousand verses upon two or three Battles.[42] It is diverting[43] to hear them say *old England*.[44] Sir old England old Scotland & old [F]rance have experienced quite a different effect from that ...[45]

---

[1] MS. Possibly 'Ferney', with an extra downstroke on the 'F'.

[2] The *salon*, which JB calls 'drawing room'

in his letter to WJT.

[3] The contrast between the English and the French had interested Voltaire since his

stay in England, where he had recognized that the English enjoyed greater liberty than his own people. He had been struck by the British system of two houses of Parliament restraining each other and jointly restraining the monarch, in tacit contrast to the French system which accepted the arbitrary rule of the monarch (*Letters Concerning the English* VIII and IX; also *Lettres philosophiques*, 1734, VIII and IX). In speaking of 'slaves' and no longer of liberty, Voltaire reveals himself as aware of the limited freedom of both nations.

[4] MS. 'an anvil or' inserted above 'a hammer'

[5] Presumably Voltaire meant to distinguish here between one who beats and one who is beaten.

[6] MS. 'low' written above 'mean'

[7] 'Garnet ... Wednesday' written along the left margin.

[8] For Dupont, see Journ. 23 Dec. n. 4 and 31 Dec. n. 8. Antoine Maurice (1716–95), Professor of Theology and amateur physicist, had just completed a six-year term as rector of the Geneva Academy (Borgeaud, ii. 637, 642). He had spent several years in Amsterdam, London, and Paris while in his twenties. Since then he had written a number of theological treatises and had just published his *Contra polygamiam* opposing polygamy (Montet, ii. 133–34). Maurice came from a distinguished family of Protestant clergymen, originally from the Provence. His grandfather, Charles Maurice, had come to Geneva in 1699 after the Revocation of the Edict of Nantes. His father, Antoine Maurice (1672–1756), also a pastor, had preceded him as professor of *belles lettres* and history, from 1710, of oriental languages from 1719, and of theology from 1724 (Galiffe, iii. 327).

The older Maurice had owned two houses close to each other in the 'rue couverte' parallel to the rue du Rive in the lower town (*Plan Billon, 1726*, repr. 1986, no. 20 on pl. 23–24; no. 18 on pl. 33–34). Possibly both the present Maurice and his grandfather had lived in one of these houses, and perhaps Dupont had lodged there.

[9] Stanislas-Catherine de Boufflers (1738–1815) was a talented young nobleman who owed his first names to his godparents, Stanislas Lezczynski (1677–1766), Duke of Lorraine and twice King of Poland (1704–09 and 1733–35), and his wife Catherine Opalinska (1680–1747); see Gaston Maugras, *Dernières années de la cour de Lunéville*, 1906, 1925, p. 218 and n. 1. Boufflers' mother was the lively, sociable Marie-Françoise-Catherine (de Beauvau-Craon) de Boufflers (1711–86), who in 1747 had become the acknowledged

mistress of Stanislas. The young Boufflers had been destined for the church but had left the seminary of Saint Sulpice when his worldly verses and the publication of his elegant tale, *Aline, reine de Golconde* (1761), had met with the disapproval of his superiors. By affiliating himself with the Knights of Malta, a quasi-religious order, he had been able to retain the benefices (two abbeys) granted him by Stanislas I and to adopt the title 'chevalier' (see Vaget Grangeat, *Le Chevalier de Boufflers et son Temps*, 1976, pp. 19–31). By 1762 he had also found a place as captain of hussars in the regiment of Esterhazy and had served for a few months on the French side before the Seven Years' War ended in Feb. 1763 (DBF, vi. 1284; Maugras, *Dernières années*, pp. 310–18, 413). He was now on his travels, using the assumed name 'M. Charles' and amusing himself by painting attractive young women of good society. On arriving at Ferney in mid-Dec., he had been welcomed warmly by Voltaire, who had known his mother, and soon he was joining Adam, Mme Cramer, and Voltaire in exchanging witty verses and recording his experiences in lively letters to his mother (published as *Lettres de Monsieur Le Chevalier de Boufflers pendant son voyage en Suisse a Madame sa Mere*, 1771, Letters VI–VIII, pp. 20–25). In one of these, Boufflers mentions the arrival of an Englishman who never tires of hearing Voltaire speak English and quote Dryden—undoubtedly JB (Letter VIII, p. 26). Although Boufflers is described only briefly in JB's journal, JB acquired several souvenirs from him, including mocking verses (MS. Yale C 551; Grangeat, p. 49 n. 4); two lyrics entitled 'chanson'; and a small sketch of a woman's head, possibly Mme Rilliet's (MS. Yale C 552; *Catalogue*, ii. 516; for Mme Rilliet, see the next note). For a balanced comparison of Boufflers and JB, so similar in temperament, talents, interests, and experiences, see *Earlier Years*, pp. 192–95.

Boufflers' subsequent attempts to find a useful occupation would take him to Senegal to oversee the slave trade from 1787 to 1789, to Paris to represent the nobility at the French National Assembly later in 1789, and to Poland, to find refuge from the revolutionists. He would continue to write essays, tales, and verses, and when he returned to France in his last years, he would be accepted as a man of letters, and a member of the French and Berlin academies. His translations, chiefly of classical authors, would include *Recueil de poésies, extraites des ouvrages d'Hélène-Maria Williams*, published in 1808 (see DBF, vi. 1285–86; Grangeat,

pp. 47–111, 175–97, 206–12). JB and Boufflers would never meet again.

[10] Lucrèce Angelique (de Normandie)
Rilliet (1734–74), born in Rotterdam, was
unhappily married to Théodore Rilliet (1727–
83), an attorney active in Genevan politics
on the side of the représentants (see Journ.
24 Dec. n. 24; Choisy, pp. 372–73). Choleric
and unstable, he would demand a legal separation from his wife in 1766 and would
obtain a divorce in 1771 (see Six siècles
d'existence Genevoise: Les Rilliets 1377–1977,
1977, pp. 64–67). The following year she
would marry Philippe Antoine de Claris de
Florian (b. 1709), a former captain of cavalry, who had been married to a niece of Voltaire's from 1762 until her death in 1771.
Because Florian was Catholic while Mme
Rilliet was a Calvinist, the couple would
choose to be married in Germany, thereby
circumventing the disapproving clergy, and
they would live at Ferney in a small house
built for them by Voltaire (see To Card. de
Bernis, 28 Jan. 1772, Corres. Voltaire, D17571
and 'Commentary'; 'Florian', Inventaire Voltaire, pp. 554–55).

[11] Henri Rieu (1721–87) was a close
friend of Voltaire, who had nicknamed him
'le Corsaire' either because of his ability to
procure rare books or because of his adventurous life. A Huguenot, born in Paris, Rieu
was a godson of Henry St. John (1678–1751),
1st Viscount Bolingbroke, the English statesman who had lived in France from 1715 to
1725 and again from 1735 to 1742, and whose
second wife was French (Burke's Peerage, i.
305). Rieu had lived in Amsterdam from
1735 to 1742 and had then worked for the
Dutch East India Company in Batavia. On
his return in 1744, he had joined a French
regiment and fought in Flanders, whereupon
he had gone to Martinique as captain in the
French navy and had become governor of St.
Martin in the Antilles. In 1750 he had married Marie Jeanne Guischard, a Creole of
good family in Guadeloupe (Charles Wirz,
'L'Institut et Musée Voltaire en 1984', Genava, n.s. 1985, xxxiii. 176 nn. 84, 85, 86;
Galiffe, iv. 318–19; see also Ira O. Wade, The
Search for a New Voltaire, 1958, p. 13).

Rieu, who had strong literary interests,
copied Voltaire's manuscripts and collected
published works by or about him. Later Rieu
would translate novels (chiefly English) and
travel accounts, including possibly SJ's Journey to the Western Islands of Scotland (published anonymously in 1785 as Voyages aux
montagnes d'Ecosse). Voltaire would bequeath
his English books to Rieu, who would
choose 227 volumes and subsequently sell

these, along with 101 bound volumes of the
Voltairean writings he had copied, to Catherine the Great (see Journ. 29 Dec. n. 11; Jean-
Daniel Candaux, 'Précisions sur Henri Rieu',
Le Siècle de Voltaire, ed. Christiane Mervaud
and Sylvain Menant, 1987, i. 210–14, 218–
21; Cat. Ferney, Introduction, p. 16).

[12] 'Every man soap his own beard',
meaning 'Let every man indulge his own
humour', was the motto of the 'Soaping
Club' which JB and several companions had
founded for their amusement in Edinburgh
in 1760 (see Corr. 9, pp. 39–40 n. 1).

[13] For this game, which dates from the
fourteenth century, see Alice Bertha Gomme,
The Traditional Games of England, Scotland,
and Ireland, 1898, ii. 192–94). JB had played
it in Utrecht with Nanette Kinloch (French
theme, c. 2–3 Nov. 1763, Yale MS. M 87,
quoted in Holland, Heinemann pp. 58–59,
Mc-Graw Hill pp. 59–60).

[14] An eight-volume edition published in
1744 was in the library (see Cat. Ferney, 'List',
no. 2740).

[15] Voltaire welcomed so many guests that
he would later complain of having become
'l'aubergiste de l'Europe' (To Marie de Vichy
de Chamrond, marquise Du Deffand, 30 Mar.
1768, Corres. Voltaire, D14897; see Pomeau,
Voltaire, ii. 286–92). To improve the life of
local villagers, he had already ordered the
draining of swamps and the breeding of silk
worms, and was encouraging the existing
manufacture of pottery and watches. A
factory for silk stockings and a tannery
would be established a few years later (Ferney-
Voltaire, pp. 133, 203–08, 230–42, 258).

[16] One of Père Adam's primary functions.
As Voltaire wrote about him to the abbé de
Sade (not to be confused with the libertine
de Sade): 'Il n'est point du tout gênant; il
joue très bien aux échecs [et] … dit la messe
fort proprement' (12 Feb. 1764, Corres.
Voltaire, D11694). Voltaire did not like to
lose, they quarrelled frequently, and Voltaire
would dismiss him in 1771. Adam would
spend the rest of his life with a curé friend in
a nearby village ('Antoine Adam', Ferney-
Voltaire, p. 323).

[17] Evidently Voltaire still had difficulty
understanding English in conversation, and
may have had particular trouble with JB's
Scottish accent (see Journ. 24 Dec. n. 16).

[18] JB made such notes on 'eight quarto
pages' (To Voltaire, 15 Jan. 1765), but they
have not been recovered except for a few
comments quoted elsewhere and the two
pages given here. The fullest surviving account of JB's visit appears in his letter to
WJT dated 28 Dec. (see Corr. 6, pp. 122–30).

[19] Expressing his well-known disapproval of Shakespeare, Voltaire here likens him to a crude entertainer at the annual Bartholomew Fair in Smithfield, which Voltaire had possibly attended while in England. For his earlier, positive view of Shakespeare, whom he had prided himself on introducing to the French, see *Letters Concerning the English*, XVIII; *Lettres philosophiques*, XVIII. His harsher view here reflects his disapproval of the growing popularity of Shakespeare in France—a popularity which, he feared, might eclipse the admiration for Corneille, in whom his new edition had given him a vested interest. In addition, the competing claims of Shakespeare and Corneille had become for Voltaire a serious cultural war that echoed the actual conflict between England and France in the Seven Years' War (see D. Williams, 'Voltaire's War with England', *Voltaire and the English*, SVEC 179 [1979]: 82–99).

[20] Voltaire had also criticized Shakespeare for basing his plots on novels ('old stories'), by which he presumably meant Saxo Grammaticus's *Historia Danica* (c. 1185) or Giraldo Cinthio's *Hecatommithi* (1565–66) as used in *Hamlet* and *Othello* (Ahmad Gunny, *Voltaire and English Literature*, 1979, p. 42).

[21] MS. Vowel in 'God', omitted three lines earlier, here half obliterated by a blot.

[22] Perhaps Voltaire recalled the story or ballad about an unchaste widow who, wishing to inherit her husband's property, was forced to ride into court 'backward upon a black ram, with his tail in her hand' while uttering a crude jingle (*The Spectator*, No. 614, quoted in *Grand Tour I*, Heinemann p. 291 n. 2, McGraw-Hill p. 299 n. 9). Voltaire evidently considered this 'low' story typical of English taste. It is possible also that he had in mind Iago's line, 'an old black ram is tupping your white ewe' (*Othello*, i. 1. 89).

[23] Possibly an allusion to Falstaff's resemblance to Don Quixote. There is no Spanish source for Falstaff.

[24] MS. 'Because … taste' inserted above the line.

[25] 'The Britons wholly cut off from all the world' (Virgil, *Eclogue* I, l. 66).

[26] MS. 'drives' inserted above deleted 'has'

[27] JB would report Voltaire's *bon mot* to SJ and record the latter's comment: 'Why, Sir, the truth is, they both drive coaches and six; but Dryden's horses are either galloping or stumbling: Pope's go at a steady even trot' ([12] Feb. 1766, *Life*, ii. 5). Voltaire's succinct contrast between Dryden and Pope does not appear in his *Letters Concerning the English* and *Lettres philosophiques*, in which, treating the two writers separately, he had described Pope as the most 'elegant' and 'correct' poet in England (Letter XXII) and Dryden as 'exuberant' but overly prolific (Letter XVIII).

Voltaire had especially admired the *Essay on Criticism* and *The Rape of the Lock*, and he had translated Canto IV, ll. 13–36 from the latter into French. However, far from accepting the so-called optimism of the *Essay on Man*, he had mocked it in *Candide* (*Letters Concerning the English* XVIII).

[28] In writing highly visualizable descriptions, notably in his *Seasons*. The quoted line condenses a passage in *Winter*, ll. 113–17 (James Thomson, *Poetical Works*, ed. J. Loge Robertson, 1908, repr. 1971). JB would recall this snatch of conversation in his *Hypochondriack* essay 'On Memory', no. LXVII (Apr. 1783), Bailey, ii. 269).

[29] MS. 'there … perfect' inserted above the line.

[30] In his 'Essay upon the Epic Poetry', the first of his pieces written in English, Voltaire had given a long, primarily favourable account of *Paradise Lost*, although he had criticized the allegorical figures of Sin and Death in Book X. In *Candide*, however, he had described the poem as a long commentary on the first chapter of Genesis in ten books of harsh verse, a disparaging judgment also expressed in subsequent works (see *Candide*, 1759, ch. 25, addition of 1761, ed. André Morize, 3rd ed. 1957, pp. 193–94 and n.). Voltaire's comment to JB is milder than his other pronouncements on Milton.

[31] Voltaire had seen such Restoration and early-18th century comedies during his stay in England, and had included brief appreciations of Wycherley, Vanbrugh, Congreve, Steele, and Cibber in his *Letters concerning the English*, XIX (also in *Lettres Philosophiques* XIX). His single-sentence summary here is more critical.

[32] A controversial topic. *Fingal* had been published late in 1761 (with the date 1762) by James Macpherson (1736–96) as an 'ancient epic poem' in six books (*CBEL*, ii. 343). It was supposedly a 'translation' of a Gaelic poem by the mythical bard Ossian, as heard by Macpherson while visiting the Scottish highlands after the success of his first volume, *Fragments of Ancient Poetry, Collected in the Highlands of Scotland and Translated from the Gallic or Erse Language* (publ. anon. 1760). JB had been aware of *Fingal* as soon as it was published (To AE, 17 Dec. 1761, *Corr. 9*, pp. 170–72). He had declared Macpherson 'a man of great genius and an honest Scotch highlander' on meeting

him in London, and had dubbed him 'the sublime savage' (Journ. 11 Dec. 1762, 23 May 1763). JB's epithet echoes the praise of Hugh Blair (1718–1800), Professor of Rhetoric and Belles Lettres at Edinburgh University, the first champion of Macpherson's Ossian, who had written enthusiastically about the sublimity of Ossian's sentiments and style in A *Critical Dissertation on the Poems of Ossian, the Son of Fingal*, 1763, 2nd ed. 1765, pp. 120–211 (misprint in page numbers). But JB was also aware of the questions being raised about the authenticity of the Ossianic poems, including *Fingal*, and the doubts harboured by SJ, who had declared these works lacking in merit as well as antiquity long before his famous quarrel with Macpherson in 1775, when he would insist on documentary proof (see 24 May 1763, 20 Jan., 2, 18, 25 Feb., 21 Mar. 1775, *Life*, i. 396; ii. 292–302, 308–11).

³³ MS. 'The Homer ... Scotland', possibly sarcastic, inserted above 'There are in both', interrupting the point about the 'noble passages' to be found in a Biblical psalm and *Fingal*. Voltaire, whose comments these are, had presumably read Fingal in the 1762 edition, which he owned (see *Cat. Ferney*, 'List', no. 1903). He was evidently aware of the Biblical echoes in Macpherson's Ossian, which had also been mentioned by Blair (A *Critical Dissertation*, pp. 112–13) and which had been recognized especially by French readers (P. Van Tieghem, *Ossian en France*, 1914, repr. 1967, pp. 155, 203, 215–16; see also Fiona Stafford, *The Sublime Savage: A Study of James Macpherson and the Poems of Ossian*, 1988, pp. 89–92). By tradition, David was held to be the author of the psalms, and the Old Testament was coming to be valued as primitive poetry thanks to Robert Lowth's *De sacra poesi Hebraeorum praelectiones*, 1753 (see Van Tieghem, p. 203 and n. 3). The parallels between Ossian and Homer had been discussed by Blair, who had found Ossian superior on several counts (A *Critical Dissertation*, pp. 38–66, 97–112). However, Voltaire was unenthusiastic about *Fingal*, which he disparaged along with other 'fatras barbares'; see Voltaire to Anne-Robert-Jacques Turgot, 22 Feb. 1764, *Corres. Voltaire*, D 11718).

³⁴ For Voltaire's command of English, see Journ. 24 Dec. n. 16.

³⁵ MS. 'O no' inserted above the line.

³⁶ Voltaire had particularly admired Addison's Cato—'the greatest Character that was ever brought upon any Stage'—while acknowledging some weaknesses in other characters and the love plot in the play (*Letters concerning the English* XVIII; *Lettres philosophiques* XVIII).

³⁷ The last phrase is presumably Voltaire's comment; the rest concerns Samuel Clarke (1675–1729), a leading English deist whom Voltaire had met and admired in England. Clarke had been a friend of Newton, whose work he had explicated and brought to Voltaire's attention. Clarke had been an Arian (see Journ. 30 Dec. n. 4), positing a supreme deity but rejecting the notion of the Trinity, for which he found no basis in the New Testament (*Scripture-doctrine of the Trinity*, 1712). A man of principle, Clarke would not allow himself to be considered for the position of Archbishop of Canterbury because he could not subscribe to orthodox Anglican beliefs. Voltaire, who had admired Clarke's character, had found support for his own deism in Clarke's writings, and had characterized him as 'more fond of his tenets than desirous of propagating them; and absorb'd so entirely in problems and calculations, that he is a mere reasoning machine' (*Letters Concerning the English* VII; *Lettres philosophiques* VII; see also W. H. Barber, 'Voltaire and Samuel Clarke', *Voltaire and the English*, SVEC 179 [1979]: 49–61; 'Deistes Anglais', *Inventaire Voltaire*, p. 368).

JB had recently read Clarke's *Discourse Concerning the Being and Attributes of God, the Obligations of Natural Religion, and the Truth and Certainty of the Christian Religion*, the Boyle sermons which he had delivered at St. Paul's in 1704–05 (To JJ, 20 Jan., *Corr. 1*, p. 118 and n. 3). SJ had recommended them to JB, though with reservations (*Life*, iv. 416 n. 2). JB had been so reassured by Clarke's rationalistic 'proofs' in the *Discourse* that he had urged WJT to read the work to overcome his religious doubts, especially concerning Revelation (Journ. 24 May 1763; 22 Oct. 1763, *Holland*, Heinemann p. 49 and n. 2, McGraw-Hill p. 50 and n. 7; To WJT, 9 Nov. 1763, *Corr.* 6, pp. 75–77; for Clarke's basic tenets, see Ezio Vailati, *Samuel Clarke, A Demonstration of the Being and Attributes of God and Other Writings*, 1998, pp. ix–xxxi). Neither SJ nor JB accepted Clarke's anti-Trinitarian theism, which presumably appealed to Voltaire.

³⁸ MS. 'but very learned ... worth' inserted above the line with a caret after 'is'. Presumably the first comment about SJ is JB's, the next is Voltaire's disparagement.

³⁹ SJ's remark that in his prose Frederick II wrote like Voltaire's 'footboy' or 'valet', is recorded in JB's journal of 18 July 1763. In the *Life* JB would clarify the scene with Voltaire: 'When I was at Ferney, I repeated this to Voltaire, in order to reconcile him somewhat to Johnson, whom he, in affecting

the English mode of expression, had previously characterised as "a superstitious dog;"
but after hearing such criticism on Frederick
the Great, with whom he was then on bad
terms, he exclaimed, "An honest fellow!'"
(18 July 1763, *Life* i. 434–35).

[40] A sign that contact with the Jacobites
was still dangerous for a British subject, and
that JB knew it.

[41] For JB's awareness of this behaviour of
Charles Edward Stuart's, see Journ. 6 Dec.
and n. 5.

[42] A more succinct judgment than in
Voltaire's *Essay upon the epick poetry*. It is
also more pointed than the comments in
*Candide*, ch. 25, which emphasize the boredom produced by the *Iliad*.

[43] MS. 'divering'

[44] MS. 'We have ex' deleted, a start of
the thought expressed in the next sentence.

[45] MS. The second page of the surviving
notes ends here. The last sentence in this
interchange is presumably JB's.

## Friday 28 December

[MEM. dated 29 Decr.] Yesterday awak'd baddish even here. Sent off Jacob. Out
& air clear'd you. Ran like the Cantab in Grays Elegy — to Church — heard a
little mass. Then in garden. Then wrote all morning — All at ease in their rooms.
Sent him verses — Ode &c. Most humbly presented to M. de Voltaire the glory of
France the Admiration of Europe by Mr. Boswell, who has had the honour of
regarding & loving him in private life at his Chateau de Ferney. After dinner
dullish [—] read Mahomet in his own house. He was not in humour at Supper.
This day — Finish Temple — Write Father — D'Hermanches Dupont &c. Fine
dress clean. Maurice &c Sunday.

[J] Last night M. de Voltaire treated me with polite respect. 'Je suis fâché
Monsieur que vous serez si mal loge.' I ought to have a good opinion of
myself; but from my unlucky education I cannot get rid of mean timidity as
to my own worth. I was very genteely lodged. My room was handsom. The
bed purple-cloth lined with white quilted sattin, the chimneypiece marble
& ornamented above with the picture of a [F]rench toilet.[1] M. de
Voltaire's Country house is the first I have slept in since I slept in that of
some good Scots family (Kelly indeed).[2] I surveyed every object here with
a minute attention and most curiously did I prove the association of ideas.
Every thing put me fully in mind of a decent Scots house, & I thought
surely the master of the family must go to church & do as public
Institutions require, & then I made my transition to the real master — the
celebrated Voltaire, the Infidel, the Authour of so many deistical pieces &
of the Pucelle d'Orleans.[3] I awaked this morning bad even here. Yet I
recovered, & as I was here for once in a life-time, & wished to have as much
of Voltaire as possible, I sent off Jacob to Geneva, to stop my coach today,
& to bring it out tomorrow. I then threw on my cloaths & ran like Cantab
(in the imitation of Gray's Elegy) with hose ungarterd[4] to Voltaire's
church, where I heard part of a mass & was realy devout. I then walked in
his Garden which is very pretty, & commands a fine prospect. I then went
to my room[,] got paper from Voltaire's Secretary[5] & wrote to my Father,
to Temple, and to Sir David Dalrymple.[6] I sent to M. de Voltaire a
Specimen of my Poem called Parliament. I also wrote a fair copy of my Ode
on Ambition for him,[7] & inscribed it thus:

323

'Most humbly presented to M. de Voltaire the glory of France, the Admiration of Europe, by Mr. Boswell, who has had the honour of regarding and loving him in private life at his Chateau de Ferney.'

He was bad today & did not appear before dinner. We dined well as usual. It was pleasant for me to think I was in [F]rance.[8] In the afternoon I was dullish. At six I applied to the Secretary for a Volume of Voltaire's plays, & went to my room, & read his Mahomet in his own house.[9] It was curious this. A good decent trusty Servant had fire & Bougies & all in order for me. There is at Ferney the true hospitality. All are master of their rooms, & do as they please. I should have mentioned yesterday that when I arrived, M. Rieu carried me to a room where the maids were and made me point out which of them I meant in my letter to Madame De Nis. M. de Voltaire was sick & out of spirits this evening, yet I made him talk some time. His Conversation shall be all collected into one Piece. I may perhaps insert it in this my Journal.[10] I supt at the table tonight. It hurt me to find that by low spirits it is possible for me to lose the relish of the most illustrious Genius. Hard indeed!

[1] Evidently much better than the garret he had offered to occupy (Journ. 25 Dec. n. 7). The picture showed either a dressing table or, more likely, a lady receiving visitors while in the last stages of dressing (see OED, s.v 'toilet', 4, 5b).

[2] JB had spent five days at Kellie, in Fifeshire, in the company of AE and AE's three sisters (30 Oct.–3 Nov., 'Journal of my Jaunt, Harvest 1762'). Possibly JB was recalling the easy sociability of this visit rather than the house, which was larger and gloomier than Voltaire's chateau. Kellie castle, which had come into the Erskine family in 1613 some years before Sir Thomas Erskine (1566–1639) was created Earl of Kellie, had been built from the 14th or 15th to the 17th century, boasted two towers from different periods, and was decorated with heraldic designs (A. H. Millar, *Fife: Pictorial and Historical*, 1895, pp. 433–37; *Scots Peer.* iv. 84–86).

[3] For church-going believers, Voltaire was an 'infidel' both in his attacks on organized religion, epitomized by the motto 'Ecrasez l'infâme' he began to use from 1761, and in the ideas he expressed in his many published works (see 'Infâme(L')', *Inventaire Voltaire*, pp. 715–16; Pomeau, *Voltaire*, ii. 189–91). These were 'deistical' in the pejorative sense expressed in SJ's definition: 'Belonging to the heresy of the deists' (*Dict. SJ*, s.v. 'deistical'). The 'heresy' included the deists' questioning the Trinity, revelation, the divinity of Christ, the immortality of the soul, and other beliefs deemed essential by orthodox Christians, and would lead SJ to remark on the 'iniquity' of Voltaire, which he declared to be as great as that of Rousseau (*Life*, 15 Feb. 1766, ii. 12). But Voltaire, whose interest in deism had been awakened soon after leaving his Jesuit school and intensified by his experiences in England, unabashedly regarded himself a deist in a philosophical sense (see Renée Pomeau, *Le Religion de Voltaire*, 1969, pp. 81–84, 137–45, 218–22; 'Déisme', *Inventaire Voltaire*, pp. 365–67; for Voltaire's own explanation of his beliefs, see Journ. 29 Dec. n. 4). *La Pucelle d'Orléans* (1762) was a burlesque retelling of the story of Joan of Arc (1412–31) that emphasized the superstitions and corruption of the clerics who opposed her.

For JB's continuing distrust of proponents of unorthodox religious views, even those whom he would meet socially, see Mary Margaret Stewart, 'Boswell and the Infidels', *Studies in English Literature, 1500–1900*, 1964, iv. 477–83.

[4] Short for 'Cantabrigian', a student at Cambridge University. JB is quoting from an affectionate parody of the 'Elegy Written in a Country Church-Yard' (1751). Published two years after Gray's elegy by 'Another Gentleman of Cambridge' and attributed to John Duncombe (1729–86), it includes the following lines:

Haply some friend may shake his hoary head
And say 'Each morn, unchill'd by frosts, he ran
With hose ungarter'd, o'er yon turfy bed,
To reach the chapel ere the psalms began'.

(*An Evening Contemplation in a College, Being a parody on the Elegy in a country church-yard*, 1753, p. 10, its author identified in the BL catalogue.)

[5] Jean-Louis Wagnière (1739–1802), who had worked for Voltaire from the age of fifteen and after only a year had become Voltaire's copyist, was now his trusted helper. He had a room above Voltaire's from which he could be summoned at any time, even though he had been married since 1763 and had just had the first of his two children (*Inventaire Voltaire*, p. 1401). He would remain with Voltaire for the rest of the latter's life and take care of the library even after Voltaire's death. Eventually he would become a minor functionary in Ferney, served as its mayor, and would survive the French Revolution ([Lucien Choudin], 'Wagnière', *Ferney-Voltaire*, 1990, p. 320; 'Wagnière', *Inventaire Voltaire*, pp. 1401–02).

[6] The letters to Lord Auchinleck and Dalrymple have not been recovered. The one to WJT, 8 sides of 4 folio leaves, is the main source of information about JB's meetings with Voltaire (see *Corr.* 6, pp. 122–30).

[7] For 'Parliament', see *Journ.* 6 Aug., n. 7. Neither the excerpts from this poem nor the 'Ode on Ambition' has been recovered. What is known of the Ode, however, is that JB was proud of it, that it was in Eglinton's possession in 1763 (*Journ.* 13 Jan. and 21

Mar.), and that it consisted of forty-eight lines when listed in the Plan prefixed to a manuscript collection of verse (Douce 193, Bodleian Library, Oxford). JB would later quote four lines in his letter to William Julius Mickle (1735–88) in 5 Aug. 1769 (Yale MS. L 964.1; see *Corr.* 7, pp. 209–11 and n. 8), and in his sending a copy to Lord Lyttelton later that month (28 Aug., Yale MS. L 89, *Catalogue*, i. 298–99).

[8] Ferney was in Gex, a small district which had become part of France in 1601 ('Gex (Pays de)', *Inventaire Voltaire*, p. 599).

[9] JB had either seen this controversial play in performance in The Hague on 6 May or had read it there (see *Holland*, Heinemann p. 233, McGraw-Hill p. 239). Entitled *Le Fanatisme ou Mahomet le Prophète* and first staged in Lille in 1741, then Paris in 1742, this tragedy presents Mahomet as a tyrant and hypocrite who misleads a young follower into becoming a fanatic. The piece was recognized as an attack on the austere Jansenists, or on Christianity, or on religion in general (Pomeau, *Religion de Voltaire*, pp. 154–56; *Inventaire Voltaire*, pp. 875–76). Mahomet was taken off the stage after its third night in Paris but could presumably be performed in countries not subject to French censorship, and it could be read in editions published in Amsterdam in 1742 and 1743, Berlin in 1751, Brussels in 1752, and Amsterdam again in 1753 (Bengesco, Nos. 131–139, i. 35–37).

[10] Most of these notes have not been recovered.

## Saturday 29 December

[MEM. dated Sunday 30 Decr.] [Y]esterday morning waited on Pere Adan who said Je fais mes prières pour M. de Voltaire tous les jours. Peutetre Dieu lui touchera le Cœur. Worthy amiable Jesuit. Then saw Theatre genteel — Then Library. Memoires Eclesiastiques (Contres les Jes: par les Jans) *Sotises Ecles.* Tragedies Barbares [—] Cleone, Elfrida, Caractacus. Was splenetic at dinner. After it saw him in Salle. When I came to see you I thought to see a very great, but a very bad man. You are very sincere. Yes, but the same makes me own that I find the contrary. Only your Dictionnaire Philosophique. For instance *Ame* the Soul — 'that is a good Article' — no — excuse me: Is it not a pleasing imagination? Is it not more noble? — Yes. You have a noble desire to be king of Europe. I wish it & I ask your protection but it is not probable — No, but all cannot be the one & may be the other. 'It must be so'[1] — till Immortality. But before we say that this soul will exist let us know what it is. I know not the cause I cannot judge I cannot be a Juryman. Cicero says — potius optand quam proband.[2] We are ignorant Beings — We are the Puppets of Providence[3] — I am a poor Punch. Would you

325

have no public worship — Yes with all my heart. Let us meet four times a year in a grand Temple with music & thank God for all his gifts. There is one Sun. There is one God, let us have one Religion. Then all mankind will be Brethren.[4] May I write in english & youll answer? Yes. Farewell. Home — Voltaire high[5] — Rouss profound. Supt Gauss after Maurice. This day Letts all day — till 6. See Tronchin — Be engage tomorrow. Pay Brackel — boots wash feet.

[J] I this morning visited M. Rieu and M. de Belle-Pré a Gentleman Painter. They lived in the same room.[6] I then visited My excellent Père Adan who gives lessons to some of the young servants & is in all respects obliging. I talked of Religion, & found him to be a sincere Christian. He said 'Je fais mes prierres pour M. de Voltaire tous les jours. Peutetre il plaira á Dieu de lui toucher le cœur et lui faire voir la vraye religion. C'est dommage qu'il n'est pas Chretien. Il en a bien des Vertus. Il a la plus belle ame. Il est bienveillant, Il est charitable; mais il a des prejugés le plus fortes contre la Religion Chretiênne. Quand il est dans serieux Je tache de lui dire un mot, mais quand il est dans l'humeur de jetter ses traits de ridicule, Je me tais.'[7] Worthy Father! how strange is the System of human things! I reasoned with him against the æternity of Hell's torments. He could not escape from the opinion of the Church: but his humanity made him say 'Je serais charmé s'il sera autrement.' I then went with Rieu and saw the Theatre of M. de Voltaire. It is not large, but very handsom.[8] It suggested to me a variety of very pleasing ideas. One circumstance rendered M. de Voltaire's particularity agreable to me. My Association of ideas was such that I constantly thought of Temple. I can account for this. Some years ago he wrote to my Father proposing that He & I should go together to study at Geneva, & should see 'Voltaire! Rousseau! immortal names!'[9] Besides we used to talk much of Voltaire with Nicholls and Claxton.[10] Such little circumstances which recall my dear freind are valuable. I next went with the Secretary and saw M. de Voltaire's Library which was tollerably numerous & in very good order.[11] I saw there the Elements of Criticism & by the Secretary's denying it I was perswaded that Voltaire had written the severe letter upon this book in the Gazette Literaire.[12] The Jansenists used to publish against the Jesuits what they called Memoires Eclesiastiques. Voltaire has got a thick Volume of them bound up with the title of *Sottises Eclesiastiques*.[13] I saw upon a Shelf an octavo with this title *Tragedies Barbares*. I was sure they must be english. I took down the Book, & found it contained *Cleone, Elfrida, Caractacus*.[14] I was mightily amused with these little sallies which were quite in the taste of Sir David Dalrymple. I heartily wish Voltaire had titled more of his Books. I was drest the first time at Ferney in my Seagreen and Silver, and now in my flowered velvet. Gloom got hold of me at dinner, in so much that I thought I would not be obliged to stay here for a great deal of money. And yet in reality I would be proud & pleased to live a long time chez M. de Voltaire. I was asked to return when I should be at Lyons. I took an easy leave of the Company. M. de Voltaire was very ill today, & had not appeared.[15] I sent my respects to him, & begged to be allowed to take leave of him. He sent to me his compliments & said he would see me. I found him in the drawing-room where I had near half an hour more with him at least more than a quarter. I told him that I had marked his conversation. He seemed pleased. This last conversation shall also be marked. It was truly singular & solemn. I was quite in enthusiasm, quite agreably mad to a certain degree. I asked his Corespondence. He granted it.[16] Is not this great? Well I must here pause, and as an impartial Philosopher decide concerning myself. What a singular Being do I find myself! Let this my Journal shew what variety my mind is capable of. But am I not well received everywhere? am I not particularly taken notice of by men of the most distinguished Genius? And why? I have neither profound knowledge, strong judgment, nor constant gayety. But I have a noble Soul which still shines forth, a certain degree of knowledge, a multiplicity of ideas of all kinds, an original humour and turn of expression, and I realy beleive a remarkable knowledge of human nature: this is different from a knowledge of the world as much as is the knowledge of a florist who understands perfectly the works of nature from that of him who understands flowers formed by art. The florist perceives in general that the artificial flowers are not natural; but whether they are made of gum'd linnen, of china, or of copper he cannot tell. So I know in general your men of the world to be artificial: But am not able to develope their different qualitys. What is realy man I think I know pretty well. With this I have a pliant ease of manners which must please. I can tune myself so to the tone of any bearable man I am with, that he is as much at freedom as with another self & till I am gone cannot imagine me a Stranger. Perhaps my talents are such as procure me more happiness than those of a more elevated kind. Were it not for my black Hypochondria, I might be a practical Epicurean. I departed from this Chateau in a most extraordinary humour, thinking hard, & wondering if I could possibly when again in Scotland again feel my most childish prejudices. When I got to Geneva I was visited by young Chappuis[18] to whom I said: M. de Voltaire est Poete c'est un Poete sublime,[19] et va bien haut [—] M. Rousseau est Philosophe et[20] va bien profond l'un vole, l'autre plonge. This is clumsily said; but the thought is not bad. I supt at M. Gaussin's where I found Lord Stanhope[21] & Lord Abingdon and his Brother.[22] I was so so. I had first been at Professor Maurice's, where I saw his Lady his Son & his Daughter.[23]

---

[1] The opening line of the famous soliloquy in Addison's *Cato* (V. i), in which the hero wonders about the immortality of the soul while holding a copy of *Phaedo,* Plato's treatise on the subject. Voltaire had translated this speech into French for the 1751 edition of his *Lettres philosophiques* (Ahmad Gunny, *Voltaire and English Literature,* 1979, pp. 67–70). JB had quoted this passage on arriving in London on 19 Nov. 1762.

[2] Potius optandum quam probandum ('rather desired than proved by demonstration'). JB would continue this argument with Voltaire a few weeks later, again maintaining his belief in the afterlife of the soul: 'You must forgive my zeal for immortality. I am a melancholy man, I know not how. In this world my prospect is clouded. I cheer my hours of gloom with expectations of a brighter scene after death and I think I have a strong probability that I shall not be deceived' (To Voltaire from Rome, Yale MS. L 1262, 24 Apr. 1765).

[3] MS. 'the' inserted before 'Puppets', 'in the hand' deleted after 'Puppets'

[4] A clear expression of Voltaire's deistic belief in a universal religion that worships one God, unites all human beings by fra-

ternal bonds, and allows public expressions of gratitude to God but not complaints or pleas for personal favours. In the absence of JB's account of this meeting, the only other known record appears in JB's letter to WJT of 28 Dec., which provides further details of this scene: 'He exprest his veneration his love of the Supreme Being, and his entire Resignation to the will of Him who is allwise. He exprest his desire to resemble the Author of Goodness, by being good himself. His sentiments go no farther. He does not inflame his mind with grand hopes of the immortality of the Soul. He says it may be; but, he knows nothing of it. And his mind is in perfect tranquillity.' To JB's question 'Are you sincere ...?', Voltaire replied: 'Before God I am'. And he declared: 'I suffer much. But I suffer with Patience & Resignation; not as Christian — But as a Man' (*Corr.* 6, p. 125). Summarized here are the deistical ideas that Voltaire was setting down at about this time in the article 'Théiste', using a term that he preferred to 'deist' after the 1750s to distinguish himself from other *philosophes* (see his *Dictionnaire philosophique portatif*, new ed. 1765, Bengesco, #1402; *Inventaire Voltaire*, p. 1318).

⁵ MS. 'hig'

⁶ Belpré was an officer in the life guards of King Stanislas Leszczynski at Lunéville and also an amateur painter. He had met Boufflers in Solothurn six weeks earlier and had become his travelling companion (Guy Cabourdin, *Quand Stanislas regnait en Lorraine*, 1980, p. 373; *Lettres de Monsieur le Chevalier de Boufflers ... a Madame sa Mere*, 1771, p. 9). Since Voltaire's chateau had not yet been extended by wings and the theatre building had not yet been remodelled to accommodate guests, Belpré must have been sharing a room with Rieu. The latter, a frequent guest at Ferney, lived in Geneva in a large house owned by his mother and in the family's country house at Chouily nearby. In 1774, he would build a house for himself and his family at Ferney on a property sold to him by Voltaire and Mme Denis (Jean-Daniel Candaux, 'Précisions sur Henri Rieu', *Le Siècle de Voltaire*, ed. Christiane Mervaud and Sylvain Menant, 1987, i. 205–07).

⁷ This passage confirms the suspicion of d'Alembert and others that Adam was trying to win Voltaire back to the Church (D'Alembert to Frederick II of Prussia, 1768, cited in Ennemond Trillat, 'Voltaire et le Père Adam', *Le Crocodile*, 1761, p. 7; see also 'Adam, Antoine, père', *Inventaire Voltaire*, p. 19).

⁸ In a separate building between the chateau and the church, this was modelled on the theatre just completed by Soufflot in Lyon. Voltaire's theatre, built between 1760 and 1761, compensated for its small stage by a skilful use of perspective that made the actors seem more distant than they were. Rieu was among the friends of Voltaire—along with the Constant-Pictets, Cramers, Angelique Rilliet, and Marie (Corneille) Dupuits—who performed Voltaire's plays here, replacing professional actors whom the disapproving Genevan authorities discouraged from accepting roles at Ferney (Candaux, 'Précisions sur Henri Rieu', p. 226; 'Corneille, Marie Françoise', *Inventaire Voltaire*, p. 327). The theatre, closed in 1765 to make space for more bedrooms, would be replaced ten years later by a new theatre in the centre of the town of Ferney (*Ferney-Voltaire*, p. 38 and n. 14).

⁹ The passage makes clear that the initial idea for the visit to both Rousseau and Voltaire had come from WJT, that WJT had actually approached Lord Auchinleck for permission, and that the very phrase 'Voltair, Rousseau, immortal names!', used by WJT in his first letter on the subject, had been a motto which had remained with JB (see From WJT, ?Spring 1759; see also 9 Aug. 1759, *Corr.* 6, pp. 17, 20 n. 1). WJT's letter to Lord Auchinleck has not been recovered.

¹⁰ Norton Nicholls (?1742–1809) and John Claxton (d. 1811) were close friends of WJT's from his days at Trinity Hall, Cambridge (see From WJT, 10 July 1763, *Corr.* 6, pp. 38 n. 4, 16). WJT had introduced them to JB in London (Journ. 13, 15 May 1763).

¹¹ The books—7,500 titles by the end of Voltaire's life—were grouped loosely by topic and were catalogued primarily by Wagnière (*Cat. Ferney*, Introduction, pp. 16–17).

¹² Listed as 'Elements of Criticism par juge Kames', *Cat. Ferney*, 'List', no. 1542. For the anonymous review, see Journ. 27 Sept. and n. 10.

¹³ Not listed in *Cat. Ferney*.

¹⁴ *Cleone* was a tragedy by Robert Dodsley (1703–64), first performed at the Theatre Royal in Covent Garden in 1758 and published the same year (CBEL, ii. 437). For William Mason's poetic dramas *Elfrida* and *Caractacus*, see Journ. 8 Nov. n. 7. The entry '2 Tragédies barbares, c:a:d. [c'est à dire] anglaises' is in Voltaire's handwriting (see *Cat. Ferney*, 'List', no. 2814, and Introduction, p. 13).

¹⁵ Voltaire suffered from constipation and diarrhoea, as well as from apoplectic fits, the first of which he suffered in 1759. He was also troubled by unspecified imaginary ill-

nesses (see Jacques Bréliant and Raphäel Roche, *L'Envers du roi Voltaire (quatre-vingts ans de la vie d'un mourant)*, 1989, pp. 105–40.

[16] For their continued correspondence, see To Voltaire, Yale MSS. L 1261–63; From Voltaire, Yale MS. C 3045; *Grand Tour I*, Heinemann pp. 308–12, McGraw-Hill pp. 318–22.

[18] Probably Paul Chappuis (1737–1809), son of JB's bankers Chappuis et fils (see Journ. 24 Dec. n. 6; Galiffe, ii. 109). He was a great admirer of Rousseau, whom he was just trying to meet (see *CC Rousseau*, Letter 3732 [12 Dec.], xxii. 221 and 'Note explicative').

[19] MS. 'un' inserted before 'Poete', 'sublime' after 'Poete'

[20] MS. 'est'

[21] Philip (1717–86), 2nd Earl Stanhope, was the son of James Stanhope (1673–1721), who had been created 1st Earl Stanhope for his valour in the War of the Spanish Succession, notably in the capture of the port of Mahon on Minorca that had allowed him to add 'Mahon' to his family name (*Comp. Peer.*, xii. 229–31 and note f). Philip Stanhope, orphaned at the age of seven, had been brought up with the guidance of his kinsman Lord Chesterfield and had been educated in Utrecht and Geneva. Although discouraged from studying science and mathematics, which were not considered gentlemanly pursuits, he had become an esteemed mathematician and Fellow of the Royal Society (*Oxford DNB* [DNB Archive], s.v. 'Stanhope, Charles, 3rd Earl Stanhope'). He had returned to Geneva in 1760 with his wife and two sons. After the older one, Philip (1746–63), succumbed to consumption, Lord Stanhope kept his surviving son Charles, *styled* Viscount Mahon (b. 1753), close to the famous Dr. Tronchin (for whom see Journ. 1 Jan. 1765 and n. 5; Ghita Stanhope, rev. by G. P. Gooch, *The Life of Charles Third Earl Stanhope*, 1914, pp. 1–5). Hospitable and public spirited while in Geneva, Lord Stanhope and his son would be offered bourgeois rights after the latter won a much prized archery contest in 1771 (Louis Dufour, 'Les Stanhopes à Genève 1720–1795', *L'ancienne Genève 1535–1798, fragments historiques*, 1909, pp. 75–96).

[22] Willoughby (Bertie), Earl of Abingdon (Jan. 1739/40–99), had been educated at Westminster School and in Geneva, had then studied at Oxford from 1759 to 1761, and had succeeded to the title in his final year. He was now in Switzerland to join the pro-Rousseau *représentants* (for whom see Journ. 24 Dec. n. 24; *Voltaire's British Visitors*, ed. G. R. de Beer and André-Michel Rousseau, SVEC 49 [1967]: 123). He was an acquaintance of JB's friend the Rev. Charles de Guiffardière, who had recently sent regards from The Hague (22 Nov., Yale MS. C 1407). Abingdon would visit Voltaire at Ferney in the company of John Wilkes in July 1765 but would not impress Horace Walpole, who would describe him as 'a singular young man, not quite devoid of parts, but rough and wrong-headed, extremely underbred but warmly honest' (Walpole, Journal, Sept. 1777, quoted in *Comp. Peer.* i. 48). Lord Abingdon's brother, the Hon. Peregrine Bertie (1741–90), had attended the Westminster School from 1750, had joined the navy in 1759 with the rank of lieutenant, and had been appointed commander in Jan. 1762, captain ten months later (*The Commissioned Sea Officers of the Royal Navy 1660–1815*, 1954, i. 65). He would represent Oxford as M.P. 'on the family interest', usually voting in opposition, from 1774 to the end of his life (Namier and Brooke, ii. 88). For an anecdote supplied by Bertie, see *Boswelliana*, p. 239.

[23] The 'lady' was Sophie-Dorothée (Bonet-Dupan) Maurice (dates not found). Her fourteen-year-old son Frédéric-Guillaume (for whom see Journ. 23 Dec. and n. 8) would develop intellectual and political interests, publishing *Observations botanico-meteorologiques* (1789) and a *Traité engrais* (1800). He would also found the *Bibliothèque britannique* with Marc-Auguste and Charles Pictet (DHBS, iv. 694; Galiffe, iii. 327–28). The daughter is not identified.

## Sunday 30 December

[MEM. dated Monday 31 Decr.] Yesterday at home all morning writing letters — at 3 Prof Maurice with you. Was amus'd to think Geneva Minister. Own'd gloom with Pride. Then went to Monot's. Good Societé [—] was hyp'd with Hunger. Danc'd one minuet — Great supper — threw Bread at each other. All taking other by hands, & Parson too — Rampag'd till 1 & Parson [—] wild idea — Saw nothing frightning — Geneva Sunday dancing &c. This day visits and prepare all well.

[J] I sat at home all forenoon writing. At three Professor Maurice called upon me & sat an hour. We were chearfull. It was a curious idea 'this is a Geneva Minister.'[1] I talked vastly well; yet I talked of my gloom with Pride. He was amazed at it. He asked my Corespondence. I shall write to him.[2] Van Eck was now at Geneva with his good Governour Monat who invited me this afternoon to the *Societé* of his Wife. He lived in the Maison de Ville.[3] I found here a very genteel company with true Geneva looks. After tea & Coffee was a Ball. The fiddle or fiddles fairly played and the Company fairly danced. Was not this enough to break my most stubborn association of gloom with a Sunday at Geneva? To compleat the thing there was a Clergyman in the Company. This is the second young Geneva Minister that I have seen. I do not at all like them. I know not if they are Arians & Socinians,[4] but I am sure they are Fops. I played a hand at whist, & after we had played and danced enough, we went to Supper. I say *we* danced, for altho' I was not much in spirits, I danced a minuet with Madam Rillet whom I had seen and grown fond of at Ferney, & thus I solaced myself with the downfall of Presbyterian Strictness. However the Geneva Clergy are different from the Scots. M. Maurice insisted 'Nous ne sommes pas des Puritains. L'archeveque de Canterburry est en liaison avec notre venerable Compagnie, et toujours quand l'Eglise Anglicane fait quelque chose d'importance, il nous en donne notice.'[5] We supped in a great Town-hall,[6] & eat and drank considerably. After which they pelted each other with the crumb of their bread formed into little balls. This was rather rude in a large company & in presence of a Stranger. I however threw with the rest partly to keep them in countenance, partly to indulge my whim. I asked if this was the common custom at Geneva. They said they did so only among freinds. They were monstrously familiar, the men pawing the sweaty hands of the women, & kissing them too, as the minister slabbered the greasy unwashen hands of a married woman.[7] Had I been the husband, I should have kicked the fellow down stairs. I was disgusted much, & only consoled myself that I beheld a nauseous example of the manners of Republicans. I was glad to get home.

[1] Maurice had been ordained in 1737, as was required for an academic position.

[2] Although JB would not correspond with Maurice, he had already received a letter from Maurice's son (for whom see Journ. 23 Dec. n. 8) and would reply from Genoa on 6 Dec. 1765 (an extract survives as Yale MS. L 958).

[3] JB had met Gaspard-Joel Monod with his pupil in Brunswick (see Journ. 11 Aug. and n. 5). Monod's wife, Suzanne-Madeline (*née* Puerari; 1737–99), whom he had married in Jan. of this year, belonged to a highly respected family, originally from Cremona, who had settled in Geneva in the mid-sixteenth century and had produced professors, magistrates, and military men (Galiffe, ii. 802, 805; Henri Puerari, *Souvenirs de famille, 1562–1909*, 1934, pp. 33–37). On his

marriage Monod had been granted a living by his employer, Sir Joshua Vanneck, in the parish of Huntingfield that he would hold *in absentia* for the rest of his life (Montet, ii. 186; J. Monod, *Cent-soixante-quinze ans 1793–1968*, 1969, pp. 8–9). Whether, and if so why, the young couple lived in the town hall, a large complex of buildings in the old city above the Bastion, is unclear. Only a few officials actually lived there (see Barbara Roth-Lochner and Livio Fornara, *L'Hotel de ville de Geneve*, 1986, pp. 3–7, 21–29). Possibly the Monods had moved into one of the adjacent houses on the rue de l'hôtel de ville (*Plan Billon 1726*, repr. 1986, pl. 3 and 4).

[4] The Arians, who took their name from the Greek (originally Libyan) priest Arius

(250–336 A.D.), questioned the divine nature of Christ (see 'Arianism', NCE, i. 791–92). The Socinians, who followed the teachings of Laelius Socinus (1525–62) and his nephew Faustus Socinus (1559–1604), also questioned the notion of the Trinity, rejecting doctrines not clearly based on the Bible and accessible to reason (see 'Socinianism', NCE, xiii. 398; 'Socinianisme', *Dict. de Rousseau*, pp. 861–62). In short, both Arians and Socinians reflected the spirit of deism with its emphasis on a rational religion (see Norman Sykes, *Church and State in England in the XVIIIth Century*, 1962, pp. 343–52).

Recently, Genevan clergymen had been called Socinians by d'Alembert, with the concurrence of Voltaire, and had been praised for no longer believing in hell or the eternity of punishments ('Genève', *Encyclopédie*, 1751, vii. 578).

[5] Only a few cordial but inconsequential exchanges of congratulations from the Archbishop are preserved in the BPUN and Archives d'Etat of Geneva (AEG) and in the library of Lambeth Palace, London. Important messages might have come by personal emissary, however, or possibly through the chaplain of the English embassy in Constantinople communicating with the Protestant Genevans residing there (AEG, Cp. Past. 29, pp. 169–70, suggested by Jacques Barrelet, Asst. Archivist, AEG, letter of 3 Apr. 2001).

[6] Probably in the tour Baudet, the oldest part of the hôtel de ville, dating from the fifteenth century (Lochner and Fornara, pp. 5–7; further information from Fornara, Sept. 2004).

[7] Evidently JB was not used to the Continental custom of hand-kissing. Altogether, the Genevans' behaviour confirmed young Buisson's observation that good manners had greatly declined in their town since Calvin's days (Journ. 28 Nov.; see also Linda Kirk, '"Going Soft": Genevan Decadence in the Eighteenth Century', *The Identity of Geneva: The Christian Commonwealth, 1564–1864*, 1998, pp. 143–54).

## Monday 31 December

[MEM. dated Tuesday 1 January 1765[1]] Yesterday had been up all night. Young Maurice came & you went & saw Library and Great Clock — & sounded one. Payed visits — Had young Maurice at dinner — Then payd visits — Lord Stanhope's [—] Pembroke. King[2] damn sail allow me to add mine?[3] Supt Mad Gaussin [—] dispute on Religion. Rousseau deep Volt high. At night so opprest could write but not think at all — quite oerpowr'd. To bed — This day send to Tronchin — Put letters right & addresses. Buy a quire of Paper to have it equal.[4] <Send>[5] letts from 1st stage.

[J] All last night I sat up & wrote letters.[6] I do not mark in this my Journal the various fluctuations of my extensive Corespondence. It would be an immense labour, and my Bundles of letters will explain it sufficiently. At ten young Maurice came to me, & we went & saw the Geneva Library, which is in good order, and tollerably provided with Manuscripts.[7] The Professor who shewed it me, talked of honest M. Du Pont. We then mounted the tower of the Church de St. Piêrre and saw the famous great Clock of which I have heard M. Dupont talk so much. I wrote to the good old Gentleman from his favourite town of Geneva, and gave him an account of All this.[8] Young Maurice dined with me at my inn. He was a very fine lad sensible and obliging. I found at my Banker's a letter from my worthy Father, in which he said 'he longed to see me, to have my assistance in his affairs, and to explain to me every point concerning them.' Altho' I was uneasy to think how little my distempered mind could apply to the sober business of life, this way of writing to me so warmed my heart that I felt a sudden spring of resolution, and hoped to give satisfaction to the worthiest of men.[9] I called on young Chais, who was sick & could not receive me.[10] I was received at Lord Stanhope's, and presented to My Lady.[11] I sat some time there. I then went to Gaussin's, where I was kept to supper. I was so so. When I got home, I was so fatigued with writing last night, and walking today that I could hardly think. I sunk to sleep most sound.

[1] MS. '1764'. Most of this memorandum, disfigured by smudges, is based on the transcription of earlier Yale editors.

[2] MS. 'King' inserted above 'damn'

[3] Unidentified anecdote, possibly told by or about Henry Herbert, 10th Earl of Pembroke (1734–94). Pembroke, who had travelled abroad, had also served in various regiments during the Seven Years' War and, an expert horseman, had published his *Method of Breaking Horses* in 1762. He had been appointed lord of the bedchamber in 1756 to the Prince of Wales, soon to be George III, but had lost his positions because of his scandalous elopement. However, he had just been reinstated, and had been appointed also as colonel in the 1st royal dragoons (*Oxford DNB*).

[4] A quire is made up of 24 or sometimes 25 sheets (OED, s.v. 'quire'). In his 'Ten Lines' of 25 Oct., JB had complained about having to write on sheets of uneven size.

[5] MS. damaged by a hole; 'Send' known from a transcription by an earlier Yale editor.

[6] To WJT, Lady Northumberland, Burnett, Mitchell, Madame de Spaen, Van Sommelsdyck, Hübner, d'Hermenches, M. de Zuylen, Belle de Zuylen, and Lord Marischal (see Reg. Let., 31 Dec.).

[7] The library was in the collège de Calvin, the school situated near the cathedral of Saint-Pierre in the old part of the town. The collection had started with the purchase, from 1547, of the books and MSS of the prior of Saint-Victor, François de Bonivard (c. 1493–1570), the 'prisoner of Chillon' later to be made famous by Lord Byron for being incarcerated from 1530 to 1536 in the middle of Lake Geneva during the struggle between Geneva and Savoy (DHBS, ii. 235). Bonivard's books had been transferred in 1559 from the ruling *Seigneurie's* holdings in the town hall, and more had come from Calvin's library on his death in 1564. Since 1539 the Geneva library had also been the repository for all books printed by Geneva booksellers (Bernard Gagnebin, 'Les Origines de la bibliothèque de Genève', *Archives, Bibliothèques et Musées de Belgique*, 30/2 [1959]: 228–33). The library's manuscript collection, also initially Bonivard's, had been enriched by important gifts in the mid-

eighteenth century, including papers concerning the siege of Orléans and Joan of Arc donated by Rousseau in 1756 while he was still on good terms with his Genevan countrymen (Gagnebin, 'Le Cabinet des manuscrit de la Bibliothèque de Genève', *Genava*, n.s. 2 [1954]: 73–95). In 1872 the library would be transferred to a site in the Bastion, next to the new buildings inaugurated as the University of Geneva (information sheet from the library itself, 1999).

[8] The 'clock' was presumably the famous great bell, 'La Clémence', named after Pope Clement VII and installed in 1407. It had an especially deep tone (W. Deonna, *Cathédrale de Saint-Pierre de Genève*, 1950, pp. 104–13). For JB's previous use of 'clock' for a bell, see Journ. 16 Oct. and n. 4.

Dupont (see Journ. 23 Dec. n. 4) had spent seven years in Geneva before going to Edinburgh. JB's letter would not survive, but his warm feelings toward Dupont would continue. When Dupont was reduced to poverty because his French-speaking congregation had dwindled, JB would try to help him gain an augmentation of his stipend by submitting a request to the Town Council on 15 Jan. 1777, unfortunately rejected two weeks later (see JB's copy of Dupont's letter to Sir David Dalrymple, Lord Hailes, 21 Feb. 1777, Yale MS. C 1165; information also from John Hamilton of Edinburgh to F. A. Pottle, 5 Sept. 1938).

[9] JB already knew on 26 Dec. that he had his father's consent to go to Italy, and had expressed similar affectionate sentiments about him in a letter to Andrew Mitchell of 26 Dec. (BL Add. MS. 6858, ff. 15–17).

[10] Jean-Antoine Chais (b. 1735) was the son of the Rev. Charles Pierre Chais (1700–85), a Genevan who had been pastor of the Protestant French church in The Hague since 1728 but who had retained the rights of bourgeoisie for his children (*Recueil genealogique Suisse*, 1st. ser. 1902, i. 78; DHBS). JB had had an introduction to him from the Rev. Pierre Dupont (?Nov. 1763, Yale MS. C 1161) and had met him in The Hague on 8 and 13 May (*Holland*, Heinemann pp. 234, 237, McGraw-Hill pp. 240, 243). 'Young' Chais, born in The Hague, had studied law in Leiden, had earned a doctorate in law there

in 1755, and had been admitted advocate in Geneva in 1759. He was now settling permanently in his father's native city (*Recueil*, i. 80).

[11] Grisel (Hamilton), Lady Stanhope (c. 1719–1811), daughter of Charles, Lord Bin-

ning, had married Lord Stanhope in 1745 when he had 'at last lifted up his eyes from Euclid, and directed them to matrimony' (Horace Walpole to Sir Horace Mann, 28 Feb. 1745, *Corres. Walpole*, xix. 19 and nn. 18, 22; *Comp. Peer.*, xii. 233–34).

## Tuesday 1 January 1765

[MEM. dated Wednesday 2 Jan. 1765] Yesterday waited on the famous Dr. Tronchin to whom Gaussin had sent. Said un homme en bonne santé pour faire ses respects. Rousseau coquin — orgueilleux ambitieux mechant — fille — pas pour sa severité de mœurs — enfants touts exposés — Je le sais — Je vous ai oté une plume de votre Bonheur. Il recroitra. Voltaire aimable — mais pas un deux[1] jour la même. Quelquefois bon Deiste — mais s'il a eu des chagrins. Il lance des traits contre la providence. Je le regardois comme un Astronome regarde un Phenomæne, J'ai marqué les nuances de cet Ame, Je l'ai vu quand il se croit mourant et moi aussi en horreurs? — non le plus malade il est, il est le meilleur Deiste. Sa maladie le fait penser plus de Dieu[2] comme un ètre misericordieux — Je puis dire cela [—] Oui — mais il est fou — car un homme qui na points de principes fixes pour le servir comme Bou<ssole>[3] est fou — et c'est l'homme le plus faible qui existe. Tronchin noble.

[J] Voltaire had solemnly assured me that he never was affraid of death, & had desired me to ask the famous Dr. Tronchin his Physician if he had ever seen him so.[4] Gaussin sent a card to Tronchin asking permission for me to wait upon him, which was granted. I was to set out this morning, so went to him in boots at eight o'clock. I found him a stately handsom man with a good air and great ease.[5] I said: 'Je ne suis pas malade Monsieur, mais si un homme en bonne santé peut vous faire ses respects.' He replied: 'Il faut bien voir des tels' & smiled. He said Rousseau was un Coquin orgueilleux ambitieux mechant qui a ecrit avec un Poignard trempé dans le sang de ses Concitoyens.[6] Un homme gaté par des maladies veneriennes, un homme qui affecte une severité de mœurs, et au même tems entretient une maitrêsse. J'etois son Ami:[7] — mais quand Je trouvois que plutot que d'avoir une obligation á Personne il exposoit ses propres enfants, Je ne voulois plus le voir.[8] This shocked me; but I recollected that Tronchin was connected with the Geneva Magistracy whom Rousseau has so keenly attacked.[9] Tronchin saw that I was hurt at hearing such a character of my admired Rousseau, and said. 'Je vous ai oté une plume de votre Bonheur.' I replied 'Il recroitra.' I then talked[10] of Voltaire. He said: 'Il est fort aimable, mais pas deux jours la même. Quelquefois il est un tres bon Deiste. Mais s'il a eu des chagrins, s'il a recu une lettre qui la piqué il vous lance des traits contre la Providence. Je l'ai regardé comme un Astronome regarde un Phænomêne. J'ai marqué toutes les nuances de cette Ame. Je l'ai vu quand il se croioit mourant et Je le croiois aussi.' Oui? Il etoit donc en horreur — 'Non. Le plus malade qu'il est il devient le meilleur Deiste. Sa Maladie le fait penser plus de Dieu[11] comme un Etre misericordieux.' 'Eh bien Je puis donc dire cela de la meilleure authorité. M. de Voltaire m'a chargé de vous demander s'il craignoit la mort comme les Ministres ont dit.' 'Vous pouvez dire cela, Monsieur.[12] Mais il est fou. J'appelle un Homme fou qui n'a point de principes fixes qui lui servent comme un Boussole dans les grands evenements de la vie. C'est l'homme le plus foible qui existe.' 'C'est curieux quand on voit des prês les grands hommes' — 'Monsieur, il y a peu d'hommes qui peuvent conserver leur gloire, quand ils sont regardés avec le microscope. J'ai envoyé mon fils á voyager. Il verra tous les grands hommes en Europe, et il apprendra de juger sans prejugé.[13] Je demandois, á M. de Voltaire pourquoi il n'agissoit pas plus constamment selon ses principes? Il me repondoit "Si J'avois le Corps aussi fort que vous, Je serois plus constant."' This Interview was of no small value as it enabled me to have allways a hold upon the Bigots who forge storys of The great Luminary of France. I set out at eleven in a Chaise mounted so high before that I was thrown back like a Bishop in his studying chair. All the Chaises for passing the Alps are hung in this way.[14] I jogged on mighty deliberate.

[1] MS. 'deux' inserted above the line.

[2] MS. 'Dieux', with final 'x' deleted.

[3] MS. damaged by a hole after 'Bou', the rest of the word revealed in Journ. of 1 Jan. 1765. Five more words are illegible.

[4] The question of how others behaved when facing death would long fascinate JB. He had made a point of observing an execution (Journ. 4 May 1763), and would do so frequently in later life. He would interview David Hume during his last weeks to learn whether the philosopher still held his atheistic beliefs (Journ. 3 Mar. 1777, Yale MS. M 117–18). Possibly JB had broached the subject with Voltaire not only because of the latter's much-vaunted questioning of an immortal soul but also because of the stories told in Utrecht by the Rev. Robert Brown, who had visited Voltaire several times in the early 1760s (see n. 12 below; Voltaire's British Visitors, ed. G. R. de Beer and André-Michel Rousseau, SVEC 49 [1967]: 49–50).

[5] Theodore Tronchin (1709–81) was six feet (1.8 m) tall and strikingly handsome. He presumably lived in the Bourg-de-Four, close to the cathedral, in a house long in the possession of his family (H. Tronchin, pp. 25, 76–77). His forebears, Huguenots who had left their native Provence in the sixteenth century, had been prominent Protestant clergymen, bankers, and members of the various councils in Geneva for several generations. Tronchin had attended school in Geneva and had studied at Cambridge, having gone to England in the hope of finding a place through his distant relation Lord Bolingbroke (Galiffe, iii. 367). When that plan failed, largely because Bolingbroke had retired from public life, Tronchin had studied medicine in Leiden from 1728 and had qualified as doctor in 1730, submitting a dissertation De nympha. Befriended by Hermann Boerhaave (1668–1738), he had become that great physician's successor and had established a successful practice in Amsterdam. But he had disapproved of the prevailing manners and morals, and so, encouraged by his wife Hélène de Witt, whom he had married in 1740, he had returned to Geneva in 1754. There he had faced unexpected jealousies on the part of the entrenched physicians, who had rejected his appointment as honorary professor of medicine at the Geneva Academy in spite of the approval of the academic senate and the Vénérable Compagnie des Pasteurs, who oversaw the university (Borgeaud, i. 589–90). When a hall was found for his lectures, he attracted enthusiastic students as well as an international clientele of patients, especially from the French and English aristocracy (for details about his career, see H. Tronchin, pp. i–ii, 1–30). He would move to Paris in 1766 to become the personal physician of the Duke of Orléans and to treat a new group of aristocratic patients (H. Tronchin, pp. 165–91, 303–05). In his practice, Tronchin rejected the bleedings, purgatives, and other violent treatments favoured by his colleagues, advocating instead a moderate diet, exercise, and fresh air (H. Tronchin, pp. 35–64). He also favoured inoculations to prevent smallpox and had just returned from treating the Duke of Parma's children (Biographisches Lexikon der hervorragenden

*Ärzte*, ed. E. Gurlt and A. Wernich, 1934, v. 643–44; *CC Rousseau*, xxi. 186–87 and note d).

[6] An indignant accusation that by his writings Rousseau had caused the hostile factions now dividing Genevans (see Journ. 24 Dec. n. 24).

[7] MS. final 'e' of 'Amie' erased.

[8] Tronchin had offered his friendship to Rousseau when they met in France in 1754 and had tried to persuade Rousseau to return to Geneva as librarian at the Academy (H. Tronchin, pp. 251–53, 270–72; Rousseau to Théodore Tronchin, 27 Feb. 1757, *CC Rousseau*, Letter 476, iv. 161–62). But Tronchin's political conservatism and strict Calvinism caused him to consider Rousseau's glorification of passion in *La Nouvelle Héloïse* dangerous for the young, and he had been offended by Rousseau's criticism of Geneva as well as by the unorthodox religious views expressed in *Émile* and *Le Contrat Social* (H. Tronchin, pp. 273–78). To attribute Rousseau's illnesses to venereal disease was malicious gossip not verifiable by Tronchin, who had never examined Rousseau. To state that Rousseau had abandoned the children he had fathered with Thérèse Levasseur was even more shocking, but was based on the knowledge Tronchin had possessed for some time that Rousseau had allowed his infant children—five of them, unnamed and not further identified—to be taken to the Paris foundling hospital between c. 1746 and c. 1752 (R. Trousson, 'Enfants de Rousseau', *Dict. de Rousseau*, pp. 297–98). But Tronchin exaggerated in giving the impression that the infants had been left unprotected outdoors. This and his other accusations echoed the assertions made in the *Sentiment des citoyens*, an anonymous eight-page diatribe, circulated on 27 Dec., which had just made public the damaging information that Rousseau had 'exposed' his children. Either Tronchin was merely selecting especially shocking details from the *Sentiment* or, more likely, it was he who had furnished these details to the unacknowledged author, who was, very likely, Voltaire. In any case, Rousseau, who believed Jacob Vernes to be the author of the diatribe, would vigorously deny the aspersions, disproving some (including one that he had killed Thérèse's mother, who was still alive) and resorting to sophistry to argue that the infants had not been left literally at the door of the hospital (see 'Voltaire, "Sentiment des citoyens"; Jean-Jacques Rousseau, "Déclaration relative à M. le pasteur de Vernes"', ed. Frédéric Eigeldinger, 1997, pp. 62–63 and note a; Rousseau

to Pierre Alexandre Du Peyrou, 31 Dec., Letter 3812, *CC Rousseau*, xxii. 337; *Confessions*, Bk. XI, *OC Rousseau*, i. 558; see also J. D. Candaux, 'Sentiment des citoyens (1764)', *Dict. de Rousseau*, pp. 212–13; for Vernes, see Journ. 3 Dec. and n. 40).

[9] Six close relations of Tronchin were members of the *Conseil des Deux Cents* at this time (Galiffe, ii. 263–67). One of these, Jean-Robert Tronchin (for whom see Journ. 24 Dec. n. 24), was also public prosecutor from 1760 to 1768, reporting to the Council.

[10] MS. 'taught'

[11] MS. final letter, presumably 'x', added then deleted.

[12] Voltaire had become Tronchin's patient shortly after arriving in Geneva in Dec. 1754. Suffering from numerous ailments and often convinced that he was dying, Voltaire had frequently turned to Tronchin for advice, invariably addressing him as 'mon cher Aesculape'. But Tronchin, who disapproved of Voltaire's attacks on religion as well as love of the theatre, remained reserved (H. Tronchin, pp. 197–98). His reports concerning Voltaire's attitude about death, quite apart from being professionally indiscreet, were contradictory, for his account here of his patient's calm deism differs markedly from the one he had given previously to the Rev. Robert Brown, which JB also recorded:

Mr. Tronchin, physician at Geneva, an intimate friend of Mr. Voltaire, told Mr. Brown, the English minister at Utrecht, that one time when Voltaire was very bad, he was under the greatest terror of death, and he used this strong expression to Mr. Tronchin, — 'Sir, if I were put upon the rack at three o'clock in the afternoon, and had both my legs and both my arms broke, if I had my choice either to die immediately or to live till seven at night, I would choose to live till seven.' A fortnight after, when he was quite recovered, he was talking against religion with as much wildness and extravagance as ever, and seemed highly delighted with shaking the faith of all the company.

Mr. Tronchin, who was present, got up with indignation, went round to Voltaire, and catching him by the breast, said, 'You pitiful wretch! are you, for a little gratification of vanity, endeavouring to destroy the only pillars which can support mankind at that awful hour which made you so lately tremble like a coward?' In contradiction to this story, see in my Journal the account which Tronchin gave me of Voltaire. (*Boswelliana*, pp. 221–22)

[13] In 1753 Dr. Tronchin had sent his son Louis François (b. 1743) with his older brother Jean Robert (b. 1741) back to Geneva to escape the supposedly lax morals in Amsterdam (CC *Rousseau,* iv. 153 note f; H. Tronchin, pp. 24, 382–83). In 1766, François would travel as expected by his father, preparing for a diplomatic career in London, then staying with Adam Smith in Glasgow and making the acquaintance of David Hume. A few months later he would become secretary to Sir Andrew Mitchell in Berlin (Galiffe, ii. 861; H. Tronchin, pp. 290, 292).

[14] This chaise, with a semi-circular back extending arm-like on both sides, seems to have looked like a glorified 'arm-chair for a library, or a reading chair' (Thomas Sheraton, *Cabinet Dictionary,* 1803, repr. 1970, pp. 17–18 and plates 5–6). Such a chair, made of wood or wicker, could be carried on poles by four or six porters (see Tobias Smollett, *Travels through France and Italy,* Letter 38, ed. Frank Felsenstein, 1979, pp. 323, 467–68) or could be horse-drawn, as JB's seems to have been since he offered the use of his horse to a needy fellow traveller. Only on the last stage, in traversing Mt. Cenis, did JB use a primitive 'Alps-machine' that provided seating on twisted cords extended between two tree trunks (Journ. 5–6 Jan. 1765, *Grand Tour II,* Heinemann pp. 22–24, McGraw-Hill pp. 21–23). On such vehicles did JB make the arduous trip over the Alps into Savoy and Italy.

# Appendix 1

## Foreign Tour Papers and other Miscellaneous Writings, June–December 1764

The following pieces, some in prose and some in verse, were written at the same time as JB's journal and memoranda of 1764. They are given here in chronological sequence, most of them following the order listed in the *Catalogue* as Foreign Tour Papers (M 93–97). Also included are two short lyrics of the Berlin period (JB's verses addressed to Caroline Kircheisen and his translation of a lyric by Ewald von Kleist), as well as JB's verse exchange with Garrick about Strasbourg Cathedral.

The 'Abregé', written on the eve of JB's departure for German territory, provides a character sketch of his travel companion, Lord Marischal, the Scottish nobleman who dominates the opening pages of the journal. It also gives the only glimpse JB offers of the Rev. Robert Brown, who had been JB's teacher and host in Utrecht.

The next items deal with practical details of JB's travels after leaving Prussia. The list of addresses refers to persons in Leipzig, Dessau, and Gotha, as well as to the beautiful laundress who charmed JB during his second stay in Brunswick. The two itineraries show JB giving careful thought to the stages of his travels after leaving Prussia to fit in as many courts as possible. The first begins in Dessau, the second revises the time schedule.

The miscellaneous fragments that follow were composed en route, either during long carriage rides or lonely stays at inns. The Rochefoucault maxims were inspired by JB's purchase of a volume of that aphorist, and the Hints and the Jottings are the fruits of boredom. At about the same time, JB also composed the Ten Lines a Day (inserted in their appropriate place in each entry). All these pieces show JB's urge to occupy himself with writing.

The two charming little lyrics show him rethinking his days in Berlin. The lines on Caroline Kircheisen reveal that he was fonder of Caroline than his journal indicates, either at the time of their frequent meetings in the Kircheisen household or in retrospect. The translation of Kleist shows JB exploring amorous feelings without a particular personal object.

The lines on Strasbourg Cathedral were inspired by verses recently composed by Garrick (supplied here to contextualize JB's). Not only are JB's lines a witty reply to Garrick's, but they are also a sign of JB's interest in public monuments. More serious are the notes on Holbein, a record of JB's intense emotional experience of a painting.

337

## I. 'Abregé d'un Voyage en Allemagne', June 1764

MS. Yale (M 93).

Je suis parti d'Utrecht Lundi le 18 Juin. J'avois eté assez embarrasse comment faire ce voyage. De le faire seul aurroit eté extremement triste. Quelquun des anciens a dit que pour vivre dans la solitude il faut etre ou un Dieu[1] ou un Bête.[2] Moi Je ne me trouve pas Dieux. Je ne me trouve pas Bête non plus; mais Je le deviens dans la Solitude. Cela me montre que Je ne suis ni plus ni moins que l'homme cet etre curieux qui a tant pensé et tant dit sur sa propre nature et qui pourtant en est si ignorant. De trouver un bon Compagnon de Voyage est fort difficile. Je n'ai point de Tuteur ou Gouverneur comme on l'appelle. Mon Pere dit tres sagement: Pendant que mon fils a besoin d'un Gouverneur, il restera chez moi. Quand il est en etat de gouverner soimême, Je l'enverois[3] en des Païs etrangers. J'avois cherché quelque Monsieur qui vouloit aller en Allemagne; Mais Je n'avois pas trouvé une occasion convenable. Par le plus grand Bonheur Mi Lord Marischal devoit aller á Berlin, et il avoit la Bonté de me faire un offre de m'y mener avec lui. J'acceptois l'offre avec beaucoup de remerciemens. Son excellence arrivat á Utrecht mercredi[4] le 13. Il avoit avec lui [M]adame de Froment la Dame Turque[5] qui etoit prise á la siêge d'Ockzakow par M. le [M]arechal Keith; ensuite elle demeuroit avec Mi Lord Marischal, qui a eu soin d'elle et l'a elevé comme sa propre fille. L'année passée elle etoit mariée avec M. de Froment françois d'origine, qui a servi quelque tems sous le Roi de Sardigne. Cette Dame etoit un peu lasse et malade et pour cela Mi Lord restoit trois quatre jours á Utrecht, ou il s'amusoit de causer avec le ministre Brown et ses dames de Suisse et le Professeur Hahn qui venoit chez [M]adame de Froment en qualité de medecin.[6] Son Excellence etoit tres bonne compagnie. Il nous donnoit une infinité[7] de jolies histoires. Mais il fachoit un peu le pauvre Brown; car il racontoit une quantité de miracles Espagnoles qu'on ne pouvoit jamais deprouver. J'ai dit á Brown Je craigns en verité que Mi Lord [M]arischal a eté trop long tems en Espagne pour etre bon Chretien. Brown me paroissoit d'etre des mêmes sentimens. Pourtant il respectoit beaucoup Mi Lord, et il le trouvoit un tres galant homme, qui ne pourroit pas avoir un mauvais sort dans l'autre monde. Ainsi nous voyons que les hommes ont des sentimens de la vraye Charité quand ils ne sont pas agités par le Zêle d'un Parti. Je pourrois gager que ce même Brown seroit echauffé extremement si [M]i Lord [M]arischal lui parleroit aussi librement qu'il pense et jen doute beaucoup si á la fin le bon ministre ne delivreroit pas au Diable son excellence pour le Chatiment de son Chair et le salut de son Âme. C'est un Bon mot tres vraye que les Prêtres de toutes Religions sont les memes. Les Calvinistes qui recrient tant contre les Catholiques Romains a cause[8] de leur esprit d'Intolerance, sont aussi intolerants qu'eux quand ils ont le pouvoir. S'il y a de la moderation dans aucune eglise, c'est assurement dans l'Eglise Anglicane qui de toutes eglises est la meilleure a touts egards. Mais Revenons á mon Voyage. Pendant les deux premiers jours nous etions assez tranquilles. Mi Lord parloit peu.

Madame de Froment parloit peu aussi; et moi par consequent Je gardois silence comme les autres. Mon sang circuloit tres lentement et Je me trouvois un peu triste. Mais ensuite, nous nous connoissons. Mi Lord parloit pas beaucoup mais passablement et avec une vivacite surprenante.[9] Il est assurement un homme singulier. Il a soixante et quinze ans et pourtant il a toutes ses facultés en plein vigeur. Son Jugement est fort & penetrant. Sa memoire est extraordinaire. Il n'oublit rien et tout ce qu'il sait est bien Arrangé. Il a assez d'imagination pour animer ses histoires mais il n'en a trop et en cela il a un grand avantage. Ceux qui ont trop d'imagination n'en ont pas le propre usage. Ils ont une foule des idées[10] mais ils ne sont pas arrangees ils ont une brilliance irreglée qui vous eblouit et confond au lieu de vous eclaircir. [M]i Lord [M]arischal est bien maitre de soi qui est un tres grand Bonheur. Il a naturellement une force d'esprit extraordinaire; et il a tant vu le monde qu'il a acquis toute la Connoissance qu'on puisse avoir des hommes. Il lui reste pourtant une simplicité des mœurs. Il n'a point d'affectation. Il a passé vingt ans en Espagne, et il aime ce païs sur tous les autres. On remarque qu'il a un peu de la reserve et la gravité espagnole. Il faut ajouter qu'il a aussi la generosité de Cœur qui a cette nation illustre qui est certainement la plus noble race qu'il y a dans le monde. Jamais a-t-on[11] trouvé un Espagnol qui etoit faux. Ils ont sans doute[12] les passions fortes, et en cela ils sont quelquefois aussi emportes au mal qu'ils ne sont au bien. Ils aiment la revange. Ils sont Jaloux. Ils sont orgeilleux Mais avec tout cela ils sont des grands hommes. Je les admire tant, que Je ne serais jamais content sans avoir fait un petit tour en Espagne. Mi Lord [M]arischal pourroit me donner des avis pour mon voyage. Si Je passe en Italie, J'irai directement de Genes a Barcelone. Ensuite J'irais a Madrid, ou se promenoit autrefois avec tant de plaisanterie le Diable Boiteux.[13] J'irais voir la noble Université de Salamancha,[14] le superbe Palais de Granada ou on voit un[15] reste distingué[16] de la magnificence des maures. Je compte d'avoir un plaisir romanesque de parcourir les champs ou etoient les Chevaliers errants de me mettre a mon aise sur une belle montagne ou le Soleil donne et d'indulger une indolence et des reveries delicieuse. Cela est vraye luxe. Presque tout le monde se moque de moi pour avoir un plan si singulier. Mon Dieu disent ils. Voyager en Espagne. Quelle idée! Oui, vous y verrez assurement une societé brillante, beaucoup de science et beaucoup de liberté, et cest assurement un excellent païs pour les Anglois pour s'y defaire de leurs prejugés, de leur fierté de leur air sombre et de leur Taciturnité. Je ne reponds a cela qu'en deux mots Je veux aller en Espagne pour voir le plus beau païs et les plus braves Gens du Monde. Avec le Visage noir[17] que la Nature m'a donné et l'air serieux que J'ai acquit cette reponse est toujours suffisante, au moins les autres se taisent, et moi Je reste Maitre du Champ. Je ne suis pas si embarrassé de soutenir ma These que Je fais bien de voyager en Espagne que Je serai embarrasse de soutenir ma vie si J'y va actuellement. Car, en premier lieu il faut beaucoup d'argent et en second lieu il est souvent difficile même d'acheter de quoi vivre. Les Espagnols ont une paresse incroyable. Si vous venez a un[18] Cordonnier pour ordonner un pair de Souliers. Il demande á sa femme questce qu'elle a pour nourrir la famille? S'il y a de quoi manger pendant deux jours. Il dit tout gravement: A present, Je ne veux pas travailler et il tiens sa parole et se remue pas jusque a ce que le faim le force. Et pourquoy non Je vous prie. Si un Espagnol se trouve plus heureux de rester dans une tranquillité orgeilleuse que de travailler comme un vif françois il n y a point de doute qu'il fait bien de suivre ses inclinations. Il y a pourtant une chose en Espagne dont Je ne veux pas entreprendre le defense cest a dire leur Malpropreté.[19] J'avoue que c'est une grande faute. Jespere que mes dignes Amis s'en corrigeront et ils seront des etres parfaits.

[1] MS. 'Dieux', final 'x' deleted.

[2] Aristotle, Politics, I. i. 12: 'It is clear therefore that the state is also prior by nature to the individual; for if each individual when separate is not self-sufficient, he must be related to the whole state as other parts are to their whole, while a man who is incapable of entering into partnership, or who is so self-sufficing that he has no need to do so, is no part of a state, so that he must be either a lower animal or a god' (Loeb ed., trans. H. Rackham, 1972).

[3] MS. 'l'enverais', with 'a' erroneously written over 'o'

[4] MS. 'mecredi'

[5] MS. 'prise' deleted after 'Turque'. For this romantic story, see Journ. 18 June n. 7.

[6] Robert Brown (1728–77) was pastor of the English (Presbyterian) church in Utrecht. A Scot, he had been educated at Marischal College, Aberdeen, and had been in Utrecht for the past seven years (Archief van de Engelsche Kerk, 'Notulen van den kerkraad 1657–1779' [Resolutions of the Consistory of the English Church], no. 848, 22 July 1757). Brown had advocated, to use Robert Warnock's words, 'a rational Christianity within a Calvinist framework' and had written the preface to the Lettres critiques d'un voyageur anglois sur l'article Genève du Dictionnaire Encyclopédique (1761) by Jacob Vernet (1698–1789), a Swiss theologian who defended Calvinism against Voltaire (for Brown, see also Journ. 19 Nov.). JB had dined frequently with Brown and his wife in order to improve his French, and although he had found Brown 'vulgar and rude', had also acknowledged him to be 'a generous and clever little man' who had become a mentor (Mems. dated 5, 7 Apr. of this year; Earlier Years, p. 125).

For 'the Swiss ladies', Brown's wife Catherine (Kinloch) Brown and her sister Nanette, see Journ. 12 Dec. nn. 1, 3.

Johannes David Hahn (1729–84), M.D., had studied medicine in his native Heidelberg and in Leiden, where he had earned his degree in 1751, and had served as professor of philosophy, experimental physics, and astronomy in Utrecht from 1753, additionally of botany and chemistry from 1759. He would be appointed professor of medicine in Leiden in 1775. Hahn had written several treatises on chemical and toxicological subjects: Diss. de efficacia mixtionis in mutandis corporum voluminibus (1751); Diss. mechanica de potentiis oblique agentibus (1755); Orat. de chemiae cum botanica conjunctione utili et pulchra (1759); and Explicatio quaestionum mathematicarum de maximo et minimo in scientia machinali (1761). He would soon publish his Diss. de igne (1765), followed by Oratio de mutuo matheseos et chemiae auxilio (1768), and Oratio de usu venenorum in medicina (1773, new ed. 1775), this last opposing the use of toxic medications (Biographisches Lexikon der hervorragenden Ärzte, 1934, iii. 18). Hahn had offered JB medical and common sense advice in Utrecht about how to overcome his debilitating depression (Mem. dated 25 May; Journ. 8 June, Holland, Heinemann pp. 252–53, 269, McGraw-Hill pp. 258, 276).

[7] MS. 'infinté'

[8] MS. 'a cause' written above deleted 'pour'

[9] MS. 'surpenante'

[10] MS. 'I dare say my fair freind' written upside down between the lines in a different pen, an earlier use of the sheet of paper.

[11] MS. 'J'amais at on'

[12] MS. 'doutes', final 's' deleted.

[13] In Le Diable boiteux (1707) by Alain-René Lesage or Le Sage (1668–1747), an imitation of the Diablo cojuelo (1641) by Luís Vélez de Guevera (1579–1644), a devil, freed from a bottle, rewards the hero by lifting the roofs of the houses of Madrid to reveal the behaviour of the inhabitants (Oxford Companion to French Literature, ed. Paul Harvey and J. E. Heseltine, 1959, p. 201).

[14] JB had recorded a compliment to the University of Salamanca by SJ in London, made in the context of SJ's encouraging him to visit Spain (Journ. 28 July 1763): 'Mr. Johnson persisted in advising me to go to

Spain. I said it would divert him to get a letter from me dated at Salamancha. "I love the University of Salamancha," said he, "for when the Spaniards were in doubt if they should conquer the West Indies, the University of Salamancha gave it as their opinion that they should not.'" JB added in the margin: 'This he said with great emotion'. In the *Life*, JB would add that SJ spoke 'with that generous warmth which dictated the lines in his "London," against Spanish encroachment' (see *Life* i. 455 and n. 3, and SJ's *London*, ll. 170–73).

[15] MS. 'une', final 'e' deleted.
[16] MS. 'distingué' inserted above deleted 'superbe'
[17] That is, dark complexioned.
[18] MS. 'un' inserted before 'Cordonnier'
[19] MS. 'Malpro' written over an indecipherable word.

## II. Names and addresses, September–October 1764

MS. Yale (M 94).

Mr. Meinart Gouveneur du Comte Molk[1] Danois est le Traducteur des Elements de Critique en Allemand. On peut lui addresser une lettre *bey* Madame Dyck Buchhandler Leipsig.[2]

Á Monsieur Bel Professeur de la Poesie et Bibliothecaire de l'Université á Leipsic.[3]

Á Monsieur Gotsched Professeur en Philosophie dans l'Université de Leipsic.[4]

M. de Neitschutz Grand Ecuier du Prince d'Anhalt Dessau[5]

Belle Blanchiseuse Brunsvic. Sandelmans auf der coes-straas in fresen hausen.[6]

Le Baron de Thungen Maréchal de la Cour de Saxe-Gotha[7]

Le Baron de Helmolt Chambellan et Ecuyer du Duc de Saxe-Gotha.[8]

[1] Not identified further. The translator was Johann Nicolaus Meinhard (*Catalogue*, i. 72).
[2] See Mem. dated 7 Oct.
[3] See Journ. 4 Oct. and n. 7.
[4] See Journ. 4 Oct. and n. 5.
[5] See Journ. 24 Sept. and n. 14.
[6] See Journ. 13 Aug. and n. 2.
[7] See Journ. 17 Oct. and n. 5.
[8] See Journ. 17 Oct. and n. 13.

## III. Plan for an itinerary through Germany to Geneva, c. 1 October 1764

MS. Yale (M 95).

1

| | |
|---|---|
| Septr. 24 | *Dessau* to Octr. 1 |
| Octr. 1 | Halle to 2 |
| 2 | Leipsic to 5 |

2

| | |
|---|---|
| Sund. 7[1] | *Dresden* to 10 |

3
12      *Weimar* \<to\> 15²

4
16      *Saxe Gotha* to 20

5
22      *Cassel to* 26³

28      Francfort to 29

6
30      *Darmstat* to Novr. 2⁴

Novr. 3      Heidelberg — to 5

7
6      *Mannheim* to 9

8
11      *Durlach* to 13

9
14      *Stutgard* to 18

10
19      *Bade-Bade* 22
24      Basle to 25
25      Soleure to 27
27      Berne to 29
29      Neufchatel to Decr. 5
5      Colombier et milord Wemys to 8
8      Iverdun to 11
15      Genêve

Plan Renewed.

| | |
|---|---|
| Leipsic | to Octr 7 |
| Dresden | to 12 |
| Gotha | to 16 |
| Cas\<sel\> | to 24 |
| Fra\<nc\>fort | to 27 |
| Darmstadt | to Novr. 1 |
| Heidelberg | to 5 |
| Mannheim | to 10 |
| Durlach | to 14 |
| Stutgard | to 20 |

| Bade Bade | to 24 |
|-----------|-------|
| Basle | to 25 |
| Soleure | to 27 |
| Berne | to 29 |
| Neufchatel | to Decr. 3.[5] |
| &c. | |

Feronce
Major

[1] MS. 'Sund.' written over 'Sat.'

[2] MS. Entire line deleted, 'retabli' written above the line; 'to' obscured by a large ink blot.

[3] MS. Entire line deleted, 'retabli' written above the line.

[4] MS. Entire line deleted, 'retabli' written above the line.

[5] MS. 'museum' written vertically along the right margin, directly below 'Decr. 3'

## IV. Verses written on a Post-Wagon, 1 October 1764

MS. Yale L 837; MS copy, Bodleian Library (Douce 193). Part of JB's letter to Caroline Kircheisen, dated 2 Oct. 1764, written the preceding day on the way to Halle. Previously printed in *Grand Tour I*, Heinemann p. 120, McGraw-Hill p. 123; and *Boswell's Book of Bad Verse*, ed. Jack Werner, 1974, p. 59.

Vers ecrits sur un Chariot de Poste
addressés á Mademoiselle Kircheisen

Autrefois J'etois Poête,
  Et Je faisois tous les jours
Des chansons sur une Brunêtte
  Qui m'inspiroit de l'amour.

La Brunêtte etoit galante,
  Elle avoit un tendre cœur;
Et (comme Cavalcabo[1] se vante)
  'Elle m'aimoit á la fureur.'

Ces jours sont passés comme un Ombre.
  Adieu l'Amour! adieu ma Lyre!
Je ne suis que froid et sombre,
  Je n'ai plus mes beaux desirs.

Ah! ma jolie Caroline![2]
  Qui me charma[3] tant de soirs:
Par vos yeux doux je devine
  Que[4] Vous ne *voulez* pas me croire.

[1] Footnote in Douce: 'Un marquis Italien qui se servoit de cette phrase en parlant d'une Dame'. For George Cavalcabò, see Journ. 13 Aug. n. 3. Since he was staying in Brunswick, he presumably knew of Caroline Kircheisen only from JB's report.

² Footnote in Douce: 'Mademoiselle Caroline Kircheisen de Berlin'. See Journ. 12 July and n. 3; 18 July.

³ MS. 'me a charmé', altered to 'me charma'
⁴ MS. 'Que' squeezed in before 'Vous' at a later time.

## V. 'Maximes á la maniêrre de la Rochefoucault', 15 October 1764

MS. Yale (M 96); English translation previously printed in *Grand Tour I*, Heinemann p. 136, McGraw-Hill p. 140. Written at Rippach on the way from Dresden to Gotha, these pithy maxims are modelled on La Rochefoucault's *Maximes*.¹ JB had purchased this book in Halle on 2 Oct.

### Maximes á la Maniêrre de la Rochefoucault.

1. C'est n'est pas a ceux qui nous aimons le plus a qui nous faisons l'Amour. C'est a ceux qui ont l'hazard d'etre vis a vis de nous, quand notre passion est dans sa force.

2. Le Regret qui nous sentons de quitter nos meilleurs Amis, n'est que la Paresse qui nous le rend dissagreable de changer d'endroit.

3. L'Empressement de joye avec laquelle nous allons voir nos meilleurs Amis n'est que le plaisir d'etre relevé de l'inquietude que nous sentons de rester long tems dans un endroit.

4. On a beau prêcher la Patience comme une Vertu. Il ne le peut etre jamais. Quand nous voyons un homme malheureux² qui se plaint, il faut dire voila un homme dont la force mal³ proportionné aux souffrances et quand nous voyons un homme malheureux⁴ qui ne se plaint pas il faut dire Voila un homme dont la force est bien⁵ proportionné aux souffrances. C'est la nature qui nous a donné plus ou moins de la force.

¹ JB had composed these self-deprecating maxims while waiting for fresh horses (see Journ. 15 Oct. n. 8).
² MS. 'malheureux' written above 'homme qui se plaint'
³ MS. Illegible word deleted, replaced by

'bien mal' above the line, with 'bien' also deleted.
⁴ MS. 'malheureux' inserted above the line with a caret.
⁵ MS. 'bien' written above a short word ending in 'l' ('mal'?) obliterated by a blot.

## VI. Translation into French of 'Amynt' by Ewald Christian von Kleist, c. 14 November 1764¹

MS. Yale (M 283).

1

Elle s'enfuit. C'en est fait de moi
un long espace separe Lalagen de moi
C'est par la qu'elle fuiait² — venez air
Vous venez peutetre d'elle.

2

Elle s'en fuit. ⌈D⌉ites á Lalagen o Ruisseaux
Que sans elle l'emaille des pres se fletrit
Votre course est plus rapide pour la suivre — dites que le
Boi souffre de son absence
Et que son Berger meurt.

3

Quelle Vallé fleurit mieux sous ses regards
Ou dance t'elle un labyrinthe? ou est ce qu'un[3]
chant remplit le bosquet. Quelle onde
heureuse devient plus belle par son
Image?

4

Seulement un serrement de Main — seulement
un demi œilade. Ah un baiser tel
qu'elle m'a autrefois donné⌈.⌉ Accordez
moi d'elle — et donc oh fortune
mettez moi quand vous voulez au tombeau.

5

Ainsi lamente[4] Amynt — les yeux plein
de larmes. Aux environs[5]
la fuite de Lalagen.
Ils paroissoient avec lui de la desirer
Et soupiroient Lalagen.

---

[1] Written on or shortly after 14 Nov., when JB heard this song (*Catalogue*, i. 120). The German text is quoted below (Kleist, *Sämtliche Werke*, Erster Theil ⌈Reuttlingen, 1775⌉, p. 62; for Kleist, see Journ. 14 Nov. n. 6):

Sie fliehet fort! Es ist um mich geschehen!
Ein weiter Raum trennt Lalagen von mir.
Dort floh sie hin! Komm Luft, mich anzuwehen!
Du kömmst vielleicht von ihr.

Sie fliehet fort! Sagt Lalagen, ihr Flüsse,
Daß ohne sie der Wiese Schmuck verdirbt;
Ihr eilt ihr nach, sagt, daß der Wald sie misse,
Und daß ihr Schäfer stirbt.

Welch Thal blüht ißt, von ihr gesehen, besser?
Wo tanzt sie nun ein Labyrint? wo füllt
Ihr Lied den Hain? welch glückliches Gewässer

Wird schöner durch ihr Bild?

Nur einen Druck der Hand, nur halbe Blicke,
Ach! einen Kuß, wie sie mir vormals gab,
Vergönne mir von ihr; dann stürz, o Glücke,
Mich, wenn du willst, ins Grab.

So klagt Amynt, die Augen voll von Thränen,
Den Gegenden die Flucht der Lalage;
Sie schienen sich mit ihm nach ihr zu sehnen,
Und seufzten: Lalage!

[2] MS. 'ai' of 'fuiait' squeezed in as an afterthought.
[3] MS. 'quon'
[4] MS. 'se pligoit' deleted and 'lamente' written above the line.
[5] MS. 'ou senfuioit Lalagen' deleted after 'environs'

### VII. 'Paper on Writing: Hints', c. 15 November 1764

MS. Yale (M 97). All that survives is this page, a side of the memorandum of c. 15 Nov.

## *Paper on Writing.*

## Hints.

Notwithstanding the immense length of time since mankind first began to communicate their thoughts & discoveries to each other by the means of written signs so that to us one should imagine it should appear no longer strange, yet there is still something mysterious in the name of Authour. It is true the art of Printing is carried on somewhat privately so that multitudes of the Species pass over this Globe without ever seeing the operations of that Art to which they have been daily indebted for Instruction & Entertainment. But in reality the other mechanical arts are carried on in the same manner and if multitudes have never seen a Printing Press, they have also been equally ignorant of the Arcana of the Loom. Yet, so it is that [...]

### VIII. Jottings, 21 November 1764

MS. Notes written on the reverse of a sheet used for the journal entry dated 21 Nov.

### Hypochond[1]

## Simple Sublime

#### In Expression
In Thomson — thy voice in dreadful Thunder *speaks*[2]
& in another Author where one would hardly expect it —
Pope [—] There St. John nobly pensive sat & thought[3]

#### Sentiment
Revelation There was silence in heaven[4]

---

No 1 Hypochond No. 2 Strange dread of being Authour &c
No 3 — Swearing to be encouraged as the only means to
continue religion[5] —

---

Write Johnston as from Rats — & here[6] — If you *swear*
not conduct you fall back to Eglint — Blair — Hamilton[7]

---

[1] Written at the top of the page, probably as an afterthought. The heading suggests that JB was already thinking about writing essays on hypochondria, or in the persona of a hypochondriac, before his stay in Milan in 1765, mentioned in the opening paragraph of his *Hypochondriack* essay no. X, 'On Truth', and assumed to be his starting point by Margery Bailey, twentieth-century editor of *The Hypochondriack* (Bailey, i. 3, 170). He would eventually compose seventy such essays as 'The Hypochondriack' for the *Lond. Mag.*

from Oct. 1777 to Aug. 1783.

² 'A Hymn on the Seasons' (1730), l. 11 (James Thomson, *Poetical Works*, ed. J. Loge Robertson, 1908, repr. 1971, p. 245). For JB's early interest in Thomson, see Journ. 24 July and nn. 6–8.

³ Pope, 'Verses on a Grotto by the River Thames at Twickenham', l. 10 (*Twickenham Edition of the Poems of Alexander Pope, Vol. 6: Minor Poems*, ed. Norman Ault, completed by John Butt, 1954, p. 383).

⁴ 'And when he opened the seventh seal, there was silence in heaven about the space of half an hour' (Rev. 8:1).

⁵ This section of the jottings lists topics for projected essays.

The oaths of allegiance, supremacy, and abjuration declared George III the supreme ruler of Great Britain, and rejected both Roman Catholicism and the Stuarts' claim to rule. These oaths were required, though not always enforced, for participation in universities, law courts, and public offices. JB seemingly favours them here, but because of his conversion to Catholicism, however brief, he would continue to be troubled by them on other occasions, notably at the prospect of taking the 'Formula Oath' to vote in the parliamentary election of autumn 1774 (*Later Years*, pp. 107–08). JB would eventually write a *Hypochondriack* essay 'On Swearing' as the second-to-last one in his series (no. LXIX [June 1783], Bailey, ii. 286–97).

⁶ Rastatt. JB had left this town in Baden-Baden on 19 Nov. and arrived in Strasbourg the next day. He wrote to JJ from Strasbourg on 22 Nov. and noted: 'I must ask your pardon, My Dear Johnston, for having neglected to write to you from Ratstat where I past three days at the court of Baden Baden .... It is the court in Germany where a man is most at his ease. You would have loved it dearly .... You see Johnston how Imagination carrys me back from Strasbourg to Ratstat' (*Corr. 1*, p. 144).

⁷ An admonition to himself not to revert to his earlier frivolous life, as with Eglinton, Blair, and Hamilton. For Eglinton, see Journ. 28 June and n. 6 (and also Mem. dated 27 Aug. n. 1). 'Blair' is possibly 'Captain Blair', a young Army officer mentioned in letters of 18 Sept. 1762 and 10 Mar. 1763 from JJ to JB, probably John Blair (d. 1772) of Dunskey, then an ensign in the 3rd Regt. ('Scots') of Foot Guards (*Corr. 1*, pp. 14–16, 56–58, and 15 n. 8). His mother was a first cousin of Lord Eglinton. JB records meeting him socially in London several times in 1763. After their final meeting JB wrote: 'He is a good worthy lad. But he has not enough of imagination, and mixes too much in the common rough intercourse of society for me. So we are very seldom together' (Journ. 24 July 1763). John Hamilton (1739–1821) of Sundrum was an Ayrshire neighbour of the Boswells who had been a friend of JB and WJT at Edinburgh University, and had matriculated with JB at the University of Glasgow in 1759 (*Earlier Years*, p. 474). JB wrote of him that he 'is like fire of a certain species of Coal which has a deal of heat, but no flame. He is warm: but wants free expression' (*Boswelliana*, p. 285; see also *Corr. 6*, p. 3 n. 2).

## IX. Garrick's and Boswell's verses on Strasbourg Cathedral

Previously printed in *Corr. 4*, App. 1, pp. 433–34.

### Upon seeing Strasbourg Cathedral
### Extempore by a Stranger
### (By Mr. Garrick.)

That hallow'd Spire which rises to the Skies,
Fills ev'ry heart with wonder and surprise.
Approach the Temple.—Round it's rev'rend base
Vile traffic Shops God's Edifice disgrace.
Are there still Goths in this enlighten'd age,
Who dare oppose and scorn the sacred Page?
Who by one Impious Act at once Express
Their want of Virtue, Taste and Righteousness?

Boswell's reply:

Answer of The
Shop-keepers round Strasbourg Cathedral
(By Mr. Boswell.)

Stranger, why storm so fierce, because arround
This grand Cathedral our poor Shops are found?
Why call us Goths? Why rank us among those
Who would the Sacred Oracles oppose?
  In times of old, the greedy Sons of gain
Their Booths set up in Judah's lofty Fane,
The Place of Prayer most impiously made
A crowded Scene of bustling, babling, Trade,
Till the Messiah came with awfull rod
And drove the Thieves from out the House of God.
  But we the Temple would not dare defile;
We hold in honour this majestic Pile:
With humble rev'rence by it's Walls we stay,
In honest Bus'ness to employ the day;
And, while thus cover'd by the holy shade.
Say, to do wrong who would not be affraid?

**X. Description of Holbein's altar-piece, 'The Sufferings of Christ', Bâle, 26 November 1764**

MS. Yale (M 98).

Holbens's Picture of the Sufferings [—] formerly Altar piece of great church.[1] In 8 divisions.

1. Moonlight Jesus praying in Agony well exprest the Disciples asleep — at a distance the Priests &c — An Angel holding the cross.
2. The Priests fully seen &c arround Jesus – He a mild figure. Judas gives him a kiss with a sly villainous smiling look. A Soldier has his hand fixed in the hair of Jesus. Below is Malchus on the ground. Peter has a leg on each side of him & one hand on his head & in the other a saber to cut off his ear.[2] He looks to his Master to receive his Approbation.[3]
3. Jesus before the High Priest. He looks at him with a piercing eye & a mild disdain. A Priest rages[3] against the high Priest rends his cloaths angry but without great expression.
4. Jesus is tied to a Pillar & whipt. It is in A temple there are only four other figures. He is ill done. He is a poor figure & with a sheepish look shrinks from the lash. He has the air of a real Malefactor. Nothing of the divine Christ.
5. Jesus with his hands bound is sitting amidst four figures. He is crownd with thorns. They hold Palms before him. A soldier with iron gloves

presses his head. He suffers with calm dignity.

6. A full piece view of calvary at a distance. The procession to the execution. Cimon bears the cross.[4] It is large. Jesus is made to be under the shade to support also the cross. He is very dark & much older than in the other figures

7. Jesus on the cross finely exprest — groupe below very well. One Apostle weeps – One in agitation stretches out his hand to the Saviour as if to seise him – Mary stands with hands folded in grief — Her face is hid by a large coiffure. Wonder & expectation reigns in the soldiers — One looks at one of the thieves — natural that they should have freinds.

8. Jesus taken down from the cross supported by 3 disciples face more clumsy flesh not pale the same colour with one of the disciples arms. Cross not seen — Mary eyes red bursting with grief. A figure by her in Anguish — I suppose Joseph — richly coloured varnish on wood

---

[1] 'The Sufferings of Christ' seen by JB on 26 Nov. in the town hall of Basel (see Journ. 23 Nov. and n. 11). JB's notes, scrawled in lead pencil, would be transcribed in ink later by JB's clerk James Brown (both copies in M 98; see *Catalogue*, i. 73).
[2] For Malchus, servant of the High Priest, and Simon Peter, who cut off Malchus's right ear, see John 18:10.
[3] MS. 'rges'
[4] MS. an initial letter S is visible under the stronger C in Cimon. The reference is to Simon of Cyrene, who carried Jesus's cross (Matt. 27:32).

# Appendix 2
## Rousseau

THIS section brings together the writings related to JB's meetings with Rousseau: the request for an interview (in three versions), a cover letter for the 'Ébauche de ma vie', and the 'Ébauche' itself. This document is followed by an unfinished first draft, two outlines, and two discarded paragraphs. Included as well is a list of topics discussed with Rousseau, providing a partial record of JB's conversations with Rousseau on 13 to 15 December.

### I. JB's letter to Rousseau (in three versions) requesting an interview

### To Jean-Jacques Rousseau, 3 December 1764 (first draft)

MS. Yale (L 1104). Previously printed in CC *Rousseau*, Letter 3694, xxii. 155–56.

[3 Dec. 1764]

MONSIEUR: Je suis un ancien[1] Ecossois qui fait ses voyages.[2] J'ecris mal le francois. Je le parle encore pire.[3] Je suis venu ici dans l'Esperance de vous voir.

Monsieur. On m'a decouragé de venir ici. Au moins on á taché de le faire. Mais tout ce qu'ils ont dit m'a rendu plus fêrme dans ma resolution de demander hardiment la permission d'entrer chez vous. 'Monsieur Rousseau est singulier.' Fort bien.[4] 'Il est misanthrope.' Vous vous trompez. 'Il a refusé les visites de Monsieur le Marquis de ——— de Monsieur ——— de Monsieur ——— &c &c.' Tant mieux. Tant mieux. Je ne resemble á aucun de ces messieurs. Si Monsieur Rousseau lassoit entrer chez lui tout tout le monde, surtout le Beau monde, sa maison ne seroit plus la Retraite du Genie et de la Pieté. Et Je ne m'empresserois avec enthousiasme d'y être recu.

---
[5]

Je suis Un Jeune Homme de vingt quatre Anns. Demandez vous si J'ai des recommendations? En est il donc besoin pour vous? Une recommendation guarantit des gens sans penetration contre des Impostures. Mais vous Monsieur qui avez etudié la nature humaine: Vous qui savez annalyser ses principes et traçer leurs effêts, pouvez vous vous tromper sur un Caractêre? Ma fois J'aurrois de la peine de la croire. Pourtant Monsieur J'ose me mettre á la preuve; A la preuve la plus forte qui a jamais soutenu un Homme. Voulez vous de Louanges? Je vous donne des faits. Vos Ecrits m'ont attendri le Cœur, m'ont elevé l'Ame m'ont allumé l'imagination m'ont donné des idées de la vie qu'un Esprit melancholique mais vif a recu comme des lumiêrres celestes. Croyez moi Je suis un Charactêre digne de votre attention. Je n'ai pas eté long tems au monde: mais J'ai beaucoup eprouvé. J'ai beaucoup á vous dire.

Ne craignez pas des fades recits des avantures d'un jeune Etourdi qui a la vanité absurde de se croire un Heros Romanesque. [M]ais attendez des circonstances embarrassantes sur lesquels [—][6]

350

Il n'y a Personne au monde qui est capable de me donner des conseils que l'Auteur de la Nouvelle Heloise. Ne voulez vous pas me reçevoir? Il sera a regretter pour vous et pour moi. Excusez une Sailie subite. Ah cher St. Preux![7] Ah Mentor sensible! J'ai un presentiment qu'une Amitié bien noble va naitre aujourdhui:

Ouvrez donc votre porte Monsieur á un jeune Etranger. Je vous prie ne me refusez pas. J'attends votre reponse.

BOSWELL

[1] MS. 'ancien' written above deleted 'bon'
[2] MS. 'qui fait ses voyages' written above deleted 'Je voyage pour m'amuser et m'instruire'
[3] MS. Two lines inserted between 'parle' and 'encore' but struck out by a single deletion stroke: 'mais Je crois que Je suis capable de vous donner mes pensees — Quand vous le'
[4] MS. 'fort bien' written above deleted 'Certainement'
[5] MS. A line drawn across the page, followed by a new start.
[6] MS. Abrupt end of a six-line indentation starting with 'Ne craignez'
[7] The hero of *La Nouvelle Héloïse*, a man of feeling who is the tutor and lover of the heroine Julie.

## To Jean-Jacques Rousseau, 3 December 1764 (second draft)

MS. Yale (L 1105).

⌊3 Déc 1764⌋

MONSIEUR: Je suis le fils ainé d'un ancien Gentilhomme Ecossois. Vous savez mon rang. J'ai vingt quatre Ans. Vous savez mon age. Il y a seize mois que Je suis sorti de la Grande Bretagne, comme un bon Insulaire, sans savoir presque un mot de françois. J'ai eté en Hollande et Allemagne, mais pas en ⌈F⌉rance. Vous excuserez donc mon langage.[1] Je suis á voyager avec une veritable desir de me perfectionner. Je suis venu ici dans l'esperance de vous voir.[2] J'ai entendu tout ce quon pouvoit dire pour me decourager dans mes esperances mais elles ne sont pas moins fortes. 'Monsieur Rousseau est singulier et Capricieux. Il a refusé les visites de M. le Marquis, M. le Comte M——— de &c &c.' Assurement, si Monsieur Rousseau laissoit entrer chez lui tout le monde, sa maison ne sera plus la Retraite du Genie exquis et de la Pieté elevé et Je ne m'empresserois pas avec enthousiasme d'y etre recu. Je sais bien Monsieur que vous ne voudrez pas vous montrer comme un Homme a deux[3] têtes et quatre jambes. Je sais bien que votre sensibilité delicate ne pourroit soutenir ni des flatteurs grossiers, ni des vains gens du monde qui viendront chez vous pour pouvoir dire[4] qu'ils ont eu cet honneur la et peutetre — ma foi cest possible — pour vous faire les admirer.[5] Mais s'il vient[6] un Jeune Homme de merite[7] qui vous etes la plus chêre Je ne saurrois douter que vous ne le recevrez grasieusement. Monsieur Je suis un tel.

Demandez vous si J'ai des recommendations? En est il donc besoin pour vous? Une Recommendation est[8] necessaire dans le comerce du Monde pour garantir des gens sans penetration, contre des Imposteures. Mais vous Monsieur qui avez tant etudié la nature humaine pouvez vous vous tromper sur un Caractêre. Si on devroit[9] envoyer un Tableau a un Raphael, devroit on lui assurer de ses perfections de dessein et de coloris? Non. Un Raphael decouvrira[10] ses perfections et ses fautes aussi[11] mieux quun autre ne les lui dira.[12] Envoyez donc votre Tableau á un grand

Juge sans rien dire. Vous devinez Monsieur mon idée. Croyez moi Je m'imagine qu'apres avoir tant tant etudie la nature humaine vous en avez un connoissance parfaite. Lessence[13] incomprehensible de l'ame apart. Vous savez toutes les principes du corps et de l'esprit avec leurs mouvements leurs sentiments tout ce quils peuvent acquerir. Vous voyez un homme. Vous l'annalyserez.[14] Vous le connoissez parfaitement. Et pourtant Monsieur J'ose me presenter devant vous. J'ose me mettre á la preuve. Dans des villes ou dans des cours ou il y a des Societés nombreuses on peut se deguiser, on peut quelquefois ebloui les yeux aux plus grands Philosophes. Mais, pour[15] moi Je me metts a la preuve la plus forte. C'est dans la silence et Solitude de votre Bois sacré que vous me jugerez, monsieur. Pensez vous que dans des tels circonstances Je puis echaper de votre œil pereant.

Vos ecrits Monsieur mont attendri le cœur, m'ont elevé l'ame, mont allumé lImagination. Jai un esprit vif mais melancolique. Et vous savez combien un Homme peut souffrir de cela, sans avoir eu des grands Malheurs externes. J'ai eu pourtant des Malheurs. Je me trouve.[16]

[1] MS. 'language' with the 'u' before 'age' deleted.

[2] MS. 'Je sais mon' and the rest of the line (now illegible) deleted, probably by JB.

[3] MS. 'curiosite naturelle' inserted above 'Homme a deux'

[4] MS. 'dire' inserted above the line, between 'pouvoir' and 'qu'ils'

[5] MS. 'et peutetre … admirer' deleted by a single line.

[6] MS. 'vient' written above 'un jeune'

[7] MS. Illegible word deleted before 'merite', 'distingué' scored out after it; 'de merite' inadvertently repeated.

[8] MS. 'fort' deleted.

[9] MS. 'devoit' with 'r' added as superscript.

[10] MS. 'decouvrira' written above a scored out word, possibly 'saura'

[11] MS. 'aussi' written above deleted 'aussi'

[12] MS. 'Monsieur Rousseau decouvre ainsi ce qui est un Homme' deleted by a single stroke. JB had seen paintings by Raphael and other major artists in the museums of Sanssouci and Dresden (Journ. 7 July and n. 4, 10 Oct. and n. 2).

[13] '1' above 'essence and '2' above 'vous en avez' in the preceding sentence, suggesting a desired transfer.

[14] MS. 'annalyserz' with the final 'e' inserted above the verb.

[15] MS. 'pour' deleted here and also at the beginning of the next page.

[16] MS. Here the draft breaks off.

## To Jean-Jacques Rousseau, 3 December 1764 (final draft)

MS. BPUN, R 307, fol. 3–4. Previously printed in *Letters JB*, i. 58–61; and *CC Rousseau*, Letter 3694(*bis*), xxii. 156–59.

Val de Travers ce 3 Decembre 1764.

MONSIEUR: Je suis un ancien Gentilhomme Ecossois. Vous savez mon rang. J'ai vingt quatre ans. Vous savez mon age. Il y a seize mois que Je suis sorti de la Grande Bretagne comme un bon Insulaire, sans savoir presque un mot de françois. J'ai ete en Hollande et en Allemagne, mais pas encore en [F]rance. Vous excuserez donc mon langage. Je suis á voyager avec un veritable desir de me perfectionner. Je suis venu ici dans l'esperance de vous voir.

J'ai entendu Monsieur que vous êtes fort difficile, que vous avez refusé les visites de plusieurs gens de la premiêre distinction. Pour cela, Monsieur, Je vous respecte de plus. Si vous laissiez entrer chez vous tout ceux dont la vanité souhaite de pouvoir dire 'Je l'ai vu' votre maison ne seroit plus la Retraire du Genie exquis et de la Pieté èlevé; et Je ne m'empresserois pas avec enthousiasme d'y etre recu.

Je me presente Monsieur comme un Homme d'une merite singulierre. Comme un Homme qui a un Cœur sensible, un Esprit vif et melancolique. Ah! si tout ce que J'ai souffert ne me donne pas une merite singulierre auprês de Monsieur Rousseau, pourquoy ai je eté tellement creé? pourquoy at il tellement ecrit?

Demandez vous si J'ai des Recommendations? En est il donc besoin pour vous? Une Recommendation est necessaire dans le commerce du monde pour garantir des Gens sans Penetration contre des Imposteures. Mais vous Monsieur qui avez tant etudie la Nature humaine, pouvez vous vous tromper sur un Caractêre? Voici mon idee de Vous. L'essence incomprehensible de l'Ame apart, vous avez une Connoissance parfaite des toutes les principes du Corps et de l'Esprit de leurs mouvements, leurs sentiments, enfin de toutce qu'ils peuvent faire, de toutce qu'ils peuvent acquerir qui influ veritablement sur l'homme. Et cependant Monsieur J'ose me presenter devant vous. J'ose me mettre á la preuve.

Dans des Villes et dans des Cours ou il y a des Societés nombreuses, on peut se deguiser, on peut quelquefois eblouir les yeux aux plus grands Philosophes. Mais moi Je me metts a preuve la plus forte. C'est dans le silence et la solitude de votre Retraite sacrée que vous jugerez de moi, et pensez vous que dans des telles circonstances Je serais capable de dissimuler?

Vos ecrits, Monsieur, m'ont attendri le Cœur m'ont elevé l'Ame m'ont allumé l'Imagination.

Croyez moi vous serez bien aise de me voir. Vous savez l'orgueil des Ecossois.— Monsieur, Je viens chez vous pour me rendre plus digne d'etre d'une Nation qui a produit Un Fletcher de Saltoun,[1] et un Milord Marischal. Excusez moi, Monsieur. Je me sens emu. Je ne puis me retenir. O cher St. Preux! Mentor eclaire! eloquent et aimable Rousseau! Jai un presentiment qu'une Amitié bien noble va naitre Aujourdhui.

J'apprends avec beaucoup de regret Monsieur, que vous êtes souvent incommodé. Peutêtre vous l'etes a present. Mais Je vous supplie que cela ne vous empeche pas de me recevoir. Vous me trouverez une Simplicite que ne vous derangera point, une Cordialite qui peut contribuer a vous faire oublir vos peines.

J'ai beaucoup á vous dire. Quoique Je ne suis qu'un Jeune Homme J'ai eprouvé une varieté d'existence[2] dont vous serez frappe. Je me trouve dans des circonstances serieuses et delicates, sur lesquelles Je souhaite ardemment d'avoir les Conseils de lauteur de la Nouvelle Heloise. Si vous etes l'homme bienfaisant que Je vous croye, Vous ne saurez hesiter de me les accorder. Ouvrez donc votre Porte Monsieur a un Homme qui ose vous assurer qu'il merite d'y entrer. Ayez de la confiance dans un Etranger singulier. Vous ne vous en repentirez point. Mais Je vous prie, soyez seul. Malgre toute mon enthousiasme, apres vous avoir ecrit de cette maniêrre, Je ne sais si Je ne voudrois plutot vous ne voir jamais, que vous voir pour la premiêrre fois, en Compagnie. Jattends avec impatience votre Reponse.

BOSWELL.

---

[1] For Andrew Fletcher, see Journ. 3 Dec. nn. 37–38.

[2] MS. 'd'existence' inserted above the line with a caret.

## II. Cover letter sent with the 'Ébauche de ma vie'

## To Jean-Jacques Rousseau, 4 or 5 December 1764

MS. BPUN, R 307, fol. 5–6. Previously printed in *Letters JB*, i. 62–63; *Correspondance générale de J.-J. Rousseau*, ed. Théophile Dufour (et Pierre-Paul Plan), 1924–34, xii. 114–15; and CC *Rousseau*, Letter 3704, xxii. 170–71.

HEADING: A Monsieur Rousseau

MONSIEUR: J'ai toute la reconnoissance possible de votre Accueil reellement gracieux.

S'il est possible Je vous prie de m'aider. Je vous laisse une Ebauche de ma vie. Je l'ai ecrit á la hate. Vous avez des faits. Les Sentiments aurroient etés trop diffus. Vous n'aimez pas d'etre gené par la compagnie de Personne. Mes Papiers peut-être peuvent etre recus.

Apres toutce que J'ai fait — J'ai encore de la Sante; J'ai encore un Esprit pour la plupart tres sain. J'ai une ame qui m'incite d'etre un Homme. O daignez de conserver un vraye Ecossois. Milord Marischal est vieux. Cette Chêne illustre de l'Ecosse doit bientot tomber. Vous aimez cet ancien Païs. Conservez en un arbrisseau.

Je reviendrais avec le Portrait[1] de Milord. Vous me        ² et Je partirais de chez vous pour le monde avec deux ou trois principes simples et nobles, et Je serais un Homme la reste de ma vie. Vous serez assez genereux de garder mon Secret.[3] Imparfait comme Je suis, Je me trouve un excellent Homme dans le monde comme il existe. Mais J'ai une idee qu'il m'est possible d'etre au dessus du monde comme il est; et avant que Je suis comme cela Je ne serais content.

Vous aurrez la bonté de me rendre mon Ebauche.

Pendant ma melancholie á Utrecht; Je fis connoissance avec une Demoiselle de la premierre Noblesse et bien riche. Je me comportois tellement qu'on m'honore de la reputation d'etre Philosophe. Ah! combien les Apparences sont trompeuses. Si vous voulez vous amuser de lire quelques pièces par cette Demoiselle, Vous les trouverez dans un petit pacquet apart.[4] Je voudrois bien avoir vos sentiments sur son charactêre. Vous êtes le seul a qui J'ai montré ses papiers. Je pouvois vous confier tout au monde.

Je suis avec un Respect et une Affection dont vous ne devez douter Votre Admirateur êternel.

[1] Either a written character-sketch, or an engraved print.

[2] MS. A single word rendered illegible by a blot or stain. Tinker, in *Letters JB*, gives the word as 'verrez'.

[3] A reference to JB's affair with a young married woman, described in detail in the 'Ébauche de ma vie' below.

[4] Presumably JB was leaving whatever papers of Belle de Zuylen he had taken with him from Utrecht. These were known to have included the prose 'characters' of Belle herself and of Catherina Elisabeth (Hasselaer) Geelvinck (1738–92), a young widowed friend of Belle, and perhaps some verses but not those he received a few days later from Anne-Susanne ('Nanette') Kinloch (for whom see Journ. 12 Dec. n. 3). Rousseau evidently returned these together with the 'Ébauche', since they were recovered among JB's papers.

## III. 'Ébauche de ma vie', 5 December 1764

### A. Final Copy

MS. Yale (L1107).

Je vous presente Monsieur une Ebauche de ma vie. Pour les Gens du monde qui sont charmés de lire des vies, il ne seroit rien. Car on y trouvera peu d'avantures amusantes. Mais si Je ne me trompe, il sera un tresor pour Monsieur Rousseau. Vous qui aimez tant l'Etude de l'homme, vous y trouverez des faits pour vous fortifier dans vos sentiments. Vous verrez en moi un exemple extraordinaire des effets d'une mauvaise education. J'ai une tres bonne Memoire pour ce que m'interesse, J'ai une Imagination vive. Je puis rapeller tout le[1] Progrês de mon Existence, depuis que J'etois capable de penser. Je vous donnerais des idées principales. Je ne cacherais pas des foiblesses et des ridicules. Je ne cacherais même des crimes.

Philosophe illustre! vous me verrez parfaitement. Vous me jugerez avec indulgence. Vous me donnerez des Conseils. Peutêtre vous m'en trouverez digne.

Je suis né d'un temperament melancolique. C'est le temperament de notre famille. Plusieurs de mes Parents en ont souffert.[2] Pourtant Je ne regrette pas que Je suis Melancolique. C'est le temperament des Cœurs tendres des Ames nobles. Mais des tels temperaments demandent une education tres soigneuse. Il est á craindre qu'ils ne tombent dans une foiblêsse qui les aneantit, ou qu'ils ne prennent une habitude d'envisager[3] tout d'une maniêrre qui leur rend la vie Amêre.

J'etois elevé fort delicatement par consequent Je commencois á bonne heure d'etre incommodé, et on me plaignoit comme un Enfant bien tendre. Ma Mere etoit fort aimable mais trop inquiête quand J'avois quelque petite maladie. Si Je ne me portois pas bien J'etois traite avec tous les egards possibles. Je n'etois pas forcé d'aller á l'ecole que Je detestois. Elle me donnoit des bon-bons et toutes sortes de jolies choses pour m'amuser. Quand Je me suis retabli, mon Esclavage recommencoit. Je savois cela et J'aimois plus d'être foible et malade que vigoureux et en bon Sante. Quelle idee denaturelle. La Nature doit etre terriblement choqué avant qu'elle se change comme cela. Selon la Nature, un Enfant doit sentir la malheur d'etre incommodé, et les agrements de la Santé. C'est par cela qu'il est encouragé de luter contre des Maladies. Moi Je les encourageois et au lieu de sauter et courir, Je restois dans un fauteil. J'etois mecontent & capricieux. Il est etonnant que Je ne me disois souvent malade quand Je me portois bien. Mais Mon Digne Pêre m'avoit imprimé un respect pour la verité qui m'a toujours resté fêrme. Ainsi Je ne mentis jamais. Mais Je me suis panché la tête vers la terre, jusques a ce que J'y sentois du douleur. Alors Je me suis plaigt comme un[4] malade.

Ma mere etoit extremement pieuse. Elle m'inspiroit de la devotion. Mais malheureusement elle m'enseignoit le Calvinisme. Mon Catechisme en renfermoit les doctrines les plus noires. L'eternité de Punition etoit ma premierre grande idée. Combien en aije fremi. Comme le feu etoit quelque chose de materiêlle J'en avois une idee. Je pensois peu de la beatitude du Ciel, parce que Je n'en avois aucune idée. J'avois entendu qu'on y etoit sans cesse á louer Dieu[,] et

Je m'imaginois qu'on chantoit des Pseaumes comme á l'eglise et cela ne m'incitoit pas. Je n'aurrois pas souhaité d'aller au Ciel, s'il y avoit eté quelque autre moyen d'echapper l'enfer. Je m'imaginois que les Saints passoient toute l'Eternité dans l'humeur des Gens nouvellement sauvés d'une Incendie qui se consoloient d'etre en sureté pendant qu'ils entendoient les cris lugubres des tourmentés.[5]

Ma mere fut de cet Secte qui croit qu'il faut une conversion marqué de chaque particulier pour être sauvé. Elle m'a donc pressé beaucoup de ceder aux operations de la grace de Dieu, et elle me mit entre les mains une petite livre ou Je lisois des conversions des enfants tres jeunes.[6] Je me souviens il y en[7] avoit un de[8] trois ans. Les Servantes m'amusoit d'une infinité de contes de Voleurs, de Meutriers, de Sorciêrres et de Revenants.[9] De sorte que mon Imagination etant continuellement effrayé Je devenois l'etre le plus craintif le plus meprisable.

Pourtant de huit a douzte Je me portois assez bien. J'avois un Gouverneur qui ne manquoit pas du Sentiment et de la sensibilité. Il commençoit de me former l'Esprit d'une manière qui m'enchantoit.[10] Il me fit lire le Spectateur et c'etoit alors que Je recu mes premiêrres idees du gout pour les beaux arts, et du plaisir qu'il y avoit de considerer la varieté de la vie humaine.[11] Je lisois les Poetes Romains et Je sentis un enthousiasme classique dans les ombres romanesques[12] de notre Campagne. Mon Gouverneur me parloit quelquefois de la Religion mais d'une manierre simple et agreable. Il me dit que si Je me[13] comportois bien pendant que Je vivois, Je serois heureux dans l'autre monde. J'y entenderois de la belle Musique. J'y apprendrois les sciences sublimes que Dieu accordera aux justes, et J'y rencontrerois tous les grands hommes dont J'avois lu, et tous les chers Amis que J'avois connu. Enfin mon Gouverneur me fit aimer le ciel, et quelque esperance se meloit avec ma Religion.[14]

Mon Pêre qui est un des plus habils et des plus dignes hommes au monde, avoit beaucoup d'affaires et ne pouvoit pas prendre immediatement beaucoup de soin de mon Education.[15] Il faisoit[16] comme les autres et me confioit a des maitres. De cinq á huit J'allois á une Ecole ou J'etois fort malheureux.[17] De huit á douze J'avois mon premier Gouverneur et pendant ces quatre Ans Je puis dire que J'etois heureux excepté les dimanches quand on me faisoit souvenir de l'Etre terrible qu'on appelloit Dieu. Les Presbyteriens Ecossois sont excessivement rigides á legard d'observer le Dimanche. On me menoit a l'Eglise ou J'etois obligé d'entendre trois discours par jours avec beaucoup de prièrres impromptu et beaucoup des Psaumes chantés et tout cela se faisoit d'une manièrre melancolique. Au soir on me faisoit dire mon Catechisme et repeter des Psaumes mis en vers les plus basses. J'etois obligé par ma Religion 'de ne pas faire mes propres ouvrages, parler mes propres mots ni penser mes propres pensés, le jour de Dieu.'[18] J'ai taché en honneteté de cœur de me conformer á cela; surtout de ne pas penser[19] Mes propres[20] pensés. Voila un joli exercise pour l'Esprit d'un Enfant. Quand J'avois douze ans mon premier Gouverneur recut le charge de Ministre, et on me donnoit un autre Gouverneur, un fort honnet homme, mais dure et sans aucune connoissance de l'esprit humain. Il avoit passé par la route ordinaire des ecoles et des Collêges.[21] Il avoit bien appri ses leçons et tout ce qu'il avoit appri faisoit un parti de luimeme. Il etoit dogmatiste sans jamais douter. Il sentit et agissoit[22] par Système. Quand Je disois un jour que J'avois un ami que J'aimois plus que mes frêres. 'Lourdaut' (repondoit il) ne savez vous pas le progrês de l'Affection. Premierrement vous aimez vos Parens, ensuite vos frêres, puis vous vous repandez sur le reste du Genre humain.' Il me faisoit lire les auteurs anciens mais sans aucun agrement. Il n'avoit aucune autre idée que de me faire[23] remplir un tache. Quand Je lui faisoit des questions sur les Poêtes, pour m'instruire ou pour m'amuser,—pourquoi non? Il etoit faché et crioit avec l'hauteur d'un maitre d'Ecole. 'Allons, allons, travaillez, travaillez; ne nous interrompez pas. Le tems s'ecoule.' Ainsi Je pris l'habitude de lire sans aucun proffit. C'etoit assez de dire J'ai lu un tel auteur. Dans ma douzième Année, J'attrappois une Rheume fort severe; on me donnoit beaucoup de remedes et mon estomac naturellement foible fut gaté en sorte que Je n'avois presque point de digestion. J'avoue que la crainte de recommencer mes etudes comme on les appelloit me faisoit souhaiter de rester malade. Les plus grands medecins d'Ecosse[24] furent appellés. J'avois la mechanceté de faire en sorte que leur remedes n'avoient aucun effet sur moi. J'etois maitre en quelque façon des mouvements de mon Estomac et Je fis sortir bien vite tout ce qu'on me faisoit prendre. Je souffrois même des vesicatoires[25] en me felicitant de n'etre pas obligé de travailler. La Faculté trouvoit en moi une maladie nerveuse bien extraordinaire et J'avoue que Je me mocquois bien de leurs consultations. J'etois affoibli en corp et en Esprit, et la melancolie que J'avois naturellement s'augmentoit. On m'envoyoit á Moffat le Spa d'[E]cosse. On me permettoit beaucoup d'amusement. Je voyois beaucoup de Gens gayes.[26] Je voulois être gaye aussi; et insensiblement Je me suis retabli; aprés avoir imaginé qu'assurement Je serois malade toute ma vie. A treize ans on m'envoyoit á l'université. J'y etois plus libre. Je m'y plaisoit[27] assez, et pendant trois ans que j'etudiois les langues, Jetois fort distingué et mes Professeurs disoient que Je serois un tres grand Homme.[28] Mes desirs de Jeunesse devenoient forts. J'avois l'horreur de crainte que Je pecherois e<t s>erois[29] danné. Il me venoit dans l'esprit troublé que Je devois suivre l'exemple d'Origen.[30] Mais cette folie se passoit. Malheureusement une Hypochondrie terrible me saisoit á l'áge de seize ans. J'apprenois La Logique et la metaphysique — Mais Je devenois methodist.[31] J'allois encore á Moffat. Il y avoit la Un Vieux Pythagoréén. Je me joignois á lui. Je m'obstinoit[32] de ne jamais manger d'aucun chair et J'etois resolu de souffrir tout comme un Martyre de l'humanité.[33] Je regardois tout le Genre humain avec horreur. Cela se passoit Je ne sais comment. Je crois en cedant aux opinions recues. Car, encore Il ne me paroit pas claire. A dix huit Je devenois Catholique.[34] Je lutois contre l'affection Paternelle l'ambition l'interet. Je les vainquois et Je m'enfuyois á Londres dans l'intention de me cacher dans quelque retraite melancolique de passer ma vie en tristêsse.[35] Milord — me fit Deiste. Je me livrois aux plaisirs sans borne. J'etois dans une delire de joye.[36] Je voulois entrer dans les Gardes.[37] Mon Pere me ramenoit en Ecosse. J'y passois deux ans á etudier le droit civile. Mais mon Esprit fermenté ne pouvoit jamais s'appliquer aux Sciences sollides.[38] Je n'avois point d'inclination pour le droit civile. Je l'appris tres superficiellement.[39] Mes Principes devenoient plus et plus embrouillés. Á la fin J'etois un Sceptique Universelle. Je meprisois tout, et Je n'avois aucun idée que pour passer agreablement le jour que s'ecouloit. J'avois des Intrigues avec des Actrices mariés.[40] Mes beaux sentiments s'effacoient absolument. J'aimois une dame la fille d'un Homme de la première distinction en Ecosse. Elle se marioit avec un Gentilhomme tres riche.[41] Elle me fit voir qu'elle m'aimoit plus que son Mari. Sans aucune difficulté, elle m'accordoit tout. Elle etoit Philosophe subtile. Elle disoit

J'aime mon Mari comme un Mari et vous comme un amant chacun dans sa place. Je luis fais tous les devoirs d'une bonne femme. Je me livre avec vous aux plaisirs delicieux. Nous gardons notre secrêt. La nature m'a tellement fait que Je n'aurrais jamais des Enfans. Personne soufre de nos Amours. Ma conscience ne me reproche pas: et Ma fois Je suis sure que le bon Dieu n'en saurroit etre offensé. Une telle Philosophie dans la bouche d'une femme charmante me paroissoit bien jolie. Mais Son Pere m'avoit accablé des bontes. Son Mari etoit un homme le plus honorable. Il me fit venir passer dans sa Campagne.[42] Les Regrets les plus Amêres me saisissoient. J'etois triste. J'etois presque au desespoir et souvent Je voulois avouer tout a M. de — pour l'engager d'oter la vie d'un Malheureux. Mais cela aurroit eté une folie la plus funêste. Je m'ouvrois le Cœur á Madame de — Quoique tendre et genereuse elle etoit ferme dans ses idées. Elle me Rapprochoit ma foiblêsse. Que pouvois Je faire. Je continuois mes Amours criminels et les plaisirs que Je goutoient faisoient un contrepoids a mes remords. Quelque fois même dans mes transports Je m'imaginoit que le Ciel ne pouvoit qu'applaudir un Bonheur si grand entre deux Mortels.[43]

A vingt deux Mon Pere me permettoit d'aller á Londres. J'etois bien aise d'echapper l'endroit ou etoit Madame de —. Je fis resolution de ne lui jamais ecrire et depuis deux ans Nous n'avons en point de nouvelles l'un de l'autre, excepté que nous nous portions bien. Á Londre J'avois une Intrigue avec une femme usée dans la Gallanterie.[44] Pour cela Je ne pouvois pas me reprocher. Mais Je donnois dans un libertinage sans sentiment avec les filles qui etoient á tout le monde qui avoient de l'argent.[45] Pour cela Je me reproche. Je fis connoissance avec un Savant illustre qui me demontroit la verité de la Religion Chretiênne, mais d'une espece un peu sevêre.[46] Mon Pere etoit toujours inquiet. Il vouloit me faire Avocat en Ecosse. Á la fin J'y consentis á condition qu'il me permettroit de voyager. J'allois á Utrecht. Je m'y forcoit d'etudier beaucoup mais Je proffitois peu. Je n'ai jamais appri á m'appliquer veritablement. La melancholie la plus noire m'accabloit. Mes tristes idees de la Religion retournoient, et quelquefois Je ne croyois rien. Je pensois avec un horreur irresolu de quitter la vie.[47]

Milord Marischal me menoit en Allemagne. Sa conversation me donnoit la changement d'idées, les Vertus donnoient du feu á mon ame gelé. Je lui avouoit ma melancholie. Il a ecrit á mon Pere pour me laisser voyager en Italie. J'attends á Neufchatel la reponse de mon Pere.

Monsieur Je vous ai donné á la hate tout ce que J'ai du mauvais.— Je vous ai dit tout ce que J'ai[48] du bon. Dites moi est il possible de me faire encore un Homme? Dites moi si Je puis etre un digne Seigneur Ecossois. Si Je Puis — Mon Dieu que je craigns! Si je puis etre verteux auprès de Madame de — Peutetre Elle a changé aussi. O Philosophe bienfaisant! Je vous supplie de m'aider. J'ai un Esprit foible; mais une Ame forte. Allumez cette Ame et le[49] feu sacré ne sera jamais etteint.

---

[1] MS. 'es' deleted at the end of 'tout', 's' deleted at the end of 'le' (i.e., changed from 'toutes les').

[2] For details concerning this trait, see the unfinished first draft of the 'Ébauche' below (App. 2, III.B and n. 3).

[3] MS. 'envisger'

[4] MS. A single word, now illegible, deleted before 'malade'

[5] As a young child, JB had been encouraged to read the catechism and other religious texts without comprehension, even without grasping the meaning of difficult concepts. In a 'French Theme' of 29 Jan.

1764, he wrote: 'Je me souviens parfaitement que ma mere m'accordoit de me faire
present d'une Confession de foy de l'Eglise
Ecossoise pourvu que je le liroit du commencement jusque au fin.... Jai lu dont [sic]
aussi vite que je pouvois cette collection des
obscurités absurdes mais mon esprit n'en
recu la moindre impression, lelection & la
reprobation & la grace irresistible etoient a
moi aussi inconnus que les systemes des
votaries de Vistnou [i.e., 'Vishnu'] Eswara
[i.e., 'Ishvara' or 'Shiva'] & Brama dans les
indes orientales. Neanmoins jai lu le livre &
ma mere en etoit contente' (Yale MS. M 87).

⁶ Lady Auchinleck's Calvinistic piety
seems also to have been influenced by the
Methodism founded by John Wesley (1703–
91) and Charles Wesley (1707–88), which
emphasized personal conversions. F. A. Pottle
has suggested that she may have been influenced particularly by the Wesleys' rival
George Whitefield (1714–70), an enthusiastic Methodist preacher who had attracted
large crowds during his several appearances
in Edinburgh between 1741 and 1757 (Earlier
Years, pp. 33, 462; Harry S. Stout, The Divine
Dramatist: George Whitefield and the Rise of
Modern Evangelism, 1991, pp. 136, 138–55).
One of his strongest supporters in Scotland
had been Lady Auchinleck's brother-in-law,
Dr. Alexander Webster (Stout, pp. 139, 150).
The little book to which JB refers has not
been identified.

⁷ MS. 'en' inserted above the line.

⁸ MS. 'dé'

⁹ MS. 'de' inserted above the line before
'Voleurs', 'Meurtriers', 'Sorciêrre', and 'Revenants'

¹⁰ MS. 'm'enchantoit' written over deleted
'menchantoit'

¹¹ The tutor, John Dun (c. 1723–92), a
native of Eskdalemuir, Dumfriesshire, had
studied for the ministry at the University of
Edinburgh. He had been appointed to the
parish of Auchinleck in Aug. 1752 and had
been ordained its minister in Nov. of that
year (Fasti Scot. iii. 4; Book of Company, p.
190; Corr. 6, pp. 396–97 n. 1). While JB's
tutor, Dun had indeed shaped many of JB's
literary tastes, especially his interest in
Addison and Steele, whose 'Mr. Spectator'
furnished him with a model of a man-about-
town in London (see Journ. 5, 11 Dec. 1762,
8 Jan., 13, 23 Apr., 29 May, 28 June 1763).
For the influence of Addison's Remarks on
Several Parts of Italy, see Journ. 28 Nov. and
n. 5.

¹² 'Romanesque', in antithesis to 'enthousiasme classique', could mean 'romantic', as
translated in Earlier Years (p. 2), or it could

mean 'novelistic', suggesting an imaginative,
literary intensity, as in Rousseau's Nouvelle
Héloïse.

¹³ MS. 'me' inserted above the line between 'Je' and 'comportois'

¹⁴ For a harsher judgment of his boyhood
'governors', see the discarded page of the
final draft of the 'Ébauche' (Yale MS. L 1111,
App. 2, III.E); see also Earlier Years, p. 18.

¹⁵ Lord Auchinleck had been admitted
advocate in Edinburgh in 1729, and had been
appointed Sheriff of Wigtownshire for two
years in 1748 (Fac. Adv., p. 18; Earlier Years,
p. 9).

¹⁶ MS. 'faisoit', changed from 'fait'

¹⁷ Starting in 1746, JB had attended the
private school of James Mundell (d. 1762)
where boys from the age of five or six were
taught Latin, English, Writing, and Arithmetic. The school was situated in Edinburgh's
West Bow, an old part of the city associated
with ghosts, and criminals on their way to
the gallows—frightening ideas for the sensi-
tive young boy (Earlier Years, pp. 15–16, 457).

¹⁸ A literal interpretation of the fourth
commandment, which teaches that it is sin-
ful to profane the Lord's day by 'needless
Works, Words, and Thoughts about our
worldly Employment and Recreations' ('The
Larger Catechism', Questions 117 and 119,
in A Collection of Confessions of Faith, Edinburgh, 1719, i. 276–77). For a description of
typical Calvinist Sunday services as experienced by JB in his youth, see Mary Margaret
Stewart, 'Boswell's Denominational Dilemma', PMLA 76 (1961): 504–05; see also
James J. Caudle, 'James Boswell and the Bi-
Confessional State', in Religious Identities in
Britain, 1660–1832, ed. William Gibson and
Robert G. Ingram, 2005, pp. 119–46.

¹⁹ MS. 'penser' written above an illegible
deleted word.

²⁰ MS. 'propres' inserted after 'Mes'

²¹ Dun would remain the parish minister,
a benevolent presence at Auchinleck, treated
with respect and affection to the end of his
life (see To WJT, 2 Sept. 1775, Corr. 6, pp.
396–97 and n. 1; Great Biographer, p. 189).
JB's new tutor, Joseph Fergusson (c. 1719/
20–92), was a minister licensed by the Presbytery of Edinburgh in 1759, ordained in
1761 and after a delay presented to Tun-
dergarth parish on 17 Sept. of that year (Corr.
1, p. 4 n. 2; Earlier Years, p. 20; Fasti Scot. ii.
223). Presumably he had studied in Edinburgh.

²² MS. 'agissosit'

²³ MS. 'me' inserted before 'faire'

²⁴ The doctors have not been identified,
but JB's family had close medical connec-

tions as his uncle Dr. John Boswell (for whom see Journ. 19 Sept. n. 2) became President of the Royal College of Physicians in Edinburgh.

[25] Blister-causing ointments made of dried flying beetles, which were applied to the skin to treat 'nervous Disorders' as well as such varied complaints as acute fevers, smallpox, and measles (OED, s.v. 'Vesicatory'; Robert James, A Medicinal Dictionary ... with a History of Drugs, 3 vols., 1743–45, s.v. 'Vesicatoriam', 'Cantharides').

[26] Moffat, a small, rustic village in Dumfriesshire in the picturesque southern highlands, had a sulphur spring whose water, used for drinking and baths, was helpful in treating JB's scorbutic complaint. Joseph Fergusson accompanied him there (Earlier Years, p. 22). Though Moffat offered only simple amusements, it gave JB a first experience of easy sociability with grown-ups. It also allowed him, at the age of thirteen, to fall in love—with a Miss Mackay, as he recalled ten years later when he met her in London (Earlier Years, pp. 21–22; Journ. 3 Jan. 1763).

[27] MS. final 's' written over final 't' in 'plaisois'

[28] At Edinburgh University, where JB had started in autumn 1753 and had excelled in Latin, which he had studied every term to 1758 with Professor George Stuart either in 'public' lectures or in smaller 'private' classes. He could read and quote Latin texts with ease, although F. A. Pottle has suggested that he may have learned more from his earlier teachers Mundell and Dun than from Stuart. JB had also studied Greek with Professor Robert Hunter, starting in 1756 (Pottle, 'Boswell's University Education', in Johnson, Boswell and their Circle, 1965, pp. 234–39; Earlier Years, p. 24). He seems not to have taken French at this time.

[29] MS. A hole in the page.

[30] Guilt feelings caused by his awakened sexuality had evidently led JB to consider following the example of Origen (184 or 185–253 or 255 A.D.), who reportedly castrated himself. An early Greek Church father, Origen was said to have taken literally the words of Jesus approving those who 'have made themselves eunuchs for the kingdom of heaven's sake' (Matt. 19: 12; see Henri Crouzel, Origen, trans. A. S. Worrall, 1989, pp. 8–9 and n. 32).

[31] In the 'Arts' course in which JB was enrolled at Edinburgh University, logic and metaphysics were two of the four general areas, the others being moral philosophy and natural philosophy (the sciences). He had studied metaphysics with John Stevenson, who had deeply disturbed him by abstract questions such as how to reconcile divine foreknowledge with human free will (see F. A. Pottle, 'Boswell's University Education', p. 231; Earlier Years, p. 32; see also Journ. 3 Aug.). In reaction, as his 'mais' suggests, he had accepted the emotional teachings of the Methodists, possibly influenced by George Whitefield (for whom see n. 6 above).

[32] MS. 't' written over 's', changing the correct first person to a third-person verb form.

[33] John Williamson, the self-educated sheepfarmer whom JB had met at Moffat, had introduced him to Pythagorean beliefs, for which see Mem. dated 9 Sept. n. 1.

[34] For F. A. Pottle's conjectures about this episode, see Journ. 5 Dec. n. 4.

[35] JB's wish for a life in seclusion, possibly even as monk, is restated in Outline 2. For the exclusions he would have suffered if he had persisted, see Earlier Years, pp. 45–47, 569–70; see also Journ. 24 June and n. 4.

[36] 'Milord', written as 'Milord E' in Outline 2, refers to Eglinton. He had made JB a Deist not in the philosophic sense, for which there is no evidence, but in the libertine style of life which JB had come to relish during his first stay in London in 1760 (Earlier Years, pp. 47–50). At that time, Eglinton had introduced JB to the Duke of York and beyond that to 'the circles of the great, the gay, and the ingenious' ('Memoirs of James Boswell, Esq.', Eur. Mag., May 1791, in Lit. Car.', p. xxxi; see also Earlier Years, pp. 48–50). In 1762–63 Eglinton, though somewhat less available to JB, had continued to act as social guide.

[37] JB had tried to pursue a commission in the foot guards in 1762–63 through influence, hoping to find a pleasant, gentlemanly occupation in or near London, though the actual profession of war tended to disturb him. His 'guards scheme' had come to nought with the end of the Seven Years' War. The suggestion that he seemed fit for the guards had been made first by Eglinton (see Journ. 11–13 Dec. 1762, 25 Jan., 27 Feb., 21 Mar. 1763; Earlier Years, pp. 50–55, 82–85, 106–08).

[38] MS. 'sciences sollides' almost obliterated by a large blot.

[39] But he had passed the private examination in Civil Law at the end of July 1762 (see To AE, 23 July 1762, Corr. 9, pp. 304–08 and n. 22; Journ. 30 July 1762; and Earlier Years, pp. 85, 481).

[40] From at least May 1761 in Edinburgh to 1763 JB carried on several clandestine intrigues, using code names in his journal entries for the actresses and certain of his other

partners. The 'A' mentioned in the journal of 8 May 1761, and 21, 23 Dec. 1762, was perhaps Mrs. Brooke (?1730–1782), a minor actress in Edinburgh who had left an abusive husband in London (*Earlier Years*, pp. 78, 478; John Taylor, *Records of My Life*, 1832, i. 31–32). Another woman, designated by JB only as ф, has been assumed by F. A. Pottle (noting that the symbol was 'the initial letter of one of the Greek nouns meaning "love"') to be the actress Mrs. Love, wife of James Love (for whom see Journ. 18 Aug. n. 5); see *Earlier Years*, pp. 77, 82, 93, 477. F. A. Pottle thought, however, that she was Elizabeth (Hooper) Love (d. 1783), whom Love had married in 1739. But Dorothy Stroud has suggested that Love had left his wife in the early 1750s and formed an alliance with another woman, an actress whose name may have been Catherine L'Amour. 'Mrs. Love' appeared with James Love on stage in Edinburgh from at least as early as the 1753–54 season, and apart from some time in Dublin, the Loves seem to have acted continuously with the Edinburgh company from the summer of 1756 until their departure for Drury Lane in 1762. In London in 1762–63, JB tried without success to renew sexual relations with Mrs. Love (see Mems. dated 28–29 Nov. 1762, 29 Mar., 21 Apr. 1763; *Earlier Years*, pp. 77, 477). She continued on the stage, under the name Mrs. Love, until 1790, and died in 1807 (*A Biographical Dictionary of Actors, Actresses, Musicians, Dancers, Managers & Other Stage Personnel in London 1660–1800*, ed. P. H. Highfill, Jr., K. A. Burnim, and E. A. Langhans, 16 vols., 1973–93, ix. 357, 363–65; Dorothy Stroud, *George Dance: Architect, 1741–1825*, 1971, p. 47; *Oxford DNB*, s.v. 'Dance, James').

[41] MS. Scored out from 'que pour passer' to 'riche' but the words are still decipherable. On a separate slip of paper referring to this passage or its verso, 'very Reprehensible' was inserted by JB's literary executor, Sir William Forbes (Yale MS. C 3106, see *Catalogue*, ii. 662).

[42] MS. Heavily scored out from 'Mais son Pere' to 'triste' but deciphered by an earlier Yale editor except for two illegible words preceding 'dans sa Campagne'. This passage is the verso of the one identified in the preceding note.

[43] The foregoing paragraph, containing JB's most explicit account of his guilt-ridden affair with the young married woman he had been planning to discuss with Rousseau, led F. A. Pottle to identify her as Jean Heron, daughter of Lord and Lady Kames, and wife of Patrick Heron (c. 1735–1803) of Kirroughtrie (see Journ. 14 Dec. n. 16; *Earlier Years*, p. 78). JB had written about Jean Heron on earlier occasions in a very different tone. He had addressed her admiringly in 'An Epistle to Miss Home' (before Nov. 1761, Bodleian Library, MS. Douce 193, *Corr. 9*, pp. 116–18) and had recorded a few of her pithy comments in his 'Boswelliana' of about the same time (i.e., autumn 1762). Several references to her appear in JB's 'Journal of My Jaunt, Harvest 1762', at the time of the actual affair, but conceal the affair from the journal's intended readers, JJ and William McQuhae, a tutor in Lord Auchinleck's household with whom JB had formed a friendship (Journ. 18 Sept., 1, 4, Oct. 1762; *Earlier Years*, p. 93; *Corr. 9*, p. 315 n. 1).

Omitted from this seemingly full account of JB's amorous experiences is his relationship in Edinburgh with 'a curious young little pretty', Peggy Doig, who had given birth to their son, whom JB named Charles, on about 7 Dec. 1762 (*Earlier Years*, pp. 80, 84, 94, 98, 482; to JJ, 17 Aug., 13 Sept., 24 Nov. 1762, *Corr. 1*, pp. 13–17, 24–25). JB had been delighted to hear of his son's birth.

[44] Presumably Anne Lewis (?1738–d. after 1791), the actress called 'Louisa' in JB's journal, with whom he had carried on an intrigue recorded stage by stage from 14 Dec. 1762 to 20 Jan. 1763 (see *Earlier Years*, pp. 98, 483–84; for her roles, see *Lond. Stage*, pt. 4, pp. 952, 957, 989, 995, 998).

[45] For such encounters, see Journ. 13 Apr. and 18 June 1763. But JB did not tell Rousseau of his meeting with other young women of the street, recorded in Journ. 9 Apr., 19 May 1763.

[46] JB met SJ several times in London after their first meeting, 16 May 1763, and in some of these meetings SJ advised him on the Christian religion (see Journ. 24 May, 14, 22, 28 July).

[47] JB's depression had mounted after hearing the news of the death of his infant son, whom he had never seen but for whom he had had high hopes (Journ. 9 Mar. 1764, *Holland*, Heinemann p. 173, McGraw-Hill p. 177; To WJT, 23 Mar., *Corr. 6*, p. 87; To JJ, 9 Apr., *Corr. 1*, pp. 121–25).

[48] MS. 'que J'ai' written above deleted 'J'avois'

[49] MS. 'il' deleted before 'le'

## B. Unfinished first draft

MS. Yale (L 1108).

*Pour Monsieur Rousseau.*

Voici un Sujet digne de vous. Je vous offre Monsieur l'ebauche d'une Vie sur la quelle vous pouvez faire bien de Reflections. Pour commencer au fond et plus recherché que vous, Je suis Le[1] fils d'une famille singulièrre.[2] Mon Grand Pêre Paternel avoit de sa Mêre un degré de l'hypocondrie.[3] Quand il etoit jeune il etoit oisif, mais son Pere le forçat aux coups de Baton de s'appliquer á ses etudes, et il devint un Jurisconsulte tres distingué et gagnoit beaucoup d'argent.[4] Cependant il fut rarement content, quoique il avoit toute sorte des avantages. Il etoit souvent attaqué d'une Melancolie noire et comme il a eté elevé de cacher ses mauvaises humeurs et non pas de les vaincre, quand il n'avoit plus son Pere á craindre, il ne les cachoit plus. C'etoit un tres digne homme. Il avoit beaucoup de Religion. Mais il avoit malheureusement appri dans son enfance, les plus tristes dogmes presbyteriens et par consequent ses craintes l'emportoit[5] sur ses esperances. Il pensoit toujours á se retirer du monde, mais [M]adame sa femme l'empechoit. Elle etoit un Caractêre le plus respectable. Elle avoit aussi beaucoup de Religion. Mais elle avoit l'esprit plus sain, plus gaye que n'avoit Son Mari.[6] Après la mort de madame, il[7] se retiroit veritablement, et vivoit sur ses terres, ou il menoit une vie fort simple. Il devoit aussi etre une vie tranquille. Mais son humeur noire et les ideès sevêres de Religion qui lui restoient jusques á sa mort otoient en grand parti le repos d'un des meilleurs hommes au monde. Je nen doute pas qu'a present il est recompencé.

Il avoit trois fils. Deux souffroient de melancolie.[8] L'autre qui est mon Pere a le temperament le plus heureux. Outre un corps des plus robustes, Il a un esprit extremement fort. Mais Il se marioit avec une Demoiselle tres delicate qui etoit fort Hypocondre et qui avoit eté elevé tout á fait hors du monde avec des notions pieuses visionnaires et scrupuleuses. Elle pleuroit quand on la forçoit d'aller une fois au Theatre et elle n'y retourna jamais.[9] Elle a fait la mêre de famille la plus aimable. Heureusement elle s'a fait un devoir d'avoir soin des choses temporelles. Ainsi elle a eu beaucoup d'amusement, Les interêts de la famille ont etés soutenues, et ma chêre mêre n'a rien de la mechançeté des devotes desœuvrés. Avec des tels Parens pourtant J'ai eté fort mal elevé. De mon premier enfance on m'enseignoit les dogmes les plus abstraits. La chute de l'homme, la peché originelle et l'incarnation de Jésus Christ m'etoient soigneusement repetes. A la fin Je les repetoit moimême: mais avec quelles idees.[10] O Philosophe eclairé dites moi, comment peut un enfant concevoir que des millions meritent d'etre punis pour la faute d'un seul. Theologiens profonds. Avouez en hommes. Ce sentiment ne choque t il pas l'Esprit naturel. Vous avez des raisonnements pour le faire convenir avec la Justice divine. Mais pensez vous qu'un Enfant est capable de les comprendre. Mais vous dites c'est toujours bon de fixer dans l'esprit tendre des verités importantes, et quand votre Elêve sera en etat de les comprendre il aurra l'avantage de les avoir imprimés sur sa memoire.[11] Mais mes amis laissez cela. Ne craignez pas que des Verités importantes seront rejettés parce que on n'en a pas appri par cœur les Mots. Non quand un jeune homme qui a l'esprit sain entend une verité, il[12] le reconnoit tout d'abord. Il s'en saisit avec un joye mâle. Il le garde, il le gardera toute sa vie si vous n'avez pas soin de lui confondre la memoire en entassant une foule de choses l'un sur l'autre.[13]

[1] MS. 'Les', final letter deleted.
[2] The information about his family had come to JB not only by word of mouth but also from the memoirs of his paternal grandfather, James Boswell ('old James', 1672–1749), 7th laird of Auchinleck, who began the family tradition of extensive autobiographical record keeping in his 'Memoirs of the family of Boswell of Auchinleck …', Yale MS. C 338.7 (hereafter cited as 'Auch. Memoirs'), continued by Lord Auchinleck.
[3] In this version of the 'Ébauche', JB emphasizes the hypochondria (depression) that, he believed, had afflicted several generations of his paternal family. His oldest forebear mentioned in this connection was his great grandmother, Anna (Hamilton), who had died in 1611 (Auch. Memoirs, p. 32). She was the wife of the sixth laird, David Boswell (1640–1712), in the branch related to the royal line of Stuart (Ominous Years, Chart III). Her eldest son, JB's grandfather James Boswell ('old James'), would be remembered for 'a melancholy and fretful temper' (Journ. 7 June 1779). His own memoirs emphasize the piety and frugality of his immediate family (Auch. Memoirs, pp. 25–27), but JB makes more of his grandfather's 'Melancolie noire', which he attributes to 'les plus tristes dogmes presbyteriens'. JB felt a particular affinity to him for 'a great Anxiety of temper' they supposedly shared (Journ. 7 Jan. 1763).
[4] The story of old James introduces the pursuit of the legal profession by three generations of Boswells. Old James had studied in Leiden from 1695–97 (Yale MS. C 338), had passed advocate in 1698 (Fac. Adv.), and had become respected in the legal profession as juris consultus. He would be remembered as 'a great lawyer though slow' (that is, given to careful deliberation) and for freely advising Lord Kames on difficult cases early in Kames's legal career (see 'Materials for the Life of Lord Kames', 20 Dec. 1778, Yale MS. M 135, section 1).
[5] MS. 'l'emportoit', final 's' deleted.
[6] Lady Elizabeth Bruce (d. 1734) was the daughter of Alexander Bruce, 2nd Earl of Kincardine (c. 1629–80). She had been brought up as an Episcopalian but had converted to the Church of Scotland. As a girl, she had lived in affluence, but once married, she had adapted quickly to a more frugal style of life. Her death, fifteen years before her husband's, had contributed to his melancholy (Auch. Memoirs, pp. 28, 33).
[7] MS 'madame. Il'
[8] Lord Auchinleck's younger brothers, the twins James (1710–?54), a 'writer' (solicitor), and John, M.D., had been mentally unstable (Earlier Years, pp. 21, 458–59).
[9] The date of Lady Auchinleck's visit to the theatre has not been ascertained.
[10] See App. 2, III.A n. 5.
[11] Rousseau had discussed this pedagogic point in Émile.
[12] MS. 'verité. Il'
[13] MS. 'Pour', a catchword pointing to another page, now missing or never written.

## C. Outline 1

MS. Yale (L 1109).

Pour Mr. Rousseau.

Vie digne de vous. Changements d'esprit plus que de situation de corps. Un homme dans le meme pais[1] qui a eté de sentiments differents qui â eu des idees variés, plus digne detre lu que celui qui a parcouru le monde avec une tete & cour de bois[2] aussi peu de changement que son Vaisseau. Née hyp. Grand Pêre Auch. ut in 1 folio.[3] Les fils un oisif — á la fin lié[4] melan. & au lit. Autre long tems harrasse de religion — a la fin assez bien.

Autre fort — mais[5] demoiselle fille d'un Pere Paralytique[6] eleve &c. Aîmable — active — mais triste. Eleve tendrement mal estomac.[7] Dabord triste religion dogmes myster. Imagination effraye la premierre grande idée punition eternelle — comme feu etoitt sensible pensoit peu de la beatitude parceque on ne savoit pas comment — meme entendoit qu'on chantoit des Psaumes[8] ne souhaitoit que par craint de horreurs esprit casse nulle oble esperance. Effraye terriblement des esprits. Jusque a 18 Ans ne pouvoit etre seul nuit. Quitte par coutume ne pas penser, et non raison. Craignoit froid et tout — grand Poltron á Edinbourg en des rues. Un Enfant ne doit etre elevé dans une ville confondû des objets. Pere digne Juge — mais ne se soucit pas de mon education immediatement. Envoyé á une ecole. Même si jeune des idees noires — Ignorance toutce que Je ne comprenoit — effrayant. Avare — veritablement triste de payer de l'argent. Avarice severe Horace le compare a une peine infernale Tantalus. Molier le montre vraye Tragedie.[9] A huit Precepteur assez joli homme — mais mal sain basse — point du monde mais un peu d'imagination. Goutoit les Poetes Romains. La mythologie allumoit Imag — en promenant dans des lieus romanesques d'Auchin. Pris des Amusements. Assez bien excepté le dimanche longues Sermons — ni occupation ni amusement — tout peché Pseaumes Catéchisme. Ennui á la mort — horreurs [—] se couchoit bientot. Quelles chaines! Predit Je serois heureux — soutenu par cela. A 12 Gove[10] á ordonner ministre. Nouvel Gouverneur Gros Lourdaut honnet homme avec savoir formel point de Gout — point de delicatesse. En hyver rhume attaqué mal tete estomac &c Lache — aimoit fauteil lutoit contre des remêdes. Hypochond. desespoir — Tout scorbut — Moffat mineraux. Deja en grimpant arbres plaisir. Ne pouvoit pas le concevoir. Pensoit du ciel — retournoit souvent grimpoit — sentoit me laissoit tomber des hautes branches en extase — tout naturel.[11] Parloit en áu Jardinier.[12] Lui rigide ne l'expliquoit pas. Amoureux á huit anns.[13] Sur honeur sentoit les plus fortes emotions excepté celles de la grand cause dont J'etois en ignorance — ou plutot n'en avois pas des idees claires. College — bon santé 14 la même — 15 aussi Collêge græc. La Guerre commençoit. Quoique timide le feu des Armes allumé vouloit aller parmi[14] les Montagnards en Amerique. C'etoit un rage. Mon Pere l'empecha.[15] J'etois elevé donc bassement. J'avois la mauvaise honte sans modestie. J'avois donc[16] lu des livres. Je savoit les rites de Venus. Mais malheureusement Japprenoit d'un camarade la funeste pratique.[17] J'etois toujours effrayé pour la damnation Je croyois que faire ainsi n'etoit qu'une peché bien legere au lieu que la fornication etoit horrible. O hommes en noire! O Pretres! O Ministres! comment avez vous acqui sur nous une si grande Influence. Comment vos decisions peuvent ils nous faire frêmir.[18]

---

[1] MS. 'dans le meme pais' inserted above the line.

[2] MS. 'avec une tete … bois' inserted above the line.

[3] MS. 'as in 1 folio'—i.e., as in the preceding draft, a sign to return to the place in Yale MS. L 1108 dealing with his grandfather James Boswell.

[4] MS. 'lie', bound; translated as 'in a strait jacket' by F. A. Pottle (unpub. note), a reference to James, one of the twin sons of old James (*Earlier Years*, p. 458; see L 1108, n. 8).

[5] MS. 'maise'; phrase 'se marioit avec' understood though omitted (unpublished emendation by F. A. Pottle).

[6] For the 'demoiselle', Lady Elizabeth (Bruce), see App. 2, III.B n. 6. The ailment of her father, the Earl of Kincardine, is not specified in Auch. Memoirs. His wife, Lady Elizabeth's mother, was Veronica van Aerssen, van Sommelsdyck (d. 1701), the first of

JB's Dutch relations (see *Burke's Peerage*, i. 963).

[7] A shift to JB's own experiences.

[8] MS. 'Pseemes'

[9] Horace had compared avarice to the punishment of Tantalus in *Satire I*, i. 68–79. Molière had dramatized a miser in *L'Avare* (1668), which is not, however, a tragedy but a dark comedy. JB would combine Horace's and Molière's depiction of the miser in *Hypochondriack* no. LVI, May 1782 (Bailey, ii. 170–71).

[10] 'Gouverneur'. For the change of tutors from Dun to Fergusson, see App. 2, III.A and n. 21.

[11] JB's frank disclosure of his first feelings of sexual arousal were in the end not discussed with Rousseau.

[12] The gardener was James Bruce, overseer of the Auchinleck estate, who had succeeded his father, also gardener at the estate, in 1741 (see Mem. dated 1 Sept. n. 2; Auch. Memoirs, p. 35; *Corr. 8, passim*).

[13] The object of JB's affection has not been identified.

[14] MS. 'pami'

[15] See Journ. 21 June, n. 11.

[16] MS. changed from 'dont'

[17] Masturbation. JB's unease on this subject continued. In Dec. 1758, he asked WJT to purchase for him in London a copy of 'the little pamphlet against Onania, a crime too little regarded' (To WJT, 16 Dec. 1758). The pamphlet was *Onania: or, the Heinous Sin of Self-Pollution and all its Frightful Consequences in both Sexes, Considered*, which was first published in 1710 and ran to twenty editions by the end of 1759 (see *Corr. 6*, pp. 14–16 and n. 13).

[18] At the bottom of the last blank page, the beginning of an earlier letter: 'To His Highness the Marcgrave of'; on the next line, 'Sir. Basle 25 Novr. 1764'—another sign that JB was short of paper. JB ends this outline with a flurry of Rousseauistic exclamations against priests and ministers.

## D. Outline 2

MS. Yale (L 1110).

En peu de mots — Est il possible de faire quelque chose — trop foible pour etre puni.[1] Temperament Melancolique. Mal elevé. Triste Calvinisme. Severité extravagante comme Origen. Methodist. Pythagoréen. Compagnon de comediens. — Eperdement amoureux d'une Actrice voulois l'Epouser.[2]— Devenois Catholique. Echappais á Londres.[3] Pensois devenir Pretre — ou moine. Milord E. fit Deiste. En delire me livrois aux plaisirs. Retournois en Ecosse — mecontent. Triste — Des Intrigues — Toutes principes confondues. La fille dun digne Ami de distinction et la femme d'un galant Homme. Croyois tout plaisir bon — retourné á Londres — harassé des Grands. Devenoit sage — voulois contenter Pere — Allois á Utrecht — Hypochondrie horrible. Tout desespoir. Retournois voulois etre parfait Chretien toujours á souffrir mort horrible[4] — tout l'hyver cachois — A la fin Noire melancholie — Pensois serieusement se tuer[5] —Toute existence ombre — Fils meurt[6] — Ne pouvois jamais acqueri des sciences — Mi Lord et Dame Turque — commencoit á changer. Priois Dieu contre triste Religion — Etourdi á Berlin — Voyage par cours — bien recu — a present — quoy faire — Supplie des conseils. Orgueilleux d'etre homme encore.

[1] MS. 'faire ... puni' inserted as separate line.

[2] JB had become friendly with theatre people in Edinburgh in 1759–60. He had been attracted particularly to a Mrs. Cowper, an actress to whom he gave favourable notice in his first separate publication, 'A View of the Edinburgh Theatre during the Summer Season, 1759'. She was a widow, virtuous, and a Catholic, and she may have been responsible for JB's interest in the Catholic church in 1759 (*Earlier Years*, pp. 40–41, 45, 61, 465). JB did not mention her by name to Rousseau, but her existence—and performance in Newcastle—were noted by WJT, who was not impressed by her talent nor by her good judgment in marrying her music master (25 Dec. 1759, *Corr. 6*, p. 30 and n. 9).

<sup>3</sup> MS. 'echappais á Londres' inserted between the lines.

<sup>4</sup> MS. 'mort horrible' inserted above the line.

<sup>5</sup> JB's most explicit statement in the 'Ébauche' papers that his depression had made him consider suicide.

<sup>6</sup> MS. 'Fils meurt' inserted above the line. For the news that his illegitimate infant son had died, which had contributed to JB's depression, see App. 2, III.A, n. 47.

## E. Discarded portion of the final draft (following JB's page 8)

MS. Yale (L 1111).

... Ans on m'envoyoit á l'université. J'etois la plus libre. Je m'y plaisois[1] assez. Je me portois assez bien mais de tems en tems ma melancolie me tourmentoit. Mes Gouverneurs avoient eté tous deux des Gens sans mannierre,[2] des Gens d'une Education la plus basse. Ils etoient comme des Domestiques de mon Pere. Ils mangeoient á la table mais ils n'osoient presque ouvrir la bouche. Je les voyois[3] meprisés. Pourtant ils avoient d'autorité sur moi pour m'inspirer des sentiments laches. Je croyois que tous les Gens qui etoient un peu mieux habillês et pouvoient parler sans crainte etoient mes Superieurs. Je tremblois devant un Lord et Je m'aurrois cru honoré d'etre le Coché d'un Duc. Des telles idées pueriles et indignes occupoit l'esprit d'un Etudien á l'Université. Je jouissoit pourtant d'une grande reputation. J'aimois les langues. Je m'y appliquois et mes Professeurs me donnoient des louanges distingués en me mettant en tête que J'etois un Genie extraordinaire que Je serois assurement un tres grand Homme qui feroit beaucoup d'honneur á sa Patrie. Je me trouvois toujours un peu different de me compagnons; et comme J'avançois[4] en age, la difference s'augmentoit. Je n'en trouvois aucune qui avoit Je ne sai quelles idées de Grandeur d'Ame et de delicatesse de Gout que Je croyois d'exister dans l'humanité et que J'esperois pourroient exister en moi un jour. Á la fin, Je me suis lié avec un Anglois nommé Temple d'un Caractère le plus digne le plus aimable, et avec un Ecossois nommé Johnston d'un Caractére male et cordial. Ces deux Hommes m'ont toujours etés fêrmes, m'ont toujours adouci la vie. Mais Je deviens trop ennuyant par la longueur de mes recits.

Des temperaments melancoliques sont des temperaments amoureux. Je vous jure qu'avant l'age de douze Ans, J'eprouvois tout ce que l'Ame peut sentir de cette passion.

Les desirs corporelles n'avoient pas encore leur force. Ils se developoient en moi d'une manierre tout a fait singulièrre.

<sup>1</sup> MS. 's' written over final letter 't', changing the third-person to the correct first-person verb ending in 'plaisois'

<sup>2</sup> MS. 's' at the end of 'mannierre' deleted

<sup>3</sup> MS. 's' written over final 't' in 'voyois'

<sup>4</sup> MS. 's' written over final 't' in 'avançois'

## F. Discarded portion of the final draft (following JB's page 8)

MS. Yale (L 1112).

Philosophe singulier & hardi, aimable et eclairé. Je vous offre un tresor. Vous avez etudié avec une curiosité ardente la nature de l'homme. Vous avez fait en cette etudes[1] des progres bien grandes. Mais dites moi avez vous eu assez de lumieres. Est il possible qu'aucun homme peut en avoir assez. Vous qui entrez en detail vous qui developez les penses les plus intimes qui tracez le progrês d'une etre humaine du commencement de son existence.[2] Dou tirez vous vos reflections? Estce de votre propre experience? Ne vous fiez trop á cela. Vous avez oubli bien de choses qui ont contribué a vous former tel[3] que vous vous trouvez et pour y suppleer il faut l'aide de L'imagination. Cela n'est il pas dangereux. Cela ne peut il vous tromper sur vos speculations fins? Croyez moi que de recueillir tous les traits de votre existence il aurroit fallu que vous etiez toujours un Sage même en Enfance, ou d'avoir deux esprit, l'un pour voir[4] naturellement, lautre pour en marquer les …

[1] MS. 'en cette etudes' inserted above the line.

[2] In his *Émile*, Rousseau had traced the development of the central character from early childhood to maturity.

[3] MS. final 'le' deleted from 'telle'

[4] MS. 'voit'

## IV. Topics considered with Rousseau, 14 or 15 December 1764[1]

MS. Yale (M 99). Previously printed in *Grand Tour I* (in English translation and in excerpts), Heinemann pp. 245–46, 250–51, McGraw-Hill pp. 251–52, 256–57.

Am I not worthy? Tell me. You have no interest no menagement. If I am — take care of me. I tell you that the idea of being Attaché meme[2] par un fil le plus mince a le Philosophe le plus eclaire l'Ame la plus noble me soutiendra toujours — toute ma vie.[3] Allons faisons accord. Je vous rencontrerais au Ciel.[4] Dites cela et c'est pour toute ma vie.

---

Crown poor woman[5]

---

De tems entems une lettre pour me rallumer — I am a fine fellow — realy I am so [—] not own ridicules — yet tell & assure me as to women — Be honest & I'll be firm.[6]

As to prayer what shall I do?
How do with my neighbours.
Emile is it now practicable?
Could he live in the world[7]
Young man with Savoyard[8]
You or not
Voltaire Rogue[9]
Journal 700 pages[10]
Must I force study
I appear instruit[11]
Zelide's character[12]
Pronounce at once
What is she?
Worthy Father
May I travel even tho[13]
Mahomet what[14]

is there expiation or not by Christ
may I just hold my peace in Scotland
not to offend tennants[15]

Vaut il la peine un individu
tout pour moi — Je ne suis qu'un[16]

[NEW PAGE, probably written before the 14 Dec. meeting with Rousseau]

Suicide — Hypochondrie[17] mal réel — Family madness.[18] Se tuer — vos arguments — not answered. Was Poet prais'd in Journals[19] — Suppose not slave to Appetites more than in marriage but will have Suiss Girl amiable &c. quite Adventure.[20] Marischal B— Rousseau B—[21] anxious to see if children sound cer marry. Hurt nobody — If clear against this can Abstain — can live as Templar in Malta.[22] Would have no deceit all clear — Scots familiarity & sarcasm — us'd to repress it by reserve & silence but this render'd hyp — may I not be gay — & fight the first Man who is rude with me — Coward from youth — how could it be otherwise? now firm. His Sentiment of Duels[23] — Court of London? no. Envoy? no. Parlmt or Home & Lawyer[24] — Old Estate good principle propagate family — Great thing of all — Shall I suffer gloom as evil & you o great Philosop will you befreind me[25]

[1] Though *Catalogue* (i. 73) states that this list of topics preceded JB's conversations with Rousseau (the first section written 13 or 14 Dec. for the meeting of 14 Dec., and the second written 14 or 15 Dec. for the meeting of 15 Dec.), several phrases in the list clearly indicate that it follows the conversations.

[2] MS. 'meme' inserted above the line.

[3] A summary of the high point in JB's farewell visit to Rousseau, affirming the bond between them (see Journ. 15 Dec.).

[4] JB's recollection of his words to the Jesuit 'Père Monier' (name uncertain) in Mannheim (see Journ. 7 Nov. n. 5).

[5] MS. A separate note, set off by straight lines across the page. For the episode, see Journ. 14 Dec. and n. 23; see also Exp. Acct., 14 Dec., where the amount is given as one écu.

[6] JB's hope for reassurance about how to deal with the young married woman with whom he had had an adulterous affair, as described in the 'Ébauche de ma vie' (see Journ. 14 Dec. and n. 16).

[7] Questions raised by the sheltered life and idealistic upbringing of Rousseau's young hero.

[8] See Journ. 25 Nov. n. 7.

[9] Evidently JB was aware of Voltaire's bad reputation, which had forced him to leave Berlin for financial speculations, and more recently Geneva for putting on plays.

[10] The numbers recorded at the head of each page show that the journal had reached page 767 for JB's first encounter with Rousseau.

[11] For a complimentary reference to JB as 'instruit', see Journ. 9 Oct.

[12] See Journ. 18 June n. 3.

[13] MS. The reading 'even tho' is speculative. F. A. Pottle rendered this sequence: 'Worthy father, may I travel even though [he disapproves?]' (*Grand Tour I*, Heinemann p. 250, McGraw-Hill p. 256).

[14] For Voltaire's play *Le Fanatisme ou Mahomet le Prophète*, which JB evidently knew of and would succeed in reading at Ferney, see Journ. 28 Dec. and n. 9.

[15] MS. 'is there expiation ... tennants' squeezed into twelve short lines in the right-hand margin. JB had just discussed expiation with Rousseau (see Journ. 14 Dec. n. 17).

JB's wish to be on good terms with his tenants contradicts his seeming lack of interest in them when speaking to Rousseau. For JB's later activities as laird, see *Corr.* 8.

[16] MS. 'Vaut il ... qu'un' written in three lines in the fold of the paper.

[17] A recurring theme in this journal. For JB's depression, which took him close to suicide in Holland, see To WJT, 16 Aug. 1763, 23 Mar., *Corr.* 6, pp. 61, 87.

[18] JB had recently described mental instability in his family in the unfinished draft of the 'Ébauche de ma vie' (L 1108, App. 2, III.B) not sent to Rousseau.

[19] Presumably a reference to JB himself as a poet. For JB's early verse, see *Lit. Car.* pp. 6–16, and for a favourable review, see *Critical Review*, June 1762, xiii. 495–99.

[20] For the 'Swiss lass' who had come to JB's mind in Leipzig, see Mem. dated 7 Oct. and n. 8.

[21] JB's fantasy about sons, as yet unborn and illegitimate, to be named after two men he greatly admired.

[22] Perhaps suggested by JB's memory of Count Schaffgotsch (see Journ. 25 July n. 7), or Sir Alexander Jardine (1712–90) of Applegirth, who had converted to Catholicism and been elected one of the Knights of Malta, and whom JB had discussed with friends in London (see Journ. 29 Mar. 1763).

[23] For JB's conversation with Rousseau concerning his dislike of Scots familiarity, and the idea of fighting a duel with a Scotsman rude to him, see Journ. 15 Dec. and n. 33. For JB's memory of his threatened duel with Capt. Durand (see Journ. 15–17 Sept.).

[24] Alternative occupations JB had been brooding about.

[25] MS. 'turn', for the verso, which provides a copy of Belle de Zuylen's poem 'Du Lac Leman Je connois les rivages', sent to JB by Nanette Kinloch.

# Appendix 3
## Expense Accounts

JB's record of his payments in the latter half of 1764 consists of two lists. The first (Yale MS. A 32) covers his expenses from 8 July to 22 Sept. during his stay in Berlin and excursions to the neighbouring Charlottenburg and Spandau. The second (Yale MS. A 33) covers his expenses during his further travels in German and Swiss territory starting in Potsdam on 19 Sept. and going as far as Geneva, and Ferney in nearby France, up to his departure on 1 Jan. 1765. The almost daily entries in these accounts vividly show the cost of travel in JB's day: transportation by public and private conveyances, lodgings, meals, wages and gratuities to servants as well as other incidentals such as paper and the franking of letters. All expenses are noted in coins, since paper money was not yet in use.

In Prussia, JB records his payments in the coins with which he was familiar from his stay in Holland, notably 'D' for Daalder (Dutch for Taler), but then uses the German Groschen ('Gr') for smaller coins. His count of 24 Groschen for each Taler reflects the valuation proposed by Johann Philipp Graumann (1690–1762) in his plan for currency reforms adopted by Frederick II in his edicts of 1750–51 and confirmed in his edict of Mar. 1764 (see Herbert Rittmann, *Deutsche Geldgeschichte 1848–1914*, 1975, 17a, pp. 161–64). JB does not mention the fact that in June 1764, debased coins were being replaced by better ones in Prussia, so that older coins of questionable value and 'good' new ones (*gute Groschen*) were presumably both in use during JB's stay. The valuation of 24 Groschen for a Taler is in the so-called 'accounting' currency, the unchanging hypothetical Taler (Rechnungstaler) useful at a time when the value of coins was not stable.

After Prussia, JB records the currency of the places he visits. From Dessau to Rastatt, he sets down écus ('é') and Groschen, counting an écu as the equivalent of a Taler. In Dresden he also mentions louis, guilders, and florins, without, however, dwelling on their particular value. In Strasbourg (France), he finds the local currency to be the livre, worth a third of an écu (see Journ. 23 Nov. and n. 3). Then, in Swiss territory, he records écus and Batzen (usually 40 per écu, but varying slightly from one canton to another). For the most part, he sets down unchanging 'accounting' currency, as if the value of the coins were stable.

JB is remarkably careful in recording his expenses. He writes 'oubli' next to any charge he has forgotten, and he adds up his expenses at the bottom of each page as well as at the end of his visit to Berlin. Although often inaccurate in his calculations, he keeps track of his expenses, probably to try to live within the allowance granted by his father.

In addition to focusing on money, JB's entries in the Expense Account refer to the places where he stayed, whether for weeks or for days or even just for hours. Some of these places, quite small, are not even mentioned in the journal, but are of interest in establishing his route, notably between Potsdam and Coswig on 23–24 Sept. and between Gotha and Frankfurt from 21 to 30 Oct. Such entries do not give distances, which are often as difficult to determine as the value of the money (see 'A Note on Distances and Currency'). But the numbers inserted above or following some of the place names indicate how many stages a coach had to pass through to reach the specified destination. These stages, each necessitating fresh horses, were determined by the time, distance, and difficulty of the journey and so give an impression of the effort required to go from place to place.

## I. 'Depensés a Berlin'

MS. Yale (A 32).

### Depensés á Berlin

| 1764 | Recus 90 Ecus[1] | | D | Gr |
|---|---|---|---|---|
| Juliet 8 | Sur le Voyage a Berlin | | 7 | – |
| | Cinq Semaines a Jacob | | 13 | 18 |
| 9 | Billiards et Caffé | | – | 6 |
| 10 | Billet de Rufin[2] | | 6 | – |
| 11 | Billiards et Caffée | | –[3] | 4 |
| | Cerises | | – | 14 |
| | Diner | | – | 18 |
| 13 | Tour á Potzdam | | 3 | – |
| 14 | Diner | | – | 18 |
| | Cerises | | – | 12 |
| | Billet de Semaine | | 4 | 18 ½ |
| | Jacob | | 2 | 18 |
| 17 | Diner | | – | 18 |
| 18 | Pour voire des choses &c | | 1 | – |
| 19 | Charité aux Noces | | 1 | – |
| | Diner | | – | 18 |
| | Fruits | | 1 | 8 |
| | Vies des Philosophes[4] | | – | 16 |
| 20 | Cerises | | – | 4 |
| 21 | Carosse a Charlottenbourg | | 5 | 12 |
| | Billet de Semaine | | 4 | 12 |
| | Jacob | | 2 | 18 |
| | Portez | D | 58 | 4[5] |

[NEW PAGE]

| | Portez | | D | Gr |
|---|---|---|---|---|
| | | | 58 | 4 |
| 22 | Carosse a Charlottenbourg | | 4 – | 8 |
| 23 | Mois des armes | | 3 | – |
| | Galon pour veste de Jacob | | 5 | 12 |
| | Taileur pour un habit á Jacob | | 40 | – |
| 24 | Diner | | – | 18 |

371

| | | | |
|---|---|---|---|
| 25 | Diner | – | 18 |
| 26 | Diner | – | 18 |
| 28  Omis | Palefrenier[6] au manêge | 2 | – |
| | Des Gands | – | 7 |
| | Bierre á Charlottenbourg | – | 7 |
| | Domestique[7] de M. Stoltz | – | 4 |
| | Billet de Semaine | 5 | – |
| | Jacob | 2 | 18 |
| Augustus 3 | Diner | – | 18 |
| 4 | Pair de grands Pigeons[8] | 4 | – |
| | Billet de Semaine | 3 | 20 |
| | Jacob | 2 | 18 |
| 25 | Tour á Brunsvic | 90[9] | – |
| | Jacob 2 semaines | 5 | 12 |
| 27 | Pair de Bottes | 6 | – |
| | Genouliéres | 1 | 16 |
| 29 | Etuis pour Madll. Kircheisen | 18 | – |
| 31 | Fruits | – | 12 |

| | | | |
|---|---|---|---|
| | Portez | 256 – | 18[10] |

[NEW PAGE]

| | | D | Gr |
|---|---|---|---|
| | Portés | 256 | 18 |
| 1 Septr. | Diner | 1 | 6 |
| | Fruits | – | 2 |
| | Cire | – | 6 |
| | Billet de Semaine | 4 | 20 |
| | Jacob | 2 | 18 |
| 3 | Encouragement á Jacob | 2 | 18 |
| | Bibliotheque du Roy &c | 1 | – |
| 4 | Au Soldat foueté | – | 4 |
| | Diner pour Stoltz & moi | 2 | 14 |
| 6 | Tour a Potzdam | 6 | 22 |
| 7 | Domestique de M. Burnet | – | 16 |
| 8 | Soldat Irlandois[11] | – | 16 |
| | Billet de Semaine | 4 | 10 |
| | Jacob | 2 | 18 |
| 10  Omis | Perdus au Jeu | 18 | – |
| 11 | Du Sois pour un habit | 21 | 6 |
| | Façon Doublure &c. | 24 | 12 |
| | Un Riding-coat | 28 | – |
| | Manêge un moi | 9 | – |
| | Aux ecuiers | – | 16 |
| | Demimois des Armes | 1 | 12 |
| Omis | Feux d'Artifice | 1 | 4 |

| | Portez | 391 – | 22 |
|---|---|---|---|

[NEW PAGE]

| | Portés | D | Gr |
|---|---|---|---|
| | | 391 – | 22 |
| [Septr.] | | | |
| 11 | Perdus au Jeu | – – | 10 |
| | Des Estampes | 2 | 14 |
| 15 | Tour á Stralo[12] | 3 | 4 |
| | Billet de Semaine | 7 | 21 |
| | Jacob | 2 | 18 |
| 19 | Logement á Berlin deux mois | 30 | – |
| | Aux domestiques de M. le President | 15 | – |
| | Un Coffre | 3 | 8 |
| | Un Bonnet de Voyage | 2 | 18 |
| | Lettres | 2 | 12 |
| | Bas de laine | 1 | 16 |
| 21 | Deux pairs bas de fils | – | 22 |
| 22 | Billet de Semaine | 4 | 5 |
| | Jacob | 2 | 18 |

| | | |
|---|---|---|
| Depensés en tout avant de quitter Berlin | 471 | –[13] |

| | £ | – |
|---|---|---|
| Recus a Berlin pour trois mois | 90 | – |
| Depensés | 76[14] | |
| | 14 | |

E   E
6 / 471/ 76
  42
  ̄41[15]
  36
  ̄4

| | £ | | | |
|---|---|---|---|---|
| Recus pour mon Voyage | 60 – | | a Berl. | 90 |
| Credit á Genêve | 30 – | | Voyage | 60 |
| | 90 | | Genêve | 30 |
| | | | En tout | 180 |

[1] Presumably from the allowance granted JB by his father (From Lord Auchinleck, 23 July, C 219).

[2] Owner of JB's inn in Berlin (see 5 July n. 2).

[3] MS. '–' written over '4'

[4] Presumably a book (not identified) purchased by JB.

[5] Error in addition; the correct total is 58 D, 16 Gr.

[6] Not identified.

[7] Not identified. Hereafter unnamed personel (e.g., servants, coachmen) will be given no further comment in a footnote.

[8] Perhaps for dinner on 4 Aug. with Kircheisen, who was president of police as well as JB's landlord.

[9] JB's estimate of expenses on his trip to Brunswick from 8 to 22 Aug.

[10] The correct total is 256 D, 14 Gr.

[11] Not identified.

[12] Stralau. For this important episode, see the journal entries for the same date.

[13] The correct total is 471 D, 20 Gr.

[14] The figure of £76 is calculated (incorrectly) from 471 D, the total of JB's expenses, by using an exchange rate of 6 D per £1 (a rate accepted by JB in equating 600 Taler to £100 in Journ. 1 Oct). The correct result is £78 10s.

[15] Here JB makes two mistakes in long division, writing '41' for '51' ('42' subtracted from '47' being '5') and writing '4' for '5' ('36' subtracted from '41' being '5').

## II. 'Depenses d'un Voyage de Berlin … á Genêve'

MS. Yale (A 33).

## Depenses d'un
## Voyage de Berlin
### par plusieurs Cours et Villes d'Allemagne
### á Genêve

| 1764 | Recus 68 Louis d'or[1] | E | Gr |
|---|---|---|---|
| Septr. 19 | Post[2] et Baggage de Berlin á *Potzdam*[3] | 2 | 16 |
| | Chevaux pour moi | 5 | – |
| 20 | Transport des Coffres | – | 18 |
| 21 | Logement de Jacob | – | 18 |
| 23 | Domestiques de M. Scott | 1 | 8 |
| | Servante de [M]adame Froment | 1 | – |
| | Lettres franchies | – | 16 |
| | Transport du Coffre | – | 6 |
| | De Potzdam á *Breitzen*[4] | 1 | 12 |
| | Coffre | 1 | 9 |
| | Maitre de Poste | – | 4 |
| | Postilion á Prelitz[5] | – | 6 |
| | Postilion | – | 4 |
| | á Bostorf paile pour dormir[6] | – | 4 |
| | Wagon M. & Postilion[7] | – | 8 |
| 24 | De Breitzen á *Coswig*[8] | 1 | 22 |
| | Wagen m. et Postilion | – | 8 |
| | De Coswig á Dessau[9] | 1 | 3[10] |
| | Postilion et transport du Coffre | – | 8 |
| | Papier | – | 2 |
| 25 | Des Gands | – | 16 |
| 26 | Des Plumes | – | 4 |
| | Papier | – | 2 |
| 27 | Pomade | – | 8 |
| | Lettres franchises | – | 6 |
| | Concierge du Chateau[11] | 2 | – |

| | | | |
|---|---|---|---|
| 28 *[12] | Perdus á Pharon | 6 | – |
| 29 | Poudre | – | 4 |
| | Dejeuner | – | 2 |
| | Papier | – | 2 |
| | Des Gands | – | 8 |
| | Jacob | 3 | – |
| 30 | Chevaux á Wittemberg et de retour | 5 | 15 |
| | Passage Gelt[13] | – | 8 |
| | Voir les tombeaux[14] | – | 12 |
| | Diner et Brandewyn pour moi et tambour[15] | – | 14 |
| | Postilion | – | 12 |

| | | | | |
|---|---|---|---|---|
| | Portez[16] | 40 | – | 21 |

[NEW PAGE]

| | | E | | Gr |
|---|---|---|---|---|
| | Portés | | | |
| 1764 | | 40 | – | 21 |
| Octr. 1 | Au Coché de la Cour | 3 – | – | |
| | Domestique | 2 – | – | |
| | Ecuier | 2 – | – | |
| | Billet á Dessau | 7 | | 12 |
| | Fille | 1 | – | |
| | Garçon | 1 | – | |
| | Lavage | 1 | | 6 |
| | Bas et linge accommodés | – | | 13 |
| | Lettres franchies | – | | 7 |
| | Papier | – | | 5 |
| | Poste de Dessau á *Halle*[17] | 1 | | 6 |
| | Wagin Meester | – | | 4 |
| | Coffre transporté | – | | 4 |
| | Coffre fraught[18] | 1 | – | |
| | Soratstat Station's Gelt | – | | 16 |
| | repas | – | | 4 |
| | De la Paile | – | | 2 |
| | Halle Station's Gelt | – | | 16 |
| | Postilion | – | | 4 |
| 2 | Transport du Coffre | – | | 4 |
| | Papier | – | | 3 |
| | Du Gros Linge pour couvrir le Coffre | 1 | | 12 |
| | Maximes de Rochefaucault[19] | – | | 16 |
| | Des fruits | – | | 1 |
| | Pour voir les salines[20] | – | | 8 |
| | oubli Grammaire Allemand[21] | 1 | | 8 |
| | Des Cordes | – | | 4 |
| 3 | Billet á Halle | 3 | – | |
| | De Halle á *Leipsic*[22] | 1 | | 6 |
| | Coffre Transporté | – | | 6 |

|  |  | E | Gr |
|---|---|---|---|
|  | Coffre fraught | – | 16 |
|  | Station's Gelt | – | 16 |
|  | Postilion | – | 8 |
|  | Pain et Biêrre | – | 2 |
|  | Extra-Gelt | – | 23 |
|  | Visiteur des Coffres | – | 8 |
|  | Transport des Coffres | – | 8 |
|  | Domestique de l'auberge | – | 8 |
|  | Fruit | – | 3 |
| 4 | Logement | 3 | – |
|  | Dejeuner | – | 9 |
|  | Porte-feuille | – | 4 |
|  | Papier | – | 2 |
|  | Diner | 1 | 6 |
|  | Fruit | – | 2 |

| | Portez | 81 – | 16[23] |
|---|---|---|---|

[NEW PAGE]

1764

| | Portés | E – | Gr |
|---|---|---|---|
| | | 81 – | 16 |

| | | E | Gr |
|---|---|---|---|
| Octr. 5 | Dejeuner | – – | 1 |
|  | Diner | 2 – | – |
|  | Logement | 3 – | – |
|  | Papier | – – | 2 |
|  | Semêles de laine | – – | 5 |
|  | Meisneri Hortulus Romanus[24] | – – | 4 |
|  | Pour voir la Bibliotheque de l'Université | – | 12 |
| 6 | Petit repas au Professeur Bel | 1 | 9 |
|  | Logement | 3 | – |
|  | Jacob | 3 | – |
|  | Fille | – | 6 |
| 7 | Poste de Leipsic á *Dresde*[25] | 3 | 4 |
|  | Transporte des Coffres | – | |
|  | Coffres | 1 | 20 |
|  | Wurtzen Station's Gelt | – | 20[26] |
|  | Postilion | – | 4 |
|  | Wirtzburg[27] Station's Gelt | – | 12 |
|  | Postilion | – | 4 |
| 8 | Stauchtz[28] Station's Gelt | – | 12 |
|  | Postilion | – | 4 |
|  | Meissen Station's Gelt | – | 12 |
|  | Postilion | – | 4 |
|  | Diner | – | 7 |
|  | Charite | – | 2 |
|  | Fruit Pain et Bierre | – | 4 |

| | | | E | Gr |
|---|---|---|---|---|
| | Dresden Postilion | | – | 4 |
| | Transport Des Coffres | | – | 8 |
| | Visiteur des Coffres[29] | | – | 6 |
| | Citron conservé | | – | 4 |
| 9 | Fourreau d'Epeé | | – | 20 |
| | Lettres franchies | | – | 14 |
| | Cartes chez l'Envoyé de Danemarc[30] | | – | 8 |
| 10 | Chaise á Porteur | | – | 7 |
| | Papier | | – | 4 |
| | Valet de louage[31] | | – | 16 |
| | Craipe pour me faire officier[32] | | – | 9 |
| | Pour voir le Cabinet de Tableaux | | 3 | 16 |
| | Un Baton | | – | 4 |
| | De la Cir | | – | 4 |
| | Petite Avanture[33] | | – | 8 |

| | | | | |
|---|---|---|---|---|
| | Portez | E— | 112 – | 17[34] |

[NEW PAGE]

| | | | E – | Gr |
|---|---|---|---|---|
| | Portés | | E – | Gr |
| 1764 | | | 112 | 17 |
| | | | | |
| Octr. 11 | Cockade | | – | 4 |
| | Des Poires | | – | 2 |
| | Chaise á Porteur | | – | 4 |
| [?][35] | Perdus á Pharon | | 1 | 12 |
| | Pour voir le muséum | | 2 | – |
| | Valet de Louage | | – | 16 |
| | Comedie | | – | 16 |
| | Petite Avanture[36] | | – | 6 |
| 12 | Billet á l'Hotel de Pologne pour 3 jours | | | |
| | Logement 2 diners Limonade et Pain[37] | | 7 | – |
| | Garçon | | – | 8 |
| | Chaise á Porteur | | – | *4[38] |
| | Lettres franchies | | – | 6 |
| 13 | Retour de Dresde á Leipsic | | 8 | 22 |
| | Jacob | | 3 | – |
| 14 | Billet á Leipsig pour | | 2 | 16 |
| | Logement et Souper[39] | | | |
| | Garçon | | – | 8 |
| | Lettre franchie | | – | 6 |
| | Extra Post de Leipsic a *Rispah*[40] | | 3 | – |
| | Wagen | | – | 16 |
| | Smear Gelt[41] | | – | 4 |
| | Postilion | | – | 10 |
| 15 | Extra Post de Rispah á *Naumbourg*[42] | | 3 | – |
| | Wagen | | – | 12 |

| | | |
|---|---|---|
| Wagen Meester | – | *2[43] |
| Smear Gelt | – | 4 |
| Postilion | – | 10 |
| Extra Post de Naumbourg á *Oversted*[44] | 2 | – |
| Wagen | – | 8 |
| Wagenmeester | – | 3 |
| Smear Gelt | – | 4 |
| Brandewyn á Naumbourg | – | 3 |
| Des Cordes | – | 2 |
| Postilion[45] | – | 9 |
| Extra Post d'Oversted á *Bottle-sted*[46] | 2 | – |
| Wagen-meester et Smear Gelt | – | 7 |
| Lettres franchies | – | 6[47] |
| Du vin á Oversted | – | 7 |
| Postilion | – | 8 |
| Extra Post de Bottlested á *Erford*[48] | 3 | – |
| Wagen meester et Smear Gelt | – | 6 |
| Postilion | – | 10 |
| Souper et coucher á Bottlested | – | 13 |

| | | | |
|---|---|---|---|
| Portez | E | 150 | –[49] |

[NEW PAGE]

| | | | |
|---|---|---|---|
| | Portés | E | Gr |
| 1764 | | 150 | – |

| | | | |
|---|---|---|---|
| Octr. 16 | Extra Post d'Erford á *Gotha*[50] | 3 | – |
| | Wagen | – | 6 |
| | Wagen-meester et Smear Gelt | – | 6 |
| | Postilion | – | 12 |
| | Diner á Erford | – | 8 |
| | Pour voir la grande Cloche | – | 3 |
| | Garçon de louage | – | 4 |
| | Perdus sur de Louis[51] | – | 12 |
| 17 | Garçon de Louage | – | 8 |
| 18 | Garçon de Louage | – | 16 |
| | Chaise á Porteur | – | 4 |
| | Hof Calender[52] | – | 5 |
| 19 | Ruband de cou | – | 4 |
| | Des Epingles | – | 1 |
| | Perdus aux Cartes | 1 | 8 |
| | Cordes de Chapeau | – | 4 |
| 20 | La Poudre | – | 4 |
| | Papier | – | 4 |
| | Lavage | 2 | 6 |
| | Jacob | 3 | – |
| | Domestique du Bibliothecaire du Duc | 1 | 8 |

| | | E | Gr |
|---|---|---|---|
| | Billet á l'Estril pour 5 jours logement un | | |
| | Souper Pain et Limonade[53] | 6 | – |
| | Garçon | – | 8 |
| | Fille | – | 8 |
| 21 | Poste de Gotha á *Langsaltz*[54] | | |
| | avec Coffre &c.[55] | 1 | 6 |
| | Porteur de Coffre | – | 6 |
| | Postilion | – | 7 |
| | Logement et petit Repas | 1 | 12 |
| | Porteur de Coffre | – | 8 |
| | Poste de Langansalza á *Cassel*.[56] *Hesse Poste*[57] | 4 | – |
| | Coffres | 1 | 9 |
| 22 | Milhausen Station's Gelt | – | 12 |
| | Postilion | – | 6 |
| | Wagen meester | – | 4 |
| | Wanfred Postilion | – | 6 |
| | Repas | – | 7 |

| | Portez | E | 182 – | 6[58] |
|---|---|---|---|---|

[NEW PAGE]

| | Portés | E | Gr |
|---|---|---|---|
| 1764 | | 182 | 6 |
| | | | |
| Octr. 22 | Bischausen Postilion | – | 6 |
| | Brandewyn | – | 3 |
| | Helsé[59] Postilion | – | 4 |
| | Veilleur des Coffres | – | 4 |
| | Guide ala Village | – | 4 |
| | Logement et Brandewyn | – | 6 |
| 23 | Cassel Postilion | – | 6 |
| | Porteur des Coffres | – | 5 |
| | Lettres franchies | – | 12 |
| 24 | Pour voir la maison[60] de modêles | – | 12 |
| 25 | Du Pain | – | 3 |
| | Garçon de Louage | – | 10 |
| | Papier | – | 12 |
| | De la Cire | – | 3 |
| | Lettre de Brunsvic | – | 3 |
| | Lettres franchies | – | 6 |
| | Brosse á razer | – | 3 |
| | Chaise á Porteur | – | 12 |
| | Perdus aux Cartes | – | 15 |
| 26 | Garçon de Louage | – | 10 |
| | Pour voir la maison de Sciences | – | 12 |
| | Pour voir le Bain | – | 8 |
| | La Comedie | – | 16 |
| | Aiguiser des Rasoirs Ciseaux et Caniffe | – | 15 |

| | | | |
|---|---|---|---|
| | Du Pain | – | 1 |
| 27 | Billet au Stockholm pour | | |
| | 5 jours logement 2 dinés Limonade &c[61] | 7 | – |
| | Garçon | – | 12 |
| | Fille | – | 6 |
| | Garçon de Louage | – | 17 |
| | Transport des Coffres | – | 5 |
| | Des Livres | – | 13 |
| | Lettres franchies | – | 5 |
| | Du Pain | – | 2 |
| | Jacob | 3 | – |
| | Werkle Postilions | – | 6 |
| | Souper vin et Paile | – | 10 |
| | Place dans l'ecurie | – | 3 |
| | Garde des Coffres | – | 5 |

| | | | |
|---|---|---|---|
| | Portez | E | 203 – 17 |

[NEW PAGE]

| | | E | Gr |
|---|---|---|---|
| 1764 | Portés | 203 | – 17 |
| Octr. 28 | Elsberg[62] Postilions | – | 6 |
| | Dejeuner | – | 7 |
| | Obzdorf[63] Postilions | – | 6 |
| | Diner | – | 10 |
| | Marpurg Postilions | – | 6 |
| | Lits pour moi et Jacob | – | 6 |
| 29 | Petite Village[64] *Appfibley* i.e. soupe | | |
| | de la farine du lait et des pommes avec des paysans[65] | – | 3 |
| | Giesen Postilions | – | 6 |
| | Eutropius[66] | – | 6 |
| | Du Pain | – | 4 |
| | Du fruit | – | 4 |
| | De la Biêrre | – | 3 |
| | Naumheim Postilions | – | 6 |
| | Souper logement et dejeuner | 1 | 4 |
| | Garde des coffres | – | 4 |
| | Fille | – | 4 |
| 30 | Transport[67] des Lettres de Berlin | – | 4 |
| | Pair de Gands du lain | – | 7 |
| | Transport des coffres | – | 3 |
| | Pauvre femme danoise[68] | 1 | – |
| | Poste de Cassel á *Francfort*[69] | 10 | 12 |
| 31 | Billet á Cassel un Nuit logement | | |
| Diner[70] | Souper Pain Limonade &c[71] | 2 | – |
| | Fille | – | 6 |
| | Poste de Francfort á *Hanau*[72] | 2 | 12 |

380

| | | | E | Gr |
|---|---|---|---|---|
| | Wagen-meester | | – | 4 |
| | Passage Gelt | | – | 2 |
| | Hanau Postilion | | – | 6 |
| | Des Bas de laine | | – | 15 |
| | Eau de Lavande[73] | | – | 6 |
| Novr. 1 | Billet á Hanau un nuit logement | | | |
| | diner limonade &c[74] | | 1 | 21 |
| | Garçon de Louage | | – | 8 |
| | Fille | | – | 6 |

| | | | E | |
|---|---|---|---|---|
| | Portez | E | 228 | – 22[75] |

[NEW PAGE]

| | | | E | Gr |
|---|---|---|---|---|
| 1764 | Portés | E | 228 | – 22 |
| Novr. 1 | Poste de Hanau á *Francfort*[76] | | 2 | 12 |
| | Francfort Postilion et des cordes[77] | | – | 18 |
| | Lettres franchies | | – | 3 |
| | Transport des coffres | | – | 5 |
| | Du feu[70] en Bateau | | – | 1 |
| | Passage de Francfort á Mayence[79] | | – | 9 |
| | Les Coffres | | – | 8 |
| | Diner en Chemin | | – | 10 |
| | Transport des Coffres | | – | 8 |
| | Garçon de Louage | | – | 4 |
| | Billet á Mayence un nuit | | | |
| | Logement Souper &c[80] | | 1 | 12 |
| | Garçon | | – | 6 |
| | Transport des Coffres | | – | 5 |
| 2 | Poste de Mayence á *Manheim*[81] | | 3 | 10 |
| | Coffre | | 1[82] | – |
| | Village du Vin | | – | 3 |
| | Diner á Worms | | – | 18 |
| | Passage Gelt Manheim | | – | 9 |
| | Manheim Postilion | | – | 6 |
| 3 | Jacob | | 3 | – |
| 4 | Principes de Negociations[83] | | – | 15 |
| 5 | Grammaire Espagnol[84] | | – | 20 |
| 8 | Billet au Prince Eugene[85] | | | |
| | 6 jours logement plusieurs diners &c[86] | | 9 | – |
| | Bourse | | – | 18 |
| | Porte chaise Rhubarb et du fil | | – | 17 |
| | Poudre Papier Grossier Plumes | | – | 13 |
| | Clous pour raccommoder le Coffre | | – | 2 |
| | Diachylon[87] et Eau de Senture | | – | 10 |

| | | | | |
|---|---|---|---|---|
| | Drink Gelt á P. Frederic | | 1 | 20 |
| | Blanchissage | | 1 | 6 |

| | | | | |
|---|---|---|---|---|
| | Portez | E | 259 | – 16 |

[NEW PAGE]

1764

| | | Portés | E | Gr |
|---|---|---|---|---|
| | | | 259 | – 16 |

| | | | | |
|---|---|---|---|---|
| Novr. 8 | | Extra Post a *Carlsrou*[88] | 9 – | 8 |
| | | Postilions en Chemin | 1 | – |
| | | Depenses en Chemin | – | 1 |
| | Oubli | Dejeuner á Manheim | – | 15 |
| 9 | | Jacob | 3 | – |
| 11 | | Pour voir le Decoye | 1 | 17 |
| 13 | | Concierge du Chateau | 1 | 10 |
| 15 | | Charité | – | 10 |
| | | Almanac de la cour | – | 6 |
| | | Pomade et Poudre | – | 11 |
| | | Change de Louis | 2 | 14 |
| | | Ecuier de M. de Muntzischein[89] | – | 12 |
| 16 | | Coché de la Cour | 5 | – |
| | | Pour luimême | 3 | 3 |
| | | Domestique de Louage[90] 9 Jours | 5 | 15 |
| | | Blanchisage | 1 | 12 |
| | | Billet á Carlsruhe pour 10 Jours logement Souper &c[91] | 15 | – |
| | | Domestique et fille | 2 | 12 |
| | | Coureur Italien[92] | 1 | – |
| | | Poste de Carlsruhe á *Ratstat*[93] avec Postilion[94] | 3 | 3 |
| 17 | | Jacob[95] | 3 | – |
| 18 | | Perdu á Pharon | 5 | – |
| 19 | | Lettres franchies | – | 10 |
| | | Fourier de la Cour | 3 | – |
| | | Cocher et Domestique de la Cour | 3 | – |
| | | Billet au Cigne[96] 4 jours logement diner & | 4 | 14 |
| | | Domestiques | – | 18 |
| | | Six pairs de Souliers 1–10 pair[97] | 8 | 12 |
| | | Garçon | – | 12 |
| | | Extra-Post de Ratstat a *Strasbourg*[98] | 7 | 15 |
| | | Postilions et des autres Depenses | 2 | – |

| | | | | |
|---|---|---|---|---|
| | Portez | E | 314 | – 9[99] |

[NEW PAGE]

## Argent de Suisse et France[100]

| 1764 | | E | Bat |
|---|---|---|---|
| Novr. 20 | Valet de Louage | – | 10 |
| 22 | Comedie | – | 6 |
| | Charité | – | 5 |
| 23 | Billet á Strasbourg Esprit[101] 4 jours | | |
| | logement diner &c[102] | 2 | – |
| | Garçon | – | 3 |
| | Servante | – | 4 |
| | Porteur des Coffres | <–>[103] | 4 |
| 24 | Carosse de Strasbourg á *Basle*[104] | 8 | – |
| | Depenses en route | – | 27 |
| 26 | Pour voir maison de ville Bibliotheque | | |
| | de College Cathedral &c | – | 20 |
| | Dance des morts | – | 20 |
| | Billet á Basle *Trois rois* pour | | |
| | 3 jours logement, 3 repas &c[105] | 3 | – |
| | Garçon et fille | – | 8 |
| 27 | Deux places en Carosse de Bale | | |
| | a *Soleure*[106] | 4 | – |
| | Postilion | – | 10 |
| | Depenses en chemin | – | 20 |
| 29 | Billet á Soleure 3 Jours Logement Souper &c | 2 | – |
| | Domestiques | – | 12 |
| | Carosse de Soleure á *Berne*[107] | 2 | 10 |
| | Cocher | – | 10 |
| 30 | Pour voir Arsenal | – | 10 |
| | Domestique de Louage | – | 18 |
| | Etuis | 2 | – |
| | Manchon[108] | 1 | – |
| Decr. 1 | Billet a Berne 3 Jours Logement 3 Repas &c | 2 | 20 |
| | Domestiques | – | 4 |
| | Oubli Arsenal á Basle | – | 20 |
| | Porter les Coffres | – | 10 |
| | Diner á Walbertswiel[109] | – | 15 |
| | Carosse de Berne á *Neufchatel*[110] | 3 | 30 |
| | Cocher | – | 10 |
| | Jacob 2 Semaines | 3 | 30 |
| | Portez     E | | 38 | 26[111] |

[NEW PAGE]

| | Portés | E | Batz |
|---|---|---|---|
| 1764 | | 38 – | 26 |
| Decr. 3 | Depenses en chemin á Motiers | – – | 10 |

| | | | |
|---|---|---|---|
| oubli | Perdu aux cartes | 1 | – |
| 5 | Depenses a la Maison de Ville a Motiers 3 jours logement 3 diners et entretien d'un Cheval[112] | 2 | – |
| | Peruquier[113] | – | 10 |
| | Servante | – | 10 |
| <6>[114] | Billet á Bro[115] un nuit logement, souper et entretien d'un Cheval[116] | – | 14 |
| | Domestiques | – | 6 |
| | Cheval 4 jours | 1 | – |
| | Garçon de l'ecurie | – | 4 |
| | Domestique du M. de Sonbrun[117] | – | 5 |
| | Lettres recues | – | 31 |
| | Perdu aux Cartes | 2 | – |
| 8 | Peruquier[118] | – | 12 |
| | Domestique de Col. Chaillet[119] | – | 6 |
| 9 | Jacob | 1 | 30 |
| 10 | Blanchisage | – | 34 |
| | Offrand aux autels &c | – | 17 |
| | Billet aux treise cantons 10 jours Logement 4 diners 2 Soupers &c[120] | 5 | 10 |
| | Domestiques | – | 20 |
| | Pair de bas de Soye | 1[121] | 7 |
| 11 | Domestiques de M. Borel[122] | – | 20 |
| | Billet de maitre Ott[123] pour diner &c | – | 20 |
| 12 | Carosse[124] de Neufchatel á *Yverdun*[125] | 4[126] | – |
| | Billet á la maison de Village un nuit logement souper &c[127] | 1 | 4 |
| | Perdu aux Cartes | – | 10 |
| 13 | Perdu aux Cartes | – | 18 |
| 14 | Pauvre femme á Motiers[128] | 1 | – |
| | Portez | 64 | –[129] |

[NEW PAGE]

| | Portés | E | Batz |
|---|---|---|---|
| 1764 | | 64 | – |
| Decr. 15 | Manchettes d'entoilage | 3 | – |
| | Deux pairs | 5 | – |
| | Billet á la maison de ville une nuit logement diner &c[130] | 1 | – |
| | Pour une *certaine affaire*[131] | 4 | – |
| | Chevaux pour [M]otiers Jour | 3 | – |
| 16 | Domestique de M. le Baillif[132] | – | 12 |
| | Perdu aux Cartes | – | 6 |

| | | | | |
|---|---|---|---|---|
| 17 | | Perdu aux Cartes | – | 12 |
| 18 | | Caniffe et de la cire | – | 8 |
| | | Pour accommoder mes Coffres | – | 20 |
| | Oubli | Domestique de M. Kinloch[133] | – | 20 |
| | | Domestique de M. du Foin[134] | – | 10 |
| 20 | | Domestiques de M. le Baron de Brackel[135] | 5 | – |
| | | Carosse d'Yverdun á Lausanne | 4 | 20 |
| | | Cocher | – | 10 |
| | | Depenses en Chemin | – | 15 |
| 21 | | Poudre et trousser un Chapeau | – | 8 |
| | | Domestique de Louage | – | 20 |
| | | Billet au Lion d'or deux jours logement Souper et diner[136] | 1 | 14 |
| | | Domestiques | – | 10 |
| 22 | | Jacob 3 Semaine | 5 | 10 |
| | | Carosse de Lausanne á Genêve | 4 | – |
| | | Cocher | – | 10 |
| | | Depenses en Chemin | – | 20 |
| | | Visiter les coffres en [F]rance | – | 16 |
| 23 | | Chocolade | – | 8 |
| 24 | | Chocolade | – | 8 |
| | | Carosse á la Campagne de M. de Voltaire | 1 | 20 |
| | | Cocher | – | 16 |
| | | Lettres de la Montagne[137] | 1 | 6 |
| | | Domestique de Louage | – | 20 |
| | | **Portez** | **109** | **– 17**[138] |

[NEW PAGE]

| | | | |
|---|---|---|---|
| | Portés | E | Batz |
| 1764 | | 109 | – 17 |
| | | | |
| Decr. 24 | Domestique de M. Constant[139] | – | 10 |
| 26 | Exprés á Ferney | – | 19 |
| 29 | Domestiques a Ferney | 1 | 19 |
| | Carosse á Ferney 27 & de retour 29[140] | 2 | 19 |
| | Cocher | 10 | – |
| | Pomade | – | 6 |
| 30 | Pour faire tourner un Habit de rouge Galon des Culottes &c[141] | 32 | – |
| 31 | Domestique de M. Gaussin[142] | – | 10 |
| [143] | Demidouzaine de Chemises toile de la Suisse Manchettes de Mousline &c[144] | 20 | – |
| | Deux Pairs de feues Manchettes d'entoilage[145] | 8 | – |

# 1765

| Janry 1 | Billet Aux Trois Rois[146] | | |
|---|---|---|---|
| | 10 Jours Logement dix | | |
| | Repas &c[147] | | |
| | Domestiques | 1 | – |
| | Collier de Grenats pour | | |
| | Mademoiselle[148] | 8[149] | – |
| | Plusieurs Petites Depenses | 2 | 21 |
| | Des Lettres recues et expediés | 5 | – |

191 – 7[150]

[1] A louis d'or is recorded by JB as worth 5 écus or Taler (see Journ. 17 Nov.; Exp. Acct. 16 Nov.). Hence his 68 louis amounted to 340 Taler or écus, a sum with which he had hoped to cover the total expenses of his German and Swiss travels (Journ. 30 Oct).

[2] A large coach or stage coach, called 'Post' for 'Postkutsche' (Langenscheidt, s.v. 'Post' 8). It transported passengers as well as letters and packages (*Poststrassen*, pp. 16, 20).

[3] MS. '4' inserted above '*Potzdam*', very likely referring to the number of stages needed for changing horses to reach this destination. A small 'x' inserted below '*Potzdam*' is not explained. In the following notes, interlineations above or below place names, or numbers following place names, are recorded without comment.

[4] MS. '*Breitzen*' with unexplained 'x' below it, followed by '4'. Presumably JB meant Treuenbriezen, 37 km (23 miles) from Potsdam.

[5] Beelitz, between Potsdam and Treuenbriezen.

[6] Bossdorf, between Treuenbriezen and Coswig. The straw bought by JB was perhaps for use in the night between 23 and 24 Sept.

[7] MS. Inserted as a separate line. The 'Wagon M.' ('Wagenmeister') was in charge of greasing the wheels of a coach (see *Poststrassen*, p. 16).

[8] MS. 'x' inserted below '*Coswig*', followed by '5'

[9] MS. '1½' following 'Dessau'

[10] MS. Uncertain numbers written with a thick pen or brush, possibly '1' written over '–' écus, '3' Gr. over an indecipherable figure, possibly '7'

[11] The palace in Dessau (see Journ. 27 Sept).

[12] Asterisk marking JB's loss at cards.

[13] Apparently a tax or toll demanded of travellers.

[14] MS. A squeezed-in line. The fee was to see the tombs of Luther and Melancthon.

[15] The drummer is not further identified .

[16] MS. 'Portés', but still showing a final 'z' erased by JB.

[17] MS. '5' inserted above '*Halle*'

[18] Fee for transporting goods, usually by water but here by land (OED, s.v. 'fraught'). The charge is for taking JB's trunk .

[19] A book that would inspire JB to formulate maxims of his own (see App. 1, 'Maximes á la maniêrre de la Rochefoucault'; Journ. 2 Oct. n. 8, 15 Oct. n. 2).

[20] MS. Inserted as a single line. For the salt manufactory, see Journ. 2 Oct. n. 4.

[21] Another book purchased by JB, but not further identified.

[22] MS. '5' inserted above '*Leipsic*'

[23] The correct total is 81 E, 15 Gr.

[24] To judge by the title, a book about Roman gardens, but not further identified.

[25] MS. '13' inserted above '*Dresde*'

[26] MS. '20' changed to '–'

[27] Not identified (a place not reported for this region).

[28] Stauchitz.

[29] Not identified.

[30] Werner von Schulenburg (see Journ. 9 Oct. and n. 14).

[31] The first of such special servants engaged by JB to demonstrate his gentlemanly status.

[32] See Journ. 12 Oct.

[33] Not identified.

[34] MS. Correction of Groschen, illegible at the bottom of the page but clear at the top of the next. However, the correct total is 112 E, 16 Gr.

[35] Unidentified private symbol in the left-hand margin marking JB's loss at cards.

[36] Not identified.

[37] MS. Brace linking this line to the preceding one.

[38] MS. Unexplained asterisk.

[39] MS. Brace linking this line to the preceding one .

[40] Rippach. MS. '3' inserted above '*Rispah*'. This and the following four entries begin with the phrase 'Extra Post'.

[41] The cost of greasing the wheels of a vehicle (*Poststrassen*, p. 16).

[42] MS. '3' inserted above '*Naumbourg*'

[43] MS. Unexplained asterisk before '2'

[44] MS. '2' inserted above '*Oversted*'. The correct name is Auerstedt (see Journ. 15 Oct. n. 3).

[45] MS. 'Postilion' inserted as a separate line.

[46] MS. '2' inserted above '*Bottle-sted*'. The correct name is Buttelstedt.

[47] MS. '6' written over an indecipherable figure.

[48] MS. '3' inserted above '*Erford*'

[49] The correct total is E 160, 3 Gr.

[50] MS. '3' inserted above '*Gotha*'

[51] Perhaps in the exchange of large gold coins for coins of lesser value.

[52] Written in Gothic script.

[53] MS. Brace linking this line to the preceding one.

[54] MS. '2' inserted above '*Langsaltz*'

[55] MS. Brace linking this line to the preceding one.

[56] MS. '*Cassel*' written over an illegible word, '9' inserted above it.

[57] The Leipziger Fahrende Post, a regional coach service run under the aegis of the Hessian landgraves. The Post-Tabelle (timetable) of 24 Oct. 1754 gives the route from Langensalza to Kassel taken by JB.

[58] The Groschen amount is written over an illegible figure, possibly 9.

[59] Helsa (see Journ. 22 Oct. n. 6).

[60] MS. 'maison' inserted above deleted 'chambre'

[61] MS. Brace linking this line to the preceding one.

[62] MS. 'Elsberg' written over 'Werkel' but not identified. JB seems to have continued with the Hesse Post, taking its Frankfurter Fahrende Post, which went from Werkel by way of Jessberg and Halsdorff (not mentioned by JB) to Marburg, Giessen, and after two more stops to Frankfurt (Post-Tabelle of 24 Oct. 1754).

[63] Not identified.

[64] Not identified.

[65] '*Appfilbley*': not a place but a peasant dish, 'Apfelbrei', made of the ingredients listed on the second line (written in a smaller handwriting, with the two lines linked by a bracket).

[66] 'Inversion of the eyelids', a medical condition of having the eyelashes turned in toward the eyeball (OED, s.v. 'entropion', 'entropium'). JB's use of the term precedes the examples in the OED by more than a hundred years. Whether JB was experiencing this possibly painful condition is not clear from the journal.

[67] MS. Erroneously recorded as 'Francfort'

[68] Not further identified

[69] MS. '18' inserted above '*Francfort*'

[70] MS. 'Diner' inserted in left margin.

[71] MS. Brace linking this line to the preceding one.

[72] MS. '2' inserted above '*Hanau*'

[73] MS. '*LaVande*'

[74] MS. Brace linking this line to the preceding one.

[75] MS. Total smudged, but clearer on the next page.

[76] MS. '2' inserted above '*Francfort*' and followed by another '2'

[77] MS. 'cordes' inserted above the line.

[78] Perhaps to provide warmth for the passengers.

[79] For the boat trip from Frankfurt to Mainz, see Journ. 1 Nov. n. 6.

[80] MS. Brace linking this line to the preceding one.

[81] MS. '6' inserted above '*Manheim*'

[82] MS. '1' written over '–'

[83] Evidently a book (not further identified) purchased by JB in Mannheim.

[84] A book, also purchased in Mannheim, attesting to JB's renewed interest in things Spanish (see App. 1, 'Abrégé d'un voyage en Allemagne').

[85] Presumably JB's inn, not named 'Prince Eugene', for which there is no record, but 'Prince Frédérique' (see Journ. 2 Nov. and n. 5).

[86] MS. Brace linking this line to the preceding one.

[87] Medicine to cure JB's cold sore (see Mem. 5 Nov. n. 1).

[88] MS. '8' inserted above '*Carlsrou*'

[89] MS. 'Unts' correcting spelling of 'Munzesheim' (for whom see 10 Nov. n. 14).

[90] 'Old Seyffert' (see Journ. 11 Nov. n. 1).

[91] MS. Brace linking this line to the preceding one.

[92] Frederico Baduano (see Journ. 17 Nov. n. 4).

[93] MS. '2$\frac{1}{2}$' inserted above '*Ratstat*'

[94] MS. Brace linking this line to the preceding one.

[95] MS. Inserted on a separate line.

[96] The name of the inn where JB stayed in Rastatt.

[97] MS. '1–10 pair' inserted above the line in smaller letters.

[98] MS. '6' inserted above 'Strasbourg'

[99] MS. Total 314 or 374, left ambiguous by JB's correction. The correct total is 356 E, 6 Gr.

[100] For expenses in Swiss and French territory, JB records écus and Batsen, the latter instead of the 'Groschen' used in German territory.

[101] MS. 'Esprit', JB's inn, inserted above 'Strasbourg' with a caret.

[102] MS. Brace linking this line to the preceding one.

[103] Hole in MS.

[104] MS. '24 L' inserted above '*Basle*', perhaps a reminder that this sum, presumably paid in Strasbourg and so in French currency, equals the 8 écus listed as expense (3 livres equalling 1 écu).

[105] MS. Brace linking this line to the preceding one.

[106] MS. '10' inserted above '*Soleure*', bracket linking this line to preceding one.

[107] MS. '8' inserted above 'Berne'

[108] A mutt (dog), not further identified.

[109] Walperswil (see Journ. 1 Dec. n. 3).

[110] MS. '10' inserted above 'Neufchatel'

[111] The correct total is 40 E, 16 Batz.

[112] MS. Brace linking this line to the preceding two.

[113] Not identified.

[114] MS. '6' half obliterated by a hole.

[115] That is, 'Brot'.

[116] MS. Brace linking this line to the preceding one.

[117] For Sombrun, see Journ. 6 Dec. n. 7.

[118] Not identified.

[119] For Chaillet, see 1 Dec. n. 2.

[120] MS. Brace linking this line to the preceding two.

[121] MS. '1' written over an indecipherable figure.

[122] Not identified.

[123] For Otz, see Journ. 10 Dec. n. 2.

[124] MS. 'Carosse' written over 'Billet á'

[125] MS. '8' inserted above '*Yverdun*'

[126] MS. '4' written over indecipherable figure.

[127] MS. Brace linking this line to the preceding one.

[128] See Journ. 14 Dec. and n. 23.

[129] The correct total is 65 E, 4 Batz.

[130] MS. Brace linking this line to the preceding one.

[131] Not further identified.

[132] For Gingins de Moiry, bailiff of Yverdon, see Journ. 13 Dec. n. 5.

[133] For Sir James Kinloch, see Journ. 13 Dec. and n. 2.

[134] For De Faugnes, see Journ. 18 Dec. and n. 1.

[135] For Brackel, see Journ. 12 Dec. and n. 1; 18 Dec. and n. 8.

[136] MS. Brace linking this line to the preceding one.

[137] Rousseau's most recent publication (see Journ. for this day and n. 24).

[138] The correct total is 108 E, 39 Batz.

[139] For Constant, see Journ. 24 Dec. n. 23.

[140] JB's return date, linked to the preceding line with a brace.

[141] MS. Brace linking this line to the preceding one.

[142] For Gaussen, see Journ. 23 Dec. and n. 8.

[143] MS. Partially erased '17' in the left margin under the preceding date.

[144] MS. Brace linking this line to the preceding two.

[145] MS. Brace linking this line to the preceding one.

[146] JB's inn in Geneva.

[147] MS. Brace linking this line to the preceding two.

[148] MS. Brace linking this line to the preceding one. 'Mademoiselle' refers to Thérèse Levasseur, whose wish for a garnet necklace JB was fulfilling (see Journ. 15 Dec. n. 53).

[149] MS. '8' written over '–'

[150] The correct total is 201 E, 1 Batz.

# Maps

THE following maps are drawn from the *Carte de l'Empire d'Allemagne*, which offers a detailed presentation of 'les routes des postes', the coach services for which the designees of Thurn und Taxis held a monopoly. The *Carte*, dated 1750 and so preceding Boswell's travels by fourteen years, was created by 'Le Sr. Robert'—that is, Gilles Robert de Vaugondy (1686–1766), geographer and map maker, who with his son Didier Robert de Vaugondy (1723–86) was a professional geographer and royal cartographer in Paris. The map of the Kassel area is augmented by a later map, the *Neue Geographische Carte der Kayserlichen Reichs und angraenzenden Posten*, 1794, by H. F. von Haysdorf, who was Ober-Postamts-Director (head postal director) in Aachen (Kneschke, iv. 261). In addition, for Map 3, the surviving timetables of the Hessen Post with its Leipziger and Frankfurter Fahrende Posten clarify Boswell's itinerary to and from Kassel.

All these maps can be read as a consecutive account of Boswell's journey, for instance from Utrecht to Berlin and later from Kassel to Frankfurt and on to Karlsruhe, Strasbourg, and Swiss territory down to Geneva. They point also to the various sidetrips from Berlin to Charlottenburg, from Brunswick to Wolfenbüttel and Salzdahlum, from Frankfurt to Hanau, and from Geneva to Ferney. These maps reflect some of the geographical features of the terrain, notably the location of Môtiers in the Val de Travers behind a ridge of the Jura Mountains. Where no coach service was available, place names are inserted here.

These maps have been prepared by Stacey D. Maples of the Yale Map Collection.

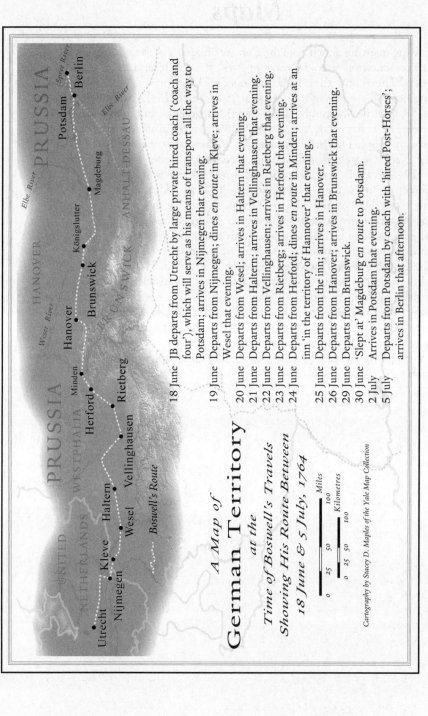

*Maps*

*A Map of*

**German Territory**

*at the*

*Time of Boswell's Travels*

*Showing His Route Between*

*18 June & 5 July, 1764*

```
            Miles
 0    25   50      100
 0   25  50    100
          Kilometres
```

*Cartography by Stacey D. Maples of the Yale Map Collection*

18 June    JB departs from Utrecht by large private hired coach ('coach and four'), which will serve as his means of transport all the way to Potsdam; arrives in Nijmegen that evening.

19 June    Departs from Nijmegen; dines *en route* in Kleve; arrives in Wesel that evening.

20 June    Departs from Wesel; arrives in Haltern that evening.

21 June    Departs from Haltern; arrives in Vellinghausen that evening.

22 June    Departs from Vellinghausen; arrives in Rietberg that evening.

23 June    Departs from Rietberg; arrives in Herford that evening.

24 June    Departs from Herford; dines *en route* in Minden; arrives at an inn 'in the territory of Hannover' that evening.

25 June    Departs from the inn; arrives in Hanover.

26 June    Departs from Hanover; arrives in Brunswick that evening.

29 June    Departs from Brunswick.

30 June    'Slept at' Magdeburg *en route* to Potsdam.

2 July    Arrives in Potsdam that evening.

5 July    Departs from Potsdam by coach with 'hired Post-Horses'; arrives in Berlin that afternoon.

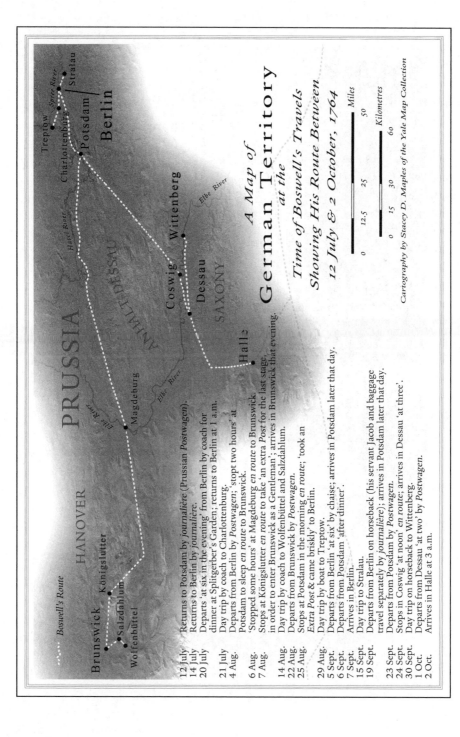

*···· Boswell's Route*

HANOVER

PRUSSIA

Brunswick

Königslutter

Salzdahlum

Wolfenbüttel

Magdeburg

*Elbe River*

*Elbe River*

ANHALT-DESSAU

Coswig

Dessau

SAXONY

Wittenberg

Halle

*Havel River*

Charlottenburg

Potsdam

**Berlin**

Treptow

*Spree River*

Stralau

*A Map of*

**German Territory**

*at the*

*Time of Boswell's Travels*

*Showing His Route Between*

*12 July & 2 October, 1764*

Miles

0    12.5    25    50

Kilometres

0    15    30    60

*Cartography by Stacey D. Maples of the Yale Map Collection*

| | |
|---|---|
| 12 July | Returns to Potsdam by *journalière* (Prussian *Postwagen*). |
| 14 July | Returns to Berlin by *journalière*. |
| 20 July | Departs 'at six in the evening' from Berlin by coach for dinner at Splitgerber's Garden; returns to Berlin at 1 a.m. |
| 21 July | Day trip by coach to Charlottenburg. |
| 4 Aug. | Departs from Berlin by *Postwagen*; stopt two hours' at Potsdam to sleep *en route* to Brunswick. |
| 6 Aug. | 'Stopped some hours' at Magdeburg *en route* to Brunswick. |
| 7 Aug. | Stops at Königslutter *en route* to take 'an extra *Post* for the last stage', in order to enter Brunswick as a Gentleman'; arrives in Brunswick that evening. |
| 14 Aug. | Day trip by coach to Wolfenbüttel and Salzdahlum. |
| 22 Aug. | Departs from Brunswick by *Postwagen*. |
| 25 Aug. | Stops at Potsdam in the morning *en route*; 'took an Extra *Post* & came briskly' to Berlin. |
| 29 Aug. | Day trip by boat to Treptow. |
| 5 Sept. | Departs from Berlin 'at six' by chaise; arrives in Potsdam later that day. |
| 6 Sept. | Departs from Potsdam 'after dinner'. |
| 7 Sept. | Arrives in Berlin. |
| 15 Sept. | Day trip to Stralau. |
| 19 Sept. | Departs from Berlin on horseback (his servant Jacob and baggage travel separately by *journalière*); arrives in Potsdam later that day. |
| 23 Sept. | Departs from Potsdam by *Postwagen*. |
| 24 Sept. | Stops in Coswig 'at noon' *en route*; arrives in Dessau 'at three'. |
| 30 Sept. | Day trip on horseback to Wittenberg. |
| 1 Oct. | Departs from Dessau 'at two' by *Postwagen*. |
| 2 Oct. | Arrives in Halle at 3 a.m. |

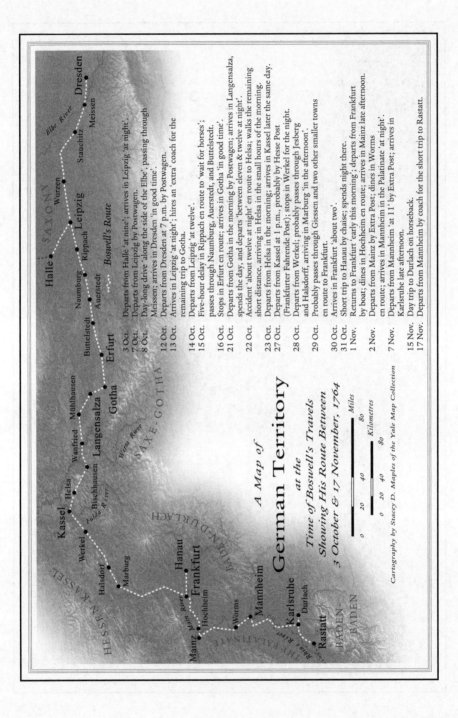

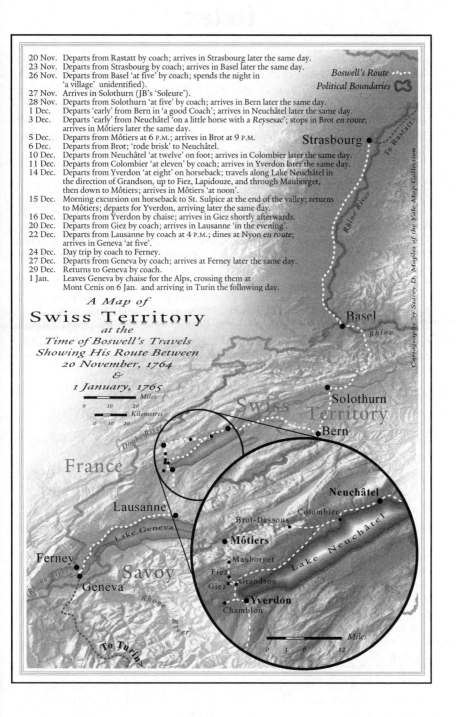

20 Nov. Departs from Rastatt by coach; arrives in Strasbourg later the same day.
23 Nov. Departs from Strasbourg by coach; arrives in Basel later the same day.
26 Nov. Departs from Basel 'at five' by coach; spends the night in 'a village' unidentified).
27 Nov. Arrives in Solothurn (JB's 'Soleure').
28 Nov. Departs from Solothurn 'at five' by coach; arrives in Bern later the same day.
1 Dec. Departs 'early' from Bern in 'a good Coach'; arrives in Neuchâtel later the same day.
3 Dec. Departs 'early' from Neuchâtel 'on a little horse with a *Reysesac*'; stops in Brot *en route*; arrives in Môtiers later the same day.
5 Dec. Departs from Môtiers at 6 P.M.; arrives in Brot at 9 P.M.
6 Dec. Departs from Brot; 'rode brisk' to Neuchâtel.
10 Dec. Departs from Neuchâtel 'at twelve' on foot; arrives in Colombier later the same day.
11 Dec. Departs from Colombier 'at eleven' by coach; arrives in Yverdon later the same day.
14 Dec. Departs from Yverdon 'at eight' on horseback; travels along Lake Neuchâtel in the direction of Grandson, up to Fiez, Lapidouze, and through Mauborget, then down to Môtiers; arrives in Môtiers 'at noon'.
15 Dec. Morning excursion on horseback to St. Sulpice at the end of the valley; returns to Môtiers; departs for Yverdon, arriving later the same day.
16 Dec. Departs from Yverdon by chaise; arrives in Giez shortly afterwards.
20 Dec. Departs from Giez by coach; arrives in Lausanne 'in the evening'.
22 Dec. Departs from Lausanne by coach at 4 P.M.; dines at Nyon *en route*; arrives in Geneva 'at five'.
24 Dec. Day trip by coach to Ferney.
27 Dec. Departs from Geneva by coach; arrives at Ferney later the same day.
29 Dec. Returns to Geneva by coach.
1 Jan. Leaves Geneva by chaise for the Alps, crossing them at Mont Cenis on 6 Jan. and arriving in Turin the following day.

Boswell's Route ·····
Political Boundaries

*A Map of*
**Swiss Territory**
*at the*
*Time of Boswell's Travels*
*Showing His Route Between*
*20 November, 1764*
&
*1 January, 1765*

Miles
0   10   20
Kilometres
0   10   20

Strasbourg

To Rastatt

Rhine River

Basel
Rhine

Solothurn

Swiss Territory
Bern

France

Doubs River

Lausanne

Lake Geneva

Ferney

Rhône River

Savoy

Geneva

Rhône River

To Turin

Neuchâtel
Colombier
Brot-Dessous
Môtiers
Mauborget
Fiez
Giez   Grandson
Yverdon
Chamblon
Lake Neuchâtel

Miles
0   3   6   12

Cartography by Stacey D. Maples of the Yale Map Collection

# Index

SOVEREIGNS and members of royal families are entered under their first names, and all other persons under their surnames (with cross references to their titles where appropriate). The following abbreviations are used: B. (Baron), Bt. (Baronet), C. (Count, Countess), D. (Duke, Duchess), M. (Marquess), E. (Earl), P. (Prince, Princess), V. (Viscount), JB (James Boswell), GD (George Dempster), SJ (Samuel Johnson), JJ (John Johnston), MM (Margaret Montgomerie), WJT (William Johnson Temple), *Life* (Boswell's *Life of Johnson*). The index was compiled by Nancy E. Johnson.

421

432